Conflict over the Columbia

CANADIAN PUBLIC ADMINISTRATION
SERIES

COLLECTION ADMINISTRATION PUBLIQUE
CANADIENNE

J. E. Hodgetts, *General Editor/Directeur général*
Roch Bolduc, *Directeur associé/Associate Editor*

The Institute of Public Administration of Canada
L'Institut d'administration publique du Canada

This series is sponsored by the Institute of Public
Administration of Canada as part of its constitutional
commitment to encourage research on contemporary
issues in Canadian public administration and public
policy, and to foster wider knowledge and understanding amongst practitioners and the concerned citizen.
There is no fixed number of volumes planned for the
series, but under the supervision of the Research
Committee of the Institute, the General Editor,
and the Associate Editor, efforts will be made to
ensure that significant areas will receive appropriate
attention.

L'Institut d'administration publique du Canada
commandite cette collection dans le cadre de ses
engagements statutaires. Il se doit de promouvoir la
recherche sur des problèmes d'actualité portant sur
l'administration publique et la détermination des poli-
tiques publiques ainsi que d'encourager les praticiens
et les citoyens intéressés à les mieux connaître et à les
mieux comprendre. Il n'a pas été prévu du nombre de
volumes donné pour la collection mais, sous la direction du Comité de recherche de l'Institut, du Directeur
général, et du Directeur associé, l'on s'efforce d'ac-
corder l'attention voulue aux questions importantes.

Canada and Immigration:
Public Policy and Public Concern
Freda Hawkins

The Biography of an Institution:
The Civil Service Commission of Canada,1908–1967
J. E. Hodgetts, William McCloskey, Reginald
Whitaker, V. Seymour Wilson

An edition in French has been published under the
title *Histoire d'une institution: La Commission de la*
Fonction publique du Canada, 1908–1967,
by Les Presses de l'Université Laval

Old Age Pensions and Policy-Making in Canada
Kenneth Bryden

Provincial Governments as Employers:
A Survey of Public Personnel Administration
in Canada's Provinces
J. E. Hodgetts and O. P. Dwivedi

Transport in Transition:
The Reorganization of the Federal Transport Portfolio
John W. Langford

Initiative and Response:
The Adaptation of Canadian Federalism to
Regional Economic Development
Anthony G. S. Careless

Canada's Salesman to the World:
The Department of Trade and Commerce, 1892–1939
A. Mary Hill

Health Insurance and Canadian Public Policy:
The Seven Decisions that Created the Canadian
Health Insurance System
Malcolm G. Taylor

Conflict over the Columbia:
The Canadian Background to an Historic Treaty
Neil A. Swainson

Conflict over the Columbia

The Canadian Background to an Historic Treaty

NEIL A. SWAINSON

The Institute of Public Administration of Canada
L'Institute d'administration publique du Canada

McGill–Queen's University Press
Montreal

© The Institute of Public Administration of Canada/
  L'Institut d'administration publique du Canada 1979

ISBN 0-7735-0325-0 (cloth)
ISBN 0-7735-0326-9 (paper)

Legal deposit 2nd quarter 1979
Bibliothèque Nationale du Québec

Printed in Canada by John Deyell Company

This book has been published with the help of a grant
from the Social Science Federation of Canada, using
funds provided by the Canada Council

To the Memory of
My Parents

Contents

Tables

Figures

Preface

The world has changed since, almost four decades ago, Canadians first began to consider seriously the manner in which they might develop their portion of the Columbia River's watershed. Indeed, it has changed in some very significant ways since the author began working on this case study some fourteen years ago. The record which follows is presented, nevertheless, in the belief that much of the Canadian experience with the development of the Columbia River is still very relevant, and in the belief that it can contribute something to our understanding of policy-making in Canada—especially when the process involves the utilization of a magnificent natural resource, on-going association with another country, and the cooperation of the two basic levels of government in this federal state.

It is my hope that this work will help to clarify the background to and the considerations involved in the negotiation of the Columbia River Treaty and related agreements, about which there has been much misunderstanding in recent years. Inevitably I have developed a perspective with respect to this entire set of arrangements, which the reader will find in the last two chapters. But advancing one has not been a basic objective of mine; this book is not a commentary on, or a critique of, the detailed provisions of the treaty. Rather it is an examination of the Canadian political system in action as it responded to a specific challenge and produced a related set of public policies.

I am especially indebted to Professor Hugh Marshall of Stanford University, for the wisdom and the patience with which he supervised the preparation of an earlier version of this work as a doctoral dissertation. And I am almost equally indebted to my former colleague, the late Professor G. Reid Elliott, who was of great assistance as he read successive drafts, offered sound advice, and helped keep me at it when my enthusiasm waned. Professor E. R. Black and a group of anonymous readers for McGill-Queen's University Press, and the Social Science Federation of Canada, read my manuscript and advanced useful suggestions which I have tried to incorporate. At several stages in the research, I have been much indebted to Professor Vincent Ostrom of the University of Indiana, to Professor Irving K. Fox of the Westwater Research Centre at the University of British Columbia, to Dr. John Krutilla of Resources for the Future, inc., and to Dr. Hugh L. Keenleyside (in a variety of capacities) for suggestions, and for their sensitizing me to the nuances of resource policy formation.

Without exception, the major Canadian and American decision-makers and their advisers whom I approached made themselves available for interviews. There were so many of them that I have decided it would be invidious to single out a few. Thus none are identified by name. But I do wish to put on the record my indebtedness to two prime ministers, to a provincial premier, to at least six cabinet ministers, to the chairmen of an international commission and two provincial power authorities, to deputy ministers, their technical advisers in government, to the consultants to government, to the economists, engineers, journalists, and laymen interested in this subject who gave freely of their time and frankly of their knowledge and opinion. I am especially grateful to two former ministers for permission to examine records under their control; without it this study could not have been written. (By the way, I did not have access to the files of the International Joint Commission, or to the papers of the late General A. G. L. McNaughton. The general's family was quite willing to make his records available, but they are still under a security classification in the National Archives.)

Naturally, none of the individuals mentioned or referred to above bears any responsibility for the views which I advance.

The research on which this record is based was supported, initially, by a fellowship award and a research grant from Resources for the Future, inc., of Washington, D.C. I should like gratefully to acknowledge this help, as well as subsequent grant assistance from the Department of Energy, Mines and Resources in Ottawa, and the Research Committee of the University of Victoria. My thanks also go to the Social Science Federation of Canada and to the Institute of Public Administration of Canada which are assisting with publication subventions, as well as to Mrs. F. M. Bird, Mrs. D. Robertson, and Miss J. Ransom for their excellent stenographic assistance.

Finally, I want to put on the record my gratitude, beyond measure, for the support and encouragement of my wife, and for the manner in which, during the course of this very time-consuming project, she carried a disproportionate share of the responsibility for raising four sons.

Chronology

March 9, 1944——Joint Canadian-American Reference re the Columbia River to the International Joint Commission (IJC).

May–June 1948——Great Columbia River flood.

January 12, 1951——First American application to build the Libby Dam filed with the IJC.

August 1, 1952——W. A. C. Bennett became premier of British Columbia.

April 8, 1953——Withdrawal by the USA of its first Libby application.

1954——Proposal of the Puget Sound Utilities Council to build, and donate to British Columbia, a major storage dam at Mica Creek.

1954——Proposal of the Kaiser Aluminum and Chemical Corporation to build a storage dam on the Arrow Lakes, upstream of Castlegar, B.C.

May 22, 1954——Second American application to build the Libby Dam filed with the IJC.

July 11, 1955——Royal assent given to the International River Improvements Bill, Ottawa; "Kaiser Dam" vetoed.

March 26–27, 1956——Prime Minister St. Laurent proposed some examination of the Columbia's development at the diplomatic level to President Eisenhower.

July 4, 1956——Ottawa and British Columbia agreed to halt public intergovernmental debate on the Columbia, and to commission independent studies of developmental alternatives.

May 20–21, 1957—Discursive diplomatic talks pursued on the Columbia, Washington, D.C.

June 10, 1957——Electoral defeat of the St. Laurent administration.

October 7, 1957——Memorandum of agreement signed between the government of British Columbia and Wenner-Gren interests concerning surveys and a feasibility study of a major hydro electric development on the Peace River.

October 14, 1957——Federal Speech from the Throne alluded to "a joint programme with the province . . . to develop the immense waters of the Columbia River."

November 1957——Submission of Montreal Engineering Company Report to the government of Canada.

December 1957——Study commissioned by the Diefenbaker administration from a new Committee on Economic Studies of Columbia River Development.

March 31, 1958——Federal general election; major Progressive-Conservative victory.

November 1958——Formation of the Peace River Power Development Company.

November 1958——"Briggs Affair."

November 1958——Receipt by the government of Canada of the Report of the Committee on Economic Studies.

December 1958——B.C. Power Commission informed by the government of British Columbia of its future role as the agency destined to develop the Columbia River in Canada.

January 29, 1959——Further Canada-U.S. reference to the IJC asking it to recommend principles to be applied in determining the benefits stemming from cooperative development, and to be applied in their apportionment.

January–March 1959——Creation of Canada-British Columbia Technical Liaison and Policy Liaison Committees.

January 1959——Crippen-Wright Report submitted to the government of British Columbia.

March 1, 1959——International Columbia River Engineering Board Report submitted to the IJC.

February–December 1959——International and Intranational (Canadian) negotiation over the IJC "Principles."

December 29, 1959——IJC Report on the "Principles" submitted to governments of Canada and the United States.

December 30, 1959——Peace River Power Development Company Report submitted to the government of British Columbia.

January 14, 1960——Federal speech from the throne presaged an imminent move to international treaty negotiations.

February 11, 1960——First meeting of Canadian-American treaty negotiators.

September 28, 1960——Joint progress report submitted by negotiators to Canada and the USA.

October 19, 1960——Progress report released, Ottawa and Washington.

December 28, 1960——Referral of proposed development of the Columbia and Peace Rivers to the B.C. Energy Board for a comparative analysis by the government of British Columbia.

January 17, 1961——Columbia River Treaty signed in Washington.

January–May 1961——Modification of British Columbia's position with respect to the disposal of its entitlement to downstream energy on the Columbia.

May 1961——Caseco Consultants Ltd. Report on Columbia River Development delivered to the B.C. Power Commission.

May 1961——Montreal Engineering Co. report on the cost of Columbia River Power delivered to the government of Canada.

August 1, 1961——Legislation introduced at Victoria to expropriate the B.C. Electric and Peace River Power Development companies.

August 1, 1961——Report of Sir Alexander Gibb and Partners, Merz and McLellan to the B.C. Energy Board tabled in the provincial Legislature.

September 18–November 22, 1961——B.C. Water Comptroller's hearings concerning proposals to build storages at Mica Creek, Duncan Lake, and on the Arrow Lakes.

November 17, 1961——Meeting between Premier Bennett and President Kennedy, Seattle, Wash.

September 16–November 28, 1961——Competitive speeches by Messrs. Bennett and Fulton, respectively, in Prince George, B.C.

March–April 1962——Near détente between Ottawa and Victoria.

April 6, 1962——General McNaughton announced his involuntary retirement from the IJC.

June 18, 1962——Federal election. Progressive Conservatives returned in a minority government. Federal Social Credit party acquired the balance of power.

August 19, 1962——New portfolio assignments for Messrs. Donald Fleming and E. D. Fulton.

September 11–December 20, 1962——Exploratory meetings of officials at Washington, D.C., Portland, Ore., Vancouver, B.C., re possible sale of Canadian entitlement to downstream Columbia power.

September 27, 1962——Nominal reversal of the Canadian ban on long-term large scale power exports in the federal Speech from the Throne.

April 8, 1963——Electoral defeat of the Diefenbaker administration.

May 10–11, 1963—Prime Minister Pearson and President Kennedy agree to negotiations leading to a protocol to the Columbia River Treaty, at Hyannis Port.

July 8, 1963——Signing of first Canadian-British Columbia Agreement with respect to the implementation of the Columbia River Treaty.

August 1–January 13, 1964——Concurrent negotiations over a protocol and a sale of the Canadian power entitlement.

January 13, 1964——Second Canada-British Columbia Agreement signed.

January 22, 1964——Signing of the protocol and terms of sale, and Exchange of Notes, Washington, D.C.

April 7–May 21, 1964——Hearings on the Columbia River Treaty before the House of Commons' Standing Committee on External Affairs.

September 16, 1964——Ratification and proclamation of the Columbia River Treaty.

Glossary

Acre-foot—a volume of water equivalent to one acre covered to a depth of one foot (43,560 cubic-feet).

Cfs—cubic feet per second, a measure of flow or discharge of water.

Dead Storage Capacity—the volume of a reservoir below the entrance to the lowest outlet; the capacity which cannot be evacuated by gravity.

Drawdown—the distance that the water surface in a reservoir is lowered from a given elevation; commonly, the difference in elevation between the high and low operating levels of a reservoir.

Energy—that which does or is able to do work; measured in terms of the work it is capable of doing. Electrical energy is usually expressed in kilowatt hours.

Firm Power—power intended to have assured availability to meet all of or any specified portion of a customer's load requirements.

Flowage Cost—the costs associated with the preparation of a reservoir for flooding—including the costs of land acquisition, clearing, building replacement, compensation to displaced persons.

Interruptible Power—power available under agreements which allow the curtailment or the elimination of delivery by the supplier.

Kilowatt—one kilowatt is equal to 1.341 horse-power.

Load Factor—the ratio of the average load over a designated period to the peak-load in the same period.

Live Storage Capacity—the volume of a reservoir minus its dead and surcharge storage capacity.

Machining—the process of installing generating equipment at a hydro project, often carried out over a number of years subsequent to completion of the dam and initial impoundment of water in the reservoir.

Moulding—the action of forming or shaping the supply of power and energy to approximate the demand curve.

Peaking Capability—the maximum peak load which a system, generating station, or unit can supply during a specified time period.

Pondage—limited reservoir storage capacity providing only daily or weekly streamflow regulation.

Prime or Continuous Power—hydroelectric power continuously available from a plant under the most unfavourable hydraulic conditions contemplated.

Primary Energy—hydroelectric energy available from prime or continuous power.

Reservoir Storage—the volume of water in a reservoir at a specified time, often expressed in acre-feet.

Riparian—the proprietor pertaining to, or situated on, the banks of a river.

Run-of-the-River Plant—a hydroelectric power plant which utilizes the flow of the river as it occurs, or pondage.

Secondary Energy—all hydroelectric energy other than primary energy.

Wheeling—the transfer of power and energy from one utility over the transmission system of a second utility for delivery to a third utility, or to a load of the first utility.

Key Personnel

Basset, Edward—Deputy minister of lands, British Columbia; one of four Canadian negotiators of the Columbia River Treaty, 1960.

Bennett, W. A. C.—Premier of British Columbia, 1952–72.

Bonner, Robert—Attorney general of British Columbia, 1952–68.

Briggs, Lee—General manager, B.C. Power Commission, 1955–58.

Chantrill, R.—Engineering adviser to the Peace River Power Development Company.

Davis, John—Director of research and planning, B.C. Electric Company, 1957–61; member of Parliament, 1962–74; parliamentary secretary to the prime minister, 1963–65, etc.

Diefenbaker, John—Prime minister of Canada, 1957–63.

Dill, Clarence—Sometime U.S. senator; spokesman for Pacific Northwest power interests.

Dinsdale, Walter—Minister of northern affairs and national resources, Canada, 1960–63.

Fleming, Donald—Minister of finance, 1957–62; minister of justice, 1962-63, Canada.

Fulton, E. Davie—Member of Parliament, Kamloops Riding, B.C., 1945–63; minister of justice, 1957–62 and public works, Canada, 1962–63; chairman of Canadian Negotiating Team, 1960.

Grauer, A. E.—Chairman of board and president, B.C. Electric Company and its parent, the B.C. Power Corporation, Ltd., 1946–61.

Green, Howard—Member of Parliament, Vancouver South and Vancouver-Quadra, 1935–63; Minister of public works, 1957–59 and secretary of state for external affairs, Canada, 1959–63.

Hamilton, Alvin—Minister of northern affairs and national resources, Canada, 1957–60; co-chairman 1959–60 of the Canada-British Columbia Policy Liaison Committee, etc.

Howe, C. D.—M.P. 1935–57; minister of railways, canals, transport, munitions and supply, reconstruction, trade and commerce, Canada, (successively).

Johnson, Byron—Coalition and Liberal premier of British Columbia, 1947–52.

Jordan, Len—Chairman, American Section, International Joint Commission, 1955–57.

Keenleyside, H. L.—Chairman, B.C. Power Commission, 1959–62; co-chairman, B.C. Hydro and Power Authority, 1962–69.

Kennedy, W. Denis—1960–62, Adviser to the B.C. Power Commission, 1962–75, successively manager, major resources division; manager, Canadian entity services; chairman, Canadian entity (Columbia River Treaty) for the B.C. Hydro and Power Authority.

Kennedy, Gilbert—Deputy attorney general, British Columbia, 1957–72.

Kidd, G. J. A.—Project engineer, B.C. Water Resources Service, B.C. Power Commission, and B.C. Hydro and Power Authority; comptroller of water rights, B.C., 1964–65.

Ladner, Leon—Lawyer, former M.P.; prominent Progressive Conservative in British Columbia.

Laing, Arthur—Leader of Liberal party of B.C., 1953–59; Canadian minister of northern affairs and national resources, 1963–72.

Lesage, Jean—Canadian minister of resources and development, 1953–57.

Lloyd, Woodrow—Premier of Saskatchewan, 1961–64.

MacNabb, Gordon—Hydraulic engineer, Department of Northern Affairs and National Resources, 1954–57; assistant and adviser to Canadian Treaty negotiators, 1958–64; deputy minister, Department of Energy, Mines and Resources, 1975–78.

McKay, Douglas—Chairman, American Section, International Joint Commission, 1957–59.

McNaughton, A. G. L.—Chairman, Canadian Section, International Joint Commission, 1950–62.

Mainwaring, William—Vice-president, B.C. Electric Company, 1958; president, Peace River Power Development Company, 1958–61.

Martin, Paul—Secretary of state for external affairs, Canada, 1963–68.

Paget, Arthur—Comptroller of water rights, British Columbia, 1954–64; deputy minister, water resources, 1962–69.

Pearson, Lester—Secretary of state for external affairs, Canada, 1948–57; prime minister, 1963–68.

Perrault, Ray—Leader of B.C. Liberal party, 1959–68.

Ritchie, E.—Assistant undersecretary of state for external affairs, Ottawa, member of Canadian Negotiating Group, Columbia River Treaty, 1960.

Robertson, Gordon—Deputy minister, Department of Northern Affairs and National Resources, Ottawa, 1953–63; member of Canadian Negotiating Group, Columbia River Treaty, 1960, 1962–63.

Sinclair, James—Minister of fisheries, Canada, 1953–57; member of B.C. Energy Board, 1959–72.

Shrum, G. M.—Chairman, Royal Commission re B.C. Power Commission, 1958–59; chairman, B.C. Energy Board, 1959–72; chairman, B.C. Electric Co., 1961–62; co-chairman, B.C. Hydro and Power Authority, 1962–69;

chairman, B.C. Hydro and Power Authority, 1969–72.

Smith, Sidney—Secretary of state for external affairs, Canada, 1957–59.

Sommers, Robert—Minister of lands and forests, British Columbia, 1952–56.

Stephens, Donald—Chairman, Manitoba Hydro-Electric Board, 1951–68; member, International Joint Commission, 1958–68.

Stevens, Jack—Engineering adviser to Puget Sound Utilities Council, 1954; to Peace River Power Development Company, 1959–61.

Strachan, Robert—Leader of the official opposition, British Columbia, 1956–69.

Thompson, Robert—Leader of the National Social Credit party, 1961–67; member of Parliament, 1962–72.

Williston, Ray G.—Minister of lands and forests, British Columbia, 1956–72.

PART ONE

Chapter One

INTRODUCTION

It's always wise to raise questions about
the most obvious and simple assumptions.
C. West Churchman, *The Systems Approach*

On January 18, 1961, Prime Minister John Diefenbaker and President Dwight Eisenhower signed the Columbia River Treaty on behalf of Canada and the United States. The treaty provided that Canada was to build three storage projects in its section of the Columbia River's watershed, and detailed the manner in which they were to be operated over its sixty-year lifetime. It gave the United States an option to build a fourth project, with a reservoir which would flood back into Canada, and it included some guarantees of and some limitations on the right to divert within the watershed. The treaty also made provision for Canada to receive the monetary equivalent of one-half the flood control benefit which Canadian storage would produce in the United States. As well, it credited to Canada and made provision for the return to Canada of one half the power which (in treaty terms) would be provided in the United States as the result of the operation of Canadian storage. Three years later, on January 22, 1964, another president and another prime minister witnessed the signing of a protocol modifying this treaty, and an agreement whereby Canada sold its downstream power entitlement for cash (prepaid) over a thirty-year period starting with the completion of its three reservoirs. Finally on September 16, 1964, this entire bargain was ratified via a formal exchange of appropriate instruments.

This study is an examination of the events, actions, and circumstances whereby Canada finally became a party to this set of arrangements; it thus deals primarily with the policy formation process in Canada. But it does much more than this, for the object of its attention was a landmark in the technology of developing a major hydraulic resource in an age of

1

major technological change. In addition, it was a unique exercise in the sharing of such a resource, and in sharing it across an international boundary. Finally, it was an exercise which involved a fascinating set of adjustments between a national and a provincial government in a federal state. All of these perspectives will be of concern to us as we review the twenty-year evolution of a public policy in Canada.

Although for most Canadians the prospect of cooperatively developing the Columbia River never acquired the visibility accorded earlier in this century to the Alaska Boundary dispute, or to the potential implications of trade reciprocity with the United States, it was certainly viewed by those Canadians who faced up to it as of great, indeed of comparable importance to these earlier questions. As a consequence, between 1944 and 1964, two levels of government in Canada devoted a great deal of effort, first to attempting to understand the problems associated with Columbia River development in the context of an international agreement, and then to identifying a preferred and mutually agreed-upon Canadian approach to their solution. Indeed, the extensiveness of the effort of these governments to generate relevant knowledge and insight, and to insert it at the appropriate time and place, has had few if any parallels in recent efforts at Canadian public policy-making. It is thus a matter of very considerable irony, albeit one which conceivably tells us something about the policy process itself, that ultimately the Canadian decisions on Columbia River development should have been so difficult to arrive at, and domestically should have become the subject of so much continuous and often acrimonious debate.

To some degree at least, just how and why this happened should become clear to the readers of the following pages, as they examine the Canadian approach to developing the Columbia River from two quite different, but complementary perspectives. Much the longest section of this study (in Part II—chapters 3-9), seeks to trace the complex evolution of Canadian policy concerning this river from those early stages when Canadian decision-makers first dimly perceived a benefit for Canada in some form of cooperative development with the United States, to the ultimate drafting of a very precise treaty, and three years later, to the final ratification of this treaty, a related protocol, and an agreement of sale. Here an attempt is made to identify the most directly involved individuals, groups, and organizations, to identify their goals or values, to suggest, where possible, the impact of popular demands and political culture on the decision-making, to define and assess leadership roles. Here also attention is focused where possible on the "points of leverage"[1] in this decision-making—sometimes personal, sometimes institutional, sometimes constitutional. In Part II a good deal of attention is devoted to the interdependence of the decision-makers, to their explicit identification of the moves and motives of others in conflict situations, and to the modification of their own behaviour in the light of these analyses. In an attempt to unravel a very complex process, we shall also be concerned in this section with the manner in which the "problem" as originally defined was or was not progressively redefined as time went on. In like manner we shall try to develop a feeling in this section for the broad range of goals and issues addressed by the Canadian decision-makers along with Columbia River development. Finally, we shall try to reflect the realities of the environment from which decisions came by suggesting how the overt decision-makers were influenced by the repertoires, programs, and regular operating procedures of the organizational subsets of their governments, how they reacted to deadlines, to past positions taken by themselves and others, to the impact of personality, to the dictates of political accommodation and efficiency. Thus one of our goals is to sketch in broad outline and in some inevitable detail the manner in which a significant set of public policy decisions evolved.

In our second approach to this decision-making, which is reserved for Part III (chapters 10–11), we seek to review analytically the strategy, or better the strategies utilized in Canada, to shape or influence the creation of this policy. At this stage answers are sought to two sets of questions derived from the astringent and perceptive thinking of Professor Charles Lindblom concerning the way in which complex public policy is actually made.[2] How, on the one hand, were the activities, contributions, roles of the individuals, groups, and organizations involved actually coordinated? Was the coordination centrally educed and often hierarchically controlled, or was it the result of the by-play of the adaptive behaviour which Professor Lindblom labels as the processes of partisan mutual adjustment?[3] Were there significant differences between the ways in which Canadian decision-makers were coordinated when they were located within single jurisdictions, and those utilized when personnel from several jurisdictions were involved? Did, for example, different approaches to coordination "fit" different subsets of the problems which emerged?

A second set of questions to be pursued in Part III directs our attention to the manner in which information was generated and incorporated into the decision-making process. Here we shall be concerned to determine the extent to which comprehensive assessments of the policy problem, involving goal identification and ranking, as well as the identification and evaluation of alternative forms of behaviour available, preceded the Canadian decision-makers' acts of deliberate choice. Alternatively we shall be concerned to ascertain the extent to which holistic analysis did not precede decision, the extent to which, again utilizing Lindblom's terminology, the approaches of the Canadian decision-makers by design or accident (or a mixture of both) involved a recourse to the making of successively limited comparisons, in a strategy which he describes as disjointedly incremental. This latter enquiry into the place which comprehensive analysis played in the Canadian approach to the Columbia is particularly appropriate for two reasons. The first is that it was in the crucible of water resource policy-making a generation and more ago that a good many of our most useful analytic techniques were first conceived and then refined. And the second is that there has been a widespread theoretic and practical acceptance of the case for preliminary "rationally comprehensive" analysis wherever the magnitude of the resources being committed by policy decisions is great, and when many of the consequences of decision are largely irreversible.

To repeat, then, there are two separate thrusts to this book, and it will be helpful if the reader keeps both in mind from the outset. This is particularly so because, while most of the time the two are pursued in separate sections, on occasion they are examined concurrently. Thus some aspects of the way in which the Canadian policy unfolded are reserved for Part III, and some references to strategic behaviour will be found throughout Part II. The serious student of this policy-making will also derive much assistance from a parallel reading of Dr. John Krutilla's impressive work, *The Columbia River Treaty*, published a decade ago.[4] Dr. Krutilla approaches the treaty from a systemic perspective, assessing it as an instrument for generating and distributing benefits to two riparians sharing an international watershed. But he does much more than this, as he casts much light on the complexities of international river development, and draws attention to the considerations which, in the light of the Columbia River experience, should be met if joint or cooperative development is to be in the economic interest of all the parties to it.

The general reader may also be helped if this introductory chapter draws attention to, or flags, a number of the basic features of much of the Canadian decision-making which we are about to reconstruct. One, to which Dr. Krutilla quite properly draws attention, is that when the prospect of jointly developing the Columbia River with the United States first emerged over a generation ago, it involved a watershed which seemed to be ideally suited to the derivation of a model approach to such a program. The two countries shared a long tradition of friendly relations and similar political systems. Both were well endowed with extensive technical expertise and capital resources. Time constraints did not pose a threat to careful investigative effort. The Columbia valley, furthermore, is not one in which viable consumptive use by an upstream riparian produces threats to the very existence of the downstream watercourse—

a complexity which greatly aggravates reaching agreement on the joint use of some shared drainage basins, such as those of the Rio Grande and Colorado Rivers. A second consideration to keep in mind is that a generation ago the Columbia's watershed was one in which, up to a point, the regulation of stream-flow produced via upstream storage could bestow very significant benefits on the downstream riparian. Note the wording of this generalization, which does not suggest that the upstream storage added to that already existing in this valley had to be Canadian. Indeed, the thrust of much of Dr. Krutilla's work is to suggest that had the United States pursued a policy of enlightened self-interest in the late stages of the Columbia decision-making, *and had it restricted its assessment of participating in cooperative development to the economic consequences directly attributable to it,* then it would not have become a party to the treaty *as it finally emerged,* but would have provided much of the additional storage which was being sought in its own section of the watershed.[5] But this is to anticipate, and must not be allowed to becloud the issue. For at least fifteen years prior to the negotiation of the Columbia River Treaty the governments of Canada and British Columbia were convinced that storage provided in the Canadian section of the watershed almost by definition would produce a massive benefit for the United States. Hence the reader will want to watch for the moves whereby over this period of time these two Canadian governments, and their agents, sought to win from the United States a recognition of what they came to call the downstream benefit case, and a crediting to Canada of some reasonable share of the wealth which they were convinced could be created in this way.

A second technical consideration which characterized the Canadian decision-making involved identifying the physical sites at which Canada might wisely be prepared to provide storage in the context of an international agreement. This required acquiring much knowledge concerning the hydraulic and physical characteristics of the Canadian portion of the watershed, but the question was more involved than this. On one Columbia tributary, the Kootenay, for instance, some of the options for Canadian storage were directly competitive with alternative American storage which could extend north of the international border, and in fact in one form would overlap at least one major Canadian reservoir site. Thus the assessment of Canadian sites also had to take into account American construction desires, the benefit-streams from Canadian and American storage, and how they were likely to be divided. Complicating the matter still further was the fact that the Canadian storages with the greatest potential for producing benefits in the United States often were capable of producing downstream benefits in Canada as well. In some cases, additionally, they were capable of producing major benefits, normally in the form of hydroelectric power, at-site in Canada. A still further consideration was that the identification of preferred storage locations (from the Canadian perspective) was also a function of one's ultimate objective. As Dr. Krutilla demonstrates so clearly, and as the following pages reveal to some degree, site selection in the context of maximizing the net gain to be shared by the two riparians was not necessarily the same thing at all as site selection pursued in the context of maximizing the net benefits to Canada, especially when these were measured in the light of a broad range of economic and non-economic criteria. Selecting the storage projects which Canada should put forward for construction in the context of an international agreement, and of almost equal importance, specifying the terms under which they should be operated, were to be continuing challenges for the Canadian decision-makers. They remain matters about which disagreement continues to this day.

There was a third technical challenge which Canadian decision-makers had to face up to in time, stemming from the fact that the sequencing of projects in river basin development, and the timing of their construction within any given sequence, have a significant bearing on the benefits which can be attributed to them. This proposition had been appreciated in general terms for some time prior to the Columbia River decision-making, but it was to be clarified and refined considerably while the studies on the Columbia's development proceeded, especially with reference to benefits produced other than at-site. Dr. Krutilla and associates, in fact, were to make a major contribution to this heightened understanding.[6] The significance of project sequencing and timing stems in part from the consideration that the addition of identical quantities of storage has diminishing incremental effectiveness for flood control management, and, as Dr. Krutilla observes, "other things being equal,"[7] diminishing effectiveness for hydro electric power production as well. During the later stages of the Canadian decision-making, for instance, it was calculated that if equal increments of 5 million acre-feet of storage were added to that already existing in the Columbia River system, the fourth added addition of 5 million acre-feet would be worth (for power production purposes under 1970–75 conditions) only about 20 percent of the value of a first identical increment of storage.[8] The significance of sequencing and timing stems in part from complex distributive and substitutive effects concerning power and flood control benefits which settling upon any one set of developmental arrangements involves. The addition of a project in a sequence, for instance, or a change in the timing of elements in a sequence, may well displace values otherwise inhering in other projects. This can happen in a shared watershed across an international boundary. (The technically inclined reader should examine chapter 3 of *The Colum-*

bia River Treaty for further details.) What all this adds up to is that when detailed negotiations leading to a treaty began, a further major Canadian objective was to have the most favourable *assumed* sequencing (and hence the greatest quantum of benefits) associated with the projects which Canada was advancing for construction. The most favourable assumption, of course, even though it might not be reflected in real world events, would be that each new Canadian storage be treated as if it were "first-added" to that already existing. The reader will want to check on the extent to which the Canadians succeeded here.

A still further set of technical questions which the Canadian decision-makers had to face up to was associated with defining and measuring the downstream benefit, and then deciding how to divide it fairly. During the years 1944 to 1954 when technical personnel in the two countries pursued joint and separate studies on alternative forms of development, a considerable number of potential benefits was examined. It soon became obvious, however, that the United States as the downstream state on the river (or riparian) was not likely to enjoy a significant recreational benefit, or a benefit in the form of improved consumptive use for domestic, municipal, and industrial purposes, as a result of upstream storage. Much the same was true concerning a potential irrigation benefit in the American portion of the Columbia valley itself. Indeed, by 1959, American representatives were able to point out that their irrigation effort associated with the Columbia Basin Project (south of Grand Coulee) would become more, not less, expensive for them as a result of Canadian regulation upstream.[9] Thus the definitional exercise with which Canadian and American personnel had to deal was concerned fundamentally with power generation and flood control management benefits.

Neither task turned out to be easy, although eventually a Canadian-American agreement was reached on the definitions themselves. This again is a complex subject, one involving a measure of genuine uncertainty, and one about which some of the treaty's continuing critics in Canada have had a good deal to say. Once again the reader is referred to Dr. Krutilla. The technical intricacies are not pursued at length in this book, which is primarily concerned with the process whereby the definitional and distributional policy emerged, rather than with its technical provisions. What the reader should be alert to from the beginning is the extent to which the definitional exercise, which in a fundamental sense was initially sponsored by technical personnel, ultimately was subsumed within and influenced by a web of international and national political relationships. How and why this happened is also a key part of the account which follows.

A word is appropriate at this point concerning the contribution of technical personnel to the decision-making we are about to review. Inevitably and properly, it had to be great. The competence of politicians does not normally extend to distinguishing between capacity and energy power benefits, to assessing the long-term contribution which upstream storage makes to the generation of peaking power, to assessing the substitution and displacement effects of project selection in river system development. What has to be kept in mind, however, is that all analytic effort involves assumptions—many often technical but some frankly value judgments. The utility of analysis, particularly if it is to be used comparatively, may be very much a function of the assumptions which it incorporates. The reader as a consequence will want to watch for signs to the effect that the Canadian decision-makers did or did not appreciate this, and for indications that different political jurisdictions in Canada periodically entered into controversies with each other as to just what the analysts' assumptions should be. The reader will also want to watch for one of the most significant features of this record—the manner in which some of the most crucial of the analysts' assumptions incorporated into the negotiations which led to the signing of the Columbia River Treaty in January 1961 were outflanked by developments over the next two years, before the treaty itself, in somewhat modified form, was ratified.

It will come as no surprise to the knowledgeable reader to discover that the creation of Canada's policy with respect to the Columbia River's development was a classic illustration of executive federalism in action. Executive officials, elected and appointed, play a crucial role in Canadian policy formation. When, as was the case with the Columbia, two basic sets of them at two different levels of government are legitimately involved in the preparation of a policy, extensive interaction between them is necessary; in a fundamental sense their contributions do have to be reconciled. The point to be kept in mind here is that the roles of the Canadian executives were complementary, and the officials in Ottawa and Victoria pursued them in the knowledge that each group of them had a capacity to facilitate or frustrate the actions of the other. Many of the most significant decisions, of course, ultimately came from elected executive officials, the Cabinet ministers. These decisions, and, where possible, the contributions of ministers, are recorded in Part II. The roles of the Cabinets per se, and the interaction of their members with each other, with their own and each other's appointed officials, and the direct interaction of the appointed officials become one of our concerns in Part III. Most of the appointed officials who played key analytic and advisory roles were located (in Victoria and Ottawa) in departments—those organizational structures which still constitute the basic anatomy of Canadian executive government. In British Columbia for long the key advisory staff were drawn from its Department of Lands, first from the deputy minister's office, and then from that department's Water Rights Branch. After 1961 the provincial Water Rights Branch became part of a Water Resources Service in an expanded three divisional Department of Lands, Forests, and Water Resources. Eventually personnel from other departments, such as that of the attorney general, were incorporated into the provincial advisory group, but its core remained in the Water Rights Branch. In Ottawa, more departments were involved. The international dimension to Columbia River development naturally concerned the Department of External Affairs from the beginning. In time, spill-overs of the decision-making were to have extensive federal implications, for example, for the Departments of Finance and of Fisheries. The major sources of technical advice, in Ottawa, however, were to come from the federal Department of Public Works, and, particularly, from the Dominion Water and Power Bureau of the Department of Mines and Resources. This latter agency became the Water Resources Division of the Department of Resources and Development in 1950, and part of the Department of Northern Affairs and National Resources in 1953. (In 1955 it was renamed the Water Resources Branch.) There was one interesting difference between the federal and provincial departmental arrangements. Whereas the bulk of the province's departmental staff work was produced in its capital, Victoria, that of the federal resource departments emerged both from the national capital, and significantly, from field offices in Vancouver. Thus the staff work which had to be interwoven in Canada was produced in three centres. Not all of it, of course, came from departments. Two non-departmental governmental agencies, one federal and one provincial, were to make a significant contribution to this decision-making as well. Both of them—the Canadian Section of the International Joint Commission, based in Ottawa, and the B.C. Power Commission—absorbed in 1962 into an expanded B.C. Hydro and Power Authority with head offices in Vancouver—are introduced to the reader in chapter 2. The point which the reader should keep in mind here is that the staff input to the final decision-making, which properly will be a major focus of our attention, was diffused on this issue in both jurisdictions, but significantly more so in federal Canada.

The twenty-year period (1944–64) during which most of the decision-making we are about to turn to took place can be divided rather neatly in half, if one concentrates on the nature of the relationships which emerged between the governments of Canada and British Columbia. During the first decade, 1944–54, on the whole the two governments worked closely together. Deliberately careful, rather measured cooperative effort seemed to be required, and was produced. Time constraints during this period were not felt to be excessive. During the second ten years, the record of the Canadian intergovernmental relationships changed, as, intermittently, it was characterized by a good deal of dissonance. Practically, however, the most useful breaks in the record of decision-making fell at somewhat different times. One certainly emerged with the defeat of the St. Laurent government in June 1957. Another coincided with the Diefenbaker government's decision to move ahead to negotiate a treaty on Columbia River development, with the United States, at the end of 1959. A third natural break occurred when the treaty itself was signed in January 1961, and a fourth followed when the Diefenbaker government went out of office in 1963. Still another is associated with the final exchange, in September 1964, of the instruments which formally ratified the complex bargain so long in the making. All of these developments mark the end of chapters in the account which follows. In addition, two of the stages in the decision-making just identified—the negotiation of the treaty itself in 1960, and the two year deadlock between Ottawa and Victoria which followed in 1961-63—became so complex that they have been subdivided for our examination. In each case the beginning of new chapters marks a significant shift on the part of at least one of the Canadian governments involved in the policy formation.

There are two additional considerations which it is appropriate to raise in an introduction to the chapters which follow. One concerns the interesting fact that we are about to review a decision-making exercise in which a single Canadian province ultimately brought the national governments of two countries to accept a pattern of resource development with which neither was in complete agreement. Why and how this should have happened is discussed in Part III. But the reader may wish to reflect on it from this point onward, especially in the light of the not unreasonable hypothesis that small jurisdictions often have a degree of behavioural flexibility open to them which is just not possessed in the modern world by large ones. The other consideration returns us to an observation made earlier in this chapter—to the effect that in the early stages of the analytic effort in which the two countries jointly engaged there was a widespread assumption among the Canadians involved that out of it would be identified a pattern of development which would be optimal for both countries. One of the most interesting features of water resource policy-making in the 'fifties, in fact, especially as it concerned the generation of hydro-electric power, was the extent to which neighbouring utilities came to appreciate how an intelligently integrated approach to project construction and operation could take the form of a positive sum game, producing considerable benefits for all concerned. It was in the context of an integrated approach, in which Canadian decision-makers were genuinely concerned with the best interests of all the parties involved, that the Canadian planning effort on the Columbia began. Nor was this perspective ever completely abandoned in Canada. As the reader will discover shortly, there was a genuine perception of mutual responsibility, for instance, incorporated in the Diefenbaker government's approach to the difficult issue of site selection in the first half of 1960, just as there was, later in that year, when British Columbia's technicians tried to make the rapidly emerging treaty somewhat more flexible. To ignore this is to be less than fair to the individuals involved.

What, once again, the reader will want to be on the watch for are signs that over the two decades the shared sense of mutual responsibility in designing a system for cooperative development was attenuated in Canada. For it was, as the policy problem increasingly became the subject of national and international bargaining. It is a truism that the bargaining route to decision so beloved of modern man is an inherent and major part of the process whereby we adjust to the mix of conflicting values, benefits, and costs associated with the public choices which we have to make, and that the intellectual case for having recourse to it is impressive. What is also a truism, of course, is that bargaining has its associated costs. One of its consequences is that it often does relax a sense of shared responsibility, as the bargainer seeks to maximize his own gain, fairly narrowly defined, in the light of an assumption that other parties to the bargaining are doing the same, and an assumption that the final point of argument reached after a reciprocal exchange of demands and offers reflects the best that can be expected from the combined perspective of all those involved. This often makes sense, although increasingly today it hardly appears to be the road to a stable social consensus. What the student of the Columbia River decision-making may well wish to ponder is whether bargaining itself puts a premium on a recourse to strategic or tactical behaviour which unwittingly may inhibit either an appreciation of, or a successful recourse to forms of agreement which might increase the gains available to all associated with cooperative effort. Equally, the student may want to reflect on the extent to which the political process as now pursued in Canada does or does not facilitate an integrated approach to policy-making, and, in the light of this account, whether, in fact, it should.

Chapter Two

The Constitutional, Political, and Physical-Developmental Setting

From one point of view, the principal strategy
of the policy sciences can be summed up as guiding
the focus of attention of all participants in
decision.
Harold Lasswell, *A Pre-View of Policy Sciences*

The opposing pulls of the decision-making strategies referred to in chapter 1 apply to the reconstruction of public policy-making quite as much as to the original exercise itself. The reconstructive effort has to be made manageable and readable, even though it involves removing one discrete issue, as an object of enquiry, from the context in which it actually emerged, was shaped, and ultimately resolved. The hazards associated with this process are great, as they invoke some genuine uncertainty; they certainly make caution in the drawing of conclusions imperative. These same hazards also require that every reasonable effort be made to identify and assess the most significant features of the environment, including the already referred-to points of "leverage," from which or whereby the policy emerged. Most of these characteristics of the "policy environment" will be revealed as the record unfolds in chapters 3–9, and a good many are dealt with again in the concluding chapters. Three categories of them, however, warrant some examination at this point, if what follows is to be read with understanding.

1. THE LEGAL-CONSTITUTIONAL SETTING

Whenever uncertainty prevails and issues are in dispute between individuals and governments, those who seek to maintain competitive positions inevitably have recourse to the rules of the game, whether they be found in conventional practice, or in that "body of dogma or systematized prediction which we call the law."[1] If in fact the contest extends over any length of time, the parties to it may seek to sustain interpretations of the operative rules favourable to them, and to oppose, modify, or replace—where possible—those believed to be inimical to their interests. Hence the need to establish with some precision just what were the working rules under which the Canadian federal system approached the prospect of developing the watershed of the Columbia River in concert with the United States.

Under Canadian domestic law both the national and provincial governments have significant legislative authority relevant to the development of water resources. Proprietary or "ownership" rights to water, however, indeed to all resources, are vested in the provinces, which have been free to develop their own concepts of relevant law. In British Columbia, for instance, the presently operative Water Act declares that "Property in and the rights to the use and flow of all the water at any time in any stream in the province are for all purposes vested in the Crown in the right of the province."[2] Note that the common law doctrine of riparian rights is thus rejected. No right to use or divert water may be obtained by prescription (long or immemorial use). Anyone who wishes to divert, to use beneficially, to store water, to alter or improve stream flow, and to construct, maintain, and operate works which do any of these things must receive a licence from the supervising provincial comptroller of water rights. The statute makes licences subject to cancellation,[3] makes retention subject to beneficial use, and requires that rentals be paid and the orders of the comptroller be observed.

Clearly the authority of the province in the sphere of water resources is great, and that authority is augmented by powers conferred on the province under Section 92 of the British North America Act. Those powers include legislative competence over the management and sale of public lands, the incorporation of companies with provincial objectives, the regulation of local works and undertakings, property and civil rights, and matters of a local or private nature within the province.[4] As students of Canadian government well know, the process of judicial interpretation in Canada has gone a considerable way to converting the grants of authority over property and civil rights and over matters of a local or private nature into *de facto* residual power clauses of the Canadian constitution—save in times of grave national danger. The provinces of Canada exercise great power and their fundamental jurisdiction over the licensing and regulation of watershed developments is unquestioned.[5]

On the other hand, the powers of the Parliament of Canada with respect to water resource development are also significant. Under section 91 of the British North America Act, Parliament has an exclusive authority over navigation and shipping (subsection 10). It can "require its sanction to any works which would interfere with navigability"[6] and probably can order the erection of works designed to create or maintain it. Indeed, an extremely hesitant opinion by the Supreme Court of Canada in 1929 appears to have indicated that works projecting beyond the limits of a province, or connecting two provinces, even if constructed for power-generating purposes, would fall under federal control.[7] Concurrent federal and provincial jurisdiction certainly exists over projects wherein the energy-producing and navigation functions are combined. In addition, Parliament has the right to acquire jurisdiction over any work, although wholly situated within a province, by declaring it to be for the general advantage of Canada or two or more of the provinces.[8] It has exclusive jurisdiction over interprovincial and international trade, transportation, and communication. It shares a concurrent jurisdiction with the provinces over agriculture, and hence over irrigation. A still further federal competence exists with respect to international rivers, derived from the premise that Parliament has responsibility for domestic acts which would affect the property, and the civil and other rights of those resident outside Canada.[9] Finally, basic responsibility for seacoast and inland fisheries has been vested in the federal government, although the administration of federal regulations concerning inland fisheries has been left to provincial officials.

Some caveats need to be added here. While the government of Canada has great influence over the Canadian economy, there has been no expansion of its jurisdiction over water resource development at all comparable to that effected in the United States via the provisions, and successive interpretations of that country's constitution. (The American government's competence in water resource development stems, in part, from its defence and general welfare powers, and to some degree from its treaty-making capacity. Primarily, however, it is derived from the property and commerce clauses of the U.S. constitution. In the United States, for instance, the federal Power Commission has had a broad power, since 1920, to license non-federal hydro-electric projects. The commerce clause has been the source of the American government's authority over navigation. This authority has been extended to the non-navigable sections of navigable streams—and to a broad range of functions, such as power production, pollution abatement, storage for consumptive use, recreation, fish and wildlife control, which are incidental to navigation but broadly related to modifications of stream flow.) Some Canadian legal authorities proclaim the existence of an expanded federal jurisdiction over interprovincial rivers, but this remains in doubt, and in any case the Columbia River is not in this category.[10] Furthermore, the "navigation" and "fisheries" powers did not really warrant a major role for the government of Canada in the development of the Canadian section of the Columbia River Basin. The headwaters of neither the Columbia nor the Kootenay rivers had great navigational significance in 1945, and both had been cut off from the anadromous fishery resources of the lower watershed since construction of Grand Coulee Dam in the 'thirties.[11] But a federal involvement was certain when, in the late 'fifties, it became apparent that the international development of this river was to be made the subject of a treaty between Canada and the United States. There was, in addition, at least a potential federal involvement with this issue stemming from the breadth which Canadians have attributed to the federal spending power, and from the likelihood of a direct federal investment on the Columbia. When finally attention was turned from the rules governing domestic policy formation to those operative at the international level, a further—indeterminate—federal role was assured when the two countries invoked the assistance of the International Joint Commission. Limited comments on these follow in turn.

The Treaty Power. Over the course of the last one hundred years, Canada's approach to the treaty power has undergone some significant changes. A century ago the negotiating, signing, and ratifying functions were exercised on her behalf by Britain. Progressively, but especially after World War I, responsibility for them was transferred to or preempted by Canada. Canada adheres to the British tradition in regarding these functions as part of the prerogative power of the Crown. They are exercisable exclusively by the governor general, acting normally on the advice of the federal Cabinet, and do not require Parliament's approval—although by convention this is now almost invariably sought, albeit by no means always prior to ratification. Also in the British tradition, Canada regards treaties simply as contracts or formal understandings between nations; they do not as in American practice automatically become part of the supreme law of the land, and will not normally be regarded as binding by the courts unless implementing legislation has been passed.

While the British North America Act is silent on the power to contract international obligations, it does refer explicitly (in section 132) to the implementing function, and grants to the Parliament and government of Canada "all powers necessary and proper for performing the obligations of Canada or of any province thereof, as part of the British Empire, towards Foreign Countries, arising under Treaties between the Empire and such Foreign Countries." There really was no question as to what this meant as long as treaty responsibilities were incurred by Canada as part of the Empire. But when, from 1919 on, Canada began to sign treaties in her own right, when these obligations were no longer incurred on her behalf as part of the Empire, doubt immediately arose as to the continuing relevance of or the interpretation to be placed on section 132. After some period of uncertainty the Judicial Committee of the Privy Council decided in the famous Labour Conventions Case in 1937 that where legislation is required to implement treaty obligations involving "provincial classes of subjects" these must be dealt with "by the totality of powers, in other words by cooperation between the Dominion and the Provinces."[12] Joint federal-provincial action is therefore required in such cases; there can be no federal government trenching, via the treaty route, on the sphere of provincial competence.

The implications of such a decision for treaty enforcement are obvious. In the absence of appropriate action by from one to all ten provinces (depending upon the scope of the treaty) the federal government could, with respect to certain treaties, find itself party to international responsibilities which in the light of domestic law it is unable to meet. To avoid this embarrassment, Canadian practice for over a generation has required that, under such circumstances, "prior consultations are had, and agreements reached, with the provinces before Canada enters into international agreements."[13] Such was the operative interpretation of the treaty power under which the governments of Canada and British Columbia approached the international development of the Columbia River.[14] Whether an agreement had been reached between them prior to the signing of the Columbia River Treaty was to become the subject of a major controversy in 1961.

The Spending Power. Prior to World War I, the federal government restricted its activities principally to the fields of defence, external affairs (chiefly matters commercial), and economic development. In the years since that war, and particularly since 1945, it has assumed a new role. Gradually, as Anglo-Canadians became reconciled to the notion of the positive state, they became less concerned about strict interpretations of the constitutional division of powers, and were conditioned to expect federal intervention. By the late 'fifties, Ottawa's initiative had been extended into almost every field which traditional interpretation of the constitution would have designated as a sphere of provincial jurisdiction.

This expansion of federal activity reflected neither formal constitutional amendment nor startlingly new judicial interpretation. It was a classic example of conventional change, and was justified, by the very few in English-speaking Canada who reflected on it,[15] by references to the importance of the matters with which the federal government was dealing, and to a perceived competence which that government enjoyed to dispose of its revenues as it chose, subject, of course, to parliamentary approval.[16] "In pressing for federal participation in matters within the legislative jurisdiction of the provinces," wrote Professor Smiley perceptively in 1964, "Anglo-Canadians have normally not ordinarily felt it necessary to demonstrate the administrative or other disabilities of exclusively provincial action or the constitutional appropriateness of their proposals; the case usually goes no further than a demonstration that the subject under discussion is of great importance and *ipso facto* Ottawa should do something about it."[17] In English-speaking Canada this rather pragmatic approach to the distribution of power was seen as a reflection of a "nationalising" of Canadian sentiment.[18] This illustration of Canadian constitutional flexibility is relevant to a study of the process of policy-making with respect to the development of the Canadian section of the Columbia River Basin. As the years of the 'fifties passed, and the prospect of massive investment in the Canadian Columbia River watershed emerged, so did the prospect of some federal participation on grounds other than those related to the formal constitutional division of powers. After 1957, the federal government anticipated receiving a direct request for financial help, and eventually British Columbia's premier did not disappoint it. What form the assistance should take, however, and what prerogatives in policy formation and administration should accrue to the federal government in the light of it, were to become issues which helped turn the Canadian response to the challenge of international development from an exercise of cooperative into one of, intermittently, competitive federalism.

The International Joint Commission. In the twenty years during which the prospect of a cooperative approach to the development of the Columbia River was actively investigated in Canada and the United States, policy-makers were able to derive singularly little help from the texts of international lawyers. In the International Joint Commission (IJC), however, they had an instrumentality to which they quite reasonably turned, for it had been created by them following the signing of the Boundary Waters Treaty in 1909 expressly to resolve and, as far as possible, to forestall, disputes with respect to water use and to deal with other matters of mutual concern which might arise anywhere along the 4,000 miles of common border.[19]

Actually the commission may serve in a number of capacities. It must give its approval to uses, obstructions, or diversions affecting the natural level and flow of boundary waters (Article III), and to works on transboundary rivers downstream from the boundary or on waters flowing from these rivers, with transboundary effects (Article IV). It may fill administrative and arbitral roles as well. Furthermore, under Article IX of the Boundary Waters Treaty, it possesses a broad investigative power, exercisable at the request of either country, to examine and report on "any other questions or matters of difference arising between them involving the rights, obligations or interests of either in relation to the other or to the inhabitants of the other along the common frontier."[20] The Boundary Waters Treaty very explicitly insists that under Article IX the commission's findings are in no way decisions of fact or law, and "in no way have the character of an arbitral award." It was under this article that the two nations referred the question of jointly developing the Columbia River to the commission in March, 1944. Here then was a body which, with an absolute jurisdiction under Article IV of the 1909 treaty over only a very few—albeit crucial—works in the Columbia River basin, was to be heavily involved for a good many years with policy-making concerning this watershed as a fact-finding and advisory instrumentality.

The IJC is composed of two sections—one American and one Canadian —each with three members, one of whom is the Section chairman. The members are, of course, appointees of the government for which they are deemed to speak or on whose behalf they act. But over some fifty years the commissioners have generally been regarded as quasi-international public servants. They have been free, in the words of a late chairman of the Canadian Section, "to act, not as separate national delegations under instruction of their respective governments, but as a single body seeking common solutions in the joint interest."[21] This is not to say that there are no ties between the sections and their respective national governments. The commissioners hold office at the pleasure of their governments, which meet their expenses, pay their salaries, and provide the legal, engineering, and other assistance which each section requires.[22] The Canadian Section's annual estimates are always presented to Parliament along with those of the Department of External Affairs, although for over two decades now the commission's activities have been reported directly to the appropriate Parliamentary committee by the Canadian Section chairman himself. These considerations notwithstanding, it must be re-emphasized that the two nations have conceded much independence to their representatives on the commission, and have generally regarded it as a means whereby the resolution of problems on which they have had differing and even opposing views would be sought, not via bilateral negotiation, but "by an objective process of joint investigation and deliberation in the joint interest."[23]

One additional feature of the frame of reference in which the commission functions should be noted, for the authors of the Boundary Waters Treaty did try to give the commission some agreed-on principles in the light of which they were to pursue their dispute resolving and forestalling missions. One of these, embodied in Article II, reserves to both countries, with respect to transboundary rivers and those flowing into boundary waters "exclusive jurisdiction and control over their use and diversion" save that any parties injured across the border as a consequence are assured of "the same rights . . . and legal remedies as if such injury took place in the country where such diversion or interference occurs."[24] In the face of a Canadian assertion during the period 1954–59 of a right to divert the Upper Columbia and its tributary headwaters, this article was at the centre of a very considerable debate, conducted within the International Joint Commission and other agencies of government, and the legal communities of the two countries.

Fundamentally two questions were at issue. Did Article II embody, as Canadians generally argued, the celebrated Harmon Doctrine, the concept of the unrestricted sovereignty of the upstream riparian over waters within its boundaries? And, if so, what precisely was the nature of the remedy available to the injured party in the other country? Secondly, and more significantly, did it provide an effective basis for a working agreement with respect to the Columbia—an agreement which very likely would be operative into the next century? It is sufficient to note here that Canada objected to the inclusion of Article II very strenuously in 1909,[25] and only accepted it at that time because of the belief that, in the words of Sir Wilfrid Laurier, along "a three thousand mile boundary the application would cut both ways."[26] During the 'fifties a good many Canadians were to become convinced that, with respect to the Columbia River's watershed, Article II had conferred on their country options to divert of considerable intrinsic and great tactical value.

2. The Political Setting

All generalizations about politics are hazardous, and those concerning political moods, tempers, or perceptions (especially in the absence of empirical data) are even more risky. Nevertheless, despite these limitations, a few observations will be advanced at this point to indicate the overtly political environment in Canada wherein two levels of government concurrently approached each other, and the United States as well, in the process of striking a bargain for the development of an international watershed. They will be advanced, in the main, as brief comments on two generally unanticipated political upheavals in Canada during the decade of the 'fifties.

One of these took place in British Columbia in 1952. Provincial politics there had been structured on party lines since early in this century, with two groups, Liberals and Conservatives, alternating in office until 1941. After an election in that year left the incumbent Liberals without a clear majority, the two parties formed a coalition, for provincial purposes only, which governed the province until 1952. During this period the Cooperative Commonwealth Federation (CCF), a fusion of democratic socialist groups established on the Canadian prairies in 1932, constituted the official legislative opposition. The coalition was dissolved early in 1952. Although the last coalition premier, Byron Johnson, was then able to form a new Liberal party administration with an absolute, if narrow, legislative majority, he chose not to serve out the more than two years remaining in the government's term, but rather to seek in June 1952, a vote of confidence through an election. What neither Liberal nor Conservative party leaders realized at this time was the extent to which their popularity had declined in the last days of the coalition, and the opportunity which a newly introduced system of alternative voting had provided to the Social Credit movement,[27] appearing as a major force for the first time on the provincial political scene with a simple platform endorsing free enterprise, and the need for fiscal conservatism and honesty in government.

Actually the arrival of Social Credit in British Columbia, as previously in Alberta, involved something of a political and sociological revolution, for it organized vigorously democratic constituency associations (in contrast to the leadership dominated ones of the traditional cadre parties), and recruited to political participation very many who had previously played no such role.

The election of 1952, in any case, resulted in a major political upset, for when the complex ballot counting was over in July 1952, the Social Crediters had won nineteen seats, the CCF eighteen, with the Liberals and Conservatives sharing the other eleven. Only when the result was known did the newly elected Social Credit members of the legislature meet to select as leader, and in effect the new provincial premier, W. A. C. Bennett, a man who had been twice a candidate for the leadership of the Progressive Conservative party in British Columbia, and who had been an active Progressive Conservative MLA for a decade prior to 1951, when he had become an independent. He had identified himself with the Social Credit cause only in December 1951, and had played a significant role in bringing about the collapse of the coalition government. After forming a minority administration in August 1952, nine months later Mr. Bennett went to the electorate again and succeeded in obtaining a clear majority.

The events of 1952–53 were to change the tone of political behaviour in British Columbia; always sharply competitive, it now became noticeably more abrasive. Mr. Bennett soon proved himself to be very much the dominant personality in his government and one who relished direct confrontation. Financially independent, supremely confident, much abler than many realized initially, and very toughminded, the new premier from the outset was sharply and often devastatingly derisive of the defeated opposition parties. All of their leaders resigned their positions. Not a little of his invective was directed against his erstwhile Conservative colleagues, whose party he believed to be a spent force, at least in provincial politics, and whose representation in the legislature of the province was soon to disappear entirely. In their turn, scornful of the economic unorthodoxy to which the Social Credit government then gave occasional (if only nominal) approval, chagrined at their own displacement, convinced of the new government's administrative incompetence (only one of the nineteen Social Credit MLA's elected in 1952, apart from the premier, had been in the legislature before, and none of the first Cabinet had had extensive or publicly-appreciated administrative experience), and perhaps above all incensed at what they regarded as at best half-truths in the premier's accounts of past and current government action, the opposition parties replied in kind. They became, to a very significant degree, almost reflexively hypercritical of many of the new government's policies.

Labels, at least those from the liberal-conservative continuum, fit badly here. Almost from the beginning the Social Credit government proved to be both conservative and radically innovative.[28] To many it appeared querulous, often aggressive, and on occasions frankly antagonistic in its approach to the central government, as it complained of its treatment by Ottawa in a manner which made its predictions into self-fulfilling prophecies. Three features of the policies which it endorsed are of particular concern to this study. Much stress was placed in the 'fifties on the need for economy in government, and much effort was directed to the eradication of the provincial debt. At the same time, Mr. Bennett and his colleagues were very much committed to establishing a reputation for getting things done. And they were anxious to project an image of large scale thinking. They placed great emphasis on the development of a transportation and communications network whereby industrial and resource development, then concentrated in the south and west, might be spread over the entire province. Small mindedness in power to its critics,[29] a portent of the New Jerusalem to its friends, over most of the 'fifties at violent odds with its political opposition, and suspect by most of the metropolitan news media and by the older provincial elites—such briefly was the government of British Columbia which in 1952 inherited responsibility for the articulation of a Columbia River development policy, and which gradually produced one, as it attracted some able recruits to the Cabinet, and established an effective working relationship with a competent senior bureaucracy.

The other political upset took place in 1957, when, after twenty-two years in office, the Liberal administration in Ottawa was defeated in a general election, and replaced—for the most crucial years in the policy formation on the Columbia River—by one drawn from the Conservative party which Mr. Bennett had abandoned and had largely written off in the early years of the decade. While Mr. Bennett had cut his ties with the Conservatives in 1951, he made no secret of his satisfaction at the Conservatives' defeat of the Liberal St. Laurent government. He was then, and remained, on a friendly basis with the new Progressive Conservative prime minister, John Diefenbaker. Indeed, their two administrations were to have much in common. Both had come to power unexpectedly. Both, within a year, were to seek and obtain working majorities in an appeal to their electorates. Between 1956 and 1958 the *federal wing* of Mr. Diefenbaker's party re-established a strong base in British Columbia, as is evidenced by the fact that its record-breaking majority in 1958 included eighteen of the province's twenty-two seats in the House of Commons. Both administrations were to be dominated by their atypical Conservative heads, albeit, as will be evident later, through very different leadership styles. Both owed much to their leaders' ability to evoke enthusiasm for accelerated resource development.

The two governments applied many of the same perspectives to the Columbia River problem, although their fields of reference were strikingly different. In both capitals it was viewed as a challenging technical exercise which could yield great economic and political dividends; in both it was viewed as a matter which had general as well as regional economic significance. There was still another direction from which the two governments examined this question, for it was also a matter which directly involved Canada's relations with the United States. From this perspective many of the attitudes expressed in Ottawa inevitably were echoed in Victoria. For a long time Canadians have regarded the continuance of harmonious relations with the United States as—next to maintaining the integrity of their bicultural country—a primary objective of Canadian foreign policy. At the same time, whether validly or not,[30] Canadians for several generations have had the impression that their country was rather badly done by in a series of nineteenth century disputes with the United States. As a consequence, both Ottawa and Victoria approached the prospect of international cooperation on the Columbia River very much aware of the fact that the dividing line between negotiation and bargaining is a narrow one; they rather expected it to be crossed, and they were very conscious of the power of their neighbour.[31] This view was widely shared, inside and outside governing circles in Canada. The assumption that it prompted Canadians to sharpen their pencils and do their homework in preparation for the international bargaining is a valid one.[32]

On the other hand, there were some notable differences between the approach to the United States from Victoria after 1952, and that from Ottawa, especially after 1957. Although quite capable of being a very hard bargainer in its own way, the Social Credit government, with its strong commitment to expanding the economic base of the province, took no delight in plucking the American eagle's feathers, and consistently denounced some of its opponents who, it claimed, were prone to do just that. The perspective at the Canadian federal level reflected the fact that after World War II the two countries entered into a relationship which, not unfairly, Professor Maxwell Cohen was to describe as " 'The Period of Maturing Continental Partnership'—irascible but inevitable."[33] Difficulties were bound to develop between the two neighbours, and did, over a number of issues—such as the control of the Distant Early Warning (Radar) Line and the basing of American servicemen in Canada. At the same time a good deal of concern developed in Canada over such matters as the pervasive influence of American culture, and the strength of American economic penetration. These were widely held to be questions for federal, not provincial action, and were reflected in the "mild but widespread anti-Americanism"[34] which Professor Meisel saw prevailing in Canada in 1957, and which played some part in the triumph of Mr. Diefenbaker in 1957 and 1958. Caution is imperative here, and indeed one hesitates to raise this matter lest inaccurate conclusions be drawn. It would be grossly unfair to suggest that the federal government which represented Canada in the negotiations leading to and beyond the signing of the Columbia River Treaty did so with an anti-American bias. But to appreciate some of the actions of the Diefenbaker administration on this question, it is necessary to keep in mind the fact that Mr. Diefenbaker himself, and Mr. Howard Green, the secretary of state for external affairs after 1959, very deliberately sought to establish a distinctly independent foreign policy for Canada, and made no secret of their determination to resist American aggressiveness when it was perceived, and to ensure that Canadian decisions were made in Canada.[35]

3. THE PHYSICAL-DEVELOPMENTAL SETTING

The Canadian portion of the Columbia Basin (see Figure 1) which is located in south-eastern British Columbia, contains some 39,500 of the

FIGURE 1. Location and Major Subdivisions of the Columbia River Basin. (Adapted from: The Bureau of Reclamation, *The Columbia River*, A Comprehensive Report on the Development of the Water Resources of the British Columbia River Basin. Washington: U.S. Government Printing Office, February 1947.)

259,000 square miles in the entire watershed of this river. The main river has its origin at Columbia Lake (Figure 2) in the Rocky Mountain Trench in Canada at an altitude of 2,655 feet and falls 1,360 feet over a distance of 480 miles before it enters the United States. As it leaves Columbia Lake it is a modest stream with an average flow of 400 cubic feet per second (cfs), but by the time it crosses the international boundary, with an average flow of 94,000 cfs, it has become a major river. Numerous minor tributaries join the Columbia main stream as it first flows 210 miles north-west from Columbia Lake before turning at the Big Bend to run almost due south some 270 miles to the American border. In addition two major tributaries, both of real significance to the Columbia River Treaty, join the main stream in Canada.

25

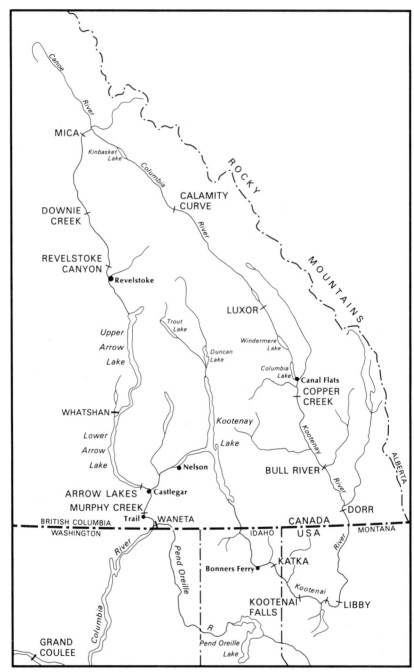

FIGURE 2. The Northern Portion of the Columbia River Basin.

One of these, the 464 mile long Kootenay (Kootenai in the United States) rises in the Rocky Mountains in Canada, passes at Canal Flats within a mile of Columbia Lake as it falls into the Rocky Mountain Trench, and flows in a south-easterly direction into the United States before looping to the west and north, returning to Canada to enter Kootenay Lake. From this natural reservoir it drops to join the Columbia River at Castlegar, twenty-nine miles north of the boundary. The other major river joining the Columbia main stream in Canada is the Pend d'Oreille, known in the United States as the Pend Oreille. Almost all of its watershed is in the United States, but the final seventeen miles of its course prior to its junction with the Columbia are just north of the international boundary in Canada. Overall, some 30 percent of the average annual run-off of the Columbia River is provided by the watershed which drains into the main stream above the junction with the Pend d'Oreille.[36]

Three characteristics of the river and its basin are particularly relevant to its development in Canada. One is that its combination of high flow[37] and great head makes its over-all potential for hydro-electric development unrivalled by that of any other river system on the North American continent. A second is that its run-off pattern is highly variable from region to region within the watershed, from month to month, and from year to year. Precipitation varies widely throughout the river basin. As has been noted already, the 13 percent of the watershed which drains into the Columbia River above Trail, B.C., produces 30 percent of the average annual flow. Actually, *in Canada* the Columbia and its tributaries are rather typical snow-melt rivers. In a normal year from 70 to 90 percent of the total annual discharge passes downstream in the five month period from April to August; on the main stream, peak flows normally occur during late May and June. It is the concentration of high flows during this period (when Pacific northwest power requirements are at their lowest level), the magnitude in the range of flow,[38] and the threat of major flood-damage which the concentration of flow entails that make storage so very significant on this river system. Actually, on the Kootenay River north from Bonners Ferry (in the United States and in Canada), and on the Columbia's main stream downstream from The Dalles (Figure 4), dyking operations which were begun in the closing years of the last century and were greatly extended during the first four decades of this one provided a considerable measure of protection to the flood plains. By 1940, for instance, they were capable of containing medium-sized floods, involving a run-off amounting, at The Dalles on the lower main stream, to about 800,000 cubic feet per second. The point of course is that periodically the river's discharge can greatly exceed this figure; it reached

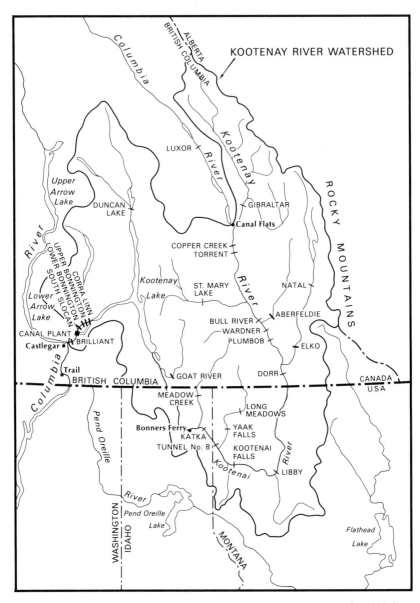

FIGURE 3. The Kootenay River Watershed. (Adapted from: International Columbia River Engineering Board, *Water Resources of the Columbia River Basin*, Report to the International Joint Commission, United States and Canada, 1959, Appendix II, Plate 1, after p. 55.)

1,240,000 cubic feet per second in the greatest flood of historic record in June 1894, and 1,010,000 cubic feet per second, in the second largest which occurred in May–June 1948. By 1959, storage provided on the American watershed in multi-purpose projects, developed since the early 'thirties, and amounting in all to 8,000,000 acre-feet by the latter date, did effect major relief from flood damage.[39] But the Corps of Engineers still calculated that between 8,000,000 and 11,000,000 acre-feet of additional storage, depending upon location, would be required to reduce a flood of 1894 dimensions to the primary manageable level of 800,000 cubic feet per second. Whether part or all of this storage—and more to provide streamflow regulation for power generation downstream—should be provided by Canada, from the 23 million acre feet which it had potentially available,[40] were to be the basic questions faced by Canadian policy-makers when they considered the prospect of the cooperative development of the basin.

The third characteristic of the Canadian watershed to keep in mind is that in it the most favourable and hence first developed damsites are found on such tributaries as the Lower Kootenay and the Pend d'Oreille, and on still smaller tributaries, the Whatshan, Bull, and Elk Rivers (See Figure 3). It is far from coincidence that, *in Canada*, prior to the negotiation of the Columbia River Treaty, there were no power developments on the main stream of the Columbia, or on the upper reaches of the Kootenay River. In both these latter water courses the rivers flow in ancient valleys, once scoured deep, but since built up over the valley floor with immense alluvial deposits of sand and gravel. Hydro-electric project construction in such valleys is difficult, but by no means unfeasible. By 1959, the record, of course, was very different in the American portion of the watershed. On the main stream itself over 780 of the 1280 feet of head below the international border had been developed in six major projects, and others were under construction or at the advanced planning stage to utilize virtually all of it (save at the marginal Ben Franklin site). About 5.5 million kilowatts of capacity had already been installed on the Columbia below the international border, and just over 2.5 million more were located in other parts of the American Basin.[41] (See Figure 4.) Overall in 1959, in the American watershed there were eleven major additional projects under construction, destined to provide a modest 1.5 million acre-feet of storage, but eventually over 4.1 million kilowatts of additional capacity.

For British Columbia there were considerations other than the difficulties of actual development which precluded for long a really serious examination of much of the hydraulic potential of this area. The population of the province was relatively small,[42] and its electric power base

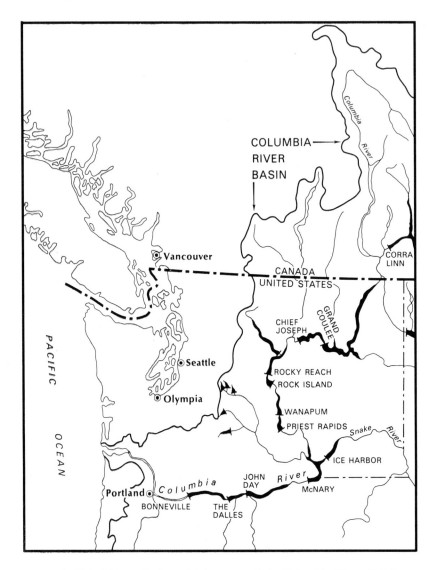

FIGURE 4. United States Projects, Mainstream of the Columbia River, Existing or Under Construction, 1960. (Adapted from: Water Management Subcommittee, Columbia Basin Inter-Agency Committee, *Report Summary of Operations, Columbia River, 1965 Flood*, March 1966, Exhibit 1.)

load was not large, especially when independent generation integral to electro-metallurgical operations is disregarded. Provincial power requirements increased rapidly during and after the Second World War, expanding at a rate of 9 percent per annum until 1954, and at almost 10 percent per annum between 1954 and 1962.[43] But, with one exception,[44] until 1955 and even later, the demand was met by comparatively modest in-scale developments on streams relatively close to the main load centres,[45] and by small thermal installations. A second additional explanation for the undeveloped state of the resource was the comparative isolation of the major power-producing sites in the area. The Mica Creek development, the largest projected for the Canadian section of the Columbia's watershed, is at least 400 transmission line miles from the major provincial market in Greater Vancouver. The cost of power production at such locations, the modest annual increments in provincial power demand, and the cost and very real technological problems associated with long-distance power transmission, all served as major deterrents to exploitation. Still another factor delaying Columbia River development in Canada was the existence of a national policy which effectively forestalled the exploitation of hydro electric resources ahead of domestic requirements, with surpluses committed on a long-range basis to the export market.

This last constraint on Canadian developmental planning was to be extraordinarily important in the evolution of a Canadian Columbia River policy.[46] Its origin, which will not be traced here, was rooted in difficulties which Canada experienced during the latter part of World War I, as she was attempting to reduce electrical energy exports being made under long term contract to the United States. Canadian experience at this time resulted in the emergence of a popular cliché, "Power exported is power lost!", and in a parallel conviction, which commanded very wide support in all party circles for forty years, that such exports should not be permitted in the future. The whole matter was debated in Parliament on many occasions over four decades. Eventually, with the passage of the National Energy Board Act in 1959, provision was made to license electric power exports for periods of up to twenty-five years, but an examination of the Parliamentary record makes it quite clear that this legislation did not in fact represent at that time a major change in government policy, any more than in opposition policy on this question.[47] After 1959, long-term power exports were possible, but some years were to pass before they were actively endorsed.[48]

Caution is imperative here. While the policy just referred to was primarily designed to forestall the export of significant blocks of firm power for long periods of time, it reflected a quite genuine concern with the consequences of the export of any sizeable quantity even on a short-term and interruptible basis. For example, a major effort of the Ontario Hydro-Electric Power Commission in 1937–38, when domestic capacity had outrun demand, to sell 120,000 kilowatt years of energy per annum to the United States on an interruptible basis came to naught because of that concern. And in the mid 'fifties, the federal government turned down an application from the Consolidated Mining and Smelting Company to export a large block of surplus energy from its Waneta development on the Pend d'Oreille to the Washington Water Power Company in the United States. However, the record does indicate that during the forty years after World War I, there were gradual intermittent increases in the amount of electricity exported to the United States on an annually-renewable, interruptible condition. Furthermore, after the Second World War, a number of major interconnection agreements were negotiated between neighbouring utilities in the two countries.[49]

Still, in Canada the widely held conviction remained, equating in an extraordinarily strong national consensus long-term and/or large power exports with the alienation of a national birthright. The maverick premier of Ontario, Mitchell Hepburn, had sought to challenge it in a carefully reasoned brief in the 'thirties, and had failed.[50] In the mid-to-later-'fifties a few farsighted Canadian laymen[51] began to join the increasing numbers of utility staff who felt the notion to be obsolete. But it was to take several years of explosive contact between another maverick premier (W. A. C. Bennett) and Canada's federal administration before the latter seriously questioned whether the considerations of the 'twenties or earlier were any longer relevant to those of the 'fifties and 'sixties, or, as some dispassionate observers were to suggest, whether the unfortunate consequences of the experience during World War I with early export contracts were not due "more to the 'nature of the arrangements' under which they were carried out, than to the fact that these arrangements were international in character."[52]

Finally, it is important to keep in mind that policy concerning the cooperative development of the Columbia River emerged within the context of different national approaches to the tensions so often related to the coexistence of public and private-sector power generation. Although, by 1950, public sector power was much more significant, on a national basis, in Canada than it was in the United States, this was not so with respect to British Columbia and the American Pacific northwest. The public power sector in British Columbia while growing, was small. It was much larger in the adjacent American states—in relative and absolute terms—even if at the same time it was fragmented. Thus, while some of the most widely recognized parts of the Americans' public power sector were the work of those major federal agencies, the Bureau of Reclamation and the Corps of Engineers, a good deal of it was the result of non-federal public investment by such instrumentalities as municipalities and public utility districts. During the years of the Eisenhower presidency (1953–61), the American national administration actively pursued a "Partnership Policy," which was intended to discourage throughout the United States the building of additional power plants under federal auspices. It was extended to the Columbia, and had the unexpected effect, when pursued within the framework of the American Federal Power Act, of discouraging those non-federal entities which did move ahead with new projects in the Columbia valley from building into them extensive storage capacity. During the 'fifties, as a consequence, the power system in the American watershed became "unbalanced," and in the later years of that decade a major objective of American policy became the acquisition of additional flow-regulating storage. This, of course, Canada was quite prepared to provide, under a set of agreed-upon conditions. As the reader will gather in chapter 7, this self-imposed constraint on American decision-making was to be modified in 1961 by the new Democratic administration and Congress in Washington, which were prepared to, and did, sponsor power-cum-storage project construction under federal auspices. What this policy change meant for the United States after 1960 was the revival of a number of options (such as the building of storage in the American section of the Columbia watershed, and an intertie linking the power systems of the Pacific northwest and southwest) which in part at least were alternatives to cooperative development, and which were less than enthusiastically considered by the Americans themselves during the formative years of the Columbia River Treaty.[53]

In British Columbia a different set of forces was at work. During the late 'forties and the 'fifties four major public utilities were engaged in power generation there. Three were privately owned—the B.C. Electric Company, the West, and the East Kootenay Power companies. The largest by far of these was the B.C. Electric, which serviced the province's two major metropolitan areas on southern Vancouver Island and the southwestern mainland. Its role in the public affairs of the province is difficult to describe briefly and fairly. With guidance, if not active encouragement, from the then Coalition premier, John Hart, the cities of Victoria and Vancouver seriously considered the prospect of "taking it over" during the 1945–46 winter. The B.C. Electric successfully resisted this move, and in the decade which followed actively sought to demonstrate that its previously rather lethargic leadership had been transformed. Wisely in the late 'forties it was very optimistic about load growth increases, and it successfully developed a reputation for aggressive building, for keeping ahead of, and indeed for generating demand, for technical competence, for model employer-employee relations, and for its support of good works in the community. On the other hand, to some degree offsetting these achievements, by the mid 'fifties, there was a public impression that the B.C. Electric was rather extravagant, and, furthermore, that it had become a major source of funds for the Social Credit party. By this date it had largely exploited the hydro-electric resources close to its major markets, and, indeed, as its load continued to expand, it had proposed that it develop the Columbia on its own, only to be turned down by Mr. Bennett.[54] Still, it remained very much interested in access to Columbia River power. Its ability to look at sites farther afield, and in a way Mr. Bennett's own decision-making, were complicated by the existence of the fourth of the provincial utilities, the publicly-owned B.C. Power Commission.

This instrumentality of the province had been created in 1945, and had commenced operations at that time by expropriating the properties of

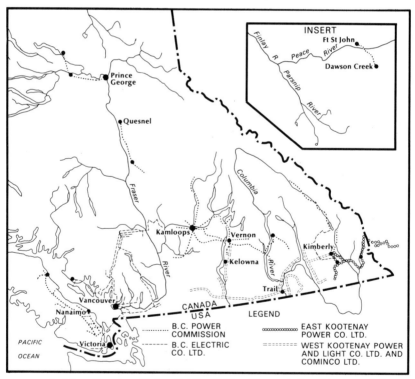

FIGURE 5. Map Showing Major Public Utility Transmission Lines, and hence Major Service Areas, British Columbia, 1960.

several small utilities, serving approximately 13,000 customers. During the next decade its customers increased rapidly in number through the expansion of existing and the acquisition of further service areas, although the customer density of its circuits in 1958 was below that of 1948.[55] By 1956, it was responsible for serving all but the lower part of Vancouver Island, and much of the mainland of the province—excepting, of course, the hinterland of Greater Vancouver, the west and southeast Kootenay areas, and the Prince Rupert market. (See Figure 5.) Between March 31, 1948, and March 31, 1958, the Power Commission's capacity increased from 14,750 to 324,735 kilowatts. After 1952 it was particularly hard-pressed to keep up with expanding demand, especially on Vancouver Island, where a large-scale expansion in the pulp and paper industry took place. Numerous small hydro-electric developments were pushed ahead, not infrequently in conflict with the fisheries resource, and an expansion of storage for its major, still modest generating plant at Campbell River, was delayed in a contest with recreation/conservation interests. Much of its load in the provincial interior was met by diesel electric generation. During this period its relations with its neighbours—the B.C. Electric and West Kootenay Companies—can only be described as correct, but rather distant. These utilities were rivals on the margins of some of their service areas. They were interconnected for emergency purposes, but were certainly not integrated in their operations. The B.C. Power Commission enjoyed a good public image for most of its existence. Some of its staff were very conscious of the much larger scale on which the B.C. Electric operated,[56] and, during the 'fifties, resented what they regarded as the rather patronizing air of the major private utility. Some of them also were passionate public power advocates and, by 1956, were prepared to argue publicly that the commission could produce much cheaper energy from the Columbia than could any private utility. In any case, by 1956, not only was the B.C. Electric expecting to add 1,500,000 kilowatts to its capacity over the next decade, but the Power Commission, also running short of energy, was looking for a new major development which would meet its needs for some years to come, and would put it in the category of a major producer.

Finally, it is important to recall that, for a variety of reasons (including the size and ruggedness of the province, the number of small thermal plants in use and the low density of distribution circuits already referred to), privately and publicly produced electricity in British Columbia was relatively expensive during the post-1945 years. Both the B.C. Electric and the Power Commission were (unhappily) well aware of this. Thus anyone reconstructing the Canadian decision-making on the Columbia two decades ago should keep in mind the desire of British Columbia's

35

utilities to obtain an assured supply of energy for the long-term market, and the appeal (especially for the Power Commission) associated with the possible assumption of major developmental responsibilities. But they should also keep in mind the extent to which an acute sensitivity to past and future power costs was likely to characterize the assessment of developmental options by decision-makers both in the province's public utility and in its political systems.

PART TWO

Chapter Three

The Canadian Approach to the Columbia
in the Pre-Diefenbaker Years

Choice, inescapably, is choice among thoughts,
and thoughts are not given.
G. L. S. Shackle, *Decision, Order and Time in Human Affairs*

Until the Second World War, and indeed later, Canadians' knowledge of
the resources of the Upper Columbia and Kootenay River valleys was
scarcely comprehensive. Fur traders and explorers had traversed the area
early in the nineteenth century, and after 1860 prospectors had combed
it for mineral wealth. It was crossed by a transcontinental railway in the
1880s, and, even before 1900, there had been considerable exploitation
of its forest resource. Nevertheless, as late as 1943, there was no good
topographical map of the upper reaches of the Columbia River watershed
in Canada.[1] The area was very sparsely settled, and much remained to be
learned concerning its geology and its hydrology.

During the 1920s the Canadian Pacific Railway Company examined
the hydro-electric potential of the Upper Columbia in connection with a
proposed electrification of its mountain division, but nothing came of this.
Hydro-electric development was, of course, not unknown in the Columbia's watershed in Canada; it dated back, in fact, to the 1890s. But, as
noted in the preceding chapter, it involved, primarily, small projects on
Kootenay River tributaries in the Rocky Mountain trench and, up to
1939, five generating stations at four dams on the Lower Kootenay River
between Kootenay Lake and the junction of the West Kootenay River
with the Columbia at Castlegar, B.C. The great majority of these were
primarily run-of-the-river plants involving little storage and no significant
change in transboundary flow. But it should be recorded that, in 1938,
after years of extended negotiations, the West Kootenay Power and Light

Company did receive the approval of the IJC to impound 670,000 acre-feet of water on Kootenay Lake in order that it, and its parent (the Consolidated Mining and Smelting Company), might increase the output of their plants on the Lower Kootenay.[2]

During the 'thirties, Canadians had watched with great interest the construction of the first of the major American projects on the lower main stream of the Columbia,[3] and some Canadians—not many—began to ponder the benefits which projects in British Columbia designed to effect significant regulation of streamflow would confer on the downstream riparian.[4] One of these Canadians was the premier of British Columbia, T. D. Pattullo, who wrote to Prime Minister W. L. Mackenzie King on May 2, 1939, asking that the whole question of Columbia River storage with extra-national significance be referred to the IJC "for study with the object of ultimately arriving at an agreement whereby the costs of the works involved would be allocated to the respective countries according to the benefits to be divided."

Mr. King, in his reply, dated June 5, 1939, declined to act at this time, as he anticipated that an extended reference to the commission would involve difficult negotiations. "In circumstances of this sort," he suggested, "it would be most desirable to have the initiative taken by the country that would secure the greater part of the benefit." In other words, he advised, let the United States make the first move. It is quite clear from these exchanges that both these Canadians and their staff advisers had a very real perception of significant benefits which might accrue to Canada from Columbia Valley storage above the forty-ninth parallel, provided the entire matter were carefully handled.

As it turned out, the American overture was not long in coming. Rapidly expanding demands for electricity in the American Pacific northwest during the middle years of the Second World War prompted a request from energy customers there that the chief of engineers, United States Army, review and if necessary augment by further studies the Army's 308 Report of 1932[5]—the first comprehensive assessment of the Columbia River resource. It soon became apparent in Washington that a consideration of the entire watershed appeared to make the most sense. A joint investigation was proposed to Canada in an American diplomatic note dated October 4, 1943; detailed consultations quickly followed, and the two countries submitted a reference on the matter to the IJC on March 9, 1944. The reference asked the commission, in the light of the investigative capacity conferred on it by Article IX of the Boundary Waters Treaty, to consider the international implications of the development of the Columbia River. More specifically, it asked that the commission determine "whether in its judgment further development of the water resources of the river basin would be practicable and in the public interest from the points of view of the two governments, having in mind (a) domestic water supply and sanitation, (b) navigation, (c) efficient development of water power, (d) the control of floods, (e) the needs of irrigation, (f) reclamation of wet lands, (g) conservation of fish and wild life, and (h) other beneficial public purposes." It required the commission, should it find further works feasible and desirable, to indicate how "the interests on either side of the boundary would be benefited or adversely affected thereby," and to estimate costs, both of damage and of remedial works. Furthermore, the commission was to indicate "how the costs of any projects and the amounts of any resulting damage may be apportioned between the two governments."[6] Note that this comprehensive reference did not ask the IJC to deal explicitly with the question of determining and apportioning any benefits which might be derived from projects within the basin having extra-national effects.

The IJC lost no time in creating investigative and advisory machinery with which to pursue this mandate. As the senior advisory body to it, it created an International Columbia River Engineering Board (referred to hereafter as ICREB), with two members drawn from each country. The ICREB, in turn, set up an Engineering Committee, made up initially of two federal government representatives from each country. This body constituted a Working Group of engineers and officials drawn from both countries, to which were assigned the twin tasks of obtaining the data required and of undertaking much of the necessary analysis. With only a modest staff of its own, and with limited resources, the IJC, in effect, turned back to the two governments much of the responsibility for the work to be done under its general direction.

1. THE FIRST DECADE

During the years 1944 to 1954 the working relationship between the governments of Canada and British Columbia, as they collaborated in this exercise in comprehensive analysis (as then understood) was, generally speaking, a close one. There was extensive consultation with the province on all significant matters—for instance, in the exchanges which led to the Columbia River reference to the IJC in 1944. Some differences between Victoria and Ottawa did emerge during this first decade, but the crucial ones (which were not numerous) were resolved, and the less significant, if not settled, were lived with quietly.

One matter which did become the subject of some intra-Canadian disagreement, although it was not pursued publicly, was the staffing of the IJC teams. In 1944, as if to emphasize its prerogative in the field of international affairs, Canada's federal government placed only personnel from its own departments on the ICREB, the Engineering Committee, and the Working Group. Four years later, apparently in response to pressure from British Columbia, it added to the Engineering Committee Mr. George Melrose, who was not only the province's deputy minister of lands, but also the province's senior civil service adviser on Columbia matters.[7] Later in the same year, a provincial engineer was added to the Working Group.[8] Subsequently Mr. Melrose attended a number of meetings of the ICREB, but neither he nor his successor was ever made a member of it, in spite of some pointed provincial government references in the mid 'fifties to the omission.

A proper appreciation of the manner in which Victoria and Ottawa cooperated in their approach to the Columbia during the 1944–54 decade can best be gained by an examination of the responses of these governments to two American initiatives which were directly related to the great Columbia flood of May–June, 1948. The torrent of waters in that year breached the dykes on the Kootenay River south of Kootenay Lake in Canada and the United States; it inundated part of Trail, B.C.; and, in the United States, it took fifty lives and caused property damage in excess of a hundred million dollars. As might be expected, the disaster evoked a number of plans designed to prevent a recurrence. One such plan was advanced by former United States Senator Clarence Dill, a consulting attorney closely associated with the Bonneville Power Administration, who was concerned not only about the recent floods but also by the decline in the firm power output at Grand Coulee as a result of its reservoir drawdown in midwinter. He proposed to Premier Byron Johnson of British Columbia that a dam be built at the foot of the Arrow Lakes to impound approximately four million acre-feet of water, without flooding above normal high water level. Such a reservoir, he estimated, would permit an increase in American firm power output downstream of up to 700,000 kw. British Columbia, he assured the premier and E. T. Kenny, the provincial minister of lands and forests, would be "well rewarded for any assistance it would render."[9]

Mr. Dill found Premier Johnson a sympathetic listener, albeit one who was convinced that further discussion of Mr. Dill's plan would be fruitless until the ICREB had endorsed it as part of the overall development of the river. The premier was obviously convinced that the approach to comprehensive planning embodied in the IJC reference should not be set aside, and accepted the assurance given four years earlier to the House of Commons by Mr. King that the investigation under IJC auspices would lead to "a complete and detailed report on the best uses to which the waters of this vast river basin can be put."[10] But he was prepared to be helpful; he went to Ottawa, discussed Mr. Dill's plan with the federal government, and seems to have taken the position, with which Ottawa agreed, that "it would be entirely advisable to accept the responsibility for speeding up the studies to see whether or not we can assist our neighbours to the south without damaging ourselves."[11] At the same time Mr. Johnson encouraged Mr. Dill to pursue the matter with his own government. This Mr. Dill promptly did, going straight to President Truman. The upshot was that the ICREB was requested to produce by April 1949, a special review of the projected Arrow Lakes Dam.

Actually the ICREB's report on the Arrow Lakes proposal dashed Mr. Dill's hopes, for it pointed out that a dam at this site would take five years to construct, and this would not help meet the immediate power shortage in the Pacific northwest states. It also pointed out that a much larger structure than the one he proposed could be built at the location in question. Mr. Dill's proposal was held to possess very limited prospects for at-site power production, and to provide only limited additional flood control. For the moment, as a consequence, Mr. Dill had to give way, although as will become apparent he did not give up.[12]

The Canadian Response to the Libby Dam Proposal. The second American proposal advanced in the wake of the 1948 flood was one for a multi-purpose project to be constructed in the United States on the Kootenay River, near Libby in Montana. (See Figure 3.) It was designed to impound over 4,000,000 acre-feet of live storage, and, as the largest American storage project in the watershed after Grand Coulee, was expected to eliminate completely the possibility of future flooding of the alluvial lands which flank the Kootenay River from Bonners Ferry in Idaho north into Canada. It was expected also to reduce materially flooding in the United States on the lower main stream of the Columbia below The Dalles, and to produce both at-site power and even more electrical energy downstream.

As the Libby Reservoir would flood above the border into Canada, the project required the approval of the IJC, and was brought to that body's attention when it held hearings on the Columbia River Basin during July 1948. Reflecting the enthusiasm of the project's sponsors, the Corps of Engineers, and a good deal of strong support from parts of southeastern British Columbia,[13] the ICREB presented a statement to the commission during a public hearing at Bonners Ferry which declared that studies concerning a high dam at Libby had proceeded far enough "to determine that this project is a desirable first step towards a comprehensive plan" for flood control and other water use. The ICREB affirmed "that the Libby Project can be adopted at this time" subject to later adjustments in the reservoir level to meet Canadian planning requirements, and subject, in addition, to a determination of costs, including indemnification for damages incurred in Canada and in the United States.[14] During the summer of 1949 the ICREB also moved to produce a more comprehensive report on the entire Kootenay.

When the seriousness of the Americans' interest in the Libby project became so apparent, two basic issues faced Canadian policy-makers. One, which was viewed as a technical problem, required an accelerated examination of the Upper Kootenay valley in British Columbia for potential damsites which might be submerged by the Libby reservoir, and then a decision as to those which, in the light of a suitable international agreement, Canada might forgo. The question to be resolved here was just how far into Canada the reservoir should be allowed to extend, and it was tackled jointly by the technical staffs of the province's Water Resources Branch, the federal Water and Power Bureau, and the federal Department of Public Works. Actually the bulk of the Canadian analysis at this time was produced by engineering personnel employed by the federal government. Their efforts were supplemented by those of at least one consulting engineering firm engaged by Ottawa before enough data had been acquired to permit the federal and provincial technicians to agree that the Libby reservoir might be allowed to stretch north to, but not to interfere with, a proposed Bull River project site on the Kootenay in Canada. At this level the Libby reservoir would inundate a number of relatively small project sites, including those at Dorr and Plumbob.

The other problem faced by the Canadians in 1949–50 was addressed exclusively by British Columbia. It had two dimensions. One involved assessing the costs of acquiring the Libby reservoir area in Canada, both in terms of direct expenditures required and in terms of income subsequently forgone. A carefully documented answer to this question was produced by a major inter-departmental effort at the provincial level between the early months of 1949 and the middle of 1950. The other dimension involved settling upon just what British Columbia's request for compensation should be if it were to consent to a Libby clearance.

A review of the province's working files for these years makes it quite evident that Premier Johnson's Coalition Cabinet relied heavily on the advice of its senior civil service advisers for answers to both these sets of questions.[15] It is also apparent that well before 1949 was over these provincial civil servants were convinced that the compensation accruing to Canada over Libby should be far more than an all-inclusive reimbursement for the costs of providing the reservoir. They were very conscious of the fact that most of the Kootenay's flow originates in Canada, that the proposed Libby reservoir, flooding back into Canada, would be up to 150 feet deep at the international border, and that virtually all of the live storage on the American side would be made possible by the correspond- ing storage in Canada.[16] They also were convinced that an agreement over Libby's reservoir would be a crucial test of the Canadian hope to obtain an American recognition of, and a willingness to share, the downstream benefits which would accrue to the United States from other Canadian Columbia watershed storage. Reasoning that the Libby decision would create a precedent, and that the province would be contributing water, head, and a significant block of storage, they came to think of the Libby project as a "joint venture," to envisage it as one in which the province might participate with respect to benefits and costs, with the province's share of the costs being met out of the sale of a block of the energy allocated to it.[17] A number of variations of this position were developed, some by mid-year 1949, and were subsequently argued out in the Cana- dian sections of the Engineering Committee and the Working Group by provincial technicians with their federal colleagues.

While not all of the records for the years 1944-54 are available, this much is clear. The commitment of the Corps of Engineers to Libby be- came firmer than ever over the winter of 1949-50, and the project was authorized by Congress in the Rivers and Harbors and Flood Control Act of 1950. Later in that year, on November 1, the ICREB presented its interim report on the Kootenay River Basin to the IJC. With reference to Libby it simply endorsed a 2459-foot reservoir level, and concluded that a Libby-Bull River combination of projects was "economically feasible"[18] and superior to a Libby-Plumbob alternative against which it had been assessed. While the accompanying letter of transmittal from the board drew attention to a number of other matters not dealt with in its report (including a consideration of benefits and costs), the overall tenor of the report was favourable to Libby, and undoubtedly it reinforced the im- pression, which the province's technical staff had already arrived at, that ultimately, if asked, the ICREB would formally recommend Libby for clearance.

The manner in which the two Canadian governments approached the formal American application for permission to build the Libby Dam which the United States filed with the IJC on January 12, 1951, is illuminating, for it reflects the differing perspectives of the national interest which so often emerge at the two basic levels of jurisdiction in a federal state. The Johnson Cabinet in British Columbia and its advisers insisted that the province must be regarded as a partner contributing essential head, water, and storage in return for a share of the output of the project. One way or another, as already observed, they were deter- mined at that point in the Columbia planning process to otbain some agreement on a "downstream benefits" principle to apply, subsequently, to other storage in the Canadian watershed. The federal government appears to have been no less keen than British Columbia to obtain a favourable agreement, but it also appears to have been much more sensitive to the potential costs to Canada as a whole of a major frustration of a strongly-held American desire. As the time for the public hearings scheduled on the Libby application approached on February 2, 1951, Prime Minister St. Laurent wrote Premier Johnson asking for the closest possible liaison between federal and provincial officials to ensure that the Canadian views presented to the commission were consistent. The liaison was effected, and the requisite coordination was obtained—although it was not complete.

On the basis of the limited record available, it is not possible to be precise either about the extent of, or the primary source of the differing emphases in the formal views of the federal and provincial governments as these emerged in 1951. The evidence does suggest that senior federal officials felt that the province was going too far when it revealed its intention to ask (1) for compensation to cover its complete reservoir-costs, (2) for a recognition of its contribution to the head, flow, and storage at Libby, and (3) for some share of the downstream benefits attributable to Libby's stream-flow regulation.[19] Certainly, when the public hearings on the Libby application were held at Cranbrook, B.C., in March 1951, the federal government simply declared that Canada did not oppose the application, but felt that approval should be conditional on the protection and indemnification of all interests in Canada, and should involve a "fair recompense to Canada for the utilization in the project of Canadian national resources."[20] The much lengthier provincial statement asked for compensation for all the direct and indirect costs which would devolve on it because of Libby. It asked also that approval be contingent on the provision to British Columbia at the international border of a block of electrical energy as deemed appropriate by the IJC "in recognition of the physical contribution of British Columbia to the project."[21] And it suggested, finally, that no order of approval be issued until the Engineering Board had reported with respect to the allocation to the two countries of the benefits to be derived from the proposed works including, by inference, those produced downstream.

While provincial spokesmen were making formal representations to the IJC, they were also arguing their case in the commission's infra-structure, for the Work Group and the Engineering Committee laboured during the 1950–51 winter on a report to the ICREB on Libby itself. Here at the Work Group and Engineering Committee levels, the province appears to have met with considerable success, for the latter body did apparently recommend to the ICREB a formula which went some considerable way to meet the province's request. The essence of this proposed arrangement was that the province would be ceded 13,300 kw years of energy per annum to cover its Libby reservoir costs,[22] and, as compensation for its resource contribution, the right to purchase up to 69,400 kw years of energy per annum at the wholesale price paid by American customers of the Bonneville Power Administration.[23] When, however, this proposal went to the ICREB that body refused to endorse it, and simply relayed it in its own report to the commission about Libby, in May 1951, as a suggestion which might prove helpful. At this time the ICREB, making little direct reference to costs, did conclude that the construction of the Libby Dam would be "mutually beneficial"[24] by referring to the manner in which it would produce a major flood control benefit and would add to power resources. It said nothing concerning the determination of or division of downstream benefits in its recommendation.[25]

The American response to the province's claim appears to have been signalled by the American technical personnel on the ICREB, and soon was made quite explicit by the Hon. A. O. Stanley, chairman, American Section, IJC, and by at least one other American commissioner. They were convinced that British Columbia was being unreasonable, and talked of withdrawing entirely the Libby proposal. The province's response to this riposte was twofold. In a brief to the IJC submitted by letter on August 31, 1951, it restated its hope to achieve a Libby settlement which would serve as a helpful precedent for other developments in the Columbia's watershed. At the same time it nominally modified its compensatory claim, eliminating the request for a share of Libby's downstream benefits, and claiming a right to purchase, at United States system prices, an increased share of Libby's at-site generation. The annual amount of energy required to meet the province's reservoir expenses was now set by the province at 14,300 kw years[26] and the block of energy which it wished to be able to purchase was raised to 109,000 kw years annually (or 44 percent of Libby's average output).[27]

The second provincial move was to reassess quietly its entire position on the Columbia. To the staff who conducted the analysis, the alternatives open to British Columbia clearly ranged between two extremes. One, regarded as the least favourable to the province, was the viewpoint advanced by Mr. Stanley and his associates. In essence it was an American undertaking (1) to pay in cash, not power, all the costs involved in constructing the Canadian portion of the reservoir, including those involved in the relocation of displaced individuals, and (2) to waive any American claim (a) to the considerable increase in potential power production downstream *in Canada* which would be made possible by the

Libby reservoir, and (b) to the protection of Canadian lands south of Kootenay Lake. The Americans did recognize that Canada was entitled to compensation for the loss of the power-producing potential in the forty-two miles of the Kootenay Valley in Canada which Libby would inundate, but suggested that this loss would be more than balanced off by the un-divided power and flood control benefit enjoyed downstream *in Canada*. The most favourable alternative, if also the most unrealistic, appeared to be the proposal of the B.C. Electric Company's chief engineer to the effect that Canada demand one-third the direct electrical output of Libby at no cost, and the right to purchase one-half its downstream power benefit at U.S. system wholesale prices. Somewhere between these positions, the province's advisers hoped to strike a bargain.

The provincial civil servants were well aware that their government was in a delicate position as it launched itself on a bargaining exercise with two national governments. As has been noted already, in southeastern British Columbia itself, parts of which anticipated securing a considerable benefit if Libby were built, there had already emerged a good deal of support for this project, and a desire to be consulted seriously about it. Furthermore, they were well aware that the greater part of the electrical energy available for public consumption in the province was the product of the three private power utilities—the East Kootenay, West Kootenay, and B.C. Electric companies (especially the last two).[28] They knew that the provincial government was prepared to consult quietly with these utilities, as well as with the publicly-owned British Columbia Power Commission, as to the tactical position it should advance vis-à-vis the Libby application. But they also knew that when the province had done this, and had privately asked these concerns for their views as to the form (cash or power) in which they felt the compensation being asked of the United States should be made available to Canada, it had elicited some very conflicting advice. The East Kootenay Power and Light and the B.C. Electric companies had come down on the side of a benefit in the form of power, and for a generally tough line with the Americans.[29] On the other hand, the provincial B.C. Power Commission was not nearly so aggressive, and suggested taking cash. And to complicate matters the West Kootenay Power and Light Company, or more accurately, its parent, Cominco,[30] pointed out in October 1951 that the Libby project was a singularly in-appropriate one on which to rest a case for a Canadian downstream benefit claim. It drew attention also to the fact that it had filed with the IJC an application to build a project at Waneta on the Pend d'Oreille *after the Americans had submitted theirs over Libby*, that the two were now being treated as one by the American Section of the commission, and that in one sense if the downstream benefits case were extended from

Libby storage in Canada to Kootenay Lake storage in Canada and Pend d'Oreille-Clark Fork storage in the United States "a logical consequence, would, if anything, give the United States grounds for claiming power from Canada."[31]

There were, of course, other difficulties. A predisposition at senior levels in Ottawa to favour a moderate stance vis-à-vis the United States was one, already referred to. Another was the fact that, while there was significant domestic American opposition to those alternative projects to Libby to which the United States did not hesitate to threaten to turn, clearly there were some limits beyond which that country could not afford to go if it also were to derive a benefit from this trans-boundary project. The reports of the Engineering Committee had made it quite apparent that Libby's construction would not be justified on the basis of the at-site benefits alone which it created. The problem lay in discerning the location of the Americans' "cut-off" point. The provincial staff advisers, furthermore, were not unaware of the complexity of the downstream benefits case which they were advancing, and of the hazards involved in associating it with a trans-boundary project such as Libby. They were prepared to concede "that there is some truth in the contention that in buying at the *system rate* we are in effect getting downstream benefits." They were also not insensitive to the hazard of claiming a downstream benefit from Libby but not agreeing to one over Waneta. On this issue their staff assessment noted tersely: "Any arguments we make for downstream benefits from Libby will backfire here."

But when they weighed all these considerations, the provincial advisers ended up by reaffirming conclusions which they had arrived at earlier. They were prepared to dedicate 13,600 acres of Canadian land to perpetual use in the Libby reservoir, "from the land use standpoint and for the best permanent welfare of the province,"[32]—provided the covering agreements were acceptable. They were as convinced that the American "offer" was unacceptable as they were insistent that the province would have to exert some leverage on the United States to upgrade it. That they had searched for other uses of the Kootenay River involving the transfer of at least part of its flow to other watersheds is evident from their observation, "there are no apparent river diversions which could be made at a profit," before they went on to enunciate the strategic position on which the Canadian position rested for much of the ensuing decade—"the only successful counter threat appears to be the withholding of agreement on Libby and the Skagit."[33]

Here, in essence, was the origin of the deadlock over the Libby application and indeed over much of the Columbia policy planning which bedevilled the IJC during the next seven years. The deadlock was made

official in March 1952, when Mr. Stanley's reply to the Canadian statements and brief was sent formally, by letter, to the chairman of the
Canadian Section, IJC.[34] It was not affected by the collapse of the provincial Coalition government in January of that year. The province was
well aware of its latent power of veto over any Columbia River arrangement to which it did not subscribe, and expected the federal government,
whether happy or not, to continue quietly adjusting or accommodating to
this fact.[35] There was, indeed, only one significant change in the manner
in which Canadian Columbia River development policy was pursued
during the first six months of 1952. General A. G. L. McNaughton, who
had become first a member of the Canadian Section, IJC, and then its
chairman, in 1950, wrote to the governments of Canada and British
Columbia, relaying Mr. Stanley's letter and asking for their views on it.
He also arranged to visit Premier Johnson in Victoria in June. The point
to note here is the extent to which the Canadian Section chairman seems
to have been overtly moving at this time to assume a role as a synthesizer
and perhaps as an initiator of Canadian policy.

General McNaughton's enquiry concerning Senator Stanley's letter in
March–April 1952, was referred by the Johnson administration in British
Columbia to its staff advisers, who prepared a carefully reasoned reply.
It had not been approved, however, before the June 1952 election in
British Columbia effectively ended that government's mandate. As a
result, a draft response to the Canadian Section chairman was placed
before Mr. Bennett and his new Social Credit Cabinet late in August, and
apparently was forwarded on August 25.[36] The evidence available would
seem to indicate that no real change was effected in the province's position,
which appears to have been argued even more vigorously than on previous
occasions. The belief that the nature of a Libby settlement would establish
a key precedent, and the province's assumption that both countries would
profit from cooperative acts were emphasized. Once again the province
requested 14,300 kw of firm power annually to cover its Libby costs, and
the right to purchase 109,000 kw of additional energy at the American
system wholesale price. It now enumerated a long series of additional
protective clauses which, to preserve its integrity, it claimed should be
inserted in any agreement. The reply sought to turn around on the Americans an argument which they had advanced with respect to the St. John
River in 1925. Much was made of the pressure under which the IJC staff
groups were required to work in the years 1949–51, and of the limited
number of alternatives which the province had been able to examine in
that time. Apparently the province's reply went on to argue that "if
Canadians are to be precluded from the benefits, it would be to our interest
to exhaustively examine the reservoir area." The implicit threat here to

search more diligently for viable alternative uses for Kootenay River water, and hence possibly for alternatives to Libby, was to be taken more seriously by the Canadian Section chairman than those at the time responsible for provincial Columbia policy formation might have expected.

Changing Perspectives in Victoria. While the new Social Credit administration appears at the outset to have accepted a position paper prepared for its predecessor, in its approach to the Columbia it soon began to develop its own emphases. The new provincial minister of lands, R. L. Sommers, was himself a resident of the Columbia Valley and knew the area well. Almost at the moment he was sworn into office he found that the preceding government had been on the verge of completing an agreement with the city of Seattle to raise the level of the Ross Dam reservoir on the Skagit River, and to flood across the border into southwestern British Columbia. (See Figure 6.) The province, indeed, had already undertaken to accept a lump sum payment of $255,508 as adequate compensation for losses incurred by that flooding. Sensing that the principle enshrined in this agreement conflicted with the evolving Canadian demand over the Libby reference for a continuing return from storage in Canadian reservoirs, Mr. Sommers and his colleagues held up final approval of this arrangement.

In December 1952, Mr. Bennett, Mr. Sommers, and colleagues received a visit from General McNaughton which in the short run, at least, resulted in a considerable meeting of minds.[37] In the course of their exchanges, the general proposed, and Mr. Bennett agreed to, the creation of a provincial Advisory Committee on the Development of the Columbia River Basin. The committee, which was not constituted until November 1953, held a number of meetings during 1954, but was then allowed to fade quietly from the scene.[38]

While the working relationship between the new Social Credit administration and the government of Canada was correct, if not close, between 1952 and 1954, it is important to note that, after they received a clear majority at the 1953 election, Mr. Bennett and his colleagues gradually became restive about some aspects of the manner in which Canadian policy over the Columbia River was evolving. They were quite prepared to continue the provincial staff contribution to the IJC's studies, and, furthermore, barring an acceptable American policy decision to concede a Canadian claim for downstream benefits, to sustain the veto established earlier over Libby. When the United States resubmitted its Libby application in 1954, the province cooperated closely with Ottawa in preparing replies to it, and, interestingly enough, now found the federal government

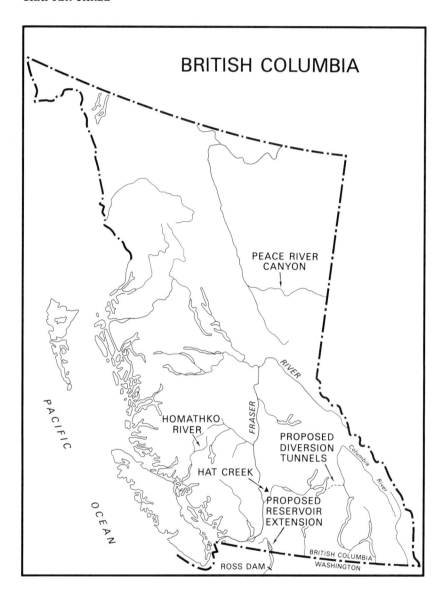

FIGURE 6. Location of Projected Developments in British Columbia.

prepared to be as tough over this question as it was. Thus both Canadian governments in their statements of response filed with the IJC referred to the possibility of diverting the Kootenay River (in effect, making the Libby project unfeasible), and requested a share of Libby's downstream benefits, compensation for losses incurred in the Libby reservoir flooding, and payment for the use of Canadian natural resources, which the province suggested be based on her contribution of head and storage.[39] Both governments repeated the province's 1951 claims, and British Columbia this time added a few more of its own, including a request for a board of control on which it would be represented.

In view of arguments such as these, the Canadian Section of the IJC appears to have had little difficulty in blocking any real progress on the Libby application, even to the extent of successfully opposing the holding of public hearings on it.[40] The stalemate, however, was anything but pleasing to Mr. Bennett and his colleagues as they reviewed the impasse on the Columbia in the light of their increasing determination to accelerate the pace and scale of natural resource development throughout the province. From this perspective they became increasingly disturbed at the prospect, which General McNaughton seemed to take for granted, that there would be no further exploitation of the Columbia River resource in Canada until the comprehensive ICREB Report on the Columbia River had been completed near the end of the decade.[41]

For a number of years British Columbia's minister of lands, Mr. Sommers, played a leading part in attempts to stimulate some action in the Columbia basin, while urging concurrently an acceleration of the pace at which the IJC was working. On several occasions he suggested that the province might abandon its opposition to the Libby project provided that the United States federal Power Commission gave permission to the Westcoast Transmission Company to export gas from the Peace River area of British Columbia to the American Pacific northwest.[42] He also began to argue that, as the Columbia River was not a boundary water, neither the IJC nor the government of Canada had direct jurisdiction over it. He emphasized this view when speaking before the policy group of the Pacific Northwest Governors' Power Policy Committee, with which group he sat.[43] And he seconded to the Engineering Committee of that body a project engineer from the British Columbia Water Resources Service.

The province's restiveness stemmed from yet another consideration, however, for it gradually became aware of the fact that while federal ministers were noticeably reticent in public about Columbia River development policy, from 1953 on, General McNaughton was becoming very much the reverse. In that year, for instance, he inaugurated the first of a series of annual oral presentations, which were extended over a decade, before the Standing Committee on External Affairs of the House of Commons. In them, he reported at length on the activities of the IJC, and, repeatedly, dealt with the Columbia River reference and the Libby applications. As the able, lucid man he was, he greatly impressed members of Parliament and the public at large with his passionate concern to advance Canadian interests. Increasingly, back-bench and opposition Parliamentarians and the public, too, came to assume that he was speaking for the Canadian governments concerned. During the years 1952–54 the St. Laurent administration in Ottawa seems to have been singularly insensitive about the manner in which the general's initiatives, often taken without consultation, and his increasingly categoric assessments of the merits and demerits of some Canadian watershed projects and sequences, seemed to justify this public assumption concerning his role. But such was certainly not the case in Victoria. The provincial Cabinet, as we have seen, was well aware of the scornful impression which many critics had of its capacity, was proud, and not surprisingly, very jealous of what it regarded as provincial prerogatives. Thus in late January 1954, for instance, as the basic resource owner, it was anything but pleased to hear that, before consulting it, the general had announced to an IJC meeting that Canada would formally investigate the possibility of a diversion from the Kootenay River into the headwaters of the Columbia.[44]

In a sense making amends for his unilateralism (on diversion) in January, the general visited Victoria on February 22, 1954, and reviewed his thinking with the provincial government. In the process he outlined a major program of development for the Canadian watershed, highlighted by a large multi-purpose dam at Mica Creek in the Upper Columbia Valley. (See Figure 2) Mr. Sommers was as enthusiastic as the general about this project when the two met the press, and was equally enthusiastic about the prospect of deriving a significant and continuing downstream benefit from it. He believed that energy derived from the Mica Dam would attract aluminium and titanium refineries, pulp and paper mills, and other forms of large-scale industry. And he indicated that British Columbia was following closely the attempts to create interstate compacts among the seven American states in the Columbia watershed, which would have recognized the downstream benefit principle for upstream construction *in the United States.* Any such agreement, he declared, could have a bearing on those made by British Columbia. Indeed, publicly, he seemed to accept the general's case for rational-comprehensive analysis when he declared: "We are all agreed that Mica is the first step, but we want to have the whole project laid out before we start."[45] Privately, however, Mr. Sommers and his colleagues had already heard of a number of American proposals for storage development on the Canadian watershed which were soon to be presented to them, and had determined not only to let the enquiries go ahead but to encourage others. They had not been completely convinced of the general's claims for synoptic analysis, or at least were determined to speed it up. However, they kept their counsel, and the general, to his annoyance, was to hear only indirectly and through the provincial press on his return to Ottawa about one of the new alternatives which were emerging.[46]

2. Two Challenges to Synoptic Planning

The Puget Sound Utilities Council Proposal. Actually two major American initiatives directed to the provision of storage on the Columbia's main stream emerged during 1954 in Canada. The most ambitious proposal, but oddly the one which attracted the least public attention, was one made to British Columbia by the Puget Sound Utilities Council, a consortium of five public and private power utilities in northwestern Washington.[47] This agency, which was headed by Dr. Paul Raver, a former Bonneville Power Administration director, suggested that it be permitted to build a large storage dam at Mica Creek.[48] It did not offer to pay for downstream benefits directly, but they were implicitly recognized in its suggestion that it turn the dam over to British Columbia on its completion. The province, when the domestic demand for power warranted such action, would then be able to capitalize on this investment of some $250,000,000 by installing generators and developing a very large block of at-site power at very low cost.[49] The regulation in stream flow would also assist generation at several run-of-the-river sites below Mica on the Columbia in Canada (such as Downie Creek and Little Dalles or High Revelstoke), when and if such projects were constructed. Downstream generation of prime power on the American main stream would be markedly increased of course by an estimated 1,161,000 kw to start, and 1,809,000 kw when the final four dams projected there had been completed. The one condition seemingly involved in this proposal was that Mica reservoir releases be such that they would produce the maximum amount of prime power "in a coordinated operation of Mica Creek and the federal Columbia River system."[50]

Representatives of the five American utilities sponsoring this plan saw Mr. Bennett and Mr. Sommers at the end of February 1954. At the suggestion of the provincial Cabinet they interviewed the chairman of the B.C. Power Commission, and later in the year visited Ottawa for what General McNaughton subsequently described as "purely exploratory" talks.[51] The subsequent reaction to this proposal by Mr. Len Jordan, Mr. Stanley's successor as the American Section chairman, IJC, warrants recording in view of the commission's responsibilities under the 1949 Columbia River reference, and in the context of the Eisenhower administration's reservations about expanding the public power sector in the United States. The enterprise of the American utilities, Mr. Jordan declared in 1956, was not "a matter with respect to which this Commission was officially concerned, although any such proposal is of interest to the members of the Commission."[52]

In view of the magnitude of the benefit to Canada which this offer involved, including relief from the burden of raising such a large block of capital, it is surprising that it did not then and there become the subject of intensive analysis and serious consideration. Just why this is so is not clear. Neither Mr. Bennett nor Mr. Sommers recalls many details of the proposal. Mr. Sommers' impression is that the fact that the Puget Sound Utilities Council had not even been formally established when its representatives first came to Victoria impaired its case.[53] Perhaps quite incorrectly, Mr. Jack Stevens, the Utilities Council's consultant, believes that the proposal was killed in General McNaughton's office.[54] It certainly faced some real hurdles in the United States. One difficult problem was the determination of a formula whereby the Utilities Council would be able to recoup its investment from the incremental power produced downstream without the other customers of the federal and non-federal generating authorities on the American main stream being seriously disadvantaged.[55] Another was the outright skepticism concerning the desirability of integrating private and public power initiatives advanced by such champions of American public power development as Senator Richard L. Neuberger.[56]

The crucial decisions concerning the Puget Sound Utilities Council, however, do appear to have been taken in British Columbia. In spite of the fact that the council had made much of its belief that the releases it would require from the Mica reservoir should be compatible with the needs of British Columbia's utilities, since "the load shapes and streamflow patterns are substantially the same in both areas"[57] Canadian utility men and government officials were not so sure that this was true of neighbouring systems of very different magnitude and at different stages of development.[58] And there was an even more important consideration. During the year 1954, the prospect of American contributions to Canadian development on the basis of a seemingly better formula than that of the Puget Sound Utilities Council began to emerge. This new option for British Columbia had three basic ingredients. The sponsors of storage development in Canada would provide the entire cost of the storage project, but they would undertake a commitment also to pay annual tax and licence fees and, in addition, they would return to Canada a stated amount of the power produced downstream. Meanwhile, negotiations over the Utilities Council scheme continued throughout 1954, but as the year progressed they became increasingly intermittent, and on December 4, citing the failure of the council's proposal to provide for a continuous downstream benefit or a tax payment in Canada, Mr. Bennett announced that the province was just not interested in the plan.[59] To all intents and purposes, the proposal was dead, although the Utilities Council's hopes were not abandoned until 1958,[60] and the premier himself was to speak optimistically of the plan in 1956.

The "Kaiser Dam" Proposal. The second American approach in 1954 to providing Canadian basin storage stemmed, in part, from the initiative of Mr. Dill, who had championed additional Arrow Lakes storage in 1948. Early in February 1954 he visited Mr. Bennett (an old friend) and Mr. Sommers, and raised with them the prospect of a non-governmental corporation building an Arrow Lakes storage dam. He found them genuinely interested and keen to know about the quantity of downstream benefit power which might be credited to British Columbia. The correspondence which Mr. Dill subsequently exchanged with W. A. Pearl, then the Bonneville Power Administration's head, indicates that Mr. Dill implied that a downstream benefit return of 30 to 40 percent of the incremental power produced might be possible.[61] The provincial Cabinet found the prospect of significant developments constructed at no cost to the province but providing it with a continuing return very appealing indeed, and allowed the impression to spread in industrial and utility circles that it would like the idea explored. The B.C. Electric and West Kootenay companies heard of it, and the former in particular followed up with some exploratory talks at the headquarters of the Bonneville Power Administration in Portland. A number of American concerns made enquiries, but it was the Kaiser Aluminum and Chemical Corporation which showed the greatest interest and made the most serious proposals to Victoria.

The province responded in two ways to the initiative from the Kaiser Corporation, which revived the prospect of increased storage on the Arrow Lakes. It told representatives of the Kaiser firm to contact General McNaughton in Ottawa, and to keep him informed of their plans and thinking. This the Kaiser people did—at least five times, through personal interviews, by letters, and by telephone between May 2 and July 22, 1954. And Mr. Sommers, after meeting with the Columbia River Basin Advisory Committee on May 24, enunciated a number of "basic principles" which might govern future investment on and thinking about the Columbia River in British Columbia. He declared that the province would insist on a share of the power produced by Libby and other such projects based on the Canadian contribution to operative head. British Columbia, he added, would require that any developments in Canada be made by Canadian companies "in such a manner as not to create any vested United States interest,"[62] that all of the province's rights under Article II of the Boundary Waters Treaty must be reserved, and that any rights conceded must be for a period not exceeding the life of any project agreed upon. Finally, he indicated that where transboundary projects such as the Libby Dam required transboundary compensation for land and property flooded, this compensation might also be made in terms of power.

In the course of an interview in Ottawa with Kaiser spokesmen on June 17, General McNaughton was asked by them if they might have access to engineering data obtained by the IJC on the site they were interested in. The general replied that before he could consider such a request "he would have to know the precise position of the companies, the privileges to be granted, and the commitments made by the British Columbia Government in the matter."[63] As a result, during the next three months the province and the Kaiser interests moved to clarify their thinking and to enter into a memorandum of understanding, which they signed on September 17, 1954.

The agreement provided that the American corporation would post a bond, and that it would proceed at once with test borings, geological and engineering field work at the site of a proposed *low* storage dam at the lower end of the Arrow Lakes near Castlegar, British Columbia. If by March 1, 1955 (later amended to September 1) the project proved to be feasible, the applicant was to incorporate a Canadian subsidiary which would apply for a conditional water licence. After public hearings on this application, should such a licence be granted by the water comptroller, the Canadian corporation was to commence constructing the dam, upon the completion of which—not later than August 1, 1959—the corporation would receive a fifty-year water licence. Basic to the understanding was a requirement that the corporation pay provincial taxes and water licence fees, and that it return 20 percent of the power generated downstream in the United States as a result of the projected 3,000,000 acre-feet of storage provided. Mr. Sommers set the net return from these sources at "well over $1,000,000 a year for 50 years with the assurance that at the end of that time the annual income would increase."[64] The Kaiser Aluminum Corporation anticipated that the Arrow Lakes project could be built in two or three years, and that it would add just over 331,000 kilowatts of prime power to the output of the United States federal plants then operating or under construction. Its proposal was that one-half of this increment, approximately 165,000 kw, be credited to it, and that from this share would come the compensation—in cash and power—to British Columbia.[65]

The plan, when revealed to the public, evoked from British Columbians a variety of responses. Active supporters of the government endorsed it; the press of the area most directly affected, the West Kootenay country, tended to be cautious, but appeared to be willing to assess the scheme on its merits. To the political opposition in the province, however, and to most of the metropolitan press, it was quickly "clear" that the alleged naiveté of the Social Credit administration had finally caught up with it, and that the province had been betrayed. As a consequence, Mr. Bennett and his colleagues were soon subjected to a heavy attack, as they were enjoined to preserve the province's birthright. The press insisted that the Kaiser plan would inhibit the full development of the Columbia and certainly would displace the much desired Mica Creek dam from a next-added position relative to existing American storage.[66] Pejorative terms such as "power-grab" and "give-away" were freely hurled at the government, which was reminded that the result would be to provide Kaiser Aluminum with a large block of very low cost firmed-up power to the competitive disadvantage of aluminum producers in Canada, and specifically to the Aluminum Company of Canada's large-scale operation at Kitimat in British Columbia. Provincial socialists regretted the departure from a pattern of public power development,[67] and newspaper columnists insisted that in a few years the province would be using a stick to beat off customers for its power.[68] One Liberal member of the provincial Legislature saw the proposal as a bad bargain, exporting capital. Numerous organized-labour groups joined in the critical chorus, and the Board of Trade in the chief population centre of the Upper Columbia Valley, Revelstoke, begged all concerned not to displace Mica from its top priority.

If much of the public comment in British Columbia was hostile, reaction from Ottawa was little better. General McNaughton received a telegram from Mr. Sommers on September 17 indicating that an agreement with Kaiser Aluminum was imminent. His responding telegram, asking for postponement in the light of "remarkable possibilities of advantage to British Columbia which are indicated by new topographical studies in progress" (presumably a reference to feasibility studies examining a Columbia to Fraser River diversion), did not succeed in stopping the signing.[69] Thereupon, he quite candidly revealed a decade later, he moved to block any such development by persuading Minister of Trade and Commerce C. D. Howe, of the folly of allowing it to move ahead. Mr. Howe, he recalled, was skeptical at first, but soon came round to his way of thinking. The general also called in representatives of the Aluminum Company of Canada to alert them to a perceived threat to their position.[70]

It is impossible to be absolutely precise about the magnitude of the leverage which General McNaughton exercised over the federal decision-making on the Kaiser Dam proposal, but the evidence does suggest that it was considerable. And, of course, it did reinforce a predisposition of some in the federal administration to be especially critical of the Social Credit government, for the Liberals' memory of the 1952 political debacle in British Columbia was still fresh. In any event, Ottawa's reaction was not long in coming. By October 13, 1954, news dispatches from the national capital were predicting that the federal government would veto the arrangement unless its terms were radically altered.[71] On November 6, James Sinclair, the federal minister of fisheries and M.P. for North Vancouver, declared that the deal was a bad one for the province and for Canada, and announced that Ottawa was going to stop it.[72]

Mr. Bennett's government was not prepared to take such opposition lying down. Mr. Sommers, for example, held that if the engineers cleared the project, British Columbia would go to the courts if necessary to enforce its determination to push it through.[73] He was, of course, advancing again his belief that, as the proposed development was one *above the boundary* on a trans-boundary river, neither the federal government nor the IJC had any jurisdiction over it. He also indicated that British Columbia itself could build the dam, but sought to show that it would be financially unwise to do so. The premier soon moved into the fray, observing that all the "Communists and Socialists" were against the Kaiser Dam, classifying the Liberals as "only socialists in a low gear," and denouncing Mr. Sinclair's position and Ottawa's as a "cheap political trick."[74] Members of the provincial Cabinet sought, in scores of speeches, to show how the "Kaiser formula," whereby the province received 20 percent of the downstream power *in addition to having the storage built and receiving annual licence and fee income*,[75] was superior to one which would entitle the province to one-half the incremental power produced by Canadian built and paid for storage. Thus, intemperately, the debate was joined. Mr. Sommers announced on November 29, 1954, that the province's Columbia Basin Advisory Committee had approved the project, but opponents quickly discounted its endorsement as biased.[76]

While these exchanges were taking place, a further riposte to British Columbia, and certainly to the United States, was about to be launched from Ottawa. It should be recalled that in the IJC the American position to this time had been to place significant limits on the value of the Kootenay flow into the Libby reservoir, and that, as we have seen, in January 1954, General McNaughton had advanced, as an alternative to be examined, the prospect of a diversion from the Kootenay into the

Columbia River headwaters. On September 28, 1954, the State Department had actually informed the IJC that it was prepared to "consider equitable recompense to Canada through the sale of power or otherwise for the value which Canadian natural resources would have to the production of power, taking into account the extent to which the project will result in a compensatory benefit to Canada."[77] What this actually meant has never been revealed, but three years later General McNaughton was to imply that the "offer" was based on the assumption that the water in question would not leave its natural channel (ie. that Canada would not divert any of it from the Upper Kootenay to the Columbia) and that, as a consequence, it was unsatisfactory.[78]

A new Canadian move was revealed on December 20, 1954, when Mr. Jean Lesage, the minister of northern affairs and national resources, announced that his department, in conjunction with the IJC, would begin in the summer of 1955 a study of a still further diversion, this time from the reservoir behind the projected Revelstoke Dam on the Columbia, through the Monashee Mountains into the watershed of the Fraser River. (See Figure 6.) Nine days later Mr. Howe made it very clear that the federal government had been quite unmoved by the province's arguments over the Kaiser agreement. It was, he declared, a "cock-eyed and improvident deal,"[79] as he reflected unhappily on the low cost of power to the United States which would be a result of it, and affirmed that Ottawa did not favour arrangements of this sort with private interests in the United States. Early in the new year, the province informally sought to outflank some of the opposition with a plan whereby the provincial government would take advantage of the lower financing rates available to it, and would build the $30,000,000 dam itself, with the Kaiser Company providing a proportionately larger cash return.[80] But this proposal failed to satisfy the critics and was quickly set aside.

The federal government imposed its veto on the agreement with the Kaiser Company through a measure which was introduced into Parliament the moment the new session began on January 10. The instrument it used, the International Rivers Improvements Bill, required a licence from the government of Canada to construct, operate, and maintain any improvement altering the natural flow of rivers running from Canada into the United States. When Mr. Howe spoke to the bill on the second reading, he justified Ottawa's action by referring to the obsolescence of single-project planning and invoked the national interest in his argument that long-term considerations must not be prejudiced "by immediate local purposes that may be inconsistent with the longer view."[81] General McNaughton's support of the measure was made clear. The Parliamentary debate at this stage was short. Only the Social Credit members of Parliament overtly dissented; the Progressive Conservatives reserved their position pending committee investigation.

Two features of the External Affairs Committee hearings on this bill stand out. One was the manner in which General McNaughton made his position explicit as he argued that the federal government had not only a right but a duty to pass the measure, and made clear his lack of enthusiasm for any storage dam on the Arrow Lakes.[82] The other was the nature of the provincial presentation to the committee. Mr. Bennett was invited to appear but declined, and sent instead Mr. Sommers, Attorney General Robert Bonner, and Mr. Arthur Paget, the water comptroller. Mr. Bonner, with some technical support from Mr. Paget, presented the province's case, and basically sought to eschew any argument on the Kaiser proposal; indeed, he indicated that there was a real possibility that American authorities would veto it as the price was too high. What he did concentrate on was the invocation of the British North America Act's section 92, sub-section 10 (c), in clause 9 of the proposed federal bill, seeing it as a move whereby Ottawa would be able to expropriate much of the province's (or other provinces') water rights. He assured the committee that his province was just as enthusiastic about the Mica project as was Ottawa, but that it regarded the Columbia to Fraser diversion as of "only academic interest,"[83] and he affirmed that British Columbia was not in favour of a complete standstill until every nook and cranny had been explored. He made it very clear, as had Mr. Bennett earlier in the year, that the provincial government felt that it had a legitimate grievance with federal authorities over their failure to communicate directly with the British Columbia government. It was about time, he suggested, that British Columbia was directly represented on the International Columbia River Engineering Board. He was careful to insist, at this time, that British Columbia was not interested in exporting power, save in unusual or temporary circumstances. In the last analysis he conceded Ottawa's right to impose a veto,[84] and Ottawa duly withdrew clause 9, although it maintained its outright opposition to the Kaiser plan.

While Parliamentary examination of the International Rivers Bill continued in Ottawa (with no question but that the measure would be approved), in British Columbia there were some very sharp exchanges in the provincial Legislature between the Bennett Cabinet and Mr. Arthur Laing, the leader of the provincial Liberal party. In one sense, the strife was continued in another way as well, although contact between Ottawa and Victoria on this issue was almost non-existent officially. Minister of Northern Affairs and National Resources Lesage, in the first half of 1955, did advance in the province two significant explanations or affirmations of federal government policy. In January, in one of those long letters which ministers sign, but civil servants often have to draft, he assured the Revelstoke City Council that "Kaiser's is a minimum project, and yet it might well preclude a more extensive development of what is the most 'natural' storage reservoir in the whole Columbia basin." He also took exception (i) to the manner in which he felt the proposal made a Murphy Creek Dam downstream from Castlegar unfeasible, (ii) to its coopting a first-added position, and (iii) to its providing the American aluminum industry with a block of power "at a price little more than half what it costs to a Canadian producer." After asserting that Canada could reasonably expect a 50 percent downstream power benefit settlement, his letter concluded with some highly imaginative projections. The downstream power benefit was estimated as amounting in time to the equivalent of some 17.5 billion kilowatt hours annually—"the annual value of which would be in excess of $85 millions at present values."[85] He went on to suggest that this amount of power could support as much as $1.5 billions' worth of manufacturing equipment and plant, the resulting annual output of which might be of the order of $8 to $9 billions. Such was the stuff of which Canadian dreams and understandable American caution and wonder were born!

In May 1955, Mr. Lesage delivered a speech in Vancouver in which he presented the most careful exposition of federal government Columbia River policy advanced to that date. He made it quite clear that Canada believed it had a right to divert flood-waters from the Kootenay to the Columbia Basin, that it felt it had a very good case for insisting on an "adequate and fair share"[86] of the downstream benefits produced from upstream storage, that resolving this matter would not be easy, but that it could be settled through the IJC. He went on to argue further that the economies of British Columbia and the American Pacific northwest were in many ways competitive, and that Canada could not allow the sale in America of at-site or downstream benefit power from British Columbia at a cost corresponding to the present average cost in the American northwest. He was well aware, he indicated, of the subsidized nature of federally produced power in the American northwest, and its depression-cost base, and felt that Canadian power could not be sold there for much less than the cost of the then cheapest domestic American alternative. He did not close the door to the prospect of selling in the United States part of a Canadian downstream power entitlement on a progressively recapturable basis, but did emphasize that, as parts of southern British Columbia were doubling their power requirements every seven years, the province with even a normal growth rate would need all of its cheap power in two or three decades. A month later, in another statement he made it very clear also that the federal government would kill any arrangement which appeared to give American interests ownership of or control over the Mica site, although he insisted that such a stand was not to be interpreted as opposition to American investment in Canadian power schemes.[87]

The passage of the International Rivers Bill in June–July 1955, vetoed the Kaiser proposal, although it probably would have come to nothing in any event, for it is doubtful that arrangements could have been made to give effect to it in the United States.[88] Some grounds existed for questioning its legality, for instance, and officers of the Corps of Engineers—orally and in writing—conveyed to the Bonneville Power Administration their skepticism, one citing the downstream benefit which it involved as the very principle to which the United States was strenuously objecting in the IJC.[89] But this is really beside the point, for the contest in Canada, which, by May 1955, certainly had the air "blue with accusations and abuse,"[90] was joined on the assumption that the Kaiser development was a real possibility.

The positions and the arguments on the "Kaiser question" have been outlined at some length for they were to have important repercussions in the later evolution of federal and provincial policy. One of the more obvious results of the whole affair was that the active role played by General McNaughton before the External Affairs Committee seems to have enhanced his reputation, both public and parliamentary.[91] On the other hand, one of the least noted consequences was that the more perceptive members of the St. Laurent Cabinet, and of the senior federal bureaucracy, did not miss the revelation during the External Affairs Committee hearings that General McNaughton had failed to keep them informed over his contacts with the Kaiser people in the summer of 1954. Victoria's reaction to the general's role in this entire affair can only be described as a mixture of disillusionment and growing determination. The disillusionment was directed first toward the general himself, and notably was the result of a statement made during the Commons' debate on the second reading of the International Rivers Improvement Bill by Mr. Howe. In it Mr. Howe declared: "Strangely enough, General McNaughton has not been consulted by the province of British Columbia about this transaction. He tells me that he was in Victoria on the day this contract was signed, and that he did not hear about the agreement until two or three weeks later."[92] The provincial Cabinet was prepared to concede that Mr. Howe had garbled what had been told him, and that, technically, they had not "consulted" with the general. But they objected strongly to the impression conveyed by Mr. Howe's statement that they had left the general uninformed, and to the fact that this impression was not corrected. For this omission they blamed General McNaughton himself, and when the External Affairs Committee hearings were held, Mr. Bonner went to a good deal of trouble to ensure that the committee did receive documentary evidence recording the contacts between the IJC office in Ottawa and the Kaiser representatives, and making it clear that these had been initiated at the express wish of the government in Victoria.[93]

The Social Crediters' disillusionment went beyond the general, however. During the committee hearings the federal Progressive Conservative members of Parliament displayed a very considerable sensitivity to the provincial government's case, and two of them, Mr. E. D. Fulton (Kamloops) and Mr. Howard Green (Vancouver-Point Grey), had caucused regularly with the provincial delegation. Mr. Bonner and Mr. Sommers had expected these parliamentarians to place a great deal of emphasis in the committee's hearings on what the representatives of British Columbia regarded as the inaccuracy and unfairness in the positions taken by Mr. Howe and the general, and were greatly disappointed when this did not happen.[94] Instead the M.P.'s had sought, fundamentally, to play a conciliating role between two governments, and recall now that at the time they felt the Kaiser agreement, at best, to be premature.

In summary, then, the government of British Columbia resented the treatment accorded it by the federal administration, and became more determined than ever to ensure that Ottawa would never be in a position to assert a fiat over the development of the Columbia. A decade later Mr. Bennett claimed that he never really believed that the Kaiser people could deliver on their undertaking. He asserts now that he knew they could not, but that the whole point to the exercise was to get established the recognition of the downstream benefit power principle. This, he points out, it did. The federal government was stupid in not seeing this, he claims, and he adds that he told Mr. Lesage so.[95] Mr. Sommers takes much the same position.[96] However accurate these recollections, there is no doubt that the government of the province did not forget that it had been held up throughout the country as a hasty, improvident, unimaginative, and shortsighted administration.

3. THE CONTRIBUTION OF THE LAWYERS

At this juncture it will be helpful if we pause for a moment to take note of the manner in which a number of Canadian lawyers were fascinated by some of the claims advanced within the IJC, and sought to test them. In their own way, within and beyond governmental circles, they did help clarify Canadian perceptions of the technical options which were open to Canada, and what their legal consequences were likely to be.

General McNaughton had developed his strategy around a number of major contentions. One, already referred to, emphasized that Canada was quite entitled to divert the flows of the Kootenay northward into the Columbia. Another held that, if it were in her interest to do so, Canada was also entitled to divert annually some 15 million acre-feet of water, which at that time was not being utilized at American plants downstream, from the Columbia watershed entirely to that of the Fraser River.[97] Before the IJC he advanced two other major claims. Canada, he averred, was entitled to far more than compensation for opportunities forgone, should she agree to such a project as a transboundary Libby reservoir. And, furthermore, the return which she received from participating in cooperative development should be assessed in terms of the cost to the United States of producing equivalent benefits without the assistance of Canadian storage, which cost, he insisted, should take into account the expense of producing peaking electric power by thermal means.[98] At the same time, and indeed for a number of years both within the IJC and extensively in Canada, the general insisted that as the diversions which he was investigating involved waters not then put to use by the United States, they could be carried out, in a sense by applying the doctrine of appropriation to the Columbia River (the "first in time first in right" principle), without incurring a valid American claim for damages.[99]

Counter arguments to all these propositions were advanced within the IJC, but none assumed the importance of the American response to the general's diversionary thesis, over which, after October 1955, the commission was effectively deadlocked. By this date Mr. Jordan, the American Section chairman, had advanced some major responses of his own. One affirmed that the proposal to divert out of the basin, in particular, would result in "very great injury"[100] to the United States. A second, involving an interesting application of the doctrine of appropriation, held that existing American projects on the lower main stream of the Columbia with unutilized capacity, and plans which had been widely discussed to build additional projects, although construction on them had not yet started, together gave his country a vested right to the entire flow of the river. His third contention was that the injuries inflicted downstream as a consequence of diversion above the border would be suffered by a sovereign, one of the "High Contracting Parties" to the Boundary Waters Treaty, and that the United States, as a sovereign, would not be "limited to redress provided for an injured party [spelled with a small letter 'p'] by Article II."[101]

The section of the Canadian legal community which was interested in the legal position of riparians on international rivers attended American seminars, held seminars of their own, searched the record, wrote and argued in labyrinthine fashion on the major issues raised by these arguments, from 1955 onward.[102] Without exception, they concluded as a result of their investigation that Article II does indeed confer a right to divert on the upstream riparian, which right Canada, in this position on the Columbia, should seek to retain. Not a few of them waxed indignant, as Canadian nationalists, over what they perceived to be an American tendency to invoke Article II when it seemed to be to its advantage, and on other occasions to set it aside. At one stage, the deputy minister of justice (Mr. F. P. Varcoe) and a prominent Canadian legal scholar (Professor Charles Bourne) developed a startling interpretation of the application of British Columbia's Water Act to the adjudication of American claims for damages as a result of an upstream diversion, which would have had the effect of rendering all such claims invalid.[103] The longer the Canadian lawyers probed into the doctrine of appropriation, the more conscious they became of its inadequacies as an adjudicative principle on international rivers. They watched with interest the development in the United States of the thesis that the operative rules for adjudication on the Columbia ought to lie in an emerging doctrine of equitable apportionment, but concluded that the whole point to the Boundary Waters Treaty in the first place had been to remove the uncertainties associated with such a vague general principle.[104]

Interestingly enough, the Canadian lawyers became very conscious of the fact that, whatever Canada's rights associated with Article II, they could be abrogated by the United States giving a one-year notice of intent to cancel the treaty. At least one (Professor Cohen) asked for some "dialectical modesty" on both sides of the border, as he found the Varcoe-Bourne thesis not entirely reasonable. Almost all of them ended up in print calling for a practical display of international cooperation, whereby through negotiation each country would secure a fair share of maximized benefits from "this common store of power,"[105] or, if one will, propounding a viewpoint which had its foundations in equity rather than in strictly legal relationships. Overall, as a result of its concentration on the problems associated with international river basins after 1955, Canadian legal opinion appears to have developed a new consciousness of the very limited usefulness of generalized legal principles in the resolution of international disputes in this field. On the other hand, during the last half of the decade it certainly did nothing to qualify the widespread conviction in Canada that the request for a share of the downstream benefits produced on the Columbia was reasonable, and it may well have hardened the conviction of those who had become convinced that the concept of diverting water from one watershed to another, and, in particular, the diversion from the Kootenay to the Columbia, was far more than a bargaining ploy.

4. Moves to Further Analysis and Diplomatic-Level Negotiation

The 1954–55 conflict between the governments in Ottawa and Victoria concerning the development of the Columbia River was a salutary experience for both. They now realized that each was in a position to forestall the other—that agreement between them had become a *sine qua non* of any development of the Canadian watershed of that great river. Hence both governments moved quietly over the 1955–56 winter to seek an understanding. The federal government faced an immediate problem, for the Department of Fisheries under Mr. Sinclair was openly alarmed at the proposal to divert water from the Columbia into the Fraser River, and was very unhappy that Mr. Sinclair's colleague in the federal Cabinet, Mr. Lesage, had endorsed General McNaughton's proposal to study that project. The institutional response to this need for coordination in Ottawa was the usual one; before the end of 1955 an Advisory Committee on Water Use Policy was established there, chaired by the deputy minister of northern affairs and national resources, and including representation from the Departments of External Affairs, Finance, Fisheries, Trade and Commerce, Mines and Technical Surveys, and from the Privy Council Office. The Canadian Section, International Joint Commission, provided observers. Representatives from British Columbia were not included.

The major problem facing Ottawa and Victoria, especially after the October 1955 meeting of the IJC at which the two Section chairmen took such diametrically opposed views, was the deadlock which had emerged there. Ottawa was especially concerned about the sharpness of the exchanges between General McNaughton and Mr. Jordan, and about the manner in which the whole matter seemed to be escalating into a considerable dispute between two close neighbours. And Victoria was more unhappy than ever over the lack of progress on the issue of downstream benefits. On November 14, 1955, General McNaughton by letter did invite the province through Mr. Sommers to make its views on the downstream benefits question known to him, and undertook to relay them to the federal government's Advisory Committee on Water Use Policy. Mr. Sommers' response (of January 10, 1956) was to inform General Mc-Naughton that the province's own advisory committee, through its working group, was undertaking a "complete study of potential developments of the Columbia basin, and at the same time dealing with the general question of upstream-downstream benefits." At this time he did not accept the offer to relay the province's viewpoint to the federal government via the desk of the IJC Section chairman. In any case, the upshot, after close liaison between the two Canadian governments, was a decision taken early in

1956 to raise with the United States the prospect of transferring some of the matters at issue from the IJC to the diplomatic level. Mr. Bennett, well briefed on this development, actually revealed that talks with the United States might begin shortly when, in a genial mood, he announced on March 11, 1956, that he was willing to take another look at the province's position on the Columbia River's development, and that he expected Mr. Lesage and his advisers to visit Victoria during the spring for a conference on this issue and related river problems.[106]

There really are just two points to make about the diplomatic-level talks as they were pursued in 1956. In that year they actually amounted to very little indeed. Prime Minister St. Laurent raised the prospect of such exchanges with President Eisenhower at White Sulphur Springs on March 26–27, 1956. In the House of Commons, on April 9, he explained that the goal of any discussions, in view of the IJC level deadlock, would simply be "to try to get at something which would make for the expeditious use of these waterways." After a meeting between diplomatic representatives on May 23 in Ottawa, a statement was issued in the name of the two governments which declared their intention of examining together the subject of transboundary waters,[107] mentioned the intermix of difficult engineering, economic, and legal questions in such basins as those of the St. John, Columbia, and Yukon Rivers, and referred in complimentary terms to the International Joint Commission. The statement revealed that the commission was to continue working on its Columbia and other references, and expressed the hope that an additional full and confidential exchange of views would help, although it did not expect answers to be easily or quickly obtained. It affirmed that "the studies may reveal that the Boundary Waters Treaty of 1909 is sufficiently broad to meet present problems."[108]

The other point to note is that General McNaughton was greatly perturbed about the move to the diplomatic level; he interpreted it as evidence of a lack of support by his national government, and considered resigning.[109] He took great exception also to the inclusion in a draft of the statement on the Columbia which Mr. St. Laurent was to take on his visit to the American president, of an indication that Canada recognized that it might be wise to consider updating the provisions of the Boundary Waters Treaty, particularly Article II, which dealt with diversionary rights.[110] Indeed he took credit for having the reference in question, which he felt threatened much of his case, deleted.[111]

During the late spring of 1956 other issues crowded those concerning the Columbia from the centre of the public stage in Canada. Nevertheless three developments should be noted. Both Canadian governments watched closely the joint hearings of the Senate (United States) Interior and

Insular Affairs Committee and a special sub-committee of the Senate Foreign Relations Committee on Upper Columbia River development. Close attention was paid to the severe grilling of Mr. Jordan by Senator Neuberger, who had conducted his own survey in British Columbia between October 17 and October 24, 1955, and apparently had come to the conclusion that a good deal of the responsibility for the delay in reaching an agreement with Canada could be traced to the American Section chairman himself, and to the American administration's lack of enthusiasm for an expansion of public power development—which seemed inherent in any settlement with Canada. Some very effective deflating of the Americans' 1955 Interagency Report on which Mr. Jordan had based a significant part of his evaluation of Canadian storage was duly noted, as was the enthusiastic advocacy of the Corps of Engineers and some Congressional spokesmen for the Libby Dam. General McNaughton did not come before the Canadian External Affairs Committee for his annual presentation until June 1956, at which time he claimed to see an improvement in the American attitude. He assured the committee that the feasibility of a Mica Dam had been proved, and expressed the opinion that the need for power in British Columbia, with its exceptionally high rate of load growth, would make impossible the reservation of the lower main stream of the Fraser and most of its tributaries to the fisheries resource.[112] One week later Premier Bennett publicly replied to the general, insisting that he was convinced that the Columbia to Fraser diversion proposal was a mistake, and that Ottawa now knew it.[113] The premier made three other announcements of importance at this time. He denied that the B.C. Electric or any other company was in "on the ground floor" of the Columbia, and said that it had not yet been really decided whether or not the provincially-owned B.C. Power Commission would be involved in its development. American money, he felt, was still available to build the Mica Dam. And he could not forbear observing that under the Kaiser formula not only would the storage dam at Mica have been built, but the 20 percent downstream benefit coming at little or no cost from it would have provided the generating facilities which were now to be a financial charge on British Columbia.[114]

Unquestionably the most important development in 1956 came out of the meeting finally held in Victoria when Mr. Lesage got there on July 4. Mr. Bennett subsequently claimed to have met him with a bargaining agreement whereby either British Columbia would get the United States to build the basic Columbia dams in Canada on the Kaiser formula, or, alternatively, if Ottawa felt able to do better, it could go ahead on its own and reap any benefits above those which British Columbia felt were available to it under the first alternative.[115] Mr. Lesage later—a year later—denied that the "offer" was a firm one.[116] Sparring exchanges aside, Mr. Lesage, Premier Bennett, and Mr. R. G. Williston, who had succeeded Mr. Sommers as the provincial minister of lands and forests, quickly reached agreement. They undertook to halt further public debate between the two governments on the subject of the Columbia's development, and in an announcement released to the press the federal government declared its willingness to make the results of its engineering studies to that point available to the government of British Columbia and other interested parties. Obviously both governments had decided that the time for highly reliable analyses of the river's potential and of the manner in which it might best be developed had arrived, whether it was to be developed independently or in association with the United States. Both governments had also concluded that these examinations should be made by external consultants in no way subject to direction from the Canadian Section of the IJC. On July 17, 1956, the Department of Northern Affairs commissioned the Montreal Engineering Company to undertake a power-system study with particular reference to the Columbia River. Four days later Mr. Williston revealed that the province had contracted for a similar one on the Columbia basin's potential by the Crippen-Wright Engineering Company of Vancouver.[117] Almost immediately, furthermore, the B.C. Electric Company announced that it would take advantage of the federal government's offer of engineering information.[118] As a consequence, no less than four groups of engineers were to be at work on the Canadian Columbia watershed before the year was over—those continuing the ICREB studies, and representatives of the two consulting engineering firms and of the B.C. Electric's engineering subsidiary.

The Diplomatic Exchange of 1957. Having just committed themselves to extensive and costly independent reviews of the alternatives open to them, the governments in Victoria and Ottawa did not move very rapidly to diplomatic level exchanges with the United States.[119] During the 1956–57 winter federal Progressive Conservative party spokesmen became increasingly interested in and articulate about Columbia development problems; at various times they were to endorse the concept of an equal sharing of downstream benefits, to express concern at any American utility involvement with the construction of the Mica Dam, and to support the proposition that Ottawa help underwrite a provincial initiative.[120] Premier Bennett, while in Ottawa in November 1956, pressed for early negotiations with the United States, and publicly declared that there was "nothing but goodwill" between the Canadian governments on the subject.[121] In the January–April 1957 session of the provincial Legislature, the CCF party sought to pin the premier down on the government's

Columbia River policy, and to advance the case for the B.C. Power Commission, but he refused to be drawn out. However, he made it clear that "the government is not opposed to public power," and that discussions had not yet advanced far enough to enable him to give an opinion as to whether his government did or did not favour a joint federal-provincial agency, which at least one of his back-benchers and the CCF had recently endorsed.[122]

Actually it was not until January 1957 that the Department of External Affairs finally approached the Department of State again on the subject of diplomatic-level talks, and not until March 19, 1957, that at a meeting of Canadian and American officials in Ottawa, arrangements were made, and a set of terms of reference was drafted, for the long proposed international meetings. Finally delegations from the two countries did meet in Washington on May 20–21, 1957—almost a year after the formal announcement of a decision to convene such a gathering. Mr. Lesage and five senior federal civil servants represented Canada; Mr. Williston, British Columbia's minister of lands, was present, also, accompanied by Mr. A. Paget and Mr. G. J. A. Kidd,[123] but the British Columbians did not sit in on the formal exchanges with the Americans. When the Canadians caucused before the first international session, Mr. Lesage informed those present that, with British Columbia's approval, he was going to propose that the two countries each nominate three men to a technical committee, which would gather "basic data and prepare reports upon which diplomatic discussions about development of the river could be based."[124] Mr. Williston agreed to the proposal, and to Mr. Lesage's suggestion that Mr. Paget sit on the group, as he emphasized that "it was desirable to establish policy on Columbia matters as soon as possible." He went out of his way to stress to the federal representatives that British Columbia wanted to avoid indefinite delay, and that its goal was maximum economic development, which would probably be somewhat less than ultimate potential development in the light of transmission costs and the economies available through total integration. He agreed that diversion rights should be maintained, but felt that Canada should guarantee to hold off for specified periods of time.

In the formal negotiating sessions the United States representatives early presented a discursive working paper, but did agree to concentrate on two or three major river basins, such as the Yukon and the Columbia. The two countries agreed not to change the 1909 treaty. When the concept of a technical committee was first broached, the Americans demurred; subsequent discussion indicated that the State and Interior Departments felt that such a body might be useful, while the Corps of Engineers did not. The final American position here was that a reply to this proposal would come through diplomatic channels,[125] and that if the committee were agreed to, the American membership on it might well come solely from the ranks of federal officials.

When the British Columbians returned home from these first exploratory contacts with the United States, they prepared a summarizing memorandum which is important, for it reflects very explicitly the perceptions in May 1957 of three men who were to play a very important role in the province in selecting the scheme for developing the Columbia ultimately incorporated in the Columbia River Treaty. They recorded that the problems to be cleared before decisions were made on Columbia River development "are not as great as are often indicated," that the passage of time certainly destroyed some economic values of upstream storage—while increasing others, and that the Columbia is not a "particularly huge source of power." They were quite clear that Columbia River development in Canada was not economic at that time without an agreement for a return of "substantial amounts" of downstream benefits, and that, to produce advantage to both sides, compromise and departure from optimal development would be required. They were sure that British Columbia must have an "official technical position where its views may be immediately reflected to the negotiating diplomatic group," and that an engineering committee which could "receive, evaluate and pass on" to diplomatic groups reports from American, British Columbian, Canadian public and private sources was as necessary as was close provincial liaison with Ottawa. Similarly they felt a Canadian committee with active western representation could maintain effective unofficial contact with corresponding American officials across the boundary. Also recorded was a conviction that an agreement on principle and procedure between the two countries would help create a favourable atmosphere for the receipt in due course of the IJC report. Categorically they asserted that "the final decision relating to the form that any Columbia River development in Canada takes must be made by British Columbia"; the federal representatives, they felt, had acknowledged that "on all points . . . the British Columbia position must be the dominant one," and could see little point in developing one not satisfactory to the province. The notes record a federal conviction that the United States would use delaying tactics, and that British Columbia could help overcome this, especially because of its ability to discuss water resource development informally with American agency personnel in the Pacific northwest. The British Columbians believed that the Corps had assumed the dominant position as far as the United States was concerned, that the Corps felt time was on their side, that the Fraser diversion was not practicable, and that they (the Americans) would soon be able to pick up the downstream benefits without cost (when Canada built upstream installations entirely on its own account). Mr. Williston and his associates sensed that on technical grounds the Corps would stress the declining value of storage for power producing purposes (as hydro-electric generation in the American system moved from a base-load to a peaking role), and, whatever happened, would certainly not want assistance to upstream entities to run beyond the amortization period of their installations. It seemed logical to them that "British Columbia representations should be carried into as high a level as possible consistent with the protocol of international discussions."[126] Their introspective document concluded with the affirmation that British Columbia should demonstrate to the United States that it did have hydro potential other than the Columbia available for immediate development, referring specifically to the Clearwater, secondary power on the Kootenay, and the resources of the Pend d'Oreille, which might well be able to meet provincial needs until 1966 or 1967.

5. THE 1957 FEDERAL GENERAL ELECTION

The Washington conference on transboundary river problems was held in the midst of a Canadian federal election campaign, which must be looked at briefly, for during it once again the development of the Columbia River became a subject of considerable intergovernmental tension in Canada. As the Progressive Conservative and CCF parties were in no sense bound by the Bennett-Lesage "understanding" of July 1956, some debate on the issue was inevitable in any case, but the initiative of Mr. James Sinclair, the federal minister of fisheries, was to ensure that the exchanges were sharp during the 1957 March–June campaign. In its very early stages, on March 24 in Vancouver, Mr. Sinclair informed a press conference that he expected an early Canadian-American agreement on the downstream benefit problem, and viewed the river's development as the "biggest public works project" in Canada to date—one which would be able to meet provincial power needs for from fifteen to thirty years. He went on to declare that, if, "after international agreement had been reached, the provincial government should decide on public development . . . and should need assistance in financing, the federal government will be prepared to assist in the same way it has joined with Ontario in constructing the interprovincial gas pipe line across northern Ontario."[127] He outlined three methods of development available if the federal offer were taken up. One possibility envisaged was the creation of a joint federal-provincial Columbia River authority to construct and develop all phases of the power generation-transmission network; another was that the federal government would give direct financial assistance to the B.C.

Power Commission, which would handle the development. The third prospect outlined was that a federal crown corporation might undertake some part of the development, such as the construction of transmission lines. These could then be rented to the B.C. Power Commission, which would be free to buy out any federal interest once profits were realized from the resulting power. Mr. Sinclair also referred to the way in which an early agreement with the United States would save the Fraser River fisheries from a power development there.

Mr. Bennett's reaction to Mr. Sinclair was not long in coming. Initially he refused to discuss Mr. Sinclair's "political campaign" and affirmed with respect to Ottawa's role, "I shall discuss it with the Prime Minister."[128] But two days later, when quizzed in the Legislative Assembly about the matter, the premier exploded. He declared that he had heard from neither Mr. Sinclair nor Mr. Laurent; he called the former's press conference "an insult to the premier" and its contents "political propaganda which will boomerang."[129] In the next two months Mr. Bennett campaigned very actively on behalf of his party's candidates in British Columbia, and sought to light a Social Credit brushfire as far away as Ontario. As he flailed the incumbent Liberals he decried the lack of any formal communication from Ottawa with him on the Columbia River's development, and denounced Mr. Sinclair for discussing publicly an issue which Mr. Lesage had asked not be debated during the international negotiations. Ignoring some of his own earlier pronouncements, he charged Mr. Sinclair also with impairing Canada's negotiating position by downgrading the attractiveness of a Columbia-Fraser diversion.

Mr. Sinclair's response to all this, both in the House of Commons and on the hustings, was to deny that Ottawa was being dictatorial over the development, and to argue that the ultimate decision was British Columbia's. He continued to stress the gains inherent in federal participation (money raised at 3.0 as opposed to 4.9 percent interest), and added "we won't permit the Americans to build it."[130] What he sought to do was to impale Mr. Bennett on a private power development stake, but the premier was much too adroit for this. Mr. Sinclair was obviously nettled, not without reason, at what he felt to be the province's monopolizing of credit for the Trans-Canada Highway, then under construction as a shared-cost project. Ottawa was prepared to help British Columbia, he insisted, but "we are not going to shovel our money to the provincial government to use or abuse."[131]

Mr. Sinclair's colleagues in the federal Cabinet were somewhat more sensitive to Mr. Bennett's reaction; at least they were to modify Mr. Sinclair's position. Two days after Mr. Sinclair's initial announcement, Mr. Lesage read it into the House of Commons record. He affirmed that it represented government policy, but denied on Mr. Sinclair's behalf any mention of a commitment to a specific amount of federal aid. He added two qualifications: Mr. Sinclair had over-simplified when referring to federal assistance to the governments of Nova Scotia and New Brunswick to link their thermal and hydro electric developments, and Mr. Lesage insisted that it should not be assumed that the possibility of a Columbia-Fraser diversion had been abandoned. On April 6 in the House of Commons Prime Minister St. Laurent sought to play down the whole issue, imagining that if British Columbia wished to proceed with the Mica project they would communicate with Ottawa, but feeling that the province might well consider the work a provincial one which should be handled alone. When in Vancouver on May 3 he repeated the essence of Mr. Sinclair's offer, including the reference to the project's self-liquidating nature, and the province's opportunity to buy Ottawa's interest out. A reference, however, to the need to look carefully at bargains appearing "attractive in the short run but that would sign away great blocks of power into the indefinite future"[132] and a failure to visit Mr. Bennett on the following weekend while in Victoria, did not mollify the premier. By May 6 the power question seemed to have become the major election issue in British Columbia, and the press generally and the CCF party were welcoming the federal stand. Mr. Bennett dug in his heels at this time and threatened to veto any downstream benefit negotiations over the Columbia "unless they are entirely satisfactory to the people of British Columbia."[133] The major qualification to Mr. Sinclair came from Minister of Trade and Commerce C. D. Howe on May 13, when, in a reference to the proposed limitation of federal assistance to subsequent public ownership, he declared in Vancouver, "I wouldn't have gone that far . . . until I knew what the province wants to do," and stressed that Ottawa had no quarrel with private development so long as it was by Canadian money for Canada.[134] Mr. Bennett announced on hearing this that he was prepared to see Mr. Howe, but the latter, although he visited Victoria, did not make the call, suggesting that it would not be appropriate, since the purpose of his trip was political, as had been Mr. Bennett's recent journey to Ontario.

One final characteristic of the election campaign which must not be forgotten was the extent to which the Progressive Conservative party sought to present itself as a group which, over the Columbia, would co-operate with, not attempt to dictate to the province as, it suggested, the incumbent Liberals had already done. When Mr. Diefenbaker made a triumphal speech in Vancouver on May 23, he drew heavily on Mr. Leon Ladner, the Vancouver lawyer and a prominent member of his party, for the comments which he made concerning the Columbia River. The policy which Mr. Diefenbaker advanced had four features. (i) There was to be no permanent alienation of the power and other resources of the Columbia, and (ii) American payments for irrigation, flood control and other downstream benefits should be applied to the costs of dam construction in Canada. Mr. Diefenbaker insisted (iii) that the Canadian entitlement to a downstream power benefit should be payable in power, although surpluses could be sold to the United States for cash, but for a fixed period of years. The proceeds of these sales were also to go to meet upstream dam construction expenses. Finally, while endorsing the most efficient means of development within the ambit of the Progressive Conservative's National Development Policy, he suggested (iv) that "responsibility for and financing of the Upper Columbia in whole or relevant parts be allocated on the most efficient basis possible . . . as revealed by detailed engineering and hydraulic studies."[135] The ambiguity of the last assertion, while significant, was little appreciated at the time. The whole served its purpose, and comment on the highly generalized nature of the policy statement was not forthcoming until after June 10, when Mr. Diefenbaker and associates scored as big a political upset as had the Social Crediters provincially in 1952, and assumed responsibility in a minority government for the formation of national policy on the Columbia's development.[136] As the long period of Liberal party rule in Ottawa came to an end the new Progressive Conservative administration appeared to have committed itself to a heightened appreciation of British Columbia's objectives and role with respect to the development of the Columbia River. That it had come to power with, on this question, some latent objectives of its own which might be anything but complementary to those of the province, was not at all appreciated in 1957, and indeed was to become public knowledge, only slowly, over the next two and a half years.

Chapter Four

Approach to a Treaty:
July 1957 - December 1959

> The *scientific basis* for ascertaining the
> valuations in society is poor.
> Gunnar Myrdahl, *Objectivity in Social Research*

There were two outstanding features of the manner in which the new Diefenbaker government approached this policy-making during those heady days in the last six months of 1957. It moved cautiously, and it did not establish a close working relationship with British Columbia despite its strong endorsement of federal-provincial collaboration on the question during the election campaign. This behaviour seems to have been the result of quite deliberate choice, although some explanations for it can be found in the environment in which Mr. Diefenbaker and his associates found themselves. There was a widely held view in Ottawa that more reliable information was required before sensible planning could be advanced. The Montreal Engineering Company's report commissioned by the previous administration had not yet been received, the widely anticipated ICREB study was not expected until the later months of 1958, and federal government personnel were heavily involved in its preparation. Offsetting this factor, on the other hand, was a growing realization by senior Canadian technical personnel that the ICREB report would not be the all-inclusive document which many were expecting; as 1957 advanced, they were to urge on their superiors the need for some clear Canadian thinking prior to its release. But a very significant factor contributing to the new government's deliberateness can be found in its tactical situation politically, for it was understandably eager to capitalize on the disarray of the federal Liberal party, to consolidate its position by implementing promptly the most attractive of its campaign promises, and to obtain a working majority in the election campaign which need not be far off. In the summer and fall of 1957 and the winter that followed, there was little political advantage to be derived from a major investment of time and effort in the very complicated Columbia River question.

1. Federal Caution Before Mounting Complexity

It is not clear to what extent, if at all, the rather celebrated hesitancy with which some of the new federal Cabinet ministers established effective working relationships with their senior advisers in the bureaucracy may have affected their early approach to this policy issue. What is clear, however, is that the new administration soon found itself receiving widely differing advice from its departmental advisers as to what features of a Columbia River settlement would be in Canada's best interest. The Department of External Affairs, for instance, made no secret of its conviction that, with respect to the Columbia and its problems, "the best permanent solution is one which permits of the minimum number of sources of international difficulty in the future,"[1] even if this meant facing in mid-year 1957 unpleasant differences with the United States and other Canadian departments of government. It held that a serious injury to international relations and to United States interests would be of rather questionable merit, and a high price to pay for a slight financial gain. The Department of Fisheries remained as opposed as it had been earlier to the suggested Columbia to Fraser diversion. Within federal departments there were almost as many views on how to calculate downstream benefits, and the Canadian entitlement thereto, as there were individuals with opinions. Between and within departments there was widespread disagreement on General McNaughton's reservations concerning the merits of large-scale electrical integration across the international border.[2] Engineering personnel in the Water Resources Branch of the Department of Northern Affairs and National Resources had real doubts about some of the general's policy preferences with respect to project selection and about the leverage which he sought on this subject. In an interpretation of jurisdictional responsibility which was to have singularly little effect on the new federal Cabinet, the Department of External Affairs was prepared to assert, with reference to engineering decisions on the Columbia: "Indeed, this is a matter almost solely a provincial responsibility."[3] Shrewdly, the civil servants drew to the Cabinet's attention the fact that two of the crucial issues still to be resolved had largely been skirted to that time. These were (i) the international consequences of diversion from one watershed to another in Canada, and (ii) the manner of calculating the downstream benefit. But when the form in which any downstream benefit compensation was raised, the Department of Finance was quite willing to accept at least a part in cash; the Department of Trade and Commerce, on the other hand, leaned to a return of energy.

Complicating matters still further for the new government was the fact that it had to decide on a continuing role for General McNaughton and the IJC in the next stages of the policy formation. There were conflicting forces at work here. At first the general was close to no new members of the new Cabinet. Mr. Diefenbaker and Mr. Howard Green, the new minister of public works and a senior parliamentarian from British Columbia, had been responsible for a good deal of the general's discomfiture during his short term as minister of national defence in the winter of 1944–45. Some members of the Cabinet seem to have had real reservations concerning what they later were to describe as the general's penchant for getting enmeshed in technical details at other than his own level of responsibility. On the other hand, there were influential members of the Progressive Conservative party, such as Mr. Leon Ladner, who were close to General McNaughton, and who were convinced that the St. Laurent government had erred in moving international discussions beyond the IJC, and during the summer of 1957 urged the new Cabinet to reverse this move. Indeed Mr. Ladner spent some time in Ottawa briefing new Cabinet ministers on the legal issues at stake, and introduced General McNaughton to such key decision-makers as Mr. Green.[4]

Viewed against this background, the rather measured pace of the early Diefenbaker administration when it dealt with the Columbia River in 1957 is not surprising. Actually, before December 1957, it appears to have taken only four significant decisions with relevance to it. The discussions begun at the diplomatic level by the St. Laurent administration over a year earlier were quietly allowed to lapse. A Cabinet Committee on Columbia River Problems was established (subsequently referred to as the Cabinet Committee).[5] The interdepartmental Advisory Committee on Water Use Policy, first established in 1955, was reconstituted and a statement on Columbia River development was included in the Speech from the Throne read at the opening of the new session of Parliament on October 14. The reference to the Columbia followed immediately on indications, in the same speech, that under the umbrella of a National Development Policy, Parliament would be "asked to authorize, in joint action with the provincial governments [of the Maritime provinces], the creation of facilities for the production and transmission of cheaper electric power in those provinces," and an indication that the federal government hoped that new discussions with Saskatchewan would make possible an early start on the South Saskatchewan Dam. The reference to the Columbia declared simply: "My Ministers are pressing for a favourable settlement of international problems in connection with the Columbia River to clear the way for a joint programme with the province of British Columbia to develop the immense power in the waters of the river."[6] Finally, in the same speech, the federal government announced the creation of a Royal Commission on Energy, although its terms of reference implied a concentration on the coal, oil, and natural gas industries.

The Emergence of New Options in British Columbia. In contrast to these decisions in Ottawa which, aggregated, amounted to little more than a holding action, some very important ones for the Columbia River's development were taken during the last half of 1957 in British Columbia. In mid-September the B.C. Electric Company announced that it was commencing construction of the Burrard Thermal Plant in suburban Vancouver which, built in stages, would eventually cost over $100,000,000 and be able to supply over 900,000 kw. Prospectively, at least, thermal energy was pre-empting a market which Columbia River energy might expect to service. Not the least interesting consequence of this move was the extent to which it effectively foreclosed the development of a major project by the publicly-owned B.C. Power Commission on the Homathko River (Figure 6), and added to the frustration of some key Power Commission personnel.[7]

To appreciate the second major decision taken at this time in British Columbia, and one which involved the appearance of a new bargaining counter and policy option for the province, it is necessary to return briefly to 1956. In that year, Swedish financier Axel Wenner-Gren and some associates became impressed with the potential wealth of the largely undeveloped northern half of British Columbia, and incorporated the Wenner-Gren B.C. Development Company to investigate it. Subsequently, on November 16, 1956, representatives of Mr. Wenner-Gren signed a memorandum of intention with Mr. Bennett whereby the Wenner-Gren interests undertook to develop about 40,000 square miles of the northern part of the province, to seek forestry rights to support a projected pulp mill there, and to build a railway north from the Rocky Mountain Trench to the Yukon Border. The memorandum also included an agreement calling for a reserve to be placed on the lands and timber within the proposed development area, and for a general survey of the resources of the area, including the possibilities for hydro-electric generation.[8]

When this imaginative plan was presented to the provincial Legislature by the premier in February 1957, Mr. Bennett and his colleagues were highly optimistic and at the same time careful to give assurances that due caution was being observed. But the enthusiasm of the government was hardly contagious. From the beginning the opposition parties were hostile, and reservation if not skepticism was widely expressed in succeeding months throughout the province. The facts that Mr. Wenner-Gren had made a fortune as an armaments manufacturer, and that he had been on an Allied black list in the early part of World War II were regularly paraded. Much criticism was directed by opposition parties in British Columbia at the appointment of Mr. Einar Gunderson, a close associate and former colleague of Premier Bennett, as a Wenner-Gren vice-president. Some took exception to the land reservations, holding them to be part of a massive "giveaway" of Crown assets.[9] Many of no political affiliation reacted uneasily because of the still very cloudy image surrounding government-sponsored resource development as a result of the Trans-Canada Pipe Line Company debacle in 1956, which had served to reinforce across the country a very unfavourable impression of promotional ethics. Still others were skeptical because of the projected railway, involving a possible expenditure of the order of $1 billion. The apparent ingenuousness of a government prepared to consider seriously such an investment in a wilderness area caused more than a few heads to shake.

During the spring and summer of 1957, Ralph L. Chantrill, in charge of the hydro electric survey for the Wenner-Gren Company, became impressed with the prospect of a major power development on the Peace River (Figure 6), a tributary of the Mackenzie River which ultimately discharges into the Arctic Ocean. He became convinced that a major dam there would create in the northern Rocky Mountain Trench, the largest man-made reservoir in the world. Its very size, he declared in a memorandum to his principals, would enable it to avoid the cyclic variations so often the bane of hydro-electric systems. He was convinced that "power from the Peace will not only be greater than the potential on the Columbia River within the Province, but it is calculated that the cost of the capital investment in the project should be less than the cost of the dams and plants on the Columbia." And he added that present calculations "indicate that power from the proposed development can be delivered to the Southern areas of the Province at less cost than the far smaller developments in such areas now in operation, or contemplated for the future."[10] He was confident that new techniques of transmission would permit moving the power the distances required.

It was in the light of these recommendations that the Wenner-Gren group returned to the provincial government and, on October 7, 1957, signed a second memorandum of agreement, undertaking this time to pursue intensive surveys to determine the feasibility of a major hydro-electric project on the Peace River on or before December 31, 1959. The memorandum looked forward, if the engineering and economic analysis was favourable, to the finalization of a construction commitment. On the following day, Mr. Bennett was able to tell a press and television conference that the Wenner-Gren concern would build the world's largest hydro-electric development on the Peace River. The results would be manifold: the Fraser's salmon would be preserved, and power would be developed in abundance, four million horsepower of it, first for the north, and then "right down to the south end and even over to Vancouver Island." His enthusiasm knew no bounds; that day, he declared, was "the most important that B.C. had experienced in its whole history." He extolled the tax revenue which would be produced, the absence of a need to involve public funds, the absence of concessions. The Columbia was not forgotten. In even more typical fashion he added: "Surely now both Ottawa and the U.S. will realize we mean business. This means the development of B.C. won't be held back while the U.S. and Ottawa hold pink teas."[11] At the same time, supporters of the Mica Dam were reassured that it would proceed just as quickly as possible. As Ottawa and Washington quickly realized, when coupled with the B.C. Electric's move into thermal generation, this plan raised the possibility that storage on the Canadian Columbia need not be developed for a decade or more.

One other development on the West Coast at this time should be noted. On October 15, Mr. Bennett informed newsmen that he was not at all happy either about the indefiniteness of the reference to the Columbia River in the federal Speech from the Throne, or about its reference to "joint development." If Ottawa wanted a joint plan, he informed a press conference, it could put up the money to build the projects, and collect the costs from the downstream benefit, but not from what he regarded as British Columbia's 20 percent share. There had been far too much delay on the Columbia already, he insisted; what was needed, and needed quickly, was an agreement with the Americans on downstream benefits. And he made his terms quite clear; they were, in essence, the "Kaiser formula" of 1954. British Columbia expected the United States to build the requisite storage facilities in Canada, to transfer title to them to the province on their completion, and to credit the province with at least 20 percent of the power produced downstream by them in the United States. No one in Ottawa appeared to hear him.

Progress within the IJC. Actually, before October 1957 was over, prospects for an international agreement on the Columbia brightened considerably within the IJC itself. When the IJC assembled for its semi-annual meeting in that month, the new United States Section chairman present was Mr. Douglas McKay, President Eisenhower's former secretary of the interior who had resigned in 1956 to run, unsuccessfully, against Senator

Neuberger. Although every bit as convinced a private power man as his predecessor, Mr. McKay made an immediately favourable impression on Canadian officials. He was also fortunate, in that the American government had begun to make some of the policy decisions so long delayed.[12] Thus he was able to announce that the American Section was agreeable to having the ICREB report on three alternative schemes of development: one would involve no diversion of the Kootenay River and would assume the building of Libby, but the second, while retaining Libby, would provide for a limited diversion, and the third would encompass a maximum Kootenay to Columbia diversion, with Libby made unfeasible. And he was able to request a special meeting of the Commission "for the purpose of clarifying the United States' position on possible terms of settlement of the Libby application, about which many misconceptions appear to have arisen."[13] At this October gathering General McNaughton once again advanced the proposal he had made in the spring of 1955 that the United States apply for a Libby structure which would flood only to a depth of thirty-seven feet at the border, which would not preclude the building of a Dorr Dam, or a maximum Kootenay to Columbia diversion, but which was widely recognized as economically unfeasible. When the special meeting on the Libby application was held in New York on January 16, 1958, the United States Section, again in Mr. McKay's words, "gave assurance to our Canadian colleagues of our willingness to proceed with discussions of terms of settlement for the Libby project in the spirit of a willing buyer and a willing seller, and that we expected that recompense for use of natural resources of Canada in the Libby project could be arranged on the basis of consideration of all pertinent factors." But the American Section chairman was more specific than this, for he went on to say: "We recognize you have an equity in this reservoir. If we are allowed to build this reservoir about 20 percent of the capacity is on Canadian soil. . . . So naturally you have an equity, to be paid either in money or power." When Mr. McKay was questioned about this meeting before the United States' Senate Committee on Interior and Insular Affairs in May 1958, he reported that all commissioners felt progress had been made, but that the official Canadian attitude relayed through the Canadian Section, was, simply, that it wasn't ready to reply. Mr. McKay did add that the commission had received "continued frank and discouraging statements from the Canadian chairman to the effect that the Libby project is unlikely to be favourably regarded by Canada."[14]

General McNaughton before the External Affairs Committee. While General McNaughton continued with his "hard" approach in the IJC, he was matching it before the External Affairs Committee, where he made his 1957 appearance in December. Once again he reviewed the story of the Libby application. He emphasized at length the merit of a plan of development to which his commitment seems to have hardened progressively after 1954. The Libby project was dismissed before the committee (in favour of Upper Kootenay-Columbia storage and diversion) as having "no advantage to Canada whatsoever," and the Mica Dam was endorsed as was one at Murphy Creek on the Columbia main stream just north of Trail, B.C. He was as critical of a High Arrow proposal as he was of Libby; referring to Murphy's 1,402 feet maximum elevation of storage on the Arrow Lakes (in contrast to High Arrow's 1,446 feet level) he declared flatly "we have no Canadian interests to be served by more storage than that." General McNaughton saw nothing for Canada in the international Columbia Valley Authority, twice proposed in that year by Senator Neuberger, reminded the committee that by the Americans' own statement "the repetition of the flood of 1894 would do something over $300 million worth of damage," and was as enthusiastic as ever about the merits of diversion.[15] Twice he sought to argue the compatibility of high dams and fish. He was questioned about the significance of the Peace River project, and was rather more cautious in his replies than Mr. Ingledow of the B.C. Electric had been a few weeks earlier. Mr. Ingledow had not been at all sure that the surplus power from the north could be transmitted economically and prudently to the lower mainland.[16] The general, who had seen Mr. Chantrill for what he called purely exploratory talks, simply indicated that there were real problems technically with long distance transmission.

Analysis Received and Commissioned. General McNaughton's willingness to be so categoric in his project evaluations before the External Affairs Committee in December was especially significant in view of the recommendations which the Montreal Engineering Company had forwarded to the federal government with its confidential report just a month previously. The Montreal company's analysis had emphasized the uneconomic nature of independent development of the Columbia in Canada. It had come out strongly for cooperative development, and the complete integration of power systems on both sides of the southern British Columbia border if maximum benefits were to be derived. And, in the integrated program, it had held the Arrow Lakes Dam to be "the most productive project that could be undertaken as an initial stage to serve the power needs of both countries." It recommended favourably on a limited Kootenay River to Columbia diversion at Canal Flats, where an inexpensive work could re-route as much as 25 percent of the Kootenay flow otherwise available to the Libby reservoir. The prospect of much greater

Kootenay diversion and storage in this area—as favoured by General McNaughton—was recognized, but the projects which it would entail were not included in the two alternative plans for development in Canada, integrated with the American system, which it advanced.[17] (See Table 1 and Figures 2 and 7.) (Central to General McNaughton's emerging concept of an optimal plan for Canada was a major high altitude reservoir which would straddle the Columbia-Kootenay height of land in the Rocky Mountain Trench and would discharge north into the Columbia. As finally detailed it would stretch from a dam at Luxor on the Columbia to one at Bull River on the Kootenay. In addition, to effect a maximum diversion of the Kootenay, a further dam was envisaged at Dorr, just north of the international boundary on that river, backing water up to the Bull River Dam for pumping into the Bull River-Luxor reservoir, which, in all, would provide over 4 million acre-feet of usable storage.)[18] Libby's high cost to the United States was made very clear by the Montreal report, but it did suggest that "any settlement that would result in

TABLE 1

Alternative Programs for Integrated Development of the
Canadian Columbia (Montreal Engineering Company)

Project	Cumulative Benefits to both countries *Billions of KWH*	Cumulative Capital Costs *Millions of Dollars*
Alternative No. 1		
Arrow Lakes—storage	13.9	112
Mica Creek f.s.l. 2435—power & storage plus		
Canal Flats—diversion	32.5	466.5
Revelstoke Canyon—power	35.5	535.5
Downie Creek—power	40.1	626.5
Murphy Creek—power	41.7	709.5
Alternative No. 2		
Arrow Lakes—storage	13.9	112
Surprise Rapids—power & storage plus		
Canal Flats—diversion	20.5	208.5
Mica Creek f.s.l. 2285—power & storage	29.4	417.5
Revelstoke Canyon—power	29.8	486.5
Downie Creek—power	35.8	577.5
Murphy Creek—power	38.6	660.5

Canada's getting the benefit of Libby storage without charge would be to Canada's advantage."[19] The lack of coincidence between these views and those of General McNaughton, who was strongly opposed to major storage on the Arrow Lakes and to the electrical integration of power systems across the international border, and who was already convinced that under no circumstances could a clearance for Libby be advantageous to Canada, was, to put it mildly, striking.

It was against this background of positive action in British Columbia, of a growing willingness to negotiate and not a little restlessness in Washington, D.C., and of General McNaughton's disagreement with much of the technical advice which the federal government was receiving from the Montreal Engineering Company and its own staff, that in December 1957 the federal Cabinet Committee decided to call for yet another evaluation of the alternatives for Columbia River development. Several features of this approach to policy formation are noteworthy. The province of British Columbia was not involved in the study, although Mr. Williston was informed, belatedly, that it was being undertaken. Reflecting its own desire for objective advice and readily legitimized conclusions, the Cabinet Committee sought to have the new investigating group chaired by Mr. Graham Towers, the widely respected former governor of the Bank of Canada. The effort failed; Mr. Towers was approached, but declined; in the end General McNaughton became the chairman. And in its search for the best possible assessment, for one on which to base supportable conclusions, as one minister put it at the time, the Cabinet Committee appears to have asked for a fundamentally economic analysis. (The group in question is referred to subsequently as the Economic Committee.) The general was the only engineer involved and he was no economist. Initially, the Department of Northern Affairs and National Resources' Water Resources Branch was not represented directly on the committee at all. Two members of the reporting group were to be senior economists from the Department of Public Works and Trade and Commerce. One was to be the deputy minister of finance (or his nominee), and one a nominee of the governor of the Bank of Canada. Specifically this high-level committee was enjoined both to work out principles for determining the downstream benefits which Canadian storage could produce in the United States[20] and to apply them to the alternative schemes of Columbia River development available.

As it turned out, the Economic Committee soon discovered that the task it had been assigned was highly complicated, that the work would take minimally four to six months to complete, and that assistance would be required from an economist with hydro-electric utility experience. One such on the staff of the Department of Northern Affairs joined the Com-

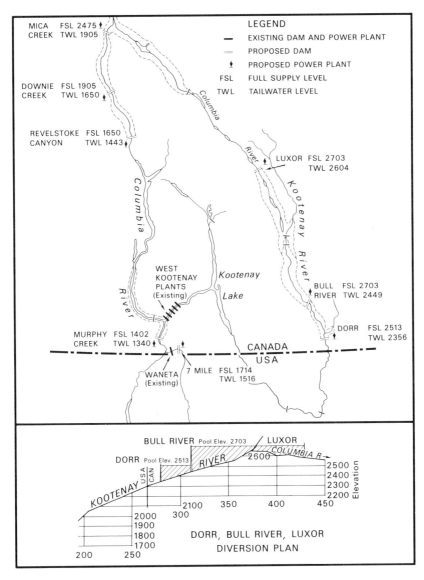

FIGURE 7. The Proposed Dorr-Bull River-Luxor Diversion and Associated Development, with a Related Profile. (The Development Map adapted from: The Montreal Engineering Company, Ltd., *Columbia River Studies*, March 1964, Appendix I. The Profile adapted from: *The Columbia River Treaty and Protocol*, issued by the Departments of External Affairs and Northern Affairs and National Resources, April 1964, p. 40.)

89

mittee, and, in addition, the services of Mr. Larratt Higgins, an economist who had worked for Ontario Hydro, were obtained. The record clearly indicates that, during the Economic Committee's deliberations, although several members of the group fought hard to present alternative points of view, and to sound warnings, General McNaughton dominated the direction of the committee's research, and greatly influenced the derivation of its conclusions. The prescience of at least two members of the committee was striking. One, from the first meeting he attended, kept drawing to the committee's attention the probability that, initially, there would be downstream benefit power for which there would be no domestic Canadian market, and that, crucial to any evaluation, would be the price that the United States would pay for this energy. Regularly also he reminded the committee of the absence of any consideration of sequence and timing in the ICREB studies, and of the strong case for Arrow Lakes storage already made by the Montreal Engineering Company, and emerging among technical circles in British Columbia. He wanted his colleagues' conclusions on this last issue submitted to a power system analyst for study. General McNaughton made clear his lack of enthusiasm for damming the Arrow Lakes, and vetoed the idea. Also insightful was the economist who, at the very last meeting of the committee, appeared disturbed at a conclusion in the report referring to the maximum use within Canada of Canadian resources without reference to costs. But once again the chairman had no doubts, and said so.

2. THE ARMS-LENGTH AND STRUCTURED RELATIONSHIPS BETWEEN VICTORIA AND OTTAWA, 1957–1959

As it turned out, the Economic Committee worked until late November 1958 before its report was complete. In the meantime, the federal government had other goals in mind. Parliament was dissolved on February 1, and an election called for March 31, 1958. Once again Columbia development was to be debated on the hustings, but only in British Columbia, and then really in a very minor way. The Columbia was simply ignored in eastern press coverage of the election. Mr. Diefenbaker with his National Development Plan and northern vision and his call for a working majority were the key issues. Mr. Howard Green's tactics were interesting, for he raised the river's development in a speech at Vancouver on February 25, in a baiting of Mr. Bennett which he was to repeat in the following month. He criticized British Columbia's failure to seek an agreement providing for joint federal-provincial Columbia development, and insisted that the province appeared to be more interested in the Wenner-Gren development. British Columbia, he maintained, should make the first move. He affirmed that Ottawa was prepared to go ahead jointly, while conceding that the downstream benefits question had not been settled.[21]

Almost at once Mr. Bennett replied to this in the provincial Legislature. Whereas the Liberals had done little to negotiate on downstream benefits, he declared, the Conservatives had done nothing at all. He went on to decry the now popular criticism of the United States. James Sinclair's 1957 declaration was described as "110 percent politics." And now, the premier added, "my very good friend Howard Green is making a similar one in this election."[22] When Mr. Diefenbaker came to the province during the campaign, Mr. Ladner was called to Revelstoke and asked to write the Columbia section of the prime minister's March 13 speech to be delivered in Vancouver. Mr. Ladner prepared a considerable memorandum on the subject—after phoning General McNaughton—and the speech duly reflected the previous year's emphases on assisting and cooperating with the province, while safeguarding its rights, especially those under the Boundary Waters Treaty. This time no one appears to have reacted unhappily, and on March 31 the Progressive Conservatives received their working majority—in fact, the greatest in Canadian history—winning 208 out of 265 House of Commons seats, and a plurality of the representation in every province save Newfoundland.

As soon as the election result was clear, messages were received in Ottawa from Victoria and Washington, quite obviously designed to produce some more positive action on the Columbia. Mr. Williston wrote both to Mr. Alvin Hamilton, the minister of northern affairs and national resources, and to Mr. Sidney Smith, the secretary of state for external affairs, asking for direct contact and collaboration between the two Canadian governments in the derivation of a Columbia River development policy. In an aide-mémoire, the United States once again raised the prospect of a clearance for the Libby project. And on May 8, by letter, General McNaughton was able to inform Mr. Hamilton that the United States had recognized the equity in the Canadian request for a share in the benefits created "from the services rendered and resources committed by Canada, and it has been agreed in the International Joint Commission that the bargain to be sought should represent agreement between 'a willing buyer and a willing seller'."

In the after-glow of their remarkable electoral success, however, the Progressive Conservative ministers were in no mood to hurry. Indeed, the Cabinet Committee did not even meet to consider the American aide-mémoire until May 15, and when it did, it quickly agreed that a Libby project should not be considered outside the context of a general Columbia River agreement. On this occasion the Cabinet Committee engaged in a broad-ranging discussion which revealed some most significant differences in the perspectives of its members. Mr. Sidney Smith, for instance, made no secret of his concern at the manner in which General McNaughton, as the only individual at the federal level then publicly discussing specific Columbia River projects, was leaving the impression that he was outlining government policy. Mr. Smith and Mr. Hamilton both wished for an effective liaison with the province of British Columbia, and Mr. Hamilton felt some such contact imperative before any reply to the United States was made. But another minister spoke in a very different vein. He felt that neither the American note nor the Williston letter ought to be treated with much consideration, and that the Columbia question was a highly political issue in B.C. where Mr. Bennett was fighting for his political life. It would be unwise to sit down on "an around the table basis" with the province, he maintained, particularly since the objective of the federal government had not yet been decided. This same minister was additionally very unhappy at the United States' move, via the aide-mémoire, in going back to the diplomatic level. To him this action was "fantastic," a by-passing of General McNaughton, of whom the Americans were afraid. As far as can be determined, responses to the aide-mémoire and the Williston letters were indefinitely postponed.

For some months, with the federal government obviously marking time and remaining aloof, there was not much that the government in British Columbia could do, save wait for its own final engineering report, and fend off charges that it was private-power oriented and "dragging its feet" on the Columbia. But one important decision was taken during this period. On June 2, 1958, Premier Bennett announced that the river would be developed by "public power."[23] At the same time he insisted that his government believed in both public and private enterprise in energy generation, and indicated that if the Columbia were too large for the B.C. Power Commission, the province would be prepared to enter into a partnership with Ottawa. A spokesman for the B.C. Electric Company, on hearing of this decision, described it as logical in the light of federal offers and other complications. By mid-summer the premier was becoming restive. He had his reservations about comprehensive analysis (not least because it had been underway for over a decade without producing a solution), and knew that the IJC's efforts were going to leave many questions unanswered. Hence on July 31 he proposed a top level conference of President Eisenhower, Mr. Diefenbaker, and himself to clear away the roadblocks to progress on the river. The prime minister rejected the suggestion in the House of Commons, suggesting a need to leave the matter with the Department of External Affairs, and to wait until the ICREB report had been filed.[24]

In the last ten days of July the entire IJC, with a large supporting party, made a 2,000 mile traverse of the Columbia River basin. When it was over General McNaughton paid a call on Mr. Williston in Victoria, and reviewed with him the steps still to be taken before agreement was reached with the Americans. Crucial to the general's view of the situation was an assumption that the entire set of negotiations with the United States, still ahead, would be conducted under IJC auspices. The position which the general advanced in this conversation was synopsized by an IJC staff member in this fashion: "After the Commission had all the factual data required, indicating the development possibilities of the Basin, detailed analysis, consultation and negotiation within the Commission would be required in order to arrive at a plan of development which would be equitable to both countries and which could be recommended for acceptance by the Governments. He emphasized when he referred to Canada he included British Columbia." It is quite apparent that Mr. Williston was perturbed at this suggestion that a reconciliation and coordination of federal and provincial objectives take place under the IJC umbrella, but for the moment he seems to have been restrained in his reply to the Canadian Section chairman. He referred to the Crippen-Wright Report, which he expected would be tabled in the provincial Legislature at an early date, stressed the need for a united front before the Americans, and was "concerned lest the consultations between British Columbia and Canada be delayed so long that Canada might find itself committed to a specific plan without prior discussion and agreement with British Columbia on the policy questions."[25] Quietly, also, he drew attention to the embarrassment impending if, when the Crippen-Wright Report was made public, he had to admit to almost total ignorance of federal Canadian objectives for the development of the Columbia.

Less than three weeks after this Premier Bennett sought publicly to clarify his government's position. At Nelson in the Kootenays he declared, exaggerating considerably, that British Columbia was ready to let a contract for Columbia River development the moment the downstream benefit question was settled. He referred to a Columbia report expected in two months, and to one on the Peace (about which he was optimistic) due in a month. "We think it would be unwise to divert the Columbia into the Fraser," he declared. And he added, "In fact, General McNaughton . . . now agrees with me on this." He reaffirmed the policy of public development of the Columbia "by the B.C. Power Commission or by some other authority to be set up."[26] The province would be happy to accept grants, he announced, or money at low interest rates.

On August 25, 1958, Mr. Williston's concern at the manner in which formal Canadian policy seemed to be evolving led him to write a long letter to the minister of northern affairs and national resources (Mr. Hamilton) in which he expressed his "alarm at the apparent lack of understanding and total absence of any cooperative effort towards an agreed-upon policy approach on this matter between our two governments." He left no doubt about the danger that the general's public pronouncements would be construed as official policy, and expressed reservations about some of the general's statements. Mr. Williston was concerned about "the impracticability of extremes in planning" because of the many political and economic problems involved, and continued, in a seeming reference to the work of the Economic Committee: "Yet General McNaughton stated to me that in the final analysis this extreme planning of the hydro-resources of the Columbia in Canada would in all probability be a statement of the Canadian position, and I can only assume that the position would be taken in spite of, or possibly without previous discussion with the province of British Columbia."

Mr. Williston reminded Mr. Hamilton that he had never been officially notified of these latest federal government studies on the Columbia, and had heard only unofficially of inter-departmental study groups. He expressed particular interest in the Economic Committee, indicating how different it was from what he had first understood it to be, and how, on April 1, he had suggested provincial representation on any such body. He drew attention to the dangers involved, if no prior agreement between the two Canadian governments had been arrived at, in a suggestion from the External Affairs Committee, then sitting, that in 1959 public hearings on the Columbia's development be held—after the receipt of the ICREB Report. Insisting that the Columbia was a "provincial resource," he suggested that any federally sponsored public hearings "to justify use of its own natural resource would be to place the province in an intolerable position." He also warned of the limitations of the ICREB Report, indicating that it probably would contain no answers and set forth no recommendations. Further he said that the report "will likely give no useable measure of the benefits accruing for the use of Canadian storage." Mr. Williston returned to the fact that General McNaughton, although stressing his unofficial status, had left him with the impression "that all reports and all data were being funneled through his hands and that he personally would be entrusted with negotiating the best possible settlement on behalf of Canada and the province of British Columbia." Before closing, he reemphasized the need for agreement at the ministerial level.

Mr. Williston's letter appears to have brought matters to a head in Ottawa, where Mr. Smith was not alone at the Cabinet level in his concern over the general's role, and where senior staff in the Department of Northern Affairs and National Resources and the Department of Finance were especially perturbed. In any case, Mr. Hamilton replied on October

10, confirming that the Canadian Section chairman was acting without direction, and quite unofficially. Further, he agreed to the requests for inter-governmental coordination, suggesting that perhaps its first form should be engineering liaison at the technical level. Mr. Williston, in reply, agreed to the technical contacts on October 22. Thus formally for the first time in thirteen years of planning as to how the Columbia should be developed, Victoria and Ottawa undertook on a continuing and structured basis to coordinate their search for a common Canadian policy.

As the year wore on, the metropolitan press in British Columbia found it increasingly difficult to appreciate the premier's unbounded optimism about the province's ability to handle the two major river developments simultaneously. Even *The Province*, by no means Mr. Bennett's sharpest critic, on October 25, attributed to him a definite preference for Peace River development, and warned that this would "rob the province of the almost providential opportunity now before it to get cheap power for future development." But the premier scoffed at all fears expressed. There would be no delay on the Columbia, Peace River or no Peace River, he affirmed. Yet he was sure that the province would get both together, and, blandly—his critics felt—argued that British Columbia power needs would grow so much that such a program would be justified.[27]

Controversy in British Columbia and a Clarification of Responsibility. "Power" politics took a very dramatic turn in British Columbia on November 12, 1958, when Premier Bennett went to Vancouver to meet the board of directors of the Wenner-Gren group's newly formed Peace River Power Development Company, and attended a press conference at which that company made some very significant announcements. Spokesmen for the new corporation declared that power from the Peace River could be delivered in the lower mainland area more cheaply than power from any existing or other new source within British Columbia. They suggested that even if the Mica Creek resource on the Columbia were immediately developed, the province would be power deficient by 1968; they asserted categorically that Peace River power could be transmitted efficiently to the lower mainland, that it need not be exported to the United States, and that navigation downstream from a Peace River dam would not be affected adversely. Finally, and this attracted much attention, it was announced at this time that the B.C. Electric Company had taken an interest in the Peace River Power Development Company, and that the B.C. Power Commission had been invited to acquire an equal share. Dr. Dal Grauer, the president of the B.C. Electric Company, issued a formal statement also, explaining his company's association with the northern project as a hedging operation in case the Peace turned out to be cheaper than thermal power on the coast, and as necessary since "the Peace is the only river which can be counted on and built to completion"[28] by the time his utility needed additional energy.

These revelations, however, were quickly overshadowed by news from Victoria, for also on November 12 the general manager of the B.C. Power Commission, Mr. Lee Briggs, issued a three thousand word statement in which he declared that he would not stand idly by "while those charged with the administration of the fiscal affairs of this province prostitute the 80,000 customers of the B.C. Power Commission to fulfil election promises."[29] The issues which prompted this unprecedented outburst were two. The government wished to refinance some of its borrowings on behalf of the Power Commission in its effort to eliminate all direct debt—making them instead direct obligations of the power utility. Also the government had requested that a rate increase which the Power Commission had intended to implement in September be held up, and had instituted an investigation of the commission's finances. Mr. Briggs on November 13 issued a further statement which included a direct attack on Mr. Einar Gunderson's directorship on the Wenner-Gren company, and on the stock options granted to senior B.C. Electric executive personnel.[30] On November 14 came two more of his exceptional press releases[31]—and the news that Mr. Briggs had been fired—as he turned his attention on the treasure in natural resources in the north "worth more than King Solomon's mines"[32] allegedly being given to the Wenner-Gren interests, on the financial policies of the B.C. Electric, on personnel links between it and the Peace River Power Development Company, and on the B.C. Electric Company's allegedly hostile attitude to the Power Commission.

Mr. Briggs' charges (which had not been cleared with his superiors, the power commissioners, who shortly resigned) need not be detailed further here. On November 17 Premier Bennett announced that the charges were to be made the subject of investigation by a royal commission chaired by Dr. Gordon Shrum, a prominent Canadian physicist, and dean of the faculty of graduate studies at the University of British Columbia. In two interim reports issued early in 1959, and a final one presented on August 14, 1959, the Shrum Commission largely discounted the charges of Mr. Briggs as they pertained to the Power Commission. It found the suggested financing not unreasonable as a basis for discussion, and held that the basic rate increase suggested by the Power Commission was unnecessary at that time. The Shrum Report did reveal that it was not until December 1958, after Mr. Briggs' departure, that the province gave a first formal intimation to the Power Commission that it was to be the agency to undertake Canadian developments on the Columbia River, and that on one occasion Premier Bennett had told the power commissioners verbally not to plan any further power developments "because in future the Commission's power was to be supplied to it."[33] It conceded that the Power Commission had not had a clear indication from the government as to its intended role, but did not agree that this or the aforementioned verbal instruction constituted political interference.

There were a number of important features to or sequels of the "Briggs Affair." For a while at least the provincial opposition parties championed Mr. Briggs' cause with great enthusiasm, as they sensed here a quite unanticipated vindication of their suspicions of the provincial government and its enthusiasm for the Peace River development. For instance, the leader of the B.C. Liberal party, Arthur Laing, announced on November 28, 1958, that he had talked with General McNaughton, who saw a 1960 start on the Columbia as a real possibility. Mr. Laing, referring to the forthcoming ICREB study as the "Sequence 9" report, was confident that Columbia power would cost two to three mills compared to the Peace's seven to eight mills cost per kwh delivered to the lower mainland.[34] Mr. Robert Strachan and Mr. Deane Finlayson, the provincial leaders of the CCF and Progressive Conservative parties respectively, joined Mr. Laing in praising Mr. Briggs and flailing the government. For a time, Mr. Briggs was a considerable popular hero. As the weeks passed, however, and the Shrum Royal Commission hearings revealed that his undoubted, indeed passionate, sincerity might have led to some genuine misconceptions, and certainly had involved him in some mighty personality clashes,[35] his support waned.

In spite of a widespread and lingering impression that the provincial government had not been entirely candid or fair in its response to Mr. Briggs, it is not at all clear that the entire episode did Mr. Bennett and his associates any real harm. The federal government was to give a last interesting fillip to Mr. Briggs' departure, when on August 10, 1959, in a move hardly designed to conciliate British Columbia's premier, it made Mr. Briggs one of its initial appointees to the newly-established National Energy Board.[36]

The B.C. Power Commission came out of this experience with ultimate responsibility for developing the Columbia River, with a new chairman, Dr. Hugh L. Keenleyside,[37] and with two ministers of the provincial Cabinet sitting on its board. In the excitement, one possibility open to it was not taken up, the opportunity to purchase an equity holding in the Peace River Power Development Company.[38] A final development takes us back to the Shrum Report, for that document recommended strongly the establishment of an over-all provincial authority "to control and direct the generation, transmission, and distribution of all electric power in British Columbia." It felt that such a body with a small research staff should be strong and independent enough "to assume the role of adviser to the government on all matters of policy pertaining to power development, generation, transmission, and distribution, and to other uses of water resources."[39] The premier accepted the suggestion by announcing the creation of the British Columbia Energy Board on August 19, 1959. Dr. Shrum became its first chairman, and Mr. Sinclair, now associated with the province's fisheries industry in a private capacity became one of its members.[40]

Late 1958 and Early 1959 Developments in Ottawa. The month of November 1958 was also to see some important new developments in the approach to Columbia River policy formation at the federal government level. Toward the end of the month, the federal Cabinet received the confidential report of the Committee on Economic Studies of the Columbia River Development. Several features of this document are significant. It sought to work out the principles for sharing the downstream benefits, and concluded that the benefits of cooperation should be divided equally between the buyer and the seller. Specifically it suggested that the two countries should contribute in money to the costs of storage in Canada in proportion to the benefits received therefrom. And it noted that under the principle it here endorsed, Canada would pay to the United States in money the incremental costs of generation and transmission of Canada's half-share of the downstream power benefit. When it turned to a division of the flood control benefits, the report suggested that Canada receive in money one-half the downstream flood control benefit calculated actuarially as an average annual saving in flood damage. In addition it recommended that the cost to Canada in energy lost and other expenses incurred in meeting requests for flood control operation of a reservoir be computed after the event and returned to Canada in energy or cash as found expedient.

The Economic Committee also applied the principles, briefly outlined above, to four selected alternative forms of Columbia River development. In each case it indicated for the alternatives being compared, the cost of delivering a uniform quantity of energy to the major provincial market in Vancouver. Summarized, the results of its analysis appeared as follows:

1. Independent development of the Columbia River without a diversion to the Fraser River and without regard to effects downstream.   5.31 mills

2. Cooperative development—based on interconnection and coordinated operations.
    (a) A proposal submitted in the Montreal Engineering Report.   4.31 mills[41]

(b) A proposal studied by the International Columbia
River Engineering Board.   3.84 mills[42]

3. A development based on the premise that when the
dams have been constructed on the Fraser River System, there would be a diversion of 10 or 15 million
acre-feet of water from the Columbia to the Fraser.
Cost before diversion to the Fraser: 3.63 mills[43]

4. A development based on proposals involving the construction of works in Canada by United States interests
in return for downstream benefits. Cost: 4.55 mills

The report went on to observe that the sequences of development apparently most favourable to Canada, 2(b) and 3, were not real alternatives, and that indeed 2(b) could become 3 with Kootenay diversion
through the building of dams at Luxor and Dorr. Significantly Arrow
storage was considered in one alternative only, 2(a), and Libby was
included in none. Lest this latter fact be overlooked, the report concluded
with the observation that the Libby project proposed by the United States
was not compatible with maximum development in the interest of Canada.
And it emphasized also that for the maximum development of electrical
energy in the Columbia basin in Canada a Kootenay diversion with
projects at Luxor and Dorr was required. One other feature of the report
should be mentioned. In an appendix it reviewed likely patterns of development in the future when the proportion of thermal generation had risen
to that point where the hydro plants economically would be transferred
from a base load to a peaking function. After a period lasting from two
to two and a half decades it expected not only that the peaking function
would be the major use for hydro, but also that the value of storage under
these circumstances would be very much enhanced.

Here then was a technical evaluation for the government of Canada
which in some notable respects ran counter to the study received a year
earlier from the Montreal Engineering Company. It certainly seemed to
suggest that, in terms both of the quantum of power made available to
Canada and of the unit cost of that power, the optimal development for
Canadians was one which closely followed General McNaughton's well
known preferences.

Assessing the impact of this confidential report is difficult, not least
because in November some key members of the Cabinet Committee
received advice of a very different sort from another very able member of
the Canadian Section of the IJC. The individual in question was Mr.
Donald M. Stephens, the chairman of Manitoba Hydro, whom Mr. Lesage
had considered placing on the international group of technical advisers

which he proposed in 1957. At the beginning of 1958 the Diefenbaker administration appointed Mr. Stephens to the IJC, where he soon became very concerned at what he regarded as jurisdictional confusion, both within Canada and internationally, over the handling of the Columbia River Reference. He became concerned also at "the apparent reluctance upon the part of the Canadian and United States commissioners to open their minds to one another."[44] In addition, as the year 1958 advanced, he had become increasingly disturbed at the fact that the IJC had reached no agreement upon some basic principles from which it could reason in assessing the great mass of technical information shortly to be put before it by the ICREB. During the summer he had a number of informal conversations with one American commissioner (Mr. Weber) and one prospective commissioner (Mr. Adams) which had convinced him that there was a genuine appreciation on their part of the need to clarify the commission's role—and indeed that, if the downstream benefits were fairly defined, there was a good chance that the United States would agree to an equal division of them. When, however, nothing was done to produce the interpretations he felt so necessary, on November 11, 1958, while in Ottawa on a visit, he spoke to three of the federal government's senior public servants about his concern. They (Messrs. R. B. Bryce, G. R. Robertson, E. Côté)[45] in turn urged him to see two Cabinet ministers, Mr. Alvin Hamilton and Mr. Green (the acting prime minister in Mr. Diefenbaker's absence). And this he did on November 13, after first outlining his views to General McNaughton, and getting from him a seeming and rather surprising endorsement of them.

The substance of the position which Mr. Stephens advanced at this time in Ottawa was as follows: Canada, he urged, should tell the Canadian Section of the International Joint Commission to quit doing British Columbia's business (in planning its future power supply) and get on with its own. The province should be urged, he suggested, to create a new agency to coordinate all of its efforts in this field, or to give this task to an existing one. What he went on to argue was that neither the province nor its agencies could at that time determine the character and the quantum of the downstream power and flood control benefit, that this would require international discussions and agreement, and that here was surely the proper concern of the Canadian government and the IJC. It was here that his informal contacts with his American colleagues strengthened his case, for when he urged that Canada suggest in an aide-mémoire to the government of the United States that the two governments make a further reference to the IJC asking it to produce principles which could govern the determination and the apportionment of the downstream benefit, he was able to add the categoric assurance that if the American government referred the suggestion to the American members of the IJC, in view of their evident desire to clarify the commission's role, a favourable response could be expected. Mr. Stephens, however, went further in the proposition he advanced, for he urged that both countries quickly designate the entities which would be responsible for producing the anticipated benefits, that these work closely with the commission on the derivation of the principles, and that once the IJC had produced them and they had been tentatively accepted by the national governments, the principles should be relayed to the entities in question. Mr. Stephens envisaged that the utilities subsequently, in the light of the now governing principles, their own load requirements, system planning and resources available, would jointly propose certain agreed-on projects (which had been properly cleared by all local authorities) to their national governments for inclusion in a treaty. The treaty as he conceived it would make provision for still other projects, agreed upon by the entities, to be approved later, and would make provision also for a continuing role for the IJC in reviewing and modifying the principles (where necessary), and in all cases approving such additions.

When the Cabinet Committee reassembled in Ottawa on December 2 and 3, it was to accept completely and to move to implement at once Mr. Stephens' suggestion concerning another reference to the IJC. As a consequence, on December 5, Canada proposed to the United States in an aide-mémoire that, if it were agreeable, the IJC be asked to report on three additional issues: the method to be used for determining the nature and quantity of the downstream power benefit; the method or principle to be followed in dividing this benefit; and the method to be used in assessing the value of storage for flood control, and in determining how it should be used and paid for.[46]

On the other hand the Cabinet Committee did not in any way concede Mr. Stephens' second point that the detailed planning of the utilization of the Columbia River resource was essentially a provincial responsibility. The aide-mémoire of December 5, in fact, was sent without any prior consultation with British Columbia, and it is quite clear that the Cabinet Committee at this time still assumed that the IJC would continue to be heavily involved with engineering and technical aspects of the river's development.[47] Nor was it prepared to abandon a role for itself here, as it spent much of the December 2 and 3 meetings seeking to assess the Economic Committee's Report—although in the end it went no farther than endorsing the concept of internationally cooperative development, and the need to preserve Canada's diversion rights. Its concern with project selection was manifest, and its determination to extract the maximum political advantage from a close association with the entire development was made doubly clear when, on December 6, 1958, Mr. Howard Green publicly announced the receipt of the Report of the Committee on Economic Studies and the federal government's decision to seek an agreement with the United States. His press release, which mentioned British Columbia's government only once, placed great stress on the benefits which would accrue to the Kootenay and Okanagan districts of the province, on the less than four mill cost of Mica and downstream benefit power combined, delivered in Vancouver. His statement included, as well, this paragraph: "Furthermore the postponement of such development in favour of some other power scheme could well result in making the development of the Columbia River in Canada impossible." When this was read to Mr. Bennett in Victoria his reaction was to stress the leverage value of the Peace, and the fact that both rivers were needed. The premier's comment, when relayed to Mr. Green, elicited the observation from him: "I wish we could be really sure Premier Bennett really wants to go ahead with the Columbia plan." Whereupon the process was reversed once more, bringing from Mr. Bennett the retort: "The best way he can be sure is to hurry up and arrange the downstream benefits."[48]

Actually, the federal government kept its distance from Victoria on Columbia River development policy throughout December 1958, and January 1959, until it had agreed with Washington on and jointly with it had relayed to the IJC the additional reference which Canada had proposed. On January 29 the two national governments asked the commission to report "at an early date its recommendations concerning the principles to be applied in determining":

(a) benefits which will result from cooperative use of storage of waters and electrical interconnection within the Columbia River system, and

(b) apportionment between the two countries of such benefits, more particularly in regard to electrical generation and flood control.[49]

In contrast to the practice followed in 1944, the wording of this reference was established without any contact whatsoever with the provincial government. Thus Mr. Williston, in addressing the provincial Legislature on January 27, discussed the absence of any effective liaison with the federal government as follows: "I have met with General McNaughton who explained in detail his concept of Columbia development. I have also received official correspondence from Ottawa to the effect that the General's opinions do not necessarily reflect federal government policy. This is as close as I have been able to get to responsible federal authority to discuss the Columbia River since the change in administration."[50] Additionally, Mr. Williston informed the Legislature that he had neither received a copy of the report of the Committee on Economic Studies, nor at that date had he been officially informed about the diplomatic exchanges then under way with the United States. In a second provincial initiative Mr. Bennett raised the entire question with Prime Minister Diefenbaker while on a visit to Ottawa on January 30, 1959. The upshot was an informal agreement to begin some effective collaboration on Columbia River policy—though not, the premier insisted, when he spoke to the press, at the cost of abandoning the Peace, for the province, he contended, needed both.

It was not until February 9, at a meeting in Ottawa attended by Mr. Alvin Hamilton, Mr. Williston, and a number of their colleagues and advisers, that a Canada-British Columbia Policy Liaison Committee on Columbia River Development was established. At the same time a Technical Sub-Committee of federal and provincial government personnel, which had already begun to function, was associated with the policy committee in a staff/advisory capacity. Schematically this administrative arrangement, which worked remarkably well over the next two years, appeared as follows:

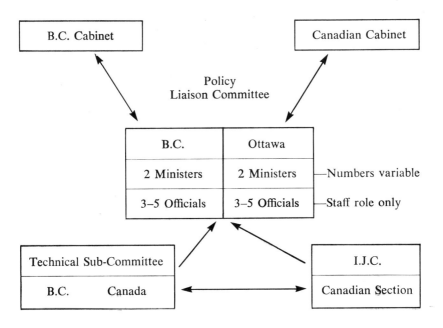

It was understood at this time that there would be minimal publicity given to the inter-governmental deliberations, and that Messrs. Hamilton and Williston would be co-chairmen, presiding in their respective capitals as the Policy Liaison Committee meetings alternated between them.

The Policy Liaison and Technical Liaison Committees were actually faced with two major tasks in 1959. One was determining an agreed-upon federal-provincial perspective concerning the principles which the IJC had been asked to establish, for it soon appeared that these involved questions of public policy ranging far beyond the ambit of the IJC itself. This challenge was met and handled successfully. The other involved establishing agreement upon an optimal plan of development which Canada might seek to obtain in the international bargaining expected to follow. This latter task was devolved by the policy committee, at its inaugural meeting on March 2, upon its technical staff advisers.

One move to significant intergovernmental cooperation in Canada came in February 1959, when the federal and provincial governments did share with each other the technical analyses which earlier they had commissioned individually. Furthermore, in March, both governments received the substance of the long awaited ICREB report, on which their personnel had collaborated with the Americans. The Montreal Engineering Company's Report and that of the Economic Committee went to Victoria, and copies of the massive Crippen-Wright study, which the province had received on January 12, were sent to General McNaughton and to the Department of Northern Affairs and National Resources in Ottawa.

3. FURTHER ANALYSES

There were three aspects of the Crippen-Wright Report which merit particular attention here. As Dr. Krutilla has pointed out, it was "unique at the time among engineering studies on the Columbia, being sensitive to problems of scale, sequence and timing of individual components of the development."[51] It enthusiastically favoured cooperation rather than independent Canadian development; "the fruits of cooperation," it declared, "confer immense benefits on both British Columbia and the United States."[52] It made no attempt to minimize the investment which developing the Columbia River in Canada would entail. But it envisaged the Columbia-Clearwater River development which it outlined ultimately producing 31,195 million kwh of potential firm power annually at a cost of 2.86 mills per kwh at load centres. It set the cost of the downstream power produced by Arrow Lakes storage as low as 2.39 mills per kwh.[53] The complete annual downstream benefit in the United States derived from Canadian storage regulation it estimated could amount to 20,000 million kwh, worth, if valued at 5.5 mills, something of the order of $110,000,000 per annum. It was unqualified in its enthusiasm for interconnections with the American system much more extensive than those required to return the downstream power benefit, and opted flatly for a fully integrated province-wide network of power plants as well. At the same time it recommended against the suggestion (endorsed by the federal Economic Committee) that each country bear an agreed-upon share of the development costs incurred in both countries. Its advice here was that Canada and the United States bear their own domestic expenses entirely.

The Crippen-Wright Report had much to say concerning a preferred scheme of development and construction sequence. Assuming that a satisfactory agreement could be reached with the Americans on downstream benefits, it advanced a High Arrow Dam as "the recommended first project on the Upper Columbia main stem" and suggested that under these circumstances "there would be no need to proceed with the Clearwater."[54] After High Arrow would follow, in order, a Kootenay Canal plant, an expansion of Lower Kootenay facilities, and projects at Seven Mile on the Pend d'Oreille (for power), at Kinbasket on the Upper Columbia (for storage at first), at Murphy Creek (for power), at Duncan Lake (for storage) (see Figure 8). Then would come generation at Kinbasket, a power-cum-storage Low Mica project and essentially power producing works at Revelstoke Canyon and Downie Creek. The Crippen-Wright group were very cautious concerning the headwaters of the Columbia and Kootenay Rivers. In an interim report they commented very favourably on a partial Kootenay to Columbia diversion effected by works at either Canal Flats or Copper Creek, and declared that in terms of power economics a large diversion effected by a project at Bull River (see Figure 9) was "not recommended."[55] The final report drew attention to the need "to establish provincial policy on the flooding of valleys," and held that "an unqualified recommendation in favour of any particular scheme of diversion is not possible until the terms of the agreement are known and the outlines of the overall scheme of developing the Upper Columbia River have been finalized."[56]

In summary, this was a report which reminded its readers of the merits of hydro electric generation in periods of inflation, which saw few combinations of projects elsewhere in the world of this magnitude which were capable of delivering power to large established land centers of population "at so low a delivered cost"[57] and which outlined a scheme of development for the Columbia which would be able to meet southern provincial power requirements from 1965 for a period ranging from thirteen to twenty-five years, depending upon load growth assumptions and the possible attraction of special industries. And finally, it was one which, by strongly endorsing the High Arrow project and by assessing benignly the Libby Dam under the circumstances of a favourable agreement with the United States, strongly reinforced the provincial government's predisposi-

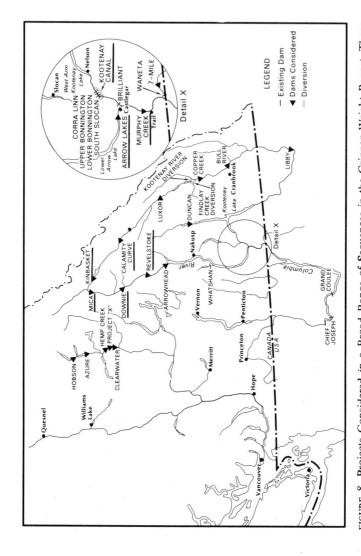

FIGURE 8. Projects Considered in a Broad Range of Sequences in the Crippen-Wright Report. Those endorsed for the recommended plan of cooperative development are underscored. (The Clearwater projects were recommended adjuncts to but not inherent in cooperative development.) (Adaptation of: Crippen-Wright Engineering Limited, *Report Hydro-Electric Development of the Columbia River Basin in Canada*, January 12, 1959, III-2.)

tion to forgo Upper Kootenay–Upper Columbia Valley storage, which under the Dorr–Bull River–Luxor scheme would flood over 70,000 acres, would impair a significant wildlife resource, would flood out much road and rail mileage, and would create a barrier to east–west transportation over 150 miles long.

The ICREB Report. The ICREB Report was formally presented to the IJC, in draft, at a meeting in Chicago on March 16–17, 1959. In the report itself and in the oral presentations made by the engineers present, the IJC was officially told that further development of the Columbia resource was "practicable and in the public interest from the point of view of the two governments,"[58] and that cooperative development of certain waters would permit greater use for flood control, irrigation, and power production purposes. The report sought to evaluate some sixty potential projects, most of them in the United States. It was a point-in-time study which examined all the proposed projects, assuming them to have been constructed in no particular order, and regarding them as all operating within "an interconnected system with cooperative use of storage to meet 1985 load with a minimum of thermal generating capacity."[59] Its perspective was system-wide; in effect, it assumed that the international boundary did not exist.

Three preliminary plans of cooperative development were subjected in the ICREB Report to a tentative evaluation, and were found to achieve "about the same degree of water resource development."[60] They were Sequence VII, providing for no diversion of the Kootenay River; Sequence VIII, providing for a modest diversion from it to the Columbia via a dam built at Copper Creek; and Sequence IX, incorporating a "full" or "Dorr" diversion of the Kootenay (see Figure 9). All three sequences provided for the construction of a High Arrow Dam, although a variant of IX, labelled IX A, provided for its elimination, and a lesser degree of Arrow Lakes storage provided by a project built downstream at Murphy Creek. (Sequence IX A, of course, was championed from the outset by General McNaughton, and in 1964 was to be labelled by him the "Canada plan.") In the light of a series of specified assumptions the report indicated that Sequence VIII, the Copper Creek diversion plan, "would provide the highest level of development of the water resources of the basin." The report added, however, that "the apparent superiority of this plan takes into account only physical and economic factors, and the margin on which this superiority rests is small. In view of these factors, and having regard to the practical limits of accuracy of the studies, no one plan of development can be selected as representing the optimal use of sites and water resources."[61]

107

The technical personnel from Ottawa and Victoria who had worked for so many years on the ICREB studies joined in stressing the limitations of the report which they were handing over to the IJC. One of the most extensive presentations at the Chicago meeting was that made by a British Columbia engineer, who, on behalf of his colleagues, argued the need for caution, as he drew attention to a number of considerations, such as project ownership, transmission costs, the economic consequences to his province of coordinating system operations, jurisdictional and flowage problems, which, in its analysis, the ICREB had not taken into account. Furthermore, he pointed out to the IJC that, since the ICREB power studies had been finalized, other schemes and sequences of development had appeared which were as good as or better than those reported on.[62] Perhaps most important of all, this British Columbian urged the IJC not to attempt to cover all contingencies in its search for rules to govern the determination and division of downstream power benefits. This viewpoint —that guidelines established to help with policy formation not be allowed to rigidify the process or to inhibit the flexibility required to resolve what was an already very complex problem—was to remain a characteristic of

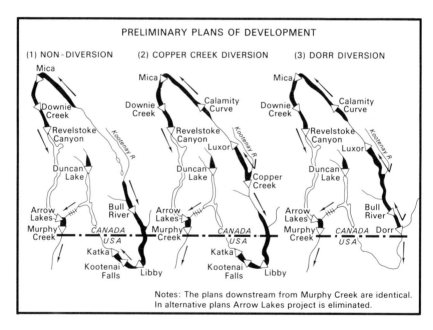

FIGURE 9. Alternative Plans of Development Advanced by the International Columbia River Engineering Board. (Adapted from: ICREB, *Water Resources of the Columbia River Basin*, Report to the International Joint Commission, United States and Canada, 1959, p. 67.)

the provincial government's position. Throughout 1959 it was clearly expressed in a number of additional ways.

4. THE SEARCH FOR NEW WORKING RULES UNDER IJC AUSPICES

One of these manifestations of the province's sensitivity to the hazards inherent in potentially inflexible guidelines and planning emerged when the IJC turned its attention to the January 1959 reference requiring it to suggest how the downstream benefits from upstream storage could first be determined and then be divided. The IJC had relatively little difficulty over the division per se. As has been indicated already, official American thinking had been changing for some time, and by May 1959 agreement on an equal division of benefits seemed to be a foregone conclusion.[63] Agreements did not come nearly so easily, however, over what was to be divided, especially over how the downstream power benefit should be calculated. Two alternative approaches to resolving this problem were apparent to all concerned with it.

One approach, indeed the one eventually endorsed by the IJC and incorporated in the Columbia River Treaty, regarded the benefit to be shared simply as the increase in dependable hydro-electric capacity and in the average annual usable electrical energy made possible by upstream storage. The assumption here, utilizing a "grossing" procedure, as it is called, was that each country would be expected to handle all of its own costs. There are a number of approaches to "netting," as the alternatives to the grossing perspective are collectively known. All stem from the unchallengeable proposition that no one knows what benefit he derives from participation in any cooperative arrangement until he determines the consequences of pursuing his best available (non-cooperative) alternative. The difference between the two represents, in effect, the net worth (or liability) of the former to him. This proposition applied to adjacent electric power systems suggests that each utility, once projects to be developed in cooperation are agreed on, very carefully evaluate the cost of meeting comparable objectives—without cooperation—by the least expensive means. For each then, the saving between this cost and the cost of acting together represents the net gain from cooperation. Summed, one has the total gain from the agreement, which may then be equitably divided. Some utilities make such calculations at present, and review each other's—albeit not across international borders. What this process guarantees, of course, is that a true benefit is shared. Without the application of a netting formula, so its proponents maintain, a party to a cooperative arrangement need not enjoy any benefit at all,[64] and certainly if mutual benefits are created under grossing and divided without reference to costs, an equal division of them would be purely coincidental. There were other approaches to netting canvassed by the Canadians. One, overwhelmingly favourable to them, after an international agreement had been reached, would have split the downstream power benefit produced in the United States in proportion to the investment *subsequently* required on both sides of the border to produce it. Another, not unnaturally advanced by the Americans, suggested a split in terms of the *total* commitment required to produce it, thus raising for consideration the more than $2 billions already invested by the United States on the main stream of the Columbia. Still another approach, considered more seriously, would have had the two countries pay equal shares of incremental costs upstream (that is, equal shares of the costs fairly chargeable to producing the downstream benefit), and of incremental costs incurred for the same purpose in the downstream state. The power produced would then be shared equally.

In the meetings which the IJC had on the January 1959 reference from February through May 1959, American spokesmen made very clear their preference for netting, and the Canadian commissioners were not unsympathetic to the principle which, it will be remembered, had been endorsed both by the Montreal Engineering Company and by the Economic Committee reports. Agreement was not reached on details, however, and some first-class arguments developed over whether or not the already existing American investment in Columbia River installations should be included in any netting formula adopted. When, however, the Canadian Intergovernmental Policy Liaison Committee met on May 29, 1959, to review the progress of the IJC deliberations, a considerable debate ensued over the policy which Canadians should pursue on this question. General McNaughton, who was present, was cautious; he seemed to feel that netting would be beneficial to Canada if the United States were not able to charge its sunk costs against regulation benefits. On the other hand, other federal spokesmen were vigorously in favour of netting.

Messrs. Bonner and Williston, representing the British Columbia Cabinet, and their technical advisers registered strong dissents. Netting across this international boundary, they insisted, was politically and probably technically unfeasible. Mr. Williston foresaw political turmoil if either of the two netting approaches being considered by the IJC were applied, and argued strongly that the Americans must be told at a forthcoming IJC meeting that grossing was being considered as well by Canada. Numerous illustrative objections were raised by him and his colleagues. What would happen, they asked, if nationalist regulations were applied on one side of the boundary to cut out low bids for equipment from foreign suppliers? How would Canadian or American legislatures react to requests for appropriations to be sent across the border? How, argued Mr.

Williston, could British Columbia politically justify paying part of the cost of an American installation which would have a continuing value after the term of an agreement, although the province could not demand a continuing benefit from it? Mr. Williston's technical advisers drew attention to differences in the two nations' financing and accounting practices, to the frequent absence of prior data on costs and benefits, to the often notorious variations between estimates and costs, to the difficulties which lay as much in interpreting as in obtaining data. The upshot was that British Columbia insisted at this time, and the Canadian Section chairman seems to have agreed, that both approaches be examined with the Americans.[65]

While the province's plea for the simplest approach to defining the downstream power benefit ultimately carried the day, the matter was not all that quickly resolved. General McNaughton, a key figure here, by July 13 had accepted the provincial position. Mr. Green, who on July 6 became the secretary of state for external affairs, may also have been a significant early convert to it. But for most of the rest of 1959 the Americans remained dubious about abandoning netting and in addition the case for it was vigorously made by a few senior members of the federal government's bureaucracy, by at least one federal minister (Mr. Hamilton), and by Mr. Donald Stephens of the IJC, who regarded grossing as senseless.[66]

Mr. Stephens and his associates notwithstanding, British Columbia's decision-makers were convinced that they were right, and refused to modify their position. Increasingly, they received support from the members of the Technical Liaison Committee. This body, in an April 28, 1959, report to the Policy Liaison Committee had pointed out that netting could have a favourable result for either side, depending on the assumptions it invoked, and that as a procedure it "equalized the natural advantages and disadvantages of each country."[67] In its third (September 1959) report to the Policy Liaison Committee it stressed the need to be careful when applying a common interest rate to calculations when different ones actually applied to the same entities involved as going concerns. Otherwise it simply listed the arguments for and against applying attributed costs to downstream generation. Quite properly, the final decision was left to the politicians, who at a Policy Liaison Committee meeting on September 29, on the grounds of simplicity and in the light of the possibility that a netting approach might lead to an American insistence on a recognition of its attributed costs, definitely opted for a grossing approach.

Even then the matter was not resolved, for the American commissioners and Mr. Stephens remained unconvinced, and they were, of course, not formally subject to direction. Drafts of the principles being circulated from the IJC offices as late as October 31 still contained provision for netting. Ultimately when a crucial Policy Liaison Committee meeting was held on December 4 to review the October 31 IJC draft of the emerging principles, the Technical Liaison Committee faced the issue squarely. The technicians reviewed the hazards involved in netting, and repeated their earlier observation that under it by reasonable calculation it would be possible to allocate greater costs to both sides. Once again, and now definitely, the policy committee opted for grossing; it simply rejected Mr. Stephens' argument that such a policy legitimized, as he put it, a "one horse, one rabbit" principle, that is it was inequitable, and that it might lead to an improvident agreement from the Canadian (or the American) point of view.[68] By this date the federal and provincial ministers had reached agreement on the question, and their real concern was not with Mr. Stephens' rearguard action, but rather with the American commissioners' reluctance to accept the position that grossing could lead to an equitable international agreement. But they were confident that "once the question was considered outside the Corps of Engineers and the Federal Power Commission, it would be so recognized."[69] Before December was out, their contention had been accepted.

The province's stress on the importance of preserving flexibility and room to manoeuvre was expressed in another way during 1959. When the British Columbians who were members of the Technical Liaison Committee turned their attention to the task of identifying an optimal plan of Columbia River development from the Canadian perspective, they seem to have concluded quickly that the difficulties involved in this analytic exercise were immense, if not insuperable, pending some clarification of the principles on which the IJC was then working. Their reasoning was relayed to their Cabinet superiors. The latter, the evidence suggests, were not at all sorry to receive it, for they were well aware of the extent to which a few months' delay here might improve the prospects for the rapidly maturing plans of the Peace River Power Development Company. The federal Cabinet ministers were equally aware of this consideration; they repeatedly urged that serious and cooperative work on an optimal plan get under way, but were held off by the province. Paraphrasing his technical advisers, Mr. Williston rejected by letter to Mr. Alvin Hamilton on July 20 a federal proposal that a cooperative assessment of the merits and demerits for Canada of a Libby Dam, a Kootenay to Columbia diversion, and of alternative forms of Upper Kootenay storage be launched immediately. The Policy Liaison Committee did again agree on September 20 that a start be made on such an effort, but little had been accomplished on it by the end of the year.

It is quite evident that, by mid-year, 1959, ministerial personnel in

Ottawa and Victoria were well aware of the fact that different perceptions of what the public interest required with respect to power development in British Columbia were emerging in the two capitals. It is evident that in this year both sets of ministers felt their positions to be strong. Neither group had a clear impression of what the difficulties inherent in, and the consequences of, a partly cooperative, partly rivalled approach to this decision-making, were going to be. But this is to anticipate. It is enough to remind ourselves again that, at this point in time and from the perspective of the provincial ministers involved, technical and strategic considerations neatly reinforced each other. At British Columbia's insistence, the cooperative search for an optimal Canadian plan simply had to wait.

One other distinctive feature of British Columbia's approach to this policy-making was a re-emphasis of a position which it had advanced four years earlier. By July, it was obvious to Mr. Williston in Victoria that the IJC was close to producing a tentative draft of the principles upon which it was working, and that General McNaughton, on behalf of the Canadian Section, intended to send it to the two Canadian governments, along with a request for their comments. The general did this in fact on September 1. Mr. Williston took the position that, if the two governments were to reply unilaterally to the Canadian Section chairman, they in effect would be allowing the Canadian Section to adjudicate any differences in the federal and provincial positions. He went on to maintain that such adjudication, if it were required, should take place within the Policy Liaison Committee. His point was agreed to; Policy Liaison Committee meetings were held throughout the fall, and the federal and provincial governments filed identical replies to the successive IJC drafts.

As has already been suggested, the United States Section did ultimately accept the grossing approach. Mr. Stephens' resistance to it continued to the end, but was outflanked. Agreement on the entire set of principles was finally announced on December 16, they were submitted to the two national governments on December 29, and from that point on the IJC's direct involvement with the formal negotiation of a Columbia River agreement ended. In view of the fact that Dr. Krutilla has reviewed the principles in detail,[70] attention will be drawn here only to those features of them which must be kept in mind when the interaction between the two Canadian governments during the negotiation of the Columbia River Treaty is reviewed over the next two chapters. The IJC advanced three general, seven power, and six flood control principles, each followed by an explicatory discussion. General Principle No. 1 provided that cooperative development designed to provide optimum benefits to each country "requires that the storage facilities and downstream power producing facilities . . ., to the extent it is practicable and feasible to do so, be added

113

in order of the most favourable benefit-cost ratio, with due consideration of factors not considered in the ratio." The proposition that cooperative development should result in an advantage to each country when compared with the domestic alternatives available to each was endorsed in General Principle No. 2. General Principle No. 3 dealt with transboundary projects such as Libby, and recorded simply that "entitlement . . . to participate in the development and to share in the downstream benefits resulting from storage, and in power generated at site, should be determined by crediting to each country such portion of the storage capacity and head potential as may be mutually agreed."

The seven power principles dealt at length with the intricacies of regulating stream flow for downstream hydro-electric generation, with the calculation of a resulting benefit, and with its division. Here Power Principle No. 6 was basic, for it incorporated the approach which the government of British Columbia and later that of Canada had insisted on. It provided for an equal sharing of the downstream power benefit (technically defined in Power Principles Nos. 3 and 4), and suggested that each state be responsible for the domestic expenses required in producing it. At the same time this principle required that General Principle No. 2 not be overridden in the process, and that where the prospect of either party being denied a genuine net advantage appeared, "there should be negotiated and agreed upon such other division of benefits or other adjustments as would be equitable to both countries and would make the cooperative development feasible."[71] The flood control principles specified that, reflecting the effectiveness of upstream storage, a flood control benefit be estimated on the basis of an assured plan of operation, and that it be paid for either in a lump sum or periodically, as agreed. The crucial provision here, embodied in Flood Control Principles Nos. 3 and 4, was that, expressed in monetary terms, the benefit be the estimated annual value of the flood damage prevented by upstream storage, and that one half of it be paid to the upstream state.

The brevity of this summary is really less than fair to the principles, which incorporated agreement on many complex issues, and which, when specific, did remarkably closely guide the course of the subsequent treaty negotiations. But the review will suffice at this point, and is detailed enough to enable the reader to appreciate a major dilemma which the representatives of both Canadian governments faced in 1959. Canadian decision-makers were well aware that in the light of benefit-cost ratios (ignoring the border, and timing) the projects which they had to offer for development on a cooperative basis outranked any available in the American portion of the Columbia River Basin. The major qualification at the end of General Principle No. 1, however, the basic reservation in

General Principle No. 2, and the complete absence of any real direction at all in General Principle No. 3 meant that, in the light of the grossing approach and the fifty-fifty split of benefits adopted, it was quite unclear as to what extent the United States would be prepared to let benefit-cost ratios determine project selection in an agreed-on plan for cooperative development. Indeed, the Canadians became quite aware during the fall of 1959 that the principles might well serve only as recommendations for subsequently guiding international decisions. The Technical Liaison Committee thus viewed them in December as "sufficiently broad to allow for international agreements,"[72] but also as giving enough latitude to each country to avoid or delay reaching a firm international agreement if it so desired.

Other Aspects of, and Inputs to, Canadian Columbia River Policy Formation in 1959. While technical and strategic considerations inhibited any effective cooperative effort by the two Canadian governments during 1959 to settle on a plan of development to which they could both subscribe, discussions of this question in Ottawa and Victoria and the shaping of some unilateral preferences, continued apace. Technical advisers and Cabinet-level policy-makers alike in Victoria remained uncommitted to any one plan, but certainly they took very seriously, through 1959, the Crippen-Wright Report's endorsation of a major early-stage storage on the Arrow Lakes, and that report's reservations concerning large-scale storage and diversion in the Upper Kootenay River Valley. Opinion ranged rather more widely in Ottawa. Most of the engineering personnel there were convinced that the case for a High Arrow project was unanswerable on economic grounds; they had had not a little to do with its inclusion in the IJC Sequences VII, VIII, IX, over General McNaughton's objection. At the same time, however, their ministerial superiors were of two minds about High Arrow, often conceding the case for it in engineering-economic terms, but tending to recoil from the political cost of flooding out some 2,000 people.[73]

Among technical personnel in Ottawa there were mixed feelings concerning proposed storages in the Upper Kootenay Valley. They were well aware of the potentially high cost of the increment of power which could be produced in Canada by building the storages at Bull River and Dorr—with or without diversion to the Columbia. But there was a good deal of concern amongst them also that an approval of Libby, the major alternative to Dorr-Bull River, would materially reduce the quantum of system benefits produced and available for international distribution.

These doubts were echoed at the Cabinet Committee level; indeed by December 1959, federal ministers had gone a long way toward accepting

General McNaughton's position apropos the Kootenay. The Cabinet ministers were well aware of Libby's low benefit-cost ratio, realizing that its inclusion would conflict with the spirit, at least, of General Principle No. 1 as it was about to be approved, and feared that accepting it would be tantamount to endorsing a sub-optimal development of the river system viewed either from an international or from a Canadian perspective. They had also been very much impressed by the general's claim that storage on the Canadian reaches of the Upper Kootenay was necessary to ensure Canadian control over that river's flow. In all, while the project preferences of the two governments' technical advisers were not that far apart, those of the ministerial-level policy-makers were anything but identical, and clearly called for some reconciliation. It was effected, rather painfully, in circumstances detailed in the next chapter.

There were three additional considerations which must not be overlooked if one is to appreciate the manner in which the two Canadian governments approached the crucial decision-making on Columbia River development during 1960. One of these was the slowdown in the Canadian economy which became evident by mid-year, 1957, and which was to become progressively more acute over the next four years. As a consequence, the Diefenbaker administration, in particular, became increasingly conscious of the stimulus to the economy which major developments in the Columbia River watershed would involve. The deliberate, unhurried, measured pace which had characterized its approach to the Columbia River during 1957 and 1958, therefore, gave way in the years which followed to a growing impatience on its part to get on with the job.

A second point to remember is that at Policy Liaison Committee meetings on September 29 and again on December 4, 1959, federal government representatives raised with provincial spokesmen the nature of the entity which would develop the Canadian watershed of the Columbia. On the first occasion they suggested that a sub-committee of representatives from the two Canadian governments be established to sketch its framework. Mr. Williston's reply reserved the province's position, promising to let Mr. Hamilton know. Nothing seems to have come of this. When asked about the matter again in December, provincial spokesmen simply indicated that it would have to be deferred until the IJC principles had been approved. Quite clearly Ottawa was anticipating a role for itself in any such body, and equally clearly the province was determined to forestall such a development. Having already informed the British Columbia Power Commission that it would be responsible for the Columbia River's development, and having already involved Power Commission personnel in planning at the Policy Liaison and Technical Liaison Committee levels, Mr. Bennett and his colleagues just were not prepared to concede at this time the need for another federal-provincial instrumentality in either an operational or a supervisory capacity, or for a direct federal government role in the operation of the Power Commission itself.

Finally, it is important to remember that during 1959, as the prospects brightened for an international agreement which might lead to a start on Columbia River development, some very prominent Progressive Conservatives (including members of the federal Cabinet) joined the ranks of those Canadians who were becoming increasingly concerned at Mr. Bennett's unwavering enthusiasm for the Peace River's development, and began to challenge him openly on the matter. Their perspective was a simple one. Assuming as they did that there would be no change in the prohibition of long-term power exports, they viewed the projected developments on the two rivers as being directly competitive; domestic markets then in sight just did not, to them, make credible the concurrent development which Mr. Bennett espoused. They were convinced also that power produced on the Peace River, bearing the cost of private financing and a transmission line 600 miles long, and without any assistance from downstream benefits, could not be genuinely competitive with energy from the Columbia River. Few of the Progressive Conservatives went as far as Mr. Deane Finlayson, who in October seemed to regard the Peace River proposal as the chief manifestation of the "complete moral bankruptcy"[74] of the Social Credit administration. Rather they were inclined to refer to British Columbia's seeming preference for the Wenner-Gren plan, or to raise doubts as to whether the province really desired to do anything on the Columbia at all.[75] Provincial Cabinet ministers either denied or ignored such allegations and did not take all of the critics (such as Mr. Finlayson, who never won a seat in the provincial Legislature) very seriously. But they were nettled all the same, especially when members of the federal Cabinet, with whom they were working quietly on the Policy Liaison Committee, or others close to that Cabinet, publicly questioned their handling of provincial power development.

One reason for the agitation of those keen to block the Peace River project at this time was that the Wenner-Gren proposal not only had an understandable appeal in North-Central British Columbia, but as 1959 advanced it acquired some significant public support elsewhere. In March, Dr. Grauer, the president of the B.C. Electric Company, suggested that the wise thing to do would be to develop both rivers and to export any surplus on a recoverable basis.[76] Six months later he quietly took a more important step while attending a meeting of the Board of the Peace River Power Development Company in London, England. There he agreed that, in preparing the report which the Peace River Company had to submit to Mr. Bennett's government by December 31, it could be assumed that the

B.C. Electric Company would purchase a block of Peace River energy.[77] There were a number of interesting sequels to this move. Mr. W. C. Mainwaring, the president of the Peace River Company, was greatly encouraged by it. He felt that it had removed the last real obstacle to the Portage Mountain (Peace River) development, which had turned out to be technically feasible. Dr. Grauer and his own staff, on the other hand, seem to have quickly come to the conclusion that the B.C. Electric Company could safely live up to its verbal purchase commitment in view of its size only if a sizeable export of energy from British Columbia were permitted. As a consequence, on September 30, 1959, he once again publicly endorsed a major sale to the United States, suggesting this time that it involve 500,000 kilowatt-years per annum of Peace River energy.[78] Privately his staff began to sound out adjacent American utilities. The consequence of all this activity was that the federal Cabinet Committee spent some time on November 24 reviewing reports of the Peace River Company's determination to have power on line by 1967, and of the way in which the B.C. Electric Company's hydro and thermal projects would meet the increase in provincial load up to that time. The prospect of a pre-emption by the Peace River project of the market which the Columbia River might serve, in the absence of a power export which the province had not requested and which the federal Cabinet does not seem to have seriously entertained, just no longer seemed all that improbable.

As 1959 drew to a close, neither Canadian government appeared willing to budge from the seemingly irreconcilable positions over the province's hydro-electric resource development which they had assumed. On December 4, just as the Policy Liaison Committee was about to assemble in Victoria, Mr. Bennett reaffirmed his determination to see the Columbia go ahead as rapidly as possible, and repeated his conviction that British Columbia needed the development of both rivers. When asked what would be done with all the energy, he replied cryptically, "Create jobs." Mr. Green, in Victoria for the Policy Liaison Committee meeting, issued his own statement on the same day in which he initially committed Ottawa to a 1960 start on the Columbia, although almost at once he modified this to a 1960 start "on the engineering phase." He envisaged the federal government sharing costs equally with British Columbia in a Columbia River development costing roughly one billion dollars.[79] Two weeks later the federal minister of justice, Mr. E. D. Fulton, affirmed that the Columbia should be the "next logical power development."[80]

To say that the Peace River Power Development Company disagreed with these latter contentions is to draw attention to the obvious. Mr. Mainwaring made his deadline, and presented to the government of British Columbia on December 30, 1959, a highly imaginative report

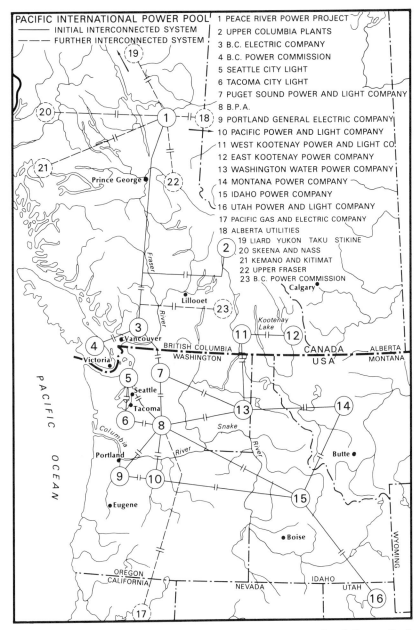

FIGURE 10. The Peace River Project and Suggested International Power Pool. (Adapted from: R. L. Chantrill and J. D. Stevens, *A Report on Power Capabilities and Operating Aspects of the Peace River Power Project and a Pacific International Pool* [Vancouver: Peace River Power Development Company, May 1960], p. 6.)

which proposed that his principals be allowed to construct not one dam but two on the northern river, with a combined generating capacity of 3,145 megawatts.[81] The tone of the analysis was unabashedly optimistic; no insuperable technical or financial difficulties were anticipated as it asserted flatly that load growth in the service areas of the B.C. Power Commission and the B.C. Electric Company would absorb the output of the entire project between 1968 and the mid 1970s. It made no reference either to power export, or to the energy which might be made available from the Columbia River's watershed.

A short five months later, in 1960, when negotiations for the Columbia River Treaty were well advanced, the Peace River Company somewhat modified its approach as it issued a further report,[82] this time from its consultants, who argued that the Peace River project should be viewed as complementary to Columbia River and, indeed, to all other projects in the Pacific northwest. All, they proposed, should be linked in a Pacific northwest international power pool. (See Figure 10.) In this May 1960 report, attention was drawn to the magnitude of the reservoir behind the projected main Peace River Dam (85 million acre-feet, 45 million of it live), and to the already well proven utility practice of storing surplus energy from one project or system in the storage facilities of another. The Peace River Company's consultants reminded their readers of the fact that all of the existing reservoirs in the Pacific northwest had relatively short drawdown periods (mid-September to mid-April), with energy remaining in them at the end of this time being wasted as the reservoirs refilled. Thus the Peace River project was presented to a skeptical political and rather startled engineering community, by virtue of the size of its main dam and reservoir, as a vast energy bank.[83] This also, however, is to anticipate. As will be seen, the two analyses met anything but an enthusiastic response from Columbia planners in both Canadian capitals. But there were exceptions, and one, notably, was W. A. C. Bennett.

Chapter Five

The Negotiation of the Treaty: Phase One

Policy is often a resultant of decisions rather than a decision.
C. E. Lindblom, "Tinbergen on Policy Making."

As 1959 drew to a close, and it became clear that the IJC was going to complete a report on the downstream benefit principles, the federal government found itself faced with two conflicting tactical policy choices. One involved halting the exchanges with the United States which had been pursued throughout 1959 under IJC auspices for a few weeks or even months, while a reasonably precise understanding was reached with British Columbia on a number of basic issues. There was a strong case for seeking substantial federal-provincial agreement, first on what the basic Canadian objectives were in this entire developmental exercise, and secondly, on what, in this context, an ideal international agreement on the Columbia would look like, before getting involved in difficult negotiations with the Americans. There was an equally strong case for agreeing, insofar as this was possible ahead of time, on the Canadian "fall-back" position should the international bargaining require some retreats. The constitutional position of the provinces with respect to international agreements bearing on their role as resource proprietors and managers, and British Columbia's only too evident determination to preserve what it regarded as its competence and its prerogatives in this regard, served to underscore the logic of pursuing this course of action. A still further consideration in its favour was that the province could no longer reasonably defer participating in a joint effort to identify an optimal Canadian position. Indeed, on December 29, 1959, Mr. Williston instructed Mr. Paget, his chief technical adviser at this time, to launch the studies required to produce such a plan "consistent with the best interests of the province."[1]

The more it reflected on this procedure, however, the more perturbed the federal Cabinet became, for it was acutely aware of a number of complications—almost all of which, in fact, have been alluded to already. One was the rapid pace at which the planning for the development of the Peace River was proceeding. The Cabinet Committee was well aware of the fact that Mr. Mainwaring had, on September 2, 1959, categorically assured the Fort St. John Board of Trade, in the heart of the Peace River country, that the project on the northern river was going to go ahead whatever happened to the Columbia negotiations—which, presciently, he suggested would carry on at least until 1963. Although the Diefenbaker government was not of one mind concerning the Peace development, and some of its members at that time were quite prepared to leave the final decision on it to the province, there was general agreement among them that Ottawa could not allow the Columbia's development to be forestalled. And two of its members from British Columbia, Mr. Green and Mr. Fulton, were very much convinced that the latter development was the superior one, and continued to say so publicly. Mr. Green, indeed, went so far in December as to reveal that the Department of External Affairs had a draft treaty on the Columbia ready.[2] Obviously reconciling federal and provincial viewpoints in this area of disagreement was not going to be easy.

The federal Cabinet, as we have seen, was already well aware that on a technical level British Columbia leaned toward the Crippen-Wright position favouring a High Arrow project, and at least keeping open the prospect of an international agreement which provided a clearance for Libby. Reconciling this point of view with its own reservations concerning both of these projects was another source of unavoidable difficulty, and it was reasonable to assume, considerable delay ahead. Trouble was already brewing, furthermore, concerning the obligations and responsibilities which the two governments would assume both during the international negotiations, and after their completion. Premier Bennett had written on December 8, 1959, to Finance Minister Donald Fleming, requesting clarification with respect to the prospective federal financial assistance which Mr. Green had spoken of to the press in Victoria four days earlier, and which Mr. Bennett suggested, in the light of Mr. Green's remarks, might amount to $500 million. But the premier had done more than this; in the same letter, he had clearly conveyed the impression that he was rather less than enthusiastic about what he saw as attempts by Mr. Green to make political capital of any federal financial involvement. Sarcastically, he had added to this letter: "I assume, of course, that such a contribution would not involve a guarantee from the province of British Columbia, and I would appreciate you confirming this is the intent of the federal government."

The second tactical option before Ottawa placed great weight on the possibility that discussions with British Columbia on the aforementioned matters were likely to be strained, and might be protracted. It stressed the argument that Canada stood to lose more than it would gain if it allowed the momentum of the 1959 contacts with the Americans to drop off. Implicitly, those in the federal government who were impressed with the case for moving ahead immediately to international negotiations, seem to have assumed that the constraints of imminent deadlines would facilitate agreement with the province, even on a federally-preferred sequence of projects, and would expedite final decision. Badly needed construction employment would be brought forward, and the perceived threat from Peace River planning would be countered.

It is not possible at this stage to reconstruct the manner in which these considerations, and the risks associated with both options, were weighed by the federal government. Clearly, the second course of action was potentially hazardous, and the fact that it was considered at all seems to have reflected perceptions of domestic, parliamentary, and political strength, as well as of great federal competence in the international arena. All that can be said with certainty is that, for six weeks, the Cabinet decided to ignore Mr. Bennett's letter, and once agreement on the IJC principles (ambiguities and all) became a certainty, it moved to launch discussions with the Americans—*for the second time in twelve months, without letting British Columbia know.*

Meanwhile, unaware of these developments, on January 13, 1960, Mr. Williston wrote to Mr. Hamilton stressing the need for agreement on a position which the two Canadian governments could support. He referred to his commission to Mr. Paget, and suggested that the resulting report might well become the subject of examination by the Technical Liaison Committee. Mr. Williston acknowledged a deliberate stress on the procedural in his letter, and explicitly argued for "prior mutual agreement of our two governments" before any meetings with the Americans. Significantly, he added:

> There is a further concept, of course, that most certainly the secondary and formal phase of negotiations with the United States should in no way usurp the sovereign powers of the province [including the right of the public to make representation or appeal any proposed development] by in effect agreeing under treaty or formal agreement in respect to specific projects on which the right to license the use of water is a British Columbia prerogative. Matters of this nature certainly point out the necessity of further study by our Canada-British Columbia Liaison Committee.

Incidentally, the financing aspect of this matter could be simplified if the confusion created by Mr. Green's announcement as reported in the Press on December 4 last could be clarified by a reply from Mr. Fleming to my Premier's letter addressed to him under date of December 8, 1959.

The die, of course, had already been cast; Mr. Williston's request for agreement with respect to tactics and objectives, and for recognition, at the outset, of a basic provincial prerogative on this question, was not going to be conceded. Indeed, on the very next day, the Speech from the Throne read at the opening of Parliament in Ottawa, in a one paragraph reference to the Columbia River, revealed that discussions seeking a satisfactory basis for the cooperative development of the river "have now been initiated with the government of the United States,"[3] and within days the press began to speak of an imminent move to detailed negotiations. The result was a telegram from Mr. Williston to Mr. Hamilton on January 19, which referred to these reports "regardless of fact basic information not yet formulated as per agreement," and again asked for a reply to Premier Bennett's letter—"urgently required to preclude any possibility of a delay in negotiations." This time a response was forthcoming; on the same day Mr. Hamilton confirmed by letter to Mr. Williston that the United States was ready to begin negotiations, adding "we think it would be very unwise to delay." The federal minister went on to suggest the holding of a Technical Liaison Committee meeting on January 26, one of the Policy Liaison Committee three days later, and a first negotiating session with the United States on February 8. In short, just three weeks were designated as the time available to harmonize the federal and provincial positions. The provincial government expressed its concern at this turn of events, but concluded in the end that it was faced with something of a *fait accompli*. It accepted the arrangement, and the international meetings began on February 11, only three days later than the date first suggested by Mr. Hamilton.

Two considerations, at least, contributed to the province's acquiescence. It was, if anything, even more confident of the strength of its bargaining position than was the federal government. Mr. Bonner was to make this very clear during the following month when, addressing a Social Credit group in Vancouver, he referred to British Columbia's ability to proceed unilaterally with the Peace if a satisfactory agreement on the Columbia was not forthcoming. "We hold five aces on this deal," he suggested, "and we intend to use them to maximum advantage."[4] In addition, British Columbia was assured that its viewpoint would be directly represented at the international negotiations, when, on January 25, Mr. E. W. Bassett, the province's deputy minister of lands, was appointed as one of four

Canadian negotiators in a group headed by Mr. Fulton. (Other interests as well, of course, were reflected in the make-up of the Canadian team. The additional negotiators for Canada were Mr. R. G. Robertson, deputy minister in the Department of Northern Affairs and National Resources— the organizational home, it will be remembered, of Canada's Water Resources Branch—and the assistant under-secretary of state for external affairs, A. E. Ritchie. In like manner, the perspectives of the agencies most intimately associated with the development of the water resources of the United States were reflected directly in the American negotiating team. It consisted of Mr. E. F. Bennett, as chairman, the under-secretary of the Department of the Interior (the department with administrative responsibility for the Bureau of Reclamation and the Bonneville Power Administration) and the chief, United States army corps of engineers, Lieutenant General E. C. Itschner, as well as an assistant secretary of the Department of State, Mr. Ivan B. White.)

1. EARLY STAGE INTRA-CANADIAN AND INTERNATIONAL NEGOTIATION

Two sets of decisions had to be taken in Ottawa before the federal government could begin to seek the still-necessary accommodation with British Columbia: Mr. Bennett had to be answered; and it still had to refine its own concept of what the national interest implied for the coming negotiations with the United States. Mr. Fleming replied to Mr. Bennett on January 20, citing the Speech from the Throne of January 14 which had affirmed the willingness of the government of Canada "to participate with British Columbia in the joint development" of the Columbia's potential. He went on to remind the premier of a similar declaration in the October 1957 Throne Speech, and declared that the amount of assistance involved "would depend on the projects jointly undertaken which would, of course, be self-liquidating," and he expressed the hope that there would be no difficulty in working out suitable arrangements.[5] The implications of the reference to "self-liquidating" and the apparent association of the availability of assistance with project selection were not missed in Victoria. On the same day Messrs. Green and Fulton made appearances before the press in Ottawa, and left no doubt about their concern over the impact which the Peace project might have on the development of the Columbia. The former took particular exception to the role which he felt Mr. Mainwaring had played. Mr. Fulton referred to the occasional speculation concerning power export as the means of resolving the problem of a limited domestic market; he saw it as "irrelevant" and stressed that "if Peace River (sic) goes ahead, B.C. will be saddled with high cost power at least until 1975."[6]

January 20 was also to see the federal Cabinet Committee on the Columbia meeting to consider a report which it had called for from the federal members of the Technical Liaison Committee on the various sequences of power project development available in British Columbia. The Technical Committee members submitted a number of charts, listing as their first choice:

Chart 1   (In order of development)
High Arrow Dam
Two Units to Steam Plants
Mica Storage
Mica At-Site Power Development
Dorr, Bull-River and Luxor Dams

and as their second:

Chart 6   Units to Existing Steam Plants
Bull River-Dorr non diversion
Mica Storage
Mica At-Site Power Generation
Bull River-Dorr-Luxor with diversion

The charts are worth noting. Both, it should be observed, proposed upper Kootenay-Columbia storage—storage which British Columbia's technical advisers had so strenuously opposed. On the other hand, Chart 1 proposed that the first project be the High Arrow Dam, which the engineering consultants of both governments had designated as the logical starting point. Not surprisingly, in the general discussion with the Cabinet Committee which accompanied this presentation, General McNaughton favoured Chart 6. Representatives of the Departments of Finance and Trade and Commerce liked both, while those from the Department of External Affairs reserved their comments. The federal ministers made no decisions at this time, but rather asked for more charts to show the effect of introducing Low Arrow[7] and the various East Kootenay alternatives on sequences with limited Kootenay to Columbia watershed diversion, to show Mica constructed in two stages, to rework Chart 6 with Low Arrow at the beginning, and to outline the effects of Libby under the various plans for sharing the downstream benefits.

If hard conclusions were elusive on January 20, they proved to be even more difficult to come by when the Cabinet Committee met on January 27 and February 2. The massive complexity and interrelatedness of so many of the assumptions being considered gradually came to impress themselves on the political decision-makers. One of the papers presented to them at their January 27 gathering served to complicate matters further by reinforcing the case presented earlier for Chart 1 with High Arrow as the first project. But the federal ministers, in their sensitivity to General McNaughton's views, were reluctant to endorse a sequence involving High Arrow, and ended up by listing seven criteria—ranging from amounts of power produced to benefit-cost ratios, and effects on the United States—on the basis of which their advisers were to evaluate the alternatives and recommend the most promising. At the same time, a committee of four senior officials was struck to consider appropriate strategy to be pursued at the forthcoming meetings with British Columbia.

When the Cabinet Committee reassembled on February 2 it had before it a memorandum which outlined a whole series of alternatives concerning physical development, one of which included Libby. The document made very clear, for instance, the opinion of the federal Water Resources Branch that the first phase of a two-stage Mica development, while economically feasible, would take seven years to build. And it clearly reflected a conviction that Libby would have great and generally adverse effects on Canadian resource development. This view of the implications for Canada of the Libby project impressed itself on the Cabinet Committee; then, and for some months thereafter, Libby to them appeared basically unacceptable from a Canadian point of view. It is important to refer again, however, to the Committee's now growing realization that sequence evaluation is not easy at the best of times, even in the absence of the complication of multiple jurisdiction. Rather understandably, its members decided to seek the assistance of a hydro systems analyst, and shortly thereafter engaged as a part-time consultant, Mr. Matthew Ward, the director of planning for Ontario Hydro.

Meanwhile the press had begun to carry under Ottawa by-lines purportedly inspired news dispatches on the decision-making to come, which, more often than not, were to annoy greatly the British Columbia Cabinet. One such story, for instance, dated January 30, reported that Ottawa officials had been told unofficially that British Columbia was in favour of a High Arrow project in spite of local opposition and declared that federal officials interpreted this as a political move to justify the earlier provincial stand on the Kaiser proposal.[8] Dispatches from British Columbia, often quite accurate, were to raise their own share of disquietude—in some federal circles at least. Typical of these was the account, published on February 2, of a speech by Dr. Shrum who suggested that the Columbia's power should be earmarked for the Vancouver area, and that of the Peace River for the north, stressed the dangers involved in simultaneous development, but went on firmly to advocate power export—with specific provision for "recoverability."[9]

On February 3, Mr. Williston presented a lengthy review of the province's hydro power development in a speech addressed quite clearly not only to the provincial Legislature which heard it, but also to the federal government which was expected to read it. Of considerable significance was the inference drawn from the compounding of the province's electricity load, which had increased in 1959 by some 10 percent. He forecast that the power requirements of the province by 1975 would be almost four times the current figure. Projects built, planned, or under construction, he felt, could meet requirements until 1966–68, but he predicted a race against time to prevent brown-outs by 1968. After referring to Peace and Columbia River potential output he declared: "Unless this province is to become more dependent upon relatively expensive thermal generation, these two rivers must be developed with power on line by 1975."[10]

Essentially, his address was a plea for expansive thinking. He made it clear that the province quite appreciated the generality of some of the IJC principles. The case which he outlined against a "netting procedure" in dividing power benefits left no doubt that the province had had no second thoughts on this score. He very deliberately drew attention to the answers which the 1959 ICREB report did not provide, although he endorsed no sequence or combination of projects. Actually, in a most significant sentence he suggested that the whole matter of the international negotiations might well be resolved by a general agreement under which the province would provide "a cited amount of water storage to provide flow regulation on a scheduled basis to effect both power and flood control benefits in the United States." The leeway which British Columbia might thus retain was made quite clear as he continued: "The actual projects involved in such an arrangement might be dealt with and water use licensed by the province in the regular manner."

Finally, an obvious and deliberate emphasis was placed on the financial implications of the Columbia's development. Attention was drawn to the fact that "all of the capital expended will not lead to the construction of works which are immediately productive," a seeming reference to the possibility that the Mica Dam might well sit "unmachined" for some years after completion.[11] In such terms the need for caution was presented, and used to justify Mr. Bennett's search for a clarification of the federal government's role in financing before the province was committed by a treaty ratification. Mr. Williston concluded this section of his review by again referring to the fact that certain projects would not be immediately self-liquidating, and stressing that this raised uncertainties with respect to financing.

A further indication of provincial government thinking was advanced (at least to the Peace River Company) on the following day—February 4—when Messrs. Chantrill and Stevens visited Mr. Williston and his advisers to discuss the report which they had almost completed on the integration of the water power resources of the Pacific northwest. At this time they discovered that British Columbia was certainly prepared to advance the High Arrow project for consideration, and would like it included in the Chantrill-Stevens analysis.[12]

When the provincial and federal members of the Technical Liaison Committee met on February 7 and 8 to produce some quite crucial recommendations for the political decision-makers, they were able to reach agreement on some significant issues, in spite of the time-squeeze with which they were faced. They endorsed the High Arrow and Duncan Dams as the initial stages of a cooperative development. They agreed that major storage on the Columbia above Revelstoke (Mica or an alternative) or in the East Kootenay Valley should be second-added in time and credit, and that the right to divert the Kootenay into the Columbia should be retained. There was no consensus among them with respect to East Kootenay storage. Their report recognized that the Bull River and Dorr projects could provide storage at less capital cost than Libby, that Kootenay to Columbia diversion would increase Canadian power production, and that a Libby project would reduce overall Canadian power development and Canadian downstream benefits. If Libby were considered essential for non-technical reasons, the report felt that it "should be included in not better than a second added" position, pooled with a second major storage in Canada. Even under these circumstances it held that the right to a partial Kootenay diversion should be retained, that downstream benefit power from it generated in Canada should be retained, and that Canada's only contribution to Libby be a provision of land "for which payment in power would be required."[13]

While the technicians were meeting, the Cabinet Committee was considering a long memorandum from General McNaughton, which argued that a major Kootenay to Columbia storage/diversion would be of great advantage to both countries, would raise by some 704,000 kw generating capacity in Canada, and, unlike High Arrow, would be of continuing usefulness to Canada.[14] At the same time, the committee was told that British Columbia remained unconvinced of the McNaughton position, that Mr. Bassett had instructed British Columbia's technical representatives not to consider any report which contemplated a Kootenay diversion, and that the province was willing to go some way via a pooling of benefits to make Libby possible. *It was informed also by its technical advisers that, Mr. Williston's recent legislative speech notwithstanding, their opposite numbers in British Columbia felt that the Peace and Columbia developments should not proceed simultaneously, that the Columbia should take precedence.* In the light of this intelligence the committee was prepared to agree on only one specific conclusion apropos the selection of alternative projects—that Libby should be opposed. In general terms, otherwise, it recorded as its goal the none too helpful concept of a maximum return of benefits to Canadians.

The Policy Liaison Committee assembled at Ottawa on February 9. (At precisely the same time, incidentally, power planning in British Columbia was given a new twist when the B.C. Electric Company announced that, as a hedge against delays in the development of the Peace and Columbia Rivers, it was purchasing at Hat Creek (see Figure 8) a coal deposit large enough to fuel a 2 million kw thermal plant for at least twenty years.) On the basic issue of project selection the position agreed to by the committee was that Canada should accept the IJC principles as the basis for negotiation. The province's representatives were not unaware that on the basis of benefit-cost ratios, Kootenay Valley storage in Canada appeared to rank ahead of and preclude any major development at Libby, and the record indicates that they did express their concern at the flooding which such Canadian storage would require. The British Columbians also agreed that they favoured an early start, but with the qualifications that initial projects should provide early returns, should be low cost, and be "generally acceptable to the public."[15] They emphasized at this time, also, the need for close coordination with other British Columbia power resource development; the Fraser, Pend d'Oreille, and West Kootenay watersheds were all mentioned. There was general agreement that roughly ten million acre-feet of storage could be provided in the Arrow Lakes region in four to five years, that this should be established in a first-added position,[16] and that from ten to fifteen million acre-feet, which could be provided upstream from Revelstoke (in both the Columbia and Kootenay Valleys), deserved next-added ranking. The entire package was felt to be superior to any domestic alternatives in the United States, and was to be presented as an initial bargaining position.

Much intra-governmental conflict in Canada over the next five months might have been forestalled had the two Canadian governments been completely frank at this time about their assumptions concerning this decision. British Columbia's representatives to this day insist that they agreed to the offer of this large block of storage to assist in establishing an initially superior bargaining position. They hold that it was obvious that the United States would not be prepared to accept all of the storage offered, and maintain that there was an implicit understanding that when the initial proposals had to be modified, the first to go would be the storage to which their reservations, they felt, had been articulated. Federal government spokesmen, on the other hand, draw attention to the fact that the record contains no reference to any such assumption; rather they argue, at least as vigorously, that a provincial reservation was not made clear. The British Columbians, who never were reconciled either to the merits of, or to the constitutional propriety of the federal Cabinet's developmental preferences for this watershed, do appear to have been somewhat less than candid at this point, as they fought for time (without mentioning the fact) in which to ensure that the Peace River's development would not be blocked. In any case, the federal representatives came out of the session with the British Columbians still convinced of the pre-eminent merits of East Kootenay storage in Canada and of the fact that, one way or another, in the context of a generally favourable settlement, British Columbia might certainly be constrained to accept it.

The other major issue dealt with by the Policy Committee on February 9–10 was financing. The Cabinet Committee had agreed on February 6 that Messrs. Hamilton, Green, and Fulton should try on this occasion to determine the province's proposals for "joint development"—including its proposals concerning project sequence, and the financial assistance it expected. On February 6 the Cabinet Committee had also decided that the British Columbia government could be told that the federal government was prepared to consider storage costs—with the final decision on whether Canada would pay half the storage expense (to be repaid from power revenues on a *pro rata* basis until cleared off), to be made, however, after discussion with the province. At the Policy Liaison Committee the federal spokesmen relayed the substance of this; they did indicate "that the federal government would be prepared to consider a proposal whereby it would participate to the extent of one-half the cost of providing the storage (including flowage costs). . . . The suggested rate of interest for such a loan would be the then current rate plus ⅛ percent."

While they disavowed any intent "to dictate a sequence of development," the record of these exchanges makes it quite clear that the offer of federal assistance at this time was conditional. The federal spokesmen did refer to a possible conflict between short and long term interests, and did not deny that a federal decision on financing might possibly be influenced by the selection of projects. The record includes the statement: "It was thought that B.C. could not, on its own, be committed to large and costly developments which might not produce adequate revenues for several years." It contains this also: "The extent of federal participation would be measured by the extent to which the federal government would consider that the development would be the best plan available for the good of the nation."[17] Interestingly, at this time, the Policy Committee members hoped that the international negotiations would be over in two months, and that the treaty would be ratified before Congress adjourned in June.[18]

The Beginning of Formal International Negotiation. Just prior to the first meeting with the Americans on February 11, the Canadian negotiators caucused in Ottawa to refine further their objectives. They agreed on the desirability of bringing out the American position on Libby, on the sale of downstream benefit power, on any special agreements required concerning non-federal American plants, and on the type of understanding to be sought. They also undertook to make a formal offer of cooperative development, and to set out specific storage possibilities thus:

TABLE 2

Increments of Storage

	Time Involved	Related Costs
Kootenay Lake and Lower Columbia Basin 8–10 million acre-feet	Within 4 years	$8–10 per acre-foot
Upper Columbia above Revelstoke 10–12 million acre-feet	Within 8–12 years	about $20 per acre-foot
East Kootenay above the Boundary 3–5 million acre-feet	In 5 years	about $25 per acre-foot

When the negotiations began, the offer to develop this storage was duly made and re-emphasized in the Canadian chairman's opening statement. The form of the final settlement was raised in the first session, but produced few difficulties. It was quickly agreed that there should be a treaty—probably on a fifty year term—and it was also agreed that technical data could be added in a schedule or appendix, perhaps later. The question of power sales was raised, the American delegates asking whether or not Canada was interested in marketing any power surplus to its needs; a twenty-year sale was suggested for part of a block, but no Canadian reply was made at the time.

The first sparring developed when the negotiators turned to the basic issue, the relevance of the IJC's principles to the process of project selection. Over two days the Canadian chairman stressed Canada's willingness to accept them, expressing Canada's hope that they would be the basis for negotiation. He emphasized especially the merits of General Principle No. 1, as an objective technical standard for evaluation, and sought an agreement to delineate first an "ideal array" of projects, which then would be followed by an examination of those made relevant by other factors. This was not forthcoming, however, as the American negotiators appreciated the tactical hazards for them which such an agreement might involve. They pointed out that some United States agencies interpreted the principles differently from the Canadians and "in some cases had strong objection to the application suggested by the Canadians."[19] At the outset, for instance, they made it very clear that a block of some 450,000 kw of very high grade secondary power, currently being profitably sold, would not be available for inclusion with other such power firmed up as a result of Canadian regulation.[20] Two days of discussion did not move them from their initial assertion that the time required to build projects and the availability of Congressional approval should be considered in addition to benefit-cost ratios in the evaluation of alternative projects.[21] In the end, the negotiators agreed that the principles need not be formally approved; they were designated as guides to both governments in the course of the negotiations.

The jockeying became more specific when the Libby project was raised. The representatives of both the Canadian governments felt the American pressure here, and the British Columbians subsequently reported to Mr. Williston their conviction that the United States wanted a clearance for Libby as "an essential development"[22] from the American point of view. Initially the Americans indicated a desire to pool Libby with High Arrow on a first-added basis; subsequently they conceded that Mica might be brought into the pool before agreeing that High Arrow, if constructed first, might be granted a preferred position over-all. They referred to studies by the Corps of Engineers, then underway, which left Arrow out because of its reservoir preparation or flowage problems. The Canadian chairman, however, made it clear that even with these disadvantages High Arrow had such great merit that Canada was prepared to offer it. He also insisted that consideration be given to the financial implications of any agreement, to problems of short-run financing until the development had become self-sustaining, and drew attention to British Columbia's need to relate any Columbia basin development to that of other provincial power resources. All in all, Mr. Fulton's performance in this difficult situation (for as we have seen he was seeking to persuade two governments, not one) seems to have been skilful, and was praised by the British Columbians present in their report to Mr. Williston.

When the Cabinet Committee met on February 15 to evaluate the first negotiating round with the United States, Mr. Fulton presented a review which acknowledged the American pressure for Libby, and the merits of High Arrow as a counter. He raised several questions, including the practicability of a limited diversion (to make Libby economic), whether or not there was any reasonable basis for Libby, and whether there was any real prospect of selling that portion of Canada's downstream power benefit entitlement which might be surplus to Canada's needs on the basis of a twenty-year contract. No decisions were taken. At a further meeting of the Cabinet Committee on February 24, however, considerable time was spent on the question of a federal commitment to High Arrow; the committee was decidedly nervous about the undesirability of ending up with it and Libby as well—the two projects which General McNaughton had publicly opposed for years as harmful to Canada. On this occasion the federal ministers agreed to continue to base Canada's case on General Principle No. 1, to oppose Libby, and to try to get British Columbia to agree to Bull River-Dorr, Mica, and High Arrow. A paper prepared by an officer of the Department of Trade and Commerce on the sale of the downstream power benefit was also discussed. Its author could see that the province might want to sell some of the downstream power benefit, but probably only for periods of three to five years, and because of load growth slowdowns or an acceleration of other provincial development to meet flood control requirements. On a 7.3 percent per annum load growth rate, the report anticipated that British Columbia would be able to absorb the downstream power benefit from High Arrow in one and one-half years (by 1965), and that from Mica by 1971. The Cabinet Committee sensed that, as a sale of surplus downstream benefit power was likely to be equated publicly with a power export, any such proposal could be domestically embarrassing; hence it agreed not to raise the matter, but to discuss it if the province did.[23]

On or just after February 24, members of the Cabinet Committee also received a lengthy memorandum from one of their senior advisers in which the need for complete agreement with British Columbia was stressed and re-stressed. This memorandum also insisted that High Arrow could not be dislodged from a first-added position on technical arguments; if it was to be excluded it would have to be on human and political grounds, and on the basis that its storage value would eventually disappear. Two additional points were emphasized for the Cabinet ministers in this document. One was the desirability of persuading British Columbia to accept East Kootenay storage. The other was a reminder that while the prime minister had endorsed limited sales of power, if required, with the returns being applied to the domestic market, there clearly should be no long-term sale of downstream hydro benefits because, so far as could be seen, all hydro power would be required in British Columbia in the short term. There would be no purpose, the report maintained, in Canada and British Columbia financing these developments for a long-term export.

At the same time, British Columbia's technical personnel were far from idle; their attention had been concentrated on the economic implications of the initial project sequences which appeared to be available, especially when either Mica or High Arrow was involved. Indeed, at this time, the province's decision-makers received from them a report which so stressed the superiority of High Arrow over Mica as an initial project that the preferred initial sequence outlined did not contain the latter project at all. The elements of the sequence (See Figure 8) were:

(1) Construction of High Arrow Storage by December, 1964.

(2) Construction of Duncan Lake Storage by December, 1966.

(3) Construction of Kootenay Canal and Brilliant Extensions by June, 1968.

(4) Construction of Two Units at Waneta by June, 1969.

(5) Construction of Seven Mile Plant (on the Pend d'Oreille) by June, 1970.[24]

Libby's construction by 1967 was assumed, and the report suggested that after the above five projects a number not on the Columbia might be added. With such a plan, the provincial Water Rights Branch argued, "The capital outlay would be less, the revenue surplus for a number of years would be much greater, a surplus position quickly established."[25] (It did advance a sequence which had the Mica storage project built in two stages, and its power house added later.) Quite obviously, this staff group had not been mesmerized by big dam thinking, nor did it feel that attention should be directed solely to the Columbia. What is interesting, however, is that the technical personnel at neither level of government were taking seriously the impact which a Peace River development would have on the province's power supply, and on project viability in the Columbia valley.

Provincial technicians notwithstanding, the Policy Liaison Committee agreed when it met at Victoria on February 27, 1960, to adhere to the position which it had endorsed earlier in the month. Specifically it decided to offer High Arrow and Duncan Lake, Mica or its equivalent, and the Bull River-Dorr projects firmly and definitely pooled in a first-added position, with construction to begin as early as possible. Federal representatives argued the merit of continuing to try for the ideal sequence first, and suggested that, while the Corps of Engineers would press for Libby, other United States agencies might support lower cost projects. They argued persuasively enough that the province's representatives accepted the position that Canada should stand on the principles, make the above offer, and listen to objections but not retreat from this position. Permission was given to members of the Technical Liaison Committee to examine a Corps of Engineers' report at Washington on March 1 and 2.

The Canadians filed a telegraphic evaluation of this American effort declaring that they could see no reason for altering the Canadian position as agreed on at Victoria.

Mr. Bennett intervened once again on March 4, when he wrote to Mr. Fleming on the subject of financing. He observed that the minutes of a Policy Liaison Committee meeting contained the only suggestion which he had received since Mr. Fleming's January 20 letter on financial matters, and proceeded to restate the minutes' contents. He stressed the reference in them to Ottawa's willingness to "consider a proposal" (which he underscored twice) to provide "such a loan," and to the fact that British Columbia could not on its own be committed to large and costly developments "which might not produce adequate revenue for several years" (both underscored once). He noted the reference to self-liquidation in the record, and wondered about the effect on provincial revenue if downstream benefits were insufficient to meet debt carrying and redemption costs. His December 8 letter had not been replied to, he insisted, nor, in his opinion, had a responsible financial offer been made. He went on to express concern at the absence of specific fiscal data in the financing references made to that point by federal spokesmen, and found perplexing both the generalizations in the minutes on cost and project financing, and the proposed limitation of assistance to the provision of storage. At the same time he could not see how domestic financing arrangements in any way affected the international negotiations. As a final challenge he asked for copies of the federal-provincial financial agreements concerning the South Saskatchewan Dam and New Brunswick power developments, along with information concerning any direct grants to them.[26]

On the same day, March 4, the second set of international meetings on the Columbia began in Washington, D.C. The American representatives made it quite clear that they felt it wrong to start with an ideal sequence, and one of them certainly indicated a doubt if there was a net advantage to the United States in Canadian storage at all. A good deal of attention was directed to the fifty-fifty split required by Power Principle No. 6, as some of the Americans sought to revive the concept of net benefit sharing, and to counter equal gross sharing. Specifically they suggested long-term sales of Canadian power and/or Canada bearing the cost of transmitting its share of the downstream benefits to the border. A second feature of the session was Mr. Fulton's re-statement of the Canadian position which, referring to the Libby project, declared that all of its benefits could be provided at lower cost on the Kootenay in Canada, and declared that Canada could not agree to the construction of a Libby project ahead of more advantageous storages, wholly situated within Canada. When the American chairman enquired if British Columbia was prepared to construct High Arrow and Kootenay storages simultaneously, the Canadian chairman replied in the affirmative.

Subsequently, the American representatives appeared to wish to back away from the grossing principle. They also indicated a real interest not only in purchasing downstream benefit power but also in lending Canada money to develop Canadian at-site generation ahead of domestic requirements, which power could be sold to the United States until needed. And they advanced proposals involving a pooling of Libby with High Arrow, or High Arrow and Mica.[27] Furthermore, they made it clear that if Libby were really not acceptable, the United States would require compensation for the flood control and power generation forgone, and that storage somewhere on the Kootenay to resolve the Bonners Ferry-Creston area flooding was a *sine qua non* of an international agreement. The pooling proposals were rejected by Canadian spokesmen, who also made the point that there were insurmountable political barriers against American investment in Canadian developments. Though the bargaining continued, very little progress was made toward a resolution of the basic issues. Once again American representatives indicated that they did not feel bound by that part of Power Principle No. 6 which dealt with the United States bearing the costs of returning the downstream benefit power to Canada.

A fifty year treaty term was agreed upon at this time, as was, basically, the proposal that Canada accept the flood control benefit in lump sum form. The issue which a year later was to be causing such disagreement in Canada, the possible sale of downstream benefit power, was discussed at length. Canadian spokesmen gave no real support to the possibility that power might be exported on a long term basis. Their reaction to the possibility of developing and selling the produce of Canadian basin run-of-the-river sites was to allude to the implications of selling to the United States at prices below those charged to domestic consumers.[28] Mr. Bassett, furthermore, did point out that some other developments, for example on Fraser River tributaries, might have for his province greater attraction than at-site Columbia generation. The impression which the Canadians left was that the sale of power was not unfeasible, but that there were very awkward political obstacles to an American-encouraged acceleration of Columbia generation in British Columbia, and to external sales therefrom. In any case it was made clear that with a load growth rate often over 10 percent per annum, British Columbia would need all its downstream and at-site power by 1975. The prospect of the Peace River modifying these assumptions was just not considered. The American negotiators had no idea at this time of the extent to which the Canadians were using the international negotiations, not only to identify the significant issues at stake internationally, but also to test the strength of the commitment of the two jurisdictions within Canada to policy options, and indirectly to policy goals, which had not yet been reconciled domestically.

When Mr. Bassett returned to Victoria, he drew Mr. Williston's attention to "(1) the evident determination of the Americans to avoid the implications of the IJC principles and to proceed primarily by a direct 'horse-trading' procedure and (2) the very clear desire of the Americans to obtain just as much Canadian power, both downstream and at site, as possible."[29] He also told Mr. Williston that more flexibility would have to be allowed to the negotiators, that the Canadians could not remain absolutely rigid on the position endorsed by the Policy Liaison Committee.

An additional and unexpected meeting of the international negotiators was to take place, however, before the Policy Committee could meet to assess the state of the negotiations from a Canadian viewpoint. The initiative for this gathering came from a representation of the United States Department of State to A. D. P. Heeney, the Canadian ambassador at Washington, to the effect that progress might be greatly accelerated if the problem of Libby could be resolved. Hence two proposals were suggested as reasonable topics for an informal unannounced exchange. Mr. Heeney relayed them to Ottawa by telegram on March 15, whence they were read to Victoria over the telephone on March 16.

One proposal (A) referred to the various ways in which Libby could be brought into a cooperative development, (i) as a second stage after High Arrow, (ii) jointly with Mica after High Arrow, and (iii) as a third stage after Mica and High Arrow. The other alternative (B) was the major surprise, for it assumed that Canada would construct three storages (High Arrow, Mica, and Bull River),[30] that Libby would be forgone, and enquired as to the volume of hydro-electric power which under this arrangement would be available to the United States. The American enquiry assumed that Canada would take its downstream power benefit from the Bull River and Arrow projects in energy, but wondered if, when Mica was machined, Canada would be willing to take the larger block of its downstream benefits power from Mica in cash rather than kind.

A meeting of the federal Cabinet Committee was held on March 18 to consider both the Heeney telegram and the reports on the international negotiations to date. The committee agreed here that Canada should oppose Libby and be prepared to consider a sale of surplus power if the United States would let Libby go; it also felt that the exportable power could be produced most advantageously by an acceleration of Mica generation. But its nervousness over the political implications of the possibility was only too evident; it agreed that such a move would need the concurrence of British Columbia, and that it would be desirable, if possible, that the suggestion of a power sale come from the province.

A secret meeting between the international negotiators (without technicians present) was held on the outskirts of Ottawa on March 21. At the outset the United States representatives made it very clear that A (i) was their first choice, that Libby would be sub-marginal to them under A (iii), and would be very difficult to justify under A (ii). The Canadians insisted that they could not go higher than A (iii), if they could entertain the proposal at all. Much jockeying took place on the question of a power sale to cover the 275–300 kilowatts of energy which the United States would have to do without if Libby were abandoned. The Americans wanted at least a twenty year power sale, with a minimum cut-off period of three years, and raised the prospect of an amortized cash payment for the power to accelerate payment. When they raised the question of price they argued their need to maintain the Bonneville Power rate structure (then involving sales at less than three mills) while the Canadians claimed that the only reasonable price should be one related to the costs of the most reasonable domestic alternative open to the United States. At the same time the Americans made it clear that if Libby were to be excluded not only would a compensatory power sale be required, but storage providing adequate flood control on the Kootenay, either in Canada or the United States, was in effect, one price of a treaty. Mr. Fulton stressed the great concession which a Libby clearance would involve; he did seek to find out just how long the downstream benefit would last, but was no more successful in obtaining an explicit answer than the Americans were when they sought to probe the length of any period during which the Canadians might be willing to forgo the diversion of the Upper Kootenay.

Ottawa's reaction to this meeting was dispassionately summarized on the same day, March 21, by one of the federal Cabinet's senior advisers. He recorded that while the United States clearly wanted Libby, it was not prepared, apparently, to build it under any circumstances. General Itschner, an American negotiator whose predisposition to it was marked, had conceded that even first-added it would be expensive. Thus the impression had been created that the United States would give it up, on a tough though friendly basis, but only if assured of power sufficient in quantity and low enough in price to make the "loss" defensible to the American public. Someone in Ottawa, however, who was very much opposed to the provincial position, acted in a different manner, for on the next day, March 22, an Ottawa columnist, Tom Gould, broke the story of the informal meeting, released the substance of the American proposals, and indicated that federal officials had been "astounded" at the change in the American position. He also reported a British Columbia predisposition to both Libby and High Arrow, adding "Ottawa firmly believes that High Arrow although attractive enough from a short-range point of view (it is the old Kaiser dam in different form) is not in the long-term interest of British Columbia or of Canada."[31]

Further Intra-Canadian Bargaining and Analysis. Between March 16 and 25, General McNaughton, in his annual presentation to the External Affairs Committee, surveyed the alternatives facing the decision-makers, reviewed the case for High Arrow while restating his opposition to it, reaffirmed his enthusiasm for a major Kootenay to Columbia diversion, and declared that a Libby Dam would be so "wrong," such a gift of Canadian resources, that Canada should go it alone if the United States were to insist upon it. Withal he still testified on March 18: "It is not our business to determine the projects for storage. Those are matters for the governments to determine."[32]

Two days after the Gould story was published Mr. Williston publicly announced (on March 24) that Ottawa had offered to lend the province one-half the cost of constructing the required storage works at the going interest rate plus ⅛ percent. He observed that there had been no offer of a grant, but otherwise gave no hint of the province's reaction and did not discuss the international negotiations. Speculative press stories in British Columbia, however, did indicate that the provincial government had been rather shocked at Ottawa's position on financing, and drew attention to the massive federal involvement in the South Saskatchewan and Canso Causeway projects. The leaders of all three opposition parties in British Columbia were far less inhibited; they publicly welcomed the federal offer on March 25.[33]

The Cabinet Committee on the Columbia met on the same day, March 25, to review the informal international negotiating meeting, and concluded that Ottawa should continue to stick with the proposed three Canadian storages. It decided to consider further a twenty-year 275,000 kw years per annum power sale, possibly covered by a prepayment at the start of construction. One day later, however, it and the government of British Columbia received a written document from the Technical Liaison Committee which called for some hard thinking. There was no doubt for the technicians about High Arrow; it and Mica were accepted as part of any cooperative development, and the only choice to them was seen as that between Libby and Bull River-Dorr. When the Technical Committee assessed the Canadian negotiating position, it noted that Canada had presented three storages to obtain first-added credit, and hence maximum downstream benefits, and to provide for future major diversions of the Kootenay. It went on to stress that if the three storages were to be built to the best advantage, it would be necessary to accelerate them to meet United States' requirements, and that this would produce power, surplus to Canadian needs, which would have to be sold. The difficulty envisaged here was that to meet Canadian demand such power would have to be recaptured well before the twenty years which any American sale contract seemed to require. The report drew attention to the prospect, in the interest of getting a good sale price, of providing an alternative more expensive source of power to meet domestic load growth. Thus the Technical Committee insisted that if all three projects were to be built under cooperative development "a policy of allowing long-term export of surplus power, or of leaving in the United States some portion of Canada's share of the downstream power benefit must be adopted."

The technicians' analysis drew attention to a still further problem when it insisted that, unless the Kootenay were diverted, any sale to the United States greater than 300,000 kw would leave Canada with less power than it would possess in a plan accommodating Libby. Further, the report held that, assuming storage on the East Koo'enay in Canada, with diversion, it might be possible to sell a 300,000 kilowatt block of power for about four mills per kwh; without it the price would have to be at least six mills "in order to place Canada in as favourable a position as with a plan including Libby." Hence a decision on diverting the Kootenay was called for, as little was seen to choose between Libby and Dorr-Bull River storage if diversion were not effected, and such a decision was obviously basic to a satisfactory negotiation concerning the price and the amount of power which might have to be exported. Dr. Krutilla, who has reviewed this document in his careful study of this decision-making,[34] is quite correct in observing that it did not demonstrate a clear-cut superiority for one course of action. It is difficult to read it, however, without sensing that the technicians were trying their best to draw to the attention of policy-makers at the federal level a conviction that the incremental merits of East Kootenay storage with diversion were not so great as to make Libby quite unfeasible within the context of a reasonable bargain. The report saw the Dorr-Bull River-Luxor scheme as meaning a heavier financing burden in the early stages, but producing more power in the long term "at a unit cost competitive with a plan including Libby." On the other hand, it noted, providing for Libby would ease the financing burden on Canada and obviate the need to make a long-term power export decision. It concluded: "If a decision is made to adopt maximum development in Canada, the financial implication of this plan, especially the price at which power should be sold to the United States, must be considered carefully."[35]

It must be noted that the Technical Committee did not go nearly so far as its provincial members apparently would have wished. By this time, the province's Water Rights Branch had submitted to its minister (R. G. Williston) a report which had reviewed a large number of sequences, which had assumed that if Canada desired first-added credit for all the storages it had offered, the United States would insist on an acceleration of Canadian project construction to meet United States load requirements, and which had come to the conclusion that any such acceleration would result "in a large financial deficit even with the export of 275 M.W." Any acceleration of the Mica project had been seen as particularly disadvantageous financially, and the provincial analysis had concluded that a sequence of development "with High Arrow first-added followed by Mica-Libby pooled appears to be the most advantageous from a financial point of view."[36]

Something of a standoff developed when the Policy Liaison Committee finally met on March 30. On the one hand, the federal spokesmen revealed their continuing commitment to East Kootenay storage; they suggested that Alternative B in the American proposals (excluding Libby) was a profitable one to explore, as it put the three Canadian storages in a first-added position, preserved the fifty-fifty split of downstream benefits, provided help with initial capital costs through the sale of surplus power, and preserved the position which gave the greatest long-term benefits to Canada. Mr. Williston, on the one hand, drew attention to the potentially serious economic and financial implications to British Columbia of constructing three projects simultaneously. He expressed again his doubts about the merit of flooding so much of the upper Kootenay-Columbia Valleys in order to obtain the incremental power to be extracted from Dorr-Bull River-Luxor storage, and, notably, was doubtful also about "the advisability of long term export of power to [the] U.S. with the possibility of having to replace the same amount of power later at a higher cost."[37] British Columbia's representatives drew attention to the questions raised by the March 26 Technical Liaison Committee Report, and repeated, with reference to Upper Columbia-Kootenay storage, the water-barrier, scarcity of usable land, and financial deficit arguments. They conceded that on February 27 the province had agreed to the offer of the three storages, but stressed now the consequences of this proposal if it were accepted. Actually they made it quite clear at this time that the province could not contemplate flooding both the East Kootenay-Columbia and Arrow Lakes valleys, and that it would not consider dropping High Arrow. As both sides remained adamant, however, it was ultimately agreed simply to explore further the reaction to all of the alternatives which had been broached, to try to determine what concessions the United States was willing to advance in order to have Libby accepted, and also to investigate the price which the United States might be willing to pay for a 275,000 kw block of power on a twenty year sale—stressing meanwhile the difficulties involved in such a proposal.

The United States Moves to Break the Deadlock. The third international negotiating session was held at Ottawa between March 31 and April 2. In keeping with the Policy Committee's directive, early in the exchanges Canada's representatives raised "certain political problems" associated with any long term export of power, and maintained that Canada would have to receive at least five mills for any such sale. The American chairman, in reply, stressed the importance of this block of power, and mentioned the role as scrutineers of the negotiations being played by certain influential congressmen and at least one senator; he made it quite clear that no such price would be paid. The Americans, he indicated, were thinking in terms of Bonneville's 2.5 mills at 100 percent load factor rate, but preferred Libby to Dorr-Bull River. They might have to let Libby go, he suggested, but not without a commitment from Canada to build Dorr-Bull River in a comparable time. Unproductive as this task had been, little more success awaited the Canadians when they sought to determine just what concessions the United States might be prepared to make for Libby.

The well known tendency of the bargaining process to put a premium on a search for new or jointly acceptable solutions was neatly illustrated on the second day of the negotiations, when the Americans, hoping to break the stalemate, advanced a proposal featuring:

(1) High Arrow and Duncan Lake first-added.

(2) Mica second-added.

(3) The United States given an option for a reasonable period—such as five years—to decide on the construction of Libby. If the option were not exercised Canada would be required to build Dorr-Bull River expeditiously.

(4) The postponement of a major Kootenay to Columbia diversion for the term of the agreement.

(5) Dorr-Bull River, if constructed, enjoying a credit position depending upon existing conditions, and certainly not better than Libby's as third-added. Canada was to have no claim to downstream benefits if non-storage plants were built on the American Kootenai.

Notably, this plan did not require that Canada make available a block of power for export, but it did maintain that Canada should bear the cost of transmitting the downstream benefit power from the American generating plants to the border. And it repeated the stance taken early in the negotiations that a block of already-sold high-grade secondary power would not be available for combining with power produced by upstream storage releases when the Canadian entitlement to a downstream benefit was calculated.

In the exchanges which followed, much attention was directed to the position accorded in the American proposal to Mica. Mr. Bassett, reflecting another study of his province's Water Resources Branch, was candidly nervous about the prospect of the Mica Dam having to operate as a storage project only for some time as the domestic electricity load was built up. Federal Canadian spokesmen did not seem to share these concerns, but were very unwilling even to consider the Libby option until the practical significance of Mica second-added was made clear. Both national groups parried; the Americans ventured that even the second-added position for Mica might have to be shaded if Mica were deferred, while the Canadians felt that without a hard understanding on Mica little progress could be expected. The upshot was that an international technical work group was established to deal with a number of issues, including a determination of the power accrual from High Arrow and Duncan, first-added, and Mica in a second-added position. The Americans also indicated that they would be in a position to make a firm offer at the next meeting, and wanted to learn the Canadian reaction to their secondary energy and return transmission positions. More favourable alternatives, they hinted, might be possible if the fifty-fifty split of benefits were set aside.

Mr. Bennett, Columbia and Peace River Development. Three days after these negotiating sessions ended, Premier Bennett returned to Victoria and was immediately questioned by the press—on April 5—about the relationships between the Peace and Columbia River developments. These enquiries were inspired by the release of a report to Mr. Williston by Water Comptroller A. F. Paget on March 25 in which the plans of the Peace River Power Development Company were found to "appear to provide for the maximum economic development of the Peace River potential upstream from Hudson Hope, B.C.," and to be, with some minor technical reservations, "entirely feasible from an engineering standpoint."[38] Mr. Paget had been at pains to point out that his report did not mean an automatic start on the Peace, that his examination had not involved an examination of Peace generation and transmission costs, nor a comparison of them with available alternatives. Such an enquiry, he had indicated, would be made when the Peace River Company applied to the province's Public Utilities Commission for a certificate of convenience and necessity. If such were granted, a further hurdle to clear would be an application to him for a water licence, a step again involving public hearings. The curiosity of the press had been particularly aroused, however, by one sentence in Mr. Paget's report which read: "The energy generated under these proposals could be marketed in British Columbia within the times expressed [1968–76] provided no other resource development, either hydro or thermal, absorbs part of the market."[39] Mr. Paget had been questioned about this by the press on March 25, and had suggested that he did not mean that the development of the Columbia would jeopardize the Peace planning. But he had indicated that it could mean a stretch-out of the northern river's development.

This was the assertion which was raised with Mr. Bennett on April 5. The premier praised Mr. Paget's report, but made it quite clear that he differed with its author on the issue of policy implications. "That's his opinion; that's the beauty of democracy," he was quoted as declaring.[40] Once again he emphasized that if the Peace died "today" the Columbia would expire "tomorrow," and insisted that British Columbia would not delay the Columbia. He repeated his contention that without the provincial initiative on the Peace, Ottawa would still be doing nothing on the Columbia.

Continuing Federal-Provincial and Intra-Provincial Exchanges. One week later, on April 11, the confidential nature of the intergovernmental exchanges was breached again, this time in an Ottawa story by Alex Young, who declared that the federal government apparently had been manoeuvered into a spot by British Columbia.[41] When Mr. Williston labelled this effort as mischief-making, and denied any downgrading of Mica, and Mr. Hamilton called it purely speculative, Mr. Young repeated the substance of his earlier article, and added: "According to the most knowledgeable people in the North American Continent, the High Arrow dam will increase the costs of the power output in Canada and decrease it in the United States."[42] On April 13 the depth of the rift between Ottawa and Victoria on the question of financing the Columbia's development was revealed when the intergovernmental correspondence on this subject was tabled in the House of Commons.

As April progressed, the opposition political parties in British Columbia seemed determined to justify Mr. Young's analysis. Mr. Perrault, the Liberal leader, viewed High Arrow as a threat to Mica, and by April 28 was assailing the Peace River Company for employing a Seattle based engineer as a lobbyist against the Columbia.[43] Mr. Finlayson of the Progressive Conservatives criticized the British Columbia government for its failure to develop a long-range plan and Mr. Strachan called for a B.C. Electric take-over.[44] On April 13, Mr. Finlayson, who had talked to General McNaughton, wrote to Mr. Diefenbaker relaying his own fears that Mr. Bennett's two river plans and the building of High Arrow could be effected only at the expense of the Mica project.

The federal Cabinet Committee on the Columbia met twice in April to review the state of the international negotiations. On April 26, the date of the second meeting, it agreed to meet soon with British Columbia to reach a firm understanding. It was told that Messrs. Williston and Bonner had agreed to a joint press release reaffirming the centrality of Mica. In view of British Columbia's unwillingness to agree to simultaneous construction of three major Canadian storage projects, including one on the Upper Kootenay, or to agree to the 275,000 kilowatt sale called for in the Alternative B proposal, the Cabinet Committee, by the time it adjourned on April 26, was close to a reluctant acceptance of Libby, provided the terms of that acceptance were not inimical to Canadian interests.

Actually, however, the Libby decision was anything but a certainty, and had to wait. But answering Mr. Bennett's letter of March 4 could not be further postponed, and agreement upon the manner in which this should be done was not to come easily. There seems little doubt that the federal Cabinet ministers from British Columbia were trying to secure for the Columbia River's development a direct non refundable grant. Ultimately, after extended inter-ministerial correspondence, and the final clearance with the prime minister which this Cabinet never omitted, the federal reply was sent by Finance Minister Fleming on April 21. The letter itself denied that Canada had withheld specific information on financing, insisted that there was a necessary fiscal interrelationship with the international negotiations, and drew attention to the oral indication of a federal willingness to discuss terms, conditions, and implications of federal assistance at the February 9 Policy Liaison Committee meeting, and at similar meetings on February 27 and March 30. It also pointed out that on these dates the province's representatives had not been willing to engage in such exchanges, and insisted that Ottawa had made a definite offer "to negotiate an arrangement." The letter went on to point out the legitimate grievance of other provinces if Ottawa became involved in the financing of hydroelectric generation in British Columbia. Before concluding (and sending along the agreements concerning the federal role in the South Saskatchewan Dam and New Brunswick power projects which Mr. Bennett had asked for) the letter declared "that the government of Canada, in order to assist the government of British Columbia, is willing to advance one-half the capital cost of providing storage which in turn will provide the greatest and least expensive return by way of downstream power benefits and at the same time make possible the provision in British Columbia of very low cost power sufficient to meet the forecast needs of the province until approximately 1975."

The implicit comparison between the Columbia and Peace River projects in this statement was quite clear, but in the reply to Mr. Fleming, which he signed on May 6, Mr. Bennett ignored it. Instead he sought to "rub in" again Mr. Green's December 5, 1959, reference to an equal federal-provincial sharing of costs, and asked for confirmation. Further, he argued: "whereas that initial undertaking suggested that Canada would pay 50% of the overall cost, I now take it to be your position that Canada would lend a portion of the capital required only for dams whose storage features would make them of primary benefit to the United States." He went on to cite his principal economic adviser, Dr. J. V. Fisher, in holding that this would have Ottawa carrying 13.25 percent, not 50 percent, of the total cost and added for good measure some pointed citations from the South Saskatchewan documents.

Another letter received by members of the Cabinet Committee at this time was one written on May 10 by General McNaughton sharply and critically reviewing an April 6 synopsis of the Chantrill-Stevens Report on the case for an international power pool. General McNaughton doubted the practicability of transmission over such a distance, noted the absence of a local market or of cost figures, and felt in essence that Messrs. Chantrill and Stevens had sought to create a market for Peace River power by truncating Columbia River storage. A memorandum expressing similar views from the chief engineer of the Canadian Section of the IJC was enclosed.

By May 11, when the Cabinet Committee met once more, it was obviously very unlikely that a treaty could be ready before the adjournment of the then current session of the U.S. Congress, and American proposals already had been received informally that, instead, an agreement in principle or a memorandum of understanding might be arrived at before June. At least one federal minister thoroughly disliked the idea, observing that, having signed one, the United States would be free to do nothing until after its presidential election, British Columbia would be free to press on with the Peace, and only Canada would be tied. At this time the Cabinet Committee decided to press for High Arrow and Mica, and for the elimination of the Libby option. It had a May 9 report of the International Work Group before it, however, and it also resolved to tell British Columbia that, if the United States continued to write down the benefits credited to High Arrow as it had appeared to do during the sessions of the Work Group, the federal government believed that High Arrow should be dropped and Mica and East Kootenay storage included instead in the first-added position. The committee also decided that Mr. Hamilton should invite representatives of the province to Ottawa to discuss financing, and that Mr. Fleming should write in the same vein.

147

Mr. Fleming did reply to Mr. Bennett repeating the offer to "negotiate with your government on the most realistic and practical basis"[45] and expressing astonishment at Mr. Bennett's claim that Ottawa was willing to assist with the construction of structures whose storage could be of primary benefit only to the United States. He mentioned that on the occasion of an April 21 visit to Victoria, Mr. Fulton had seen Messrs. Williston and Bonner to urge British Columbia to send one or two persons to Ottawa specifically to clear up any misunderstanding. All he could add was that, to date, this proposal had not only not been accepted; it had not been responded to. With this letter all real contact between Mr. Bennett and Mr. Fleming on the question of financing was broken off and was not to be resumed for five months.

2. Final Stages of Federal-Provincial Bargaining on Project Selection

The Policy Liaison Committee met at Victoria on May 14 to hear a report on the third round of international negotiations, a review of the findings of the International Work Group, and a commentary on these findings by the Canadian technical staff who had helped produce them. The gathering concentrated on the crucial issue of East Kootenay storage. British Columbia's representatives outlined once again their reservations about flooding there, as they had done on March 30, while federal spokesmen presented the case that the right to divert the Kootenay-Columbia should be retained, and the construction of the Dorr and Bull River storages was necessary to demonstrate it. At this point the province displayed a huge map to scale showing the relative amounts of land which would be inundated by the High Arrow and East Kootenay projects respectively. Mr. Williston maintained that "a firm proposal to construct storage on the East Kootenay would create so much organized opposition that the whole Columbia River development would be jeopardized."[46] He conceded that British Columbia had agreed to include it at the beginning to create the strongest possible negotiating position, but maintained that it was clear from the outset that such flooding would have to result in a net advantage to the province. He did not feel that evidence that such would be the result had been provided.

In the sharp discussion which followed, federal spokesmen were concerned about what they saw as a retreat from a previously agreed-to position, and feared it would mean that the United States would not accept the High Arrow, Duncan Lake, and Mica projects as first-added. Mr. Williston frankly stated that his province preferred Libby to upstream Kootenay storage in Canada, if satisfactory arrangements could be made as to the net benefit position with the United States. The upshot was that the Canadian negotiators were instructed to reject the proposal that the United States be given an option to build Libby, with Canada committed to build at Dorr and Bull River if the option were not taken up. They were also to strive for High Arrow and Duncan first-added, Mica in a following position, and were to consider Libby on a third-added basis. The Policy Committee authorized the negotiators to modify, if necessary, the previous Canadian position that Libby reservoir costs and the cost of returning the downstream benefit should be borne by the United States, and that the secondary energy currently sold in that country should be included in calculating the quantum of firm power produced by the Canadian regulation when determining the downstream benefit. The basic Canadian position on Libby was that the United States retain all at-site and downstream power produced in the United States, and that Canada not have to share the downstream benefit produced by it in Canada. The negotiators were instructed finally to seek a joint progress report to be submitted to the two national governments at the next meeting.

Substantially, the British Columbia position had been accepted; one federal minister in fact remarked that there was now no alternative to Libby. The record indicates, however, that the meeting concluded in a mood of some uncertainty, as two federal ministers at least were obviously perturbed, and one declared that he would report the whole situation to the Canadian Cabinet. Before the meeting ended, federal representatives once more sought, unsuccessfully, a reaction to Mr. Fleming's February 9 proposal on financing. It was agreed that an understanding was desirable, and the committee undertook to recommend to the respective finance ministers that governmental representatives meet informally to consider the terms, degree, and form of federal fiscal participation in the Columbia's development. It was also felt that they might discuss such questions as the designation or creation of a Canadian entity to develop the river, power pricing, and the downstream benefit accruing from upstream Canadian or American storage at the plants of the Consolidated Mining and Smelting Company (Cominco) on the Lower Kootenay.

Within a very few days of this Policy Liaison Committee meeting, the federal Cabinet asked the United States for a two week postponement of the next international meeting, due to be held on May 23–24, only to discover that this would be unfeasible. Furthermore the Americans pressed for a meeting on the previously designated dates, as they had a firm proposal which they wished to bring forward. Sometime before May 20 the federal Cabinet agreed to attempt to hold such a meeting, and at the same time decided that its position would be to oppose further negotiations with the United States if storage at Dorr and Bull River were precluded from consideration. It also agreed that the province be asked to send a representative to explore possibilities of reconciliation and that the minister of finance should make new overtures to British Columbia on the subject of financial assistance. Mr. Fulton phoned Mr. Williston, appraised him of the United States' request, and invited him to Ottawa to discuss the situation. Mr. Williston in reply indicated that neither he nor the other provincial members of the Policy Committee could go on such short notice and left no doubt about his unhappiness at the position which was developing. However, on May 19 he did give Mr. Bassett a memorandum telling him of a possible meeting with the Americans during the next week, and instructing him to attend it. Mr. Williston was careful to record, however, that he had been informed "that the purpose of such a meeting would be solely to hear a new proposal which the Americans wish to advance for consideration" and directed Mr. Bassett "that at such a meeting you will restrict your participation to a listening brief on behalf of the government of British Columbia. . . . You shall not negotiate or participate in discussion of matters other than on the basis of the direction given to the Canadian Team by the Canada-British Columbia Policy Liaison Committee meeting in Victoria on the 14th instant."

The substance of the proposal advanced by the United States in Washington on May 23–24, as one which it would commit itself to, was that Canada build the Dorr and Bull River, and either (1) the High Arrow and Duncan Lake, or (2) the Mica projects. Specifically it suggested that:

(1) Canada was to build expeditiously storage dams at Bull River and Dorr (with a 1 million acre-feet per year diversion into the Columbia permitted), and High Arrow and Duncan, or Mica, or High Arrow alone. These developments were to have a next added existing position to American projects, unless the International Work Group found *a higher benefit-cost ratio for the United States* . . . in projected Corps projects in the United States over Bull River-Dorr.

(2) The downstream power benefit was to be equally divided but, as indicated in Report No. 1 of the International Work Group,[47] allowance would be made for a decline in the resulting marketable secondary energy resulting from Canadian storage.

(3) Each country would be responsible for the transmission costs from the generating plants to market associated with its share of the downstream power benefit. The United States would make available wheeling facilities at between $2 and $3 per kw annually depending upon where the power was returned to Canada.

(4) The United States would pay Canada annually one-half the estimated average flood damage prevented—discounted to a present value capital sum if Canada wished.

A long discussion of the implications of these proposals followed. When the Canadian chairman raised the question of the American position if Canada found a downgraded Dorr-Bull River scheme uneconomic, the American response was that then Canada would have to permit Libby, and would have to allow enough benefits adjusted against Mica and High Arrow to make it attractive. Before the first day's session ended Mr. Fulton made it clear that Canada might be prepared to consider the United States' proposal, but not until the clause (italicized in proposition (1) above), which could downgrade the Dorr and Bull River projects, was removed.

When the Canadians caucused that evening, a senior Canadian technical adviser reported on the meeting of the International Work Group at which Dorr and Bull River had been placed in American figures behind High Mountain Sheep and possibly other projects, and the Americans had doubted the efficacy of Arrow storage as a re-regulator for Mica. He felt the latest American proposal was much worse than any of their previous ones. Mr. Bassett then read a statement which he had just written in which he deprecated the shading out of one of the best Canadian projects (either Mica or Arrow) and deplored the departure from where he felt the Canadians could have been—had they gone forward on the basis of the May 14 Policy Liaison Committee decisions. He suggested that more questions needed to be asked of the Americans about their proposal, but that unless the Canadians put forward their May 14 position, the meeting should be terminated.

As a result, when discussion was resumed the next day, Mr. Fulton made it clear to the Americans that Canada regarded the earlier American proposals A and B (with and without Libby respectively) as still open for examination. The Canadian representatives revealed their unhappiness at the rather modest volume of Canadian storage which the Americans seemed to be willing to credit (some 13 million acre-feet), and were rather disturbed to hear that it might be even less under some circumstances. Eventually American spokesmen did concede that they could use 16 million acre-feet, but returned to a position they had established earlier, that if Canada got a first-added position for two storages, it should be prepared to accept decreased benefits accruing to its East Kootenay storage, and that a second-added position should also go to some United States storage. At least one federal Canadian spokesman seemed to be prepared to accept a second-added position for Bull River and Dorr, if the United States would remove the conditional clause in its offer which could have seen it further downgraded. When, however, American spokesmen asked directly if Canada could answer "yes" or "no" to their proposal, and later if it could answer should the Dorr and Bull River projects be confirmed in a second-added position, Mr. Fulton had to answer that he had no such authority. Hence the meeting ended with the Canadians being asked to come to the next session with a concrete proposal.

The American proposal clearly had the federal ministers in a dilemma, for it opened up the prospect of an agreement incorporating the very projects which they wanted. But it involved also such difficulties as the possibility that some of this storage would get at best second-added credit, and Canada paying for the return of downstream benefit power from American plants. Thus by June 9 the federal Cabinet Committee was divided, as some of its members had begun to wonder about the wisdom of opposing the province and its wishes.

At this point the reader may be wondering, quite legitimately, how it was that three months of meetings, with a strong and continuing technical staff input, could have produced so little evident modification of the views held in Ottawa and Victoria. Actually, the disagreement between the federal and provincial Canadian technicians, which had been marked enough in the earlier months of the year with reference to the relative merits for Canada of a Libby clearance or building Upper Kootenay storage in Canada, had stemmed from differing but quite defensible views or fears as to the costs which, in bargaining exchanges, the United States was likely to associate with the various policy options. By late May these costs had been significantly clarified, and, as will be seen shortly, the Canadian technicians had come very close to a complete meeting of minds. But at the ministerial level, the situation was different. Some accommodation had begun to emerge, as we have just seen in the preceding paragraph. But a few key ministers in Ottawa through May, and indeed, through June, remained convinced that the national interest required a major Kootenay to Columbia diversion, and maximizing Canadian power generation on this watershed year by year into the future. Their disagreement with Victoria was intractable because, although it was set in the context of a debate over means, it really involved a fundamental disagreement over ends.[48]

Frustration of another sort characterized the decision-making in Victoria, where there was a real conviction that the strength of the Canadian position in the international bargaining had deteriorated significantly. When the Policy Liaison Committee met for a climactic meeting at Ottawa on June 15 and 16, Mr. Williston in a formal statement took strong exception to the manner in which the federal government refused to accept the decisions which British Columbia felt had been agreed to, had cancelled the scheduled negotiating meeting, and had then moved (he asserted) to another phase of the international negotiations without further Policy Liaison Committee discussion and direction. Mr. Hamilton replied to this by denying that a firm and explicit direction had been agreed upon at the last meeting, and by emphasizing that Ottawa had not moved unilaterally to the Washington meeting which, he emphasized, was an exploratory, not a negotiating, one.

Mr. Williston maintained that "the federal representatives have overlooked the position of this province and seem prepared to disregard provincial planning for development unless it happens to dovetail with the viewpoint of the national government." Indeed he argued that the Americans had seized the initiative. As he reviewed the negotiating position he agreed that if a choice had to be made between Mica and High Arrow the latter would go, but he insisted—referring in the process to the endorsation of the governments' engineering consultants and technical advisers—that it was "the most efficient practical and logical development in Canada." Again he returned to the province's contention that

> it is not realistic, practical or proper for the federal government in Ottawa to plan the development of the Columbia River at long range and to disregard overall provincial planning and the local problems that can only be adequately assessed by close, on-the-spot observation and dealt with constitutionally by provincial decision. The provincial viewpoint must be given every consideration in this matter. . . . I must restress the Columbia River is a provincial resource and provincial planning should be paramount in what is finally decided.

Mr. Williston made it very clear that he felt the Canadian bargaining position of High Arrow-Duncan first-added and Mica second, with flexibility to make concessions to allow for a third project of mutual benefit, had been eroded so that the Americans were now arguing that Bull River-Dorr was a concession on their part for which Canada must concede either benefits of Mica or High Arrow-Duncan.

The federal reply to this on the same and the following day was to stress Ottawa's concurrent jurisdiction over an international river, its responsibility to protect the national interest, and to deny that federal action had done irreparable harm to the Canadian case. Any weakening of it, in fact, was attributed in a statement read by Mr. Hamilton, to the unwillingness of British Columbia to stand by the original bargaining offer. Mr. Hamilton made it quite explicit that Ottawa still felt the goal ought to be the production of "the largest amount of power for Canada over the life-time of the agreement . . . keeping in mind at the same time the capital costs involved and the unit cost of power produced."

When attention was directed in heated exchanges to the problems which could no longer be deferred, British Columbia's representatives asked for a return to the position which they felt had been firmly and explicitly decided upon at the May 23-24 meeting. Once more federal spokesmen asked the province to reconsider its objection to East Kootenay flooding, as federal representatives introduced a federal Department of Agriculture statement showing that only about 28,000 of the 91,000 acres in the Dorr-Bull River-Luxor reservoir were being used. Mr. Hamilton's second day statement outlined three alternative objectives for Canada as Ottawa saw them:

(1) The three storages (Mica, High Arrow, Dorr-Bull River) plus a major Kootenay diversion, still seen as the best in the Canadian interest.

(2) Failing (1), a position based on the American May 23 offer— specifically Mica and Duncan plus Bull River and Dorr storage— all first-added.

(3) Failing (2), a position based on the American April 1 proposal— namely High Arrow-Duncan first-added, Mica next, and the decision as to whether Libby or Dorr were to be built to be decided "on the basis of economics." "The federal government, in this approach," Mr. Hamilton declared, "would reluctantly be accepting the British Columbia position with regard to High Arrow."[49]

Mr. Williston repeated once more his government's views of the present and future value of the East Kootenay and Arrow Lakes valleys, its unwillingness to flood both, and its view that High Arrow, Duncan, and Mica should all be first-added storages. Even at this late date, he noted, the U.S. reaction to his province's position really was not known. He did agree, when pressed, to present Ottawa's proposals to the provincial Cabinet but felt there was little chance it would shift ground.

In all the foregoing, the strength of Ottawa's attachment to East Kootenay storage and its aversion to Libby are very clearly reflected. It is all the more striking because the Canadian Section of the International Work Group—all members of the Technical Liaison Committee (federal and provincial)—had produced a study on June 10 which compared a form of Plan A—on the assumption that the United States built Libby—and Plan B—based on the American proposal of May 23, with Canada providing 18.1 million acre-feet of storage (13.9 million of it live) at Mica Creek, Duncan Lake, Dorr and Bull River. The study had listed the advantages and disadvantages of both approaches without specifically endorsing one over the other. But a dispassionate re-reading of the document certainly conveys the impression that the combined federal-provincial technical group by this time was very skeptical about East Kootenay Valley storage.[50] It calculated, for example, that in 1972, the year in which it assumed at-site generation would begin, Plan A would have an operational deficit of $27.4 millions, but annual revenues then exceeding costs by $2 millions—while Plan B would have an operational deficit of $50.3 millions and costs which would be exceeding revenues by $4.5 millions. Consequently it is not surprising that, when Mr. Williston wrote to Mr. Hamilton on June 24, conveying the information that the British Columbia Cabinet had considered at length its views and had decided not to change its position, he was able to add that he and his colleagues would be very interested indeed to see the technical analyses substantiating the economic superiority of the plan involving the East Kootenay storage to which Mr. Hamilton had referred at the last Policy Liaison Committee meeting.

On June 24 also Mr. Hamilton phoned Mr. Williston (presumably after hearing of the provincial stand) and indicated that Ottawa was going to go back to the American option over Libby (ie. to abandon the construction of Bull River-Dorr), with High Arrow and Mica credit left inviolate. He also suggested that Ottawa did not want to *ask* the United States to build Libby, fearing a downgrading of Canadian storage, but did think (and Mr. Williston seems to have agreed with him) that in view of the impending American election the Americans just might go for Libby even if it were uneconomic and had no large storage credit reservations. Even at this stage at least one member of the Cabinet Committee, who was reluctant to see Libby cleared, prepared for the prime minister, and reviewed first with his Cabinet Committee colleagues, a detailed assessment of the three courses of action which he felt were now open to the federal government. One alternative, a refusal to continue negotiations, was seen as unfeasible. The advantages and disadvantages of giving the province what it wanted—the second alternative—were also specified. The third alternative canvassed raised the possibility of seeking a bargain with British Columbia whereby, if the province would accept Ottawa's preferred sequence and set of projects, which he maintained best served Canada's long-term interests, the national government could agree to build the entire development and operate it until it was self-sustaining. Then it would be turned over to the province on condition that an agreed portion of the federal contribution be repaid. Quite clearly this was a very long shot, and, as it turned out, it involved risks which neither the Cabinet Committee nor the prime minister was prepared to take.

Thus by mid-summer, 1960, after their invocation of a variety of mechanisms of adjustment, the federal and provincial governments finally resolved their painful dispute over project selection. Some hard bargaining concerning a number of quite basic details of the embryonic international agreement lay ahead, but it was not expected to generate any major inter-governmental stress in Canada. Still to be faced domestically, however, and presumably to be resolved prior to the completion of an agreement with the United States, was a clarification of the financing responsibilities of the two Canadian governments, and the task of agreeing upon the necessity, not to mention the form, of a Canadian agency to supervise the implementation of an on-going international commitment.

Chapter Six

The Negotiation of the Treaty: Phase Two

> Every politician, or public man, is the prisoner of his
> advisers. He can only be liberated by his values.
> Dalton Camp, to the Progressive Conservative
> Party Conference, Montmorency, August 1967.

Before proceeding further with our attempt to unravel the main threads in the Canadian decision-making directly related to the Columbia River, we should pause for a moment to bring ourselves up to date on the decision-making environment, by identifying a number of developments in British Columbia concerning the Peace River project. When Mr. Paget gave his feasibility clearance to the Peace River Company's plans at the end of March,[1] Mr. Mainwaring quickly set out to get both the B.C. Power Commission and the B.C. Electric to sign letters of intent to purchase blocks of power from the northern project. He soon found that the B.C. Power Commission was quite unwilling to move until assured that the B.C. Electric had done likewise, that it wanted to purchase a smaller block at a lower price than he proposed, and that with the Columbia development ahead, the commission had no reason to hurry. The B.C. Electric had made plans for thermal power sufficient to meet its anticipated needs for a decade; it also wanted a smaller block at a lower price. Further, Dr. Grauer now told Mr. Mainwaring that his advisers reported a flattening in the load-growth curve which made the proposed Peace River energy purchase, at least in the quantity suggested, surplus to his company's needs. The B.C. Electric, in spite of its interest in the Peace River Company, was in a dilemma; it feared that power from the Peace might be significantly dearer than that from the Columbia, and it was well aware of the tug-of-war going on between Mr. Bennett and the federal government over the timing of the Peace development. A decision either way by it was bound to antagonize one government or the other. In any case Dr. Grauer also declined to sign, despite his undertaking of the previous September to do so.

As the summer approached, Premier Bennett became more and more eager to have a start made on the Peace River project. But he had no ready answer for Mr. Mainwaring when the latter informed him, in May, of his marketing problems, especially with Dr. Grauer. Mr. Bennett sought to contact Dr. Grauer, who had left for Europe. Shortly, however, the premier was in Britain, and, while there, put the situation squarely to Dr. Grauer and Sir Andrew McTaggart of the Peace River Power Development Company. One way or another, he indicated, he wanted the Peace River Company to have an application before the province's Public Utilities Commission by September, and work gangs on the river before the fall was over, or he would build the project.[2]

Certainly by July, and probably earlier, senior officers of the B.C. Electric Company saw to it that the federal Cabinet was appraised of the pressure on them to purchase power from the Peace River, and of their fears concerning its potential expensiveness. This information appears to have reinforced the reservations which the federal ministers on the Policy Liaison Committee held with respect to Peace River development, and may well have been one consideration which prompted them to ask at the meeting of the committee on June 15 just what were the overall plans of the province with respect to power. The record on this point reads as follows: "In answer to a question by Mr. Green, Mr. Williston advised that B.C. had no intention of timing the Peace River project between the High Arrow and Mica projects. B.C. would definitely commit itself to a sequence of High Arrow followed by Mica, provided of course that the downstream benefit returns were satisfactory." Dr. Keenleyside also declared at this time that he was completely satisfied that the British Columbia government would not defer the Columbia because of the Peace. These two guarantees must have provided some assurance to the federal representatives, although an enigmatic observation by Mr. Williston on the following day, June 16, to the effect that "it would be impossible for the B.C. government to commit itself not to license construction of other power projects in B.C. until Mica had been started"[3] may well have aroused again some uncertainty in the minds of those who heard him.

1. The Resumption of Direct Negotiations with the United States

When the Policy Liaison Committee met in Victoria on July 4 it was obvious that the impasse within that body had been resolved. Mr. Hamilton read a statement which reviewed what had happened, and accepted fundamentally the provincial position on project selection. He suggested that the Mica, High Arrow, and Duncan dams all be next-added, receiving full credit for an estimated 14.71 million acre-feet of storage, with no reservation allowed against this or displacement permitted because of Libby. The statement proposed that the United States be given an option to build Libby, with that country paying all costs associated with it, and retaining the at-site and downstream benefits produced by it in the United States. Canada, it proposed, should, without recompense, be entitled to whatever power benefits Canadian generating plants derived from Libby storage. Mr. Williston indicated basic agreement with this, although he maintained that the 14.71 million acre-feet should be regarded as a minimum objective, and that Canada initially should advance a credit claim for 20.2 million acre-feet. In all, some nine specific negotiating objectives were agreed to, including the retention of the right to divert one to one and a half million acre-feet from the Kootenay to the Columbia River. After the agreement had expired there was to be no limitation on diversion rights. It was agreed that Canada would seek to have the United States pay the cost of transmitting the downstream benefit power to Canada, and that Canada would accept a lump sum representing the present worth of the flood control benefit.[4] Should the United States decide to build Libby, it was agreed to strive for American coverage of all reservoir costs including those in Canada, although a possible need in bargaining to modify this objective (as a departure from grossing) was recognized. It was further agreed that the Canadian claim for downstream power benefits should apply to private as well as public plants, including those still unbuilt, on the Columbia's American main stream. A progress report to both national governments was to be produced at the next international meeting, if the negotiators felt it desirable. One further item agreed to was the American position on the decline in average annual saleable secondary energy, which was recognized as reasonable and in accord with IJC principles. It could be accepted, the Policy Liaison Committee agreed, but should be viewed as a tactical concession in the bargaining.

This position was advanced by Canada when the fifth international negotiating meeting was held at Ottawa on July 14 and 15. Agreement did not come easily at first, as the American representatives stressed that Libby had only a 1.13 to 1 benefit-cost ratio first-added after High Arrow, that after Duncan was also first-added the ratio fell to .9 to 1, and that, with Mica and the limited Kootenay diversion included, the position would further deteriorate. The Americans also took strong exception to the proposed credit position of Duncan Lake storage, in spite of its short construction time, because of the extent to which Libby would duplicate the production of both its flood control and power benefits downstream.

The Canadian representatives argued that, as the Columbia basin's power problems could be solved without Libby, Canada would accept it "but could not be expected to pay a price for it."[5] Eventually the Canadians cut the storage for which next-added credit was sought to 16.5 million acre-feet, and agreed to defer any Kootenay diversion until 1977, and perhaps 1980, to improve Libby's potential. Still the Americans bargained, re-emphasizing Libby's downstream benefits in Canada, and the increased generation possible at Mica and downstream-in-Canada, thanks to diversion from the Kootenay, when effected. They indicated a willingness to accept the Canadian offer, but on two conditions. One was that the flood control benefit of Duncan Lake (and the very small one of Mica) be transferred to Libby; the other involved the proposal that some 125 megawatts of capacity and related energy be withdrawn from the quantum of downstream benefit power before any division was made. To counter this move the Canadians lowered the amount of storage offered to 15.5 million acre-feet. Indeed, before the bargaining was adjourned, they offered to cut the Canadian storage to 15 million acre-feet and to recommend that Canada meet the Libby flowage costs in Canada if the Americans would reconsider their reluctance to meet the cost of transmitting the downstream power benefit to the Canadian border.[6]

Some real progress was made before the meeting broke up. The three Canadian storages did appear to have been accepted in a next-added position, credited with 15 million acre-feet of storage. The way was cleared for Libby, and it was agreed that the Canadian right to a partial Kootenay diversion was to be deferred for a period of fifteen to twenty years.[7] Responsibility for the cost of transmitting the Canadian downstream power benefit was not settled, although the Americans did point out that the United States would be prepared to make allowances if, once Canadian at-site power was developed, suitable exchange agreements were entered into with the United States.

When the Cabinet Committee on the Columbia met in Ottawa on July 21 to review this latest round of bargaining, it was quite clear that, with some of its members, there were strong and lingering regrets over the acceptance of the province's position. At least one Cabinet minister spoke warmly of Sequence IX A. General McNaughton, who was present, re-iterated his position. He conceded that the extra costs incurred through Libby's inclusion fell on the United States, but felt that the concessions made to that country helped to pass the costs on to Canada. Another minister, very critical of Libby, doubted if he could support any Canadian financial participation. Secretary of State for External Affairs Howard Green helped to keep things moving by observing that the only feasible alternative, to kill the agreement, was just impracticable. Presumably he was referring to the costs which would be associated with writing off fifteen years of analytic effort, with setting aside the ICREB Report's endorsation of cooperative development, with disappointing the United States, with subjecting south-eastern British Columbia to more years of uncertainty, and above all with the constitutional as well as technical difficulties inherent in having to sustain the proposition that, on this issue, the provincial government did not recognize its own best interest.

No meeting of the Policy Liaison Committee was necessary before the international negotiators met for a sixth time on July 23–24 in Washington. On this occasion it soon became evident that the question of downstream power transmission costs had become crucial, and that a Canadian payment for transmission in the United States was as embarrassing and difficult for the Canadians to consider as it seemed to be for the Americans. Save for the evident desire of both sides to reach an agreement, at the end of the first day of bargaining a virtual stalemate had been reached. The Americans rejected the Canadian offer to reduce their credited storage some 500,000 acre-feet if the United States picked up the transmission cost to the border; hence the storage offered and accepted returned to 15.5 million acre-feet. When the deadlock continued for a further hour on the second day, an off-the-record executive session was held (without technical staff present). This exercise in candour had its effect. The Americans ultimately advanced, as a concomitant of their delivering the benefit power at the border, the concept of their providing a stand-by east-west circuit, and the Canadian representatives agreed to recommend that Canada pay $1.50 per kilowatt per annum for its use in lieu of spending some $26–$29 million (or about some $2 million a year over the life of the agreement) to construct similar facilities on Canadian soil.[8] Libby flowage costs continued to provide difficulty, with the Canadians indicating real problems for them in meeting this charge as well as that for the stand-by transmission service. As an alternative it was agreed that should Canada not accept these costs the United States would—if Duncan flood control benefits were transferred to Libby from Duncan. As an offset here the Canadians understood that the United States would be prepared to consider increasing the flood control benefit accruing to High Arrow from 50 to 65 percent of the total flood damage which this project prevented.[9] The United States' representatives once again pressed for a deferment of the Kootenay diversion until 1985, and for a provision for subsequent discussions which would ensure that such a diversion would cause minimal loss to the United States—and still provide for the best use of the diversion waters in Canada.

The need to pursue some technical analyses of the alternatives still open, plus some staff pressures for a short break, help explain a two month pause at this time in the formal negotiations. Another factor contributing to the delay, although it should not be over-emphasized, was the calling of a provincial election on August 3 in British Columbia, with polling to take place on September 12. Mr. Bennett did not make the Columbia a central issue. But no proposed development of this magnitude could escape extensive discussion under such circumstances, and the opposition to Social Credit was not loath to debate it. All three opposition parties already had declared themselves against further private corporate projects on large rivers and had denounced the premier's plans for concurrent development of the Peace and Columbia Rivers. During the election campaign their spokesman expressed reservations about the seeming course of the negotiations, for although no details had been formally released, the inclusion of High Arrow and the exclusion of East Kootenay storage in Canada were already foregone conclusions. Mr. Finlayson, for example, accused the Social Credit government of pushing High Arrow because the investment required was much smaller than that for Mica, and because it wanted to open up a place for the Peace River's development. Progressive Conservative candidates in Vancouver were supported by Mr. Howard Green, who campaigned on their behalf, and promised that a provincial Conservative administration would see to it that Columbia River development would precede that on any other provincial river. Mr. Perrault for the Liberals stressed that his party would press for the construction of Mica first, and attacked the classification of High Arrow by Mr. Williston as the No. 1 project, although he was prepared to accept it if convinced it was in Canada's and British Columbia's best interest. He praised General McNaughton as "the greatest power thinker we know of."[10] The most vigorous attempt to make power policy a key issue came from Mr. Strachan, who openly charged that the B.C. Electric was the main source of Social Credit campaign funds, who was as critical as he had ever been of the Peace River Company, and who campaigned on a promise of a public takeover of both corporations. He promised that, on the day the B.C. Power Commission took over the B.C. Electric (as it already had taken over twenty-eight smaller private companies) there would be a reduction in electricity bills, and a beginning would be made on the "development of the Columbia to ensure low cost power."[11] He insisted that a CCF government would have no part of the Arrow project—unless engineering and economic considerations more than offset the social and agricultural costs. Such a government, he asserted, would also develop the Peace River, under public auspices through the Power Commission, when economically desirable and feasible.[12]

Almost all members of the provincial Cabinet argued against Mr.

Strachan's approach to the B.C. Electric, though the premier himself remained silent on this issue. Mr. Williston, in particular, repeated a claim he had made publicly earlier that international agreement had established High Arrow as the best Columbia development because it had the best benefit-cost ratio (which he saw as 6:1) for both countries. He drew attention to the way in which Mica Dam partisans ignored its nine-year, or longer, construction period, and re-emphasized that the government's Columbia position was based on the best engineering data available. Early in the election campaign he denied the existence of "a mythical plan for developing the Peace before the Columbia,"[13] arguing that British Columbia would need the simultaneous development of both rivers to prevent a power shortage.

After the sixth meeting of the international negotiators on July 23-24, the staff of the Water Resources Service in Victoria prepared, with great care, an extensive position paper on the options still open to Canada. One matter dealt with was the timing of Mica's construction. The technicians' recommendation here was blunt; the Mica Dam they declared "should not be constructed until all the low-cost power from the High Arrow-Duncan downstream benefits and from the West Kootenay and Pend d'Oreille development have been absorbed into the provincial load."[14] They noted that the Americans had indicated on July 14 and 15 that planning such timing for mutual benefit could be effected, and suggested that, if a Mica development by 1970 were considered necessary for non-technical reasons, careful consideration be given to a staging of construction whereby a medium Mica reservoir could be associated with one upstream at Surprise Rapids.[15] The very beneficial consequences of deferring Mica entirely for four years, and the lesser but still real gains from building a two stage alternative, were indicated. The analysts were well aware of hazards in their assumptions here. Dr. Keenleyside and other provincial spokesmen had known for months that provincial studies were revealing a strong economic case for a Mica deferment and had raised the matter at Policy Liaison Committee meetings—where the federal reaction had been that any such move was unacceptable. Furthermore, the provincial technicians were assuming, or hoping, that if Mica were deferred, it would still hold its first-added credit position relative to such projects as Libby.

While the provincial advisers were thus raising questions about the project which to so many had become the keystone of the Columbia's development, they were also careful to draw attention to possibilities of using this project as a large cyclic storage reservoir on the Upper Columbia—a reservoir which would serve as an energy bank "very similar to that proposed for the Peace River Power development." Another feature of this report was the extent to which its authors made their enthusiasm for the Columbia's development clear—in the light of the competitive situation which they well knew had developed in the province. When they referred to an assumed selling price of four mills per kwh, they observed that capital construction costs were felt to be conservatively high and pointed out that coordination benefits had been ignored in arriving at this figure. It seemed, therefore, that the assumed figure might be improved upon. They saw it as a "yardstick of the energy cost at load centres which is sufficiently cheaper than power from competitive projects to indicate real desirability."[16]

The provincial technicians assessed the American suggestion that the flood control credit of Duncan Lake be transferred to Libby, in return for the United States meeting the Libby flowage costs, (on the understanding that with such an arrangement the Arrow Lakes' flood control credit would rise also to 65 percent of the damage prevented) as worth some $410,000 per annum to Canada.[17] The willingness of Americans to make such a "bargain" was viewed by the British Columbians as a measure of their desire to allocate the full value of Kootenay River flood control to their major project. Under the circumstances, the position paper raised the question of dropping Duncan Lake (if Libby could be regulated to advantage for West Kootenay generation), and adding its storage to other sites such as Kootenay Lake, Trout Lake, and Mica. Indeed, it suggested that some $13 millions over the period to 1981 might be saved if the Duncan Lake storage for downstream power generation in the Untied States were transferred to Mica. Rather perceptively, federal technical staff evaluating this same alternative came to the conclusion that the American chairman had made a mistake, and had intended to offer the increase in Arrow Lake flood control credit as as an alternative to handling Libby flowage—if the Duncan Lake flood control credit were transferred. Finally it must be noted that the provincial report took a hard look at the merit of moving from a 15 million acre-foot sequence involving Duncan Lake, High Arrow and Mica—all completed by 1970, and Canada providing full transmission facilities for moving the downstream benefit power from the Canadian border near Oliver, B.C., to a further sequence offering 15.5 million acre-feet of storage at the projects, and accepting the Americans' stand-by transmission line proposal. As earlier studies had suggested, this last sequence proved to be quite advantageous to Canada. The advantage was seen as decreasing over time, but would of course be all the greater if, in time, as large interchanges of power across the border were effected, the stand-by charge were waived entirely.

Some clarification of American intentions, received informally, provincial reflection on the implications of the report just referred to, and provincial preoccupation with the election (which the Social Credit government won on September 12) all contributed eventually to a provincial willingness, without a further Policy Liaison Committee meeting, to have the international negotiators meet again—for the seventh time—on September 26–28 in Ottawa. Here, Canadian representatives did agree, that the marginal economic case for the unconstructed Ben Franklin Dam on the United States main stream justified its exemption from the agreed-upon sharing of benefits rule. Hard bargaining ensued over the interest rate to be used in capitalizing the flood control benefits, with Canadians arguing for the use of the lower American-level figures and the Americans pressing for a higher rate, before agreement was finally reached that a basically American-level rate would apply. The American offer to provide a stand-by transmission facility (for $1.50 (U.S.) per kw year), as the price of returning the downstream benefit power, was accepted. The provincial analyses of the Americans' "offer" concerning Libby flowage costs turned out to be based either on a misconception or a reconsideration. On this occasion the Americans offered to pay some $8 millions of the Libby flowage costs in Canada in return for a reduction of the Duncan Lake flood control benefit from one-half to one-quarter of the damage prevented, and asked in addition for a ten year option on Libby. Canada rejected this—after consultation with Mr. Williston.[18] Finally, at this negotiating meeting, agreement was reached on a progress report to the governments concerned, in the preparation of which provincial as well as federal staff were intimately involved.

2. The Progress Report

The fact that a progress report had been signed was revealed in a press release just as soon as the Ottawa negotiations ended on September 28. At the same time the chairmen of the two negotiating teams, Mr. Fulton and Mr. Elmer Bennett, predicted a 1961 start on project construction. The report itself, which was not released at this time, was submitted to the Canadian Cabinet and to the American Secretary of State on October 5. Essentially it outlined in general terms the bargain which had been struck. Its provisions need not be repeated here; what is relevant to our perspective is the manner in which it was treated by the three governments directly involved.

In Ottawa Mr. Hamilton and Mr. Fulton prepared a memorandum, parts of which were widely circulated, in which they described the proposed arrangement as a favourable one for Canada, and recommended that it be accepted as the basis of a treaty. They recommended that the Cabinet Committee together with the minister of finance be authorized to consider further the details of federal financial participation, and, subject to Cabinet approval, to carry on discussions on this subject with British Columbia. They asked also that the Policy Liaison Committee or the minister of finance—whichever in any particular circumstance was deemed the more appropriate—be authorized to work out further details required in Canada for the negotiation and execution of the river's development, and that the Cabinet Committee be authorized to make all necessary arrangements leading to the completion of a draft treaty for submission to the Cabinet. The memorandum included the following table:

TABLE 3

Benefits from Proposed Agreement

Storage credit	15.5 million acre-feet
Downstream power benefits to Canada	6.885 billion kwh
Power benefits on the Kootenay in Canada	2.172 billion kwh
Total power benefits	9.057 billion kwh

Flood control annual benefits $3,000,845 (income from capital invested in 50 year annuities @ 5½ %).

Investment cost in Canada	$529,890,000*
Stand-by service charge for transmission by the U.S.	$ 1,965,000
Net annual cost to Canada	$ 34,184,000
Cost of power in mills	$ 3.77

*Including the cost of Cominco extensions. U.S. and Canadian dollars assumed at par for calculations.

Meanwhile the United States government, which had noticed throughout the negotiations how British Columbia's representatives had maintained that no international agreement should be allowed to serve as a justification for bypassing the licensing procedure which the province's Water Act required be applied to the storage works involved, insisted that full approval of the progress report by the government of British Columbia as well as by the two national governments should precede its release. No difficulty with British Columbia was expected over the concept of a progress report per se; its production was quite consistent with Mr. Williston's insistence to this point that the process of legitimizing projects under provincial water law should and would precede the final drafting of an international agreement.[19] As, however, opinion in Ottawa and Washington now seemed to envisage moving directly to a treaty, subject to a retrospective approval of the arrangement under Canadian domestic law, Washington's nervousness was understandable. By October 12, Ottawa was able to report that the province had cleared the report. On the same day, however, it learned from Washington that the American administration was very keen to issue the progress report on October 19, along with an assessment which would include figures on the magnitude of the downstream power benefit. Here was a complication which Ottawa had not expected to have to face at this time, and it was not slow to point out that there had not yet been agreement on any such estimates. In a flurry of exchanges Ottawa got the impression that only global amounts of prime power would be referred to, but it still remained unhappy over the proposal. The American government, however, heavily involved as it was in a presidential-congressional election,[20] was not to be deterred, and went ahead as it had planned.

This then is the background to the release of the progress report on October 19 in Washington, Ottawa, and Victoria, to an accompanying exchange of diplomatic notes and to rather different official approaches. In Victoria, notwithstanding the fact that the American note of October 19 had proposed that the two national governments' representatives undertake the preparation of a draft treaty based on the report, with a view to submitting it to them by the end of the year if possible, and the Canadian reply had accepted this proposal, Mr. Williston's press release emphasized that the progress report had been accepted by Canada and British Columbia in principle for treaty purposes, and as the basis for "Water Act" licensing applications. He also estimated the cost of power which would accrue to Canada at about 4 mills per kwh, stressed the first-added position of Canadian storages, estimated the cost of the reservoirs and transmission lines required at about $450 millions, and declared that the B.C. Power Commission was to be the operative entity for the Columbia River's development. On the same day, the B.C. Power Commission revealed that contracts for locating materials for constructing the Arrow and Duncan Dams had already been let, and that, shortly, it intended to apply for water licences.[21]

The analysis of the report issued in Washington by the Department of the Interior on October 19 was an enthusiastic document which outlined in detail the benefits which accrued to the United States. It argued that capital expenditures of some $710 millions would be required without Canadian storage to match the benefits available for some $410 millions under it.[22] The clearance given to Libby, the consequent feasibility of an American project downstream from Libby at Kootenay Falls, the continuing nature of the flood control benefits, and the time which Canadian storage made available to the United States for the resolution of domestic reservoir problems were all stressed as further gains from the arrangement.

167

For Canada—and British Columbia—the enthusiasm of this American document produced some difficulties, in that its wording led the Canadian who read it carelessly, or who did not understand what he had read, to assume that the Americans had obtained much the best of the bargain. Note, for example, this excerpt from the last page of the American analysis:

TABLE 4

Power Benefits (Analysis by U.S. Negotiators of the Report to the Governments of the United States and Canada . . . , October 1960)

Additional Kilowatts of Prime Power

With 15.5 Million Acre-Feet, 1970 Conditions

	United States	Canada
High Arrow	645,000	484,000
Duncan	138,000	75,000
Mica	359,000	204,000
Libby	544,000	—
TOTAL	1,686,000*	763,000**

*One half of the increase in average annual useable energy, plus secondary energy available to the United States which is firmed up.
**One half of the increase in average annual useable energy.[23]

Meanwhile in Ottawa Mr. Fulton and Mr. Diefenbaker issued press releases which emphasized the merits of the bargain for Canada, stressing the reduction which it would permit in the current power rates in British Columbia. They were undoubtedly gratified by the largely favourable national press reaction.[24] Mr. Fulton sent copies of the report to many who had followed the negotiations closely, and enclosed a mimeographed summary of the benefits accruing to Canada in which was included a 3.77 mill evaluation of the downstream power benefit, and one of 3.97 mills per kwh representing the average cost to British Columbia of the 20.2 billion kilowatt hours of energy which eventually would be produced on the Columbia in Canada.

The enthusiastic and complimentary analysis from Ottawa, of course, was no more accidental than that emanating from Washington. Both national governments saw political advantage in association with the Columbia development, and Ottawa was especially anxious to heighten the public's favourable impression of the merits of the agreement and of its superiority to the proposals of the Peace River Power Development Company. The provincial government was anything but ingenuous on this point, of course, and Mr. Williston was realist enough to appreciate the purely hypothetical nature of mill rate cost estimates so far ahead of actual development. Privately he urged Mr. Fulton to eschew a Columbia power evaluation other than one at roughly 4 mills, and publicly he expressed his doubts about more precise estimates. British Columbia's metropolitan press did not miss the differing emphases in the Victoria and Ottawa announcements, and those sections of it which were rather consistently skeptical of Social Credit government claims emphasized that Mr. Fulton's figures held out the promise of a block of power being available to British Columbia at a cost 46 percent less than prevailing Vancouver prices. The immediate consequence, in any case, of the release of the progress report was the issuance of a series of rather sharply competitive assessments from Ottawa and Victoria concerning the validity of the evaluations of the cost of Columbia River power. To *The Vancouver Sun* on October 21, Mr. Fulton seemed to suggest that Ottawa reserved the right to see that the downstream power benefit was used judiciously, and that while the national government was agreeable to a sale of surplus downstream energy in the United States, it would not approve such an action if it meant that British Columbians would have to pay higher prices for power from alternative sources.[25] Within a few days he appeared to back away from his precise estimate of the cost of Columbia River power.[26] Also, on October 21, an Ottawa journalist produced a story which maintained that early in the international negotiations a provincial spokesman, before the entire international negotiating group, had categorically rejected the possibility of any East Kootenay Valley storage in Canada—to the extreme discomfiture of the federal Canadian representatives and the delight of General Itschner of the Corps of Engineers. This news dispatch, denied in both Canadian capitals, was very much resented by the policy-makers in Victoria.[27]

On hearing of Ottawa's optimism with respect to the cost of Columbia power and with respect to the possibility of a start on project construction in 1961, Mr. Mainwaring also entered the debate. He publicly discounted that optimism, holding that Columbia cost estimates were too low, and that the Columbia still faced two to three years of legal and technical problem-solving before physical development could begin.[28] Mr. Fulton did not agree. Privately, within a week, Mr. Mainwaring was to become very conscious of the leverage which Ottawa was exerting, when, on October 24, he met with Dr. Grauer, and the latter, in Mr. Mainwaring's own words, "took the position that the information that has been released leads the people to believe that the Columbia is going to produce a large amount of cheap power and this must be answered one way or another before the B.C. Electric can sign for Peace River Power." Indeed, Dr.

Grauer insisted that his company must not take any action "that in the eyes of the public would be wrong" and that if the B.C. Electric did contract now to purchase all of its requirements from Peace River generation they would be accused of scuttling the Columbia development. His position was that the B.C. Power Commission would have to sign a letter of intent first.[29] In reply to this Mr. Mainwaring could only reveal that immediately after November 15 he would forward the latest rate studies of the terms on which Peace River power would be available to the B.C. Power Commission and the B.C. Electric, that he would expect a reply within two weeks, and after that time would feel free to go to Mr. Bennett and tell him that his instructions had been followed.

3. FEDERAL-PROVINCIAL DISAGREEMENT ON FINANCING, A JOINT ENTITY, AND THE PEACE RIVER

When Mr. Bassett reported to Mr. Williston after the September 26–28 international negotiations he drew the minister's attention to the need for clarifying the financial obligations of the two Canadian governments in the Columbia's development. In the week which followed the release of the progress report, Mr. Williston suggested publicly that the federal government's financial position had never been put in writing. Mr. Fulton denied this, and observed that while the federal government's offer in March was only a beginning, Ottawa had no real idea of what the province intended to do in this connection. All this sparring was brought to a head on October 26 when Mr. Bennett, in Ottawa, informed the press that the federal government had made no attempt to discuss Columbia River financing with him. Before the day was over he had a meeting with Mr. Fleming, and indicated that there were five questions to which he wished answers. Four of these asked for precise details concerning the maximum loan which Ottawa would extend to the B.C. Power Commission, which he also described as "the agency which would carry out the development."[30] The fifth inquired flatly about the amount of the outright grant to be made—in view of current federal help to other provinces.[31]

The federal Cabinet Committee now had to respond to a rather categoric and well-publicized request, but it found the process difficult. Messrs. Green and Fulton had been trying for some weeks to have their colleagues reconsider the prospect of a direct grant, had not been unwilling to mention the South Saskatchewan Dam, and had emphasized the need for a significant and visible federal role in this on-going development. But Mr. Fleming's position as the minister of finance (and the only minister with whom Mr. Bennett would deal on the Columbia questions—save Mr. Diefenbaker himself) was crucial, and Mr. Fleming as early as

October 13 was inclined to view Ottawa's participation in the Columbia's development very differently. He was prepared to argue that the federal government should avoid being needlessly embroiled in construction and operations, and that there was not much point to a supervisory agency to provide for federal participation. If further supervision were required, a federal nominee on the board of the provincial entity, or a board established under IJC auspices he saw as reasonable possibilities. By October 28, Mr. Hamilton had come to a somewhat similar conclusion, and also had come to doubt the need for federal financial participation. As an individual member of Cabinet (as the new minister of agriculture he could no longer relay his former department's viewpoint)[32] he proposed that this administrative arrangement might be attained by repeating the offer to pay one-half the storage costs, but attaching to it such conditions as to encourage British Columbia to go it alone. In fairness to the ministers just referred to, it must be noted that the views mentioned, and others, were inevitably often modified quickly in the crucible of discussion required by the convention of Cabinet solidarity. All that can be said with confidence is that the view which prevailed in the Cabinet Committee was the one which maintained that close federal supervision and control would be necessary. Its advocates held that through the long process of international negitiation Ottawa had assumed not only an obligation to see that the designated storages were built, but also a legal-political responsibility involving considerations as varied as the price at which the resulting power should be sold and the responsibility to ensure that the Canadian downstream benefits were recovered in kind and not sold in such a way as to require other developments and perhaps costlier power in Canada.

The federal Cabinet ministers actually wrestled with drafts of their answer to Mr. Bennett for almost six weeks, debating many issues. To Victoria, of course, there was just one basic question—the amount and the form of any financial assistance which would be available from Ottawa. Mr. Williston's and Mr. Bennett's statements designating the B.C. Power Commission as the operating entity were felt to have resolved the question of the entity which would carry out Canadian projects on the Columbia. The federal Cabinet, however, for some time was not prepared to accept such a unilateral provincial assertion, and insisted that the entity established under the treaty would be quite as significant as the financing of the resulting projects. It viewed as inseparable the matters of financial assistance and designating an administrative entity, and seriously considered two alternative arrangements. One would have involved the creation of a joint federal-provincial agency with a broadly supervisory role (although with latent compulsive powers) over the B.C. Power Commission, which latter body would act as the construction and operating entity. The other would have involved the two governments cooperating in a single instrumentality performing all functions—construction, finance, and operation. Those who championed the first proposal felt that it still recognized the provincial decision already announced, and it seems to have been this alternative which federal representatives had in mind when they raised the question before the Policy Liaison Committee, when it met for the eleventh time on November 23–24 at Ottawa. A joint entity, they maintained, would ensure the fulfilment of international obligations, and the performance of a host of tasks, from raising funds, to approving plans and the appointment of engineers. In reply, British Columbia's Cabinet ministers gave no indication that they had been convinced of the federal case; they admitted the need for close liaison between the two Canadian governments, but not for rather intensive federal supervision, and not for another body in addition to the B.C. Power Commission. They did suggest that the federal-provincial partnership arrangement both in financing and in an entity which Ottawa was now advocating be made specific in the letter then being drafted in Ottawa in response to Mr. Bennett's direct questions.

When the reply to Mr. Bennett was finally agreed to—as late as December 7, the day it was dispatched—Ottawa's offer of financial assistance was presented as an investment in a joint self-liquidating project to cover one-half the cost of the storage projects. It suggested that capital repayment be from revenue, with each government's contributions being subject to the same maturity dates and repayment conditions. The reference to repayment from revenue was significant, for by it Ottawa was undertaking to carry its loan until revenue had begun to accrue from the capital investment, and was seeking to meet the claim made by Mr. Bennett on October 26 that the national government wished its contribution repaid before that of the province and its agency was cleared off. This was as far as the federal ministers from British Columbia had been able to push their colleagues in the direction of a direct grant. At the same time the federal letter, signed by Mr. Fleming, left no doubt that this offer was conditional; the whole arrangement was subject to "satisfactory agreement on the character and functions of a joint federal-provincial co-ordinating agency." Mr. Fleming's letter pictured the entity as a medium through which federal monies could be relayed to the British Columbia Power Commission as contracts were approved, and through which provincial contributions also might be handled. Alternatively it suggested that, in the light of a two-government guarantee, the entity might raise all or part of the funds required directly from the public. The letter contained one other interesting proposal worded thus: "Until its investment has been recovered by it, the federal government would be entitled to receive a share of the net revenue earned from the project in proportion to its contribution."[33] Ottawa's objective here was never made clear; it may have been concerned only to accelerate the redemption of the federal investment once the project had become self-sustaining. On the other hand, it may have hoped through such a proviso to prevent the creation of any net revenue at all from the Columbia's development—in short, to ensure that all power produced was sold at cost.

While an agreement on financing and one on entity identification were the major issues complicating Ottawa-Victoria relations at this time, there were a number of others which also required serious attention. When Canadian technical personnel met on November 4 to review a draft Columbia River Treaty, federal representatives had to work hard to persuade their provincial colleagues that it would be impossible to include details as to how a treaty was to be implemented in Canada, in a document requiring the approval of the United States Senate. A second consideration of great concern to the provincial staff at this time was the mechanism whereby, during the life of a treaty, the Canadian and American operating entities could enter into subordinate working agreements. Here no consensus was established among the technicians, as the provincial group challenged the wisdom of the federal contention that such agreements should be covered by formal exchanges of notes between the two national governments. Finally, it is interesting to note that by November 4, provincial representatives had begun to worry about the prospect of naming specific projects in a treaty, especially if it were to be signed quickly.

This last question was to be raised and discussed at the Policy Liaison Committee meeting on November 23–24. By this time the Eisenhower government (on November 8) had lost the quadrennial American election, but had given some indication that it would like to finalize a treaty before leaving office. Canadian federal government spokesmen stressed the significance to Canada of a rapid start in view of the severity of the unemployment problem, and all present saw merit in not having to repeat the negotiations with a new American team. Mr. Williston observed here that "if a treaty was to be formulated by January it would be necessary to include a general statement only about the location of storages to be provided in Canada." But he did not insist on this, and added that if "on the other hand, it was necessary to be specific . . . the treaty could not be finalized until public hearings had been held and licences granted." Before the two-day meeting was over, agreement between the two governments was reached on a general understanding to the effect that "the licensing procedures and hearings in both countries"[34] would have to be completed before the treaty was ratified.

One additional issue raised on November 23 and 24 concerned the ability of the province to absorb the large block of downstream benefit power, and the willingness of the United States to purchase energy surplus to Canadian needs. No agreement was reached, however, as to the basis for pricing Canadian power sales, or as to providing for some leeway in the scheduling of the Mica Dam. Because of outstanding issues of this sort, and in the absence of agreement on either development entities or financing, it was agreed at this time that no further discussion with the United States should be held until the governments of Canada and British Columbia had reached agreement on matters related to the implementation of a treaty.

When the Policy Liaison Committee reconvened on December 8 in Victoria, it had to deal with all of these issues. Authorization of sales of surplus power was a question which raised no little debate, as federal spokesmen insisted that such sales be the subject of exchanges of diplomatic notes. The province's representatives once again stressed the need for flexibility in connection with these transactions, which they felt "would normally be on a short-term basis." Their contention was that one general note outlining the basis of such exchanges ought to suffice, with the operating agencies free to work out details. There was also an inconclusive discussion on a provincial suggestion that the draft treaty refer to "British Columbia's" rather than to "Canada's" entitlement to a downstream power benefit. Similarly, a discussion of the authority and responsibility which might be devolved on a proposed permanent engineering board appears to have evoked differing opinions from the spokesmen of the two governments. The most they could do here was to concur in the statement that a thorough examination of the proposal was necessary before it could be accepted. But they did agree on a number of technical issues, such as the unacceptability of an American proposal that the Canadian downstream benefit power entitlement be returned in equal weekly amounts; they agreed, also, that flood control allocation of storage not be related to specific projects, and on the proposal that Canada not allocate reservoir capacity to the so-called secondary storage objective of the United States —reducing a flood at The Dalles from 800,000 cfs. to 600,000 cfs.— except on special calls by the United States from time to time, and with adequate compensation. They agreed also on the desirability of making some provision in the treaty for Mica's deferment should economic conditions require it, and on the proposition that, except for a guaranteed flow to the United States of 1,000 cfs., Canada retain the right of full Kootenay diversion after the treaty's termination, and also if the Libby option were not exercised.

But overshadowing everything else on this occasion was the attempt to settle upon the basic considerations to be incorporated in a Canada-

British Columbia agreement. The December 7 letter from Mr. Fleming (on financing and the joint entity) was brought to Victoria by the federal members of the Policy Liaison Committee and was delivered to the premier's office on the morning of December 8. On the same day *The Vancouver Sun* ran a reasonably accurate story on its contents.[35] What happened, however, was that Mr. Bennett held a press conference at 2 p.m. on December 8, at just the moment the Policy Liaison Committee was convening in another part of the Legislative Buildings. Reading from a prepared statement he asserted that throughout the Columbia River negotiations "the government of British Columbia has accepted and affirmed its responsibility to the people of this province to carry out this development on their behalf through the agency of the B.C. Power Commission," and went on to declare that the government of Canada has been asked "to negotiate those questions, mainly concerning downstream benefits, which required settlement by treaty." After reviewing his earlier request for a financial contribution, and other clarifications from Ottawa, he took specific exception to a number of provisions in Mr. Fleming's letter. He objected to the limitation of the assistance which had been offered to the provision of storage, to the absence of a direct grant, and to the condition that "profits" be shared. He maintained that Ottawa sought a profit of $110 millions.[36] The premier went on to declare: "The federal government proposes, through the creation of a new separate agency, to carry out the development of a natural resource which belongs to the people of British Columbia, to effectively remove control of that resource from this province."[37] And he concluded by saying that the proposal was unacceptable.

The result of Mr. Bennett's action was a resounding row, for when Mr. Fulton subsequently heard of the premier's announcement, and sought but was refused an interview with Mr. Bennett, he held his own news conference. The premier, he maintained, had mistakenly or deliberately falsified the federal offer, which he insisted was the most generous ever made by the national government to a province over hydro-electric project financing. And whatever the ultimate arrangement over treaty financing, he added: "We want to be sure no improvident arrangements are made and that nothing is done that is inconsistent with the treaty obligations." He continued: "We are not prepared to allow benefits under this treaty . . . , to be used for financing other pet projects of the premier of B.C."[38] Lest anyone had missed his point, when the Policy Liaison Committee reassembled on December 9, the minister of justice read a statement into the record which referred to the "discourteous and ill-considered rejection by British Columbia of the extremely generous offer of financial assistance made by the federal government" and asserted "it can only be concluded that either there was a deliberate attempt to mislead or that the decision to reject was made before Mr. Fleming's letter was received."[39]

There was no mistaking the chagrin and annoyance reflected here. On December 10, Mr. Fulton, now in Vancouver on his way back to Ottawa, addressed a Conservative party function, and in the course of it repeated the substance of his comments on the previous day.[40] Journalists in British Columbia were quick to note the seeming commitment of the federal government to a blocking of the Peace River project. So did Mr. Bennett, who formally replied to Mr. Fleming on December 14. Once again he held the federal proposals to be unacceptable, as he assured the federal minister of finance that the province would fulfil treaty terms. "In return," he continued, "British Columbia would, of course, expect the government of Canada to guarantee that the obligations imposed on the United States government by the terms of the treaty will be fulfilled."

One immediate consequence of this confrontation was a decision of the Policy Liaison Committee on December 9 to defer seeking a federal-provincial agreement on the treaty's implementation before continuing discussions with the United States. International negotiations were resumed on December 14 in Washington. By this time the major difficulty in the process of the international decision-making was the question of the control of the storage being provided by Canada. Canada had accepted in Power Principle No. 1, prepared by the IJC in 1959, the concept that downstream power benefits be determined on the basis of an assured plan of operation. But representatives of both Canadian governments were disturbed about the fact that operating the storage to maximize a downstream benefit in the United States might have very serious implications for the Canadian desire to maximize the combined returns of generation in Canada and downstream in the United States. With a complete integration of the Canadian and American electrical systems much of the need for concern in this respect would disappear, and the American representatives made no secret of the ease with which the matter could be solved under such circumstances. But in late 1960 the Technical Liaison Committee remained as cautious as it had been in 1959 about the consequences of integrating two systems at such vastly different stages of development. As a result, both Canadian governments cooperated closely in advancing, at this international meeting, a proposal for a rolling five-year assured operating plan which was ultimately to be accepted by the Americans. At this time also, to ensure still further flexibility for the operation of Mica generation (and any other further downstream in Canada), the negotiators agreed that the Canadian storage committed to downstream power production could be reduced by 500,000 acre-feet in any one year, or 3,000,000 acre-feet over the treaty's life. It was agreed to hold a still further meeting on January 5–6, 1961, and in the meantime to prepare and exchange further treaty drafts.

It is necessary at this stage to return briefly to the role of the Peace River Company, whose directors had been told so bluntly by Mr. Bennett in the early fall of 1960 that he expected prompt action. They certainly tried to give him satisfaction, but were blocked, fundamentally, by the unwillingness of the B.C. Electric to commit itself. The Peace River Company's prime requirement was an assured market, which it sought in a variety of ways. For example, it proposed that the B.C. Power Commission purchase its expanding requirements in the 'sixties (until 1968) from the B.C. Electric, and forgo increases in its own generation. Subsequently, both the Power Commission and the B.C. Electric would be in a position to purchase substantial blocks of Peace River power. Neither of these proposals was viewed with much enthusiasm by the B.C. Power Commission, with the development of the Columbia, and its responsibility for said development, now almost certainly assured. Furthermore, the B.C. Electric Co. was able to refer to the manner in which the Burrard Thermal Plant under construction,[41] lesser projects, and then the construction of a power plant utilizing the coal deposits at Hat Creek, could look after its needs. Additionally, it insisted that load growth over the next five years was not likely to exceed 7 percent per annum, as opposed to the 10 percent assumed by the Peace River Company's report to Mr. Paget, and in that company's letter of intent as well. It also declined to purchase Peace River energy.

Nevertheless, after a crucial meeting of the Peace River Company's directors on December 12–13 in Vancouver, Mr. Mainwaring announced publicly that he had been authorized to proceed with all plans for the Peace River Company's development, that his company hoped to apply to the Public Utilities Commission for a licence in February or early March 1961, that it would apply for a water licence as soon as it received this approval, and that it hoped to start preliminary construction in the late spring of 1961, and to raise funds by public subscription late in 1961 or early in 1962. He was quite explicit in saying that the Columbia's development would not interfere with these plans, that current Peace River planning did not call for export, and that he hoped to have the two major provincial utilities signed up to purchase contracts within six to eight weeks.[42] But there was, in fact, little to justify this exercise in positive thinking, for neither the B.C. Electric nor the B.C. Power Commission had altered its position. Nor, as we have seen, had the federal government backed off from its evident hostility to the Peace River Project, and no indication had been given that the large scale export of domestically produced electricity would be permitted. By late December, when final details on the Columbia River Treaty had been all but concluded, it had become obvious that the prospects of the sale which Mr. Mainwaring so badly wanted had faded rather than brightened.

This then was the situation when, just before Christmas, 1960, Mr. Mainwaring phoned Mr. Bennett and arranged to meet the premier in Vancouver. Mr. Mainwaring had followed the course of the international negotiations closely through an unspecified but highly-placed informant in Washington, D.C.,[43] and had become very critical of a number of features of the nearly completed international agreement. In any case, when he and Mr. Bennett met in the Hotel Vancouver, Mr. Mainwaring presented the premier with a list of eight serious weaknesses which he perceived in the draft treaty, and argued that throughout 1960 the province's chief Columbia negotiators had been well-meaning but amateurish before the tough representatives of the Corps of Engineers. In addition, the two men undoubtedly assessed the tactical position in which the Peace River Company's development had been placed. Mr. Mainwaring nearly five years later added two further recollections to his recreation of this meeting. He recalled having assured the premier that the downstream power benefit to be produced on the Columbia in the United States could be sold for five mills, that Mr. Bennett had assured him that his advisers held this to be unfeasible, but that he (W.M.) had urged both a sale and a hold-out for this sum. As he remembered the situation, before their long conference was over, the premier, obviously perturbed, had asked him what he would do in such a position, and he had replied by suggesting that the proposed development of both rivers be referred to the British Columbia Energy Board for an objective analysis. His recollection was that the premier accepted the proposal on the spot, and by telephone immediately set in motion the process of drafting an order-in-council, requiring the Energy Board to determine the costs of developing the two rivers in phases. Whether or not Mr. Mainwaring's account of its genesis is complete, such an order was issued on December 28.

The Energy Board was required by this reference to specify the assumptions underlying its determinations, to establish the cost of at-site power development on both rivers (allowing for the return of the downstream power benefit on the Columbia, but excluding consideration of the return from flood control provided by Canadian Columbia storage), and to determine the cost of transmission and standby transmission facilities to the three major markets of Greater Vancouver, Vancouver Island, and Prince George. It was asked to estimate the probable cost to customers in each of the three markets. And it was instructed finally to determine the extent to which the Columbia and Peace River developments might be related, if at all, and if they were found to be "complementary in this relationship, the legal and economic conditions under which complementary development may take place."[44] In announcing the reference, the provincial government was to place great stress on the recourse to and the reliance on comprehensive analysis involved. Its intention, declared Mr. Bonner, was to have "the most objective people we can appoint bring the facts up and let the chips fall where they may," and Mr. Bennett laconically described the reference as a means of "letting the sunshine in."[45] On the other hand, Mr. Williston has made it clear that at least part of his motivation in approving the reference was that he saw it as a means of transferring financial responsibility to an agency other than the B.C. Power Commission for some of the detailed engineering work on the Columbia itself which the Power Commission had contracted for, but at very considerable strain, and actually as the result of a personal decision made by Mr. Williston months earlier not to relay to the Commission instructions which he had received from Mr. Bennett to suspend such investigations.[46]

4. FINAL STAGE TREATY NEGOTIATIONS

When the Policy Liaison Committee reassembled in Ottawa on January 3–4, 1961, the concern of the federal Cabinet ministers about the real objective of the province's Energy Board reference was manifest, and British Columbia's ministers were questioned about it in detail. They advanced a lengthy explanation in reply, stressing the limitations on the spending power of the B.C. Power Commission concerning projects the development of which was not absolutely assured, and the freedom from such restrictions of the Energy Board as a commission of enquiry under provincial law. They made a good deal here, and indeed for a year and more thereafter, of the claim that the engineering studies to be pursued would be required in any case. Before the Policy Liaison Committee meetings were over, Mr. Fulton read a statement expressing the federal government's understanding of the situation, declaring that "the British Columbia government is prepared to proceed with the Columbia River Development" and concluding "that the studies are for the purpose of speeding up the preliminaries to ratification."[47] The province's representatives agreed to this.

Most of the time at this gathering was devoted to a detailed article by article review of the first joint Canada-United States draft of the treaty. Once again the nervousness reflected in the province's technical analyses concerning the inserting of a Mica development before a large scale market existed for its power led to a provincial attempt to have the date by which the project had to be completed moved back to some extent.

Federal spokesmen did not agree to advance the province's request.[48] Provincial representatives also argued with reference to Article VIII in the draft treaty that one exchange of diplomatic notes ought to be enough to provide for the sale of surplus portions of the Canadian entitlement to downstream benefit power, and for the governing conditions and limits— with such exchanges subsequently handled by the nominated entities. But the federal government here did not back down from its claim that the treaty would represent a continuing responsibility for the national government, which it would have to be able to control.

There was no cessation of the competitive jockeying for position in Canada during the days which immediately followed, as the international negotiators met once more (January 4–8, 1961) to produce a definitive treaty. On January 5 Mr. Fulton issued a statement declaring that the "Federal Government does not believe that the present instruction by British Columbia that its Energy Board study the Columbia and Peace River development will result in delay in concluding a Columbia River agreement" and affirming that satisfactory assurances had been received of British Columbia's readiness to implement the proposed Columbia River agreement. It added: "It is understood in Ottawa that the purpose of the study, insofar as the Columbia River is concerned, is to establish on an official basis the feasibility of the proposed treaty projects in order that the necessary clearances, under British Columbia statutes, may be given at the earliest possible date. The giving of these assurances is one of the prerequisites to ratification of the treaty."[49] Mr. Bennett's riposte to this in Victoria was his declaration that the Columbia River Treaty would not be held up "if Ottawa will give us a guarantee that the power will be delivered to Vancouver for 3.77 mills per kilowatt hour." And he added: "I am sure that they would give such a guarantee. They surely didn't bring this figure of 3.77 mills out of the air."[50]

Events moved rapidly from this point. The international negotiators agreed to a final draft of a treaty, and undertook to recommend it to their respective governments on January 8. Mr. Fulton wrote to Mr. Williston on January 9, indicating that he intended to recommend the treaty to the federal Cabinet, which would go ahead with preparations for its signature, unless he heard from Mr. Williston to the contrary. On January 10 the federal Cabinet Committee met, with advisers, to review the draft treaty, and a draft memorandum endorsing it for the Cabinet. On this occasion Mr. Fulton thanked all those who had assisted and made a special reference to the contribution from General McNaughton whose assistance on the secondary energy problem in particular he felt had secured a most advantageous limitation on American rights. It was made quite clear that the ministers saw the treaty as "the most beneficial arrangement from a

Canadian viewpoint that, with the concurrence of British Columbia, could be negotiated at that time." Mr. Fulton told the advisers that it was essential to be able to report their concurrence in the recommendation that the treaty be approved for signature if British Columbia did not dissent. He asked the technical advisers two questions. Did the treaty represent a net advantage to Canada, and did it represent advantages not otherwise obtainable? At this point, a record of proceedings of this meeting notes General McNaughton's statement that his views on the physical aspects of Columbia River development were well known, and that while he could not support the recommendation he did not oppose it. Mr. Fulton's recollection is that General McNaughton then "said words to the effect that he must maintain his freedom of expression for the future."[51] At this time the Cabinet Committee reviewed its arrangements with British Columbia. It is interesting to note that at least one minister present advanced the view that the new Permanent Engineering Board provided for in the treaty might well be a mechanism around which, without a formal joint entity, a tight agreement with British Columbia might be established. The Cabinet Committee was also told that the American negotiators had indicated in conversation that the United States might withdraw its signature if Canadian ratification were delayed, for example, by attempts to dispose of power to the U.S. The committee concluded that, if a financial agreement could not be reached with British Columbia, Canada should seek for the Columbia, as a minimum, conditions such as those which it had applied to Ontario in the case of the St. Lawrence.

The final intergovernmental exchanges leading up to the signing of the Columbia River Treaty have been the subject of so much controversy that some elaboration of them, finally, is in order. Mr. Williston replied to Mr. Fulton in a letter dated January 12. In it, he declared: "I note it is proposed that the treaty receive signature on Monday, January 16 next, and accordingly the text has received our preliminary study in that light." He continued: "In respect to the subsequent and final ratification to the treaty, however, I know that the government of Canada is aware, from proceedings of the Canada-British Columbia Policy Liaison Committee on Columbia River Development, that a number of matters must necessarily be dealt with prior to ratification. Paramount in this respect is, of course, completion of the engineering and economic studies required to establish feasibility of components of the Canadian development of the River." This information he saw as necessary to the provincial licensing procedures, and to a meeting of treaty time limits. He referred to the fact that the Americans knew of this situation, that some of these matters would be dealt with in a Canada-British Columbia agreement "to be completed prior to ratification." Some agreements involving exchanges of notes would be necessary prior to ratification, he maintained. And he added: "In this latter respect I have in mind, particularly such aspects as dealt with in Article 8 (1) of the treaty, in which respect I understand that you gave your personal assurances to Mr. Bassett and Dr. Kennedy to the effect that Canada would not ratify pending satisfactory arrangements between us."[52]

"I think, therefore," he went on, "that after signature and before ratification of the treaty, we must necessarily have another meeting of the Canada-British Columbia Policy Liaison Committee on the Columbia River Development to deal with a number of matters and particularly the context of a Canada-British Columbia Agreement. Meanwhile our respective Ministers of Finance are to meet[53] to discuss the broad question of financing the Columbia development and it would seem we should await the outcome of that discussion before convening a meeting of the Committee to deal with the general agreement." He concluded with expressions of his personal thanks and his government's appreciation for the work of Mr. Fulton, Messrs. Robertson and Ritichie, and the federal technical staff.

It is impossible to deny the subsequent federal claim that this letter gave provincial clearance to the act of signing.[54] To complicate the story, however, reference must be made to still another letter written to Mr. Fleming by Mr. Bennett only one day later, on January 13. This letter was quite enigmatic, for while it stressed British Columbia's desire to start on the Columbia's development "at the earliest possible moment" it included the qualification "assuming of course that it proves feasible from engineering and financial standpoints." Mr. Bennett went on to query the much-talked-of attractively low federal estimate of Columbia power costs, and concluded that until this had been verified by the B.C. Energy Board, a federal guarantee that the cost was firm and accurate would be necessary "before it [British Columbia] would add its own guarantee to any financial arrangements for the development."

What happened to this letter in Ottawa is something of a mystery. It presumably reached Mr. Fleming's office by Monday, January 16—the day before the treaty was signed in Washington; Mr. Fleming, in fact, has an impression that it came in on the evening of Sunday, January 15.[55] Copies, however, do not appear to have been sent by Mr. Fleming to his colleagues until January 17, and another day seems to have passed before their delivery. All that can be said with assurance about what transpired is (1) that at least one heavily involved federal Cabinet minister wistfully regrets that the letter had not been circulated more rapidly, (2) that Premier Bennett is certain that the letter and its contents were widely known in Ottawa before Messrs. Diefenbaker and Fulton left by air for

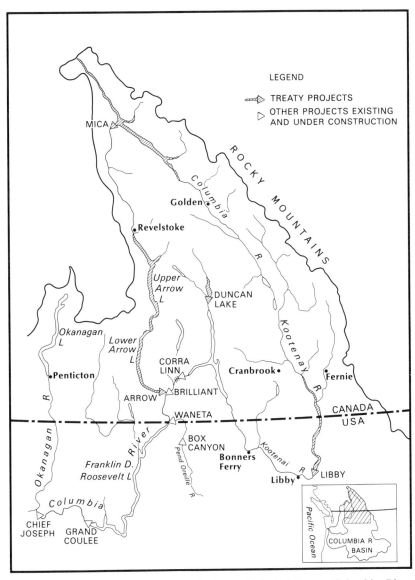

FIGURE 11. Columbia River Treaty Projects. (Adapted from: Columbia River Treaty Engineering Board, *Annual Report to the Governments of the United States and Canada*, Washington, D.C. and Ottawa, September 1965, Plate No. 1.)

Washington,[56] and (3) that Mr. Diefenbaker is categoric in saying that
the letter from Mr. Bennett had not been brought to his attention before
the signing ceremony.[57]

Here then was the background to the extraordinary position in which
the government of Canada found itself after January 17, 1961. Mr.
Bennett was subsequently to refer pointedly to his January 13 letter as a

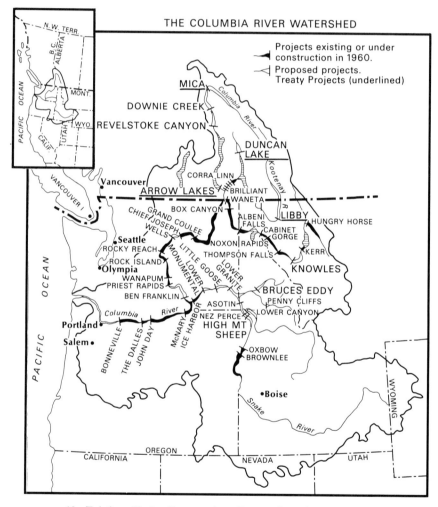

FIGURE 12. Existing, Under-Construction, Proposed, and Treaty Projects in the
Columbia River Basin, 1960. (Adapted from: J. V. Krutilla, *The Columbia
River Treaty*, p. 24. Based on 2nd Sess., Plate 1; and International Columbia
River Engineering Board, *Water Resources of the Columbia River Basin*, Report
to the International Joint Commission, United States and Canada, 1959, p. 67.)

warning which Ottawa ignored. The federal government's view, initially one of uneasy confidence, became progressively one of mystification, and then chagrin at a conviction of having been made the victim of sharp practice. Crucial to its case, of course, is the January 12 letter from Mr. Williston which, with reason, it argued, in every sense encouraged it to go ahead with the signing act. What remains to be explored is the lack of coincidence between that letter and the one which followed from Victoria a day later. It is hardly conceivable that Mr. Williston's letter was sent before some consultation with and approval from his colleagues. The possibility exists that the premier's initiative, on the other hand, was not cleared in this way at all. But, as we have seen, not all the mystery was in Victoria. It remains a matter for conjecture as to why the arrival of Mr. Bennett's letter was not reported to the prime minister prior to his departure for Washington.

Chapter Seven

1961: A Year of Stalemate

The distinguishing mark of science is not that it eliminates
trials and errors, but that it gives us a standard for
distinguishing good guesses from bad ones.
Herbert Kaufman, "The Next Step in Case Studies."

The year 1961 was to prove to be a surprising and indeed a disappointing
one for the protaganists of the Columbia River Treaty, notwithstanding
its apparently auspicious beginning. It was not to be marked, as they had
hoped, by rapid surmounting of the final obstacles on the road to the
ratification of the treaty. Indeed, it was to be distinguished by the emergence of much new uncertainty, stemming in large part from a number of
quite unexpected developments. These in turn had the effect of altering
or challenging some of the major assumptions held, during the 1960
negotiations, by the technical advisers to the governments at Ottawa and
Victoria, and by a good many Canadian Cabinet-level policy-makers as
well.

The uncertainty about British Columbia's intentions, which had per-
meated the decision-making environment in Ottawa in the weeks immediately prior to the signing of the Columbia River Treaty, was to
become much more acute in the months which immediately followed. On
January 18 Mr. Bennett released the text of his January 13 letter to Mr.
Fleming, and in an accompanying press release indicated that he was very
pleased with the signing of the treaty. At the same time, however, he made
it clear that he had doubts about Ottawa's cost estimate for Columbia
River power—the 3.77 mill figure for the downstream benefit. The province, he declared, would proceed immediately with the construction of
the Columbia projects through the agency of the B.C. Power Commission
"the moment the federal government guarantees this figure in writing."[1]
In the new session of the province's Legislature, on February 2, 1961, he

cryptically indicated that the treaty arrangements were anything but superior to those considered earlier.

Quite clearly, there was not much that the federal government could do but wait upon the province. The answer to a question asked by Mr. Lester Pearson in the House of Commons required a policy decision at the federal level, for the leader of the opposition had enquired if the treaty was to be submitted to Parliament for consideration "before the conclusion of negotiations with the province of British Columbia and the acceptance of the treaty by that province." Mr. Diefenbaker's reply was simply that the treaty would go to the appropriate standing committee, but he could not say when.[2] On January 20 the Cabinet Committee did consider the prospect that Parliamentary examination and approval of the treaty might bring pressure on the province to agree to its implementation, but discounted the idea. And, indeed, when Mr. Pearson suggested on May 31, 1961, in the House of Commons that the treaty be submitted to the External Affairs Committee before the conclusion of formal negotiations with Victoria, Mr. Diefenbaker rejected such a procedure as improper.[3]

Mr. Fulton and Mr. Fleming sought to clarify their government's position in correspondence with Victoria. Mr. Fulton, replying on January 31 to Mr. Williston, was very precise about his understanding that there had been no commitment to the effect that ratification would be held up pending a sale of power surplus to British Columbia's needs. The only undertaking on power disposal, he insisted, had been to ensure that prior to ratification there would be an opportunity to clear with United States authorities the "conditions and limits" within which, by exchange of notes, disposals of surplus energy might subsequently be made. His letter made two other points. Ottawa was perplexed by the allusions in Mr. Williston's and Mr. Bennett's correspondence to questions of economic and engineering feasibility; it had gone ahead on the assumption that the construction obligations would be met. And Ottawa was very anxious to proceed as rapidly as possible with the entire sequence of unfinished business—from the creation of a Canada-British Columbia agreement to ratification and the commencement of construction. Mr. Fleming replied to Mr. Bennett in a letter accepting the proposal that the two men meet to discuss Columbia financing, but reminded the premier of the doubts which Ottawa had had concerning the reference to the B.C. Energy Board, and of the fact that the federal government had signed the treaty on the basis of assurances given to it by provincial Cabinet ministers.

From Victoria, Mr. Williston, on the other hand, was taking a somewhat different stand on ratification. As early as January 17 he had argued publicly that there could be no Canadian ratification until the engineering studies (including those of the B.C. Energy Board) had been completed, until licensing hearings for the treaty dams had been held, until the licences had been issued, and until the two Canadian governments had reached an agreement on operating procedures and responsibilities.[4] In a long formal review of power developments before the provincial Legislature on February 8 he re-emphasized what he regarded as an informal but very real guarantee from Ottawa that ratification would not precede the act of provincial licensing. At the same time he provided a detailed explanation and defence of the treaty. He was enthusiastic, but he was also careful to emphasize that "the present arrangement with the United States will not provide an abundance of cheap electricity at this time."[5] He foresaw cheap incremental power coming later—possibly after the passage of twenty years; in the interim, he suggested, if interest rates were high, the intervening period was not going to be easy. He placed much emphasis on the fact that the engineering firms responsible for the treaty storage projects had been named, that their work was progressing, and that, in fact, there had been no delays. Once again he explicitly deplored the use of very specific values for Columbia power before much of the basic storage, generating and transmission engineering had been completed, and before the all-important cost of money was known. Implicitly, he was protesting something more—the attempt to portray the merits of the Columbia in so overwhelmingly favourable a light as to make unfeasible any serious consideration of the development of the Peace River.

Mr. Fulton made a swing through the Canadian Columbia watershed in mid-February during which he addressed eleven meetings and sought to explain and defend at length the treaty arrangements. In his own words, to Mr. Williston by letter on February 18, except in Revelstoke, and initially Castlegar, he found "a generally favourable response." He encountered a conviction that flooding costs in the area immediately south of Revelstoke had been overlooked, did his best to refute this position, and informed Mr. Williston of it. At this time all that the federal Cabinet ministers dared do was to warn publicly of the dangers to the entire Columbia agreement should the province delay action unduly, and to repeat that the federal offer of financial assistance still stood.[6] Others, less inhibited, were freely asserting that the provincial government was far from willing to let the Peace River project go.[7]

1. A FREEZE-UP IN FEDERAL-PROVINCIAL RELATIONSHIPS

Actually, as February advanced, formal contact between ministers and technical staffs in Ottawa and Victoria dwindled much as it had done over the winter of 1957–58, only this time the stand-off relationship appears to have been inspired in the province (and, many in Ottawa felt, by Mr. Bennett himself). When on February 20, 1961, the Cabinet Committee, which was well aware that Mr. Bennett and Mr. Fleming would be meeting a month later on Columbia development financing, wished to advance the prospect of a concurrent meeting of the Policy Liaison Committee, it is significant that the request for such a gathering was relayed to Victoria through the senior bureaucracy of each government. Taken to the Cabinet level in Victoria the suggestion was rejected. Similarly, when on March 1, 1961, an interim report of the B.C. Energy Board was tabled in the provincial Legislature, the federal Cabinet Committee had to rely for information concerning it on press reports and on interpretive informal soundings taken through the bureaucracy. The basic position advanced by the Energy Board was that the load growth curve for British Columbia and the whole Pacific northwest was flattening, that preliminary study had not revealed the likelihood of a substantially increased demand for power in the American states adjacent to British Columbia before 1970, and that without marketing agreements between the Peace River Company and the B.C. Electric and B.C. Power Commission, no figures could be cited as the probable laid-down cost of Peace River power in Vancouver. In view of the facts that much engineering work remained to be done, that the projections of the downstream benefit needed to be made more precise, and that there was a real case for making the commencement of storage operations coincide more closely with power requirements, the report declared that ratification of the Columbia River Treaty before these matters had been considered would not be in the public interest. Its theme, in short, was caution.[8] In the light of this document, a good many interpretations of the province's intentions, all speculative, were advanced in Ottawa. The federal Cabinet was understandably concerned, not least because the United States Senate was soon to consider ratifying the Columbia River Treaty. Indeed, on March 13, Mr. Fulton sought to allay fears concerning the treaty's future in the House of Commons in an extensive, sharply-worded statement in which he stressed the involvement of the province, including two members of the provincial Energy Board, in the detailed negotiations leading to the treaty,[9] the province's approval of the treaty prior to signature, and the impossibility of introducing absolute certainty into decision-making of this sort. His warnings at this time about the possible consequences of provincially instigated delay were to bring the customary sharp retorts from Mr. Bennett in Victoria, and a calmer assertion from Mr. Williston that "we'd be committing economic suicide if we ratified before we knew where we were going."[10] By March 11, Mr. Williston was openly prepared to attack the federal government for its opposition to power exports.[11]

190

Federal government fears about Congressional action—or rather in-action—proved to be unfounded. The Committee on Foreign Relations of the United States Senate commenced hearings on the treaty on March 8, 1961, and the agreement was ratified in the Senate itself by a ninety to one vote on March 16. At the same time, the boundaries of the decision-making began to change in both Canada and the United States in a most interesting way. Mr. Donald Fleming was able to inform his colleagues in Ottawa that, while in Washington, D.C. on March 14, he had been in-formed by a United States State Department official[12] that the new American administration was considering an electrical inter-tie between the American northwest and southwest, and that if Canadian power could be made available on a sufficiently long-term basis, the prospects of marketing surplus Canadian energy—which had been viewed unenthus-iastically by American negotiators at the end of 1960—might be signifi-cantly altered. (Actually, an American task force to examine the proposal had been set up on March 10.)[13] Clearly, the range of alternatives for consideration was increasing.

When Mr. Bennett and Mr. Fleming finally met on March 24 and 25, 1961, to discuss financing the Columbia's development, the premier advanced two alternative courses of action. One proposal suggested that the federal government might construct and operate the storage dams and transmission lines necessary to carry out the Canadian obligations under the Columbia River Treaty, meeting all costs (including those incurred already by the province for project engineering, and those involved in transmission) until its investment had been recovered. The works were then to be turned over to the province free of charge—and, in any case, were to be so transferred not later than fifty years after treaty development had begun. Excluded from the federal revenue would be the $64,000,000 flood control benefit, which was to be set aside as a perpetual endowment to reimburse the section of the province flooded as a result of the treaty. The other proposal would have British Columbia building the storage projects, with Ottawa guaranteeing that the net cost of Columbia power in Vancouver not exceed 4.25 mills per kwh and arranging with the United States that any surplus be sold there at not less than the same price. Seemingly the proposals were designed to impale the federal government on its repeated insistence on the cheapness of Columbia power, and its reported assertions that British Columbia was holding up the river's development. One way or another, Mr. Bennett was saying to Ottawa "make good your claims." He released his proposals to the press at once.

Almost two months were to ensue before the federal government replied to Mr. Bennett's tactical move. In the interim the provincial opposition parties were to become increasingly critical of the Social Credit government's position. CCF spokesmen tended to follow Mr. Strachan in seeing the province's ambivalence as "a callous means of paying off the premier's political debts."[14] A good many Liberals echoed Mr. Arthur Laing's concern that power exports would aid California but hurt British Columbia, and his conviction that the Arrow Dam should be dropped.[15] Federal government spokesmen as well blamed the province for developmental delays, the existence of which the provincial Cabinet denied. By mid-May Mr. Bennett and Mr. Fulton were releasing all of the January intergovernmental correspondence, as the former argued that he had warned the federal government of provincial doubts before Ottawa had moved to sign the treaty, and the latter stressed the import of his correspondence with Mr. Williston.[16] At the same time, in another of his unofficial but candid public addresses, Dr. Shrum delighted Mr. Bennett's supporters and dismayed his critics. Once more he made quite clear his support of power exports, and argued the wisdom—in view of the penalties in the Columbia River Treaty—of firming up planning before moving to ratification. Impressed with the magnitude of the province's planning, he felt it merited some financial support from the federal government. At the same time he sought to moderate claims about the magnitude and the cheapness of the downstream benefits.[17] Finally, on May 17, Mr. Fleming dispatched a letter informing Mr. Bennett that his suggested role for Ottawa as a constructor and operator was unacceptable, because, with a reasonable measure of assistance, the development of the Columbia was not beyond the province's capabilities. Mr. Fleming raised a number of inherent difficulties, including the vulnerability of any such federal initiative to new provincial decisions concerning other power projects. At the same time Mr. Fleming rejected the suggested provincial development with the backing of federal guarantees as impractical. He went on to call for an early agreement on financing, construction, and ratification "without considering at this time any departure in future from established export policy," and after reviewing the assumptions on which the treaty was negotiated, he advanced once again the joint entity proposal of December 6, 1960. Ottawa was making clear its determination to stick with the Columbia, and its unwillingness to take any action which might provide room for a simultaneous start on the Peace.

Hardly one to take rebuffs when convinced of the validity of his own position, Mr. Bennett apparently replied orally to Mr. Fleming when they met at the Seigneury Club in Quebec on May 25, and returned to Victoria more confident than ever that Ottawa would change its position on the export of electrical energy. Certainly, on May 26 he was convinced that eastern Canadian opinion was already being modified, as he assured the press that the Mica Dam would be machined, and its power would be used, along with that of the Peace River, to meet southern British Columbia loads, all subsidized by the revenue from the sale of the Canadian share of the downstream power benefit.[18] Here were the essentials of his strategy, and he put them in writing in another letter to Mr. Fleming on June 9. Unequivocally now he maintained that "the sound approach would be to dispose of the total amount (of downstream benefit entitlement) as firm power, for which a very favourable price could be negotiated." He insisted that "the sale of any lesser amount, or its sale on an interruptible basis, would present two dangers: first, the certainty of a lower price for the power, and second, the burden of installing expensive transmission lines to return a small portion of the benefits to Canada." The preliminaries to Water Act licensing were continuing, he maintained. And he repeated his claim for outright federal assistance to a development which would have an effect all across the country, declaring in rather dramatic fashion: "I believe that the $172,000,000 investment by the government of Canada suggested by you in our earlier correspondence should not take the form of an interest-bearing loan, but should be an outright grant."

While Mr. Bennett was thus serially unfolding a policy which would permit him to make good on his promises concerning "two-river" development, he was, at the same time, quietly moving to another major decision. As we have already seen, he had been unable during 1960 to bring the Peace River Power Development Company to the position where it could start developing its great project. Through the first half of 1961 the B.C. Electric Company remained a major stumbling block to Peace River Company financing. Although a shareholder in the Peace River Company, and prepared, actually, to expand its investment there,[19] it was still not willing to commit itself to purchase a block of its power. At the same time, although Dr. Grauer by 1961 was quite prepared to see merit in the elimination of the long-standing Canadian ban on the export of electricity, and in the export of surplus energy—on a recoverable basis—he very emphatically opposed the proposal to sell the Canadian entitlement to the downstream power benefit on the Columbia in the United States. Indeed, in the spring of 1961 he argued in a definitive essay that selling this power would be "a tragedy because most of British Columbia, unlike the states of the Pacific northwest, has never had the stimulus of really cheap power."[20] He saw the downstream benefit power as the cheapest available to the province. (The apparent cheapness of the downstream power benefit stemmed from the fact that the only costs attributed to it were a charge for a stand-by American transmission facility, and the capital costs of the Canadian storage from which ultimately the energy was derived— *but only until this Canadian storage began to produce at-site energy.* This last, of course, was a quite arbitrary and debatable assumption—as Canadian technicians often reminded their ministers.) A real if not too clearly recognized complication derived from the stress placed by Dr. Grauer and the federal ministers on the immediate benefits to be gained by selling the downstream power in Canada at its nominally low cost was that this proposal prospectively limited the freedom of action of the provincial government and its agent the British Columbia Power Commission. One alternative course of action which appealed to the Social Credit administration involved selling the downstream entitlement for a price well above the cost as just defined—whether at home or elsewhere. The additional revenue thus made available would have enabled the Power Commission both to reduce the price of some of the expensive thermal energy which at that time it was generating and marketing to some of its customers, and, ultimately, to reduce the cost of the energy produced directly in the Canadian section of the Columbia's watershed. It was in fact this latter course of action which Mr. Bennett and his colleagues decided to follow.

The Peace River Power Development Company did not give up easily. After it was frustrated by the B.C. Electric Company, early in January 1961 it proposed to the B.C. Power Commission that a direct line built from the Peace River development to the Homathko site would materially assist both agencies to launch their projects. The prospect of having plentiful energy from the Columbia's development appears to have forestalled any likelihood that the Power Commission would acquiesce in this proposal. Again, in March, representatives of the Peace River Company met Mr. Luce, the chairman of the Bonneville Power Administration, and became aware of that agency's enthusiasm for the California inter-tie. Any prospect of an assured market here in the near future faded, however, with Ottawa's refusal to budge on the question of extra-national electric power sales. In still another move, the technical consultants to the Peace River Company (Messrs. R. Chantrill and J. Stevens) were commissioned to produce another report, reviewing the prospects for Peace River development in the light of the Columbia River Treaty. This new analysis was not released until May 1961, but it merits some attention, as it was widely circulated—and read—by decision-makers in Ottawa and Victoria.

Two Further Engineering Reports. Messrs. Chantrill and Stevens' theme in 1961 was that the province faced a period of dynamic industrial expansion which the load growth estimates of the province's operating utilities did not correctly anticipate.[21] They took no exception to the Columbia River Treaty, but advanced two propositions. They were convinced that Canada's share of the downstream power benefits and Mica

at-site generation could not be effectively moulded to domestic requirements by themselves and that complete coordination either with steam
electric generation or a large storage project would be required for this
purpose. The ability of the Peace reservoir to do this most effectively, and
to convert usable secondary into firm energy, was their theme. At the same
time, they suggested that the Canadian entitlement to downstream power
might be delivered on a firm basis to United States utilities and a like
amount delivered from the Peace River project to load centres in British
Columbia. Thus a ready market for downstream energy could be obtained,
they argued, and the cost of extensive transmission facilities from the
Canadian-American border to load centres in British Columbia could be
avoided. One other observation which they made is noteworthy, for they
suggested that in the initial years, probably through 1975–76, Canadian
storage on the Columbia River would be used solely to produce prime
power in the American base system.[22] Quite obviously there was evidence
here to cheer both those who supported two-river development, and those
who were convinced that going ahead on the Peace would effectively
downgrade the Columbia.

The Chantrill-Stephens study was not the only engineering analysis
available to decision-makers in Canada in May, for during that month the
B.C. Power Commission received a major evaluation of the Columbia's
development which it had commissioned on January 17, 1961, on the very
day that the treaty was signed, from Caseco Consultants Ltd.[23] The Caseco
group had addressed itself to a number of problems. One was determining
the precise location for the treaty storages. Perhaps the most significant
issue which it faced concerned specifying the manner in which the developments in the Columbia basin in Canada should be combined "into a
system which can satisfy most economically the demand for electric
power"[24] in the light of existing plants within the basin and the availability
of the downstream power benefit. The interesting thing about this report
is that the sequence of development which it endorsed (running to 1982)
assumed the ratification of the treaty in 1961, expected the downstream
power benefit returned to Canada to meet provincial load growth requirements between 1966 and 1972 (without additional generation), and
affirmed that Columbia at-site and downstream Canadian energy combined would be capable of supplying "nearly all the developed areas in
British Columbia,"[25] really until 1982. One other point which it made
should be noted for while it saw real merit in having the Canadian
Columbia projects operated in coordination with American and other
Canadian utility systems, it insisted that economic development of the
Columbia River in Canada was not contingent upon such an arrangement.
This is important, as the Chantrill-Stephens Report issued almost at the

same time claimed very much the reverse. The technical staff of the B.C. Power Commission did not miss the contradictory nature of these recommendations, and two of them (G. J. A. Kidd and A. W. Lash) drew particular attention to it, supporting the Caseco conclusion, in an analysis of the Peace River Company's latest position which they prepared on June 26, 1961.[26] The Power Commission technicians felt that the power studies of the Chantrill-Stephens Report were of little value in the absence of any confirmation of their major assumptions. And they did not hesitate to object to a clear misinterpretation by the Peace River Company's consultants of the treaty's provisions concerning the operation of the Mica dam. They objected also to the way in which Mica at-site generation was not even considered by Messrs. Chantrill and Stephens until the Peace had been developed, and to the manner in which the report in question seemed to be designated to convince provincial policy-makers that the Columbia's development was not practical until it had been preceded by the construction of the great reservoir in the north. One must assume that this analysis ended up on Dr. Keenleyside's desk, but it has to be remembered that throughout the formation of Canadian policy the crucial initiatives did not come from the Power Commission. Indeed by the time the technical analysis just referred to had been produced, Mr. Bennett had already taken the decision which was to remove the chief obstacle to the implementation of his plans.

2. The Hardening of Federal and Provincial Positions

The first public indication that the premier was thinking of a change in the B.C. Electric's status came in the provincial Legislature on February 27, 1961, when, in a debate on the financial agreements which Ottawa had entered into with the provinces at five yearly intervals since 1947, he was questioned concerning the taxation of investor-owned utilities. At that time he referred to the exemption of publicly-owned utilities from federal and provincial corporation income taxation, and to the apparent advantage which, as a consequence, their customers enjoyed over those serviced by privately owned power producers. He specifically objected to the federal government using such utility income tax revenue—collected, as it was, differentially between provinces—to help finance equalization payments to the provinces. Actually, for some years previously, 50 percent of the federal corporation tax on gas and electric utilities had been returned to the provinces in which there were investor-owned utilities. Mr. Diefenbaker had announced that this arrangement could continue to March 31, 1962, and Mr. Bennett (and others) had chosen to interpret this as notice of intent to terminate the arrangement at that time. Mr.

Bennett declared that, in the absence of fair treatment by Ottawa, his government would have to consider taking over those utilities which were privately owned—in order to obtain, in effect, a complete remission of the taxation which they were likely to have to pay. In the provincial Legislature a month later this declaration was emphasized when government members voted without discussion, to approve a motion made by Mr. Strachan endorsing the consideration of public ownership for the privately-owned utilities of the province.

These developments caused an immediate flurry of speculative comment both in the Legislature and the press, but it quickly died and was soon forgotten by the public. B.C. Electric officers who checked could get no definite information from Victoria, and some, certainly, assumed that their company and Ottawa both were being faced with an intimidating bluff. On the other hand, Mr. Mainwaring felt otherwise, and assured his principals in the Peace River Company that public ownership was imminent.[27] (To his death Mr. Mainwaring remained convinced that as late as April 1961, a B.C. Electric contract for Peace River energy, and a consequent start on northern construction would have forestalled a takeover.)[28] Late in April a senior officer of the B.C. Electric assured Finance Minister Fleming that the threat of expropriation was a real one, as he urged upon Ottawa the importance of meeting Mr. Bennett's complaints about utility taxation in the forthcoming June 1961, budget. The premier said nothing publicly on the utility tax issue for some months—but much, it will be remembered, on his proposals for launching the Columbia development. Sometime in the spring he briefed at best a few of his Cabinet colleagues on his intentions.

(Mr. Mainwaring may well have been correct in his surmise, for the premier's concern with the B.C. Electric Company was not primarily related to its tax commitments. What he objected to were its unwillingness to purchase Peace River power, its open support for the return of the downstream power, its unwillingness to commit itself to purchase all of this benefit, and its planned move into thermal generation. All of these moves he saw as frustrating both Peace and Columbia River development, at least as he envisaged it. He appears to have been genuinely enough concerned at this time over the prospect that portions of the downstream benefit not immediately marketable in Canada would have to be sold at low dump-power rates in the United States.)

It is not easy to recreate the decision-making environment in Ottawa during the late spring and early summer of 1961. The federal government was heavily preoccupied with a number of issues other than the Columbia; indeed, the Cabinet Committee on the Columbia River did not meet for some months prior to June. But the Columbia simply could not be

197

ignored; party pressures alone saw to that. Mr. Leon Ladner, who was described in the *Victoria Daily Times* on May 29 as "the most powerful Conservative politician in British Columbia,"[29] two days later wrote a long personal letter to Mr. Fleming on the subject of Conservative government policy. The gist of it was a plea to outflank Mr. Bennett (who "always seems to be one step ahead of us and often is") by cutting the federal corporation tax on privately-owned utility income on the condition that the relief go straight to the consumer. At the same time, while endorsing the concept of returning the downstream power benefit (selling in the United States only the surplus), Mr. Ladner made it clear that he favoured export power sales generally—as did, he felt, the public at large. He indicated also his sympathy for Mr. Bennett's plans for eventual resource development in the north and for power cost reductions—subsidized by a sale of the downstream power benefit. This latter concept he described as "a good idea in a way, but not practical at the present time in a financial political way."

Three additional letters written from British Columbia ten days later were to give the federal Cabinet further cause to return to the Columbia. One from Mr. Bennett on June 9, already mentioned, asked for an outright grant of $172 millions and proposed to sell the entire downstream benefit. A second was a letter by Mr. Strachan to Mr. Diefenbaker, also written on June 9, and made public immediately, in which British Columbia's opposition leader argued it would be "a national disaster if the benefits of cheap public power from this river are denied to the people of Canada simply to facilitate the sale of uneconomic Peace River power by a foreign controlled private company." He quoted the stand recently taken by Dr. Grauer of the B.C. Electric, and appealed to Mr. Diefenbaker as the prime minister to "use your influence to prevent the sale of the power derived from downstream benefits to the United States." Although Mr. Strachan did not specifically ask the prime minister to invoke the power which the federal government possesses to bring any works exclusively under its jurisdiction, this was the interpretation widely placed upon his suggestion. Finally, also on June 9, Mr. Ladner wrote again from Vancouver. Addressing his remarks to Mr. Fleming, with copies to Messrs. Howard Green and Davie Fulton, Mr. Ladner conveyed the "amazing information," which he assured the federal Cabinet ministers was unquestionably true, that the premier was going to take over the B.C. Electric and the Peace River's development, introduce significant rate cuts, and initiate action on a grand scale. While still arguing that Mr. Bennett's proposal to sell the downstream power entitlement was a blunder, he begged once again for a Conservative initiative in being first with a plan to reduce electricity costs. At the same time in an accompanying memorandum he expanded at length on the need for Ottawa to avoid exposing itself to political attack for appropriating a provincial resource— as it well might be if, in the light of Mr. Strachan's request, it invoked Section 92, 10(c) of the British North America Act. Such an action, he insisted would be "in my opinion a colossal political mistake."[30] At this time Mr. Ladner was veritably bombarding his friends in Ottawa, where budget day was approaching. In a still further letter—this time to Mr. Fulton on June 15—Mr. Ladner pointed out that 33.7 percent of Canada's hydro-electric capacity was privately owned, that it was mostly in Quebec, Alberta, and British Columbia, that there were 114 federal constituencies in these provinces, of which the Progressive Conservatives held 85!

While pressure on Ottawa was certainly increasing from British Colum- bia, it is important to remember that in the interplay of forces upon members of the federal Cabinet, not all the resultants favoured either a reconsideration of the federal government's position on the Columbia, or a modification of it. When the letters just referred to reached Ottawa, the Cabinet Committee, as has been noted, had not met for some months. At the same time Cabinet ministers were receiving staff and consultant engin- eering studies which served only to confirm their conviction that the Columbia's development as outlined in the treaty was much superior to any available alternative. By far the most important of these studies was one commissioned by the federal government from the Montreal Engineer- ing Company in March, with the endorsation of the staff of the federal Water Resources Branch. That study can be fairly described as the result both of considerable external criticism from a member of one of the federal regulatory agencies, who had held in February that British Colum- bia would be better off accepting six mill per kwh Peace River power than the downstream benefit from the treaty as it was then drafted. In any case, the Montreal Engineering Company's Report, completed in May, esti- mated the theoretic cost of the downstream benefit alone—with no allow- ance for business risks or contingencies—at 3.6 mills per kwh, and, if the downstream benefit should turn out to be 25 percent larger than it had estimated, the 3.6 mills would become 3.0 mills.

Actually, the Montreal Engineering Company's Report very sanely listed the large number of assumptions required in making a before-the- event estimate, and drew attention to the operative necessity of providing for business risks and other contingencies. Indeed, it suggested that the theoretic cost of the whole package of Columbia power (at-site and down- stream) might well be of the order of 5.4 mills, making allowance for such considerations, and assuming an 8 percent load growth. Here indeed were grounds for caution, but attention in Ottawa, at the ministerial level, at least, seems to have riveted on the downstream benefit power figures under the most favourable set of assumptions. Further confirmation of the merits of Columbia River development was drawn from a report of a Department of Northern Affairs and National Resources official in mid-May to the effect that Caseco Consultants, Ltd. (the engineering consortium which was designing the Mica Dam, acting as consultants to the B.C. Power Commission, and also providing studies being reviewed by the consultants to the B.C. Energy Board), had come up with a figure for the cost of power derived from the complete development of the river by 1985 even more attractive than those previously produced by the Department's own Water Resources Branch. The Caseco firm, he also reported, had also reviewed the provision in the treaty whereby Canada was given permission to withdraw three million feet of storage from the 15.5 million acre-feet dedicated to cooperative utilization and had concluded that it would be more than adequate to protect Canada in its desire to obtain maximum firm-power generation.[31] In one sense at least, Mr. Bennett in Victoria also found the Caseco studies encouraging, and upon officially receiving them he moved on May 30 to have an order-in-council passed permitting the B.C. Power Commission to apply for licences to build the treaty dams. He did not overlook the opportunity to describe this act as an example of the province's doing "everything in its power" to get the Columbia development underway.[32]

The Cabinet Committee on the Columbia did not meet until June 20; in the meantime, at least one concerned member of it continued to urge upon his colleagues that the federal offer of capital assistance be extended from the storage works to transmission lines, and argued that Ottawa's inflexibility had enabled Mr. Bennett to seize the initiative. When the Cabinet Committee did assemble it interpreted the latest Montreal Engineering Company's Report as a substantial confirmation of figures and conclusions which its members had earlier used, and concluded that, taking into account private financing, the cost of Peace River power would be about twice that of Columbia River energy. The committee agreed to make public a summary of the report's findings, its satisfaction with the treaty, its seeming confirmation of earlier estimates of low cost Columbia power, and its indication of cost savings available with federal financing assistance. It listened to a colleague argue the case for capital assistance with transmission-line construction, and agreed to take the proposal to the Cabinet. On the other hand, after another member had drawn attention to Mr. Bennett's latest letter, and had reviewed the assumptions upon which the treaty was negotiated, and the centrality of cheap power to Ottawa's thinking, the committee agreed that Mr. Fleming should reject Mr. Bennett's latest request, and should endorse the exportation only of that power which was truly surplus to Canadian needs.

200

3. The Removal of a Veto Point

Meanwhile, Mr. Bennett had determined that the time for action had arrived. For some months it had been realized that during the last half of 1961, probably in the fall, a short special session of the provincial Legislature would be required to ratify the new tax collection agreement with the federal government. Now, late in June, and almost immediately after learning that the June 20 federal budget had produced no change in the corporation tax payable by privately-owned utilities, Mr. Bennett called a Legislative session for August 1, nominally to deal with the fiscal arrangement with Ottawa, but in reality, as well, to permit the take-over of the B.C. Electric and Peace River companies. Rumours concerning this latter prospect were in the air during July, and, indeed, a take-over was the subject of press speculation in Ottawa as early as June 20. But Mr. Bennett and his colleagues were not talking, and the reports were once again discounted by the general public; indeed, most of Mr. Bennett's colleagues had not been briefed as to the details of the expropriation, and the Social Credit caucus had not been consulted. As we have seen, among those who knew what the special session meant were the members of the federal Cabinet, and one of them, Mr. Fulton, decided upon a last ditch stand to forestall the now apparently inevitable. On July 25, in Vancouver, he announced in a prepared statement that the Montreal Engineering Company's statistics had confirmed that downstream benefit power, under reasonable assumptions, could be delivered to the lower mainland at 3.6 mills per kwh; he implied that the province was trying to cut out Mica, and asserted that Ottawa would veto any such move. He hoped that the British Columbia government would never seriously consider using Columbia power and flood benefits to subsidize "hydro-electric development elsewhere in the province, or indeed for purposes not directly related to power production" and repeated the earlier offer of federal assistance. He was sure that there was no need for Peace River development at this time, argued that it would come later, and suggested that questions concerning the export of Peace River power were too hypothetical to warrant discussion. He could hardly have been more critical of the premier's planning, as he called it "the greatest betrayal of Canadian interests that it would be possible to contemplate." To all this the public response of the provincial ministers was restrained, with Mr. Bennett himself simply observing "that all his dealing had been with Finance Minister Fleming."[33]

Any mystery attached to the special Legislative session disappeared on August 1, 1961, when Mr. Bennett introduced there the Power Development Act, 1961,[34] which made the B.C. Electric Company into a crown corporation, and provided that it acquire all the assets of the Peace River Power Development Company. In a drama-packed two-day debate Mr.

Bennett sought to justify the move fundamentally by direct reference to the disabilities under which the customers of privately owned utilities had been forced to live. He promised an early start on the Peace River's development, and tabled the report of the B.C. Energy Board on the Peace and Columbia River power projects—finding here also strong support for his action.

The Energy Board certainly had left him with plenty of room in which to manoeuvre. It had concluded its examination of the development of the two rivers with a discussion of the really fundamental question—whether or not they might proceed simultaneously—and had affirmed that benefits in the form of reduced power costs or an increased quantity of available power might thus be made available. It had argued that power would have to be exported to permit this—logically to the American Pacific northwest or to California, and had held it "obvious that the first power to be sold in the United States ought to be some or all of the Columbia downstream benefits."[35] Actually, while affirming that a sizeable enough market for simultaneous development did exist in the United States, it had repeated its March 1 observation that the American northwest's needs appeared to be fairly well looked after until the early 'seventies, before welcoming the proposed inter-tie with its associated possibilities of an earlier market for large blocks of firm power in California. It had foreseen no insurmountable problems with recoverability and had endorsed extensive integration and coordination of the power resources in the province and with those outside it as well. An early construction start on either river was seen as providing the province with "a much needed economic stimulus" and a contribution to "curbing unemployment."[36]

The Energy Board's comparison of the costs of power from the two river systems had also paved the way for the Peace River Company's takeover. The substance of its findings, as represented below, was that under similar conditions and public ownership, there would be little to choose between the power costs averaged over the period to 1985:

TABLE 5

Unit Cost of Power at Load Centres, B.C. Energy Board Report, July 31, 1961 (Mills/kwh)[37]

	Higher Load Forecast	Basic Load Forecast
Columbia	4.03	4.40
Peace (Private)	6.42	6.59
Peace (Public)	4.20	4.37

Again, in its review of the Columbia River Treaty, the board provided some justification for further delay before moving to implementation. It saw "great potential benefit to Canada and British Columbia"[38] in the developments envisaged by the treaty, but urged that three points be kept in mind. In view of the penalty clauses for delays in project completion, there was a case for deferring ratification until the risks associated with the obligations involved could be safely incurred. Furthermore, the interlocking nature of the treaty projects with others in the Canadian watershed would require as an economic necessity almost the full development of the Canadian Columbia River system. If export markets were not obtained, and the domestic load growth then projected were in fact realized, the report held that the Columbia's development would preclude any other major move into electrical generation for twenty years. Thus it stressed the necessity of removing the uncertainty associated with the treaty's provision for a post-ratification exchange-of-notes power-sale procedure. "Control over the disposition of downstream benefits," it declared, "should be vested in the province before ratification."[39]

Although opposition party members in the Legislature made much of the fact that in the provincial election held less than one year previously members of the Social Credit Cabinet had scorned the wisdom of the line of action which they were now endorsing, when the final vote on the take-over legislation was taken on August 3 not a single member of the Legislature dissented! Almost from the moment that the Legislative session ended, however, great controversy erupted over the reasonableness of the compensation made available to the former owners of the B.C. Electric Company[40] and over the inclusion of a privative clause in the expropriation act apparently forestalling any adjudication on the magnitude of the compensation by the courts. The opposition parties, which only belatedly had noted this latter provision in the legislation, generally joined in the outcry. Shortly, virtually all opposition members of the Legislature were to criticize the report of the Energy Board itself, especially when, as the Columbia partisans which they so often were, they came to reflect on the significance for the board's analysis of the provincial government's advice to it that the $64.4 million (U.S.) flood control payment be set aside in a trust fund to compensate "for the loss to the provincial economy of the flooded areas"—and the fact that it was thus not to be directly related to Columbia River power costs. Those who like Mr. Strachan subsequently read the report of the engineering consultants to the Energy Board[41] were more than ever outraged to discover that, as Mr. Sherman was to observe, the board had "loaded its figures to a degree."[42] Specifically, the critics were to object to the manner in which the Energy Board had ignored the not insignificant downstream benefit which accrued in Canada from the

Duncan and Libby projects. They objected also to the board's failure to indicate what import a series of favourable assumptions (concerning the attraction of additional industry, and treaty energy servicing of expanding Cominco power needs at Kimberley and Trail) might have in still further reducing the cost of Columbia River power. As the weeks advanced, critics suggested that the Energy Board's report had been guilty of a further omission in that it had made no allowance for the beneficial consequence of federal participation in the financing of the Columbia projects.

Throughout the month of August federal government spokesmen said little about the power politics of British Columbia. Official circles in Ottawa still seemed convinced that the province was out to kill or delay the Mica project. Mr. Green described the take-over of the B.C. Electric as a "great disappointment"[43] to the federal government, and suggested that the Columbia development might not take place. Some Vancouver Progressive-Conservatives urged Mr. Diefenbaker to go it alone and develop the Columbia. By August 30 the federal government was reading news despatches describing the speed with which the new board of directors of the now publicly-owned B.C. Electric Company (with Dr. Shrum as its chairman) was moving to commence development on the Peace River, of Mr. Bennett's satisfaction with this, of his confidence that similar progress would soon be made on the Columbia—but on the condition that the downstream benefit would be sold, and the fair adequate price required would have to be settled before any agreement was arrived at between Victoria and Ottawa.[44] A day later it was again reading that Mr. Bennett had confirmed to the press that the downstream benefit sale price which met his requirements was five mills per kwh.

The federal Cabinet Committee met on August 25 to consider the last two months' developments, and especially Mr. Bennett's attempt to assign to the federal government real responsibility for delay on the Columbia. The prospect of his being able to make good his planned downstream benefit power sale was immediately raised. On the basis of exchanges with the Americans at the time the treaty was negotiated, and of informal discussions recently held, most of those present were skeptical of claims as to the possibility of large scale power sales to the United States at reasonable prices. It was generally felt that three mills per kwh would be the best return available. At the same time, however, the Cabinet Committee obviously felt a new "sounding" of the market to be in order, and, subject to the prime minister's approval, agreed that informal enquiries in the American Pacific northwest would be made. It decided that the Montreal Engineering Company be asked to report on the B.C. Energy Board's figures, and its comparisons, as soon as possible. Rather significantly also, the committee felt that the federal Department of Public

Works should be asked to withhold any licence for development on the Peace River. Two months were to pass before the committee met again. In the meantime, the government of the United States was not idle. On September 12 it informed Ottawa, confidentially, that the Department of the Interior had come to feel that a very substantial amount of downstream benefit power might be sold on a long-term, fifteen to twenty year basis, within a 3¾ to 4½ mill price range. Canada was also informed that the United States government might appropriately exhibit some restlessness over any undue delay in treaty ratification. Just a month later the Canadian government (and this time that of British Columbia also) were to receive another interpretation of the American market—this time from the Bonneville Power Administration (BPA). The analysis was prepared in fact at the request of the two Canadian governments which had found themselves making informal inquiries of the same American officials, virtually simultaneously. In this market review the Bonneville Power Administration, after contacting utilities in the northwest and California which might be interested in purchasing the Canadian downstream power entitlement, declined to relay any maximum price which the utilities would be prepared to pay. It indicated that the price would only appear in negotiation, and would vary substantially with the conditions and terms of sale. Some of these were detailed. It was made clear, for instance, that the longer the term of sale, the more gradual the pull-back,and the greater the degree to which the power sold could be moulded to fit utilities' load curves, the greater the potential price.

Re-reading the Bonneville document leaves one with the distinct impression that whatever the difficulties involved, the BPA was making a real effort to open up a new range of alternatives to Canada if it wished to pursue them. One point it did make was that as a departmental agency it simply lacked the authority to purchase from the Canadian entity under the treaty; sales, in short, would have to be made to each purchasing utility. It went into considerable detail on the magnitude of the markets as it envisaged them, and did relay the information that all of the purchasing utilities had indicated that they would pay less for purchased power than they would from alternative sources which they would own.

4. FROM IMPASSE TO CONFRONTATION

There were other developments during the early fall of 1961 which must be recorded. One was the degeneration of the exchanges between Mr. Bennett and Mr. Fulton to an extraordinary level of bitterness. The mischief this time began on September 13, when in the House of Commons, Mr. H. W. Herridge asked Mr. Fulton if the federal government was giving consideration to blocking the development of the Peace River by the use of the Navigable Waters Protection Act—or any other federal statute. To this Mr. Fulton replied: "The answer is that the government is giving consideration to all measures which would bring about a logical, orderly and sensible development of the power potential of British Columbia, which, of course, means that the Columbia River development should be started first."[45]

Three days later, in an address delivered at Prince George in north-central British Columbia, the premier openly assailed the federal minister for the threat to block the Peace River project which he perceived in Mr. Fulton's Commons' statement. He was scathing in his reference to the fiat which Ottawa assumed it possessed concerning this public work because of its impact on upstream and downstream navigation. Once again he explained in detail his plan to finance Columbia River storages and to pay for the machining of Mica from the sale of downstream benefit energy. In a phrase of which he has frequently been reminded since, he continued: "This is the real meaning of cheap power, because nothing is cheaper than something that is free."[46] He left no doubt in anyone's mind that he was not prepared to examine the two projects on a mutually exclusive basis, and deplored the tendency of certain federal ministers to reduce the issue "to a head-on collision between the two projects." Federal claims of the superiority of the Columbia first proposal were, he continued, absolutely unfounded. Indeed, he assailed the Columbia River Treaty itself, citing Mr. Udall, the American secretary of the interior, to the effect that the benefits the United States was getting under it could only be provided unilaterally in that country through an investment of some $750 millions.[47] In similar vein he sought to confound the "cheap downstream benefit" thesis, maintaining that the cost of the Canadian entitlement returned to Vancouver in the first year would be some 8.65 mills. He agreed that it would be down to 4.34 mills by 1970 but had it back up to 7.80 mills by 1985 (and averaging 6.35 mills for the entire period).[48] Resistance to the production and certainly the domestic consumption of such expensive energy was thus portrayed as an obvious defence of the province's economy. With a flourish he informed his audience that tenders would be returned on October 11 for the Peace River project diversion tunnels.

This sally certainly complicated an already very involved situation. Hardly surprisingly, the opposition to Mr. Bennett responded in widely differing ways. Mr. Fulton appeared for the moment to be keen to moderate the debate. He assured the press that no federal minister had said that the Peace should not be developed, although he referred to its marketing problem and its possibly serious impact on Mackenzie River navigation. Rather, he suggested, his concern was with the sale of the downstream benefit in the United States "where it can be used only for developing that country."[49] A month later—in a speech in Spokane Washington, which was widely reported—Mr. Fulton repeated his conviction that returning the downstream benefit was the way to keep down, if not reduce, British Columbia power costs. At this time he suggested that he did not think Ottawa would change its opposition to the export of all the Canadian entitlement. Quite frankly he told the overwhelmingly American audience of his doubts concerning the existence of a market for all the entitlement, and the unreality, as he saw it, of a firm selling price.[50] To get any firm price at all, he maintained, "still well below the level talked about—it would be necessary to make very long term commitments with a high degree of permanence."[51]

Mr. Strachan was very critical of the premier's Prince George speech, and sought to focus public attention on the upgrading of Columbia power costs in the Energy Board's report, and the discrepancies between its figures and those of its own consultants. He noted that Ottawa had the power to take control of both river developments, and that if it did so, it would meet no opposition from him.[52] At the founding convention of the New Democratic Party in British Columbia (the successor to the CCF), held at the end of October, Mr. Strachan's resolution on provincial power policy was rejected as too weak; the one adopted favoured the "McNaughton plan," no firm or long-term exports, and no sale of the downstream benefit!

Mr. Pearson, in Vancouver on October 2, suggested that deadlocks such as the one concerning the Columbia "need not happen in a well-ordered federal democracy."[53] He appeared to accept the provincial position that the export price for electricity should be established before, not after, ratification. On the other hand, he urged that no province press for power export which did not provide securely for long-term provincial and Canadian needs. And in a way he was to puzzle the governments in both Ottawa and Victoria with a plea that they get together to find a common basis on which to ask the United States to renegotiate the treaty. Their perplexity stemmed from the fact that neither really felt that this would help at all. The provincial Liberals in convention on October 13 and 14 were willing to endorse a resolution critical of the treaty, and their new leader, Mr. Perrault, a month later seemed to feel that no cash payment could compensate Canada for the damage to it caused by a downstream power entitlement sale.[54]

The early fall of 1961 also saw Mr. Paget, in his role as the comptroller of water rights for British Columbia, conducting public hearings on the applications which had been filed with him for licences to permit the construction of the Duncan, Mica, and High Arrow Dams.[55] This was an entirely provincial exercise. Mr. Paget had some awkward moments, as, without complete success, he sought to restrict the arguments of those presenting evidence to a discussion of the licence applications, and to eschew a general evaluation of the treaty and the provincial government's power policies. There were some amusing incidents as well—as when an opponent of the High Arrow Dam attempted to enter as evidence, on September 27, Mr. Bennett's unflattering evaluation of the treaty made at Prince George eleven days earlier.[56] At each of the hearings Dr. Keenleyside, as the chairman of the agency applying for licences, described the general significance of the project in question, had his observations on engineering considerations supported and expanded by eminent consultants and by his own staff, and outlined in general terms the compensatory policies which the Power Commission intended to follow as it dealt with those displaced by the storage construction.

Actually, very little criticism was directed at the Mica and Duncan applications but the hearings concerning the High Arrow Dam were a different story. A great variety of arguments was advanced against the proposal to raise the maximum flood level of the Arrow Lakes almost forty feet. Some critics insisted that the range of values considered by the decision-makers had been far too narrow;[57] others expressed real doubts as to the accuracy of the engineering estimates of project costs. Much dissatisfaction was expressed over the conditions of uncertainty which had dominated the Arrow Lakes Valley for some years, and over the adequacy of the resources available to compensate and relocate the displaced. Many of the residents of the Arrow Valley emphasized the loss of the sense of community, indeed of civilization itself. The flooding of the Arrow littoral and relocation of its inhabitants was viewed by some as "immoral"[58] and comparable to the expulsion of the Acadians. Many of the general criticisms already widely advanced concerning the treaty were repeated. High Arrow, for instance, was pictured as "part of a sinister scheme to export electrical power . . . facilitating the increase of employment opportunities and the creation of new wealth, but all this outside the boundaries of Canada."[59] General McNaughton's opposition to the Arrow Dam, and Mr. Fulton's description of the treaty arrangements as "second best" were duly invoked. To all these protestations and to many others, spokesmen for the Power Commission replied at length, either at the hearings in the watershed itself, or at the final session in Victoria. Some of the objections, on the other hand, were not answered at all—as when complaints were advanced that Arrow Lakes residents had been confronted at the hearings with a "fait accompli," although they had been given to understand a year earlier by Mr. Williston that the hearings would precede the signing of the treaty.[60] As the hearings concluded, although

Mr. Paget made it clear that his authority under the Water Act left him free to adjudicate and reject government policy—and Mr. Strachan complimented him on his handling of the enquiry—no one really expected the Power Commission's application to be set aside.

Indeed, Mr. Bennett and his colleagues appeared supremely confident that their position was sound, and would be vindicated. They gave no indication of being unduly perturbed at opinion surveys which showed a small majority of British Columbians, who had opinions on the matter, favoured Ottawa's power planning rather than that of the province.[61] Nor did the provincial government appear concerned when the American under-secretary of the interior, Mr. J. K. Carr, urged publicly quick Canadian action, as he drew attention in Spokane to the costs associated with power generation forgone and with flood damage incurred or threatened. There was no immediate or subsequent provincial response to Mr. Carr's declaration that the United States would deliver to Canada any portion of the downstream power benefit entitlement which it wished returned, that the American government would assist in marketing the excess, and that some of the downstream power benefit could be returned in advance of its being produced—in a proposal to mould the return to the pattern of British Columbia's load growth which had come out of a meeting between Mr. Fulton and Mr. Luce in September. The provincial ministers were well aware of the opposition to their plans, but were equally well aware of the fragmented nature of that opposition. They did not appear perturbed when, privative clause notwithstanding, a challenge was launched in the Supreme Court of British Columbia testing the legality of the expropriation of the B.C. Electric Company. Persistently, members of the provincial Cabinet, especially Messrs. Bennett, Williston, and Bonner, sought to put the record straight—from their perspective—in numerous public speeches. They pleaded for the right to negotiate with the Americans, vigorously endorsed the wisdom of power sales, and challenged Ottawa to let British Columbia stake its future on its own plan. But they appealed to the public in another way. On October 27, Mr. Bennett announced that reductions would be made in provincial power rates, financed out of former B.C. Electric taxes and profits, to take effect on January 1, 1962. At the same time he offered to sell the Canadian entitlement to downstream power on the Columbia to the federal government for a now projected national power grid at the five mill price which, otherwise, he expected the Americans to pay.[62]

The reference to the national power grid is interesting, for this proposal clearly illustrates the case made by bargaining enthusiasts that in the reciprocal exchange of offers and demands which it entails there is a strong incentive to search out new areas of agreement. The concept was not a new one. It had been advanced by Dr. Merril W. Menzies in a significant monograph written in 1956,[63] and was endorsed in a 1960 report of the House of Commons' Standing Committee on Mines, Forests and Waters.[64] Nothing really had come of these initiatives, however, before Mr. Donald Stephens paid a visit to Ottawa late in September 1961. On this occasion Mr. Stephens raised with Mr. R. B. Bryce, the clerk of the privy council, and Mr. R. G. Robertson, the deputy minister of northern affairs and national resources, the fact that as the head of Manitoba Hydro he was interested in the prospect of selling energy to central Ontario, and wondered if such a plan might have some relevance to an all-Canadian grid. He referred directly to his hope to introduce Nelson River power from northern Manitoba via a 1200 megawatt direct-current line into the Toronto market, and he perceived major advantages to federal government participation in national grid planning and construction. Without paying any direct subsidies, he maintained, the federal government, if it assisted in financing the transmission lines, could help provincial power commissions with a very heavy burden. Furthermore, under such circumstances it could lay down technical standards which would be common to the inter-connected systems. Mr. Bryce and Mr. Robertson grasped the possibilities in the suggestion, and a considerable memorandum on the subject was prepared for Mr. Robertson's minister, Mr. Dinsdale. Out of it came an argument for going ahead with the Columbia at that time, and holding off on the Peace so that the latter might form part of a gigantic Canadian venture linking the northern portions of the provinces. Although an engineering review produced within the Water Resources Branch at Ottawa suggested that technically the proposal was questionable since reliability of supply under such conditions had just not yet been proven, Mr. Dinsdale became an active supporter of the proposal that the grid become the subject of an evaluative study.

When the Cabinet Committee on the Columbia River reassembled on October 31, it agreed to launch just such an investigation. It arrived at a number of additional decisions which are interesting. One was to take to the Cabinet a proposal that the May 1961 report of the Montreal Engineering Company be released, along with an accompanying memorandum which would highlight the magnitude of the Columbia development, its economy, and its ability to meet the load growth in the southern part of British Columbia at least until 1968. Another decision involved a change in tactics over the Peace River's development, for it was now agreed to obtain as much data as possible concerning the navigational effects of a dam at Portage Mountain, but not to oppose it. Finally, the committee rejected a proposal to pursue further enquiries concerning the prospects of a downstream power sale as constituting bad fighting ground for the federal government. There appeared to be a consensus that power could be sold in the northwestern states, and possibly in California, at a gross price of five mills or a net of 3½ to 4 mills, but once again the argument that a downstream benefit sale was contrary to the main purpose of Columbia development carried the day. Provincial optimism notwithstanding, the Columbia had all the appearances of having reached a stalemate.

New dimensions to the federal-provincial hiatus were to appear in November. Mr. Bennett, first of all, visited Seattle on November 17, and met briefly in private with President John Kennedy. Canadian journalists had a field-day over this development, as they speculated that Mr. Bennett had outflanked Ottawa, and was on very strong ground politically. Mr. Bennett has always been loath to discuss this meeting, apparently sensing that it involved some violation of diplomatic protocol. He does concede that it took place, and insists that he simply sought to put the record straight on what British Columbia's intentions were.[65] On November 17, Mr. Udall still further complicated matters when, in Seattle, he confirmed that American officials had been consulting both Ottawa and Premier Bennett, and expressed a hope for an early agreement.[66] At the same time he was candidly exasperated about the now traditional Canadian "power once exported is power lost" thesis; to him it was "stuff and nonsense"[67] that the United States would not honour a recapture provision in a power contract. On November 23 Mr. Fulton issued a press release in which he revealed his own exasperation at Mr. Udall's remarks, and indicated that the American ambassador in Ottawa had described the Bennett-Kennedy meeting as purely social. Subsequently, Mr. Udall through a press release on November 24, sought to clarify his position. He claimed that he had been misquoted, but really made no attempt to modify his earlier stand. Indeed, on November 24 he declared, "We have tried to be scrupulously careful. . . . What we're interested in is our share of the power. If Canada wants to sell its [share] that would be fine by us. . . . if Canada does not want to sell . . ., that would be fine, too."[68] Statements such as this, while making clear America's neutrality in the Ottawa-Victoria dispute, did in a way strengthen Mr. Bennett's position—and this, of course, was what Mr. Fulton realized. In a public interview on November 27, Mr. Udall made comments which were even tougher than those of three days earlier: "We've ratified the treaty. They haven't. We cannot tell them how to resolve their controversy. That would be meddlesome. All we can do is sit here and be wounded."[69] And he indicated that American patience was not unlimited. Unless the treaty was ratified within the next few months, he declared, the United States would consider dropping it.

Mr. Fulton may not have read this last statement before he left Ottawa to deliver at Prince George his long deferred reply to Mr. Bennett, but he most certainly knew that the premier on November 22 had called on Ottawa to ratify the treaty in the new session of Parliament beginning in January, and probably knew that Dr. Shrum, citing an Energy Board opinion, had just declared that the Peace would look after the province's electrical needs "for the next twenty years."[70] In any case, at Prince George on November 28 he delivered a vehement defence of the federal government's position and a bitter attack on Mr. Bennett. Once again British Columbians were told that they were being asked to sell abroad "our best and cheapest power resource." Mr. Bennett's policy was characterized as sheer madness, as reckless and improvident philanthropy, a sell-out. "The Americans haven't been offered such a windfall since the purchase of Manhattan Island," he maintained, "unless, of course, it was the Bennett-Kaiser deal." He was critical of the role he perceived the Americans as playing, referred to their reported support of Mr. Bennett, and asked rhetorically: "And why not? What they failed to get at the negotiating table is now being offered them by Mr. Bennett on a platter without regard to B.C.'s real interest."[71] Mr. Bennett's motivation was analyzed in the most unflattering terms. Before concluding, Mr. Fulton did suggest that Ottawa was willing to negotiate any reasonable settlement, including a short-term sale of part of the downstream power entitlement, but this observation seems to have been largely lost in the excitement caused by his earlier colourful imagery.

Beyond Confrontation. After this climactic riposte, the forces of accommodation in the Canadian political system seemed to induce an almost immediate moderation of the intergovernmental debate. Although Mr. Bennett had reacted strongly to Mr. Fulton's November 28 attack on him, had declared that Mr. Fulton would regret it to the end of his political career, and had described the attacks on American officials as disgraceful, when he and Mr. Fulton appeared on a national television program in turn on December 5 and 12, respectively, their long-range exchanges were quite dispassionate. Neither retreated. Mr. Bennett did predict a 1962 ratification, and did offer to sell power to the Americans in short five-year terms (as he suggested Mr. Fulton required) if Ottawa would guarantee a long-term price.[72] On December 7, in an interview, he was to make his position even more precise. To get a proper price, he argued, British Columbia should sell for a minimum twenty-year period—with a cancellation option open to the province but not to the United States—on ten years' notice. He repeated his conviction that he could get, at 4½ percent or less, the money (source unspecified) to build the treaty projects, and

212

that, overall, the Columbia would mean 3-mill power for the United States and "2,000,000 horsepower of no-mill power for British Columbia, great new industry, and jobs in B.C."[73] One point did come through from all this: British Columbia had no intention of scuttling the Columbia's development. For his part, before December was out, Mr. Fulton was publicly emphasizing again that while Ottawa would kill an outright sell-out, it was not opposed to short term sales of surpluses.

Actually, on November 27 Mr. Bennett had written to Mr. Fleming suggesting a resumption of talks on Columbia financing, and the federal Cabinet Committee members were to spend considerable time in December debating the form of a response to him. The reply finally sent accepted the proposal for a meeting, but otherwise simply restated the position which Ottawa had taken for a year as to its understanding of the treaty on power sales. Mr. Fleming's letter did enclose this time a copy of the Montreal Engineering Company's May 1961 report, and a supplementary memorandum from the federal government's Water Resources Branch which concluded that the complete development of the Columbia River in Canada would provide 60 percent more power to Canada than would the deevlopment of the Peace River—at a 25 percent lower unit cost. The letter and enclosures were released on December 27 to the press, which soon spotted not only the Montreal Company's favourable estimate of downstream energy costs, but also its emphasis on the necessary difference between the wholesale price of power (so often cited in public debate) and the figure at which it could be retailed.[74]

In their own way members of the public bureaucracies in both Victoria and Ottawa were urging their principals to continue searching for an agreement, for in both capitals there was a strong conviction among the senior public service personnel of the merits of the Columbia River Treaty, and a real awareness also of the evanescent nature of some of the benefits to be derived from upstream storage. Ministers in both capitals had this point made clearly to them. There was a broad range of opinion amongst the advisers to both governments about the Peace River project— about which neither technical bureaucracy was well-informed. But working strongly in Mr. Bennett's favour—whatever the merits of the Peace itself—was a widespread conviction among the public servants now that the provincial premier was certainly correct in his willingness to endorse power export, and in his complete rejection of the thesis that such sales could not be terminated, on due notice, when the energy was needed at home. This was a major point made in the address by Dr. Hugh Keenleyside on December 13, 1961, when he took formally his first public stance on provincial power policy since his appointment two and a half years earlier. He flatly supported Mr. Bennett's position, maintained that informed opinion no longer opposed power exports, anticipated that Peace as well as Columbia River energy might be sold abroad, and held that Ottawa's intransigence on this subject would do "direct, gross and permanent injury to B.C."[75]

As indicated, the federal government's technical staff were embarrassed by federal ministerial resistance to the thought that energy derived from a renewable resource was, in many respects, a more desirable export than the sale of, for example, hydro-carbon fuel. Highly sensitive as they were to the long list of assumptions involved in projecting power costs, they had been embarrassed for many months also by the tendency of their principals to become enmeshed in the intellectual quagmire of a debate on power costs. Certainly by the end of 1961 they were becoming further distressed by the strength of their ministers' conviction that the Canadian entitlement to downstream benefit power was low-cost. They realized that if by any chance Mr. Bennett could persuade Americans to buy at-site power at a price even close to five mills, a description of the entitlement as cheap power would no longer be valid—at least in the sense that the cost to anyone of a good consumed is the return forgone by not disposing of it.

This very point was advanced by one of the federal Cabinet's senior advisers, in a memorandum which he wrote on December 14, 1961, in Ottawa. But the memorandum went much further than this. It raised directly the wisdom of taking a new look at the sale of the downstream benefits, and advanced for consideration a proposal whereby Ottawa would agree to a sale of about one-half the Canadian power entitlement on the condition that British Columbia commit itself to approve immediately Columbia development to meet all load-growth requirements in the province. The projected sale would then be precisely a disposal of surplus power as contemplated in the treaty. A second condition in this plan was to be that the Peace River development would be deferred so that it would take its place after the Columbia River in meeting British Columbia's power needs. The memorandum's author thought that the significant thing about Mr. Bennett's recent television appearance was that he had not insisted that a twenty-year sale of the downstream benefit was an overriding condition. If the federal government appeared to be willing to meet the premier halfway, he argued, it might be very difficult for the province to refuse to consider more substantial conditions about terms of sale, the amount of power sold, and priority in execution for the Columbia over the Peace. There was the germ of a viable compromise here, even though on the prospect of deferring the Portage Mountain project the deputy minister in question did not appreciate the strength of Mr. Bennett's commitment to it, or the strength of the premier's bargaining position. Quite clearly, nevertheless, the federal bureaucracy was seeking to broaden the horizon of its political decision-making superiors. The process, however, was to be a slow one.

Just why the official federal position moved so slowly at this time is a subject which will be examined in the concluding chapters. It is sufficient to note here that Mr. Green's reluctance to make any change in the arrangements envisaged by the treaty was a major explanation, as was, at the end of 1961, Mr. Fulton's conviction that a sale of the downstream power entitlement at five mills was just not at all likely. There were other explanations. One surely was the volume and the vehemence of the correspondence reaching the federal Cabinet ministers from members of the Progressive Conservative party, and the public at large, urging no surrender on any account to Mr. Bennett. Many communications came in like vein from shareholders of the B.C. Power Corporation. Actually, however, we must record that the pressures on the Cabinet were complex, and by no means all favoured a stand-pat position. It is true, for instance, that a senior officer of the B.C. Power Corporation did leave with the prime minister on December 1, 1961, a memorandum which suggested that any further provincial legislation concerning the B.C. Electric Company be reserved by the province's lieutenant governor on federal instructions.[76] But this same man was anything but rigidly obstructionist. Indeed, he spent much time there urging, especially upon Mr. Howard Green, the obsolescence of the old power export ban. He was enthusiastic about the prospect that, via a sale of all or part of the downstream benefit, and the direct utilization of the flood control benefit, the treaty projects could be built and Mica machined expeditiously. Clearly, in his concern to promote the welfare of his own corporation's proprietors (and the general welfare of the community as he saw it) he was more than willing to promote a Canada-British Columbia agreement which went some way to meet the provincial government's wishes. At the same time he did seek a federal undertaking that no such agreement would be finalized until the dissatisfaction of the Power Corporation's shareholders had been resolved.

In summary, the state of Canada's policy with respect to the international development of the Columbia River was markedly different in December 1961, from what it had been a year earlier. A treaty incorporating some very specific commitments had been signed, but remained unratified. The deadlock which had arisen out of British Columbia's late-stage decision to sell all of its entitlement to downstream benefit power in the United States for an extended period of years continued unabated. By year-end, both Canadian governments had re-emphasized their ability to checkmate each other apropos the Columbia. If the impasse were to be broken, it remained uncertain whether this would come about as the result of a major shift on the part of one of the two Canadian governments involved, or by rather more modest accommodating moves on the part of both of them—assisted perhaps by some incremental adjustments in the United States itself.

Chapter Eight

The First Steps Toward a Federal-Provincial Détente

The philosophy of "the one best way" has been only a
way of protecting oneself against the difficulty of
having to choose, a scientist's substitute for the
traditional ideologies upon which rested the legitimacy
of the ruler's decision.
Michel Crozier, *The Bureaucratic Phenomenon*

Three points should be kept in mind about the process of Canadian
policy formation concerning the Columbia River, as it responded both to
the impasse of the previous year and to changes in the environment within
which the treaty had been negotiated, during the early months of 1962. It
was pursued in Ottawa and Victoria in the light of the knowledge that the
special task force on the California Inter-tie had reported very favourably
on the project to the secretary of the interior, and that on December 19,
1961, he had announced his department's approval of it, and his intention
to request the necessary Congressional authorizations.[1] And it was pursued in Ottawa in the light of the knowledge that the now publicly owned
B.C. Electric Company was moving ahead rapidly with its engineering
planning on the Peace, and in the light of some considerable pressure
from downstream interests on the Peace that federal controls be implemented.[2]

Overshadowing everything else, however, was the knowledge that a
federal general election could not long be delayed, and that the political
costs—in British Columbia at least—of being held responsible for inaction on the Columbia might be very great indeed. Rather understandably, the thirteen Progressive Conservative members of Parliament from
the province were acutely sensitive about this matter, and met on two

occasions with the four Cabinet ministers most concerned with the formation of Columbia policy (Messrs. Green, Fulton, Fleming, and Dinsdale), at the end of January 1962, to advance forcibly their views that the federal government's offer of assistance should be substantially increased. The press reported that some of the back-bench members favoured a modification of the federal stand on downstream power sales, and rumours certainly reached Victoria that a change in federal policy might be in the offing, but nothing, however, materialized at once. Nor did anything result from a number of informal discussions which Mr. Fulton had with Mr. Udall in January, when the latter was in Ottawa on other business, on the possibility (or impossibility) of obtaining a firm American commitment to purchase a definite portion of the downstream benefit at an at-site price of approximately five mills.

One real dilemma which faced the federal government at this time concerned the licensing of the Peace River Dam. The federal Cabinet Committee was assured by a senior deputy minister that the proposed provincial work certainly fell under the jurisdiction of the Navigable Waters Protection Act, and, hence, required a federal licence. But he added that an application when submitted very probably would have to be approved. In November 1961, British Columbia had been reminded that an application was necessary and an official of the B.C. Electric had informed Ottawa in December 1961, that one was being considered. Nothing more was heard from British Columbia on the subject, however, and the Cabinet Committee could go no further than endorsing the sending of a letter to Victoria arguing that the sooner a proper application was filed, the sooner the project could go ahead. The unspoken issue here centred on the prospect that British Columbia might ignore the federal statute—as, indeed, it has to this day.[3]

1. PUBLIC AND PRIVATE DEBATE AND NEAR COMPROMISE

The early months of 1962 were marked by a continuation of the great public debate on the relative merits of the positions which the governments of Canada and British Columbia had taken. The public continued to be assailed with a barrage of conflicting claims, couched in increasingly technical and often quantitative terms. The province's leader of the official opposition, for instance, became increasingly convinced, as he reflected on the report of the consultants of the B.C. Energy Board, that the Columbia would produce the cheapest power. Mr. Bonner, on the other hand, made much of the extent to which power exports were a fact of life in Europe.[4] Once more Drs. Keenleyside and Shrum defended the province's position, although the American Section chairman on the IJC warned that the United States would wait only three to four months longer for a Canadian decision.[5] Liberal party spokesmen revealed both a broad range of opinion on the power issue and a change of position on the part of the provincial party leader. On January 29, Mr. Perrault in the provincial Legislature, endorsed a modification of the treaty to permit the development of low-cost projects such as High Arrow and Duncan Lake first and a postponement of the expensive reservoir at Mica Creek. He indicated that the province might be wise, in fact, to turn subsequently to smaller projects elsewhere before Mica was developed. And he suggested that he and his party were now beginning to realize that Premier Bennett had a strong case with respect to power export sales. Mr. Walter Gordon, the president of the National Liberal Federation, described the treaty as a bad deal for Canada which, perhaps, should be renegotiated.[6] Mr. Jack Pickersgill, on the other hand, a leading national Liberal and a member of their federal shadow cabinet, laconically suggested that the whole issue was not "a proper basis or subject for a political battle."[7]

A complication which neither Canadian government had anticipated appeared at the end of February in the form of an uncommissioned report on the production of electrical energy in British Columbia. It was issued by seven well known and widely-respected members of the faculty of the University of British Columbia at Vancouver. The professors were perturbed about the two river plan of development to which the provincial government was committed, especially as it might mean, in their words "delaying full Columbia development for twenty or thirty years."[8] If such were likely to happen, they argued, the treaty should be analyzed simply as a source of downstream benefits. This they proceeded to do, and produced a very low cost figure for downstream energy related to the High Arrow and Duncan projects (2.07 mills per kwh), but a very high one indeed for the downstream energy credited to the Mica Dam (9.50 mills per kwh). As a consequence they concluded that, unless the installation of Mica generation could be proceeded with immediately and on-site generation there was shown to be unusually low cost, the treaty should not be ratified, but renegotiated "either (a) to postpone Mica indefinitely without altering the terms of the Treaty (thus providing Canada with 916,000 kw at a cost of approximately 2 mills per kwh), or (b) to alter its other terms so that the cost of Canada's share of the energy under the whole Treaty is reduced approximately to that of Class 1 energy (that is, 2½ mills per kwh)."[9] When they looked at the Peace River project they concluded that, as the energy produced by it would be more expensive than that which could be produced through thermal production at either Burrard Inlet (estimated cost of energy at load centre—4 mills per kwh), or that produced at a new plant at Hat Creek (estimated cost—3.70 mills

219

per kwh), and more expensive also than energy obtained through generation at an alternative (and they felt immensely superior) major project
site at Moran on the Fraser River, it should be delayed. In short, they
were convinced that "on the evidence available" the Moran project was
"more attractive than either the Peace or the present Columbia River
Treaty projects."[10] They were convinced also that the 4 mills per kwh, at
which price they believed Burrard Thermal power could be delivered,
should be the highest price paid for energy in the lower British Columbia
mainland under then existing circumstances.

For a few days the professors' analysis was on significant desk-tops in
Ottawa, as the high power cost figure associated with the Mica Dam
seemed to strike at the project which all along had been at the heart of
federal planning. Soon, however, a staff study from the Water Resources
Branch set the federal decision-makers' fears at rest.[11] In British Columbia,
Dr. Shrum, as chairman of the British Columbia Energy Board, issued a
two-page reply to the academicians. That reply had been prepared by Dr.
Jack Davis, then the director of the Research and Planning Division of
the B.C. Electric Company, and, as did the federal document which had
not been released, challenged the professors' assumptions and findings.
While the professors' conclusions were thus rapidly discounted at the
official level, their analysis disturbed party and non-party opinion for
many months to come. This was so even though their claims were, from the
outset, made somewhat implausible in view of an asserted compatibility of
fish migration and high dam construction—which they advanced apropos
the Moran site—and which had not then (and has not yet) been sub-
stantiated.

Throughout the winter months the federal Cabinet continued to receive
much advice, especially from active members of the Progressive Conservative party, as to what its power policy ought to be. The presidents of
the British Columbia Progressive Conservative constituency associations,
meeting in Vancouver on February 3, 1962, unanimously endorsed the
federal government's position. Indeed some Conservatives continued to
argue that there should be no moderation of the hard line with Victoria
until the matter of compensation for the B.C. Electric's expropriation had
been resolved.[12] Other Conservatives supported the members of Parliament who were genuinely perturbed about the inflexibility of the federal
government and who had urged that Ottawa must reach an understanding
with the province. Convinced that the Vancouver newspaper, *The Province*, spoke the truth when it declared on March 14 that "British Columbians are fed up,"[13] they warned, in effect, that power policy could well
be for the Conservatives in 1962 what pipeline planning had been for the
Liberals six years earlier. A realization that this last group just might be

right was to lead the federal Cabinet, during the months which followed, to a considerable and largely unappreciated, even if temporary, change in position.

During the first two months of 1962 neither Mr. Bennett nor Mr. Fleming was able to find a suitable time and place at which they could resume their meetings; indeed one did not emerge until Mr. Bennett accepted an invitation from Mr. Diefenbaker to attend a premiers' conference in Ottawa on the subject of a national power grid. Mr. Fleming suggested that the occasion be seized for a meeting to discuss Columbia planning. In the provincial Legislature Mr. Bennett made it clear, on February 27, that, while in Ottawa, he intended to ask for permission to export Peace River energy, and on March 1 declared that he would sooner resign than take the downstream power back.[14] Thereafter he left on a trip to the United States, as the press speculated that his objective was a written commitment from the Americans to purchase, for a period of twenty years at five mills per kwh, a block of Canadian downstream benefit power.

That such indeed had been his goal was to be confirmed, startlingly, in a story in the Vancouver press of March 10, which reported that he had unsuccessfully sought his sale in San Francisco. Undaunted, it added, he had phoned the Bonneville Power Administration's chief executive, Mr. Charles Luce, then in Washington, D.C., and had asked for a letter from Mr. Luce requesting a commitment from British Columbia to deliver downstream power from Duncan Lake storage to the United States at a price of five mills, subject to an agreement upon details. It revealed also that Mr. Luce had declined the request, had declared himself unwilling to become involved in a Canadian domestic controversy, and had referred Mr. Bennett to the Bonneville Authority's evaluation of power sales prospects made during the previous October. In reply, Mr. Bennett was reported to have declared, "If that's the way the Americans want to act, then I'm through with the Columbia River Treaty."[15] Today Mr. Bennett confirms this account with a chuckle; the confrontation, he declares, was a direct consequence of his having been "stood-up" for an appointment by Mr. Luce.[16]

Some measure of the stress in the formal relationship between Victoria and Ottawa during these years may be found in the rather extraordinary way in which releases to and interviews with the news media were used to signal the clarification or modification of policy positions. (The two Canadian governments went so far at this time as to subscribe to press clipping services on Columbia matters in an attempt to keep track of the thinking of each other.) Typical of such press stories was one from Vancouver on March 12. *The Province* reported its understanding that Ottawa would suggest allocating Columbia River power to the Lower Mainland (that is, the main provincial) market, and that of the Peace to a national power grid, with the downstream benefit being returned, a direct financial grant made to assist in the Columbia's construction, and the Columbia's development being finished sometime before that on the Peace.[17] Before that day was over, however, Mr. Bennett, now back in Victoria, called a press conference to make it clear that he would have nothing to do with this proposal. "We don't need any of their money," he indicated. "We can finance both the Peace and the Columbia ourselves very nicely. Thank you. Our credit is high, and this is a sound business proposition. I love a fight. This is the fight of my career to build these two great projects."[18] He went on to reaffirm his confidence that a five mill price could be obtained for the downstream benefit power, but that Ottawa could have it—at a price of five mills.

This assertion of the province's financial independence was not over-looked in Ottawa. Indeed, obtaining confirmation of it was one of the two major objectives which the federal Cabinet appears to have set for Mr. Fleming in his forthcoming meeting with Mr. Bennett. The other decision which the Cabinet seems to have taken at this time was to agree to sell up to 49.9 percent of the available power, subject to National Energy Board certification that the energy in question was surplus to Canadian requirements. At the same time, at least one federal minister renewed his attempt to persuade his colleagues that Ottawa should improve its financial offer. In a memorandum he cited aid given to other provinces, and pressed once again for an outright grant, suggesting that it amount to one-half the cost of a transmission line from the Columbia Valley (one-half, in short, of an estimated $110 million). He conceded that Mr. Bennett's recent observations on compromises did not make him hopeful that the proposition he was urging would be accepted, but he did suggest that something of this sort was necessary to carry the Conservatives through the next federal election, and possibly a provincial one called on the power issue.

There were three significant developments on the following day, March 17. Mr. Bennett arrived in Ottawa and had a long talk with Mr. Fleming. He appears to have been in persuasive form, and, in a revealing offer, undertook to modify his position on the downstream power benefit if the federal government's technical advisers did not agree with him. Also on March 17, and quite obviously not through sheer coincidence, the Department of External Affairs received a note from the United States Embassy in Ottawa urging that full consideration be given to an early ratification of the treaty even if purely Canadian problems had to be worked out while construction was underway. But positions were changing here also, and the American note went on to indicate that if Canada so desired, the United States would be willing to engage in discussions at that time about price and terms of disposition in the United States of any Canadian power. The theme on which the note ended was that if some substantial indication of ratification and implementation were forthcoming, the United States would be reasonable, but if not, then it would have to look to alternative solutions. On March 17, also, in opening the federal-provincial conference on the power grid, Mr. Diefenbaker spoke in a manner which indicated that the federal government was getting ready to modify its position on the exportation of power.[19]

Mr. Bennett's recollection is that he and Mr. Fleming did have the meeting with the federal technicians on March 18, and that they entered no objections to his planning; then and on Saturday, March 29, at a meeting in Vancouver, the two finance ministers went a long way toward effecting a rapprochment.[20] The result was the first meeting of senior staff advisers to the two Canadian governments since the signing of the treaty. This gathering of "technical personnel" took place in Ottawa on April 5 and 6, 1962. At the outset a difference of approach appeared, as the federal representatives indicated that their objective was to look at the real costs of downstream benefit power in relation to the cost of other power available in British Columbia, including that from the Peace River. The British Columbians responded that their directions had included none having to do with a comparison of Columbia and Peace River power costs, and insisted that such an effort would be pointless, for the Peace development was underway, and a decision had been taken that it not be stopped. Their understanding, which they vigorously presented, was that, by general agreement, Messrs. Fleming and Bennett had halted the Peace River-Columbia debate, and that the two groups had been brought together to draw up specific proposals whereby the Columbia could proceed. Their instructions, they indicated, focused on the downstream benefits, and required them "to cooperate with the federal representatives to prepare a sound and convincing case for the sale of the downstream benefits in the United States that would serve as a basis for a political decision."[21] In reply, the federal spokesmen made it clear that they had no authorization to agree to anything, but only to report back. They did agree, however, to listen.

The British Columbians thereupon introduced a carefully reasoned memorandum on the merits of a sale of the downstream benefit entitlement, argued the absolute necessity of this policy in the light of the irreversible Peace River development, and presented a number of "proposals and compromises." These latter were:

(1) Until Peace River power was available, British Columbia would

223

meet its load increase by purchasing from the Bonneville Power Authority.

(2) All downstream benefits were to be sold in the United States at about five mills per kwh on the basis of a ten-year firm contract and a ten-year notification of termination thereafter.

(3) Subject to British Columbia's needs, the National Grid was to get first call on B.C. power at rates less than those of sales to the United States.[22]

(4) The Peace was not to displace Mica at-site generation from its "natural markets" and the later stages of the Peace development would be postponed, if necessary, to assure this. Mica at-site power would be developed as soon as possible (about 1973) to meet the incremental load in British Columbia.

(5) British Columbia undertook to use the income from the sale of the downstream benefits for Columbia development.

(6) The flood control payments would be used for the rehabilitation of the flooded areas and the economic development in the Columbia basin in Canada.

(7) Furthermore, subject to agreement between the two governments and to immediate ratification of the treaty, British Columbia declared its willingness to start construction on the Duncan Dam by July 1962, on the Arrow project by September, and at Mica as early as possible in 1963.

The enthusiasm of the British Columbians for their package was manifest, and they worked hard to ensure that they were understood. They answered what questions they could. It is also clear, however, that the federal representatives, although they did not enter into a debate on the logic of the British Columbia position, held out no false hopes. They did agree to discuss the provincial proposals in detail with their ministers, and overnight did meet with Mr. Fleming. When the two groups caucused on the following morning, however, the federal representatives were able to report only that Mr. Fleming found the proposals helpful and interesting, but since they did relate to contemporary political problems, he needed some time for consideration of them. The federal representatives thus were unable to hold out any real hope of agreement, or even to say if another meeting was desirable.

For almost a fortnight in British Columbia's government there were high hopes that an agreement would be reached, substantially on the basis of the province's new position, and provincial ministers gave guarded expression to their optimism. But that optimism was to be short-lived, for only a week after the technical staff had met in Ottawa, all the signs there began to point to an imminent dissolution of Parliament. On April 9, and again on April 13, Mr. Green assured the House of Commons that ratification would not take place until after the treaty had received a detailed examination by the Commons' Standing Committee on External Affairs.[23] On April 13, Mr. Bennett revealed that in a telegram to Mr. Fleming he had requested ratification before dissolution, and at the same time, Mr. Williston expressed the opinion that it would be disastrous if ratification were to be delayed.[24] But delayed it was. Mr. Diefenbaker announced the dissolution of Parliament on April 19, and no official statement then or thereafter was made on the recent inter-governmental exchanges.

There are still uncertainties associated with the near détente. Their earlier position notwithstanding, Mr. Bennett and his associates certainly appeared in March–April, 1962, to be quite prepared to make a prompt construction start after ratification, even though a definitive sale of downstream benefit power had not then been arranged. Indeed, a year later, Mr. Williston was to declare that at the March 19 meeting between Messrs. Bennett and Fleming it had been agreed "that every effort would be made to ratify the treaty by the federal government prior to the dissolution of Parliament, which was expected to take place sometime in May."[25] He pointed out that part of this arrangement involved the completion and release of the conditional water licences for the treaty storage projects, which were, in fact, duly issued by Mr. Paget on April 16, 1962. The British Columbians were well aware that while Canada was claiming a first-added position for its Columbia storage, the restless Americans were licensing other projects which were in fact progressively reducing the attractiveness of the treaty arrangement to them. On the other hand, there was an element of the unreal about the sudden provincial enthusiasm for almost immediate ratification. While making some genuine concessions to the federal position, the province at the same time was certainly seeking to free itself from responsibility concerning the delay in the treaty's implementation, and in the process was advocating that Ottawa pursue a course of action which, if not constitutionally proscribed, certainly was an unconventional one. For it really was unrealistic to think that a treaty as controversial as this one would be put into effect before its critics had had their opportunity to challenge it, especially within two months of a general election. It is true that Mr. Diefenbaker's statements to the House of Commons on this matter had never said categorically that the examination of the treaty by the External Affairs Committee would precede ratification but his press release in Washington, D.C., immediately following the signing of the treaty, had given this assurance.[26] And this the province knew.

In other respects, it is still not clear why the federal government did not respond in a more positive way to the province's initiative at this time. Certainly, the province had gone some distance towards meeting Ottawa's objections. The proposed purchase of power from the Bonneville Authority during much of the 'sixties was in fact an advance return, in kind, of the downstream power benefit. There were here, in short, proposals the adoption of which would have enabled both governments to save face. A major explanation for the federal response, or more precisely, the lack of a positive one, appears to lie in the nature of the decision-making process within the Diefenbaker Cabinet. This will be examined later. But certainly contributing to federal inaction were three additional considerations. Late in March 1962, the British Columbia government introduced new legislation in the provincial Legislature to strengthen its position. One measure modified the 1961 legislative takeover of the B.C. Electric, replacing two key sections in the 1961 legislation with others more tightly drawn, and adding an amendment which expressly forbade the commencement or continuation of any action or proceeding against either the B.C. Electric or the attorney-general, except in accordance with the requirements of the province's Crown Procedures Act.[27] Another statute merged the B.C. Electric (which had taken over the Peace River Company) with the British Columbia Power Commission, effectively scrambling their assets in a new B.C. Hydro and Power Authority.[28] Both measures had been given final approval in an extraordinary all-night sitting of the Legislature in Victoria, and, not unnaturally, had evoked a violent reaction from the opposition parties, and, of course, from the former owners of the B.C. Electric. Early in April, federal Cabinet ministers were bombarded with letters from irate shareholders, and strong representations for federal action came from some of the B.C. Electric's former executive officers. Mr. Sherman declares that Mr. Fulton "toyed with the idea of disallowing the two bills."[29] He certainly considered this step, but seems to have been equally interested in another alternative, that the legislation simply be reserved by the lieutenant-governor of British Columbia—on instructions from the Governor General-in-Council—in order that the constitutionality of government legislation which proscribed appeals against the same government's actions might be referred to the Supreme Court of Canada for an opinion. To his colleagues he made no secret of his concern for the legal principle which he felt was at issue in both pieces of provincial legislation. In turn, his colleagues today make no secret of their belief that, whatever the principle, the political costs associated with the invocation of this over-riding federal power, not to mention those latent in the process of being labelled, whether fairly or not, as partisans for the B.C. Electric's former owners, made the adoption of such a policy in March–April 1962, unfeasible. In any event no action was taken on it. Even its consideration in Ottawa, however, hardly stimulated a sympathetic hearing for the province's compromise proposals.

Another explanation for the federal attitude may well be found, ironically enough, in letters which at this time Mr. Ladner was sending to Messrs. Fulton and Fleming. While on the one hand he urged that an agreement be reached with British Columbia as soon as possible to permit it to sell surplus power, he also informed them that recent interviews with the president of the Pacific Gas and Electric Company in San Francisco had satisfied him that that concern would certainly not pay five mills for Canadian power.

Finally, a much more important complication appeared on April 6, when General McNaughton announced that he had been "removed" on April 1 as the Canadian co-chairman of the IJC, called Mr. Diefenbaker "a dictator," and attributed this action to his opposition to the Columbia River Treaty, which, he maintained, would establish a "servitude in perpetuity of our vital rights and interests."[30] The general went on to assert that the Canadian treaty negotiators had been unskilled and uninformed, that in negotiation they presented a house divided, and that when the Americans saw this "they moved in on these people and skinned them alive."[31] The upshot was a considerable, if short-lived uproar. Mr. Herridge not surprisingly was delighted at the general's public assessment and action. Mr. Pearson saw it as further proof of the government's excessive haste to sign the treaty, and of the need to renegotiate. Quite obviously the federal government had not expected such a reaction, for the outburst was a very considerable embarrassment shortly before a general election. In any case, even if there had been any prospect of an early ratification, this was now manifestly impossible. Mr. Williston and later Dr. Keenleyside, in Victoria, declared that the general's thesis had been examined over and over again by engineers and economists in Ottawa and Victoria, and after consideration of all the implications, had been rejected. The general soon expanded his views in a series of additional press releases, made them the subject of a journal article,[32] and developed them in great detail over the next two years. Within hours of General McNaughton's initial release, Mr. Fulton had issued a statement indicating that the general apparently was having second thoughts, since he had not opposed the signing of the treaty. Subsequently Mr. Fulton complicated matters in at least two speeches in western Canada, when he asserted that Canada would have been better off with a treaty drawn in accord with General McNaughton's wishes, but that in view of British Columbia's position this had been impossible.[33] Within a short time, a memorandum produced in the Water Resources Branch in Ottawa for policy-level review appears to have set at rest the worst of the fears raised by the general's charges. It answered a good many of his points seriatim and in a way answered Mr. Fulton also by pointing out that there was not

227

at that time and there never had been any assurance that a sequence of developments, or a division of benefits as proposed by General Mc-Naughton, would be accepted by the United States. Such in any case was the environment in which the federal government decided to take no action on the provincial suggestions.

2. The 1962 Federal Election Campaign

During the May–June election, the development of the Columbia River was simply not a matter of nation-wide concern, although in British Columbia it could not be ignored, especially as the substance of the provincial offer—but without mention of the early return of the downstream power benefit—had been revealed by an enterprising journalist on May 5.[34] General McNaughton, who had issued a second statement on April 13 outlining his reason for attacking the treaty, on May 4 denied any desire or intent to get involved in the forthcoming election, but reaffirmed that the treaty would be ratified "over my dead body."[35]

The Conservatives' approach to Columbia River development during the election was decidedly low-key. Mr. Fleming confirmed on May 23 in Victoria that no federal-provincial agreement had been reached. Mr. Diefenbaker repeated that federal assistance would be available if and when the Columbia River's development was agreed upon, and at Prince George on May 28 seemed to endorse all possible hydro-electric projects, on the Peace River as well as the Columbia. Mr. Fulton described the Peace River as entirely provincial in its problems and benefits, declared that the April discussions appeared to reflect a modification of the province's stand, and held that a Conservative election victory could lead to speedy agreement and ratification.[36] Mr. Pearson characterized the treaty as "a very sad story indeed," and insisted that his party would examine it, as there was "overwhelming evidence that it was bad for Canada." He undertook to approach the United States' negotiators, declaring, "I know this will work,"[37] and undertook also to enlist General McNaughton in the work of revision. He did not come out against a sale of the downstream benefits, but did oppose a sale "without first fixing the price."[38] And he promised to get on with the job. Mr. Strachan and the New Democrats found the absence of a Liberal party condemnation of a downstream power benefit sale most disturbing and sought to belabour the provincial wing of the Liberal party for its inconsistencies with respect to Columbia development policy. Mr. Strachan endorsed, or reindorsed, the Mc-Naughton plan.[39]

The most vigorous response to the Liberals' renegotiation proposal came from the provincial Social Crediters, whose Columbia theme was one of optimism. The B.C. Hydro and Power Authority in fact announced on May 10 that Duncan Lake construction tenders would be called in a few days. They were, two days later, but the call revealed that they were for camp construction and reservoir clearing only. Mr. Bennett dismissed Mr. Pearson's position, holding that any necessary modifications could be effected quite simply by an exchange of diplomatic notes. His colleague, Mr. Bonner, directly attacked the Conservatives for calling the election before ratifying the treaty. To each party, it seemed, a victory for it would assure an end to the frustrating delay.

As it turned out, the June 18 election ended disastrously for the Progressive Conservatives. Their 202 seats were reduced to 117, with the Liberals (96), Social Crediters (30), and New Democrats (19), together significantly outnumbering them in the new Parliament. In British Columbia the Conservative strength was reduced from eighteen to six. Minority government had returned, although there was no reason to believe that a continuing Conservative administration could not survive under such circumstances, as the Social Credit group led by Mr. Robert Thompson had shown no disposition whatsoever to prefer a Liberal government.

How significant the issue of the Columbia was in determining the election result—especially in British Columbia, where, in terms of percentages, the Conservative vote fell most sharply—simply cannot be determined. Quite obviously it played some part. Interestingly, Columbia River policy was not mentioned once in a series of fifteen review papers written by academic observers on the results of the election in Canada as a whole.[40]

Reassessments of Strategy, Especially in Ottawa. Three considerations dominated Columbia decision-making during the summer of 1962. In some respects, effecting a settlement of this issue had become more urgent than ever, for the state of the economy, and especially of Canada's foreign exchange position, continued to disturb both the financial community and the makers of policy in the federal government. Those in the federal Cabinet eager to reach an agreement with British Columbia became significantly stronger, and Mr. Bennett himself continued to urge action. By July 16, one minister whose department was directly concerned with some of the technical issues involved, had become absolutely convinced of the merit of selling the downstream benefit, and so argued in a long memorandum which he sent to his colleagues. Much of it was devoted to reviewing the British Columbia proposals of April 5 and 6, and to stressing the prospect that early action on the treaty could do a great deal to simulate a substantial inflow of U.S. funds. The minister also drew attention to the fact that, in April, British Columbia had pressed only for the sale of the downstream benefit, and not for the export of domestically generated energy. He went on to suggest that obstacles in the way of a purchase by the Bonneville Administration were being cleared away, and that, if a sale of the downstream power benefit were approved, the province would probably agree to use the flood control benefit to meet construction costs. The wisdom of selling the downstream benefit was examined at length, in an argument which emphasized that the key figure to watch was the average cost of power used in Canada from the entire scheme. The average cost of Columbia power with no sale of downstream power benefits was put at 4.3 mills per kwh, and the impact on this figure of the proceeds from a downstream power benefit sale to defray project costs was represented as follows:

TABLE 6

Cost of Columbia Power as a Whole (D.N.A. and N.R. Appreciation, Ottawa, July 1962)

Sale over 20 years of half the Canadian downstream entitlement at 5 mills per kwh (U.S. funds calculated at an 8 percent premium).	3.9 mills per kwh
Comparable sale of all the entitlement	3.2 mills per kwh

This minister argued (in a manuscript which assuredly reflected much technical staff opinion) that by selling the downstream power benefits, British Columbia could reduce the cost of the entire block of Canadian Columbia River energy to that of the downstream benefit alone if the latter were returned to Canada. His recommendation, supported by further technical analyses, was that the Cabinet Committee be directed to prepare detailed proposals in preparation for negotiations with British Columbia to be resumed through the Policy Liaison Committee.

Pressure for action was mounting elsewhere. In the same month the six surviving Progressive Conservative members of Parliament from British Columbia met with Mr. Diefenbaker to express their concern over their government's seemingly continued intransigence on this issue. The prime minister gave them a fair hearing, but declined to make any promises of a change; instead, he indicated the extent to which the Cabinet relied upon Messrs. Green and Fulton on this issue, and referred the six to them. The back-benchers persisted, and with some senior provincial officers of the party met with Messrs. Green and Fulton at a closed meeting in Vancouver on August 4. Feelings ran high on this occasion as the vehemence of the back-bench members was matched, apparently, by the vigour with which the two ministers argued the merits of seeking a compromise by offering a federal contribution to the cost of Columbia transmission facilities. The upshot of this meeting was the passage of a resolution urging Ottawa to proclaim its readiness to reopen negotiations with the province.

Finally, on August 19, the strategic position of some of the key players on the federal stage was modified when Mr. Diefenbaker reshuffled his Cabinet. Mr. Fleming was moved to the Justice portfolio but retained, at the prime minister's request (not to mention Mr. Bennett's desire), continued responsibility for the coordination of the federal approach to British Columbia on the Columbia River's development. Mr. Fulton, on the other hand, was transferred to the less prestigious Ministry of Public Works. Within a day the press was speculating that he would leave federal politics for the vacant leadership of British Columbia's Progressive Conservative party.

3. A Move to Informal International Negotiations

By mid-August technical personnel in Victoria were asking Ottawa to clear a meeting between them and the staff of the federal Water Resources Branch to check some engineering details of the treaty projects, and Mr. Bennett was requesting and receiving an appointment to discuss with Mr. Fleming expediting the development of the Columbia. When the two met, the premier quite obviously made a very strong plea to be allowed to test officially the United States market,[41] and the federal Cabinet shortly agreed to allow the province to put its proposals before the Americans. Mr. R. G. Robertson and three colleagues from the federal public service were authorized, furthermore, to attend any negotiating meetings as observers. But the federal government went no further at this time than conceding that the meetings could take place and undertaking to give the whole matter further and careful consideration if the Americans were in fact prepared to respond positively to British Columbia's thinking.

While disappointed at this very limited freedom of action which it had gained, the provincial government was still decidedly optimistic, and, with Ottawa, moved to arrange the first of a new series of international negotiating sessions, beginning with a meeting in Washington, D.C., on September 11 and 12, 1962. Early in these exchanges five propositions were advanced by British Columbia's representatives. They were reducible to the suggestion that under a commercial type contract between B.C. Hydro and Power Authority and the Bonneville Power Administration, Canada's entitlement to the downstream power benefit should be sold for the life of the treaty with the provision, however, after twenty years and on ten years' notice, that there could be a reduction of the amount of power sold. The entitlement was offered at five mills per kwh, with capacity being exchanged for energy, and also being paid for at five mills— on the basis of an agreed-on formula. And either the Bonneville Administration, or some other agency of the United States government, was to make money available for the construction of the Canadian Columbian projects at the interest rate charged by the government of the United States when supplying funds for publicly constructed hydro power installation domestically.

Drs. Keenleyside and Shrum did the bulk of the arguing for Canada. When, for example, a Bonneville representative suggested that four mills per kwh at the generators for power sold in California, and three mills for that sold in the northwest was the best price that could be expected, Dr. Keenleyside indicated that, on these terms, British Columbia would not go ahead. And Dr. Shrum was quite prepared to suggest that British Columbia might be willing to firm up the declining quantity of the downstream entitlement in a sale from the Peace or other provincial sources. The Bonneville Power Authority's ability to act as a broker for, but not as a purchaser of Canadian power, posed quite obvious difficulties. On the other hand, the Canadians did gather that the American representatives would be willing to suggest financing at a rate of the order of 4 percent— although they were reminded that the United States had a balance of payments problem also. As this meeting concluded, Mr. Robertson was assured unofficially that with a downstream benefit sale the stand-by transmission charge would be waived, and the Americans agreed to consider the financing and marketing problems which the Canadians had raised.

In the three weeks which were to pass before the negotiators met again, the new session of Parliament opened in Ottawa, and in the Speech from the Throne the federal government not only declared its hope to be able to place the Columbia River Treaty and implementing legislation before Parliament for examination and approval shortly, but it announced a distinctly new policy on the encouragement of electrical energy exports. "The Government has concluded," the speech declared, "that large-scale, long-term contracts for the export of power surplus to Canada's needs, present and potential, should now be encouraged in order to expedite the development of major projects in Canada which are too large to be supported by domestic markets. Such exports can also strengthen our balance of payments."[42] Nothing could have been more encouraging to the provincial government in British Columbia. Few observers noted that informed journalists in Ottawa immediately stressed the tactical, tentative nature of the apparent reversal of policy, or that it need not apply to the downstream power benefit on the Columbia.[43] The statement was taken at face value by many—including Mr. Strachan, incidentally, to whom it was a great disappointment.

The second in a series of power sale meetings was held at Portland, Oregon, on October 2 and 3. The Canadian delegation of eight was provided in equal numbers from Victoria and Ottawa; Mr. Robertson acted as their chairman. The Americans lost no time in coming to the point as they introduced three short position papers. One of these, dealing with the prospect of financing by the government of the United States, urged caution, and cited a number of reasons for such a policy here. A second paper indicated that in the event of a downstream benefit power sale the standby transmission charge would be waived. In subsequent discussion (prompted by a question from Mr. Robertson) this understanding was extended also to the circumstances of a partial sale and partial return of the downstream entitlement, if special transmission facilities were not required. The third paper dealt with markets in the United States for the sale of the Canadian downstream power benefit, and referred to investigations which had been made in the northwest and California. Some very tentative figures, such as 3¾ to 4 mills net per kwh at 60 percent load factor for the Los Angeles market, and 3 to 3½ mills for similar power in the Pacific northwest were cited.

After some considerable and inconclusive skirmishing, the Americans then moved to a new approach, whereby they sought to delineate the four approaches, which, as they saw the situation, were open to the negotiators. The first of these simply indicated that the United States was prepared to proceed with the treaty in its original concept. Here it was emphasizing that the basic decision to sell the downstream benefit was based upon domestic Canadian considerations. Dr. Keenleyside promptly made it clear that this was not acceptable to British Columbia—and, for the record, the federal representatives indicated that this arrangement had been at the beginning and still was acceptable to the government of Canada.

The second alternative projected by the Americans was designed to take advantage of the newly announced Canadian national policy of actively encouraging power exports. It envisaged the accelerated Canadian development of the Columbia, to take advantage of this, with (1) the downstream power entitlement sold in the United States, (2) Mica machined as soon as physically possible to meet domestic loads, and (3) to facilitate this, if necessary, the Peace River postponed. It anticipated also that some surplus Mica-generated energy might possibly be sold in the United States. A considerable list of arguments in favour of this procedure was advanced by the Americans, as they suggested it could be an effective way of reducing power costs to electricity consumers in British Columbia. During the period of Mica's construction, they added, thought could be given to the means whereby potential deficits in British Columbia might be met by low-cost Bonneville power.

The third alternative drew attention to the implications of completing the Mica Dam in 1972 but not marketing power from it, if Peace River energy had pre-empted the market, until 1980. The cost of this delay was estimated at over $100 millions. That cost could be avoided by machining Mica at once and selling the whole of the power output on a long-term contract, using the proceeds to amortize Mica's cost, and leaving the way clear for downstream projects at Downie and Revelstoke to meet domestic requirements when Peace River energy had been absorbed. Finally, the fourth alternative advanced the possibility that British Columbia might be given some leeway with respect to completion of Mica, provided that it was completed in not more than seventeen years after ratification.

Several features of the exchange which followed deserve our attention. Dr. Keenleyside made it very clear that alternatives one and four were not at all acceptable to his government, drew attention to the position which he had outlined in Washington, and felt that no real progress to an agreement satisfactory to the province had been made. Only by inference, he noted, had an indication been given that all of the downstream entitlement would be purchased, and two crucial indications were absent—acceptance of the five mill price (or its equivalent), and a commitment by the United States to assist in financing the treaty projects. He was frankly disturbed by the indications that the Bonneville authority itself was a most unlikely purchaser, and disclaimed any desire on the part of B.C. Hydro to negotiate with a large number of American utilities. He did refer to the recent federal Speech from the Throne, and declared categorically that British Columbia was prepared and anxious to sell the downstream power benefit, and willing to supplement that sale with energy from provincial generators if this would improve the marketability of the Canadian entitlement energy in the United States. At this point spokesmen for the Canadian federal government warned that it was important not to assume that there had been a significant change in its attitude to the export of energy. Ottawa's representatives were merely being honest. In fact, a very considerable tug-of-war was going on in the Canadian Cabinet on the extent to which the declaration of policy in the Speech from the Throne should be literally interpreted. To a considerable degree its inclusion had been politically inspired by a desire to satisfy those in Canada who were especially concerned with Canada's balance of payments difficulties.[44]

In the exchanges which followed, the Americans clarified a number of matters. Power supply conditions in the northwest had changed, producing increasingly difficult problems associated with short-term sales. They agreed that a longer sale period—perhaps thirty years, the approximate life of a steam plant—might command a higher sale price. *There was no prospect of a sale to the United States with an escalation-in-price provision included.* Above all, Mr. Luce stressed the difficulty of getting from American utilities anything in the nature of a commitment on firm sale prices for energy, or a prepayment for Canadian energy, until the government of Canada had made a definite policy decision on the international sale of electrical energy exported from or belonging to British Columbia.

Thus this rather crucial meeting ended up inconclusively; the Canadians had found the indications of what they were likely to get from the Americans anything but encouraging. However, both they and the Americans at Portland appear to have shared a conviction that an official stalemate must be avoided and, as a consequence, it was agreed that talks might be continued by technical representatives in an attempt to find an acceptable formula on which negotiations might proceed.

As a result of the Portland meeting, Mr. Fleming concluded and informed his colleagues that the Canadian share of the downstream benefit power could not be sold for five mills, although he conceded that in the absence of a firm proposal being made to the American utilities one could not be certain. Financing at anything like the 4 percent capital cost Mr. Bennett had hoped for would not be available either. The second of the American alternatives advanced at Portland was seen as the basis of an economic arrangement, but it involved a Peace deferment felt to be unacceptable to Mr. Bennett. In the end, he recommended to his colleagues that another meeting be approved, with once again the federal representatives having no authority to make commitments on behalf of the Canadian government.[45]

On the day after this report was written in Ottawa, Mr. Bennett met the press, and reiterated his belief that the province could get by with the Peace. Without a settlement on the Columbia that was advantageous to British Columbia, he insisted, that river would not be developed.[46] He was told at this time that Dr. Davis, now a Liberal M.P., had publicly endorsed the concept of a single lump sum prepayment for a power sale, and indicated that the idea was worth exploring. Two days later, on October 12, Dr. Keenleyside phoned Mr. Robertson to relay to him Mr. Bennett's reaction to the Portland discussions. Mr. Bennett had not been prepared to accept the negative results of the negotiations as final, and felt that, once the coming American elections were over, senior American political figures could again give their attention to this problem. Dr.

Keenleyside indicated that the premier was not prepared to consider any other kind of arrangement unless absolutely convinced that the one he sought was unattainable.

Negotiation and Analysis At The Technical Level. Meanwhile, on October 10, the first of the continuing meetings of Canadian-American technical personnel had been held.[47] Some indication was given by the Americans that a stretch-out or extension of a sale contract might make possible a better price. And some inconclusive attention was given to the concept of a lump-sum prepayment for energy sold which might be made available from private purchasers and, possibly, a new public corporation, perhaps able to borrow at 4 percent. Attempting anything of this sort raised the need to estimate in advance the magnitude of the downstream benefit. The technicians appreciated the risk to both parties involved in this process. The way in which new American projects were pre-empting the markets in the northwest for the late 'sixties was reflected clearly in suggestions from the American spokesman, Mr. Goldhammer, that if the downstream power benefit was to be sold in the United States, and a sale to California did not materialize, then the United States might wish to delay Arrow Lake storage until 1968, and Mica until 1972. At the conclusion of this meeting Mr. Kidd reported to the government of British Columbia that he could see merit in continuing the technical-level discussions, but suggested that more formal negotiations at that stage would be unwise. Mr. Kidd certainly brought back to Victoria a real concern over the way in which newly authorized American developments were pre-empting the value of Canadian storage.

The technical team in British Columbia continued with their own detailed analyses of the alternatives facing the province after October 10, and directed a whole series of enquiries to the Economic Planning Department of B.C. Hydro, seeking to probe the consequences of the second American alternative of October 2 and 3, which involved the sale of the downstream benefit and some Mica generation for twenty years at 3.7 mills per kwh at 60 percent load factor. On the basis of the results, they concluded that the American alternative was unacceptable, unless, with American assistance, the capital required could be raised for not more than 4 percent. Indeed, the harder they worked the more convinced they became that increased emphasis would have to be given to an additional complication, the prospect of a continued significant annual inflation. They directed a series of studies aimed at establishing the minimum price that British Columbia could be prepared to accept, taking account, as best they could, of all the risk factors involved, including inflation. "Present indications," Mr. Kidd was to report when reviewing these for Dr. Keenleyside and the provincial government, "are that assuming inflation at 3 percent per annum, this price should be not much less than 5 mills per kwh unless it is possible to obtain low interest financing."[48]

At a second international meeting of technical staff held on November 21 and 22, Mr. Kidd and Mr. MacNabb represented Canada, and faced personnel from the Bonneville Power Administration and Corps of Engineers. On this occasion at least two of the American spokesmen stressed the need for early ratification, in the light of the new American projects which had been authorized and the pressure being mounted by non-federal agencies in the American watershed. The Americans did report that the Corps of Engineers and the Bonneville Power Administration had studies underway on the magnitude of the downstream power benefit. Mr. Kidd's impression of the results of these American agency studies was that they seemed to indicate that the estimates made in 1960 of the increase in energy which Canadian regulation would make possible appeared to be reasonable, and should be used in future analysis. On the other hand, Mr. Kidd reported to his principals an impression, derived from these studies, that the effect of a sale in the United States of the Canadian entitlement to downstream benefit power would have a much more modest influence on retarding the rate of decline of the downstream benefit than calculations made in the Water Resources Branch at Ottawa had earlier indicated. When the question of reassembling the international negotiating teams was raised, the Americans supported the proposal that the two national groups be brought together in December, if only to discuss the results of the downstream benefit studies. Apparently in response, Mr. Kidd argued that the Canadians would not be interested in discussing solely technical data, and maintained that the United States should make some definite reply to the September proposal of British Columbia, as he repeated the suggestion that the province might be willing—in return for annual payments or a lump sum which could cover the cost of the Columbia storage projects and Mica generation—to provide a constant amount of power (downstream entitlement plus an increasing block of Canadian generation) to the United States over a period of years.

The Reassessment of Options in Victoria and Ottawa. Within a week the three governments had agreed to hold another meeting on a power sale at Vancouver in late December. Mr. Green made the announcement in the House of Commons on November 27, and took the opportunity to deny Mr. Bennett's charge on the previous day that the secretary of state for external affairs was sabotaging the negotiations by not supporting with the American State Department his demand for five mill downstream benefit power sale (or its equivalent).[49]

This decision was taken at a time when a number of key technical advisers to the two Canadian governments had become deeply depressed by the extent to which unanticipated developments had invalidated or out-flanked some of the most crucial assumptions incorporated into their 1960 treaty calculations. Some of the modifications in the policy environment which had occurred have already been referred to. As Dr. Grauer's advisers had predicted in 1960, the load growth rate in British Columbia during the next two years did moderate. It declined also in the American Pacific northwest, with the result that, by late 1962, American utilities were much less concerned than they had been in 1960 about their post-1965 load increases, which, during the treaty negotiations, they had counted on Arrow Lake and Duncan Lake storage to help them meet. Another significant development had been the emergence of the Pacific northwest-California and southwest intertie as the subject of serious consideration in the United States. The Canadian technicians had anticipated this development in 1960, and had been able to prevent a drastic decline in the Canadian downstream power entitlement should it materialize (in Annex B, Paragraph 3 of the treaty), but they well realized by late 1962 that if the United States were to abandon the treaty, it would find in the intertie a significant alternative and solely domestic route to the power, if not the flood control benefit, which the treaty was expected to provide.[50]

Still another major change after 1960 had been an escalation in the projected cost of building the High Arrow Dam. Three factors, apart from continuing inflation, had made the 1957 estimated cost of $66 millions quite unrealistic by late 1962. One was the insistence by the province's Water Resources Service, after 1960, that the dam contain a major lock. A second was the fact that the provincial water comptroller made the issuance of the treaty storage licences in April 1962 conditional on a standard of foreshore clearing on the Arrow Lakes not anticipated by Canadian planners prior to 1961. Additionally, and perhaps most significant of all, the operation of the new forest products complex just above Castlegar after January 1961, had an almost immediately beneficent effect on the economy of the two hundred miles of valley between Castlegar and Revelstoke, which for decades had been a genuinely depressed area. The result once again was a further increase in flowage costs.

Perhaps the most obvious of the modifications in the assumptions which the technical advisers to the Canadian negotiators had taken for granted in 1960 were the provincial government's decisions in 1961 to move ahead immediately with the development of the Peace River, and to sell the Canadian entitlement to downstream power on the Columbia. Another was a *new* willingness of the provincial government to undertake programs involving very large-scale initial capital investments. By December 1962, the emphasis which the province's technical staff had had to place during the 1960 negotiations on starting the Columbia's development with low-cost high-return projects was just not nearly so relevant. In the two years which followed the negotiation of the Columbia River Treaty, Mr. Bennett had acquired a fresh appreciation of his government's financial capacity and its ability to guarantee the borrowing of such Crown agencies as the B.C. Hydro and Power Authority.

One of the most interesting changes in policy assumptions, and one which was of great potential significance for the still unratified Columbia River Treaty, took place in the United States. Whereas, as we saw in chapter 1, the American portion of the Columbia River basin became "grossly deficient"[51] in storage during the Eisenhower years, the Kennedy administration after 1960 introduced a number of new or modified perspectives which certainly altered some of the premises on the basis of which the treaty had been negotiated. Reflecting thus both a new American policy-making environment and the long delay over ratifying the treaty in Canada, clearance was given in the United States after 1960 to a number of domestic projects in the Pacific northwest—to the power-cum-storage project at Bruce's Eddy (Dworshak), and to the Hanford thermal plant in particular. The Boundary plant on the Pend Oreille also moved to the construction stage, strong American federal executive level support was given to the Knowles project on the Pend Oreille, and a licence was granted by the Federal Power Commission for the High Mountain Sheep project on the Snake. These American initiatives had a number of direct implications for the bargain incorporated in the still unratified Columbia River Treaty. The newly approved or likely-to-be approved American storage projects, although inferior when evaluated on a system basis to equivalent storage in Canada, promised to go some way to appropriating and displacing the downstream utility of storage located in Canada.[52] The Libby and Bruce's Eddy projects alone would provide almost as much storage as Canada, under the treaty, was making available for primary flood-control operation. And with the commencement of these new works the American case for revising the "base system" specified in Annex B of the treaty, on which the Canadian power benefits were calculated, was made increasingly impressive.

At this juncture, and in the light of the considerations just detailed, four highly confidential position papers on Canada's strategic position were prepared by Canadian technical personnel—two in Ottawa and two in Victoria. All four referred specifically to the manner in which the prospect of coordinating the Peace and Mica projects, which the treaty planners had set aside in 1960, now opened up a whole new range of possibilities.[53] Both of the provincial staff papers discussed the case which had emerged for abandoning the Duncan Lake and High Arrow projects. One ended up suggesting that the only realistic course to follow was to defer Mica, and to sell the Americans excess energy from the Peace River development to make up for the Mica downstream benefit forgone in the interim. The other provincial staff appreciation suggested that British Columbia faced two major alternatives. One was a dropping of Mica, an alternative which the author found unrealistic, although he cited a number of supporting arguments for the proposal; the other was the elimination of the High Arrow and Duncan projects, in view of the development of the Peace and of Libby. After explicitly referring to the difficulties involved in selling the entire downstream power benefit at a price high enough to meet Canadian storage costs, this engineer suggested that, failing a suitable sale, consideration be given to the alternatives he had listed, and also to the wisdom of deferring Mica storage construction until Mica at-site power was needed.[54]

The author of the first of the two papers prepared in Ottawa was equally alarmed. "The cost of the downstream benefit is therefore increasing," he wrote, "at the same time as actions by British Columbia and United States governments are removing the markets for these benefits." He went on to suggest that British Columbia should be called upon either (a) to honour the commitments made at the last Policy Liaison Committee meeting on January 3 and 4, 1961, or (b) to produce in short order an American commitment to provide the financing and to purchase the downstream power benefit at a rate which would make good the prospect of "free Mica power," or (c) to give Ottawa "its full support in the negotiation of a treaty which would contain only the Mica project in Canada."[55] Actually he saw little chance of his options (a) and (b) being met, and emphasized the strong engineering and economic case to be made for option (c) under circumstances which he specified.[56]

This officer's concern was certainly echoed by his departmental superiors in Ottawa, who, by late November, were quite convinced that a crucial and possibly decisive stage in the attempt to implement the Columbia River Treaty was rapidly approaching, and who moved to prepare a comprehensive assessment of the situation as it then appeared. The task took a fortnight, before the document was completed as a memorandum for the Cabinet on the Columbia River Treaty. In the interim, drafts were circulated to members of the Cabinet, and to some degree were modified in the light of their suggestions.

The argument in this memorandum was carefully reasoned. Correctly, it noted that the essential question had become one of determining whether or not an arrangement could be worked out that would be better than no treaty at all. It felt in the light of two negotiating meetings that it was unrealistic to think in terms of a sale at above four mills. The views of the senior departmental staff and their minister came through clearly, for the consequences of a four-mill sale of the downstream power benefit for thirty years, if associated with 4 percent American financing, were listed in detail. These ranged from payment for the three storages, to a reminder that there would be another thirty years' downstream benefit to come, to the substantial inflow of American currency, to the multiplier effect of the development on the Canadian economy. The prospect that without a treaty the development of the Canadian river might be economically unfeasible was not overlooked. Attention was drawn to the fact that the return to Canada would be substantially better than that accruing from the now anticipated international sales from the Hamilton and Nelson River projects where the American market price would be higher, but would be significantly offset by very high transmission charges. The memorandum drew attention to two additional alternatives. One indicated that, if the Peace River initially was to meet all of the province's domestic energy needs, deferring Mica storage two to three years after the treaty deadline would make the whole development cheaper to finance. The other involved abandoning the treaty, but seeking a new agreement with the United States whereby the Mica Dam would be built, but that at the Arrow site dropped. If full first-added credit could be retained for Mica, the memorandum continued, this last arrangement would have substantial economic value, although it was seen as inferior to the full treaty plan if a 4 mill sale and 4½ percent financing could be realized.

Finally, the memorandum returned to the forthcoming December meetings. It recommended categorically that the federal government support the concept of the profitable export of surplus hydro-electric energy including the sale of the downstream benefits. And it pointed out that it would be impossible for the officials representing the federal government to press and argue for better terms unless they could say—without having to commit the government—that the government of Canada was definitely ready to agree to a sale if the terms were right. If the worst materialized, and no agreement seemed in prospect, it advanced two further suggestions. One was that Ottawa approach the Americans at the ministerial level to see what could be done. The other, with an eye on a resolution in Victoria, suggested considering extending the offer of federal Canadian financing to include one-half the transmission costs in British Columbia. And, it suggested, that in view of the long-range benefits to Canada from the treaty, and the possibility that some American capital might be available, if necessary the federal contribution to the financing of the entire development might be provided at a 4½ percent interest rate.

At least one deputy minister lost no time in urging individual ministers to carry the whole matter to the Cabinet while there was still time for a decision to be taken. On December 13 he was able to tell ministerial personnel in writing that he had learned from the American embassy that British Columbia's proposal for financing at American agency interest rates was going as far as President Kennedy, and that a 4 mill net price for Canadian downstream power was a possibility only if the California intertie were to be built as a public project. Subsequently, on December 17, he was able to send forward the additional information that it was now very likely that the United States would agree to prepayments for the power sale, that it would offer probably 4 mills net for a constant block of power over thirty years, that March 1963 was its absolute deadline, and that President Kennedy was being asked to approve the intertie as a public project.

Ministerial and deputy ministerial effort notwithstanding, it is not at all clear that their memorandum did go before the whole Cabinet, but it certainly was examined at a meeting of the Cabinet Committee on December 17. The debate there was a far-ranging one, but in the end the federal sales negotiation representatives were told simply that their instructions remained as they had been for the first meeting in September.

Another Round of International Bargaining. When the international bargaining was resumed on December 19 at Vancouver, the Canadian federal representatives thus had to make it clear immediately that their role was no different from what it had been at the two previous meetings. Once again British Columbia's position was put by Dr. Keenleyside, who reviewed the negotiations to that point, outlined the difficulties for the province in the suggestions that had been made, and wondered if some purchase agreement might not be worked out. In reply American spokesmen countered with the changes which had taken place in the American power situation since 1960, and with the statement that their country could drop the treaty without major economic loss. But the possibility of effecting lower power costs in both countries with it was recognized, and the American delegation chairman went on to add that scars which would last a long time would be the result if the treaty were abandoned, and flood damage with possible loss of life were to ensue. He made it clear that the United States was disturbed by the criticism which had been associated with the delay, and felt it undesirable that the end result of all the labour be an unfriendly Canada. Against this background he presented an offer, dated December 18, which he assured those present had been cleared with five different federal agencies at the highest level.

The substance of the United States proposal was as follows: that country undertook to obtain firm assurances prior to ratification from utilities in the United States for the purchase of the Canadian share of the downstream power benefit and for an escalating amount of Canadian generated power (to keep the quantum purchased constant). The price suggested was a probable maximum of 3.75 mills per kwh (4 mills Canadian) at 60 percent load factor, and the sale was to be for a thirty year period. Furthermore, the United States undertook to do its best to obtain firm assurances of an advance payment (discounted at 4–4½ percent) for about 26 percent of the downstream benefit power, and a short-term loan—in effect an advance payment for the flood control payments (again discounted). It declared its willingness to work out a rescheduling of Mica—if Canada so desired—and to explore the prospect of an advance payment by purchasers of the remaining 74 percent of the entitlement. One additional suggestion which the Americans made was that Canada proceed to ratify the treaty—as this would considerably help United States' planning and the raising of the finances mentioned above—but withhold the exchange of the appropriate instruments until the sale and the financing had been arranged. Questioning from federal Canadian representatives elicited the information that Mica's credit position under this arrangement would depend upon the length of its deferment, and the prepayment for flood control would be made to the government of Canada. There was some discussion of the exchange of ratifications. Dr. Shrum saw no insurmountable problems here but did direct attention to the quite obvious fact that if the market for power produced in British Columbia were—save for the export referred to in the American proposal —restricted to that within the province, one or other of the major projects in the province could not be proceeded with at their normal rate of construction. His point, of course, was that the difficulty could be resolved for British Columbia if the United States would purchase more power. When the American negotiators' chairman, Mr. White, neatly summed up the alternatives facing Canada as being either the deferment of one or other of the projects or going ahead with simultaneous construction, taking a chance on future markets in the United States, Dr. Shrum seemed to feel the latter option unrealistic, and observed that the project deferred would not be that on the Peace. At one point in the proceedings the American chairman enquired as to the extent to which Canadian financial assistance was available for British Columbia, and observed that it hardly seemed reasonable to expect his country to become involved in project financing just because the province of British Columbia did not wish the assistance of the government of Canada. Reasonable or not, all present knew that nothing else than this was Mr. Bennett's objective. Both groups of Canadian negotiators, furthermore, saw substantial advantages accruing to their respective jurisdictions in such an arrangement.

Assessment and Advice From the Canadian Technicians. Quite obviously the Americans had not met the basic propositions advanced by the British Columbians on September 11 and 12, but they had gone some way toward them. Technical evaluation was clearly required before the federal and provincial officials could indicate to their principals what the offer really meant, and the significant point to note is that the evaluation was a joint federal-provincial effort. After returning to Ottawa briefly for Christmas, Mr. MacNabb joined three British Columbians (Messrs. Kidd, Kennedy, and Purcell) to produce, by January 11, a six-chapter, three-appendix report. Their analysis is important, for it represented at this point in time the considered opinion of the four technical advisers in Canada who best understood the intricacies of the proposed power sale. What they sought to do was to evaluate the American proposal in the light of the three alternatives which faced British Columbia. One of these was the development of the three Canadian treaty storage projects, the machining of Mica as soon as permitted by provincial loads, and the deferment of the Peace—charging the $29 millions already invested there to the Columbia at 5 percent. The second alternative involved the development of Duncan and Arrow only, the sale of the downstream benefits accruing from them, and the deferment of Mica's completion until it could be operative both as storage and generating project in 1978. The third alternative was the same as the second, except that Mica would serve as a storage project for the years 1971–78. Studies of each of these three alternatives were made—with and without allowances for inflation of costs. Without inflation they estimated that the revenues accruing to British Columbia over thirty years would pay the capital costs and the operating and maintenance costs of the three treaty storages. In addition, some $47 millions would be available to machine Mica if it was deferred as a storage and generation project to 1978, and some $14 millions if Mica storage and generation were made operational in 1971. Under these circumstances, the power available at the Mica site was estimated to cost between .7 and 1.2 mills per kwh—depending on the alternative selected. The marketing dilemma quite clearly bothered them, for they could see no assured sale for Mica generation until about 1978 if the Peace was constructed as scheduled to meet domestic loads. "Without inflation," they argued, "it is not prudent from an academic viewpoint to construct Mica storage dam for purposes of obtaining downstream benefits only."[57] With inflation, the American proposal was seen as still having advantages for Canada, although now over thirty years the revenues would cover all operating and maintenance expenses, but only 90 percent of the capital cost of the storage projects. Even here the cost of Mica generation at site would be only 2.2–2.7 mills per kwh, depending upon the alternative selected. They were very conscious of, and listed, the assumptions which they had been required to make concerning the uncertainties of the construction-sale period. The most obvious one was the operative interest rate, but others concerned the prospect that a deferred Mica might not hold on to its treaty credit position, and the prospect that Ottawa might not approve a power export to firm up the downstream power benefit. In all, they favoured the completion of Mica in 1971 if both storage and generating operations could commence there at that time. If no market existed for Mica energy at that time, under inflationary conditions they did not categorically endorse a deferment of Mica storage, but suggested that one should be carefully considered, and if it were to be deferred until 1978, they suggested that no commitment should be made at that time for the sale of the downstream benefit.

These men were well aware of the strength of the political commitment in Ottawa and Victoria to the Mica and Peace River projects, respectively, and of the difficulties involved in delaying either. Their report, furthermore, had not really made the politicians' decision-making any easier. They were so fearful, however, that the impasse would continue that they added a special appendix on the results of a failure to accept the American proposal or some modification of it by April 1963. They drew attention to the hydro and storage projects which the Americans would almost certainly proceed with in the face of further Canadian delay, and emphasized the precipitate way in which the flood control and power benefits accruing to Canadian storage would decline under these circumstances. Were the operation of the treaty to be delayed until 1978, they argued, American projects might well have taken up all of the flood control values, and perhaps only 50 percent or even less of the power values available to upstream storage would remain. In this situation they affirmed that the Duncan and Arrow Dams would probably not be economically justified, an entirely new agreement would be required, and almost certainly not attainable. Thus the consequence of non-ratification "in the near future"[58] they saw as the loss of the downstream benefits (a major and very economic resource). But they went further, as they stressed that no evidence existed to ensure that an independent Canadian development after 1978 would be economically feasible. The downstream benefit and the renewable resource which the treaty made viable on the Columbia River in Canada were felt to sum to approximately 4 million kw of dependable capacity. There was no prospect of misunderstanding this message, or of the warning which it really conveyed to both governments in Canada.

The three British Columbia technicians spelled it out again in a covering letter to Drs. Keenleyside and Shrum, which, also, in effect, advised acting on the American suggestion of an early Canadian ratification—with a delayed exchange of the implementing instruments. Dr. Keenleyside, who had come to play an increasingly responsible role in the negotiations as the co-chairman of the designated Canadian entity, was no less positive in his letter transmitting the technicians' report and letter to Premier Bennett. He listed at least six reasons for not allowing the American proposal to be dropped. There is no official record of the premier's reaction to the American proposal, but his public quip on January 8, 1963, in which he confirmed the 4 mill figure and described it as "good as a starter"[59] seems to have summarized his viewpoint neatly. At the same time he reaffirmed his determination to reach his well-known objectives.

In Ottawa the technicians' report was examined at the most senior levels of the public service. From this review emerged a memorandum to the Cabinet which was attached to the technical evaluation, and which unequivocally endorsed the position taken by the technicians. Whether this document ever was examined by the Cabinet or by the Cabinet Committee is not certain. What is unquestionable is that by this date the federal Cabinet had more pressing issues before it, which involved the very life of the government, and indeed, in combination, led to its defeat in the House of Commons on February 5, 1963. Thereafter an April general election was to be the major concern of all parties alike; whatever the risks, the Columbia River Treaty would have to wait. Just what the Conservative Cabinet would have done with the technical staff recommendation had the government not fallen is an interesting subject for conjecture. Mr. Fulton, one of the Cabinet ministers most vitally concerned, but one who was opting out of federal politics at this time, reflects that he "doesn't know."[60]

The 1963 Election Campaign. A final look at the manner in which the great debate on the merits of the Columbia River Treaty was conducted during the fall and winter of 1962–63 will serve as a backdrop to some concluding comments on the 1963 election campaign. During these months the Diefenbaker government, beset from many quarters, and painfully wrestling with its policy position on this issue, was clearly in no mood to do its thinking in public. Twice in the fall it successfully fended off attempts by Mr. Pearson to initiate a parliamentary examination of the Columbia deadlock. Still, opposition party spokesmen were able to attack the government on two occasions. In the Debate on the Address at the beginning of the fall Session, the freshman Liberal member for Coast-Capilano (Vancouver) Dr. Jack Davis, a parliamentarian with competence in engineering and in power economics, in his maiden speech, deplored Ottawa's failure to consider the broad range of energy sources available to utilities in British Columbia, and described the treaty, as interpreted by the Diefenbaker government, as "nothing short of a fiasco."[61] He welcomed the newly announced power export policy as realistic although "too late in coming," before advancing the suggestion to which we have already referred—that the whole arrangement might be salvaged if the downstream benefit were sold at a profit and paid for in advance by a lump sum which he suggested might be $500 millions. Two months later Dr. Davis spoke again, and on this occasion argued strongly for a complete renegotiation of the treaty. By now he was convinced that a treaty should not specify any particular projects at all.[62] Two New Democratic Party speakers in the same debate (Messrs. Herridge and Berger) made clear their party's support for the "McNaughton Plan." The Liberal member for Kootenay East, Mr. Byrne, shared their view that the treaty "should be renegotiated."[63]

Elsewhere, the quietness of the debate may well have been partly the result of the hiatus over the power sale, partly the result of sheer exhaustion, and partly the consequence of the publication of a remarkably comprehensive four-page supplement in a Vancouver daily paper written by a widely respected journalist, P. L. Sherman. In it Mr. Sherman, who had been given access to the record of the inter- and intra-national negotiations by both Mr. Williston and Mr. Fulton, went some way toward clearing the air and deflating the claims of all partisans determined to direct, or at least influence, Columbia decision-making.[64] But the public exchanges did not cease. Although the federal Progressive Conservatives rather played down the issue, Mr. Fulton, moving directly into the provincial arena, was much less inhibited, and was still prepared to suggest that the Peace River's development might be a bluff (with its markets and its power still not settled), and that British Columbia's vacillating approach to the treaty could well spur the Americans to look elsewhere for power. Mr. Williston vigorously defended his government's power policy in his annual address to the provincial Legislature on the subject on February 9. He was especially critical of the way in which, in a reference to the opposition parties' espousal of General McNaughton's claims, they had sought "to squeeze every last ounce of political advantage out of a man who has made his mark, is now past his prime, never has been an acknowledged hydraulic engineer, and now stands alone."[65]

Throughout this period Mr. Strachan maintained his critical approach to the Peace River development, and to some features of the Columbia planning. Some of his colleagues, such as Mr. George Hobbs, repeated their categorical support of the "McNaughton Plan," and condemned the treaty for giving away the control of the whole river basin.[66]

Liberal party opinion remained as variable as it had been a year earlier. Mr. Pearson, in his major election campaign in British Columbia on April 1, spoke rather vaguely of the need to reconsider the treaty arrangements, but as election day approached his comments on the adequacy of the treaty became increasingly cautious, and almost non-existent outside British Columbia. Some federal Liberals, however, were not so careful; they accepted General McNaughton's denigration of the treaty, and were prepared over the winter of 1962–63, to denounce British Columbia's "double-cross"[67] of Ottawa in the international bargaining. Mr. Perrault on the other hand, was more dispassionate. While directing a good deal of criticism at the British Columbia Energy Board, whose objectivity he challenged, he wondered at the beginning of the new session of the provincial Legislature if the time had not come for the premier to take the opposition leaders into his confidence.[68] During the 1963 election campaign, Dr. Davis went so far as to call the treaty a "sell-out of our resources"[69] in the first of five articles on the treaty published in *The Vancouver Sun*. At this time he repeated his belief that a sale of most or all of the downstream benefit was the only way to salvage something from the treaty arrangements in the short run. Indeed he argued the merit of caution with respect to building big dams anywhere in times of high interest rates and unproven markets. Direct provincial employment in construction and operation associated with such projects was greatly over-rated, he insisted, and the costs of transporting electrical energy were underplayed. He warned against the fallacies inherent in the "power brings industry" thesis; for the immediate future, he claimed, the sound thing to do was to concentrate on low power rates which would mean keeping construction costs and excess capacity at a minimum.

It cannot be emphasized too strongly that these views were Dr. Davis' alone; he was not the enunciator of party policy on this matter, and, indeed, was to revise many of his criticisms of the treaty when, shortly, he became a member of the Pearson administration. But at this time he was chairman of a Power Study Group in the Liberal party caucus, and those who were vigorously opposed to the treaty, including a number of critics clustered around General McNaughton, tended to regard his views as inspired. They certainly hoped for some form of public re-assessment of the treaty—in the manner Mr. Davis had suggested in the preceding December—before any move was made to further negotiation with the United States.

Two final developments must be recorded in this broad survey of the Canadian decision-making in the now-ending Diefenbaker years. When the federal government was defeated in the House of Commons, and an election became inevitable, the United States did give Canada another reprieve, this time until midsummer 1963, in the time limit for reaching a solution. At the same time its spokesman, Mr. Udall, left no doubt that failing action then, the alternatives facing the United States would be renegotiation or a complete pull-out, and that if new alternative American projects were launched, the equal division of downstream benefits provided for in the treaty could not be retained.[70]

And on April 4, just four days before the federal election, Mr. Bennett opened the tenders for the Portage Mountain Dam on the Peace River—which was expected to cost between $90 and $100 millions. To his pleasant surprise the government received one tender for just over $73 millions. The die was certainly cast now as the premier and his colleagues observed that this made Peace costs even more attractive. At the same time he affirmed that "the Columbia looks better today than ever before."[71]

Chapter Nine

Federal-Provincial Rapprochement

Our image of the consequences of our acts is suffused
with uncertainty to the point where we are not even sure
what we are certain about.
K. Boulding, *The Image.*

Nothing is clearer from a review of the final stages of the Canadian
decision-making apropos the Columbia River, with which this chapter
now deals, than the seminal importance to it of the April 8, 1963,
election, in which the Liberal party won the largest number of seats, 129,
but not a majority in the Commons. One of the most extraordinary periods
of indeterminacy and hesitancy in Canadian policy-formation history
was about to be followed by one marked by an equally extraordinary
commitment to action. But this is to anticipate. For a few days after April
8 there was a good deal of uncertainty in Ottawa as to just what would
happen. Mr. Bennett in British Columbia, however, had no doubts whatsoever as to the constitutional implications of the result, and on April 9
urged that Mr. Pearson be named prime minister as rapidly as possible. At
the same time he declared his confidence that agreement on the Columbia
River Treaty could soon be reached, and construction could be under way
by the fall.[1] Mr. Pearson did in fact take office on April 22, 1963, naming
Mr. Paul Martin as the secretary of state for external affairs and Mr.
Arthur Laing, Premier Bennett's old opponent in provincial politics, as
minister of northern affairs and national resources. Subsequently he
selected Dr. Jack Davis as one of his parliamentary secretaries.

Throughout April, provincial government spokesmen such as Mr.
Bonner and Mr. Williston were openly confident that the "knowledgeable"
(Mr. Williston's phrase) members of the new national administration,
after consultation with the federal government's technical personnel,
would realize that the treaty was fundamentally sound, and that renegotia-

tion was not required. They suggested that the new government might require a face-saving manoeuvre. In their confidence, at least, the Social Crediters were prescient, for, in the early days of the new government, as it planned to make good its election campaign promises to get the country moving, and to institute "Sixty Days of Decision," a considerable in-camera debate does appear to have ensued between treaty revisionists such as Dr. Davis on the one hand, and, on the other, the federal public servants who had assessed the implications of the Americans' December 1972 purchase offer, and who feared the consequences of any further delay. But the exchanges were short-lived; within a very few days Mr. Pearson and colleagues at Cabinet level had become convinced that the province's objectives were anything but unreasonable, and that a massive parliamentary review of the treaty before a sale agreement had been effected would probably jeopardize the whole arrangement. Quite clearly in the calculus which the federal policy-makers used, the potential gains from such a review were not felt to offset potential losses. Consequently, on April 23, Mr. Laing revealed that top priority would be given to implementing the Columbia River Treaty, and that any change required in it would be effected by an exchange of notes.[2] Two days later press reports from Ottawa suggested that Mr. Pearson would present a plan for action on the Columbia River and for modifications to the treaty to President Kennedy when the two met at Hyannis Port on May 10 and 11, 1963.

This was precisely the course which Mr. Pearson did follow on his visit to the American president. He left with Mr. Kennedy a memorandum which, on an illustrative basis, listed five aspects of the treaty which had been the object of domestic Canadian criticism and which, as he put it, "will require some modification or clarification,"[3] appropriately, it was suggested, via a protocol to the original agreement. And it went on to give the Americans the assurance which had never been forthcoming from the previous Canadian administration. "Subject to agreement on satisfactory terms," the memorandum declared, "the Government of Canada would be prepared to authorize the sale of downstream power benefits within the United States for a definite period or periods."[4]

Upon his return from the United States, Mr. Pearson wrote Mr. Bennett a friendly letter, dated May 17, in which he told of this meeting, and enclosed a copy of the document he had left with Mr. Kennedy. He indicated that he had neither expected nor received any commitment on the matters which he had raised, but added he thought it clear "that the United States government would be prepared to discuss items for inclusion in a protocol if and when agreement on the points that should be covered had been reached between the governments of Canada and British Columbia." Politely here Mr. Pearson was relaying the second major decision which he and his colleagues had taken at the end of April. They were not prepared to move one step further in direct negotiations with the Americans until the two Canadian jurisdictions had reached an explicit understanding, and had put that understanding in writing.

1. THE FIRST CANADA-BRITISH COLUMBIA AGREEMENT

The government of British Columbia was not in the least perturbed by the federal Cabinet's procedural position. From the province's point of view the crucial decision taken in Ottawa had been the agreement to approve a sale of the Canadian downstream power benefit entitlement, if one could be effected on favourable terms, and it soon made clear its willingness to work toward and to commit itself to a federal-provincial compact. Arrangements were quickly made for a meeting in Ottawa on June 3 and 4 between Mr. Pearson, Mr. Bennett, Cabinet associates, and technical personnel from both governments to prepare a formal Canada-British Columbia agreement on the respective responsibilities of the two jurisdictions covering the implementation of the Columbia River Treaty. Mr. Pearson did not stay long with the two groups when they assembled on the dates in question, but several matters were settled before his departure. He designated Mr. Martin as the Cabinet minister who would chair the federal group, and who would be responsible over-all for the negotiations with the Americans and for Parliamentary examination and ratification in Canada. Mr. Bennett made it very clear that the province had no objection to the points raised with President Kennedy, and emphasized both that the province was keen to get on with the job and that Mica generation would be phased in with the first stage of the Peace development. He noted in addition that there would be surplus power at times which in his opinion it would be sensible to export—if the power was not required on a national grid. Candidly he described the export ban as an anachronism. Mr. Pearson hedged on this issue, but did indicate that a new federal position would have to be enunciated. Mr. Pearson made two other major points. He stressed his government's commitment to an extensive examination of the treaty and related agreements in Parliament; he thought that the process would be difficult, that the river's development should not be a partisan matter, and indicated that he would be pleased if Mr. Bennett could forestall criticism by meeting with the leaders of the opposition parties while he was in Ottawa. And he agreed that the province should have prime responsibility for negotiating the sales agreement (with federal representatives participating). In response to a query, Mr. Bennett suggested that Ottawa should "set the goalposts" within which provincial representatives might reach a settlement with the Americans.

In the exchanges which followed on June 3 and 4 the provincial representatives drew attention to the possibility that they could get a better price than that inherent in the December 1962 American offer, and expressed the hope that it would be received in annual lump sums spanning the construction period. If the price were right, the premier indicated, the province would need no federal help in financing storage construction, and would have the cost of machining Mica wholly or partly covered as well. Provincial spokesmen discussed the rate of load growth, and its relationship to the machining of Mica. They favoured a thirty year sale, and were optimistic that it could be covered by a single contract, approved by two governments and signed by one power entity for each party. On this occasion the provincial spokesmen did show some real sensitivity to the sensitivities of others; when they returned to the issue of power exports they disclaimed any role as advocates of a change in federal policy (although they had argued for one for two years). They asserted that they would not oppose such a change, and that there was a possibility (although only subsequent negotiations could confirm this) that the right to sell firming power "might materially affect the prospects of attaining the highest price from the United States."[5] Mr. Martin raised two additional matters—letters from the premier of Saskatchewan on the treaty's provisions concerning diversion for consumptive use, and the role which Mr. Robert B. Anderson, a former United States secretary of the treasury, was playing on behalf of the province. The fact that Mr. Anderson, a friend of Mr. Bennett, was representing the premier in his search for an American corporate buyer at a satisfactory price had been revealed to the press by Mr. Bennett on May 22. Mr. Bennett appears to have described his association with Mr. Anderson and to have expressed the hope that Mr. Martin would meet with him.[6] Provincial representatives expressed some concern over possible delays involved in federal licensing procedures under the International Rivers Improvements and Navigational Waters Protection Acts, but federal representatives discounted such fears.

Although the basic decisions were made by Messrs. Pearson, Martin, and Bennett in Ottawa on June 3 and 4, preparing, exchanging, and modifying copies of the document embodying them was to take the balance of that month. The drafting was tight, and in the light of memories of recent controversy and of an absence of much helpful precedent, a good deal of it was disputed. But both parties were determined to avoid deadlock, and the final form of the highly detailed six-page agreement was settled on during a meeting between Mr. Martin and Dr. Gilbert Kennedy, British Columbia's deputy attorney-general, in Ottawa on June 26. In it, all proprietary rights, title, and interests arising under the treaty were declared to belong absolutely to British Columbia. The province for its part undertook to meet all the construction and operating requirements of the treaty, to do all it was capable of doing constitutionally to carry out its terms. Canada agreed to nominate the B.C. Hydro and Power Authority as the Canadian entity, and agreed that the province could nominate one of the two Canadian members of the Permanent Engineering Board established by the treaty's provisions. Canada undertook to obtain the concurrence of the province before pursuing a number of courses of action, such as terminating the treaty, and agreed also to endeavour to obtain the consent of the United States to a number of others—such as a diversion not provided for in the treaty, if requested to do so by British Columbia. The province, on the other hand, committed itself to indemnify Canada in respect of any liabilities to the United States save where these are the result of an action or a failure to act on the part of the federal government. The agreement expressly provided for the sale of the downstream power benefits, subject to an approval of terms by both Canada and British Columbia. Canada was declared to have no financing obligation whatsoever. The province did undertake to commit the downstream power and flood control payments to the financing of the treaty storages. Both governments agreed that the construction and operation of treaty projects should be subject to the laws of Canada and British Columbia, and resolved to do everything possible to expedite the issuance of the necessary licences and permits.[7]

Mr. Bennett, who returned to Victoria on June 5, publicly declared himself well pleased with the meeting in Ottawa, praised Mr. Pearson's approach, reaffirmed his two-river policy, and maintained that Peace River power would be laid down for 3¾ mills per kwh in Vancouver. But there was no let-up in his struggle with Mr. Fulton, who, he declared, had wrecked one government and was now after another. A decision taken by the provincial Cabinet to call a by-election for July 15 to fill a vacancy in the Columbia riding—in the Upper Columbia Valley—was to have, briefly, an unanticipated consequence for Mr. Bennett. The federal government was well aware of the extent to which the provincial Liberals had endorsed renegotiation of the treaty, and was conscious of the manner in which an agreement with the province could be used against them in the Columbia by-election. It therefore delayed giving the agreement formal, final approval. But Mr. Bennett was having none of this. Mr. Williston was sent to Ottawa, the documents were formally signed on July 8 in time for Mr. Bennett to use in the dying stages of the by-election campaign, which his party fought on the power issue, and won.[8]

Additional Federal-Provincial Staff Analyses. While basic differences were being resolved at the political and constitutional-legal level, the specialist advisers to both Canadian governments were hard at work on studies in preparation for the more technical and detailed international bargaining still to come. In British Columbia, the B.C. Hydro and Power Authority instituted an elaborate planning program to help assess and coordinate the development of the Peace, Columbia, and other river systems. As early as May 9, for instance, Hydro's senior economic analyst, Mr. J. B. Hedley, reported that, on the basis of an admittedly incomplete survey of the alternatives open to the United States should Canada not ratify, it appeared that "the benefits which the United States would obtain from their alternative program would, in the short term at least, approach the benefits which they would receive under the Columbia River Treaty."[9] He was especially concerned about what would happen to the treaty arrangement if the United States sought to insert the Knowles and Bruce's Eddy projects into their Columbia system on a first-added basis.[10] Mr. Denis Kennedy, Hydro's division manager for major resources, followed this up with a letter in a similar vein to Dr. Keenleyside on May 21. He drew attention to the fact that three United States projects (one of which Dworshak, Bruce's Eddy—was going ahead in any case) could enable the Americans to meet their full Pacific northwest power loads until 1973, and, only two to three years after the treaty projects, would provide the same primary flood control as well.[11] Assuming that capital was available for the American power projects at 2½ percent interest he estimated that the average cost of the additional power produced by these three projects (at-site and downstream, without the treaty) to be not over 3½ mills per kwh.

During May and June the Hydro planning group proposed and circulated to provincial decision-makers analyses of a number of proposals which the province might advance in the sales negotiations to come. They were synopsized as recorded in Table 7.

Writing to Dr. Keenleyside on July 3, Mr. Kennedy in effect wrote off alternatives 1 and 2 as unrealistic, in that they appeared to be asking the Americans to pay over 6 mills per kwh for the power purchased. Alternatives 3 and 4 were seen as better than the American December 1962 offer; alternative 3 was seen as a solution which could be satisfactory and might be negotiable.

While the prospective Canadian entity's staff was reasoning thus, the personnel of the federal Water Resources Branch and the provincial Water Resources Service had re-established close contact, and had resumed extensive exchanges of information. The first problem to which they devoted their attention was the preparation of drafts of the protocol to come, for it was realized that agreement with respect to it, and on the related exchange of notes, would have to precede the negotiations on a

TABLE 7

Payment Options Assessed

Alternative American reimbursement for the Canadian entitlement to the downstream power benefit (in Canadian $)	Would meet the cost of
1. 10 annual payments of $51 millions	The capital cost of all treaty storage, and Mica generation.
2. 10 annual payments of $48.4 millions	The capital cost of all treaty storage, and 75 percent of Mica generation.
3. 10 annual payments of $35.8 millions	The capital cost of all treaty storage, and 25 percent of Mica generation.
4. A modification of the American December 1962 proposal.	

sales agreement. As early as June 12 the federal technical staff took the initiative, sending to Victoria a list of seven items which might be included in a protocol. This paper realistically reviewed the criticisms which had been directed against the treaty, discounted a number, but argued the case for some clarification and refinement of earlier interpretations. One of its interesting features was its lack of enthusiasm for the proposal that Canada sell an escalating amount of Canadian generation to make up for the decline in the downstream benefit. Rapid progress was made, for there were now no major differences in approach, only some differences in emphasis, between Ottawa and Victoria.

Consistent with their 1960 negotiating position, provincial spokesmen sought to avoid including technical details in the protocol. It seems that federal government representatives were quite candid in their references to the political necessity of being able to demonstrate that some material advantage to Canada had been gained. It seems, too, that the provincial spokesmen balked at some of the federal proposals, insisting that they would create a problem for the Americans which might have the effect of unduly prolonging the negotiations to come. When, for instance, the prospect of having the Americans agree to payments for early completion of treaty storage was advanced, it was the provincial spokesmen who were skeptical that this point would be conceded, for they envisaged it as a major alteration to the treaty.[12] One of the main arguments developed over the section of the Canadian draft protocol concerning the operation of the treaty storages. Here federal representatives stressed the importance of being able to show that Canada was free to operate the storage in her own interest—to counter the charge that the amount of storage was substantially fixed while the benefits to Canada declined. The provincial representatives did not disagree with the federal goal, but they did point out that the treaty itself and its annexes contained, especially in the requirement that the two entities agree on operating plans, very considerable protection for Canada. They did not want to give the Americans the impression that they wished to avoid the 15.5 million acre-feet commitment. In any case, the important point to note is that these differences were resolved, and at a meeting of federal and provincial representatives in Ottawa on July 24 and 25, a very close working relationship was established between the two governments. It was agreed that the province would be formally represented at the forthcoming international negotiations, with Ottawa taking the initiative concerning the protocol and exchange of notes, and Victoria doing likewise over the terms of the power sale. Each government agreed to keep the other fully informed.

2. International Negotiations over a Treaty Protocol and Power Sale

Formal diplomatic talks with the United States over the protocol were quickly arranged and were held in Ottawa on August 1 and 2, 1963. Mr. Martin, Mr. Robertson, and Mr. Ritchie were joined as Canada's representatives by Dr. Keenleyside. Before the meeting was over, agreement had been reached tentatively on a draft which was not greatly changed from the one the Canadians had presented at the beginning of the meetings, although a few of the modifications made were substantial. As the Canadians had originally drafted Article 4, for instance, a potential 720,000 cfs flow at The Dalles had been included as the figure representing the level in relation to which Canada was to provide flood protection. Not unreasonably the Americans insisted that this be 600,000 cfs—to be consistent with the treaty. The Canadian representatives wanted and got in Article I a statement defining the Canadian obligation to operate its storages for flood control purposes especially for the period sixty years and more beyond initial ratification. At the same time, the Americans insisted upon a right to call for treaty storage operation for flood control if the entities together or the Permanent Engineering Board had not been able to agree to the need for such action. The Americans did agree at this time to the inclusion of a provision for a probable increase in the flood control benefit in the event of early Canadian completion of the storages.

The Canadian representatives had begun these meetings with a reference to the constraints which they faced in the light of domestic criticism, and the federal government's minority position.[13] As they concluded, the Americans reminded the Canadians of the need for a firm Canadian response to their December 1962 purchase proposal.

Unexpected Developments in British Columbia. While these exchanges were taking place at the diplomatic level in Ottawa, British Columbians had something else to think about. On July 29, in the most stunning upset which Mr. Bennett had experienced in a decade, Chief Justice Lett of British Columbia's Supreme Court[14] found the legislation which expropriated the B.C. Electric Company and created the B.C. Hydro and Power Authority to be *ultra vires*. Mr. Justice Lett devoted over one-half of his lengthy judgment to rejecting a claim that the B.C. Electric's property should be returned forthwith to its former owner, but at the same time he indicated that the compensation stipulated was inadequate, and by a complicated formula of his own devising set a new one.[15] He also expressly rejected one of the claims advanced by counsel for the B.C. Power Corporation, to the effect that the provincial government had deliberately sought to promote ends other than the public good "by assuming control of the Electric Company in order to be able to compel it to make contracts for the bringing of power to the load centres of the Electric Company from the Peace River to the exclusion of downstream benefits from the Columbia River."[16] He held that it is not the Court's function to find on the motives underlying legislation, and that the evidence had not revealed a scheme to frustrate. But even if it had, he maintained, in the light of the recently signed Canada-British Columbia agreement, the treaty had not been frustrated and was now about to go ahead.

For a few days the level of excitement and uncertainty occasioned by this bombshell was high. Although the B.C. Power Corporation almost immediately offered to arrive at a mutually agreed-upon settlement with the government of British Columbia, and this proposal was endorsed by all the opposition parties, the provincial government at first rejected any such suggestion, and announced its determination to challenge the constitutional basis of the court's interpretation.[17] On August 1, however, Mr. Bennett revealed the government's willingness to pay the additional $21 millions to reach the judicially set compensation figure, and by August 6 his administration had indicated that it was willing to negotiate with the Power Corporation. A month of behind-the-scenes bargaining ensued before, unable to agree, the provincial government and the B.C. Power Corporation once again turned to Mr. Lett. This time he established (on September 27) a final compensatory price of just over $197,000,000—

an amount between the two figures being advanced by the contending parties.

The only direct result which the Lett judgment had on Mr. Bennett's power development policies was to produce a three-week halt to construction on the Peace River. Indirectly however it had a considerable impact, for it contributed to a noticeable rise in the political temperature of the province, and to the pressure on the premier, who, on August 22, reversing a position which he had taken earlier, announced that a general election would be held on September 30. Attributing motives is always hazardous, but it is at least a reasonable assumption that among his objectives in making this decision was a desire to strengthen his bargaining position with the officers of the B.C. Power Corporation, with his critics everywhere, and not least with the Americans over the Columbia in the months ahead. Many issues were raised during that short election campaign and no empirical studies sought to determine their relative significance in influencing voting behaviour. Leadership style in general terms certainly was one, but leadership style related to power planning and the Columbia's development certainly became another, for Mr. Bennett and Mr. Fulton presented very different programs to the public. Before the campaign was over Mr. Bennett laid his two-river policy on the line, and insisted that his administration would stand or fall on it. During his campaign he watched with satisfaction the diversion of the Peace River preparatory to actual dam construction. He denounced Mr. Fulton as a wrecker, an expert at "putting sand in the gears." Once again he emphasized the stupidity of taking back the downstream benefit, as he affirmed: "We will develop the Columbia on the sound basis of making the Americans pay for it."[18] Mr. Fulton presented a very different picture, as he attacked the premier's "arrogance," and appealed for new "standards of excellence, of principle and conduct in government behaviour." He also appealed to what he described as the province's "capacity of vision," but sought to concentrate on issues other than river development. Midway through the campaign, and against the advice of his associates, he promised, if elected premier, to shut the Peace project down in spite of the investment already made there. It would be built, he argued, when the time was right.[19]

Mr. Perrault, for the Liberals, at one stage of the campaign came out for the elimination of the High Arrow Dam, and endorsed scaling down the Peace River development, although he did concede that if Mr. Williston were correct, and the Peace were beyond the point of no return, then, whatever its merits, a two-river policy was inescapable.[20] The New Democratic Party continued its opposition to the treaty, and especially the Arrow project and the downstream power benefit sale. Mr. Strachan directed much of his attention to the accounting methods of the B.C. Hydro and Power Authority, which he claimed were designed to conceal the true costs of the Peace River development. Mr. T. C. Douglas, the NDP's national leader, argued for an immediate start on the Columbia, opposed the downstream benefit sale, and categorized the treaty arrangement as a "complete sell-out to the U.S."[21]

International Negotiations Leading to a Power Sale. Meanwhile, during August, active preparations continued to be made, especially at the staff level in British Columbia, for the impending negotiations on a power sale with the Americans. The planning group at B.C. Hydro produced a number of significant memoranda exploring such future bargaining considerations as the relationship of operative interest rates to costs (and hence to sale price), the length of the amortization period used, and the implications of the Canadian demand 'hat the purchase be effected by a single American agency. On August 22, over Dr. Keenleyside's signature, the province officially informed Ottawa that the American offer of December 1962 was not acceptable. Dr. Keenleyside's message, which had been cleared at the highest levels in Victoria, went on to cite a number of reasons for the provincial response. For example, it claimed that it would be impracticable to make B.C. Hydro responsible for vending the Canadian power entitlement in the United States, even with help. It noted, also, the absence of an assurance that all of the entitlement could be so disposed of, and designated as unacceptable the proposal that Canada sell "make up" power, firming the entitlement, at a 3.75 mills per kwh and 60 percent load factor price. Dr. Keenleyside advanced on behalf of the province the concept of a thirty-year sale arranged by single entities, with no firming Canadian generation involved, and with the American payment to be made in ten equal annual instalments. Four days later Mr. Bennett restated the province's objectives: a single American purchaser, a schedule of payments to meet treaty project costs, and a sale price of five mills or its equivalent.

Once Ottawa had received an assurance from Victoria that the forthcoming election need not have any impact on the process of international negotiation, arrangements were quickly made for a new round of international meetings, to begin in Washington on September 6 and 7. As had been the case a month earlier in the negotiations on a draft protocol, the Canadian team consisted of Mr. Paul Martin, and Messrs. G. Robertson and E. Ritchie from Ottawa, and Dr. Keenleyside from Victoria. Once again the Canadian governments provided jointly the backup staff. The Canadian team caucused ahead of time, and reached complete agreement upon objectives and tactics.

The British Columbians returned from the Washington meetings convinced that progress had been made, and pleased with Mr. Martin's efforts in support of the province's position.[22] They also found the atmosphere of the international exchanges more satisfactory than they had at any of the bargaining during the previous year. One obvious reason for this, of course, was Ottawa's categoric approval of a sale of the downstream power benefit—if the terms were favourable. Another was that at the September 6–7, 1963, meeting the Canadians received an indication that the United States had taken seriously British Columbia's requirement that there be a single purchaser—although there were still major difficulties to be overcome in this connection. A good deal of time was devoted at Washington to the Mica project, as American spokesmen indicated that the Pacific northwest could probably absorb the Canadian downstream power derived from Arrow and Duncan Lake regulation, but that from Mica either would be unsaleable, or would have to go to California. The Canadian response to this was to stress how fundamental Mica was to the treaty, and to draw attention to the possibility of some rescheduling within treaty limits.

One issue which the American negotiators and other interested members of Congress and of the administration in Washington had pressed upon the Canadians concerned the sheer magnitude of the calls upon the American capital market which the simultaneous development of the Peace and Columbia rivers would entail. In conversation both with Mr. Martin and Dr. Keenleyside, Senator Magnuson, Mr. McGeorge Bundy, and the Hon. Ivan White had all expressed doubts about the ability of the American capital market to meet these demands. The bland toughness of the provincial position is nicely reflected in Dr. Keenleyside's comment on this matter in his report to the premier. "I told them," he wrote, "that in my opinion the two projects were so advantageous and promised such a satisfactory return that I was confident, as I am sure you were, that the necessary funds could be obtained."[23] Inevitably, much involved sparring over the two-day period had concerned the sale price. The Canadian representatives stressed the unattractiveness, from their perspective, of having to face at least two intangibles—future interest rates, and the rate at which in future the downstream power benefit would decline. They certainly insisted that a 3.75 mill per kwh price would be too low, and pressed hard the concept that it ought to be possible to estimate an assured though declining amount of downstream power, to raise money on it, and to regard the whole transaction as the purchase of a commodity rather than an export of capital. Out of all the exchanges had come no explicit indication that a higher price would be forthcoming from an American purchaser, but the Canadians had returned with an impression that the

American rigidity on price might be relaxed. After two days the general exchanges of views had gone as far as seemed feasible; staff groups were designated to concentrate on the technical issues which had been raised. One (Work Group No. 1) had an international technical membership,[24] and was concerned with seeking a consensus on the changing nature and the quantity of the downstream power benefits during the proposed sale period. Work Group No. 2, with a purely American membership, was set up to suggest the organization required for the conclusion of sales contracts in the United States and for their financing.

Three months were to pass before another full-scale meeting of the negotiators was to take place, but much was to happen in the interval. The Social Credit government won its fifth straight electoral victory on September 30, removing any doubts as to the direction of provincial power planning and the strength of Mr. Bennett's position. And eight days later Mr. Mitchell Sharp, the Liberal minister of trade and commerce, cleared away once and for all any ambiguities and uncertainties about the federal government's policy on the export of electrical energy. In the House of Commons he announced a new national policy as he came out clearly for interconnection agreements and interties between the utilities of Canada and the United States. Much as the Conservatives had done a year previously (as Mr. Diefenbaker quickly reminded him), Mr. Sharp categorically endorsed the wisdom of exporting large blocks of firm power "to permit the development of such large remote hydro or other power projects which would not be viable unless supported by the export for long periods of a sufficient proportion of the power generated." "The old aphorism that an export sale, once established, cannot be terminated without hardship in the export market, and danger of international friction," he continued, "is no longer valid if the export contract is made with a public utility in the United States under reasonable terms and conditions."[25]

The staff groups set up at Washington in September worked through that month, October, and November. Work Group No. 1, on which the Canadians were represented, commissioned extensive computer studies, using facilities made available by the Bonneville Power Administration in Portland. On November 27 it produced a considerable report. When faced with the task of trying to agree on a projection of the downstream benefit, the technicians inevitably had to posit a long series of assumptions, ranging from load growth estimates to the treatment of Grand Coulee pumping loads, to irrigation depletions, to service dates for Canadian storage, to the implementation of Kootenay-Columbia River diversion, to Kootenay Lake regulation, evaporation losses, twenty- and thirty-year stream flow records,[26] and the impact of generation at Hanford. These were all cited, without argument—although the work group itself had not been able to reach agreement concerning some of them "either because differing interpretations of the treaty were possible or they hinged on matters about which the treaty was silent."[27] The work group's report showed the results for a number of different assumptions, but volunteered no conclusions.

When the report was sent to the diplomatic negotiators, the Canadian technical staff prepared a memorandum on the problems involved, pointing out the need for a clarification of some of the assumptions highlighted by the work group, and the need for agreement on them, before treaty ratification. Inevitably they discussed many technical issues relevant to the measurement of the downstream power benefit and the rate of its decline. Attention was drawn to the manner in which a high rate of American load growth would accelerate the decline in the downstream entitlement, and how, in contradiction to the Americans, the Canadians, in bargaining, had found themselves predicting a lower one. The conclusion of the Canadian technicians was clear. "There is no rational method by which these forecasts can be reconciled."[28] The report dealt also with a ticklish problem which had arisen in the attempt to agree upon the method of determining the decline in the capacity benefit. If the Canadian technicians had stopped here, it is hard to see how their efforts would have greatly assisted the Canadian negotiators; uncertainty would simply have been made more explicit. In British Columbia, however, Messrs. G. J. A. Kidd and W. D. Kennedy, two of the technical advisers to the provincial government and B.C. Hydro who now were closest to the details of this intricate exercise, had come to the conclusion as early as October 17 that the long-range estimates of the downstream power benefit were simply not significant, that the benefit could not be known accurately until it occurred and was measured under the treaty,[29] and that instead British Columbia should sell the whole of it, for a fixed payment in advance, leaving the Americans free to accept the loss if the benefits were smaller, or the gain if larger than expected.

On November 27 Mr. Kidd wrote an important memorandum for Mr. Williston in which he relayed these conclusions of Mr. Kennedy and himself, and, at the same time, enclosed the report of Work Group No. 1 and the comments of the Canadian technicians. He forwarded also a memorandum which he had written to Mr. Kennedy on October 17 summarizing the difficulties which the technicians faced. In his October 17 paper he had made the point that comparison with one's best alternatives is the only way to evaluate a seeming bargain. He had noted that there were no detailed studies providing at-site costs of power from such alternative sources as development on the Peace (first stage), on the Clearwater and the Homathko Rivers, but he surmised that such at-site power would cost roughly 2½ mills per kwh. On October 17 he had felt that to provide the equivalent power cost at Mica on the Columbia during the thirty-year sale period, the absolute minimum annual payment from the United States for ten years would have to be of the order of $26 millions—or arranged otherwise, a sum having a present worth of about $250 millions. At the same time he had proposed that Canada should ask for "approximately ten equal payments"[30] with a present worth of approximately $350 millions, and that a careful study of all aspects of the sale agreement would be necessary if the United States offered less than $300 millions. He had suggested in October on the basis of the current estimates of the downstream power benefit the figure of $350 million present worth would represent a sale at approximately 5 mills, and $250 millions one at roughly 3.6 mills per kwh.

Mr. Kennedy reported by letter to Dr. Keenleyside on December 3 in much the same vein, as he referred to the manner in which the discrepancy between the Canadian and American estimates of load growth in the United States alone accounted for a variation of 17 percent in the present worth of the estimated Canadian entitlement. He also noted that the Americans would derive advantages in coordinating their generating plants—which "may not be strictly related to the Canadian capacity and energy entitlements."

The records available do not enable us to follow the Kennedy-Kidd assessment of the Canadian tactical position further than to indicate that it appears to have been accepted promptly in Victoria and Ottawa, and that arrangements were quickly made to reconvene the international negotiators for what were to be the most crucial of the sales negotiations. (Both the Canadian governments and the Americans were becoming acutely conscious of the cost of the long delay in approving the treaty.)[31] In the early stages of the negotiations which began in Ottawa on December 9 the Canadian representatives[32] made it clear that they were now unwilling to make available for sale a block of energy of constant size.[33] Soon the bargaining became specific, and the Canadian representatives, following their new tactic, advanced as a fair return which would cover costs ten annual payments of $40 millions (Canadian) beginning on October 1, 1964.[34] After some deliberation the Americans countered with an offer of $309 millions, including the flood control payments, and made in eight annual instalments beginning in July 1965—if the sale covered sixty years. At the same time the United States declared its willingness to consider buying additional power.

In this manner and from this position the bargaining advanced, with the Canadians rejecting a sixty-year sale, the Americans denigrating Mica's effectiveness, and both parties agreeing that, in future, a British Columbia-

Bonneville Power administration coordination agreement would be mutually beneficial. At one point a rather extraordinary bargaining ploy from the Canadian side helped produce an improvement in the American offer. A technical adviser from Ottawa who had discovered an error in the treaty which, as it stood, produced an extremely favourable, if unintended, advantage for Canada, argued vigorously that the treaty be interpreted as it read. Mr. Martin's bargaining position was reinforced, and the United States did move to obtain a Canadian remission of the fortuitous advantage. The American representatives reported their willingness to consider increasing the estimate of the Canadian power entitlement by using a thirty rather than a twenty-year stream flow record, and by treating Grand Coulee irrigation pumping as part of the general system load rather than as a station service load,[35] on the understanding that the United States position on the paragraph in dispute be accepted. Still later, by shifting from a high to an intermediate load growth estimate they were able to improve their offer further—making it now eight annual payments totalling approximately $342 millions (U.S.)—still including the flood control payments. Subsequently a "recalculation" raised this to $344.2 millions (U.S.) or $370 millions in Canadian funds, and the Americans suggested that this sum could be improved upon if the government of Canada acting as a fiduciary were to take the sum to be paid for the purchase of Canada's power entitlement and invest unutilized portions of it during the construction period, not least because Canadian interest rates in general were higher than those in the United States. The Canadian representatives were well aware of the possible increment to be acquired in this way, but they were aware also of the not inconsiderable investment responsibility involved, and, in any case, were not prepared to settle for this. They rejected the offer involving a receipt, over time, of $370 millions, and suggested instead payments adding up to $419 millions (Canadian)—ten of $35 millions, plus $60 millions for flood control. At this point the Americans dug in, and raised the proposition that the government of Canada assume a trusteeship role in connection with any prepayment, not least to keep interest rates down. The bargaining reached a stalemate, which ultimately was represented graphically on a blackboard table prepared by Messrs. Kidd and Goldhammer, and is here reproduced in Table 8.

Then Mr. Williston suggested that the difference be split. Eventually, *ad referendum*, and on the assumption that no further problems would arise out of the sales agreement, both the American chairman and Mr. Martin agreed to it. (Mr. Martin's role in these final negotiations appears to have been very skilfully played, and crucial. He had established an extraordinarily close working relationship with Mr. Bennett, who had confided in him, but not Mr. Williston, what, in dollar terms and from the

TABLE 8

Comparison of Late Stage Bargaining Positions
Concerning the Sale of the Canadian Downstream Power Entitlement

(In millions of U.S. dollars)	Eight Annual Payments Beginning July 1, 1965	Present Worth July 1, 1965
Canadian offer	321.6	277
U.S. offer	289.3	249
Difference	32.3	28

Excludes Flood Control Payments—Present Worth July 1, 1965—$54 millions.
Includes Canadian Trustee for funds paid to B.C.
Includes sales of Canadian entitlement from completion of each dam.
Assumes interest at 4 percent.

province's perspective, the minimum settlement figure had to be.)

Before the meeting adjourned on December 11 an overtly political consideration appeared with a vengeance as the prospect of issuing a mill rate figure arose during the consideration of a press release. The British Columbians would have liked a reference to an imminent sale at a five mill (or better) price, but the Americans present had constituents to think of also, and declared that if such a reference were made they would counter with one showing not more than 3.75 mills per kwh as the selling price.[36] As a result, the communiqué issued simply referred to substantial progress and general agreement on a report being submitted to the governments concerned.

Two days after their return from Ottawa on December 14 the negotiating group from British Columbia put before Premier Bennett a report which evaluated the results of the Ottawa negotiations in the most favourable possible light. It referred again to the 250 megawatts of low-cost generation made possible on the Lower Kootenay, to the prospect that at the end of the sale period the province would own the dams "debt free," and to the power entitlement stretching over almost thirty years after the sale with a probable value of $5 to $10 millions annually. The report went on to maintain that 80 percent of the total of $343 million revenue (from the power sale and flood control payments) "will be paid before the treaty projects are completed; therefore this sum will":

A. Pay all the capital storage project costs (Duncan, Arrow, Mica) as they occur.
B. Pay approximately one-half the capital cost of the Mica generators.
C. Produce a revenue of about 5.5 mills per kilowatt-hour of the Canadian entitlement sold in the USA.

D. Result in the production of power at Mica for approximately 1.5 mills per kwh.

E. Pay all the operating costs of the Canadian projects for thirty years —if Mica power is sold at cost at site.[37]

The technicians also referred to other staff studies dealing with the possibility of advantageous year-to-year sales of surplus power to the United States, with the resulting construction employment in British Columbia, and with the deferment of capital borrowing required to complete machining the Mica powerhouse until the major part of the Peace River development had been completed. All of these arguments in combination did not forestall some very pointed questioning by the premier, who ever since has remained convinced that a better bargain for Canada could have been obtained.[38] The negotiators recall in fact that their reception was "pretty severe," but in the end the terms agreed on in Ottawa were approved. Before the negotiators left Mr. Bennett, the question of a mill rate value for the power sale was raised, and it was agreed that the flood control payment could now be used in computing a kwh price for the power sold by Canada. It was agreed also that the provincial negotiators would seek to have Mr. Luce initial a statement to the effect that, under specified assumptions, the price which Canada had received was roughly 5½ mills per kwh.

At the penultimate meeting of the international negotiators, held in Ottawa on December 19 and 20, a number of amendments to the draft protocol which had been prepared in August were advanced and approved. Several of these simply recorded understandings arrived at during the sales negotiations (such as that concerning Grand Coulee pumping). One advanced by Canada and agreed to by the United States (subject to legal confirmation that it did not change the treaty) reaffirmed the right of both countries to divert for consumptive use. It was on this occasion that the Americans dropped their proposed payment for the Canadian power entitlement in stages, in favour of a single payment of $254.4 millions (U.S.)—discounted to October 1, 1964, at 4 percent (and subject to further discounting if still further prepaid). By far the most interesting feature of this gathering, however, was the very real nervousness apparently displayed by the American representatives. They were very conscious of the fact that with the prepayment, the entire nature of the international bargain had been modified for British Columbia over the period of a generation. The constraint on the province of its own self-interest to so operate the storage as to optimize power generation in the United States (as required by Item 6 of Annex A to the treaty) and (after the machining of Mica or other Canadian installations) downstream in Canada and the United States (Item 7) would be removed. As a consequence an item was deliberately included in the meeting's minutes to recognize that the sale of the Canadian entitlement in no way contemplated any departure from the operating criteria set out in Annex A. The Americans' nervousness and desire for a guarantee of delivery was expressed in another form as well. Lest B.C. Hydro fail to construct or to operate to produce the entitlement for which the prepayment was being made, they wanted Canada to assume the role of a construction trustee in ensuring that the funds advanced were actually utilized to construct the treaty storage in Canada. Failing this, they argued that the exculpatory clauses in Article VIII of the treaty which qualified the responsibility of each country to the other in the event of breaches of the treaty should be suspended in relation to the Canadian entitlement for the period during which it was to be sold on a prepaid basis. In a sense the requested trusteeship arrangement was resolved—negatively—outside the conference room, for Mr. Laing publicly revealed the American request. When Mr. Bennett was informed of it, he rejected it at once, and to the press, as completely unnecessary, and an impugning of the province's good name. Eventually, as Dr. Keenleyside reported by letter to the premier on December 21, "the Americans agreed without reservation that what Canada did with the money was not a matter on which they had a right to be consulted—so long as Canada as well as British Columbia accepted responsibility for seeing that the terms of the treaty and subsequent Protocol and Agreement of Sale are carried out."

Even then a good many details remained to be cleared up at a final meeting in early January 1964. One, however, was dealt with at this time —agreement on a text to be released which would publicly endorse the figure of over five mills per kwh. Some of the negotiators from Ottawa had misgivings about the Americans' willingness to subscribe to any such statement, but they were wrong, as a Canadian (British Columbian) draft was approved with no significant changes.

Before his return to the province, Dr. Keenleyside had one additional task to perform, for at Mr. Bennett's request he interviewed Mr. Walter Gordon, the federal minister of finance, to make a representation on the impact which the newly levied federal sales tax on construction materials would have on the Columbia project costs. He argued for a rebate/ exemption, citing the province's right to expect in equity some equivalence to the federal subsidies to power projects in Saskatchewan and Ontario, especially in view of the measure of flood control involved (for which traditionally in Canada the federal government is expected to and does accept a considerable responsibility). He stressed as well the general economic benefit of the power sale to Canada, but received no positive response from Mr. Gordon.

3. THE SECOND CANADA-BRITISH COLUMBIA AGREEMENT, THE PROTOCOL, AND THE TERMS OF SALE

As the international negotiations moved to a climax and conclusion, it became necessary for the federal and provincial governments to further define their respective responsibilities relative to the sale agreement, especially in view of the American concern mentioned earlier. Consequently, in the last weeks of 1963 and the early weeks of 1964 the two governments prepared and exchanged a number of draft supplements to their original July 1963 agreement. Once again the British Columbians involved[39] argued vigorously that the federal proposals were unnecessarily complex, and inclined to repeat the main agreement. They objected to what they regarded as an unnecessary brusqueness in the tone of the federal proposals. When federal and provincial representatives met at Ottawa on January 7 and 8 to finalize a supplemental Canada-British Columbia Agreement, it was agreed that the province would keep Canada indemnified, would meet the time schedule set out in the terms of sale, and would provide "at reasonable intervals . . . current reports to Canada on the progress of construction."[40] Canada, on the other hand, agreed to transfer to the province immediately upon receipt, the full equivalent of the purchase price in Canadian dollars for the downstream benefit sale. Agreement proved much harder to come by, on the other hand, when the question of the provision of an automatic means for reimbursing the federal government in the event of some provincial default was raised.[41] Provincial tempers were heightened by the very nature of the question, in view of the obligations which the province had now twice accepted.[42] Furthermore, Ottawa proposed that it be entitled to reimburse itself for any liability incurred through provincial action or inaction by direct deduction from funds owing by it to British Columbia. Indeed at one point Mr. Bennett—then in Hawaii—ordered the provincial delegation in Ottawa home. Only two phone calls to the premier, and a compromise whereby such a drawback could be instituted only if the Exchequer Court of Canada had ordered the province to make a compensatory payment to Ottawa, and it had not done so for sixty days—saved the day.

A short final meeting of the Canadian and American negotiators was held in Ottawa on January 13, 1964. The Americans' uncertainty as to the legal status of the B.C. Hydro and Power Authority was still very much in evidence, as they wanted to know if the government of British Columbia could be called upon to fulfill any contract defaulted on by the Canadian entity. The Canadian delegation was able to agree that this was so, to report that the two Canadian governments were in full agreement on their reciprocal responsibilities, and that the last signatures were being added on that very day to the latest Canada-British Columbia Agreement. One of the last significant issues raised by the Canadians at this time concerned the filling of the Mica reservoir, as they feared that initial operation for storage purposes might conflict with a Canadian desire to acquire dead storage, building up head in the reservoir for at-site generation. The Americans did not see a major difficulty here. Both sides agreed on the wisdom of avoiding a situation in which, because of the filling, American utilities were forced to drop secondary loads early in the filling period, and to spill water in the last years of it. Both parties also agreed on a definition which specified when a treaty dam was fully operable, and which was included in the second of the major agreements to which the negotiators now gave approval—an attachment relating to the terms of sale.

The last document did not actually effect the sale, but it represented an agreement on the general conditions and limits of a sale, and an undertaking in advance to approve one (within these conditions and limits) to be completed when the instruments ratifying the treaty were exchanged. The highlight of the terms of sale, of course, was the agreement that, for $254.4 millions (U.S.) as of October 1, 1964, the entire Canadian entitlement to downstream power for a period of thirty years from the completion of each of the three Canadian treaty storages was to be sold to an American purchaser. The terms of sale also made provision for a set of deadlines for storage completion, and for the payment of an extra adjustment if the storages were operative and providing flood control protection before these dates. In view of the prepayment, the Canadian entity undertook to compensate the purchaser (in money or in power—at the discretion of the Canadian entity), for any of the entitlement sold but not actually realized. Monetary compensation for power so lost was related to replacement costs, and provision was made for settling compensatory disputes by a special tribunal. Nervousness in Washington, and in Ottawa for that matter, was reflected once again—this time in a proviso requiring the application of the funds transferred to the construction of the treaty projects.

Many of the provisions of the other document which now got a final approval from the negotiators, the protocol to the treaty, have already been mentioned. Substantially the protocol reflected the desire of the Canadian government to answer the more responsible domestic Canadian criticisms of the treaty. Thus, for example, the first section of the protocol dealt with the additional calls which the United States was entitled to make under the treaty for additional flood control storage in Canada. It requires that such requests go to the Canadian entity, which can accept, reject, or suggest modifications to them, and to the Permanent Engineering Board, if agreement is not reached between the entities. The decision of the Engineering Board is to be binding, but where deadlock ensues here also, to minimize loss of life and damage to property, Canada has agreed to honour a renewed call for all or part of the storage. The right of the United States to make such additional calls was limited to a specific flow condition (above 600,000 cfs at The Dalles), and for the duration of the treaty to occasions when the American base system, the 8,450,000 acre-feet of Canadian treaty storage, and that of Libby had been fully utilized. The protocol thus provided that these additional calls would be made only in the face of the threat of a very serious flood. It sought to answer Canadian critics in another way by providing that after the initial sixty-year period, all the American storages which then existed in the basin would have to be used before such a call could be made. Some of the sections in the protocol reflected the terms of sale. One section (no. 7) sought to answer those who claimed that the Canadian entity would be unduly constrained in its operation of the treaty storages for at-site or downstream-in-Canada power production. Here, within the treaty require-ment of an operating plan agreed to in advance, Canada was given full discretion to decide from which storages to make releases, and as to the detailed operation of these storages, as long as the monthly storage quantities agreed to are met. Section 8 substituted a thirty-year for a twenty-year record of stream flow record in calculating downstream benefits, and section 9 clarified the procedure to be used in their calcula-tion. In section 10 the Grand Coulee pumping load was dealt with in the manner already indicated. In response to those who perceived ambiguities in the treaty's provisions concerning the diversion rights, section 6 (1) positively recognized a right to divert for consumptive use; section 6 (2) guaranteed in perpetuity any diversions of the Kootenay River made under Article XIII of the treaty,[43] and section 13 denied that the treaty estab-lished any precedental inhibition of Canadian freedom as an upstream riparian on other watersheds.

On January 22, only nine days after this final session was held in Ottawa, Secretaries Martin and Rusk signed the protocol and the terms of sale in Washington, and exchanged the appropriate notes, while Prime Minister Pearson and President Johnson looked on. Mr. Williston was present representing British Columbia. At the same time the federal gov-ernment issued a background paper and a news release emphasizing the gains attributable to the protocol as well as the merits of the treaty itself.[44] Mica at-site power was described as costing under 1.5 mills per kwh, and the entire four million kilowatts of eventual installation on the Canadian reaches of the Columbia were estimated to be capable of producing energy at an average cost of 2 mills.[45] Provincial Cabinet ministers were openly jubilant, as they repeated these figures and Mr. Bennett's claim to have reached and exceeded his 5 mill target for the sale of the downstream power benefit. The premier himself asserted that the new arrangement had saved the province "hundreds of millions of dollars."[46]

4. PARLIAMENTARY APPROVAL AND FINAL STAGE DETAILS

Two major hurdles still had to be passed in 1964 before decision-making with respect to the Columbia could be regarded as complete; the detailed sales contract had to be negotiated, and Parliamentary approval had to be obtained for the treaty and protocol. The province and its creature, B.C. Hydro, were expected to take the initiative over the sale, and did, but they had to wait some months, as the purchaser, the Columbia Storage Power Exchange—an instrumentality of three American Public Utility Districts—was not formally organized under the non-profit, non-corporate law of the State of Washington until May 11, 1964. On the other hand, the government of Canada accepted full responsibility for securing Parliamentary approval of the treaty, and kept in close touch with British Columbia during the process. Although a minority government, the Pearson administration unquestionably felt that, on this issue, its position was tactically strong; it could count on the support of the Social Credit and Créditiste members of Parliament and did not expect the Conservatives as a party to vote against a treaty which their leaders had signed. At the same time the official opposition was expected to make some capital of the Liberals' volte-face, and to be rather skeptical concerning the improvements claimed for the protocol. Only from the New Democrats was outright opposition expected. Such indeed was the alignment which materialized in a short debate in the House of Commons between March 3 and March 9 before, without a recorded vote, the treaty and protocol were sent to the Standing Committee on External Affairs.

Mr. Martin and his colleagues were well aware of the fact that, in British Columbia notably but to a lesser degree throughout the country, the public was anything but well informed on the issue, that the bulk of the staff analysis and the engineering studies on which the Canadian-British Columbia position was based had never been revealed, that the entire arrangement had some prestigious critics, and that the hyperbolic nature of much of the dissent had produced an uneasiness in the country which was reflected in Parliament, and would have to be taken seriously. As a consequence, an extraordinarily detailed defence of the treaty and protocol was decided upon, and the decision was made to give every critic desiring it his day in court. In preparation for the subsequent examination, in February 1964, the Department of Northern Affairs and National Resources and the Department of External Affairs jointly published in a white paper a collection of documents which ranged from the treaty and protocol to a background paper, summaries of the major engineering reports, and an explanation of the payments and prices associated with the proposed sale.[47] The report of the B.C. Engineering Company— one of the least significant technical documents in the decision-making, but one of considerable domesic tactical importance because it discounted the merits of a Columbia to Fraser River diversion, was tabled in the House of Commons at long last on February 27. Professor Max Cohen was brought in from McGill University to assist with the preparation of a detailed presentation paper which at great length sought to make clear the background to the treaty, the reason for the selection of its major projects, the best alternative uses of the Columbia River basin for Canada, and the costs and benefits associated with the entire undertaking.[48] The presentation paper, which was prepared in association also with provincial technical personnel, provided an extended commentary on and assessment of the treaty, protocol, terms of sale, and Canada-British Columbia agreements. It was introduced to the members of the House of Commons' Standing Committee on External Affairs and reviewed in detail for them by Mr. Martin when committee hearings on the treaty formally commenced on April 7.[49]

This, however, was just a beginning. Between April 7 and May 21 the committee in fifty meetings listened to and questioned some forty-seven witnesses. The verbatim record of the hearings, with twenty-six appendices alone runs over 1,500 pages. Many of the witnesses filed lengthy briefs in advance. In addition, the federal government provided committee members with a special study of the treaty and protocol which it had commissioned from the Montreal Engineering Company, and a synopsis of the engineering work carried on over the course of a decade by its own technical staff. In brief, the debate which ensued during the months of April and May in the External Affairs Committee was pursued in an environment strikingly different from that which had existed during the previous five years; no longer were parliamentarians at large and interested laymen basically uninformed. Indeed the members of the committee were almost overwhelmed with exhibits and presentations.

At the outset of the hearings Mr. Martin presented the official or federal government's case in a comprehensive low-keyed presentation which represented the treaty, protocol, and terms of sale as "the best possible arrangement from Canada's point of view," and stressed that "it reflected the wishes of the province of British Columbia."[50] He was the only federal minister to testify. Five members of the federal bureaucracy gave evidence as well—with one, G. M. MacNabb of the Water Resources Branch, presenting almost all of the technical analysis of the treaty and protocol. Two Cabinet ministers from British Columbia, Messrs. R. G. Williston and R. W. Bonner, supported the federal government's position, and two of their advisers answered questions. Dr. H. L. Keenleyside presented and supported a brief as the chairman of the Canadian entity; he had as well two technical advisers to answer questions. Mr. Fulton was invited by the committee to present a statement and to testify. He did both, and without backing away from his well-known position on the sale of the downstream benefit came out strongly for the approval of the treaty and (in the light of the decision of the people of British Columbia) for the approval of the protocol and terms of sale.[51] Four of the most prominent civil engineers in Canada gave evidence concerning the physical plan involved in the treaty and the engineering of its projects. Two internationally famous engineers were brought to Ottawa to testify as to the carefulness of the engineering review directly related to the construction of the storages. And two representatives of the Consolidated Mining and Smelting Company, the region's largest industrial concern, and electric power producer and consumer, also endorsed the government's position.

In one sense the case against ratification was presented by those who, in giving evidence, urged the committee to withhold its assent. Preeminent here was General McNaughton, who testified twice, on the first occasion for four consecutive days. Others in this category included Mr. Larratt Higgins, who had been closely associated with General McNaughton's critique for some time, four representatives of Canadian trade unions, one from a British Columbia group known as the Columbia for Canada Committee, and the national leader of the Communist Party in Canada. Some of the most effective opposition testimony came from Mr. Ritchie Deane (a Consolidated Mining and Smelting Company employee) who on his own initiative and responsibility presented a brief and personally argued for the elimination of the High Arrow project.[52] On the other hand, as the hearings were notably partisan, a good deal of the opposition case was elaborated as three New Democratic Party members (Messrs. Herridge, Cameron, and Brewin) and one maverick Progressive Conservative (Dr. Kindt) asked appropriately facilitating questions of the witnesses opposed to ratification, and appropriately embarrassing ones of those who supported it. Some Social Credit and Liberal members behaved in like (though reversed) manner throughout. The questioning from both sides on occasions gave indications of being inspired either by the witnesses or in the case of queries from a small eager group of Liberal party committee men, by the federal technical bureaucracy. The unequalness of this contest was readily apparent to the observer, for laymen without competent professional advice—especially from those who had participated in the long process of negotiation—were at a major disadvantage throughout.

Another feature of the hearings was the extent to which the debate fed in upon itself, and still another was the way in which, overall, no real dent was made in the government's case. Although some of the dissenting witnesses had engaged in long exchanges of correspondence and had had extensive interviews with the technical advisers to both Canadian governments, and both General McNaughton and Mr. Higgins (in 1958) had been in this position themselves for a while at least, none of them had had access to the entire record of inter- and intra-national negotiation, and to the detailed staff analyses which accompanied it. As a consequence the dissent tended to place disproportionate weight on that which had been made public. Furthermore, much of it was derived from a sincerely held but quite unjustified impression of Canadian technical naïveté. As a conseqence, the critics were extraordinarily vulnerable, and what concern the two Canadian governments may have had about the outcome of the hearings was entirely dispelled within a fortnight of their opening. Before they were over, in fact, committee members were almost embarrassed by the completeness of the rebuttal which Mr. MacNabb in particular was to make in precise and devastating testimony to many of the major technical issues raised and not answered to that point.[53]

Finally, attention must be drawn to the manner in which, for the first time, the official views of another provincial administration were introduced into the argument and reviewed by the External Affairs Committee. When Mr. Martin made his presentation to the committee on April 7 he tabled two sets of correspondence. One consisted of letters sent to him by General McNaughton and his replies; the other contained letters and telegrams sent by Premier W. S. Lloyd of Saskatchewan to ministers of the government of Canada (Messrs. Dinsdale, Pearson, and Martin) and their replies.[54] These exchanges on the issue of Columbia River diversions had been initiated by Premier Lloyd on June 21, 1962, and had continued until only one week previously. In his first letter Premier Lloyd had written about concern in his province over the future adequacy of the water supply of the Canadian prairies, and of the requirements in particular of the valley of the South Saskatchewan River. He had gone on to mention studies which his government's advisers had recently made into the prospect of diverting water from other watersheds to the South Saskatchewan drainage basin, before making a direct reference to the prospect of transfers across the Rocky Mountains from the headwaters of the Fraser, Columbia, and Kootenay Rivers. Mr. Lloyd's letter had conceded that such a development would be expensive, but it argued that "the costs may be returned several times both directly by power benefits and indirectly by permitting a high level of industrial, irrigation and other economic development in the future." He had called as well for a "full and early" study of such a proposal, and urged that the Columbia River Treaty not be ratified until the right to divert a reasonable proportion of this river's flow into other river basins in Canada had been explicitly guaranteed. Direct mention was also made of the possibility that allowing downstream American development on the Columbia might establish claims which would make subsequent diversions practically impossible.

Mr. Dinsdale's response to this in 1962 had been to enquire if British Columbia and Alberta had been consulted, and to ask for a copy of the Saskatchewan consultants' report. On August 22, 1962, after receiving the report, and learning that Alberta and British Columbia had not been consulted, Mr. Dinsdale had written to Mr. Lloyd declaring he could see "no justification for withholding ratification of the Columbia Treaty." He had been careful to draw attention to the diversion provisions of the Columbia River Treaty, to the fact that the Boundary Waters Treaty could be cancelled upon one year's notice, and to the possibility of some diversions being made within provinces. But his letter made it clear that he considered British Columbia one of the provinces affected in any Canadian diversion proposal; it drew attention also to the very high cost of the schemes being discussed, and to costs which had been omitted from the report submitted by the Saskatchewan consultants.

Here the matter rested until May 14, 1963, when Mr. Lloyd directed the same request to the new prime minister. Mr. Pearson, just back from Hyannis Port, promised simply to refer it to his colleagues for "careful study and consideration." As the summer of 1963 advanced, the possibility of a transfer of water across the Rockies was raised in the House of Commons by a member of Parliament from Saskatchewan.[55] There were two immediate responses to this initiative. Mr. Martin observed in the House of Commons that a diversion for consumptive purposes was already provided for in the treaty, and Mr. Bennett, when informed of the suggestion in Victoria, replied sharply: "Tell Saskatchewan to keep its cotton-picking hands off our resources."[56] Thereafter the letters from Mr. Lloyd were directed to Mr. Martin. On August 21, 1963, for instance, Mr. Lloyd informed Mr. Martin that his advisers felt that the treaty proscribed any extra basin transfer for sixty years, and asked for assurance that diversions not be precluded because on their way to a consumptive use they flowed through hydro-electric power plants. Specifically he asked for a more explicit recognition of the asserted diversionary rights in the treaty or the projected protocol. The exchanges which followed between Mr. Martin and Mr. Lloyd on this issue became increasingly sharp, as Mr. Martin argued at length in legal terms that the rights desired were already assured, and that the generation of electric power incidentally would not preclude the application of the descriptive category "consumptive" to such a use. Pragmatically also, on October 3, 1963, he insisted that there were more economic water supplies available east of the Rockies, that the treaty arrangement was a highly beneficial one, and in accord with British Columbia's wishes. Mr. Williston referred to these exchanges in the British Columbia Legislature on February 6, 1964. He wondered why the two most westerly provinces had not been consulted by Saskatchewan, and advanced as the only conclusion he had been able to reach "that at times partisan politics can overcome economic feasibility and common sense if there is even a semblance of mystic fantasy to sustain a highly improbable proposition."[57] Finally, on March 31, 1964, Mr. Martin simply made it clear that in his government's opinion the national interest required the ratification of the treaty, and that the economic development of Saskatchewan would not be hindered. Mr. Lloyd consistently disagreed and maintained that the re-assertion in the Protocol in a positive way of the right to divert had not removed his fears.

Much of this ground was reworked in the first two days of the External Affairs Committee hearings. New Democratic Party questioners were particular keen to get an answer to a question which Mr. Lloyd had repeatedly raised, an inquiry as to whether or not Canada had ascertained the views of the American government on the question of multiple use in the course of a diversion exercise. In the end, however, although not satisfied, they simply had to accept Mr. Martin's assertion that the key point was the main or primary purpose of the diversion, that the American officials were "reasonable minded people" but that "if we had pressed for further clarification to include power use specifically, I would not have been surprised if the United States would have insisted on specific limitations in the agreement with regard to consumptive use."[58] When attention was turned to the practical and economic feasibility aspects of the Columbia-Kootenay to prairies diversion proposal, the External Affairs Committee found that the federal government's presentation paper and the special submission on the treaty from the Montreal Engineering Company seemed to provide strong grounds for doubt. The Montreal Company's analysis, in fact, concluded that the proposal "could be likened to depositing one dollar in the bank in British Columbia in order to draw out fifty cents on the Prairies after paying a two dollar service charge."[59] A qualification must be added here, however, for on May 14 a presentation was made to the committee on behalf of the government of Saskatchewan in which the claim was not made that the eastward diversion was feasible, but rather that it just might be, and that this alternative form of Canadian development just ought not to be foreclosed by the treaty. The Canadian government's response to this, advanced by committee members and witnesses, was that the treaty had not closed the door to it, but that in any case the likelihood of its being feasible during the lifetime of the treaty— or ever—was extremely remote.

At the conclusion of the hearings, the committee sat in camera on two occasions and, as expected, adopted a report which recorded the approval of a resolution declaring "Your Committee has considered and approved the above-mentioned treaty and Protocol."[60] The opposition continued to the end, and the committee voted down successive amendments from Messrs. Brewin, Herridge, and Kindt which would have called for a further vindication of the right to divert up to five million acre-feet of water annually for the beneficial use of the prairie region, which would have required a further definition of "consumptive use," and which would have called for further negotiation to eliminate the High Arrow and Libby Dams. An amendment calling on the United States Army Engineers to reconsider their Lower Columbia flood control measures and to carry out a program of moving people and industry to higher ground was defeated— as was one renouncing as "dangerous and unsound constitutional doctrine" references to the right of veto of "a provincial government in which is vested the ownership of the resources to be produced by an international river in respect to the development of an international project."[61]

The Parliamentary review of the committee report was brief. Mr. Martin, who presented the report to the House of Commons on June 3, introduced the appropriate endorsing motion, and repeated seven arguments in its favour which added up to a recital of benefits not obtainable without a cooperative arrangement with the United States. Progressive Conservative spokesmen indicated their approval, with the first of them, Stuart Fleming (the member of Parliament from Okanagan-Revelstoke) reasoning thus: "Surely, if there is any validity to the federal system of government, surely if there is any validity with regard to their jurisdiction over their lands and resources, the federal government must take into account the wishes of the province concerned in an agreement of this kind."[62] Progressive Conservatives and New Democrats alike indulged in a final effort at embarrassing the Liberals, or some of them, over the contrast between their 1962 and 1964 evaluations of the treaty. Those New Democrats who spoke went on to repeat their concern over the perceived inadequacy of the guarantee concerning consumptive diversions, over Mr. Bennett, over the antagonistic reception given in the committee by some of its members to witnesses opposing the treaty. Mr. Brewin argued once more that Canada had a duty not to submit "to dictation or veto in international negotiations from any province,"[63] and expressed his concern that, short of bringing the federal government down, changes in the treaty and protocol would not be permitted. On June 5, Mr. Martin, on behalf of the government, made the final speech of the debate, the vote was taken, and approval given by well under one-half the membership of the Commons (108 Yea—16 Nay). Four days later the same motion of endorsation was introduced into the Senate. The debate there was brief and the approving resolution passed on June 10. Twenty-five minutes later, in Vancouver, Dr. Keenleyside signed the major construction contract for the Duncan Lake Dam—the first of the treaty storages scheduled for completion.

While the process of legitimization was being pursued in Ottawa, a good deal of hard work remained for the technical personnel of both countries in work associated with the sales contract. The Americans were particularly hard pressed, for after putting together the Columbia Storage Power Exchange (CSPE), they had to negotiate the sale of the power to which it was acquiring title, and to raise the very considerable sums involved. Marketing had become an exclusively American responsibility and hence Canadian personnel were not directly involved as the staff of the Bonneville Power Administration worked to arrange the contracts between the CSPE utilities, and agencies of governments in the western states, upon the completion of which the success of the financing rested. In fact, the Canadian technical personnel followed these developments closely, and were not a little fascinated by the extent to which the Pacific northwest-Pacific southwest intertie now appeared on the one hand to have made the sale possible, and on the other to have been made viable by the sale.[64]

Three highly involved technical issues had to be resolved, however, between the Canadians and Americans before the contract for the sale of power could be signed. They concerned the dates on which Canadian storage was to be operative for flood control purposes, and the detailed method of calculating damages suffered by the United States in the event of wilful or non-wilful Canadian action upstream. The problems raised were resolved in five meetings between Canadian (federal and provincial) and American technicians in Spokane and Seattle late in July 1964. One interesting feature of them was that the provincial technicians felt that their federal colleague, Mr. MacNabb, was being unreasonably tough on at least one crucial issue, about which, informally, they had already reached an understanding with the Americans. Still Mr. MacNabb appears to have forced his point. The "gain" for Canada, actually, might have been achieved in any case, for it rested on a defensible technical argument. But it does illustrate rather neatly the intricacies of a polycentric decision-making exercise—and the difficulties faced by the Americans who had two jurisdictions to satisfy. From this point on, agreement came rapidly. The Canadian Entitlement Purchase Agreement between the British

Columbia Hydro and Power Authority and the Columbia Storage Power Exchange was signed on August 13 in Seattle,[65] and shortly exchange, allocation, assignment, and coordination agreements were entered into between the Bonneville Power Administration and a large number of United States utilities and agencies. As it turned out, the sale of the Canadian entitlement was effected successfully—much of it initially going to California, and the bonds of the CSPE found a ready market at an interest rate (U.S.) of about 3⅞ percent. Thus it was possible to pay the $254.4 millions (U.S.) to Canada on September 16,[66] at which time the instruments of ratification were exchanged in Ottawa and Washington, along with another set of notes making the Purchase Agreement effective.[67] On the same day at Blaine, Washington, President Johnson proclaimed the Columbia River Treaty in the presence of Prime Minister Pearson and Premier Bennett.

Since 1964 the commitments of Canada and the United States under the treaty have been met in full, and the construction option made available to the United States has been picked up. The B.C. Hydro and Power Authority completed the Duncan and Arrow Lakes storage projects well ahead of target dates, and the Mica Dam on schedule.[68] Subsequently these facilities have been operated on the basis of detailed and assured operating plans regularly agreed to ahead-of-time by the two nations' entities. As noted already, the United States did move to build the Libby Dam, which became operational for storage purposes on April 17, 1973.[69] Power generation at Mica, with its reservoir filled, began on December 15, 1976.

Readers familiar with energy consumption forecasts will be interested to know that the high growth predictions advanced by consultants to the Peace River Power Development Company in 1960–61, and widely discounted at the time, turned out to be prescient. Indeed, especially in the 'sixties, B.C. Hydro, which generates about 65 percent of all the electricity produced in British Columbia, faced some extraordinarily large annual increases in demand. Active development of the Burrard Thermal Generating Plant during the 'sixties and early 'seventies[70] helped meet the need, and indirectly permitted the installation of larger generating units in the hydro-electric plants then under construction. Between 1968 and 1974 some 2,116,000 kw of capacity were brought into service at the Portage Mountain Dam on the Peace River, which by the latter date was providing some 58 percent of B.C. Hydro's electrical energy needs. In 1975 and 1976 the first Canadian-site generation directly associated with Columbia River Treaty developments was completed when some 529,200 kw of capacity were commissioned at a new Kootenay Canal plant on the Lower Kootenay River. (See Figure 3.) This facility was built to take

281

advantage of the regulation provided upstream on the Kootenay system by the Duncan Lake and Libby projects. By 1976 B.C. Hydro had under construction additional projects at Site One on the Peace River (twelve miles below Portage Mountain), and at Seven Mile on the Pend d'Oreille. (See Figure 8.) It had proceeded, as well, to apply for and receive (conditionally) a water licence to construct a High Revelstoke Dam, combining in effect the earlier-projected Low Revelstoke and Downie developments, and providing for a larger generating capability than that scheduled for the Mica site. (See Figure 2.) The Site One and Revelstoke projects, of course, rely heavily on upstream storage in Canada on the Peace and Columbia Rivers. That at Seven Mile is a beneficiary, outside the provisions of the treaty, of already existing works in the United States. All of these developments have been pursued since 1964 in the context of a greatly heightened public sensitivity in British Columbia to environmental considerations.

Forecasting future trends in electric power development has remained as difficult for British Columbians as it was when the Columbia River Treaty was emergent, notwithstanding at least two major comprehensive approaches to the issue pursued during the 'seventies. As this manuscript is being revised, a considerable debate is being pursued publicly between the B.C. Energy Commission (a new instrumentality created in 1973) and B.C. Hydro over two issues. One concerns the magnitude of the load which the provincial authority must plan to meet a decade and more hence. The other concerns the construction policy which is most likely to minimize costs when the risks associated with the load predictions are juxtaposed with those inherent in an age of inflation.[71]

Finally, to return to our primary concern with the decision-making process in Canada, it should be noted that the inter-governmental cooperation in Canada required for the creation of the Columbia River Treaty also has been required, and has been produced, for its implementation. This cooperation has extended across the international border as well; the two national entities under the treaty have established staff task forces which have worked closely for over a decade now on their continuing and complex exercise. As provided for in the July 1963 Canada-British Columbia Agreement, a liaison committee of ministerial representatives has been established to coordinate the actions of the federal and provincial governments concerning the implementation of the treaty, and to forestall intra-national disputes. In March 1965, this liaison committee decided to constitute a new technical advisory committee to provide it with specialist advice, with membership drawn from both governmental staffs. Also as provided for by the July 1963 agreement a British Columbian (initially Mr. Paget)[72] was appointed as one of the two

Canadian members (the other—Mr. MacNabb) on the Columbia River Treaty Permanent Engineering Board. In 1967 this body established a technical advisory committee of its own with the Canadian membership drawn from Victoria as well as Ottawa, to help it assess the progress reports and operating plans which the entities regularly file with it. In the years immediately following the ratification of the treaty there was some feeling in Victoria that Ottawa was expecting to exercise, unwisely, a rather detailed control over entity operations through its representation on the Permanent Engineering Board. With the passage of time this concern appears to have faded.

Since 1964 there have been two issues concerning the Columbia's development on which Victoria and Ottawa have clearly differed. The most important of these became a matter of direct federal-provincial concern when Premier Bennett's government lost a general election, in August of 1972, to British Columbia's New Democratic Party, under the leadership of Mr. David Barrett. As we have seen, many New Democrats had long been critical of the treaty itself, and had empathized with the appproach to it taken by General McNaughton. (Their new provincial administration, indeed, was shortly to name the reservoir behind the Mica Dam after him.) In addition, for over a decade they had questioned the wisdom of the sale of the downstream power entitlement. They had placed, and continue to place, much emphasis on the fact that in the face of mounting construction costs the proceeds of the sale did not cover all of the costs to Canada of constructing the storage projects, and certainly did not produce the "no-mill power" of which Mr. Bennett had spoken optimistically in 1961. Hence in December 1972 Mr. Barrett formally approached the Canadian government with a request that an adjustment for inflation be sought from the Americans, and undertook to file a brief on the case for a revision of the international bargain. The federal government reputedly was prepared to put the whole question before an intragovernmental liaison committee, but appeared to be manifestly skeptical of the evaluation on which the province's request was based, and concerned at the precedental implications which it aroused. The record available does not permit us to follow these exchanges further. Although the treaty came in for a good deal of partisan and hostile attention in British Columbia during the next three years, Mr. Barrett's proposal had not led to any agreed-upon Canadian revisionary initiative before his government fell in December 1975.[73]

The other matter on which the two Canadian governments have differed emerged earlier, and attracted no public attention at all. Under the International Rivers Improvements Act a definite federal regulatory function is specified not only concerning the licensing, but also the construction, maintenance, and operation of international river improvements. It so happens, however, that this act contains a provision allowing the governor-general-in-council to exempt any such improvement from the operation of the act. In the light of this, not surprisingly, British Columbia applied late in 1963 for an exemption from the licensing requirements of the act apropos the Columbia River Treaty storages. This the. federal government declined to grant. An impasse appears to have ensued, and to have been resolved as of August 1, 1965, with the issuance of federal licences for the treaty dams. The licences very explicitly require that the construction, operation, and maintenance of the treaty projects in Canada "shall comply with any orders, directions and judgments of the Permanent Engineering Board . . . and any tribunal or authority mentioned in Article XVI of the said treaty."[74] If, as appears possible, the licences were issued without an application for them being filed by the British Columbia Hydro and Power Authority, the federal action must be classified as a unilateral emphasis on a federal jurisdictional competence which ultimately the province does not deny, but the exercise of which it regarded in this context under all normal circumstances as unnecessary, superfluous, and rather provocatively implying that the public servants of a province and/ or its agent cannot be counted on to keep a bargain. On the other hand, the federal government's insistence in asserting its fiat here may well have reflected a very respectable viewpoint in law (and one understandably popular in Ottawa) to the effect that the crucial power so often is the regulatory one, rather than that derived from proprietorship per se. In this connection, only the evolving pattern of Canadian federalism will determine which interpretation (if either) prevails.

PART THREE

Chapter Ten

The Policy Formation Reviewed (A)

> Tools do not have to be perfect in
> order to be helpful.
> Roland N. McKean, *Public Spending.*

A number of impressions are readily derivable from the preceding pages. One certainly is that those responsible for the policy-making in Canada were well aware of its major technological dimensions. They were also conscious as time went on that the benefits and the costs associated with it—extending as they did to considerations of national sovereignty and political credit and risk—were likely to be great. Thus they approached the policy-making determined to anchor their conclusions in clearly supportable analysis, and to reserve whatever time was required to produce it. But a second impression surely is that as the data gathering and assessment effort continued, new values, considerations, and options emerged and had to be taken into account, although their relevance had not been appreciated earlier, and, indeed, in many cases could not have been appreciated earlier—either by the major decision-makers or by the analysts involved. Still another impression is that the policy-making inspired a wide variety of types of decision. Direct analytic computation became the basis for a good many acts of judgment. But judgment was influenced by other forms of behaviour, including bargaining, and some of the decision-making can only be described as of an "inspirational" order.[1] Clearly, furthermore, no one set of individuals was able to control the entire policy-making exercise.

1. COORDINATION AND COGNITION

Identifying such characteristics of the policy-making process as these brings us directly back to the perspective referred to in chapter 1, and associated with the work of Professor Lindblom. This approach, it will be remembered, concentrates on two dimensions of the process whereby policy is generated. One involves the range of means whereby decision-making actors are coordinated. The other concerns the range of styles or techniques used both to perceive problems and to gather, analyze, interpret, and "apply" knowledge or insight to their resolution. The former may be designated the coordinating process, and the latter the cognitive one. Following Charles Lindblom, these two dimensions are represented as continua below, and the behavioural extremes open to society are identified thereon.

The Coordinating Process

Central	Partisan
Control	Mutual
	Adjustment
(Hierarchy)^2	(Bargaining)

The Cognitive Process

Synoptic	Incrementalism
Holistic	Successive Limited
Analysis	Comparisons

The thesis of so much of Charles Lindblom's work has been to emphasize the extent to which, whatever our intent, in making complex public policy we have to move so extensively to the right-hand end of the two continua. Of course, under certain circumstances, there is a major case to be made for not doing this. Long standing theory and practice make extensive use of organizational positions (often in hierarchies) whose occupants are expected to be central coordinators. The need for such coordination reflects to some extent the factoring of problems and the specialization of labour which are correlates of large-scale organizational endeavour. It reflects also man's desire for clarity, for consistency between decisions, his dislike of uncertainty, and his belief that, especially in times of peril, certain crucial coordinating, decision-making and decision-implementing functions must not be estopped. The problem with all this, of course, is that for a long time we have been becoming conscious of the extent to which central coordinators are not masters of all that they survey, or even that they are officially responsible for. The environment in which everyone is placed talks back, and to some degree must be listened to. Further, the very claims advanced on behalf of central coordination evoke some strong counter argument. Central coordinators certainly take decisions, but whether they are as aware as they would like to be, or sometimes think they are, of the interrelationships emerging as a complex public policy evolves, is another matter. Similarly, the practical limits to any one individual's capacity to maintain an intelligent overview of the implications of system or sub-system decisions raise doubts concerning the central coordinator's ability to be consistent. And, to further complicate matters, especially when organizations approach goals serially, there can be circumstances in which to be consistent is not to be rational.[8]

If coordination in the formulation of complex public policy is not produced via the central coordinator, whence does it come? Who is involved? A very respectable case can be advanced for the proposition that we must move to the right hand end of our first continuum, and that the answer is, "everyone." Coordination takes place undeniably, but in reality often is just the end-product of the interaction of a host of individuals and groups in a variety of forms of adjustment whereby behaviour is modified. These patterns of adjustment, as Lindblom reminds us, may be grouped into two categories. One is the "adaptive," those in which a decision-maker, although adjusting to another decision-maker, expects no response from the latter. These adjustments are clearly asymmetric. The other category of adjustment is the "manipulated," where a response is anticipated and expected from the other party, and the relationship is reciprocal. The latter category in particular takes many forms —negotiation broadly defined, partisan discussion and indirect manipulation, for instance—but the best known form of manipulative adjustment is bargaining, which is technically a form of negotiation. As a term, however, bargaining may be applied descriptively, if somewhat inaccurately, to the broad range of means of partisan mutual adjustment found in the political market-place. We shall use it in this sense in the balance of this study.

What can be said in defence of mutual adjustment, of bargaining, as a coordinative device? It significantly reduces the data gathering and analytic capacity otherwise required of central decision-makers. It reduces the span of attention required of any formal coordinator. At the same time, it is a fertile source of feedback as to values, insights, options, and consequences which may be overlooked both in the earlier stages of decision-making, and in the monitoring phase of policy implementation. Bargaining, furthermore, is a fact of life, a dictate of the environment, if one will. Power is always shared. As Chester Barnard reminded us a generation ago, the most senior executive has to bargain, both within his own organization and with the organization's external clientele. The very ubiquity of bargaining may be testimony to its utility. Bargaining is endemic, furthermore, because our values conflict. Offsets between them

289

abound in all polities, and may only be reconciled in the end by trade-offs which are, in large part, bargains.

In addition, two quite fundamental claims may be made for bargaining (narrowly defined). One is that there may be a basic congruity between coalition-building and hence bargaining power on the one hand, and the extent to which one's objectives are in general harmony with society's most widely shared goals. The other suggests that the result of the bargaining process is a stimulus to go beyond the compromises of hierarchic decision-makers in a search for new areas, new propositions, on which men can agree. The end product of the "hidden hand" in bargaining is what Lindblom calls values widely shared, which he equates with the public interest.[4]

Such, in essence, is the case for bargaining. There is, of course, another side to this coin, for in numerous circumstances the utilization of bargaining as a coordinative mechanism is singularly inappropriate. Even if all significant interests are represented in the bargaining process, and this is by no means always the case, they may not be represented adequately. The race may go to the aggressive, the strong, the well-organized. In addition, where bargaining puts a premium on demagogic skill, stubbornness, or outright deception, the results can leave a great deal to be desired. Bargaining also may lead to stalemate, to the avoidance of decision, which of itself does not necessarily impose high costs on society, but it may.

When one turns to the cognitive or intelligence continuum, one has little difficulty in identifying the basic assumption underlying the synoptic, holistic, or "rationally comprehensive" strategy. It is, simply, that understanding a problem is the key to solving it. Thus the emphasis which it places on accumulating knowledge concerning past experience, on the use of the most refined analytic procedures, on the deliberate identification of the goals related to emergent policy, on a ranking of these goals, on the identification, evaluation, and interpretation of the broadest possible range of means of attaining them.[5] This multi-stage approach is as concerned with probabilities as it with certainties. It involves at all levels the need to make choices; it makes extensive use at the evaluation stage of models as simplifications of reality; and, above all else, if properly used it is continually reconstructive. Its most sophisticated devotees do not claim that it will produce perfect or near-perfect decisions, but only that it should lead to improvements on its predecessors, and better decisions than those likely to emerge if it is not utilized.[6]

What difficulties do in fact arise when reasoning man seeks to apply synopsis or comprehensive analysis to complex public policy questions? One, so the argument runs, is that he is grossly naive as to what is involved in our handling of values. Analysis assumes a capacity to reconcile values which more often than not is unattainable. Even the individual has great difficulty in attributing weights to his own values. They inhere in differing packages to differing policy options. What decision-makers do is not to analytically weight their values at the beginning of the formulation of a policy position, but to assess them in the light of their marginal utility; the appeal of one increment of value, in short, is compared with increments of others. There really is no way intellectually in which the analyst can thus weigh the value components of the options which he is studying. Individuals do not agree on values, save when stated in very general terms, but on concrete policies, and for mixes of very differing reasons. But the "anti-synoptic" case does not stop here. It places a great deal of emphasis on the costliness of analysis in time, money, available personnel, and technology utilized.[7] Once again it draws attention to man's limited intellectual capacity, and to the absence of data which the analyst requires. Much emphasis is placed on the extent to which the synoptic analyst distorts reality by "taking"it out of the context in which it will have to be resolved. In the real world the reconciliation of interests incorporated in any one policy exercise may be affected significantly by past efforts at reconciliation, and, indeed, by perceptions of what future efforts might be.[8]

The alternative to comprehensiveness is incrementalism, a strategy which deliberately eschews claims to synoptic competence. Its characteristics are clearly identifiable. The decision-maker does not get immersed here in an intensive rank ordering of values. Instead he concentrates only on the values inhering in the policy choices with which he deals, and trades off these increments at the margin. He selects a modest number of policy alternatives only for examination. Similarly, he puts a limit to the number of consequences of policy options which he attempts to probe. In both these cases he acts to reduce drastically the demands on his own capacity; the decision-making process in short, is deliberately simplified. But it is simplified and made sophisticated concurrently, it is argued, because of two other hallmarks of incrementalism. One is that it seldom views policy decisions as final, but rather as sequential steps in a continuing process of on-going decision, with the incremental adjustments which they incorporate in successive runs at the problem taking into account options and characteristics put to one side on earlier occasions. The other characteristic of incrementalism is its great sensitivity to the manner in which the policy process is a fluid, reconstructive one. Problems often change dramatically over time as goals, options, and consequences little appreciated earlier subsequently acquire great significance, and are fed back into the planning process. The incremental strategy adapts beautifully to the flexibility required here.

The defence of incrementalism is anchored in these considerations. It also is heavily pragmatic, in that it asserts that this is, in fact, the manner in which the task of formulating complex public policy is approached in the real world. Great emphasis is placed on the psychic and physiological limits to man's cognitive and analytic ability, on his bounded rationality in other words,[9] and on the manner in which incrementalism, by putting limits to the demands upon the decision-maker, keeps the entire policy-making effort manageable. Much is made of the wisdom, for both individuals and organizations, of starting off with simple models of causality, of looking for answers close to problem symptoms and to current practice, until satisfied that this procedure will not be successful.[10] And a great deal of attention is drawn to its serial, remedial, reconstructive bias, to the manner in which its deliberate utilization of short-run action permits short-run monitoring, and the almost immediate feed-back of results into reassessment effort. It is perceived consequently as an extremely logical set of decision rules with which to face a very uncertain world.

These claims have evoked much argument and counter argument, as critics have found in them an essentially conservative bias, an unrealistic assumption concerning the continuity of policy problems, an under-rating of the wisdom of periodic broad-ranging goal scanning, and, above all, a legitimization of a recourse to the use of dimmer-eyed increments, when wider-eyed ones might be within reach.[11] The debate will not be traced further here. Lindblom's thinking is seminal both because it has prompted a continuing reassessment of much of our previously conventional wisdom concerning the hallmarks of rational policy-making, and because it is so productive of further reflection.

For instance, it is apparent that the coordinative process utilized in any one exercise in policy-formation depends upon many considerations, such as the nature of the problem itself, the constitutional, institutional, and other constraints of the political culture, past experience, and the time available. It seems reasonable to assume that differing subsets of emergent policy may be approached from different ends of the coordination continuum concurrently. In like manner the extent to which the cognitive demands of the policy formation process are approached synoptically or incrementally will depend upon a broad range of considerations. The wealth of the community is one (although its impact may be ambiguous). Perceptions of the importance of the policy, of the level of potential understanding, of the time available, of the nature of the problem, of serious past failure[12]—are others. Once again, the search for answers to different subsets of a policy problem may well invoke different approaches, concurrently, this time to the cognitive process.

There is a readily evident logical and experiential affinity between the hierarchical end of the coordinating continuum and recourse to analytic procedures. Analysis, especially in the early stages of policy formation, is commonly invoked by central coordinators, and in any case, assumes a considerable control over its own procedures. In the same manner there is an apparent relationship between a recourse to bargaining and incrementalism. Juxtaposing the short-run perspective of incrementalism with the "negotiated environment" derived from mutual adjustment is a classic means of reducing uncertainty in the policy formation process to tolerable levels.[13] Additionally, very important diagonal relationships exist between hierarchy and incrementalism, between synoptic analysis and bargaining. These relationships may be represented simply thus:

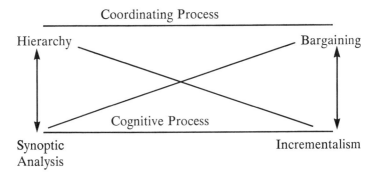

The whole thrust of Lindblom's now classic essay, "The Science of Muddling Through," was to suggest that the hierarchic coordinator himself pushes the cognitive component of decision-making to the incremental end of the scale, and that more often than not this is the rational thing to do when dealing with complex public policy. But the other diagonal, representing the reciprocal relationship between synoptic analysis and bargaining is in many respects an equally important one. Numerous generalizations concerning it can be readily advanced. Single analytic efforts are not often sponsored by large numbers of bargainers if only because they find it so difficult to agree upon the preliminary definition of the problem. The results of analytic effort may have a significant impact on the bargaining process, especially in cultures such as ours which often defer to the expert. It is no accident that in the western democratic state analytic support has become "a fundamental tactic in the play of power."[14] Obviously the impact of analysis may be a function of the resources invested in it. A significant result of analysis may be to give the bargainer clues as to how to best use his time.[15] Another may be to alter the nature of the dialogue within a bargaining system. Analysts who are sensitive to the merits of bargaining may also seek to extend its range in the policy-making process, and to move the levels in which it is pursued upward, with

293

the intent of making their own efforts more comprehensive.

Of course, those who invoke or produce analytic effort may be perturbed, in time, by the use of their efforts made by bargainers, and may seek to reimpose hierarchic control on the policy-making. Conversely, should bargainers find the results of analysis disturbing, they may seek to limit further recourse to it, and encourage moves to incrementalism. Alternatively, they may develop the capacity to produce analytic effort within their own ranks, if only to test the validity of the analyses performed by others.

If analytic effort increases the number of objectives being considered, almost by definition it may broaden the scope for bargaining. What actually happens in this respect, however, may well depend on the flexibility with which objectives or values are used in analysis, and associated under different circumstances with different alternatives.[16] Again, it is apparent that there is a likely relationship between the aspiration levels of policy-makers, who may be bargainers, and recourse to analysis. In reverse fashion, such analysis as is produced can be expected to have a variable effect on the aspiration levels of bargainers; it may stimulate the aspirations of some, and, especially to the extent that it illuminates conflicts in values and complexities, it may moderate the aspirations of others.

There are still further dimensions to the rich and varied relationships between hierarchy, bargaining, analysis, and incrementalism. Hierarchy and bargaining, as we have seen, may not be all that antithetic. The one form of coordination may complement and actively seek assistance from the other. In the same manner, analytic effort does not in fact look all that askance at incrementalism. A strong case can be made for the proposition that the most sophisticated analysis frequently ends up so conscious of the extent to which its conclusions rely on hazardous projections into an uncertain future that it calls for action with short-run and reversible implications, for, if one will, Lewis and Clark planning.[17] Furthermore, we have said almost nothing at all about communication interaction between the analyst and the hierarchic coordinator, or about the way in which values are shaped in these exchanges.[18]

Still, one hopes the basic point has been made. There is a multitude of non-static interrelationships between hierarchy, bargaining, synopsis, and incrementalism. Similarly, the mix of emphases on the primary mechanics of coordination and cognition utilized is almost infinite. It will vary from policy to policy, and during the evolution of policies. It will be influenced by personal, institutional, and strategic considerations, by the organizational and bureaucratic environments involved, by past and anticipated experience, by the polity or polities, and by the policy concerned. We turn now to a review of the Columbia River policy-making in the light of a number of questions inspired by Lindblom's incisive thinking. Specifically, we shall attempt to determine how the coordination and intelligence functions, and the relationships between them, were handled on this issue in the Canadian federal state. Such conclusions as we arrive at will be relevant to final comments on the comprehensiveness of the Columbia River Treaty itself, and on the extent to which, at least in the Canadian context and on this issue, Lindblom's initially descriptive emphasis on the strength and the merits of the "pulls" to bargaining and incrementalism has normative validity as well.

2. THE EXTENT OF THE RECOURSE TO HIERARCHIC COORDINATION

Especially when it is reviewed from a national perspective, Canada's approach to the prospect of developing the Columbia River on a cooperative basis with the United States is a classic example of what Herbert Simon labelled "the process of composite decision." No one group, no one individual, was aware of all the decisions entering into the final "Canadian approach," let alone the ultimate refinement and modification of it in the crucible of international bargaining. Furthermore, the roles of the governments of Canada and British Columbia on this question really were co-ordinate. There was no central authority above them to which an appeal could be made. Fundamentally, therefore, the difficulties which stemmed from the extent to which this exercise in policy formation led to a contest between two levels of government in Canada were not resolved via hierarchic coordination, but rather via the ubiquitous processes of partisan mutual adjustment. But, when this observation is made, it should be followed by two others. During the entire twenty-year period within which this Canadian policy was being formulated the degree of central coordination maintained over this issue *within the respective jurisdictions of the federal and provincial governments* was very great indeed. This is not surprising, of course, to anyone familiar with the decision-making strategies available to the executive and administrative branches of government in parliamentary systems which are characterized, as in Canada, by strong cabinets and prime ministers, as well as by tightly disciplined parties. In some respects the central coordination was greater at the provincial level, where the number of departments involved was much less, and for long the key offices involved were located in the capital city. Still, there was plenty of central coordination in Ottawa also, where, as has already been demonstrated, ministerial level decision-making remained crucial in the constant formulation and re-formulation of the policy involved.

The other consideration to keep in mind at the outset is the fact that it is always possible for two strong hierarchies jointly approaching the same problem, either via informal contacts or through formal coordinative machinery, to so integrate their efforts as to increase the overall degree of central control being exercised concerning the resolution of a difficult problem. This, for example, is what the Policy and Technical Liaison committees were designed to permit when established in 1959, and what, to quite a degree, they achieved, even though they became the venue of recourse to bargained coordination as well.

To repeat then, the mechanisms of hierarchic coordination were operative and significant *within* rather than *between* Canadian political jurisdictions. It will be helpful, at this point, if we look further at the contribution to the central control which was effected by the executive cabinets and public bureaucracies which were primarily involved.

The Coordinative Role of the Federal and Provincial Cabinets. At the outset here, the reader should be reminded that legislatures in Canada are not legislatures in the American tradition. Their function is not, primarily, to write the on-going law of the land, or to initiate public policy, but rather to legitimize and hold responsible the actions of their Cabinet colleagues who do. Actually the only legislation dealing with this entire issue presented to the Parliament of Canada was the International Rivers Bill of 1955, and it was not until seven years after the Columbia River Treaty was signed that, in 1968, the first statutory enactment accounted for by the international development of the Columbia River was introduced into the Legislative Assembly of British Columbia.[19] Partly this bypassing of the formal legislative process was the result of the invocation of the federal prerogative power as a result of the use of the treaty route to international agreement, and the further use of the prerogative power, federal and provincial, to create inter-Canadian governmental agreements. To some extent also the non-involvement of the Canadian legislatures stemmed from the downstream benefit power sale, which had the effect of drastically reducing the need to raise public funds for treaty project construction. Overall, Canadian policy on the development of the Columbia River was very much a Cabinet-level creation.

If this be so, it is important to seek to identify those distinctive features of the Canadian Cabinets, which appear to have influenced their coordinative roles. British Columbia's Cabinet was much the smaller of the two. During the period of intense activity over the Columbia River it was roughly half the size of the federal executive. While the provincial Cabinet uses committees as a coordinating medium and as a device for factoring complex problems, with respect to the Columbia River it seems to have operated without any such instrument and very informally. The three Cabinet ministers who took the key decisions were Messrs. Bennett, Bonner, and Williston. Mr. Bennett saw himself as the central coordinator and acted like one, leaving the details of project selection almost exclusively to Mr. Williston. Mr. Bonner was closely associated with the provincial minister of lands and forests in inter-governmental negotiations, although as the chief law officer of the province, and as a senior colleague, he was close to Mr. Bennett also. After mid-year 1959, Mr. Bennett seems to have reserved to himself policy decisions concerning the financing of Canada's treaty commitments. There is no denying that his power was great and that he used it on a number of occasions, apparently, by taking crucial decisions unilaterally, and only subsequently seeking the approval of his Cabinet colleagues. Still the point must not be overdone; the twin principles of Cabinet responsibility and Cabinet solidarity put real limits to any premier's freedom of decision and action. On this question the provincial Cabinet seems to have been subject to few internal strains, save perhaps briefly in January 1961.

The Cabinet team then in British Columbia was headed by an incisive action-oriented coordinator-cum-decision-maker, and was flexible. Certainly it was well-informed on the crucial issues. Mr. Bennett and Mr. Bonner had held their portfolios since 1952; Mr. Williston, who was responsible for so much of the detailed analysis, went to the Department of Lands and Forests in 1956. And there they stayed, through all of the Columbia decision-making. Nor should two other considerations be overlooked. In British Columbia, sessions of the provincial legislature in the years under review seldom lasted more than three months. During the most crucial years in the evolution of Canadian Columbia River policy, federal Cabinet ministers, with a broad range of national problems before them, were fortunate to get three months clear in any one year from the demands of daily appearances in the House of Commons. It is not surprising that, under these circumstances, a provincial minister such as Mr. Williston could develop a familiarity with the intricacies of this entire question which federal ministers found it hard to match. (Mr. Fulton seems to have been an exception here.)[20] The other consideration to keep in mind is that the staff from the provincial bureaucracy which worked most closely with the responsible Cabinet ministers was small. It consisted of three senior officers of the Department of Lands (and, after 1961, of Water Resources), when legal matters were involved, the deputy attorney-general (Dr. Kennedy), and increasingly after mid-year 1960, Dr. Keenleyside and one at least of his close associates in the B.C. Power Commission.[21]

At the federal level in Canada, Columbia River decision-making was spread over three administrations. In 1956, after tempers had cooled following the confrontation over the Kaiser Dam, Prime Minister St. Laurent made the minister of northern affairs and national resources (Jean Lesage) responsible for evolving federal policy on the Columbia, both because his department contained the Water Resources Branch, and because the Cabinet minister from British Columbia (James Sinclair), who might have played a leadership role here, was the president of the B.C. Liberal Association and an outspoken critic of Mr. Bennett.[22] When the Progressive Conservatives came to power in 1957, as we have seen, they created an ad hoc Cabinet committee to deal with this question, under the chairmanship of their minister of northern affairs and national resources (initially Mr. Hamilton).

There were at least three ways in which the institutional mechanism utilized in Ottawa differed from that at Victoria. Leadership in determining federal policy on sub-sets of the Columbia River problem was not allocated to individual members of the Cabinet Committee. Questions ranging from project selection to financing appear to have been dealt with collegially. Furthermore, whereas in British Columbia the key ministers involved seem to have had to go only rarely to the provincial Cabinet for an endorsement or review of their decisions, in Ottawa many questions dealt with by the Cabinet Committee and in extended inter-ministerial written communications (virtually never used in the province on this issue) seem to have been re-argued under Mr. Diefenbaker's chairmanship. In some ways, too, the Cabinet Committee was rather cumbersome. Not one of the more prestigious assignments available to Cabinet personnel, it seems to have suffered some attrition and changes of membership, although some ministers (such as Mr. Green) remained with it, and some, such as Mr. Fleming and Mr. Fulton, were added. But the point made by a minister who did leave it is that at any meeting attended by anywhere from two to six ministers there would also normally be present up to eighteen staff advisers drawn from interested federal government departments and agencies. Under such circumstances, he observed, there was a tendency to "talk for effect."

When the Liberals returned to office in 1963, Mr. Pearson made the new secretary of state for external affairs, Paul Martin, responsible for the negotiations leading to the two agreements with British Columbia and to the protocol, for the general direction of federal government policy on the treaty itself (once the basic decision had been taken at Cabinet level to agree to a downstream benefit sale), and for the presentation of the treaty, protocol, and sales agreement to the House of Commons. For the Liberals, as for the Progressive Conservatives, the greater part of the staff support came from the Water Resources Branch—from sources where the turn-over in staff had not been great, and real familiarity with the problems involved was the order of the day. Decisions came quickly out of this arrangement.

Two additional observations must be added concerning the role of Canadian Cabinets in the determination of Columbia River development policy. Interest groups, which may exist within as well as beyond institutional government, are no more ignored in the Canadian than they are in any other democratic political system. But in Canada the strong, responsible Cabinet drawn from the disciplined party is simply not faced with the need to engage in the continuous coalition building which is so characteristic of executive and legislative behaviour in the United States. As we have already seen, the perspectives of the most vitally concerned departments and agencies of government were represented in the Canadian and American negotiating teams.[23] But the manner in which executive government in the two countries dealt with their respective legislatures was strikingly different.

During the negotiation of the IJC principles in 1959, the government of the United States appears to have been prepared both to keep well informed and to accept advice from a sub-committee of the Senate Committee of Interior and Insular Affairs chaired by Senator Neuberger. When the treaty negotiations themselves began in 1960 (Senator Neuberger died in March of that year), the senators from the four Pacific northwest states, and especially Messrs. Church, Mansfield, and Morse—all members of the Senate Foreign Relations Committee—were well briefed on developments. Very much the reverse was true in Canada. At no stage either in 1959-60 or in 1963 were non-ministerial members on either side of the two Canadian legislatures involved or kept informed concerning the international bargaining. Mr. Williston did go some considerable way to providing after-the-event explanations in annual addresses to the provincial Legislative Assembly, and some sharp debates did ensue there, but there was an air of the unreal about the entire exercise in view of the limited information available to the provincial government's critics. Major debate in the House of Commons had to await the presentation to it of the treaty, sales agreement, and protocol "package" in 1964. In other words, save via what Friedrich labelled "the rule of anticipated reactions," which, after all, is a corner-stone of responsible government in the parliamentary tradition, the legislatures in Ottawa and Victoria, to repeat the point made at the beginning of this section, did not significantly restrain the degree of Cabinet control exercised over this policy formation.

The second additional observation to be made concerning the role of the Cabinets at Ottawa and Victoria is that while they did not share their knowledge, their considerable coordinating control, or even (via some form of consultation) their decision-making responsibility with their respective legislatures during the years between 1959 and 1963, they did pay far greater attention to the details of the treaty, and of the protocol and sales agreement, than did the Executive Branch in the United States. The American negotiating team in 1960 and again in 1963 actually had a great deal of freedom; as one of its members on both occasions recalls the situation, the "next level up" was swamped,and just not concerned with detail.[24] The "next level up" in Canada (especially in Ottawa) was swamped also, but more than willing, nevertheless, to wrestle with the fine print. Whether this was wise can be debated; that it happened was directly the result of the much greater relative importance of a Columbia River settlement to Canada and of the competitive approach which the two Canadian governments took to its consummation.

The Coordinative Role of the Canadian Public Bureaucracy. Just as one would expect with such an inherently technical policy question, the contribution of technical personnel in the Canadian public bureaucracy to the ultimate policy-making was very great. These were the individuals who either conducted the analytic investigation and interpreted it or, more often than not, recommended that external analytic effort be secured to supplement their own. It was at the technical staff level that many of the initial problem formulations were conceived, that many of the search procedures were conducted, and many of the policy options were identified and evaluated. Much of the data generated by these same personnel was made available to the governments' external consultants, and of course, to the IJC, whose Engineering Board, Committee, and Work Group the bureaucracies so largely staffed. Their information was important, their influence great.

There were some significant similarities and differences between the structuring of the contributions of the public services in the two Canadian governments. In both capitals the staff groups seconded to intensive technical work on the Columbia River were small, containing fewer than fifteen persons in the provincial, and probably not more than twice that number of persons in the federal service. The fact that they had an impact out of all proportion to their modest size was due to their hard work, and to the existence in both of them of some first rate analytic talent. In Victoria, as noted in chapter 1, the Department of Lands and Forests, a broad spectrum organization dealing with land, forests, water resources, and, until the 'mid 'fifties, with recreation and conservation, was the source of the great bulk of the "in-house" analytic effort, coordinated the bureaucratic contribution, and generated most of the recommendations on this question which went to Cabinet level. By the 'mid 'fifties, the

Water Rights Branch of this department, headed by A. F. Paget, the water comptroller, had acquired a key role here. Its opposite number in Ottawa was the Water Resources Branch which, as we saw in chapter 1, had several departmental homes in the twenty years after 1944, and a significant staff in Vancouver. Overall, no one public servant or department in Ottawa had quite the influence with Cabinet-level decision-makers accorded to Mr. Paget and his group in Victoria.

This distinction stemmed partly from the broader range of responsibilities which, almost by definition, a national government has to consider. It was derived partly, also, from the allocation of direct responsibility in the province for the detailed provisions of a Columbia River development plan to the minister of lands and forests, R. G. Williston. Mr. Williston worked so closely with Mr. Paget and a few senior staff members in the Department of Lands that these men appear to have achieved a real meeting of minds on a good many of the basic objectives which a Columbia River agreement should strive for, and, indeed on the basic provisions which it should contain. One result of this close association was an interesting distinction in bureaucratic behaviour between the two capitals. In sessions of the Policy Liaison Committee senior technical staff from the province on occasions felt free to join in arguments over quite crucial policy matters (such as the grossing-netting problem), obviously assured that they were representing their government's position. Members of the federal bureaucracy adhered more closely to the conventional norm which reserves the enunciation of policy positions in such situations to ministerial representatives.[25] One senses that the contact and relationship of the federal personnel with their ministers were much more formalized and hence somewhat less close than were those between the elected and selected from Victoria. (A dozen years after the treaty's ratification, the roles of these two bureaucracies appear to have changed in one interesting respect. While most of the senior members of the province's 1954–64 staff team have left the provincial service since that time, and several have died, a number of the major advisers to the federal government on Columbia policy-making prior to 1964 continue to occupy very key posts in Ottawa. Their now almost unique familiarity with the background, and terms of the treaty, protocol, and sales agreement has significantly reinforced the federal position in some recent Canadian intergovernmental exchanges concerning the treaty itself.)

A further distinction between the coordinative roles of the two bureaucracies, of course, stemmed from the impact of General McNaughton's approach to the development of the Columbia River. The general, it will be remembered, took advantage of the position which he enjoyed as an IJC commissioner to disagree privately with some of the policy perceptions of the federal line departments in the early 'fifties, and subsequently—and on his own initiative—to launch investigations of some policy options which he deemed particularly favourable to Canada. As the decade advanced, further, he quite deliberately sought to play a key role as a coordinator and synthesizer of the differing perspectives which had begun to emerge in Victoria and Ottawa. These efforts had almost no influence on the role played by the bureaucracy in Victoria, but they certainly did serve to diffuse and, in some respects, to offset or moderate the influence of the departmental bureaucracy in Ottawa.

If the coordinative function of the two bureaucracies was very significant, while somewhat different, it is important to remember that it was not unlimited. Partly this was the result of rather widespread recourse to the processes of mutual adjustment between Cabinet-level decision-makers, and between them and extra-hierarchic groups and individuals. Very largely, of course, it was the result of a recognition by the public service itself of the prerogatives of ministers, and of the limits to their own capacities, duties, and responsibilities. Both public services saw themselves as progenitors of technical analysis and as transmitters of its results and related advice. The working papers of both governments make it quite evident that this responsibility was taken very seriously, and that the advice was given.[26] But it remained advice from individuals who were fundamentally committed to analysis in terms of economic efficiency, who did not necessarily agree with General McNaughton's views on the goals of Canadian policy (to be examined shortly), and who were not committed to building large projects per se.[27] (The careers of these men were not tied organizationally to the subsequent construction and operation of the projects with which they were dealing.) Furthermore, the record indicates that it was advice which was commendably candid and forthright; it does not reveal a predisposition to tell ministerial principals what the latter wanted to hear. Far from it. For example, when provincial technical personnel felt that the claims being advanced to their Cabinet on behalf of the Peace River's development were sadly lacking in supporting economic analysis, they made their views known. Similarly, as we have seen, when not a few of the assumptions incorporated into the treaty planning in 1960 were set aside in 1961, they did not hesitate to draw attention to said fact. This same candor was well exemplified by a senior deputy minister in Ottawa late in February 1960 telling the Cabinet Committee there which did not wish to hear it, that the Arrow project could not be dislodged on demonstrable technical grounds. It was equally reflected for example in the care with which, when federal engineers produced through 1960–61 very favourable evaluations of the cost of Columbia River power, they appended lists of the operative assumptions on which their calculations were based, and tried to alert their ministers to the extent to which many of these assumptions were crucial, involving long-term projections into the future, and left much room for genuine uncertainty.

While the federal and provincial public services undoubtedly contained their share of individuals reluctant to relay unwelcome news upward, to repeat, the senior levels of the Canadian bureaucracies which dealt with the Columbia River were generally unencumbered by such individuals. It is true that both jurisdictions, within and without the bureaucracy, do appear to have produced some examples of that well known administrative phenomenon, the report signed in the interest of producing a working consensus by individuals possessing doubts about some of the derivations and recommendations included.[28] But these were rare. On the whole both Canadian governments were very well served by their careerist advisers, within their clearly delimited spheres of competence. Furthermore, both federal and provincial Cabinet personnel recognize and appreciate the fact. Several of the six senior members of the Diefenbaker administration who were interviewed made reference to the comprehensiveness and fairness of the support they had received. To their credit, not one of them sought to transfer to the bureaucracy responsibility for the ultimate dénouement.[29] Mr. Bennett recalled with a chuckle the technical advice which on some crucial occasions he ignored, and quickly went on to ask his interviewer to account for "the unimaginativeness of university-trained men."[30]

In summary, Cabinet-level personnel in Ottawa and Victoria supported by careerist technical bureaucracies in both cities did attempt to coordinate, to internalize, and to control a great deal of the decision-making associated with the evolution of this policy. In many respects they succeeded. As the range of issues involved expanded, however, and the two hierarchies ultimately found themselves in an intense if intermittently competitive bargaining relationship with each other, the degree of control which either of them was able to impose on the policy formation process was greatly modified. Decisions still came out of hierarchies, but often in the context of bargained adjustment. It is to this moderation of hierarchic control which we now must direct our attention.

3. The Extent of the Recourse to Bargaining

If hierarchic coordination played an important role in this story, it is also true that seldom if ever before in Canadian experience has the final resolution of what was a major foreign as well as a major domestic policy issue been marked by so little central direction from the national government. Indeed, the processes whereby it was resolved illustrate rather well the manner in which partisan mutual adjustment can lead, ultimately, to a reconciliation of views, and to coordinated action.

It comes as no surprise to the reader who has dipped at all into chapters 3 to 9 to learn that all of the forms of mutual adjustment identified by Charles Lindblom played a role in the formulation of this Canadian public policy. Actually those which he classifies as adaptive, and which assume that decision-maker X adapts to decision-maker Y (and Y's decisions, made and anticipated) without expecting a response from Y, were not prominent. After all, in this polycentric decision-making three governments possessed vetoes; each government realized that, in the last analysis, the others would have to be persuaded. It was the manipulative category of adjustment, where decision-maker X anticipates a response from Y, that was so much in evidence here. Intermittently, over two decades, extended use was made of the adjustments effected through *negotiation* and *bargaining*. *Partisan discussions* (a form of negotiation) played some role in the processes of international accommodation (recall the lawyers' arguments over the Boundary Waters Treaty), and not a little in federal-provincial accommodation as well. Recourse was also had to *compensation* (for example, in the federal government's attempts to educe its preferred sequence of development or an institutional supervisory umbrella in 1960). These are *symmetrical* forms of adjustment. Use was certainly made of the *non-symmetrical* forms as well. Mr. Bennett's contacts with Mr. Robert O. Anderson in 1963 were invocations of the technique of *indirect manipulation*, and the provincial take-over of the B.C. Electric Company, with its inherent modification of the responses open to Ottawa, was an example of the technique of *unconditional manipulation*. Again Mr. Bennett's move to alter a basic assumption of the treaty's negotiators by unilaterally deciding to sell the downstream power benefit, was an example of *prior decision*.[31] The refusal of the government of British Columbia to agree to the flooding of the Upper Kootenay-Columbia Valleys was by no means the only occasion in which the adjustment of *authoritative prescription* was used.

Several aspects of the Canadian recourse to the processes of mutual adjustment warrant attention. Did, in fact, these processes help make the coordinative, decision-making function manageable? Did they elicit a recognition of and consideration for a wider range of interests than would have been the case otherwise? Did, in the end, the resultant of all the mutual interacting turn out to be a widespread accommodation to broadly shared values? In this process, did most "participants" adjust extensively to the position of others? And if the latter be only partly the case, how does one account for this fact? Finally, what can one say about the roles of two representative institutions, Canadian political parties and the IJC, and the manner in which the processes of mutual adjustment operated within them, and for that matter, between them and the environment in which they were placed?

Bargaining's Contribution to the Raising of Interests, and to the Search for Agreement. At the outset, the point must be made that, in a decision-making exercise with which hierarchies were heavily involved over a twenty-year period, many interests were recognized and taken into consideration on the initiative of decision-makers within the hierarchies themselves. During the first ten years, 1945–55, for instance, when the Water Rights Branch in Victoria, and the Water Resources Branch and offices of the federal Department of Public Works were working to identify and evaluate potential dam-sites, and to develop a real familiarity with the hydrology of the river system, other sectors of these same bureaucracies were demonstrating a sensitivity to the spill-overs associated with reservoir construction. Thus, for example, when a clearance for a Libby reservoir stretching into Canada became a real issue in 1949, the transportation, forestry, recreational and wild life sectors of the provincial government's staff were marshalled to help assess what the consequences of such a move would be. At this same time, it will be remembered, the provincial government moved, quietly, to alert the obviously interested four operating utilities in the province, and to seek their advice. Well before the end of the 'fifties, but while the analytic process was still in a highly fluid state, members of the provincial public service and some members of the province's Cabinet began to consider very seriously the social and environmental consequences of flooding the Arrow Lakes and Upper Kootenay-Columbia Valleys, and to wrestle with the consequences of pursuing either or both options. But there were limits, clearly, to the extent to which the hierarchy was prepared to go in identifying and considering interests; the more of these interests seriously considered the more complicated the decision-making process was bound to be. It is quite evident that the hierarchies in Ottawa and Victoria attached weights or degrees of significance to the interests which they had identified, that these weights were not identical in the two capitals, that in some cases they changed over time, and that they related not just to the extent to which the decision-makers felt interests would have to be accommodated ultimately, but also to the extent to which groups or individuals openly associated with these interests would have to be carried along during the formulation of the public policy. It is apparent also that, as the two hierarchies approached the crucial stages of the decision-making in a competitive spirit, and at the same time prepared for tough bargaining ahead with the United States, by imposing a major degree of confidentiality on strategic thinking they significantly reduced the number of interests with which, otherwise, they might concurrently have had to deal. In some respects they limited their contacts with groups which, at earlier stages in the policy formation process, they had been prepared to consult.[32]

Even when conceding a major role to hierarchic coordinators as identifiers of interests, as we must, it remains very evident that the overt bargaining which ensued in Canada did focus attention on many interests which might not have received the same attention, or attention at the time when it was directed to them. Thus, for example, the bargaining which ensued within the Policy Liaison Committee may well have forced two sets of decision-makers to consider and reconsider the merits of policy objectives and of options which, otherwise, in one capital or the other might have been dismissed out of hand. The debate at the Technical Liaison as well as at the Policy Liaison Committee level over the merits of the grossing-netting approaches to calculating the downstream benefits, for example, put on the table and commanded a hearing for the constraints of political realism in British Columbia which, otherwise, might have been overlooked in Ottawa. It was in a bargaining context that the federal government pushed so hard in 1960 for a definitive and very specific treaty, and thus emphasized, among other values, those associated with the prospect of an early priming of the construction industry pump. As has been indicated already, provincial decision-makers began to weigh the social costs involved in constructing a major reservoir on the Arrow Lakes well before the public had any knowledge that the policy option was being considered. But there is certainly no doubt that the pressure exerted on Victoria, and to a lesser extent on Ottawa during 1960, via letter, telegram, and delegations of residents from the west Kootenay country with respect to the consequences of such a development, did serve to clarify the perceptions of the technical advisory group and cabinet-level personnel both as to the range of public views on this subject, and the intensity with which they were held, even if it did not deflect the decision-makers in Victoria ultimately from their conviction that the social and environmental costs would be worth paying.

In another sense also the processes of bargaining had a major coordinative significance, in that they broke down the whole rather cosmic issue into manageable proportions. Thus, for instance, when the government of Saskatchewan became involved, it addressed itself solely to the question of whether or not the treaty had preserved a right for Canada to divert water out of the Columbia River basin for consumptive purposes. In much the same manner, many of the most effective critiques of the treaty in the years between 1960 and 1963, by which one means critiques which prompted the most serious reassessments by the two governments' staff advisers, were those which concentrated on a limited number of issues. Overall, the bargaining which ensued does appear to have broadened the range of values considered in Canada, and, in some cases, to have raised aspiration levels (which will be dealt with later). In some circumstances, as when Ottawa and Victoria almost reached a *modus vivendi* in their near compromise of March–April, 1962, it did also lead, in classic fashion, to a search for options incorporating shared values, the glue or paste, as Lindblom correctly notes, which ties alliances together.[33]

All this having been said, however, it is still not clear that the processes of mutual adjustment, as they were invoked with respect to the Columbia River's development in Canada, did work solely to extend the range of values considered, or the number of policy options and related consequences which were examined. In some respects the bargaining involved appears to have had just the reverse effect. Of crucial importance, in this respect, was a very distinctive feature of the bargaining process as it was pursued in Canada. Much of it certainly was polycentric; many inputs from many different interests and power centres were involved. Much of it, however, was not, but consisted rather of a contest between two hierarchies, each of which within its own perceived sphere of competence had retained a very significant degree of coordinative control. Under these circumstances there were occasions when the coalition building, the seeking of allies, the constant modification of position so characteristic of ongoing mutual adjustment (and which, to be accurate, Lindblom associates in his panegyric on the merits of bargaining with multi-party rather than two-party interactions),[34] just were put aside. When during these periods intransigence reigned, there was operative a countervailing, if temporary tendency, to freeze perceptions, and to narrow, not broaden perspectives concerning values, options, and their consequences.

The Asymmetric Nature of the Bargained Adjustments. When the great mix of processes of adjustment had finally run its course, and the positions, goals, and strategic behaviour of the actors involved had been adapted in a multitude of ways to the behaviour and perceptions of others, an accommodation was reached between the Social Credit government in Victoria, and, first, in late 1960, the federal Progressive Conservative government, and then in 1963, a new Liberal administration in Ottawa. The final settlement did incorporate, ultimately, a broad range of values. Nevertheless, anyone reflecting on the significance of the impact of the processes of adjustment on the perceptions and the behaviour of the Canadian actors involved cannot but be struck by the extent to which, when the bargaining ended formally in 1964, British Columbia had received so

307

much of what it had been asking for since 1958. Why was it that so much of the crucially deferential adjusting was done by others in the direction of the province's objectives? Why, in short, was it quite so asymmetric?

A number of answers suggest themselves. It is always possible for one party in a multilateral exercise in policy formation, either by serendipity or through a combination of careful analysis and clear thinking, to hit upon, early, a genuinely superior solution, to be convinced of this fact, and gradually to bring others around to its way of thinking. One can argue fairly that to some degree something of this sort happened here. Although the provincial government did not finally settle on a set of projects until June 1960, for at least a year and a half prior to that time provincial Cabinet ministers and technical personnel alike had been much impressed with the conclusions of the Crippen-Wright study. They had thought long and hard about the East Kootenay-Upper Columbia Valley storage problem, and had taken the position that before they abandoned the Crippen-Wright preferences (including High Arrow, a limited Kootenay diversion only, and a clearance for Libby if the conditions were right) they would have to see a decidedly superior alternative. In the processes of partisan discussion and objective analysis which were inter-mixed in the proceedings of Policy and Technical Liaison committees, the province's representatives were confident from the outset, and were never persuaded that the Crippen-Wright assessments and recommendations were invalid. (We return to this perception of bargaining strength later.)

There are obvious limits to this "explanation," for some federal Cabinet ministers, and certainly General McNaughton, never were convinced that the Crippen-Wright "formula" was correct. Not a little of the asymmetric adjustment can be accounted for by the fact that the Peace River project did provide the provincial administration with a viable alternative. In the bargaining which ensued, both the United States and federal Canada became at times painfully aware of the extent to which the province was prepared to be a tough bargainer, and prepared to risk completely for-going the Columbia's development if its own terms were not met. The strength of this position was only increased, of course, when the national-ization by the province of the B.C. Electric Company in 1961 preempted for its new owner the major market for new energy in the province, and thus eliminated what slim possibility there was that a federal take-over of the Columbia's development, in the face of provincial opposition, could have been made to work.

A further and very important explanation for the asymmetric nature of the adjustment, which is rooted in the constitutional allocation of respons-ibility to the Canadian provinces for the development of their water power resources, is discussed in the final chapter. Still another explanation lies in the person of British Columbia's premier, and his extraordinary political skill. Throughout the evolution of the Columbia River development policy Mr. Bennett displayed an extraordinary admixture of tactical shrewdness and precise timing. He was also tough. Dr. Keenleyside, the co-chairman of the B.C. Hydro and Power Authority, was to bear interesting testimony to this fact when all of the decisions had been taken. "We were aware," he revealed in 1965, "that if we didn't come back with the pound of flesh and quart of blood he wanted then there would be some changes— certainly in Hydro and maybe in the government."[35] But this is not the whole story; Mr. Bennett was not infallible, and on occasion anticipated strategic moves by those with whom he was competing which, in fact, were not being seriously considered. (Over the 1960–61 winter, for example, he seems to have expected for a while a federal "take-over" of the Columbia's development. Hence for some months his attempt to prevent further B.C. Power Commission expenditures on Columbia developmental engineering.) Furthermore, at times he went to debatable lengths to sustain his position. Some of his denigration of the Columbia River Treaty in 1961–62 can only fairly be described in these terms. His willingness to join others in citing Mr. Udall, out of context, to convey the impression that Canada had been hoodwinked over the Columbia River Treaty, was a case in point. So, it may be argued, was the manner in which the conditions incorporated into the province's December 28, 1960, reference to the B.C. Energy Board requiring it to assess comparatively the merits of Peace and Columbia River developments did have the effect of down-grading the attractiveness of energy which could be derived from the Columbia, before the investigation started.[36] Perhaps the best illustration of Mr. Bennett's willingness to combine nerve and extraordinary behaviour is to be found in a computer study of the effects of the implementation of the Columbia River Treaty which he commissioned late in December 1960, and of which he subsequently made some public and private use. This investigation asserted that at the end of sixty-nine years, as a result of the treaty's operation, the province would have incurred a net debt of some $2,274,086,000. What he failed to point out to those to whom he cited or showed this study (Lester Pearson was one;[37] the author of this study another) was (1) that it assumed there would be no sale whatsoever for downstream entitlement energy surplus to domestic market requirements in British Columbia, (2) that it ignored the downstream benefits in Canada which the province would enjoy from the Duncan and Libby projects, and (3) it took no account of the downstream flood control benefits accruing to Canada from the United States. Above all, when citing the study's conclusion he failed to mention its assumption that the Mica Creek Dam would be built but would sit unmachined and delivering no energy for the entire sixty-nine year period! It is hardly surprising that the highly idiosyncratic, and at times unpredictable behaviour of this man had the federal Cabinet baffled, and made him (as the game theorists would lead us to expect) very hard to counter.

A still further explanation for the manner in which the adjusting process worked toward asymmetry lies in the fundamental decisions which the government of British Columbia ultimately took vis-à-vis two strategic factors in the Columbia policy formation. One of these concerned the crucial question of committing the Upper Columbia and Upper Kootenay valleys in Canada to storage use. When in 1958 the interim Crippen Wright reports drew attention to the apparently high cost of Canadian storage there (and of the power produced by it), and also noted the apparent merit of the High Arrow project, provincial decision-makers came to the tentative conclusion that a favourable Canadian response to the Americans' Libby Dam application might be in order. They, who with their predecessors had a primary responsibility for the holdup on this question since 1951, now began to feel that the debate over Libby would have served its purpose if the United States did in fact recognize as a general principle the case for sharing the downstream benefit produced from upstream Canadian storage. In short—they concluded that the province very likely would be better off leaving the headwaters of the Columbia and Kootenay alone (save possibly for a modest diversion to the north), and that the Americans would be keen to build the Libby project under circumstances which would make its downstream benefits in Canada available on terms attractive to the province. This in fact happened, and the Americans did offer a number of concessions to obtain what, unknown to them, the province had already decided it was prepared to concede![38] Ultimately the adamant stand which the province took in opposition to a major high-altitude reservoir in the Upper Kootenay-Columbia valleys, and to the proposition that maximizing the quantum of Canadian generation should be the prime objective of Canadian policy, forced Ottawa to adjust to British Columbia's position, if a bargain was to be struck at all.

The second crucial matter about which the province made a shrewd decision was the long-standing ban on electric power exports. Although the Gordon Royal Commission on Canada's Economic Prospects reported to the federal government in November 1957 that times had changed and that extranational sales of electricity for stated periods "are perfectly feasible in our opinion, and might be more in the public interest than any other alternative method of developing some of the very large blocks of hydro-electric power that still remain to be harnessed in this country,"[39] this view was greeted, outside technical circles, with a good deal of reserve. No political party endorsed major power exports as a policy until the Social Crediters did so in 1961. As we have seen, the Progressive Conservatives did make provision for them in the 1959 National Energy Board Act and in the October, 1972 Speech From the Throne, but never openly accepted them (when applied to downstream benefit energy on the Columbia) during their years in office.[40]

Both the provincial Social Credit and federal Progressive Conservative administrations were well aware that political myths of forty years' standing are not set aside overnight, and approached this one cautiously. Neither Mr. Bennett nor his senior colleagues publicly raised the matter at length between 1958 and 1960, even though as the Peace River Company's confidence mounted some form of export seemed to be implicit in the premier's enthusiasm for concurrent development.[41] The program of "public education" was left to the independently-minded like Dr. Gordon Shrum, to Dr. Grauer, who found himself faced with otherwise irreconcilable government expectations, and to spokesmen for the Peace River Power Development Company itself. Furthermore, it is not at all clear that the Bennett government was determined through 1960 to push the power export issue to the point of an outright confrontation. In the last analysis, the ultimate decision did rest with Ottawa. Certainly it was not seriously proposed and debated in the sessions of the Policy Liaison Committee. There was an added complication here also, for, while in the very early international bargaining meetings in 1960 the American representatives had indicated a real interest in the purchase of Canadian generated Columbia River energy (presumably from such an installation as that projected at Mica) and a willingness to help in its financing, they had also made it quite clear that they were not in the market, directly or indirectly, for Peace River energy. In other words, even if Canada had lifted the operative ban on major electrical energy exports early in 1960, it was not at all certain *at that time* that such a move would have accommodated Mr. Bennett in his desire for two-river development.[42] The American offer to purchase part of Mica's output raised the additional difficulty for Ottawa that this action might well ultimately create room for apparently higher cost energy from the Peace River to take up part of the provincial load. As the federal government was anxious to see that this did not happen, the prospect of a major power export was set aside at this time.

Nevertheless it is clear that the federal government's stance on the exportation of Canadian "surplus energy" from the Columbia was not one of absolute opposition, and that, indeed, when the possibility emerged in March 1960, that the United States would be willing to let Libby go, it did reach the position of being prepared to consider a sale to facilitate the building of three major storages (at High Arrow, Mica, and Bull River-Dorr) in Canada. But when this combination of projects was ultimately rejected by Victoria, the Progressive Conservative government's willingness to tolerate a long term power export disappeared.

Interwoven as they were in the contest between Mr. Bennett and the federal government over his plans for two-river development, the implications of the removal of the constraint on electrical energy exports for Canada generally, and for the technical planning of the Columbia River's development, in particular, were not subjected to dispassionate analysis in Ottawa and Victoria *before* the treaty's signature. It is impossible to avoid the impression that when in 1961 Mr. Bennett and his colleagues did raise the prospect of selling the Canadian entitlement to downstream power generated in the United States, and indirectly challenged the long-standing ban on major electricity sales across the border, they really had the federal government in an untenable position. The anomaly of a federal policy which called for major increases in the export of hydrocarbon fuels to the United States (where often they were sold to electricity-generating utilities), but which opposed the sale of energy from a completely renewable resource just could not be explained away. Even the technical personnel in the provincial and federal bureaucracies who were genuinely concerned about the implications of Peace River development, believing its product to be inevitably dearer than the Columbia's and fearing that its utilization, by inevitably slowing down the pace at which the Columbia River was exploited, would seriously impair the competitive advantage which they felt a Columbia-first policy possessed, had to agree with the provincial Cabinet here. Yet the fact remains that the Diefenbaker Cabinet's stand on electrical energy exports, and its position on the related, although not identical, issue of selling the downstream power benefit, underwent no operationally significant change in the years 1961–63. If we ignore for the moment the jurisdictional propriety of its becoming so involved with British Columbia's domestic power planning at all, there is no doubt that there was a great deal to be said, in terms of power system economics alone, for the priority to Columbia River development which the Diefenbaker Cabinet insisted upon so strongly in 1960–61. What happened in 1961–62, however, was that the merit of its case was largely outflanked in the context of a different argument concerning the export of electrical energy. "The substitution of conflicts" which Mr. Bennett effected proved to be, as E. E. Schattschneider suggests is normally the case, "the most devastating kind of political strategy."[43]

If the power export issue really was a strategic factor in this long complex policy exercise, and the province greatly strengthened its hand in the end by coming down on the right side of it, the question remains as to why the Progressive Conservative Cabinet was so inflexible concerning the downstream power entitlement sale. At least five explanations can be advanced. One was the continuing conviction of some of the federal ministers concerning the cheapness of the entitlement in question and the desirability of making it available, at cost, to provincial consumers. Furthermore, the political costs for a Progressive Conservative government of agreeing to a downstream benefit sale in a decision which, whatever its merits, would inevitably appear to be a giving way to Mr. Bennett and his Social Credit party were not inconsiderable. This was especially true after August 1961, when great pressure was directed on the federal Cabinet to ensure more favourable treatment for the former proprietors of B.C. Electric Company. Another source of the inflexibility may be located in the indecisiveness which seems to have beset Mr. Diefenbaker in his later years as prime minister, and which numerous observers since have commented on.[44] Whatever the explanation for this phenomenon, the fact remains that in the final two years of its life, the Diefenbaker government had great difficulty in coming to the point of decision on a number of crucially important items, one of which was the adaptation of the Columbia River Treaty to a rapidly changing environment. Some have suggested that part of its uncertainty (especially Mr. Diefenbaker's) may have stemmed from disproportionate influence attached to constituent mail, which on this issue reflected no clear public consensus. But there was a still further and much more important consideration. It is a well known fact that the function of representing regional provincial interests, which a century ago was allocated to the Canadian Senate, has gradually been transferred to the federal Cabinet, where, by convention, each province now must have one member, and the more populous ones still larger representation. Cabinet ministers are clearly expected to articulate the interests of their regions as they see them. In some administrations prime ministers have been willing to go beyond this, however, and to concede to one or more of the ministers from a province or region leadership concerning policy with unique relevance to it, whatever the portfolios they actually occupy. When the principle of Cabinet solidarity is operative, as it is in Canada, it can be seen that, under these circumstances, the adamant minister with a significant power base may acquire something close to veto power. He can, if he finds himself in a minority position and is unwilling to defer to his colleagues, compel the prime minister to defer to him or to ask him to resign. A correlative of this is the situation which exists even when regional leadership is not conceded, but the prime minister himself asserts a veto over all Cabinet decisions, and some few members of the Cabinet possess his confidence to an unusual degree. As Cabinet meetings are secret, and their records privileged, it is only possible to speculate as to the manner in which the Diefenbaker Cabinet in the last analysis reached, or decided not to reach, conclusions concerning the development of the Columbia River. But the evidence suggests that Mr. Diefenbaker had to be persuaded on all major issues, that he placed great weight on obtaining a consensus in Cabinet, that with respect to the Columbia he relied heavily on Mr. Green,[45] that, after 1960, the great majority of members of both the Progressive Conservative Cabinet and the party caucus were prepared to allow Mr. Bennett to have his way on this matter, but that the two crucially important ministers from British Columbia, Mr. Green and Mr. Fulton, succeeded, if not in completely blocking a reassessment of their government's position after 1960, at least in forestalling a definitive and major reversal to it. It is also quite evident that these two ministers were rather less than happy, with the manner in which Mr. Bennett seemed to undermine their position in the federal Cabinet by directing representations concerning the Columbia either to Mr. Diefenbaker or to Mr. Donald Fleming, successively the minister of finance and of justice.[46] Their influence seems to have been more significant negatively than positively, for they were never able to elicit from their colleagues a favourable response to their repeated requests for an outright Columbia River development grant.

One question remains. Why, if the rearguard action of these two or three men was so significant, did they not sense the magnitude of the hazards inherent in their handling of this policy issue? This is much the same inquiry as the one posed over another issue in "power politics" by Aaron Wildavsky concerning the members of the Eisenhower administration and their handling of the Dixon-Yates contract. Wildavsky suggests that part of the answer to his query lay in the manner in which the intensely held views of these men on the public-private power question in the United States filtered or skewed to some degree their perceptions of reality.[47] There really was no such ideological issue involved in the contention between the Diefenbaker and Bennett Cabinets. The stubbornness of the federal ministers is partly to be explained by their unwillingness to abandon the dream of a block of cheap downstream benefit energy with which they hoped to endow British Columbia.[48] Partly it is explicable in the light of the fact that Cabinet ministers and civil servants alike, in Ottawa, took a surprisingly long time to appreciate, after August 1, 1961, how irrevocable Mr. Bennett's commitment to the Peace River really was. It may derive to some extent from the fact that even if an unpleasant development is anticipated, it seldom influences emotions with the impact of one actually experienced. But it seems to have been rooted also in a perception of chagrin, hurt, injury, indeed almost betrayal which federal policy-makers felt after the January 1961 modification of provincial government policy. For two years their public and private communication and argument on this issue was studded with references to the "treaty as originally negotiated," "terms freely agreed to," the "bargain struck in accord with provincial wishes." Their deep-seated fear throughout the 1959–61 exchanges that some of the province's "stonewalling" was designed to make room for the Peace had indeed turned out to be true. Meanwhile their government's position on this issue became increasingly vulnerable, and they, apparently, remained quite insensitive to that fact.

In all, recourse to extended analysis and the availability of strategically strong policy alternatives, in addition to considerations of jurisdictional propriety, tactical shrewdness, much confusion, and some sound judgment on crucial issues, induced over all a great stubbornness on the part of the government of British Columbia, even though its decision-making retained some flexibility as well. Taken in conjunction with the sheer staying power of Mr. Bennett and his associates, the result was that two national governments came to realize that the wishes of this province would have to be agreed to, substantially, if any agreement was to be reached.

Canadian Political Parties and the Recourse to Bargaining. In any democracy, perhaps indeed, in any state, political parties serve as a primary mechanism whereby values are identified, aggregated, and traded-off into program packages which, one hopes, help to resolve conflict and to evoke a broad social consensus. The precise roles which they play vary enormously, of course, in the light of such considerations as the frequency, nature, and significance of elections, the manner of selecting the executive arm of government and the authority attributed to it, and the function of the representative legislature. All the forms of adjustment are operative within parties, between them, and between them and the community at large. Our concern at this stage is to determine the extent to which rank and file party members, and those members holding legislative seats, did influence the two powerful political executives which, over two decades, so dominated the decision-making on the Columbia River's development.

Two features of Canadian political parties should be kept in mind at the outset. They have adhered, broadly, to the cadre end of Duverger's famous continuum—although within the last generation, led by the CCF-NDP, all have sought to acquire some of the characteristics of the mass party. Their membership is small, much of their organizational activity between elections is routinized, their discipline is strong. Secondly, until well into the decade of the 'sixties, when the situation began to change,[49] Canadian parties have long adhered to the tradition which makes the determination of operative policy very much a prerogative of party leaders. Although the situation may be changing somewhat now, there long has been operative in the Canadian political culture, as in the British, a norm which expects the member of Parliament to act in concert with his colleagues and to endorse the prescriptions of his or her leaders. The norm appears to be rapidly internalized once one is elected.[50]

In view of the above, and of earlier remarks concerning the power of Canadian executives, it is not surprising that there were few occasions between 1954 and 1964 when the cohesiveness of Canadian parties over the Columbia River's development was broken publicly. There were no occasions when Social Credit members of British Columbia's Legislative Assembly bolted the party over it, or gave any indication of a desire to do so. Furthermore, the members of the federal Social Credit Party and of its Créditiste party spin-off consistently supported British Columbia's position in the House of Commons. The fact that these two groups held the balance of power in the House of Commons after June 1962, and felt as they did toward the Columbia, may well have helped move the Progressive Conservative Cabinet in Ottawa to its qualified willingness to permit exploratory negotiations with the Americans in the fall of that year. On the other hand, the then leader of the federal Social Credit party, Mr. Robert Thompson, is categoric in his assertion that at no time during the 1962–63 minority Diefenbaker administration did he use his bargaining power to make a clearance for the province's desires, or any action on the Columbia, a *quid pro quo* of his group's continuing support.[51]

The Progressive Conservative party was the one subjected to the greatest internal strain over this policy issue, and it seems to have felt few qualms before 1961. The flattering evaluations of the Columbia's development potential and the denigration of the Peace River project by Mr. Finlayson at the provincial level and by Messrs. Fulton and Green at the federal, were accepted in party circles with little dissent. It was really only when the deadlock between Ottawa and Victoria developed in 1961, and the slow-down in the economy continued into that year, that party loyalty began to be tested on the question, although in no consistent pattern, and seldom publicly. On the whole, those Progressive Conservatives who were perturbed after 1960 were prepared to reserve judgment on the Peace River project, and seldom became its active supporters. Some of the more thoughtful of them, however, became increasingly concerned about the dispute between the two Canadian governments, at the manner in which, in British Columbia, it seemed to threaten the federally dominant position which, for the first time in a generation, their party was enjoying. They were concerned also that the *de facto* embargo on power exports and the unwillingness in Ottawa to entertain the prospect of a downstream power benefit sale were becoming increasingly difficult to justify. They well knew that both the B.C. Chamber of Commerce and the Vancouver Board of

Trade came to favour international electrical energy sales after 1960. The whole question was complicated in Progressive Conservative circles, however, by the outrage felt in influential party circles at the compensatory features of the B.C. Electric's expropriation in 1961. Overall, the range of "grass roots" party opinion relayed to its leadership was so great that it is very difficult even to speculate sensibly as to what effect it had; its most significant result as suggested earlier, may have been a reinforcement of the federal Cabinet's indecision. The pressure for reaching a *modus vivendi* with Mr. Bennett which was generated within the Progressive Conservative parliamentary delegation early in 1962 has already been referred to, and was very real. The fact remains that it was not responded to prior to the June 1962, election, and was only partially accommodated by the clearance given to the exploratory sales negotiations with the Americans in the fall of that year. The loyalty norm continued to operate here—notwithstanding massive and increasing unhappiness within the party and the administration—and the Progressive Conservatives went down to defeat in 1963 facing no overt rebellion from the ranks on this issue.

The adjustments made in the Liberal party concerning the Columbia River Treaty have been the subject of a good deal of comment especially from those who wanted the main international agreement rewritten after 1960. While the leaders of the federal Liberal party never did take quite the antagonistic position to the Peace River's development adopted by some of Mr. Diefenbaker's colleagues, they certainly did their utmost after January 1961, to embarrass the Progressive Conservatives over the strains which had developed with the province over the Columbia. And some of them (Mr. Pearson included)[52] did seem to commit themselves to a renegotiation of the treaty, especially after General McNaughton dramatically retired. But, as has already been noted, not all Liberal leaders thought the Columbia a fit subject for partisan debate, and before the June 1962 election Mr. Pearson rather backed away from a categoric endorsation of renegotiation. His comments on the question remained highly generalized through the winter which followed and through the 1963 election campaign. "Renegotiation" quite genuinely seems to have meant different things to different people, and perhaps different things to the same people at different times, in the year prior to the April 1963 general election.[53] Meanwhile, of course, over the 1962–63 winter, Liberal members of Parliament such as Dr. John Davis and Mr. James Byrne took strong stands for a complete reworking of the treaty.

Donald Waterfield, in his book *Continental Waterboy*, is frankly puzzled over Mr. Pearson's decision not to reopen the treaty in 1963 and his decision, in effect, to give Mr. Bennett what he wanted. He refers to it as Mr. Pearson's "pusillanimous surrender"[54] and speculates that it was a decision taken in response to a United States, ever thirsty for pure fresh water, threatening to "lean on" the exports of Canadian forest products to the American market. In fact, during its first month in office, the new Liberal government simply arrived at a pragmatic decision based on substantially the same appreciation of Columbia River alternatives as was put before its Progressive Conservative predecessors in January 1963. A case for a major renegotiation was recognized, but as was noted in chapter 9, Mr. Pearson and his Cabinet colleagues in the end decided that the probable losses and the certain hazards involved in a major restructuring outweighed the likely gains. Hence the decision to approve the sale, to stick with the treaty, and to seek at the most incremental adjustments via a protocol. Mr. Byrne and Dr. Davis, soon to be named parliamentary secretaries, accepted the conclusion (despite their earlier opinion to the contrary), as did Mr. Laing, now in Mr. Pearson's Cabinet, and his successor as head of British Columbia's Liberals, Mr. Perrault. Once again the cohesion norm was at work.

The preceding chapters contain frequent references to the manner in which the CCF-NDP, as the official opposition in British Columbia, was critical of the Social Credit government's power planning from the time of the Kaiser Dam proposals in 1954. Its leaders and rank and file alike opposed the "two-river" concept; they were hostile to the Peace River Company's project and even more so to its sponsors. In the late 'fifties, and well into the 'sixties, Mr. Strachan and many of his associates shared the conviction, so strongly held by the Progressive Conservatives, that the Columbia River's development was likely to produce much cheaper power, and that the downstream benefit energy returned to Canada would permit quite dramatic reductions in the cost of electricity to provincial consumers. Indeed, it was the strength of Mr. Strachan's feeling on this question of the downstream power benefit sale which prompted him to write his June 9, 1961, letter to Mr. Diefenbaker urging that any such transaction be blocked.

There were subtleties to Mr. Strachan's position, however, which the public largely missed, although they were noted by and disturbed some of his colleagues. While prepared from 1960 to 1964 to endorse the "Mac-Naughton plan" in general terms, he tried to keep his options open. For instance, in December 1960, he warned his colleagues that their party's opposition to the High Arrow Dam might be tactically dangerous. He sensed, in short, that the Crippen-Wright and other not released reports might in fact support the provincial government's position.[55] He also drew to the attention of his colleagues the hazards implicit in doing everything possible to delay any effective intergovernmental agreement on the

318

Columbia. His point here was that such a policy would only play directly into the hands of the Peace River Power Development Company (as he also believed would a sale of the downstream power benefit).[56] Furthermore, while strongly opposing a sale of the downstream power entitlement in the United States, he was careful to avoid condemning power exports *per se* notwithstanding the antagonistic position to them of organized labour, whose influence in his party appeared to increase with the CCF to New Democratic Party metamorphosis in 1961.[57]

The unwillingness to concede an almost unchecked prerogative to the party leader to determine party policy, which has been a feature of the CCF-NDP since its founding, actually was well illustrated in this issue. It is clear that on a number of occasions the provincial rank and file, led by the MLA's from the Columbia Valley, Messrs. George Hobbs and Randolph Harding, ultimately pushed Mr. Strachan into positions (for example, involving categoric opposition to the High Arrow project) which he would rather have not taken, although he still did retain some flexibility.[58] Even though there was much indifference to the Columbia issue in the national NDP,[59] and some of its federal members of Parliament had their doubts about the wisdom of opposing the treaty even on Mr. Strachan's terms, Mr. Douglas, as the national leader, was constrained by the strength of the opposition to the Columbia River Treaty within his own ranks to go all the way in denouncing it and endorsing General McNaughton's proposals as a preferred alternative.

Overall, to a striking degree, federal and provincial Cabinet ministers were able to retain their capacity to make decisions without being subjected to irresistible pressures derived from the identification and representation of interests by their own or by opposition parties. One ironic and dysfunctional consequence of the bargaining assaults on the treaty by members of the opposition Liberal and CCF-New Democratic parties in 1961–62 should be noted. In defending the treaty against these attacks the Diefenbaker and Bennett Cabinets acquired a very considerable vested interest in retaining it substantially unmodified, notwithstanding the case which had emerged for "reworking it" by 1963. But more of this later. Within the Canadian parties, in time, the "manipulated adjustments" of partisan discussion and authoritative prescription (in addition to all the others used) began to produce the consensus required for the legitimization of the policy decision. Only among the New Democrats, where the intensity with which views were held on this subject effectively magnified their impact, and where not a few party members traditionally scorn the meliorative compromise which is so often the road to electoral success in Canada, was a refusal to adjust in the direction of British Columbia's position maintained.

The IJC and the Bargaining Process. It is quite clear that the Boundary Waters Treaty of 1909 did assign to the International Joint Commission responsibilities which could require it to act, in different capacities, in rather different ways.[60] The judicial role conferred on IJC members is not quite the same as the investigative and reporting one envisaged in Article IX, under which the Columbia River reference was handled. Nevertheless, in practice since 1912, the IJC has gone a long way to approaching these two basic functions in a consistent manner; within it the perspective outlined by the late Arnold Heeney,[61] and cited in chapter 2, has been widely accepted. The six commissioners have faced problems as a unit; they have not normally acted as national delegations, but have been absolutely candid with each other, and have sought to coordinate the interests of the two countries through a search for what Mary Parket Follett described as integrated solutions. There have been exceptions to this, but only minor ones, save for the handling, after 1950, of the Columbia River reference.

Just why the IJC departed from its traditional approach to coordinating the interests of the two countries over the Columbia reference is not all that clear; ex-Senator Stanley and ex-Governor Jordan, for instance, could be quite as stubborn, in their own way, as General McNaughton in his. The stakes were high, of course. The Canadian request for a recognition of the downstream benefits principle, which formally dated from the British Columbia response to the first Libby application, was before the IJC from 1951. To the Canadian commissioners the principle was a reasonable one; to a majority of the Americans (in view of the compensation which the United States was offering for a clearance on Libby) it was not. American Commissioner McWhorter, for instance, long a hold-out on this issue, clearly felt that Canada was being rather outrageous in its request. He did not miss the anomaly in the Canadians' 1951 behaviour whereby they held up the Libby application for a downstream benefit not ceded, and yet, three months after the first Libby application was filed, completely ignored the same principle when they applied for a licence to build the Waneta project, which would and does derive a major benefit from upstream American storage, on the Pend d'Oreille. He had a point.[62] The American appointment of an official of the federal Power Commission, and later of an official of the Corps of Engineers to the American Section of the IJC, may well have contributed to the extent to which the international debate on the Columbia was conducted within rather than before the Commission. Certainly, however, some part of the responsibility for this development must be allocated to the man who was Canadian Section chairman from 1950.

General McNaughton's influence was, on the one hand, so pervasive, and on the other, the subject of so much behind-the-scenes concern and some conflict that it is difficult to assess fairly. He was in many ways an extraordinary individual, very able, very industrious, personally gracious, and skilled in exposition—all of which qualities had much to do with the impact which he made on the External Affairs Committee of the House of Commons, on the public and press, and, for a time, on successive federal administrations. He was also a highly subjective person; problems or projects or institutions with which he was associated, especially in a directing capacity, rapidly became "his." As a technically trained man he was fascinated by the challenge which the Columbia River's development represented.[63] But it would appear at least to this writer that he was also the victim of faulty analogous reasoning, at least to the extent to which he regarded the development of the Columbia River as akin jurisdictionally to that of the St. Lawrence Seaway. From first to last he stressed that the Columbia was an *international* river; he firmly believed that the federal government's jurisdiction was therefore pre-eminent and should override that of the province concerned.[64]

To complicate matters, almost from the moment he became the IJC Section chairman in 1950, he was convinced that some of the federal government's departments were wrong in not being as toughminded as British Columbia was with the Americans over Libby. He was inclined to date a coolness towards him within the ranks of federal departmental engineering personnel from this time.[65]

His vigorous bargaining approach to the downstream benefits question has already been detailed. It ranged from his presentations within the IJC, to his championing there and elsewhere of a series of development options which involved varying degrees of diversion within and beyond the Columbia watershed (and which placed great stress on the importance to Canada of the diversionary rights in Article II of the Boundary Waters Treaty), to his role in blocking the Kaiser project in 1954–55, to his dismissal of the case for a major Arrow Lakes storage, and to his effort in 1956 in preventing an international reassessment of the place of Article II in the Boundary Waters Treaty. And it included, of course, the efforts he made to underscore the importance, as he saw it, of the case for storage on and diversion from the Upper Kootenay in Canada—as a means of maintaining "physical control" of that run-off—notwithstanding the American capacity to apply exactly the same tactics (at substantial cost to Canada) via storage on and diversion from their upstream portion of the Pend d'Oreille's watershed—directly into the Grand Coulee reservoir.

Canadians will long disagree over the consequences of these initiatives on the general's part. His numerous admirers are convinced that the Americans were not prepared within the IJC to consider the downstream benefits case in an arbitral manner, and that it was his stubbornness within and without the commission which won through in the end. Others suggest that the traditionally adjudicatory approach should have been utilized, that the commission made little headway when its members became "agents in negotiation," when instead of hearing argument they generated the case on which they then nominally sat in judgment. The latter perspective deplores the extent to which over much of the 'fifties the commissioners seemed to have abandoned their mission to consider carefully the interests, on both sides of the border, affected by the issue before them. (The writer leans to this point of view.)

What is clear is that with his very incisive and categoric endorsement of some projects and arrangements, and his rejection of others, the general did move himself and to some extent the Canadian Section, IJC, into an untenable position domestically. He really did attempt to preempt or to arrogate to himself a planning function which it would seem was, properly, one for the province, and which the IJC had neither the capacity nor the responsibility to perform, and certainly not the ability to sustain in the face of provincial opposition. Eventually he had to give way, although the impression which he had made on members of the federal Cabinet had a very considerable residual effect. Just why this should have been so has given rise to some wonder. Save perhaps for Mr. Green, eventually, the members of the Diefenbaker administration were not close to him—indeed Mr. Diefenbaker recalls vividly the leading role which he personally played in the general's political humiliation in 1944–45.[66] The tenacity with which General McNaughton advanced his views, the strength of his personality, and the weakness of the case for Libby, when it was assessed in purely economic terms and from the perspective of an international system, seem to have been major explanations for his continuing influence in federal Cabinet ranks.

Mr. Donald Stephens, who so strongly believed that IJC commissioners ought not to regard themselves as "agents in negotiation" or "conciliation officers" made a remarkable effort after he joined the commission in 1958 to return it to an adjudicatory or arbitral mode of deliberation. He did open his mind completely to United States Commissioners Weber and Adams on the downstream benefit issue during 1958, and they reciprocated. Later in that year, it will be remembered, he sought to convince senior policy-makers in Ottawa that the IJC should stop trying to do the province's job (as he put it), that British Columbia should be encouraged to name its operational entity, and that the commission should be asked to face up to those issues for which its adjudicatory competence, he felt, so admirably fitted it. The proposition which he advanced, it will be remembered, envisaged the ICREB being asked to work out the methodology of the "character and quantum" downstream benefit assessment, with the IJC itself dealing with the apportionment of the power and flood control benefit. In the light of these IJC determinations and the then current situation, he anticipated that the province would select the projects and interim sequence which best met its requirements and would clear them through its own domestic adjudicatory and licensing procedures, that it would reach a general agreement with the government of Canada, and that the two Canadian jurisdictions would then make a joint application to the IJC which itself would hold another set of public hearings. Subsequently the commission would issue an order approving the projects advanced and legitimizing the principles for the calculation of the downstream entitlement. Interestingly enough, he anticipated that while certain principles "might be assumed to be fixed for all time it would be presumed that the recommendation of the Commission, to be approved by the two governments, would contain a schedule, setting out the manner in which 'hindsight' entitlements are to be completed—and a further position . . . as to the manner in which the schedules [method] might be modified from time to time if the Commission can come up with a better plan."[67]

The reference to the IJC concerning the principles did materialize, of course, but Ottawa did not give the clear indication to the province that it and its entity were free to do their own detailed power planning in consultation with a corresponding American agency—as Mr. Stephens had advocated. Whether, if the federal government had taken this stand with British Columbia, it, in turn, would have been willing to let the IJC work out the principles on its own is an interesting matter for speculation. Mr. Stephens' own objective is quite clear; he was very keen to have jurisdictional considerations intrude as little as possible on the application of the most advanced technology to the Columbia's development.[68] To him the "character and quantum" studies were a matter for technical rather than political-level determination. But of course this was not the way in which the policy-making evolved. Both the federal and provincial governments "looked over the shoulder" of the IJC through 1959, finally in a manner which provided an exception to W. R. Willoughby's assertion that the two national governments have not attempted "to exert pressure on IJC members."[69] Accounting for this fact is not easy. Partly it seems to have reflected the province's concern that basic decisions on the ground rules not be taken without its concurrence when even project selection apparently was going to be a matter for some Canadian inter-governmental adjudication. Partly also it reflected the provincial government's belief that a policy calling for an American sharing of Canadian development costs, and a Canadian sharing of American, as one way or another a "netting" approach would have required, was just a "non-starter" given the political environment in British Columbia during the years 1959–60. Whether a netting approach might have been feasible had the preceding five years not witnessed such an extended internal Canadian debate involving so many unflattering reflections on American motivation—to which General McNaughton had certainly made his contribution—is another matter for legitimate reflection. So is the prospect that the IJC might have been allowed to maintain a continuing contact with the Columbia's development had the Canadian Section possessed a different chairman. Competent though he was in so many ways, in this role General McNaughton may well have been miscast.

In summary, when the IJC established its board, committee, and working group infrastructure during the mid 'forties in response to the Columbia River reference, it did provide an institutional framework within which the data gathering and analytic efforts of the technical personnel of the United States and Canada could be coordinated as they sought agreed-upon answers to some very basic questions. This mechanism served its purpose well for fifteen years. It also facilitated technical coordination (below the ICREB level) between the staffs of the two Canadian governments. When serious conflict as to goals and means began to emerge, however, notably with the Libby application, the IJC's capacity to contain, to internalize the coordination required by an increasingly complex public policy issue, began to wane. It declined still further, and sharply for a time in the 'fifties, when the commission itself deadlocked over the downstream benefits issue. And it was not helped, to put the matter mildly, when the Canadian Section chairman sought to play the role of an hierarchic coordinator of the positions of two Canadian jurisdictions which, ultimately, insisted upon bargaining their way to a reconciliation of their views.

Eventually, with the production of the principles at the end of 1959, the IJC moved off the scene. The legal and engineering advisers to the Canadian Section, however, were closely associated with the work of the federal-provincial liaison committees through 1960, and, in deference to his intense interest, General McNaughton himself was invited to sit in on the Policy Liaison Committee's meetings throughout that year. In his interview with this writer the general did not raise the prospect, which his supporters have since advanced, that he might have been a member of the Canadian negotiating team. (Placing him there, and leaving him on the Canadian Section would have involved a complete break with an arbitral/adjudicatory image for the commission.) All that he had to say, with some evident regret, was that "the real mischief was done at the Technical Liaison Committee level."[70] He provided a running commentary on the course of the negotiations through January 1961 within the Policy Liaison Committee, and directly to the federal government, but it did not consist of *ex cathedra* pronouncements, and was not interpreted as such. The Canadian Section of the IJC, not to mention the commissioners as a whole, did introduce perspectives into the decision-making which were not precisely those of either Canadian government—as the efforts of General McNaughton and Donald Stephens both reveal. In this sense, the commission's involvement did contribute to a recognition of a wider range of interests than might have otherwise been the case. There is no doubt also that when at least some IJC commissioners were prepared to be absolutely candid with each other in off-the-record exchanges, and at the same time were prepared to view the Columbia River in the context of the adjudication of disputes along a common frontier, perceptions were clarified in both countries, and the on-going process of international decision was thus better coordinated. The association of the federal and provincial technicians in IJC teams had much the same effect. It cannot be said, however, that the Canadian Section succeeded in accelerating the process of *mutual* adjustment between Ottawa and Victoria at Cabinet level. It might have succeeded in this respect if the general had held off attempting any such role until the later 'fifties, until, perhaps, after other coordinative routes had been tried, and had failed. But the general's attempt miscarried, preeminently, *because the province had become acutely conscious of his own preferred policy outcome,* feared that in the coordinative process he would seek to impose it, and was determined that this not be allowed to happen.

4. THE EXTENT OF THE RECOURSE TO SYNOPTIC ANALYSIS

This manuscript has already emphasized several times the strength of the Canadian policy makers' commitment, over this issue, to the merit of deriving guidance from careful analysis. This, of course, was the point to the 1944 IJC reference, and to the studies pursued under it, which were set in a system or international framework. It was the point also to the decision taken in 1956 in Canada by the governments of Canada and British Columbia, to inject a national perspective into the supporting analysis through studies commissioned from the Montreal Engineering and Crippen-Wright companies. The decision to create the federal government's Economic Committee at the end of 1957 reflected the same conviction. It was equally well illustrated in the careful deliberate studies produced for a decade after 1954 in the Water Resources Branch in Ottawa and the Water Rights Branch in Victoria, as these two agencies sought to clarify the range of options which gradually unfolded for Canada. Rather picturesque testimony to the capacity of analytic effort "to let the sunshine in" was offered, it may be recalled, by the Bennett Cabinet at the time of its December 1960 reference to the B.C. Energy Board.

Three issues are raised immediately by an enquiry into the comprehensiveness of the analysis utilized. One is crucial and fundamental. Did the Canadian analysts, in seeking to investigate the "problem," determine what the consequences for Canada would be if that country were to develop its portion of the Columbia River watershed independently, without having reached any agreement with the United States at all? And did they use these assessments as the base from which to measure the efficacy of the various approaches to cooperative development which they did examine? The answer to these questions is in the affirmative. The Crippen-Wright, Montreal Engineering Company, and Economic Committee reports all provided clear-cut perceptions of the gains Canada stood to enjoy in the context of a favourable international agreement, when assessed against the most favourable possible development in the absence of international cooperation. It is the absence of such fall-back analysis on the American side, by the way, which provides Dr. Krutilla with what probably is his major criticism of the analytic support to the United States' position in these involved negotiations.[71]

A second consideration to be probed concerns the extent to which a broad range of policy options was identified, and the extent to which the likely consequences of each were investigated. Here, of course, we run across the limits imposed by human and organizational capacities, and must concede Lindblom's case that absolute comprehensiveness is simply unattainable. But the question really is to determine how far the scanning and the examination of alternatives and their consequences were taken. And the answer here is that these processes were pushed very far indeed in Canada with respect to alternatives within the Columbia's watershed, although for reasons and in a manner to be identified later in this section, they were not moved all that far beyond it. The Montreal Engineering and Economic Committee reports also investigated the prospect of leaving the Columbia River alone, and of generating additional electrical energy by thermal means near Vancouver, the major load centre. The Crippen-Wright analysis, it may be remembered, included a number of projects in the Clearwater River watershed, itself part of the Fraser River system. But for the record it must be noted that neither in Ottawa nor in Victoria was an attempt made to identify and assess concurrently in a major exercise in comprehensive analysis all of the seemingly feasible thermal and power developments available in British Columbia. In the latter part of the 'fifties senior officers in British Columbia's Department of Lands, and in its Water Rights Branch, sought to make such an all-embracing analytic effort possible when they tried to persuade the provincial government of the case for creating a new instrumentality which would develop major remote sources of power in British Columbia, and operate a transmission grid linking all of the utility systems.[72] But nothing came of this effort, save that the province's Energy Board, when established in 1959, was given a competence to perform the comprehensive planning function, although it was not asked to pursue it prior to the virtual completion of the Columbia River Treaty (and strictly speaking, not then). The policy options examined in Ottawa and Victoria, to repeat, were extensive, but largely restricted to the various means of developing the Columbia River and its tributaries.

The third question to be examined in any assessment of the holistic character of the Canadian analytic effort concerns the extent to which goals or objectives were identified in the planning process. During the years which this study reviews, academic observers frequently suggested that, ideally, the place to start a complex exercise in river system development was with an identification and a derivation of a consensus concerning the broad range of national aims involved. These aims, naturally, would include the consumptive, power generation, navigation, irrigation, and other beneficial uses (including recreation) specifically referred to in the 1944 joint reference to the IJC. They would include also such values as income redistribution (both territorial and between income classes), other aspects of regional economic development, the control of speculation in the benefits provided, and a host of real but intangible values associated with the preservation or modification of the physical environment.[73] If such a consensus could be elicited at the beginning of a long-term analytic effort, which is doubtful, presumably it would require an extended recourse to bargaining. In any case, it was not pursued deliberately, and certainly not in this manner in Canada. The Canadian analysis, as a consequence, was not synoptic in this sense. From the outset, nevertheless, there was a widespread recognition amongst those who invoked the Canadian analytic effort that the uses to which water can be put do conflict. These same individuals fully subscribed in 1959 to the thesis embodied in the ICREB's report, which simply endorsed the proposition that the conflict between the values identified in the 1944 reference should be kept to a minimum.[74]

There was from the outset, also, a widespread conviction among Canadian hierarchic leaders and the analysts themselves that the Canadian analytic effort should be directed initially to examining the physical feasibility and consequences of project construction, and then to assessing the efficiency, in economic terms, of various combinations of projects with reference, primarily, to hydro power generation, but, to a lesser extent, to flood control and irrigation as well. This is not to say that the analysts were told to forget people or the environment. One very significant element of subjective environmental concern was the likely impact of the "McNaughton Plan's" 150-mile long water barrier in the Rocky Mountain trench between Dorr and Luxor, which concern was felt by 1957 in provincial Cabinet and bureaucratic circles, and which may well have had its reflection in the Crippen-Wright group's conclusion that the American desire to build Libby should be indulged in the context of a favourable bargain for Canada. The fact remains that some significant issues, such as those involving income redistribution effects and regional development in other parts of the province, were not incorporated into Canadian Columbia River analysis. When for instance, in 1956 the Crippen-Wright firm was commissioned to make its study for the government of British Columbia, it was enjoined to examine a long list of enumerated considerations: the engineering and economic feasibility of generation in the provincial portion of the Columbia basin; resulting downstream benefits in the United States; transmission facilities required; the requirements for integrating Canadian facilities in whole or in part with those in the United States; and the physical effects on the established population, on resources, and on transportation facilities. It was also encouraged to advance "any additional and pertinent observation which may arise as a result of the policy." But the objective of all this was made no more precise than recommending "a basis for Government determination of an optimum plan for the development of the river in British Columbia."[75] Similarly, when in 1964 Mr. Williston sought to outline the objectives pursued by Canada and British Columbia for twenty years on this matter, he perceived them in these terms:

> to provide for the maximum economic development of the Columbia in Canada: to obtain the largest possible share of the downstream benefits in the United States which would result from the development of the Columbia river in Canada, while retaining control of the Columbia river and its tributaries for future Canadian requirements: and to achieve these objectives with the minimum disturbance to existing settlement, transportation and resource value.[76]

It is important to remember that although the efficiency criterion was given great weight in both Ottawa and Victoria, and was thus a shared value, this does not mean that all who invoked or pursued analysis started from the same assumptions or came to the same conclusions. When Mr. Williston referred subsequently to "maximum economic development," the emphasis in his argument and consistently, as he saw the matter, was on the adjective "economic." He and his staff were well aware that British

Columbia had very large additional hydraulic resources still untapped, and saw little point in squeezing the last kilowatt of energy, irrespective of monetary and other costs, out of the Columbia River's flow. But there were other perspectives. As has been indicated already, the position which General McNaughton supported in the Policy Liaison Committee throughout 1959 and 1960 and which had a considerable impact on several members of the federal Cabinet, was quite different. The Canadian goal, as he saw it, should be to maximize Canadian firm power production, year by year into the future, and to secure, by implementing a Kootenay to Columbia diversion, complete physical control over the Canadian portion of that river. "Maximum economic development" came to signify for those who shared his perspective an emphasis on the first adjective— hence the federal Cabinet's unwillingness, in May–June 1960, to give up plans for building East Kootenay storages. Conversely, although very sensitive to the social and other costs of flooding 27,000 acres behind the High Arrow Dam, the Diefenbaker administration was quite willing to inundate 86,000 acres of the Upper Kootenay-Columbia Valleys behind the Dorr-Bull River-Luxor projects, and indeed to put both the western and eastern valleys under water. The province's hierarchy of values was quite different.

Ultimately the basic concern of both Canadian governments (but not of General McNaughton) prior to 1960 lay in determining: (1) the most efficient manner (in national income terms) in which the Columbia River in Canada could be developed independently; (2) whether or not in the light of alternative sources of energy this was a viable policy choice; (3) what the magnitude of the downstream benefit derived from cooperative development was likely to be; (4) what form a Canadian contribution to cooperative development might most reasonably take; and (5) what, assuming cooperative development, the significance for Canada would be of coordinating, or not coordinating the Canadian system with the American plants. For its answers to these questions, British Columbia relied heavily upon the Crippen-Wright report. The federal government was able to turn to the Montreal Engineering Company and Economic Committee reports. However it received still further analytic assistance prior to 1960 from its Water Resources Branch, which in one set of studies sought answers to question (5) above, and, in another, set out to determine the merits of the alternative forms of Kootenay to Columbia River diversion available.[77]

In some ways the most crucial of all the objectives over which federal-provincial conflict resulted was Mr. Bennett's insistence that the Peace and Columbia rivers must be developed at the same time. The basic point that Mr. Bennett was making with his contention was that the development of the north-central province, involving a considerable income redistribution, as well as a perceived stimulus to regional economic development, ranked in his scale of values right beside any reductions in power costs which might be derived from the Columbia River's development. (To complicate matters, as the year 1960 advanced, he seems to have taken quite seriously the claims of the Peace River Company that, in energy cost terms, its project was anything but a second-best alternative to pursue.) Canadian intergovernmental agreement on this issue was never obtained. What must be kept in mind is that before and during the treaty negotiations in 1960, the federal Cabinet, and senior technical personnel in *both* Ottawa and Victoria did not take the premier seriously over his "two-river policy;" they did not assume that there would be concurrent development of the Peace and Columbia Rivers. *The result of this fact was that, through 1962, in neither Ottawa nor Victoria was a comprehensive technical study ever undertaken of the implications of the policy outcome which Mr. Bennett had proclaimed as his objective since 1958.* How this came about is discussed in the final section of this long chapter. It is enough at the moment to record that it happened in spite of the fact that after 1959 at least one provincial minister (Mr. Williston) and probably a second (Mr. Bonner) received very explicit directions from Mr. Bennett to make certain that action taken on the Columbia River not have the result of deferring the development of the Peace River. (The remaining members of the provincial Cabinet do not appear to have been party to this decision through 1960. Some of them had questioned the logic of the embargo on power exports over the years, but this was a subject on which Messrs. Bennett, Williston, and Bonner remained silent through 1960. Perhaps the best that can be said about Mr. Bennett's other colleagues is that they did not quite see how he could "pull off" simultaneous development, but they shared his enthusiasm for the consequences if he could, and through 1960 were loath to let the prospect go.)

Interestingly, an attempt was made in 1962 within the newly-formed B.C. Hydro and Power Authority to launch a comprehensive study of the likely technical consequences of implementing Mr. Bennett's grand design. The effort came to naught, however, as it was deflected by the stresses generated in the amalgamation of the former B.C. Electric and B.C. Power Commission staffs.

In summary, the Canadian analytic effort was an extensive one. It started out straightforwardly, but inevitably became more complex as the 'fifties advanced, and the governments of Canada and British Columbia came to realize that the values of Canada and the United States conjointly were not necessarily those of the same two countries singly. It did involve a careful attempt to assess the implications for Canada of Columbia River development with and without assistance derived from an international bargain. The likely consequences of building many projects, in a wide variety of sequences, were carefully explored—although they were restricted primarily, to the Columbia watershed itself.[78] Some crucial but subjective values, over which much intra-Canadian debate ensued, were deliberately excluded from the analytic effort. Had greater resources been made available[79] and had the pressure of limited time not been so acute in 1960, the analysis might have been still more comprehensive. As it was, within some of the limits already indicated, it was pursued with great care and deliberation, and led to a remarkable synthesis of technical findings during the year 1959–60 in the federal-provincial Technical Liaison Committee. The manner in which this synthesis served to illuminate the processes of adjustment at the Policy Liaison Committee level will be discussed in chapter 11.

5. The Extent of the Recourse to Incrementalism

Any policy formation process may be said to be deliberately incremental to the extent to which the goals, alternative roads to these goals, and the consequences of the alternatives examined are consciously limited in number. It is deliberately incremental also to the extent that conscious limits are placed on the time and resources allocated to this examination. Frequently there is a degree of unconscious incrementalism as well associated with the evolution of a complex public policy, in that, in both the planning and implementing stages, policy formation often has to adapt serially or to unfold in response to the emergence of unanticipated developments, problems, or strategic situations. Of course, the serial or incremental development of a public policy over an extended period of time may also be the result of deliberate choice.

Examples of all of these approaches to incrementalism may be found in this case study. The limitation of the number of policy options or alternatives examined was very much the product of deliberate, and in many ways, quite understandable action. The attempt of the staff of the provincial Department of Lands to sponsor the creation of a new instrumentality charged with a responsibility for pursuing absolutely comprehensive (intra-provincial) project comparison,[80] appears to have been killed at Cabinet level in Victoria as the result of the rather acute inter-utility rivalry which existed in British Columbia in the later 'fifties, and which, it will be remembered, erupted into public view in the latter part of 1958. Both the federal and provincial governments had good cause to set aside an examination of Fraser River generation in the 'fifties; they were well aware that developments on this river system would have an indeterminate, but probably very serious impact on a major anadromous fishery. There was still another reason for concentrating much of the Canadian decision-makers' attention on the Columbia River watershed. By 1957 it had become quite evident that American technical personnel were convinced, and were going to argue strongly in international bargaining sessions, that the value of storage for power generation purposes in an electrical system declines over time, as the system moves from a condition in which its base load is met primarily by hydro to one in which it is met primarily by thermal sources. There is a strong technical case to be made for this proposition.[81] Its significance from our perspective is very clear. What Canada had to "sell" by way of stream-flow regulation on the Columbia River when assessed in the light of its value for power generation, became, in the view of this contention, very much a wasting asset. Canadians had good reason, in other words, to restrict their attention to alternative means of making viable the production of a large block of hydro-electric energy from the Columbia River's Canadian watershed which, early investigation had indicated, might remain sub-marginal economically without the stimulus derived from beneficial cooperative development.[82]

The apparently perishable nature of the value of upstream Columbia River storage to the United States was also an explanation for the fact that Canadian planners paid relatively little attention to prospects of thermal generation—involving, for example, the Hat Creek coal deposit purchased by the B.C. Electric Company early in 1960. Additionally, the significance of this privately-owned deposit was not all that clear to analysts and decision-makers in government prior to 1961. In like manner, the displacement effect which moving ahead with early development on the Peace River might have in delaying similar work on the Columbia and hence in reducing the stream of benefits attributable to the latter, was a major consideration prompting Canadian technical personnel, and the federal Cabinet, to set aside concurrent "two-river development" as a viable policy option. There were other explanations as well, of course, for the removal of Peace River development from the planners' spectrum of policy options. Not the least was the already mentioned widespread conviction at the time that the remoteness of the Peace River sites made generation there economically suboptimal for the immediate future. The technicians might have run joint development studies for the two rivers if the constraint on large scale power exports had not been so very real, or if there had been, as there was not, any clear indication that it was likely to be lifted in the near future.[83] Doubtless, the Canadian technicians would have pursued "two-river studies" if they had been expressly directed to do so, but the fact remains that in the context of the incremental strategy which Cabinet-level policy-makers applied to this question in Canada, such instructions were not given.

At this point we really move from the limitation of means examined to a limitation of ends, although in fact the two are inseparable. Within the context of intense bargaining with British Columbia, the federal government consciously limited the goals it was prepared to consider when for so long it declined to attribute any legitimacy at all to Mr. Bennett's desires with respect to accelerated development in the northern part of his province. In this sense it was incremental. But in another sense Mr. Bennett was crucially incremental also, even though his range of values was broader. What he and, ultimately, Mr. Williston did when they realized that to Ottawa and to so many staff advisers in Ottawa and Victoria the values associated with Peace River and Columbia River development were in such conflict, was to "split the problem." In essence they decided to attend to the issues raised by the Peace and the Columbia River proposals in differing environments, and at different times. They invoked, fundamentally, a classic strategic response to conflict, by resolving to deal sequentially with goals, invoking a time buffer, to use a phrase of Cyert and March,[84] and an environmental buffer as well to enable them to solve one problem at a time, even though the searches for solutions to both problems were moving ahead concurrently.

If in one way or another strategic limits were placed on the means and ends considered, what can be said about the significance of the incrementalist dimension of the Canadian strategy for the decision-makers themselves and for the policy outcome? During the years prior to 1959 the concentration on a limited number of goals and policy options certainly helped make the entire planning effort manageable; it was focused. The simplification of the issues, if one will, had the same effect also during the years of international negotiation, 1959–60, especially among the technicians. At the same time, the provincial insistence that establishing an agreed-upon Canadian policy position had to follow on, incrementally, from the derivation of the IJC principles did have the consequence of putting great pressure on the Canadian decision-makers and their advisers when other considerations, in 1960, severely limited the time available for further analysis. *But, preeminently, the incremental strategy utilized by the provincial government had one overwhelming result. In the end British Columbia did obtain a clearance for its two river developmental objective, which, had the province put its cards openly on the table in 1960, might well have been forestalled.* On the other hand, by divorcing two aspects of a developmental policy which actually were interrelated, the provincial incrementalism promoted an extended dialogue between decision-makers in Ottawa and Victoria (and their advisers) which was not based on shared assumptions, and which introduced or sustained some strategic considerations in the planning and calculations of both Canadian governments during 1960 which, shortly thereafter, were to be outflanked. Canada thus ended up with an agreement in 1961 which endowed her, as Dr. Krutilla calculated in 1967, with a demonstrable net gain of between one quarter and one half a billion dollars.[85] But it was an agreement which involved provisions for and some related Canadian concessions concerning the proposed return of the downstream power benefit which by mid-1961 had become redundant for a generation. And it was an agreement also which included provision for the High Arrow Dam, the need for which, when the decision to build the Portage Mountain project was taken, at least merited reconsideration.[86] The decision in 1963 not to seek a reopening of the still unratified treaty was itself to be a classic illustration of the manner in which incrementalism enables one to hedge against risk. The protocol and sale agreement did ensure that the major provincial objective of concurrent two-river development would be realized, and did simplify British Columbia's financial problems. At the same time they did forestall the prospect of losing all or most of the international agreement if, via a complete renegotiation in the highly fluid situation which prevailed in 1963, different ground rules from those used in 1960 had been utilized. Dr. Krutilla's reflection on the renegotiation issue in 1962–63 merits repeating.

> Doubtless, several opportunities to effect economies might have been realized, given the accumulation of new information, enlarged technical opportunities, and changes in policy parameters. But if, as is more likely, substantially different projects, sequences, and technical combinations had emerged, it is not at all clear that the resulting benefit division would have better served British Columbia's objectives.[87]

In short, incrementalist strategy helped produce for Canada very substantial benefits, although, under other circumstances, they might have been larger.

One final observation concerning the relationship between an incrementalist strategy and the retention of the High Arrow Dam is in order. By 1964 the estimated cost of the project was $129.5 millions. After the ratification of the treaty in 1964 further considerations drove the investment on the Arrow project still higher. The expenditure at the dam-site itself, by having a stimulating effect on the entire valley, added to the reservoir preparation costs. B.C. Hydro, additionally, found itself providing new or rebuilt or relocated capital works in the reservoir area, often to a higher standard than those which they replaced, and to a standard above that anticipated earlier. In any case, the combined cost of the dam and reservoir, as completed in 1968, was almost $200 millions. Now, in this inflationary age and especially in a field wherein the market price of the product is rising, project cost increases merit dispassionate treatment. But it is not unreasonable to suggest, even if one does so with the benefit of hindsight, that had the Canadian technical staff, and indeed their political masters, appreciated *in 1963* that this single purpose/storage project would absorb roughly one-half the cash being received from the flood control prepayment and the power benefit sale combined, they would have looked much more carefully than they did at the case for renegotiating the treaty, whatever the hazards which this exercise would have involved. In the context of the assumptions incorporated by the Canadian and indeed by the American technicians into their 1957–60 technical analyses, the High Arrow Dam was a most economic proposition. It is much less attractive when viewed with the wisdom of hindsight, and in the context of the concurrent development of the Peace and the Columbia rivers, a policy outcome obtained through the use of a significantly incremental strategy.

Chapter Eleven

The Policy Formation Reviewed (B)

*The pioneering work by Charles E. Lindblom should not
be wrongly interpreted as being anti-analysis, but as
a seminal effort to understand what we do when we try
to grapple with social problems.*
  Aaron Wildavsky, "Rescuing Policy Analysis from PPBS"

Anyone who has thought seriously about the place of analytic effort in
the policy-making process is conscious of the fact that two assumptions
concerning it are often taken for granted. One is that analysis can help
produce decisions which are different from those otherwise likely to
emerge, and the other is that, in the light of either initially specified or
progressively identified values, the decisions may be better. These remain
basic convictions for many, including this writer. At the same time, as
we refine our perceptions of what major policy-making is all about, and
as we become more conscious of the real difficulties inherent in hitting
policy targets, not to mention the difficulties associated with adapting
policies to the moving nature of such targets, the importance and the
difficulty of testing these assumptions is borne in upon us. There is a still
further proposition commonly associated with analytic effort, even when
its sponsors may have some doubts about the first two. This is to the effect
that analysis can be expected to influence the bargaining dialogue in the
policy-making process.[1] We shall be interested to reflect on these assumptions, and other considerations, as we turn now in this final chapter to
examine some of the relationships between analysis and the broad range
of forms of partisan mutual adjustment which emerged in Canada in
connection with the Columbia River's development.

1. The Interrelationships Between Bargaining and Analysis

Bargaining, Analysis, and Aspiration Levels. One observation can be
made at the outset with confidence. The recourse to analysis in Canada

seems to have affected aspirations there in three distinct ways. First of all, *at least for those who had access to it*, analysis served to clarify Canadians' perceptions of what they might reasonably expect as a return in down-stream benefits from their provision of upstream storage. This clarification came about slowly, and, indeed, was not complete until the international bargaining had ended in January 1961. Even by 1959, however, it had made the picture for Canadian decision-makers very much clearer than it had been as late as 1955.

Secondly, analysis seems to have tempered and eventually reduced the expectations of not a few analysts themselves, and of some official spokes-men who, like Mr. Lesage, in the mid 'fifties had been prepared to attri-bute an extraordinarily high value to the downstream power and flood control benefits available on the Columbia. During the late 'fifties, also, the skeptical work of economic location theorists (and of some utility personnel) regarding what they considered as grossly exaggerated claims being advanced with respect to the stimulus derivable from the availability of large blocks of cheap electrical energy served to moderate the aspira-tion levels of some analysts and of some federal decision-makers. It remains true, however, that the impact of the location theorists was not unlimited; some key figures, such as Mr. Bennett's chief economic adviser, Dr. J. V. Fisher, were unimpressed by their conclusions. Dr. Fisher was convinced that developing a large new source of reasonably priced elec-tricity in north-central British Columbia would stimulate a major boom there, and continued to advise the premier to this effect.[2]

Thirdly, for a few individuals, the injection of the results of analysis into competitive exchanges on the merits of alternative developmental schemes, and in some cases on the merits of apparently mutually exclusive courses of development, did appear to expand horizons or to raise aspira-tion levels. Mr. Bennett, of course, is the pre-eminent example of this phenomenon. He and his close associates, initially, may very well have viewed the overtures of the Wenner-Gren interests with respect to the development of the Peace River as a mechanism whereby they could speed up what appeared to the provincial Cabinet to be a very measured ap-proach on the part of the Diefenbaker government and the IJC to com-prehensive Columbia River planning. The premier certainly did perceive and use this proposal as a bargaining tool wherewith to obtain attractive terms for an agreement concerning cooperative development on the Columbia. But it is also true that as hard data emerged with respect to each river development scheme, the more Mr. Bennett was dazzled by the prospect of realizing them both concurrently. Interestingly enough in Ottawa, where the Diefenbaker Cabinet had won its record majority in 1958 to some degree on the strength of a vision of northern development, the spin-off from bargaining with respect to the Peace and Columbia rivers was not at all of this order. Accounting for the difference in the aspiration levels generated in the two Canadian capitals is difficult, and indeed, remains a matter for speculation. The whole question is complicated by the intense personal rivalries which were involved. It may well be that a federal government, like Canada's, with five large and quite distinct geographic areas to deal with continuously, in the interest of maintaining a reasonable balance with respect to the pace of national development, is almost forced to restrain what it perceives to be excessive growth-rate aspirations in any one of them. But perhaps Mr. Bennett was correct, and a significant consideration here was the extent to which executive and technical circles in Ottawa were staffed by university-trained men!

Finally, attention should be drawn to the manner in which analysis and bargaining together had an effect on the component of aspiration levels which is associated with decision-makers' perceptions of the time available to them. Both analysis and bargaining are time-consuming, and by 1959 the former process had been under way on this issue for fifteen years. Both, eventually, made their contribution to the emergence of a "time squeeze" in 1960, which served eventually, as Herbert Simon suggests is likely to happen under such circumstances, to moderate some aspirations.[3] This seems to have been particularly, if belatedly, true of decision-makers in Ottawa. It certainly does not apply to W. A. C. Bennett.

Analysis, Bargaining, and the "Play of Power." It is quite evident that much of the Canadian analytic effort was commissioned by decision-makers who anticipated receiving from it both a heightened general understanding of the nature of the problems involved, and, as well, strongly supportable conclusions which they expected to put to good use in future bargaining exchanges. The initial approach to analysis via the IJC in the 'forties concentrated primarily on formulating the problem and conducting a data search. There was an operative if unspoken assumption of sorts, prior to 1955, that the end result of the studies pursued under IJC auspices might be the provision of some clear-cut answers for Canada. Thus, it will be recalled, there was great unwillingness in Ottawa and Victoria in 1948–49, and in Ottawa in 1954–55, to compromise the IJC's approach to generating a comprehensive plan by allowing incremental (i.e. Low Arrow) development in the interim.

After 1955, and the confrontation over the Kaiser proposal, the two Canadian governments began to appreciate that the IJC's system-wide analytic perspective might well produce answers which need not be optimal in terms of domestic Canadian goals and Canadian political realities. Hence, it will be remembered, both governments set in motion departmental and externally commissioned analytic efforts in preparation for the tough bargaining with the United States which they perceived ahead of them. Furthermore, after 1957 in particular, part of the incentive to pursuing this analytic effort was rooted in a very strong desire to sustain positions in inter-governmental bargaining within Canada.

Attention has already been drawn in chapter 5 to the manner in which the belief that policy positions were firmly supported by highly defensible analysis did serve to strengthen decision-makers' perceptions of their power in the bargaining process. This was notably true of the British Columbians, who relied heavily on the Crippen-Wright Report, which they were convinced, at least through 1959, was more sophisticated than anything attempted in Ottawa. In like manner the legitimacy widely attached to analytic effort, and to the views of those who produced it, was very neatly underscored and utilized on occasion by Mr. Bennett, who, of course, was prepared to ignore it as well when he wished to. In March 1962, it will be recalled, he made a good deal of his willingness to be interrogated and challenged by the federal government's technical personnel with respect to his proposal to sell the Canadian entitlement to a downstream power benefit.

There is another side to this story, of course. Different analytic efforts pursued within the same jurisdiction can produce different results; technical advisers can disagree, sometimes with great vigour. As we have seen, the findings of the 1957 Montreal Engineering Company's Report to the federal government, and a good many of the analyses of federal departmental staff in 1958–59 were singularly at variance with the views advanced by General McNaughton (and the Economic Committee). From the perspective of Cabinet-level decision-makers in Ottawa the cleavage among its technical advisers over granting or not granting a clearance to the Libby Dam proposal was even deeper; here General McNaughton carried some part of the departmental analytic group with him. The significance of conflicting advice upon those who receive it, however, is variable. It may result in great uncertainty on the part of the decision-maker—a schizophrenia, if one will. Or it may sustain or even strengthen the decision-maker's assurance if it permits him to select a policy alternative from within the range of options represented by the spectrum of advice before him, which he arrives at partly on subjective grounds. Something of this latter order does seem to have happened at Cabinet-level in Ottawa during the years 1958–60, when key personnel there acquired such a strong attachment to a scheme of Columbia River development (involving ultimately a major Kootenay to Columbia River diversion) which would maximize Canadian power generation, year by year, into the future.

What can be said of the extent to which analysis reinforced bargaining positions during the Canadian-American negotiations? An examination of the minutes of these negotiations, and of the documentation prepared for the Canadian representatives, before and during them, suggests that analysis was utilized very sanely indeed to identify, especially with reference to economic considerations, what the most desirable positions were that Canada should take, and what the likely consequences of American counter proposals were. Its influence was certainly attenuated or complicated during the period February to June 1960, when at Cabinet-level a major contest ensued between Victoria and Ottawa over defining preferences and priorities. But, thereafter, in 1960, and during the 1962–63 power sale negotiations, staff analysis was used by the Canadian representatives in textbook fashion to direct the reciprocal exchange of offers and concessions in directions favourable to Canada. Dr. Krutilla bears interesting testimony to this fact when he writes:

> Canadian technicians left a voluminous record of careful and detailed analysis of the implications of alternative proposals, and Canadian negotiators generally had excellent information on the economic implications of proposals coming up for consideration; their skill in diverting the course of discussion to proposals, terms, and conditions which had the benefit of prior evaluation by the Canadian technical staff stands out in the dialogue leading to the international agreement.[4]

There was competent analysis and competent use of it on the American side as well, although Dr. Krutilla takes exception to what he perceives to have been an American tendency to sell short the insight and understanding which could have been derived from analysis in the interest of concentrating on the "resolution of conflict and achievement of consensus."[5] *The record does not substantiate the claim advanced by a number of Canadians since 1960 that the Canadian analysis was far inferior to the American, and much less adroitly used.*

The Deliberate Recourse to Bargaining as an Aid to Comprehensiveness. The extent to which Canadian decision-makers deliberately invoked recourse to bargaining as a means whereby new values and insights might be identified and accorded significance in the on-going analysis was limited. Inter-departmental committees, of course, are a traditional mechanism for pursuing this goal, and were used in both Ottawa and Victoria to some degree.[6] British Columbia's willingness to consult its utilities in 1951–52, and the Advisory Committee set up to facilitate this consultation in 1953, were modest moves in this direction also, although, by 1956, they had been dropped. Probably the two clearest examples of a willingness deliberately to pursue bargaining with the objective of increasing analytic comprehensiveness are to be found, first in the decision taken in 1956 by the two Canadian governments to commission quite independent analytic studies, and, secondly, in the 1957 proposal which came from within British Columbia's Department of Lands to create an entirely new investigatory and operational provincial instrumentality. In the former case, it was quite evident to the St. Laurent and Bennett administrations that there might be real merit in pursuing two independent and even competitive investigations to what, at their level, was still perceived to be one problem. In the latter case, it is possible, if the Department of Lands' proposal had been accepted by the Bennett Cabinet, that an adversary/competitive relationship between the four operative utilities in British Columbia might have been utilized to further illuminate the policy goals and choices open to British Columbia. This might have happened, for instance, if the agency proposed in 1957 had become responsible for a major provincial power grid, and for at least some of the province's new major hydro-electric generating projects, if it had become a party to the treaty planning, and if it, perhaps, had become the Canadian entity. It is just conceivable that if the B.C. Power Commission, the B.C. Electric, and the West and East Kootenay Power and Light companies had realized that for some time to come they would have had to purchase the bulk of their increased hydro-electric energy from this body, the interplay of market forces reflected by these utilities' perceptions might have pushed the Canadian policy formation strategy still further in the direction of combining on-going comprehensiveness with flexibility. But this, of course, did not happen.

It must be recognized also that the elaborate and ultimately effective coordinative machinery which emerged in and around the Policy and Technical Liaison committees in 1959–60 was not really perceived by either Canadian government as a means of intensifying or broadening the scope of the Canadian analysis. The operative rules of Canadian federalism with reference to the foreign affairs power required that, in some way, perceptions and actions in Ottawa and Victoria be integrated. One cannot escape the impression, however, that in many respects the two Canadian governments found this experience a rather trying, albeit inevitable one, even though, ultimately, it worked. Nor can one escape the conviction that, through 1960, each government believed that it might have been freer in its approach to the scanning and evaluation of policy options if the other government, substantially, had been out of the picture.[7] This is not to say, of course, that such a perception was necessarily valid.

This record is thus a mixed one. There were occasions when bargaining was deliberately invoked as a means of broadening the exploration of issues. On the whole, however, there was little recognition in Canada that bargaining was something to be deliberately encouraged, rather than something which just had to be lived with as a necessary element of the governmental process.

The Response of the Canadian Analysts to Bargaining. It has already been observed in chapter 10 that much of the Canadian analytic effort was initially evoked in a hierarchically controlled environment, although not all the values reflected in the final choices were laid down by hierarchic superiors. There was a strong commitment among the Canadian technicians, for example, to economic efficiency as the dominant evaluative criterion. In 1959, however, if not earlier, the analysts found themselves part of an environment which was characterized by domestic as well as by international bargaining, and hence by shifting goals. Continuously during 1959 and 1960, as members of the Technical Liaison Committee and as observer/advisers at sessions of the Policy Liaison Committee and at meetings of the international negotiators, staff personnel were made acutely aware of the strategic moves of policy planners in an on-going contest between the two governments which they were serving. Until June 1960, when agreement was finally obtained on the selection of projects which Canada would pursue in the treaty negotiations, they simply had to pursue their analytic efforts in a situation in which policy goals were indeterminate.

To some extent the Canadian analytic group found itself caught up in the rivalries and disagreements which characterized the relationships between their Cabinet-level superiors. Not all the bargaining *between* the federal and provincial hierarchies was restricted to the level of the political executives. The concern of the federal advisers during the early months of 1960 at the potential cost of granting a clearance to the Libby project, to cite an example, produced its share of misunderstanding and disagreement between them and their provincial counterparts. So did, after mid-year 1961, the provincial technicians' pragmatic if reluctant acceptance of Mr. Bennett's decision to move ahead with the development of the Peace River. One senses that on occasion both bureaucracies were hyper-sensitive in their responses to each other. Some federal staff, for instance, appear to have been rather pointed in the manner in which, late in 1960, they drew attention to what they regarded as provincial naïveté concerning the technical details of treaty drafting. Conversely, from 1958 onward, British Columbia's technical personnel on occasion seem to have bridled at what they perceived to be manifestations of an Ottawa-knows-best philosophy. The differences which did emerge were real enough, but they were the exceptions, not the rule, in the working relationship which became increasingly close after 1959. The analysts were not basically responsible for the contest waged between Victoria and Ottawa in 1960, first over project selection, continuously over financing, and finally with reference to a supervisory authority. Nor did technical personnel cause the estrangement of the years 1961–63.

Since 1945, it can be argued, the place of analytic effort in Canadian policy-making has undergone some interesting changes. During the early post-war years, many of the major policy innovations were derived from essentially political initiatives; analysis was used subsequently to refine them. During the later 'fifties and the 'sixties, however, technological imperatives incorporated in the form of advice seemed to set bounds to the bargaining pursued over some major issues at the political level. And especially within the last decade, while the earlier emphases have continued, analysts have found themselves emphasizing concurrently both the potential utility of, and the limitations to, their own efforts. Now it is obvious that when roles evolve in this way, there are possibilities for tension-producing misunderstanding between executive decision-makers and their advisers. Some in fact did emerge over the Columbia between 1959 and 1964, but it would be a mistake to overstress its significance. As has been noted on earlier pages, this policy-making did involve partisan adjustment *within* as well as between the federal and provincial hierarchies, but the Canadian analysts advanced no fundamental challenge during these years to their political masters' right to set aside their advice.

What is particularly interesting from our perspective is the manner in which these analysts were distressed, by late 1962, if not much earlier, at the extent to which a very defensible if complex technical bargain incorporated in the Columbia River Treaty had been outflanked and made partly obsolete, before work on any of the developments which it provided for had even begun. They were especially perturbed at the extent to which the prospect of going ahead rapidly and hence economically with the Mica, Arrow, Duncan Lake, and Libby projects, and of equal import, with a series of downstream projects in the Canadian watershed (at the Downie, Revelstoke, Murphy Creek, and Kootenay Canal sites) now seemed to be in real jeopardy. Much of this dénouement they attributed, and not unreasonably, to the bargaining process pursued at higher levels. Hence they pushed hard in both capitals, after mid-year 1962, to have the possibilities of a reasonable power sale explored and pushed hard, after December 1962, when the likelihood of such a sale emerged, to see that it was followed up. There is no mistaking the significance of their action here. When faced with the prospect of salvaging a still reasonable agreement, they did their best to prevent an extension or broadening of the bargaining that inevitably would have taken place had the treaty been reopened. At this point synoptic effort demonstrated its affinity for stability in the goals sought and the alternatives to be considered.

Analysis and the Bargaining Dialogue. The first observation which must be made concerning the relationship between the Canadian analytic effort and the Canadian bargaining dialogue (as well as that which ensued with American representatives) is elemental. The dialogue itself was conducted in two quite different sets of circumstances: one was private; the other public. Much of the most critical bargaining with respect to the policy outcome was of the first order, involving as it did all of the sessions of the Technical and Policy Liaison committees, the meetings of Cabinets and Cabinet committees, many of the consultations with members of these executive bodies, and all of the international negotiating sessions. The public dialogue, which involved exchanges between members of the community at large, between them and the two Canadian governments, and between sets of public figures, really began in the early 'fifties. But it was largely dominated by long range debate between ministerial-level personnel until the end of the decade, save for General McNaughton's contribution, and remained unenriched by any significant analytic input until the release of the ICREB's Report in the spring of 1959. Thereafter, a solid if limited base of factual information was available to the public, although attempts to use it in the lay community did not move into high gear until well into 1960, when the basic dimensions of the treaty became manifest. Even then, with the international negotiations continuing in camera, the debate was rather inhibited. This could not be said of the period after October 1960, and then January 1961, when some further, albeit still limited technical details were issued, first in the progress report of the negotiators, and then in a statement released by Mr. Diefenbaker at the time of the signing of the treaty itself. Thereafter the public partisan discussion escalated rapidly, as it ranged over the provisions of the treaty, over the proposal to sell the downstream power entitlement, over the expropriation of the B.C. Electric and Peace River companies, over the merits of the Peace River development, and, after April 1962, over the person and position of General McNaughton.

A second characteristic of the bargaining dialogue in Canada was that frequently it did stimulate a healthy enough willingness to check analysis with counter-analysis. Many examples of this tendency can be cited. This, fundamentally, is what the Diefenbaker Cabinet had in mind when, late in 1957, faced with very differing perceptions from General McNaughton, departmental analysts, and external consultants, it turned to yet another study which, it hoped, would be directed by an eminent and objective Canadian. This was the rationale advanced by British Columbia, also, in December 1960, when it referred both the Peace and Columbia proposals to the B.C. Energy Board for review, although clearly there was a major strategic effort involved here as well to prevent any foreclosing of action on the Peace River itself. The B.C. Power Commission's action in turning to Caseco Consultants Ltd.early in 1961 for a review of the whole Columbia River development plan, including project magnitudes, project sites, and sequencing them, was another excellent example of "double checking." So were the occasions in 1960, when British Columbia went back to the Crippen-Wright firm for an analysis of the 1959 IJC principles, or in 1961, when the federal government turned once more to the Montreal Engineering Company for a reassessment of the treaty as a bargain. The response generated within the federal and provincial hierarchies to the claims advanced by the seven University of British Columbia professors in February 1962 (which were contained in one of the limited number of analytic efforts produced outside these same hierarchies and their associated consulting groups) was another case in point.

If countervailing analysis was often utilized to check conclusions and to clarify perceptions, it must be remembered that it served in this way primarily for in-camera as opposed to open bargaining, for Cabinet-level and supportive staff personnel, not for the immediately interested public at large. The manner in which analysis served to sharpen the Canadian effort in the international negotiations has already been referred to; it served in the same way to assist the negotiations conducted in and around the Policy and the Technical Liaison committees. Here the results of technical studies did substantially clarify what the significance of policy options was, and did indicate when subjective judgment was called for, or was taking over. Dr. Krutilla, who has reviewed much of the working Canadian file, is well worth citing again on the manner in which analysis was utilized by Canadian decision-makers in a bargaining environment— "There is no doubt that Canada, and British Columbia in particular, figured with a very sharp pencil. Analysis was used to illuminate policy choices and to evaluate the magnitudes in the trade-offs when economic and political, long-run and short-run, and similar conflicting objectives were being weighed in the balance. . . . Whatever its origin, the maintenance of the distinction between technical analysis and policy choice was an outstanding Canadian accomplishment."[8]

By contrast, prior to 1964 the dominant characteristic of most of the bargaining debate conducted *in public* in Canada was the extent to which those outside the two governments' hierarchies who participated in it had no access at all to most of the relevant technical studies. For example, much of the basic technical analysis (such as that contained in the 1957 Montreal Engineering Company's Report, or the 1961 Caseco Consultants Report) was never made available for public inspection; the crucial Crippen-Wright studies, which so heavily influenced British Columbia's goals and its strategy after 1958, did not become publicly accessible until 1964; the records of the intra-Canadian negotiations and of the international negotiations have been treated as privileged documents from the outset; and the very existence, not to mention the content or conclusions of the detailed staff studies produced to back up the crucial decision-making in 1960, and again in 1962–63, was really unknown to back-bench members of the Canadian legislatures, let alone to the community at large.

It is quite evident, in other words, that the strategy utilized by the two Canadian governments concerning the Columbia River's development did not call for an on-going public debate, enriched by the introduction of the results of comprehensive analysis while the policy was in its formative stages. Thus there were no comprehensive ministerial or bureaucratic explications of the policy problem delivered to the House of Commons, or to its External Affairs Committee (with the exception of General McNaughton's appearances before the latter body between 1953 and 1960), prior to 1964. Although British Columbia's legislature has a number of standing and ad hoc committees, none was asked to examine this question. In one sense the much smaller house in Victoria permitted debate on the question in committee-of-the-whole, and Mr. Williston did make a serious effort to give his Legislative colleagues there a good deal of descriptive information, orally and in writing. But, as has been recorded already, the "technical record" was not made available to the Legislature or its committees, nor were provincial civil servants required to comment on or explain its contents in this environment. Similarly, as we have seen, the hearings conducted under the provincial Water Act by the provincial water comptroller in the fall of 1961 did not provide for a general over-view and public examination of the provisions of a draft understanding before it had been formally agreed to in apparently irrevocable form.

Even when much of the technical record was made available, belatedly, in 1964, it emerged in such quantities and over such a short period of time during the hearings of the External Affairs Committee in April–May 1964, that much of the analysis it contained was not used very effectively to clarify the debate going on within that body, and concurrently, through-out the country at large. Many of the submissions to the committee, for instance, were prepared in ignorance of the results of analytic effort which the committee had received a few days or weeks earlier. To complicate matters, only the formal submissions of the governments of Canada and

British Columbia, and of General McNaughton, were printed in the record of the committee's hearings. And of even more importance, the committee had no expert adviser, no systems analyst, available to assist members, especially opposition party members, in their interrogation of witnesses, or indeed, to direct questions to the witnesses themselves.

The institutional, conventional, and behavioural considerations which operated to limit the role played by analysis were by no means restricted to the Canadians' public dialogue. For example, the practice of some key Canadian decision-makers of soliciting advice and analysis on a very confidential basis had precisely this effect on some of the most crucial in-camera debate. Mr. Bennett, in particular, was one whose style was to range very far in search of information, perspectives, viewpoints, to put as little as possible on paper, to keep his own counsel, and to avoid the large-group approach to decision-making. There is no doubt that British Columbia's technical personnel, not to mention Ottawa's, remained substantially unaware in the early winter of 1960, and later, of some representations to the premier to which they might have responded analytically, and which did have a major impact on the evolution of the Columbia River's development. The hazards involved in such behaviour are obvious; unlike recourse to bargaining, it contains no provision for an automatic or structured response to test the assumptions on which the information thus received rests, or the logic in the reasoning by which it is derived.

Similarly there were some rather obvious structurally-induced limitations on the extent to which analytically-reinforced bargaining could be pursued in and around the Cabinet in Ottawa. Ultimately the crucial inputs to top-level decision-making there had to be relayed through a few key ministers and a synthesizing Cabinet committee. Notably absent, however, were alternative assessments of the ministers' evaluations of the analytical data they had received, which might have been produced directly for the Cabinet.[9] In like manner, in contradiction to what happens in some countries, vigorous reviews of ministerial goals and assumptions were not pursued by personnel in ministers' private offices.[10]

There were explanations for the withholding of so much of the technical information from the public debate before, during, and after 1962, just as there were explanations for the fact that a full-dress public assessment of the treaty was not staged as late as 1963. To some extent, the reticence with regard to the releasing of information stemmed from the long-standing Canadian tradition of administrative secrecy. Another explanation lay in the fact that the strictly Canadian documents referred to did contain assessments of the magnitude of the "prize" being sought in an international bargaining situation which, with the change in provincial policy in 1961, was to remain fluid for three years after the treaty was signed. A very pertinent consideration, of course, was the well known fact that the possession of information is significantly correlated with power in political contests. And to complicate the issue further, relations between Mr. Bennett and the provincial opposition party leaders could hardly have been worse.[11] When the public debate had nearly run its course, in February 1963, it will be recalled that Mr. Perrault did suggest that the premier might take the opposition party leaders into his confidence, but this never happened. Interestingly enough, the potential cost of an uninformed public debate did not go unrecognized in Ottawa, where some members of the federal Cabinet and senior members of the public service alike gave attention, early in 1961, to the prospect of preparing and releasing an explanatory white paper. The effort was finally abandoned in the face of the changing circumstances of 1961–62, and of the risk that such a release might itself become the subject of still more federal-provincial contention.

From the perspective of this study it is most important to draw attention to some of the consequences, not already identified, of the manner in which analysis and the bargaining dialogue were and were not related in Canada. In the absence of access to the complete documentary basis of Canadian Columbia River policy, those outside the governmental hierarchies who wished to trace its evolution, and to evaluate its results, were forced to rely on the data which were available. Of major significance here were the ICREB Report of 1959, the 1960 progress report of the treaty negotiators to their governments, and a public statement issued by the government of Canada at the time the treaty was signed in 1961. None of these was irrelevant, but often unwittingly unwarranted conclusions were drawn from them as their underlying assumptions were overlooked. The fact, for instance, that the ICREB Report assumed the existence of an integrated system ignoring the international border, and, for analytic purposes, all of the new projects which it evaluated being added simultaneously, was singularly misunderstood and led to much distortion. The situation was only complicated, of course, when, in the debate over the merits of the Columbia and Peace River proposals some of the Cabinet-level policy makers themselves on occasion made categoric assertions which, at worst, were an affront to common sense, and at best, were based on assumptions leaving great room for error. At the time (1960–64) the Canadian public (and not a few Cabinet ministers) had little real appreciation of the impact on final energy costs of such considerations as the rate of inflation during construction (and over the entire amortization period), the length of the amortization period assumed, the size of contingency allowances provided for, load factors, the price at which surpluses might be disposed of (if at all), and the rate of system load growth. Equally, there was little real understanding of the difficulty if not the sheer impossibility of predicting what these variables might be. Indeed, even had all of the data become a matter of public record, the most sophisticated analyst would have had trouble in making comparisons, for one of the difficulties with analyses running over an extended period of time is that differing assumptions are almost inevitably fed into the calculations. The 1957 Montreal Engineering, 1958–59 Crippen-Wright, 1959 ICREB, and the 1961 Gibbs-Merz & McLellan reports, for instance, all assumed different interest rates! In view of the above, it is not to be wondered at that there was little public recognition of the fact that the treaty represented a "package" of arrangements and accommodations, and that more often than not, reworking it on paper to introduce other projects or to exclude those provided for invoked assumptions about the range of alternatives open to Canadians (let alone about their merits) which were frequently invalid.

A rather obvious conclusion to be derived from what has been said about the Canadian public dialogue is that it was marked by a high degree of confusion. It was also characterized by an acerbity which inhibited the very dispassionateness and deferral of judgment really warranted by the complex issues at stake. The tone of the debate was in part a spill-over from bitterly-fought political contests in British Columbia, and in part both a cause and a consequence of a recourse to frequently misleading yet dramatically hyperbolic imagery. In many respects the dialogue was an exercise in irrationality. But the point has to be made also that there was confusion associated with the in-camera bargaining as well, and that this confusion is not to be explained, simplistically, as the result of the absence of an analytic input. Rather, here, it stemmed from the limited attention given by Canadians in their analysis, as well as their bargaining, to a continuing examination of goals. To repeat a point made earlier, this is not to suggest that only the value of economic efficiency was considered in the Canadian decision-making. But it is to draw attention to the fact that, during the long process of policy formation in Canada, when analysis was being generated and incorporated into preferred outcomes, there was little recognition by the decision-makers or the analysts of the wisdom of simultaneously reviewing objectives as well as production functions, or as Charles Schultze puts the case so succinctly, of the manner in which a "better understanding of production functions clarifies objectives, and a clearer knowledge of objectives stimulates the development of alternative production functions."[12] Arthur Paget, British Columbia's water comptroller, and Mr. Williston's major adviser during these years, was subsequently to testify to the resulting absence of clarity in this shrewd retrospective comment:

We can credit the present Treaty to the efforts of too many technical and legal advisors who lost all concept of the true intent of the Treaty in attempting to balance neat arithmetical calculations based on improbable assumptions. There was too much intent to placate purely personal considerations as well. It is remarkable that as good a document resulted from this confused welter of technicians. I must credit both you and myself in adding our confusion to the overall product.[13]

General McNaughton himself bore testimony to the extent to which, in a sense even the analytic effort was pursued at cross purposes when he remarked to the author in a wistful and revealing aside in 1964, "If only I had known what Bennett really wanted, I would have planned a very different sort of Columbia River development for him."[14] In a fundamental sense, many of the participants in the Canadian bargaining dialogue talked past each other.

It is quite apparent that much the most significant result of this limited attention to objectives was the widespread discounting of Premier Bennett's claim that the scale of values of his province justified placing the regional development of the north right beside the efficiency criterion so widely applied to the Columbia River's development, and warranted pursuing the two of them concurrently. (As we have seen, some members of the Diefenbaker administration and many of Mr. Bennett's critics in British Columbia felt strongly that a Columbia-first development policy involving a return of the Canadian downstream power entitlement, and its sale in Canada at cost, would be of immense benefit to the province, and should be the primary Canadian goal in the policy-making. General McNaughton was to place less emphasis on power costs, and more, as he saw the situation, on the maintenance of Canadian "sovereignty" especially with respect to the use of the Upper Kootenay River.) There was an additional result of the limited Canadian attention to policy objectives, for a concomitant of it, in logic, is a review of the basic assumptions being incorporated into the policy formation itself. It was precisely this periodic reversion to a broad scanning of major goals and assumptions, eschewing details, which was lacking on this question in Canada.[15] Thus the case for seriously reassessing the operative proscription of large-scale exports of electrical energy was not even put on the table when Canadian policy was in its nominally comprehensive and formative stage.

A still further consequence of the Canadian public bargaining dialogue with its limited analytic input was that the diffuseness and contradictions which characterized it left a strong-willed government, such as British Columbia possessed, with a good deal of room in which to manoeuvre. This, in time, was widely appreciated. On the other hand, there was another result of the public dialogue which was little recognized, although it may have had considerable strategic significance. Between 1960 and 1963, while disagreeing so vigorously on the power sale issue, the two Canadian governments each advanced some strong public defences of the treaty. To the critical section of the public, and to the political opposition, however, these defences were highly generalized and incomplete. Specifically, they were not associated in the public mind, as they might have been had the technical "case" been revealed at this time. Thus, in some respects at least, the capacity of the two governments to respond to the changes in the policy environment which emerged by 1962–63 was inhibited by the extent to which they still had not legitimized the decisions which they had taken in 1960! This is not to suggest that the processes of legitimization ought never to be deferred. It is to draw attention to the political costs which the decision-maker may incur if those who criticize decisions turn out to be at least partly right, perhaps for reasons not appreciated by the critics themselves, but for reasons which are rooted in a change of circumstances not foreseen at the time the decisions were arrived at. Something of this order does appear to have happened concerning the Columbia River in Canada after 1961.

2. CANADIAN FEDERALISM, BARGAINING, AND THE RECOURSE TO ANALYSIS

If it be a fact that the policy outcome which Canada ultimately sought and obtained was one which provided, indirectly, for the development of the Peace as well as the Columbia River, and this policy outcome was not made the subject of broad-ranging comprehensive analytic effort, one final question remains to be asked. How was it that this happened, in view of the competitive rivalry between two Canadian governments and the great credence attributed by both of them to analytic investigation? The moment one raises this question, one has to face up to the relationship between the provinces and the national government in federal Canada.

Clearly the thrust of the *Labour Conventions Case* decision, referred to in chapter 2, is that whenever in Canada a policy issue arises which normally falls within the jurisdiction of a province or provinces but which also is likely to require the negotiation of an international agreement, an understanding must be arrived at between the federal government and the province or provinces in question. The former not only has a distinct international responsibility, and plays the basic procedural role in international negotiations, but from a national perspective it has a responsibility to evaluate obligations about to be undertaken in the name of the country. Meanwhile, unless they assume a formal commitment with the federal government, the provinces retain the power, with respect to international obligations of the sort we are referring to, of *implementing* or *not implementing* them, as they please.

If the roles of the two levels of government in Canada are not to be completely blurred under these circumstances, obtaining an agreement between them which identifies the criteria in the light of which the federal government will attempt to assess the national interest, as it pursues its vetting role, becomes a matter of crucial importance. It was this agreement which was not obtained between Ottawa and Victoria for so long over this issue, with results already discussed. A number of hypotheses may be derived from the implications of this unique federal-provincial relationship for the strategies which may be applied to this order of domestic-cum-international policy formation in Canada. Two are especially relevant to this case study, with its involvement, for so long, of just two Canadian governments. On the one hand, if agreement on the evaluative criteria to be utilized by Ottawa should come easily in the context of exchanges between Ottawa and one province, then the scope for the utilization of synoptic analysis as the major route to comprehensiveness in planning *may* be greatly extended.[16] If agreement on these evaluative criteria is not readily attained, it is self evident that extensive inter-jurisdictional bargaining will be required. The result again *may* be increased understanding, and, ultimately, a greater accommodation of widely-shared goals. But a second hypothesis would suggest that, if much of the bargaining is conducted in the context of a two-party federal-provincial contest, the bargaining may lead to deadlock, or at best may have the effect of truncating or inhibiting the understanding of the participants and the general comprehensiveness of the decision-making itself.

Now in a sense the distinctive feature of federalism is the extent to which it recognizes that different values exist in society, and tries to structure on jurisdictional or territorial lines the nature of the response to them. It attempts to restrict decision-taking on broad categories of issues to certain spatial arenas, although it does not prescribe the strategies to be invoked within these jurisdictions. What it does attempt to proscribe are massive exercises in bargaining involving the national and provincial levels of government on all issues facing the polity; thus it seeks to forestall intergovernmental contests which could lead to deadlock. As Professor Lindblom suggests, it is a means of distinguishing between useful and disruptive bargaining. There are, of course, major limits to the extent to which governmental spheres can be clearly delimited, or "watertight compartments" identified. Judicial decision and conventional change have greatly blurred documentary precision; furthermore, it may be possible to approach the same policy issue legitimately from either national or provincial perspectives. Canadian constitutional adjudication long since has recognized this. Nevertheless, it remains a fact of life in Canada as a federal state, that the constitution does try to allocate jurisdictional responsibility with reasonable clarity, and does attempt to forestall the emergence of situations in which cooperative and coordinate action by two levels of government may be required, without, however, there being any clear-cut understanding as to the one whose fiat in the last analysis is to prevail, at least on subsets of the issue in question.

When we turn to the subject of this case study, we must concede, at the outset, that the government of Canada had every right to be concerned with the Columbia River. Although it does not possess a generally overriding jurisdiction concerning the development of international rivers as such,[17] as its 1955 International River Improvements Act emphasized it cannot be indifferent to the extranational consequences of provincial initiatives on them. It may well have a basic competence also vis-à-vis such rivers as the Columbia which it can invoke should provincial action or inaction appear likely to impose intolerable costs on Canada as a whole, or on other units in the Canadian federation. Furthermore, there is no question about the legitimacy of its concern with Canadian regional economic development. None of these considerations, however, really justified the role which the federal government sought to play over the Columbia between 1957 and 1962. As they emerged after 1958, British Columbia's plans for the Columbia did not have high extra-provincial significance; indeed the question of the impact of this river's development on other provinces was not raised until Premier Lloyd of Saskatchewan advanced, in 1962, what was to prove a very tenuous claim at best. Had British Columbia's actions threatened to impose high or intolerable costs on Canada as a whole, or indeed on one or a few of the other provinces, a direct federal intervention with respect to the details of British Columbia's power planning might have been both justified and constitutionally sustainable. But British Columbia was not indictable on either of these counts, nor was it holding back the transformation of an undeveloped region.

The very real competence of Canadian provinces in river basin development has already been referred to. Ottawa's extended use of its spending power to launch initiatives in many fields after 1945, of course served to complicate the issue for many Canadians, and for Canadian governments as well. The willingness of the provincial premiers (save Quebec's) to accept conditional grants, and often to ask for more, had the same effect. It can be maintained that British Columbia's request for outright federal assistance in 1960–61, and Ottawa's assumption that its offer of a major loan would be accepted, warranted the federal government's attempt to educe provincial acquiescence to its preferred sequence of projects in 1960, and then, subsequently, to a joint supervisory agency. But the argument is not very strong, and the justification for any direct federal role in British Columbia's power planning vanishes when the prospect of a federal capital investment is abandoned. It is often forgotten that Mr. Bennett publicly made it very clear at the time of the Diefenbaker administration's first public reference to its Columbia River policy and to the prospect of "joint development," on October 14, 1957, that British Columbia saw no need for any federal participation.[18] He did not change his position fundamentally on this issue until Mr. Green spoke publicly, in December 1959, of a major federal Columbia investment. A respectable claim sustaining a strong federal initiative on this issue might have emerged if Ottawa, in effect, had been offering a subsidy (which it was not) to the province to tip the scales in favour of a program which, in contrast to British Columbia's first choice, would generate somewhat lower benefits (however defined) for the province, but very much greater gains for the rest of the country. It is highly questionable, to say the least, whether such an argument could have been associated with the role which the Diefenbaker administration in particular sought to play with reference to the Columbia, but in any case it was not advanced.

The proposition which General McNaughton argued at length, and which a number of articulate Canadians who share his perspective have continued to maintain, that, with respect to international rivers, the federal government's jurisdiction must be the overriding one,[19] is dangerously simplistic. Indeed, save under the circumstances envisaged in the two preceding paragraphs, the federal and provincial governments enjoy a coordinate status with respect to rivers such as the Columbia, which are international but not interprovincial. Concerning such rivers, each has a sphere of competence within which it can exercise a veto; each can checkmate the other. Conceding this, however, gives to the federal government neither the power nor the responsibility to constrain a province to accept a development on such a river which it does not want. This was the position which Mr. Martin adhered to in 1964. It was challenged by the New Democratic M.P.'s, Messrs. Brewin and Herridge, before the same committee as "dangerous and unsound constitutional doctrine," but the challenge was rejected there by a vote of fourteen to three.[20]

It is interesting that Mr. Fulton himself agreed with Mr. Martin concerning the significance of provincial proprietary rights when he appeared before the External Affairs Committee in 1964—although he did mention the overriding federal power in section 92, 10 (c) of the

BNA Act which, in theory at least, can be invoked at pleasure. Setting aside some of the more exotic legal tangles which can be envisaged, the fact remains that, Messrs. Brewin and Herridge notwithstanding, the fundamental proprietary and licensing rights to water and its use in the generation of hydro-electric power, the determination of the selling price of electrical energy within a province, project selection, the pace and scale of project development—all matters over which the Diefenbaker administration sought in one way or another to constrain the government of British Columbia—are, within the operative rules of Canadian federalism, basically concerns of the provinces. If there had to be a contest between the prospect of a reduction of energy prices in British Columbia in the short run and a reduction deferred perhaps two decades but preceded or accompanied by a northward shift in the economic development and distribution of population within the province, it was essentially one to have been fought out in the provincial arena.[21] The Diefenbaker administration was not alone in its vulnerability on this score; Mr. Sinclair can be faulted in much the same way for his interpretation of the federal government's prospective role in 1957, with his offer of federal assistance subject to the condition that the Columbia be developed under public auspices. The resolution of the public-private power issue in Canada is also, fundamentally, one for settlement at the provincial level.[22]

Just why the two levels of government in Canada should have become so enmeshed in a contested relationship involving a fascinating escalation of vetoes is a matter for some intriguing speculation. Partly the involvement may be attributed to a "change in direction" from centralization to decentralization which was taking place across the whole spectrum of federal-provincial relations between 1956 and 1964, and which certainly produced some ambiguities in perceptions of power, as relative strengths were altered. There does seem to have emerged throughout this period of uncertainty a tendency to translate stands taken on single issues, of which the Columbia was only one, into general tests of strength.[23] A partial explanation is to be found at the level of interacting personality. This study probes no further on this front, but the reader who overlooks the strained relationships between Mr. Bennett and the federal Liberals between 1952 and 1956, and between those erstwhile Conservative colleagues in British Columbia, Messrs. Green and Fulton, on the one hand, and Mr. Bennett on the other, for the years 1958–63, runs the risk of seriously misconstruing what actually happened on this issue.[24] To a major degree, however, this confrontation developed when the Diefenbaker government succumbed to a temptation to become a competitor with the provincial Social Credit party as it sought a share of the credit from the sponsorship of a major program of resource development.

Overall, the support which this case study provides for the hypotheses advanced earlier in this section is impressive. There was a good deal of bargaining and much analysis pursued in Canada in connection with the Columbia River's development, but they were notably truncated by the dichotomous relationship which emerged between the two Canadian governments. Had agreement been reached early on with respect to the role of the two governments (and the IJC), and had the province been left free to choose the projects being advanced for development under an international agreement (or had it been conceded "design leadership" in its power planning, to use an engineering analogy,) it is at least conceivable that both the bargaining and the analysis pursued might have been significantly different. In these circumstances there might have been much wider, more open, and earlier bargaining under the province's umbrella, which might well have required those responsible for the analytic effort to give much earlier and more continuous attention to the broad spectrum of fundamental provincial objectives—and their likely implications. In short, had so much of the Canadian policy-making not been associated with a two-party contest, the end result might well have been greater biases in Canadian strategy toward accommodating widely shared goals, as well as toward initiative and decision.

Some additional and important conclusions concerning the interrelationship of Canadian federalism with bargaining and analysis can be derived from a review of this long and involved exercise in policy formation. Inevitably in federal states one does have to accept the proposition that there is, in some sense, a basic congruity between the national interest, however defined, and the perceptions of a genuinely representative national government. The experience with the Columbia River Treaty, however, does underscore the possibility that the view from the centre need not always be the clearest, and the equally important consideration that there are real hazards involved when federal states overstress, or try to overstress, the hierarchical relationship between their components. As Professors Black and Cairns suggest, the classic definition of federalism which posits some degree of coordinate status is not to be taken lightly.[25] The wise federal government must always be alert to the possibility that a province may be ahead of it either in advancing or at least in taking seriously some policy alternatives with great potential for the whole national community—as basically happened with respect to the proposal to export electrical energy.

Whatever the degree of synoptic analysis or incrementalism applied to the resolution of policy issues in Canada which involve both provincial jurisdiction and the treaty power, the viewpoints of the national government and the provincial government or governments concerned do have to be accommodated, ultimately via the processes of partisan mutual adjustment. Since the mid-sixties a number of scholars, not all located in Quebec, have maintained that the currently required approach to co-operation and agreement is inflexible and unduly constraining, at least as it affects one province. Some have gone so far as to claim that the present constitutional arrangement cannot work, and that the provinces, or at least Quebec, must be allowed to deal directly with foreign states.[26] Attention has been drawn in the course of developing this argument to the imbroglio which ensued over the Columbia River Treaty. The question can be debated in a broader context, and one would be hard put to develop the proposition in the late 'seventies, that all possible forms of federal-provincial accommodation concerning the treaty power have even been identified, let alone explored. But to draw the conclusion from this policy experience that the present arrangement is unworkable really is a non sequitur.[27] What has been emphasized by it is the wisdom of establishing the required Canadian intergovernmental agreement early in the process of international negotiation, before the negotiation begins, if possible, and in any case prior to treaty signature. That lesson has not been lost on Canadian governments.

Despite all the delay and the stress which characterized the period between the signing and the ratification of the treaty, a basic conclusion to be derived from the entire experience is that, even under difficult circumstances, federal and provincial ministerial and staff personnel can jointly and effectively work out solutions to international as well as to internal Canadian problems. The functioning of the Policy and Technical Liaison committees in 1959–60 and of the Canadian negotiating team in 1960, the factoring of the issues requiring international agreement for their resolution in 1963, and the manner in which the provincial government's representatives participated with federal personnel in the international exchanges in 1960 and 1963 were all illustrative of the fact that, when eventually the basic lines of responsibility are recognized, the "system" can work very well indeed. Mr. Bennett, it is worth remembering, in 1967 and 1968 categorically endorsed leaving the conduct of external relations "including in particular the right to negotiate treaties"[28] formally within the exclusive jurisdiction of the federal government.

Overall, the interaction between the federal and provincial governments with respect to the Columbia River's development both reflected and contributed to a reaccentuating of the role of the Canadian provinces. By helping to roll back the tendency of one level of government in Canada to overlap on the jurisdiction of the other, when the reverse was not happening, the admixture of cooperative effort and partisan mutual adjustment which linked the two levels of government in the end may well have contributed to the democratic maturation of them both.²⁹ Certainly the manner in which the lubrication of jurisdictional modesty and common sense ultimately served to eliminate in 1963 a quite avoidable and unnecessary "squeak point" in Canadian intergovernmental relations, to use Mr. Elazar's phrase, has not been missed.³⁰ It may be an exaggeration to suggest that in the process, British Columbia with its aggressive experimentation and innovative thinking, as well as its clarification of the parameters of jurisdictional competence, has strengthened the long-run viability of the Canadian community. But it is worth recalling that on this issue as on a number of others this province has been, to use Professor Tarlton's phaseology,³¹ an island of low entropy, and as such has helped maintain a reasonable balance between the symmetric and the asymmetric forces in the Canadian federation.

3. CONCLUSION

In the years since 1945 throughout the developed world there has been an historically unique increase in national wealth, which has been accompanied by an even more striking increase in public expectations. One consequence of this latter phenonmenon has been the extent to which governments, with unparalleled resources at their disposal, have been and remain hard-pressed to meet the demands upon them. Inevitably and properly they have been inspired to search for policy alternatives which are efficient, for alternatives which in some measure provide the largest social return commensurate with any given investment of resources. In this search a great deal of attention has been directed to the strategies utilized in the derivation of public policy, and some more limited attention has been given to the relationship between these same strategies and the institutional structures which would appear to reflect the approaches to decision most commonly pursued within them.

Much of this process of reassessment has sought to increase the degree of understanding, and to decrease the degree of uncertainty associated with generating and implementing policy responses to complex public problems. These attempts to improve understanding, as we have seen, have not always had the effect of curtailing uncertainty, but by identifying it where it exists, they have made possible intelligent adaptations to it. In any case, this general striving for improved efficiency has had a number of important consequences. Decision-makers who are increasingly conscious of the hazards associated with prediction in a very uncertain world have come to reaccentuate the merits of short-run policy implementation. They have sought also to capitalize on the extent to which well-informed partisan mutual adjustment, if invoked at the right time, may increase the overall level of understanding in the decision-making process. And of course, one of the hallmarks of the decision-making in our time has been the greatly extended effort made within hierarchies to produce and to utilize improved analytic techniques. The search for more effective, knowledgeable policies and policy formation processes has a long way to go; there is still a great deal to learn. But it is not unreasonable to suggest that there has now emerged from the efforts just referred to a heightened appreciation of the manner in which a judicious integration of the four ends of our continua—analysis and incrementalism, hierarchy and bargaining—invoked with due regard both to the benefits which may be derived from them, and to their limitations, may contribute significantly to "improving" the policy formation process.

Planning which is comprehensive and policy implementation which is incremental do have a unique relevance to river system development. Over the last generation the refinement of analytic techniques has greatly expanded planning horizons, and has made possible, in the context of clearly defined sets of assumptions, the anticipation of socially beneficial results from developmental decisions extending over a large part of the life of the developments themselves. Used sanely, this analysis can help make the act of choice more rational.[32] At the same time, however, two other characteristics of water resource development buttress the case for short-run approaches to policy implementation. One of these is the speed with which public values concerning the uses to which water and land may be put actually change. The other is the extent to which the pace of technological innovation associated with hydro-electric power development, and with other forms of water resource utilization, is as great as it is unpredictable.[33]

For these reasons a very few Canadians who were especially sensitive to the case to be made with respect to the Columbia River's development for giving system design techniques and technology just as much freedom as possible over as great a time period as possible, would have preferred to see their country settle for a very different type of international agreement from the one ultimately agreed upon.[34] To be precise, they would have preferred the Columbia River Treaty to have been far less detailed and specific. The case which can be made for this proposition remains impressive today, especially when viewed from a technological/analytic perspective. Pragmatically, however, the situation in 1959–60 was complicated. There were very strong pressures in the United States during these years to meet domestic American power needs after 1965 with American projects which, while inferior to a number in Canada when evaluated on a system-wide basis, if built first would have pre-empted a good many of the values inhering in Canadian storage. Although the records examined are silent on the question, it may well have been that proponents of cooperative development, in Canada and in the United States, perceived a treaty which included quite definite commitments to construct specified storages in Canada as the only way to prevent alternative American watershed development from going ahead. Yet this assuredly is not the whole story; both Canadian governments in the end had additional reasons for being prepared to accept the specific project commitments of the Columbia River Treaty. Both were keen to initiate an extensive construction program quickly, in view of the level of domestic unemployment.[35] At the same time, Mr. Diefenbaker's government envisaged a precise and comprehensive treaty as an obvious means of ensuring that what appeared to it to be a superior Canadian policy option would not be held up for the prior implementation of what, to it, appeared to be an inferior scheme of development. Even in Victoria a treaty, which until late in 1960 British Columbia still hoped would provide for extensive entity-to-entity agreement and flexibility, may well have appeared to the province as an effective mechanism for bringing to an end Ottawa's direct involvement with its power planning. But this really is to deal conjointly with two issues, the utilization of the treaty route at all, and the nature of the treaty itself. Whatever the forces or considerations which led to the striking of this bargain in this form, and the gains which stemmed from it, its very specific nature just did not facilitate the type of incremental adjustment to changing circumstances and new information which subsequent developments suggest would have been desirable. In the light of the feedback to the Canadian policy-makers generated after 1960 there is much to be said for variants of the schema which Mr. Stephens on the IJC and some senior federal and provincial staff had in mind during 1959, whereby a treaty need only have endorsed the concept of cooperative development, and assigned to some agency (perhaps the IJC) the task of specifying the on-going principles to guide it, and the responsibility of supervising their application. Leaving to the responsible designated entities the identification and planning of the projects whose benefits they wished to share, and probably wished to construct serially, might well have been the most effective means of educing the most technologically sophisticated solution to a complex problem in a highly fluid environment —if, for the moment, the Columbia be thought of only in those terms. Mr. Bennett's one publicly retrospective comment on the treaty as an instrumentality, by the way, deals with this question at best obliquely. "The thing that's at fault with the treaty," he declared in 1967, "is that it was signed too quickly."[36]

The case for a much simpler treaty may be made in another way simply by emphasizing the importance of providing decision-makers with on-going opportunities to learn. Over this policy issue virtually all of them, and not a few of the external observers who followed their efforts, ended up much wiser after-the-event. This is certainly true of the Canadian federal and provincial technical personnel (and presumably American specialists as well), who, for example, had such major reservations about the technical feasibility of the Peace River project as late as 1960, who certainly feared through that year that it so threatened the cooperative development of the Columbia River as to be likely to displace it forever, but who now are often quite prepared to concede that the Portage Mountain project on the Peace has been a first rate technical and economic achievement.

Many of these same individuals do not appear to have been cognizant through the period of the treaty negotiations in 1960, of the significance which the major Peace River project, with its massive storage capacity, could have, if it were to go ahead concurrently with the Columbia, for the technical planning of the Columbia River's development. Interestingly enough, they were not alone in this respect. Neither the B.C. Energy Board nor its engineering consultants drew attention in their published 1961 reports on provincial power planning to the potential redundancy of some of the Columbia Treaty projects should a concurrent two-river program be proceeded with. The Peace River Company's consultants (Messrs. R. Chantrill and J. Stevens) were informed in February 1960 of the likelihood that British Columbia would favour the inclusion of a High Arrow project to an international agreement on the Columbia River, and were urged to take this fact into consideration in their planning. But, in the files examined,[37] there is no record that during 1960 the technical personnel of either the Peace River Company or the provincial government drew attention to the bearing which the Peace, if, perchance, it were developed in parallel with the Columbia, might well have on the selection of Columbia projects. But if the consultants and government technicians did not stress the significance of inter-watershed inter-connection for project selection on the Columbia before and shortly after the finalization of the treaty in January 1961, they were not alone. Neither did a good many others who spoke and wrote on the treaty in the years 1961–62.[38] Dr. John Davis, for instance, raised the question only indirectly when he presented a paper on the benefit-cost ratios of Columbia River, Peace River, and thermal development before the October 1961, Resources for Tomorrow Conference held in Montreal,[39] although he was very conscious of it by the end of 1962. The seven University of British Columbia professors did not suggest modifying the development of the Columbia by excluding the High Arrow Dam when, early in 1962, they advanced their assessment of the options open to the province, and sought to advance some new ones. Indeed, even Dr. Krutilla himself did not draw attention to the potential redundancy of this project in the light of the development of the Peace when, in July 1962, he privately produced a paper in response to Mr. Davis' earlier effort.[40] Perhaps, on reflection, this should not be all that surprising, for Mr. Bennett's initiatives did add a unique dimension to power system planning.

Not all of the insights awaiting the Canadian advisers and their political masters concerned technical matters. It is quite evident that through mid-year 1961 the Canadian technical advisory group, as well as the federal Cabinet, the board of directors of the B.C. Power Corporation, and the public at large had a good deal to learn concerning Mr. Bennett's strength of will and versatility. The reverse is also true; had Mr. Bennett known rather more concerning the potential technical implications of his desire for the concurrent development of the two provincial rivers, he presumably would have seen to it that his government's technical planners took him much more seriously on this subject between 1958 and 1960 than in fact they did. (It is also true that Mr. Bennett might have been rather less averse to massive investments on Columbia River development before offsetting streams of benefits began to emerge had he possessed in 1958 the perception which he seems to have acquired by 1961 with respect to his province's financial capability.)

Cost estimates for major projects were another matter about which Canadians had some learning before them. Technician and layman alike were well aware, prior to 1960, that such estimates often involve a significant margin of error, but the Canadian experience with the Columbia River Treaty has underscored for both groups the hazards involved in underestimating the range within which it is likely to fall. Not the least of the lessons for Canadians in this policy-making experience concerns the sheer complexity of the analytic effort required to assess even a limited number of policy options in the light of a limited number of values when the physical framework for decision is a major river system. (It is to be hoped that Canadian staff advisers will not in future be expected to come up with the almost instant evaluations of development alternatives such as were asked for by the federal ministers in February 1960.)

A still further lesson concerns the relative significance of efficiency considerations in the process whereby nations sharing a watershed do or do not decide to develop it cooperatively. The experience detailed in this case study emphasizes the breadth of the range of values involved as Canada and the United States faced up to this question, and suggests that cost factors were not the critical desiderata in carrying the two countries to a position favouring the cooperative approach. Interestingly enough, the work of Professor Irving Fox and of David Le Marquand suggests that, more often than not, this state of affairs is the rule rather than the exception, with international river development.[41] (The seeming intransigence of British Columbia's premier after 1958 appears to have been based on a shrewd appreciation of the mix of values at stake, and an appreciation of the likelihood that two national governments, with an ongoing tradition of mutual self-help to sustain, would not abandon fifteen years of cooperative endeavour after it had been carried to the point of treaty signature.)

Overall, we have ended up re-emphasizing the impressive case to be made for associating learning which takes place over time (as a consequence of incremental policy formation) with the insights stemming from the utilization of the most comprehensive analytic techniques available for the development of water resources. We have also ended up conscious of the extraordinary range of combinations of hierarchic control, bargaining, synoptic analysis, and incrementalism which may be applied to the making of a complex public policy. The number of these combinations is made all the greater because of the wide variety of forms in which bargaining and incrementalism themselves may be pursued.

How to account for the degree to which any one of these four forms of strategic behaviour is involved in policy determination is a matter about which we still have much to learn. We do get hierarchic decision-making when power is centralized, and when decision-makers want to preserve as much freedom to manoeuvre as possible by keeping their cards close to their chests—although the scalar model breaks down when authority associated with position has to be correlated with the authority of knowledge. We do get bargaining when power is involuntarily shared as it is, inevitably, whatever hierarchic decision-makers like to think. We get synoptic analysis when there is no other way to approach certain problems, when decision-makers perceive that it will heighten their bargaining power, and certainly when they wish to discover best or optimal positions. Similarly, we resort to incrementalism when time and resources are limited, when the "problem" permits no other tactical behaviour because it itself is unfolding serially, and when there are sharp perceptions of the indeterminateness of the future.

Choosing a combination of these forms of behaviour, that is a strategy of decision, involves assigning weights to them individually. This is a complex process, not by any means solely the result of conscious deliberate decision at any one point in time. Partly the selection will be determined by structural considerations and by the conventional rules of the game which have to face up to the challenge of a particular policy problem. In this sense the choice will be the product of earlier individual and organizational perceptions and learning as to how best to approach the resolution of certain issues. Partly also the relative importance attributed to hierarchic control, bargaining, synoptic analysis, and incrementalism will be attributable to the style, preferences, and motives of decision-makers. In some sense the choice may be dictated, at least for part of the decision-making process, by the nature of the problem itself— although Lindblom's warnings about the need to be careful with reference to gross correlations here are well taken.[42] A very important element in the selection of a strategy at any point in time will be rooted in key decision-makers' perceptions of the type of result desired, or their perceptions of the type of outcome which the operative environment allows.

If this case study serves to emphasize that the selection of a strategy is a highly complicated, and not entirely deliberate exercise, it also highlights a point made very succinctly by Henry Rowen, to wit that, whatever the contribution which the manifold forms of partisan mutual adjustment may make to our understanding and handling of complex issues, they do not automatically educe analysis.[43] Careful and deliberate provision has to be made for it, as Canadians now realize when they review retrospectively the bargaining which went on with respect to the concurrent development of the Peace and Columbia rivers. It draws attention to a still further consideration, the extent to which, if analysis be pursued in the context of values and assumptions held by decision-makers to be congruent with the public interest, the conclusions to which the analysis points may firm up, stiffen the resolution of the decision-makers themselves. This, of course, may be highly desirable. If, however, different groups of analysts work from somewhat different perceptions of what the public interest really requires, the impact which their findings may have in reinforcing decision-makers' perceptions and commitments may make more rather than less difficult the on-going "moving compromise"[44] which the gestation of a complex policy actually requires, and which Lindblom rightly designates as the primary objective of reconstructive leadership.

This is not for a moment to downgrade the contribution which analysis can make to the solution of difficult issues. As much as anything else, however, it is to draw attention to the manner in which strategies themselves must be able to unfold or evolve, as the weights assigned to their components, and to the contributions of participants in bargaining, are allowed to change over time. We have to face up to the fact that, while so often the analyst would like to assign his own weights, and to invoke some bargaining, some incrementalism to extend the comprehensiveness of his own efforts, what we describe as the political process frequently takes over, and produces aggregations of these types of behaviour, often in far different intensities and mixes, than the analyst perceives to be wise. This is of course inevitable; the political cannot be taken out of politics, and analysts' views and values are not, by definition, necessarily those of society. There are real and not necessarily irrational pressures in society to satisfice, to settle for less, but to settle, frequently through the use of "uncertainty-absorbing contracts" and other devices, to use the terminology of Cyert and March,[45] whereby men to some degree impose their will on, or control the environment.

Of course the costs associated with selecting a satisficing policy alternative may be as high as they often are unrecognized. Suppose, for instance, the Canadian policy-makers had decided in 1959 to give an absolutely overriding priority to the evaluative criterion of economic efficiency when the IJC was formulating its recommendations concerning the determination and the division of downstream benefits. In logic they would have required the Canadian decision-makers to insist upon the adoption of some type of netting formula in the calculation of the downstream power benefit. There seems to be no other analytic approach than it, if misinterpretations of the apparent benefits of cooperative action are to be avoided.[46] Indeed, with hindsight now, it is possible to agree with the late Donald Stephens, and to concede that in a sense Canada's rejection of netting did redound to Canada's disadvantage, as he feared it might. If, under some netting formula, the United States had been sharing in the cost of building the High Arrow project when its costs began to mount so sharply, and when the launching of the Peace River project raised some doubts as to the need for this dam to re-regulate Mica's discharges, it is conceivable that High Arrow's role might have been reassessed without threatening the entire agreement. As it was, when under a grossing arrangement this possible diseconomy emerged on the Canadian side of the border, there was no incentive to remove it from the perspective of one party to the bargain, the United States, for its cost was borne entirely by Canada.

There is, however, a most important offset to this proposition which is rooted in the overtly political environment in which Canadian policy was formed. In 1959, it will be remembered, British Columbia's ministerial and technical personnel maintained that in addition to serious strategic hazards there were well-nigh insuperable political difficulties involved in attempting to apply a netting formula across at least their section of the international border. They were, and indeed remain, convinced that the utilization of anything other than a grossing approach might have paved the way for a consideration of the prior United States mainstream investment on the Columbia—to Canada's disadvantage. But they were also persuaded in 1959 that there were just no effective mechanisms in sight which would hold within reasonable bounds the *international* conflicts which might well arise over differences in estimates of costs, over operative interest rates, over the "Buy America Act," over agreeing on reasonable standards of reservoir preparation and compensation to those displaced. Opinions only can be expressed at this point, but this writer's impression of the provincial government's assessment (which ultimately the federal Cabinet came to share) is that it was an accurate if regrettable reading of the political mood and temper of British Columbia at the time, and that, had a netting approach been attempted, the entire exercise in international development might well have been written off as unfeasible.

If it has to be agreed that considerations of political efficiency are always of crucial and sometimes of overriding importance in the formation of public policy, one final observation needs to be made with reference to a form of decision-making strategy which is widely utilized to keep problems manageable, especially if a time constraint is operative. This is the technique of redefining a problem in such a way as to permit recourse to simpler techniques on the road to its solution. Not infrequently these exercises in "redefinition" are both understandable and defensible. After the widespread public and partisan debate which revolved around the Kaiser Dam proposal in 1954–55, in essence what the governments of Canada and of British Columbia did was to redefine the problem, and, for a time, to pull it back from a bargaining environment into a hierarchically controlled one. Their action may be faulted, but it has to be assessed in the light of the fact that in the real world of domestic and international politics there are strategic situations which do inhibit putting all of one's cards, even if one knows what they are, on the table before the bargaining begins. Similarly, it is not difficult to appreciate the case for simplifying or redefining the problem as was done in Canada in 1963, when the decision was taken not to risk the bargaining hazards associated with re-opening a still unratified treaty.

The difficulty with problem simplification, of course, is that one can never be sure just what the consequences of it are likely to be. It is this consideration which keeps the analyst so alert, and so concerned about the hazards of too much incrementalism, even though he uses simplifications in his own approach to understanding. Simplications of reality, however useful operationally, do at the same time distort it. In many ways Mr. Bennett and his associates, by divorcing the technical analysis and strategic planning being pursued concerning Columbia on the one hand, and Peace River development on the other, produced a strategic re-definition of the problem as they perceived it in 1959–60, and simplified its handling from their point of view. Ultimately also, they did obtain their desired two-river development. But it is interesting to note what an after-the-event assessment of the benefits accruing to Canada under the Columbia River Treaty amounts to. In the short run Canada is not so well off, and in the long run she may be little if any better off, than she would have been had she simply accepted the 1954 offer of the Puget Sound Utilities Council to build and to hand over to Canada the Mica Creek Dam, and had she negotiated, concerning the Libby project, a separate agreement with the United States which, it is reasonable to assume, would have involved no direct costs for her.

No one could have known this in 1954, of course, and this comment, made with the benefit of hindsight, is not intended to suggest that the decade of analytic and other effort which followed 1954 should not have been attempted. It is advanced as we reflect on the magnitude of the still greater benefit or savings which Canada might have enjoyed had more comprehensive analysis been applied to the two-river development proposal, and had more time been available, to emphasize the risks involved in problem simplification. Having said this, however, one must immediately add a caution emphasizing the hazards associated with simplistic perceptions of what the policy formation process is all about. The record of the preceding pages does serve to underscore Professor Lindblom's point that it is exceedingly complex; in the apt phraseology of Professors Eulau and Prewitt, "the ways of democratic governance are labyrinthine."[47] One should not forget the intensity of the Americans' opposition in 1960 to concurrent two-river development, which they correctly believed would have to be financed out of their already-strained capital market. The possibility certainly exists that no international agreement might have been reached at all, had Canada formally advanced in the international bargaining in 1960 the whole position publicly endorsed by Mr. Bennett after 1958.

The Columbia River Treaty emerged from a bargaining situation in which the participants had to reconcile differing perceptions of what was desirable and feasible, in which, inevitably, they conferred benefits and imposed costs on each other, and in which not all of the physiographic trumps had been dealt into Canadian hands.[48] From the Canadian perspective the treaty has to stand as a very considerable achievement, as one which endowed Canada with a significant material benefit. In the context of the rules of the game and the constraints which were operative two decades ago, it is possible to fault the actions of some of the policymakers. On the whole, however, the record of the efforts of both the Canadian Cabinet-level and technical personnel to serve their country well is impressive. Their task was difficult, although in one sense easier than a similar one would be today, for they did not have to respond to the challenges to executive and representative government which, within the last decade, have stemmed from the environmental movement and the participative ethic. It is unlikely now in the late 'seventies that Canada (or any other state) would commit the regulation of a resource to a rather categoric use for as long a period as sixty years. But the world of the late 'fifties was very different from today's, and, once again, we have to record that it is not at all clear that an agreement which kept many options open, and left the identification of and choice between on-going scenarios to two national entities would have been negotiable almost two decades ago. It remains true, nevertheless, that the Canadian experience with the negotiation of the Columbia River Treaty still contains much to suggest that if the members of a polity (including its analysts) are prepared to learn, over time it may be possible to so order the relationship of hierarchic control and bargaining, of synoptic analysis and incrementalism, at least in some circumstances, as to produce decisions which accommodate to more interests, not fewer, over a longer period of time. It is precisely this aspiration which, the world over, keeps the analytically-minded at their desks.

Notes

Notes to Chapter 1, Introduction

1. See Raymond Bauer, "The Study of Policy Formation: An Introduction," in *The Study of Policy Formation*, edited by R. Bauer and K. J. Gergen (New York: The Free Press, 1968), p. 21.

2. Lindblom's sensitivity to the process of social, political, and economic adjustment was first revealed in his joint effort, Robert A. Dahl and Charles E. Lindblom, *Politics, Economics and Welfare* (New York: Harper & Brothers, 1953). He developed his thinking on the processes of adjustment in "Bargaining: The Hidden Hand in Government" (Santa Monica: The Rand Corporation, 1955)—an unpublished monograph—and on both adjustment and incrementalism in his "Policy Analysis," *The American Economic Review*, 48, no. 3 (June 1958): 531–38. His now classic essay on incrementalism,, "The Science of Muddling Through," *Public Administration Review* 19, no. 2 (Spring, 1959):79–88, was followed by a collaborative effort, in A. O. Hirsham and Charles Lindblom, "Economic Development, Research and Development, Policy Making: Some Converging Views," *Behavioral Science* 7 (1962): 211–22, and later expanded into a full length work in David Braybrooke and Charles Lindblom, *A Strategy of Decision: Policy Evaluation as a Social Process* (New York: The Free Press of Glencoe, 1963). Note also his "Decision-Making in Taxation and Expenditures," in *Public Finances: Needs, Sources and Utilization* (Princeton: Princeton University Press, 1961), pp. 295–329. The most complete statement of his thinking is found in his *The Intelligence of Democracy: Decision-Making Through Mutual Adjustment* (New York: The Free Press, 1965); a more recent outline of it was provided in his *The Policy-Making Process* (Englewood Cliffs, N.J.: Prentice-Hall, Inc., 1968).

3. Lindblom, *The Intelligence of Democracy*, Part II.

4. John V. Krutilla, *The Columbia River Treaty: The Economics of an International River Basin Development* (Baltimore: The Johns Hopkins Press, 1967).

5. Ibid., chapters 9, 10.

6. See, for example, J. V. Krutilla and Otto Eckstein, *Multiple Purpose River Development* (Baltimore: Johns Hopkins Press, 1958); and J. V. Krutilla, *Sequence and Timing in River Basin Development with Special Application to Canadian-United States Columbia River Basin Planning* (Washington, D.C.: Resources for the Future, Inc., 1960).

7. Krutilla, *The Columbia River Treaty*, p. 43.

8. *The Columbia River Treaty and Protocol: A Presentation* (Ottawa: Departments of External Affairs and Northern Affairs and National Resources, 1964), p. 59.

9. Krutilla, *The Columbia River Treaty*, pp. 26–29.

Notes to Chapter 2, The Constitutional, Political and Physical-Developmental Setting

1. Oliver W. Holmes, Jr., "The Path of the Law," *Harvard Law Review* 10 (March, 1897): 458.

2. British Columbia, *Revised Statutes* (1960), c. 405, s. 3.

3. Essentially for non-compliance with the provisions of the act, or of the licence itself.

4. The provinces thus enjoy a broad authority, together with the federal government, in the sphere of economic development. Indeed, they were more active than Ottawa in this area prior to World War II, save during the periods of the creation of the national tariff and the granting of major incentives to railway building. Cf. Pauline Jewett, "Political and Administrative Aspects of Policy," in *Canadian Economic Policy*, edited by T. N. Brewis (Toronto: Macmillan Co. of Canada, 1965), p. 337.

5. Bora Laskin, "Jurisdictional Framework for Water Management," *Resources for Tomorrow, Conference Background Papers* (Ottawa: Queen's Printer, 1961), p. 219.

6. Bora Laskin, *Canadian Constitutional Law* (Toronto: The Carswell Company, Ltd., 1960), p. 517.

7. Reference Re Waters and Water Powers. In the Supreme Court of Canada (1929), S.C.R. 200 (1929), 2 D.L.R. 481.

8. The British North America Act (1867), section 92, subsection 10 (c). This constitutional provision, in particular, prompts K. C. Wheare to classify the Canadian constitution as quasi-federal. K. C. Wheare, *Federal Government* (London: Oxford University Press, 1953), pp. 19–21.

9. Canada, *Statutes* (1955) 3–4 Eliz. II, ch. 47, The International River Improvements Act.

10. See the arguments of C. B. Bourne, "Energy's Legal Framework," *Transactions of the Thirteenth British Columbia Natural Resources Conference* (Victoria: The B.C. Natural Resources Conference, 1961), pp. 38–39.

11. There is a significant sport fishery in the watershed, however, and the navigational significance of the Columbia main stream in Canada has revived

notably since a large Kraft pulpmill and a sawmill were opened at Castlegar, B.C. in 1961. In June 1977 it became the subject of litigation between the pulpmill-sawmill owner (now a crown corporation) and the Canadian entity under the Columbia River Treaty.

12. A.-G. Can. v. A.-G. Ont., in the Privy Council (1937), 1 D.L.R., p. 685.

13. "Memorandum of 21 July, 1952, from the Government of Canada," *Laws and Practices Concerning the Conclusion of Treaties*, United Nations Legislative Series (New York: The United Nations, 1953), p. 25.

14. The validity and wisdom of the Privy Council's 1937 decision has been debated for a generation, especially by those Canadians who have deplored its limitation of the central government's competence.

15. Few English-speaking Canadians raised questions about it before 1960. One was Henry Angus, a member of the Rowell-Sirois Commission of 1937–40. Another was J. A. Corry of Queen's University. See J. A. Corry, "Constitutional Trends and Federalism," in *Evolving Canadian Federalism*, A. R. M. Lower et al. (Durham, N.C.: Duke University Press, 1958), pp. 118–25. One French Canadian academic observer greatly disturbed by it was Pierre Elliott Trudeau. See his *Federalism and the French Canadians* (Toronto: Macmillan of Canada, 1968), chapter IV, and p. 137.

16. The power is derived from a broad definition of section 91 (1A) of the BNA Act, which confers on Parliament power to make laws respecting "The Public Debt and Property." See Gerard V. LaForest, *Natural Resources and Public Property under the Canadian Constitution* (Toronto: University of Toronto Press, 1969), pp. 136–43.

17. Donald V. Smiley, "The Two Themes of Canadian Federalism," *The Canadian Journal of Economics and Political Science* 31, no. 1 (February 1965), p. 86.

18. J. A. Corry, "Constitutional Trends and Federalism," pp. 92–125.

19. Not to mention the 1540 miles of frontier between Canada and Alaska.

20. The text of the Boundary Waters Treaty is printed in *The Columbia River Treaty, Protocol and Related Documents*, issued by the Departments of External Affairs and Northern Affairs and National Resources (Ottawa: Queen's Printer, February 1964), pp. 7–16. (Cited hereafter as *The Columbia River Treaty, Protocol, and Related Documents*.)

21. Arnold D. P. Heeney, "The International Joint Commission," *External Affairs* 15, no. 3 (March 1963): 142–43.

22. See W. R. Willoughby, "The Appointment and Removal of Members of the International Joint Commission," *Canadian Public Administration* 12, no. 3 (Fall, 1969): 410–26.

23. Heeney, "The International Joint Commission," p. 154.

24. *The Columbia River Treaty, Protocol, and Related Documents*, p. 8.

25. Canada, House of Commons, *Debates*, 11th Parliament, 3rd Sess., December 9, 1910, pp. 911–12.

26. Letter of George Gibbons, a chief Canadian negotiator of the Boundary Waters Treaty, cited in A. O. Gibbons, "Sir George Gibbons and the Boundary

Waters Treaty of 1909," *Canadian Historical Review* 34, no. 2 (June 1953): 132.

27. At this time it deliberately eschewed the name "party."

28. Two points might be made here. It is possible to argue that Conservatism (Canadian style)—whence much Social Credit support comes—has always had a latent radical dimension. Certainly the Social Crediters' pragmatism has been in the classic conservative tradition. See the comments of Dennis Smith, "Rhetorical Radical," *Canadian Forum* 43 (December 1963): 203–205; Gad Horowitz, "Conservatism, Liberalism and Socialism in Canada," *The Canadian Journal of Economics and Political Sciences* 32 (May 1966): 157.

29. Donald V. Smiley, "Canada's Poujadists: A New Look at Social Credit," *Canadian Forum* 40 (September 1962): 121–23.

30 G. P. de t. Glazebrook, *A History of Canadian External Relations* (Toronto: Oxford University Press, 1950), p. 245.

31. George V. Ferguson, "Likely Trends in Canadian-American Political Relations," *Canadian Journal of Economics and Political Science* 20 (November 1956): 438.

32. John V. Krutilla, *The Columbia River Treaty*, p. 201.

33. Maxwell Cohen, "Canada-United States Treaty Relationships: Trends and Future Problems," in *Canada-United States Treaty Relations*, edited by David Deener (Durham, N.C.: Duke University Press, 1963), p. 188.

34. John Meisel, *The Canadian General Election of 1957* (Toronto: University of Toronto Press, 1962), p. 4.

35. The approach to the United States of these two men has not yet been clearly explained, and perhaps not yet fairly described, although a good many have tried. (See for example: Peter C. Newman, *Renegade in Power: The Diefenbaker Years* (Toronto: McClelland and Stewart, 1963), chapter 24; Blair Fraser, *The Search for Identity* (Toronto: Doubleday, Canada, Ltd., 1967), pp. 193–97; Bruce Hutchison, *Mr. Prime Minister, 1867–1964* (New York: Harcourt Brace and World, Inc., 1964), pp. 336–49).

Perhaps George Grant comes closest when he suggests that these two Canadian Conservatives inchoately sensed that the continuation of past policies would mean an end to the Canada which they knew, or felt, could be. Cf. G. Grant, *Lament for a Nation* (Toronto: McClelland and Stewart, Ltd., 1965), p. 33.

36. With the main stream of the Columbia at Castlegar (excluding the Kootenay) providing 18.3 percent and the Kootenay basin 11.7 percent, the Pend d'Oreille adds another 10.6 percent of the total flow. In periods of major flooding, these percentages increase; during flood control operations approximately 50 percent of the flow originates in the Canadian-American watersheds upstream from the Columbia River's crossing of the international boundary. International Columbia River Engineering Board, *Water Resources of the Columbia River Basin* (Ottawa and Washington: International Joint Commission, March, 1959), p. 33 and Appendix V, p. 5. (Report cited hereafter as *Water Resources of the Columbia River Basin*.)

37. Averaging 180,000,000 acre-feet per annum, exceeded in North America only by that of the Mississippi, St. Lawrence, and MacKenzie Rivers.

38. At Revelstoke in the Upper Canadian watershed the highest flow recorded has been as much as ninety-nine times the lowest. Cf. *The Columbia River Treaty and Protocol: A Presentation*, p. 16.

39. ICREB, *Water Resources of the Columbia River Basin*, p. 56. With the addition of further upstream regulation a further two million acre-feet would automatically be made available at Grand Coulee. See also John V. Krutilla, *The Columbia River Treaty: The Economics of an International River Basin Development*, p. 23.

40. ICREB, *Water Resources of the Columbia River Basin*, p. 57.

41. Ibid., pp. 45–46.

42. 1921—522,584; 1941—809,203; Dominion Bureau of Statistics, *Canada Year Book* (Ottawa: King's Printer, 1942), p. 84.

43. *The Columbia River Treaty and Protocol*, p. 18.

44. The Aluminum Company of Canada's development at Kitimat and Kemano, on the north central coast, which commenced operations in 1954.

45. For decades, two-thirds of the province's population has been concentrated in a small section of the south-western mainland, and on southern Vancouver Island.

46. This question is well reviewed in two sources: D. M. Stephens, "Power Across International Frontiers," an Address to the Canadian Electrical Association, June 26, 1961 (mimeographed); A. E. Dal Grauer, "The Export of Electricity from Canada," in *Canadian Issues, Essays in Honour of Henry F. Angus*, edited by R. M. Clark (Toronto: University of Toronto Press, 1961), pp. 248–85.

47. Canada, House of Commons, *Debates*, 24th Parliament, 2nd Session, June 2, 1959, pp. 4249–54.

48. Note Professor Lloyd's comment. Trevor Lloyd, *Canada in World Affairs, 1957–1959* (Toronto: Oxford University Press, 1968), p. 88.

49. One major interconnection was established across British Columbia's southern border in 1948, at Blaine.

50. Grauer, "The Export of Electricity," pp. 269–71.

51. See, for example, George V. Ferguson, "Likely Trends in Canadian-American Political Relations," *Canadian Journal of Economics and Political Science* XXII (November 1956): 441; John Davis, *Canadian Energy Policy* (Toronto: Canadian Institute of International Affairs, 1959), pp. 12–13.

52. Stephens, "Power Across International Frontiers," p. 15. Many of the difficulties with the pre-World War I export contracts stemmed from the fact that in them Canadian power was supplied on a very long term basis not to American utility networks but directly to American industrial consumers.

53. See Krutilla, *The Columbia River Treaty*, pp. 12–13, 26.

54. Personal interview with W. C. Mainwaring (until 1958 a B.C. Electric vice-president), August 13, 1965.

55. *Report of the Royal Commission in the Matter of the British Columbia Power Commission* (August 14, 1959), p. 10.

56. By 1958 the installed capacity of the B.C. Electric Company was 1,029,835 h p., roughly three times that of the B.C. Power Commission.

Notes to Chapter 3, The Canadian Approach to the Columbia in the Pre-Diefenbaker Years

1. F. C. Green, surveyor-general of British Columbia, to E. Davis, comptroller of water rights, British Columbia, December 9, 1943.

2. The IJC had jurisdiction because the impoundment could lead to flooding upstream on the Kootenay, across the border into Idaho. The order of approval was dated November 11, 1938. The commission made storage contingent upon a deepening of the outlet of Kootenay Lake, and subject to regulation by an International Kootenay Lake Board of Control, which it established. It assigned to the applicant responsibility for compensation for damage done to upstream farms. No reference was made to downstream benefits, either by the appplicant or by the commission. Such a benefit was realized in the United States, nevertheless, and a major purchaser of the additional energy thus made available in the United States, the Washington Water Power Company, assisted the West Kootenay Power and Light Company in meeting the upstream damage costs.

3. The first was the Rock Island project of the Puget Sound Power and Light Company, completed in 1933. The Bonneville Dam, the first of the major American federal government projects, was completed in 1938; Grand Coulee produced its first electricity in September 1941.

4. Cf. *The Province* (Vancouver), September 30, 1937, p. 4.

5. Division engineer, North Pacific Division, USA, *Report on Columbia River and Minor Tributaries Concerning Navigation, Flood Control, Power Development and Irrigation* (Washington: Government Priting Office, 2 vols., 1933–1934).

6. L. M. Bloomfield and G. F. Fitzgerald, *The Boundary Waters Problems of Canada and the United States* (Toronto: Carswell, 1958), pp. 164–65. The text of the reference may also be found in *The Columbia River Treaty, Protocol and Related Documents*.

7. Mr. Melrose served on the Engineering Committee until 1953; in the following year his successor as deputy minister of lands, Mr. E. Bassett, was appointed to the committee.

8. J. F. Miles, who served from 1948 to 1954, when succeeded as the province's representative by G. J. A. Kidd.

9. *The Daily Colonist* (Victoria), January 7, 1949, p. 8—citing Mr. Dill.

10. Canada, House of Commons, *Debates*, 19th Parlt., 5th Sess , March 9, 1944, p. 1292.

11. The terminology is that of G. P. Melrose, writing to G. E. Webb (a federal government engineer), January 22, 1949, p. 2—describing the Johnson-Dill exchanges.

12. See Dorothy L. Moore, "The Role of the International Joint Commis-

sion in Columbia River Basin Development," M.A. thesis, University of California, Berkeley, 1962, pp. 61–65.

13. Especially from residents of the Kootenay Valley in and near Creston, B.C.

14. International Columbia River Engineering Board, *Interim Report on Kootenay River to the International Joint Commission*, November 1, 1950, pp. 4, 5.

15. Confirmed by letter to author from E. T. Kenny, minister of lands and forests in that administration, May 28, 1970.

16. Graphically they represented a cross-section of the storage in the Libby reservoir then projected as follows:

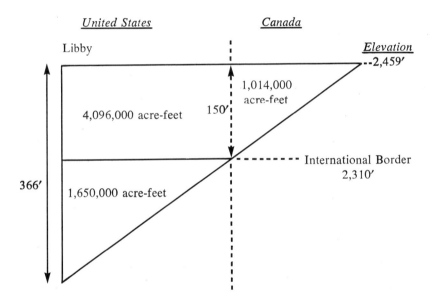

17. An undated, unsigned monograph in the province's files which appears to have been written in mid-June 1949, clearly outlines this position. It advanced the prospect of Canada receiving both a downstream power benefit and a downstream flood control benefit as well. "Preliminary Consideration of the Principles of Allocation of Costs and Revenues of Columbia River Basin Developments as between Canada and the United States," Item 20, D. Series, Microfilm File, reel 73.

18. International Columbia River Engineering Board, *Kootenay River: An Interim Report to the International Joint Commission*, November 1, 1950, p. 78.

19. George Melrose, "Re Libby Dam Proposals, Memorandum to the Hon. E. T. Kenny," April 30, 1951. Mr. Melrose recorded how he and British Columbia's assistant deputy attorney-general, Alan Maclean, had met with federal officials including Canadian ICREB members in March 1951—

"the result of which was that they would give us no support for our claim for downstream benefits and in their statement to the Commission hearings the Department of External Affairs were very non-committal on it."

20. L. B. Pearson, "Statement in Response," March 8, 1951. ("Public Hearing at Cranbrook, B.C. in the Matter of the Application of the government of the United States dated January 12, 1951, re Libby Dam"—International Joint Commission, March 1951, p. 26.)

21. G. S. Wismer, "Statement in Response by the Government of British Columbia," March 9, 1951. Ibid., p. 27.

22. The capitalized value of Canada's reservoir costs was set as $6,459,800 (Canadian dollars) or $6 million (U.S. dollars) at this time.

The 13,300 kw years were valued at the U.S. system price of $17.50 per kw year, and were advanced on the assumption that direct reservoir costs would be fully amortized over fifty years at 3 percent interest.

23. The Canadian technicians were well aware of the subsidized nature of the Bonneville rate structure. The 69,400 kw figure was derived as follows:

Libby's average output was set at 248,000 kw. Canada was estimated to provide 15 percent of Libby's storage and 41 percent of the head. The two averaged $\dfrac{15 + 41}{2}$ came to 28 percent. $248,000 \times .28 = 69,400$.

24. International Columbia River Engineering Board, *Libby Project: Kootenay River*, a report submitted to the International Joint Commission, May–July, 1951, p. 22.

25. Just what the province's response would have been had the ICREB categorically accepted the Engineering Committee's recommendation is not clear. Note that the Engineering Committee's proposal made no direct reference to a sharing of benefits produced downstream from Libby, and did not take into account such factors as the higher interest rate which British Columbia, as opposed to the United States, might well have to pay on its Libby reservoir borrowing. Attention was quickly directed to these considerations in provincial staff memoranda.

26. Calculated on Canadian dollar costs, to reflect later cost estimates and to protect the province against interest rate increases in the cost of providing the flowage area.

27. The 44 percent was derived in this manner:

—percentage of the drainage area above Libby provided by Canada   75
—percentage of the head provided by Canada   42
—percentage of the storage provided by Canada   15
                                                                        ——
                                                                        132

$$\dfrac{132}{3} = 44$$

28. The main service areas of the four major provincial utilities are represented in Figure 5.

29. G. E. Elkington (general manager, East Kootenay Light and Power Co.) to G. P. Melrose, May 25, 1951. A. E. Dal Grauer (president, B.C. Electric Co.) to G. P. Melrose, May 25, 1951. Interestingly enough Mr. Elkington felt that the possibilities of a Canal Flats diversion should not be overlooked, and Dr. Grauer hoped the province would be able to make a profit on any energy which it was able to sell to his company.

30. The Consolidated Mining and Smelting Company, Ltd. Its views were recorded in a memorandum, "Economic Consequences of the Libby Project for British Columbia," October 24, 1951.

31. Ibid., Appendix, p. 2. The Waneta project (and a further one, then unbuilt at Seven Mile on the Pend d'Oreille) stood to benefit materially from over five million acre-feet of upstream American storage. *Yet the Canadian applicant in this case had advanced no offer to pay a downstream benefit.*

32. E. H. Tredcroft (comptroller of water rights), D. B. Turner (director of conservation), J. F. Miles (project engineer), "Current International River Situation," memorandum to the Hon. E. T. Kenny, minister of lands, October 27, 1951, pp. 3, 5, 7.

33. Ibid., p. 7.

34. Chairman Stanley's response, in the form of a long letter to General McNaughton dated March 12, 1952, is printed in U.S. Congress, Senate, Committee on Interior and Insular Affairs, Hearings, *Upper Columbia River Development*, 85th Cong., 2nd Sess., 1958, pp. 284–89 (cited hereafter as *Upper Columbia River Development*, 1958).

35. Apparently a good deal of American pressure was exerted on the Canadian Section chairman, IJC, during the early 'fifties, to persuade him to sign a Libby order of approval.

Personal interview, A. G. L. McNaughton, September 10, 1964.

Those who made such efforts were really unaware of the nuances of the Canadian constitution.

36. Some caution is in order here, for the manuscript reviewed was the draft letter to General McNaughton as sent by the provincial staff to Cabinet. It may have been modified there before it was transmitted. My assumption is that, substantially, it remained unchanged.

37. Personal interviews, W. A. C. Bennett, December 6, 1965; A. G. L. McNaughton, September 10, 1964.

38. Appointed to it were R. L. Sommers (minister of lands and forests), K. Kiernan (minister of mines), W. Black (provincial secretary), S. R. Weston (chairman of the British Columbia Power Commission), T. Ingledow (vice president, engineering, the B.C. Electric Company), and R. G. Anderson (general manager of the West Kootenay Power and Light Company). Its secretary was G. J. A. Kidd, project engineer in the provincial Water Resources Service.

39. This was an adaptation of the so-called Hackworth formula first advanced before the IJC by U.S. Counsel George Hackworth in the Grand Falls Power Case, Docket No. 19. See Bloomfield and Fitzgerald, *Boundary Waters Problems*, p. 113. In 1955 General McNaughton estimated that

applied to Libby it would entitle British Columbia to roughly one-third of its at-site power; Canada, House of Commons, Standing Committee on External Affairs, *Minutes of Proceedings and Evidence*, 22nd Parlt., 2nd Sess., March 10, 1955, p. 35. (Cited hereafter as External Affairs Committee, *Minutes of Proceedings and Evidence*.)

40. U.S. Congress, Senate, Committee on Interior and Insular Affairs and a Special Subcommittee of the Committee on Foreign Relations. *Upper Columbia River Development, Joint Hearings*. 84th Cong., 2nd sess., March 22, 1956, p. 55. (Cited hereafter as *Upper Columbia River Development*, 1956).

See also *Upper Columbia River Development*, 1958, p. 269.

41. On May 12, 1954, General McNaughton told the External Affairs Committee of the House of Commons that the ICREB Report likely would require another four years of work. External Affairs Committee, *Minutes of Proceedings and Evidence*, 22nd Parlt., 1st Sess., May 12, 1954, p. 169.

42. *The Daily Colonist* (Victoria), December 18, 1952, p. 15; *The Province* (Vancouver), November 12, 1954, p. 5.

43. *The Daily Colonist* (Victoria), February 11, 1954, p. 20.

44. See the evidence of R. W. Bonner, External Affairs Committee, *Minutes of Proceedings and Evidence*, 22nd Parlt., 2nd Sess., April 28, 1955, p. 340. Personal interview, R. Sommers, December 30, 1969.

45. *The Daily Colonist* (Victoria), February 23, 1954, pp. 1–2.

46. See his evidence: External Affairs Committee, *Minutes of Proceedings and Evidence*, 22nd Parlt., 1st Sess., May 5, 1954, pp. 174–75.

47. Its power consultant was Mr. Jack D. Stevens, formerly chief power engineer, Bonneville Power Administration. It consisted of Puget Sound Power and Light, Seattle City Light, Tacoma City Light, Chelan County P.U.D. No. 1, Snohomish County P.U.D. No. 1.

48. *The Daily Colonist* (Victoria), February 23, 1954, p. 2.

49. Mr. Stevens estimated that the project might produce up to 2.8 million h.p. costing not more than .8 mills per kwh at-site. *The Province* (Vancouver), December 3, 1954, p. 3.

50. Excerpt from a letter: Jack D. Stevens to the Hon. J. E. Murray, chairman, Committee on Interior and Insular Affairs, *Upper Columbia River Development*, 1956, p. 465. See also Ibid., p. 174.

51. *The Daily Colonist* (Victoria), September 28, 1954, p. 5.

52. Excerpt from Mr. Jordan's testimony before the Committee on Interior and Insular Affairs, and a Sub-Committee of the Senate Foreign Relations Committee. *Upper Columbia River Development*, 1956, p. 55. Note that Mr. Jordan did not join the International Joint Commission until January 1955.

53. Personal interview, R. Sommers, December 30, 1969. The council was officially constituted on April 13, 1954.

54. Personal interview, J. Stevens, June 24, 1968.

55. Inherent in the proposal was the concept that the Utilities Council would receive from U.S. federal plants power to cover its investment costs, and that the remaining power increment would be shared with the United

States government. A year later Mr. Stevens was prepared to envisage having the council finance the installation of generation at Mica Creek, with this power also being equitably shared.

The Puget Sound Utilities Council proposal is described in *Upper Columbia River Development*, 1956, pp. 173–74, 364–65. It is described also in J. D. Stevens, *A Power Program for the Puget Sound-Cascade Region* (Seattle: Puget Sound Utilities Council, March 1955), pp. 70–72.

56. R. L. Neuberger, "Power Struggle on the Canadian Border," *Harper's Magazine* 215 (December, 1957): 46.

57. Puget Sound Utilities Council Statement, *Upper Columbia River Development*, 1956, May 23, 1956, p. 174.

58. They point out, indeed, that there may be substantial variations in run-off patterns on watersheds within a province as large as British Columbia.

59. *The Province* (Vancouver), December 7, 1954, p. 8.

60. See *Upper Columbia River Development*, 1958, pp. 322–23.

61. This correspondence is reviewed in Moore, *The Role of the International Joint Commission in Columbia River Basin Development*, p. 68.

62. *The Daily Colonist* (Victoria), May 2, 1955, p. 12. This attempt to relate the power rebate on transboundary projects to the upstream state's head contribution would have meant Canada's receiving credit for a 150 foot contribution to a total 344 foot head. American intransigence over this is hardly to be wondered at.

63. Excerpt from an IJC memorandum record, cited before the Standing Committee on External Affairs, *Minutes of Proceedings and Evidence*, 22nd Parlt., 2nd Sess., April 22, 1955, p. 386. Although apparently he did not keep the federal government in the picture, the general did forward precise summaries of his meetings with Kaiser spokesmen to Victoria.

64. R. E. Sommers, "The Castlegar Dam" (radio address script, mimeographed, November 29, 1954, p. 2). (The assumption was that the Kaiser interests would amortize their investment in the Arrow Dam over fifty years, and that, after that time, the downstream power rebate to British Columbia would rise.)

65. *Upper Columbia River Development*, May 23, 1956, p. 173.

66. See, for example, *The Province* (Vancouver), October 9, 1954, p. 6; October 26, 1954, p. 6; November 13, 1954, p. 6.

67. Ibid., December 24, 1954, p. 5.

68. *Vancouver Sun*, October 13, 1954, p. 2.

69. Mr. Sommers in a September 17 wire to General McNaughton indicated that British Columbia could not contemplate greater Arrow Lakes storage "which would flood agricultural and existing economic values." Both telegrams were cited before the External Affairs Committee, *Minutes of Proceedings and Evidence*, 22nd Parlt., 2nd Sess., April 29, 1955, pp. 420–21.

70. Personal interview, General McNaughton, September 10, 1964.

71. *Vancouver Sun*, October 13, 1954, p. 2.

72. *The Province* (Vancouver), November 8, 1954, p. 8. Mr. Sinclair repeated many of the contentions already featured in the metropolitan press.

73. Ibid., October 28, 1954, p. 1.

74. Ibid., November 25, 1954, p. 3.

75. To this day they remain exasperated at the alacrity with which critics ignored or forgot the additional considerations (including the reallocation of benefits after fifty years), beyond the 20 percent power return.

76. Subsequently it was learned that the West Kootenay Power and Light Company member of the committee, Mr. Anderson, had opposed it.

77. *Upper Columbia River Development*, 1956, p. 203.

78. External Affairs Committee, *Minutes of Proceedings and Evidence*, 23rd Parlt., 1st Sess., December 12, 1957, pp. 248–50.

79. *The Province* (Vancouver), December 30, 1954, p. 1.

80. Outlined by Mr. Sommers at Castlegar. *The Province* (Vancouver), January 5, 1955, p. 1.

81. Canada, House of Commons, *Debates*, 22nd Parlt., 2nd Sess., February 4, 1955, p. 871.

82. External Affairs Committee, *Minutes of Proceedings and Evidence*, 22nd Sess , 2nd Sess , March 9, 1955, p. 92. He argued that an Arrow Lakes Dam would inhibit a superior project downstream at Murphy Creek.

83. Ibid., April 27, 1955, p. 294.

84. Mr. Bonner in effect accepted the federal government's claim that it had a clear jurisdiction over works on international rivers when those works would affect property, civil, and other rights beyond the borders of the country. See the evidence of F. P. Varcoe, deputy minister of justice, External Affairs Committee, *Minutes of Proceedings and Evidence*, 22nd Parlt., 2nd Sess., March 16, 1955, p. 158.

85. His letter was printed in full in *The Revelstoke Review*, January 13, 1955, p. 1.

86. J. Lesage, Address to the Pacific Northwest Trade Association, Vancouver, B.C., May 9, 1955, and reprinted in *Upper Columbia River Development*, 1956, pp. 375–80. p. 377.

87. *The Province* (Vancouver), June 15, 1955, p. 23.

88. See *Upper Columbia River Development*, 1958, pp. 212–13; 321–22.

89. Cited in Moore, *The Role of the International Joint Commission*, pp. 72–73.

90. David Corbett, "Hydro Power in B.C.," *Canadian Forum* (May 1955): 26–27.

91. Senator Richard L. Neuberger, who visited British Columbia between October 17 and 25, 1955, on behalf of the Senate Committee on Interior and Insular Affairs, reported to that body on his return: "Canadians generally have confidence that their position in these negotiations is being represented to the full limits of their national interests under the leadership of General A. G. L. McNaughton, who is respected as Canada's most illustrious soldier." Cited in *Upper Columbia River Development*, 1956, p. 11. (The complete report is printed there, pp. 6–25.)

92. Canada. House of Commons, *Debates*, 22nd Parlt., 2nd Sess., February 11, 1955, p. 1106. Mr. Howe had gone on to declare: "I may say that the

most disturbed man about this situation is General McNaughton. He sees several years of work thrown away; he sees the program that he hoped to carry out for the Columbia River system made unworkable."

93. External Affairs Committee, *Minutes of Proceedings and Evidence*, 22nd Parlt., 2nd Sess., April 28, 1955, pp. 405–409.

94. Mr. Fulton did seek to make the point, from evidence given by General McNaughton to the External Affairs Committee *in 1954*, and evidence submitted by British Columbia in 1955, that

(a) British Columbia had a perfect right to enter into a tentative arrangement with the Kaiser Company, and indeed

(b) something of this sort appeared to be required before the government of Canada would release any engineering data to Kaiser personnel.

Federal spokesmen, especially Mr. Lesage, emphasized that Ottawa had not been consulted by the province (Ibid., March 22, 1955, p. 245), and also that General McNaughton, in his June 17, 1955 interview with the Kaiser Company's representatives, had also declared: "Before proceeding with any confidence, clearance from both the British Columbia government and the government of Canada would be needed by the companies." (Cited Ibid., April 28, 1955, p. 386.)

95. Personal interview, December 6, 1965.

96. Personal interview, December 30, 1969.

97. This diversionary case was developed by General McNaughton before the April 1955 meeting of the IJC, the minutes of which were printed in External Affairs Committee, *Minutes of Proceedings and Evidence*, 22nd Parlt., 3rd Sess., June 7, 1956, pp. 354–73.

98. Ibid., 22nd Parlt., 2nd Sess., March 9, 1955, p. 45.

99. See his evidence; Ibid., May 12, 1954, p. 172; March 10, 1955, p. 86; December 13, 1957, p. 277.

100. *Upper Columbia River Development*, 1956, March 22, 1956, p. 60.

101. Ibid., p. 58. General Itschner of the Corps of Engineers estimated that if the 15 million acre-feet were removed from the Columbia, when the main stream in the United States was fully developed the energy lost to it at federal and non-federal plants would have a fuel replacement value of slightly over $50 million annually. *Upper Columbia River Development*, 1958, p. 226.

102. See for example Leon J. Ladner and Charles Bourne, "Diversion of Columbia River Waters," Presentations to the Pacific Northwest Regional Meeting, American Society of International Law, April 19, 1956 (Seattle: Institute of International Affairs, University of Washington, Bulletin no. 12, part 4, June 1956), pp. 1–18, 26–32; Maxwell Cohen, "Some Legal and Policy Aspects of the Columbia River Dispute," *The Canadian Bar Review* 36, no. 1 (March 1958): 25–41; Jacob Austin, "Canadian-United States Practice and Theory Respecting the International Law of International Rivers: A Study of the History and Influence of the Harmon Doctrine," *The Canadian Bar Review* 37, no. 3 (September 1959): 393–433; Charles B. Bourne, "The Columbia River Controversy," *The Canadian Bar Review* 37, no. 3 (September 1959): 444–72.

103. See the testimony of Mr. Varcoe, External Affairs Committee, *Minutes of Proceedings and Evidence*, 22nd Parlt., 2nd Sess., March 17, 1955, p. 172, and Charles Bourne, "The Columbia River Controversy," p. 456.

104. The position which the Department of State was advancing by April 1958, was that, insofar as diversions were concerned, the Boundary Waters Treaty did not govern the signatory parties except with respect to the right to object to diversion on the ground of injury caused to navigation. The official American claim by that time had come to hold that other injuries resulting from diversion, such as those concerning hydro-electric development, were not "within the contemplation of the treaty of 1909. Therefore, the position of the parties, it maintained, is necessarily determined by the international law prevalent at the time injury results from a diversion." (Evidence of Richard Kearney, assistant legal adviser for European Affairs, Department of State) *Upper Columbia River Development*, 1958, April 21, 1958, p. 28. See also the evidence of Frederick Jandrey, deputy assistant secretary of state, Ibid., p. 8.

105. Cohen, "Some Legal and Policy Aspects . . . ," p. 38.

106. The Province (Vancouver), March 12, 1956, p. 1. The prospect of diplomatic-level contacts on this issue was being endorsed elsewhere. See, for example, Senator Neuberger's report to the Senate Committee on Interior and Insular Affairs . . . , *Upper Columbia River Development*, 1956, p. 23.

107. Not really looked at thoroughly since 1909.

108. Canada, House of Commons, *Debates*, 22nd Parlt., 3rd Sess., May 23, 1956, p. 4249.

109. John Swettenham, *McNaughton* (Toronto: Ryerson Press, 1969), III, p. 269. The care which Mr. St. Laurent took to avoid offending General McNaughton in his House of Commons statement was noteworthy. He declined to speak of discussions at a "higher level," and assured Mr. E. D. Fulton that the move need in no way hold up Columbia surveys and planning. Canada, House of Commons, *Debates*, 22nd Parlt., 3rd Sess., April 9, 1956, pp. 2728–29.

110. The writer has not seen either the federal government's or the IJC's documentary record on this matter, and Mr. Lester Pearson, Canada's secretary of state for external affairs, at the time, did not recall the details when interviewed on April 10, 1970. The unqualified right of the upstream state to divert (subject to compensatory claims by an injured party downstream), which Article II embodied, was twice advanced in IJC decision-making by the United States during the 'fifties. It was not, however, the operative rule in American domestic law, and had been specifically disavowed by an American government spokesman before the (U.S.) Senate Foreign Relations Committee in 1945. Furthermore, it was not invoked by the United States when it, as the upstream riparian, negotiated the 1945 treaty over the Colorado and Rio Grande Rivers with Mexico. The philosophy which it represented did and does appear to be out of joint with the times. One can only assume that it was considerations of this sort which prompted the Department of External Affairs to look hard at it in 1956.

See Charles E. Martin, "The Diversion of Columbia River Waters," *Proceedings of the American Society of International Law* (Seattle: Institute of International Affairs, University of Washington, Bulletin No. 13, June 1958), p. 5.

111. Swettenham, *McNaughton* III, p. 269. Mr. Leon Ladner asserts that the general went directly to the prime minister in this connection. Personal interview, L. Ladner, June 17, 1964. Unfortunately my notes of my own interview with the general do not refer to the matter.

112. External Affairs Committee, *Minutes of Proceedings and Evidence*, 22nd Parlt., 3rd Sess., June 14, 1956, p. 415.

113. The premier was referring here to the forthcoming engineering report on this diversion which the federal government had commissioned on June 14, 1955 from the B.C. Engineering Co., Ltd. When presented (privately) to the government of Canada in 1956 this report found the Columbia to Fraser diversion technically feasible, but the 3,394,000 kilowatts of capacity which it would produce the source of very high cost power indeed.

The cost of the power was estimated to be 7.10 mills per kwh—making no allowance for the costs of the Mica and Revelstoke dams essential to the scheme's operation, and none for the loss of a Canadian entitlement to a share of the downstream Columbia Basin benefits which would be forgone as a consequence of diversion—or, of course, for indeterminate damage to the Fraser fishery. The report is summarized in *The Columbia River Treaty, Protocol, and Related Documents*, pp. 164–67. It was not made public at this time.

114. *The Province* (Vancouver), June 21, 1956, p. 1. The Puget Sound Utilities Council was still very much interested, assuming, in Mr. Jack Stevens' words, it got "a reasonable amount of power out of the dam at a reasonable cost." Ibid., June 19, 1956, p. 14.

115. *Vancouver Sun*, May 18, 1957, p. 51.

116. In a letter to Mr. Sinclair late in the 1957 federal election campaign. *The Province* (Vancouver), June 8, 1957, p. 16.

117. The terms of reference of the Crippen-Wright Report called for a broad study on the engineering and economic feasibility of hydro-electric generation in the B.C. portion of the Columbia, a review of resultant downstream benefits, of required transmission services, of physical effects, and the requirements involved in integrating in whole or in part with the United States' system.

Crippen-Wright were given a broad authorization to recommend "as a basis for government determination of an optimum plan for development of the river in Central British Columbia."

By July 24, 1956, the terms of reference had been broadened by letter to include integrated operation with projects on the Clearwater River in central British Columbia.

When referring to the examination of downstream benefits, the terms of reference added: "this, with a view to preparing a comprehensive plan for the return of an optimum portion of such benefits to British Columbia."

Crippen-Wright Engineering, Ltd., *Report Hydro-Electric Development of the Columbia River Basin in Canada*, I, p. 2.

118. *The Province* (Vancouver), July 5, 1955, pp. 1–2. The B.C. Electric Company commissioned a major study of its own on the Columbia from its subsidiary, the B.C. Engineering Company. The latter's *Report on an investigation of the Columbia River in Canada* was completed in 1958, and sent in confidence to Mr. Bennett.

119. In the meantime, Canadian journalists and others close to General McNaughton deplored the prospect of action beyond the IJC. W. Bruce Hutchison, "The Continuing Battle for the Columbia," *MacLean's Magazine*, September 29, 1956, p. 30. See also Ferguson, "Likely Trends in Canadian-American Political Relations," pp. 440, 437–48, and Leon Ladner before the B.C. Historical Association, *The Province* (Vancouver), September 27, 1956, p. 49.

120. George Hees at Prince Rupert, *The Province* (Vancouver), October 9, 1956, p. 11; Howard Green at New Westminster and Vancouver, *The Province* (Vancouver), October 24, p. 12, November 7, p. 2.

121. *The Province* (Vancouver), November 15, 1956, p. 1.

122. The back-bencher was Robert Newton. *The Province* (Vancouver), March 7, 1956, p. 4; March 12, 1957, p. 22.

123. Comptroller of water rights and project engineer in the B.C. Water Resources Service respectively.

124. "Summary of Discussions between Canadian and British Columbia Officials: Diplomatic Discussion Between Canada and the U.S.A. Relating to International Rivers That Took Place in Washington, D.C. on May 20, 21, 1957" (typewritten), p. 2.

125. Mr. Lesage indicated to British Columbia that the Canadian members of such a committee, in addition to Mr. Paget, might well be Mr. G. A. Gaherty, president of Montreal Engineering, and Mr. D. M. Stephens, chairman of Manitoba Hydro. The last named, I believe, had first suggested the idea of a technical committee to Ottawa. His thought was not that it do any negotiating, but rather that it look at the principles which had evolved in utility practice—from the downstream benefit concept to the means of calculaing same—to see if a generally defensible principle might be enunciated therefrom which might be relevant to international river development.

126. "Notes on Diplomatic Discussions between Canada and the United States relating to International Rivers," pp. 10, 12, 13.

127. *The Province* (Vancouver), March 25, 1957, p. 1. In November 1955, in an attempt to get the trans-Canada pipeline project under way, the federal government and that of Ontario undertook to build an unproductive 690-mile stretch east of the Manitoba-Ontario border, which would be leased to the Trans-Canada Company on terms making its subsequent purchase almost a certainty.

128. *The Province* (Vancouver), March 25, 1957, p. 1.

129. Ibid., March 27, 1957, p. 27.

130. Ibid., May 8, 1957, p. 5.

131. Ibid., May 7, 1957, p. 5.

132. Ibid., May 4, 1957, p. 1.

133. Ibid., May 6, 1957, p. 1.

134. Ibid , May 13, 1957, p. 19. Mr. Sinclair denied any difference in position. He recalls that he had cleared his raising the whole matter, and the way in which he did it, with Mr. St. Laurent, but that the latter had not checked with Mr. Howe. Personal interview, J. Sinclair, October 6, 1965.

Professor Meisel observes that this lack of uniformity in the federal Cabinet's approach, just one of a number, did nothing to help the Liberals. J. Meisel, *The Canadian General Election of 1957*, p. 187.

135. *The Province* (Vancouver), May 24, 1957, p. 1. The Vancouver speech has often since been held to have marked the turning point in the campaign—because of the warmth of the response generated to Mr. Diefenbaker on this occasion. See Peter Newman, *Renegade in Power*, p. 53.

136. Election results gave the Progressive Conservatives 112 to the Liberals 105 seats; the CCF had 25, Social Credit 19, Independents 4.

Notes to Chapter 4, Approach to a Treaty: July, 1957–December, 1959

1. "Summary Memorandum for the Acting Secretary of State for External Affairs on the Columbia River, July 3, 1957," p. 5.

2. The general was strongly opposed to the concept of complete system integration.

3. "Summary Memorandum . . . on the Columbia River," p. 4.

4. Personal interview, Mr. Ladner, June 17, 1964. Howard Green, minister of public works, 1957–59; secretary of state for external affairs, 1959–63. In mid summer 1957 General McNaughton complained bitterly to Mr. Ladner about his "isolation" from the federal Cabinet which he attributed, largely, to members of the senior bureaucracy.

5. Eventually, all of the Cabinet ministers from British Columbia (Messrs. Green, Pearkes, and Fulton) were members, although Mr. Pearkes after a while became absorbed in other interests and attended only intermittently. Mr. Smith, the secretary of state for external affairs, and Mr. Alvin Hamilton, the minister of northern affairs and national resources, were also on it, as was Mr. Alfred Brooks, the minister of veterans affairs (until September 1960).

6. Canada, House of Commons, *Debates*, 23rd Parlt., 1st Sess., October 14, 1957, p. 6. (Enclosure mine.) See Dalton Camp, *Gentlemen, Players and Politicians* (Toronto: McClelland and Stewart, 1970), p. 325. Long talked of, the proposal to build a dam on the South Saskatchewan River in Saskatchewan was widely recognized as economically indefensible. Mr. Diefenbaker, however, had accepted a commitment to it in the 1957 election campaign.

7. See H. L. Briggs, "Brief Respecting the Trusteeship in Behalf of the People of British Columbia as Rendered through the B.C. Power Commission 1955–1958," Presented to the Royal Commission in the Matter of the British

Columbia Power Commission, December 30, 1958, pp. 31–32. (Mimeo-graphed.)

As noted in chapter 2, the Power Commission had been through a number of embarrassingly power-deficient years, and, since 1956 had been seriously considering developing the Homathko. But its own load was too small and diffused to support such a move unless it could be augmented with a sale. Unfortunately the Homathko energy was expensive. The B.C. Electric rejected the offer of 250,000 kilowatts of it, or more.

8. The hydraulic potential of the Peace River canyon was well known to government engineers, but the prospect of exploiting it awaited the refinement of high dam construction and a break-through in long distance power trans-mission. The canyon is 600 transmission-line miles from Vancouver. See Sherman, *Bennett*, p. 220.

9. They were, in fact, primarily a move to foil speculators.

10. Ralph L. Chantrill, "Report on Hydro-Electric Development of the Peace River" (undated, attached to the Memorandum of Agreement between Birger Strid and Bernard Gore and the government of the province of B.C., October 7, 1957), pp. 2–3.

11. *Vancouver Sun*, October 9, 1957, p. 1, and *The Daily Colonist* (Vic-toria), October 9, 1957, p. 1.

12. Probably most unfairly Canadians had viewed Mr. Jordan very harshly between 1955 and 1957. It is hard to see what else he could have done but counter the general as vigorously as he did, pending policy decisions at a higher level not made during his tenure which ended on July 18, 1957.

13. U.S. Congress, Senate, Committee on Interior and Insular Affairs, *Upper Columbia River Development, 1958*, p. 269.

14. Ibid., pp. 269–72.

15. External Affairs Committee, *Minutes of Proceedings and Evidence*, 23rd Parlt., 7st Sess., December 12, 1957, pp. 251, 253, 260. A prominent interrogator of the general at this time was H. W. Herridge, a foreshore resident on the Arrow Lakes and CCF member of Parliament for Kootenay West, who had opposed Arrow Lakes flooding from Kaiser Dam days, and was to lead the opposition of his party to the ratification of the Columbia River Treaty into 1964.

16. T. Ingledow to the Vancouver Branch of the Institute of Professional Engineers, *Vancouver Sun*, November 20, 1957, p. 15. High voltage a/c transmission he described as feasible, but at this distance "difficult to build and more difficult to maintain." He admitted that direct current transmission had been studied for thirty years, but he commented "There is as yet no assurance that such a transmission system would be economical and sound from an engineering and operating point of view."

17. Montreal Engineering Company, Ltd., *The Development of Canada's Water Power Resources in the Columbia River Basin*, pp. iv, 54, 55. The Montreal company observed that such projects could be added to the recom-mended development if justified. Its report simply observed that the larger diversion projects "would be of lesser value, and it is not necessary to com-

plicate the study of integrated development by introducing them at this time."

18. Ibid., p. 54. Alternative 1, identified by the Montreal Company provided the greater storage and benefits. Alternative 2 was seen as rather easier to finance, and more flexible in relation to the market for the power produced.

19. Ibid., p. iv.

20. The Montreal Engineering Company's Report had advanced one method of determining and dividing these benefits.

21. *The Province* (Vancouver), February 26, 1958, p. 17.

22. Ibid., February 27, 1958, p. 1.

23. Ibid., June 3, 1958, p. 15.

24. Canada, House of Commons, *Debates*, 24th Parlt., 1st Sess., August 1, 1958, p. 2938.

25. J. L. MacCallum, "Memorandum on Interview," August 4, 1958.

26. *The Province* (Vancouver), August 20, p. 15.

27. Ibid., October 31, 1958, p. 1.

28. Ibid., November 12, 1958, p. 3. Dr. Grauer issued another statement on his company's position on December 1. Current B.C. Electric power costs were described as about 5.9 mills, and he felt they would rise to approximately 6 mills with the new thermal plant. He declared that the lower mainland area would need power from either the Peace or the Columbia within a decade and the B.C. Electric was looking to the Peace because of the virtual commitment of the latter to a crown corporation, and the continuing difficulty in reaching a settlement. He noted that Mica storage, which would take ten years to build, would provide no more than 500,000 kw of energy, enough to meet provincial needs a decade hence for only a couple of years. He rather expected that, at the start, there would be one dam on the Peace and one on the Columbia. *The Province* (Vancouver), December 1, 1958, p. 8.

29. Cited in *The Daily Colonist* (Victoria), November 13, 1958, p. 1.

30. *The Daily Colonist* (Victoria), November 14, 1958, pp. 1, 6.

31. *Vancouver Sun*, November 14, 1958, pp. 1–2.

32. *The Province* (Vancouver), November 15, 1958, p. 21. It was quite a week. In another unprecedented development on November 15, Mr. Sommers was jailed for five years on a charge of accepting bribes while a Cabinet minister.

33. W. H. Anderson, J. Dunsmuir, G. M. Shrum, *Report of the Royal Commission in the Matter of the British Columbia Power Commission*, pp. 167–68, 170. Between 1956 and 1958 the government of British Columbia gave a good deal of attention to the question of the instrumentality which should further develop the Columbia River in Canada. One proposal seriously considered was that a new agency, a joint venture of all the major provincial utilities, be established for this purpose. Throughout 1958 Mr. Briggs had been privately opposed to the suggestion. He argued before the Shrum Royal Commission that in such an arrangement the public power interests of the B.C. Power Commission would be submerged. Cf. Lee Briggs, "Brief Respecting the Trusteeship," pp. 43, 65–70.

Another proposal considered by the provincial Cabinet would have seen a new and presumably public authority take over the development of major new projects and of a major transmission network linking all parts of the province.

34. *The Province* (Vancouver), November 28, 1958, p. 5.

35. With Mr. Ingledow of the B.C. Electric Company, and Dr. J. V. Fisher, Premier Bennett's chief financial adviser.

36. The creation of such a body had been endorsed by the Gordon and Borden Commissions. It was made responsible for the regulation of the construction and operation of oil and natural gas pipelines subject to federal jurisdiction, for their tolls, for the exportation and importation of gas, for the export of electricity, and the construction of transmission lines required in this connection.

For a different opinion of the impact of the "Briggs affair" see P. L. Sherman, *Bennett*, p. 200.

37. With extensive federal and international administrative experience. He took office on April 1, 1959. (He had been the deputy minister in Ottawa between 1947 and 1950 of the department housing the Dominion Water and Power Bureau.)

38. Mr. Bennett's explanation here is that the northern project was still unproven, the commission's financial position was tight, and it had to be very careful about getting tied to still potentially high cost suppliers. Personal interview, May 13, 1966.

39. Anderson, Dunsmuir, Shrum, *Report of the Royal Commission in the Matter of the B.C. Power Commission*, pp. 196–97.

40. The Energy Board was formally constituted on January 11, 1960. Its other members were Dr. Keenleyside, Mr. Paget (comptroller of water rights), and Dr. Henry Angus (chairman of the Public Utilities Commission of the province). These were not full-time appointments.

41. Components here were a Canal Flats diversion, Mica Creek, Downie Creek, Revelstoke Canyon, Arrow Lakes, Murphy Creek.

42. Components here were Mica Creek, Downie, Revelstoke, Murphy Creek, Bull River (Kootenay), Duncan Lake, Kootenay Lake. Actually 2(b) and 3, which were identified as IJC Sequences VII and IX were not identical with them, but rather with IJC Sequences VII A and IX A, which eliminated the High Arrow project.

A dam at Murphy Creek on the Columbia main stream, located two miles upstream from Trail, B.C. could store about 3,100,000 acre-feet of water upstream, to the head of the Arrow Lakes, if a High Arrow Dam were not built. Under these circumstances it was often referred to as the Low Arrow project.

43. Alternative 3 included these projects: Dorr, Bull River-Luxor, Calamity Curve, Mica Creek, Downie, Revelstoke, Murphy Creek, Duncan Lake, Kootenay Lake.

44. As he put it in a memorandum record in his file referring to this period, and dated 1-6-59. He reviewed his views and actions in 1958 in other memoranda, dated 1-6-59 and 20-4-60.

45. Clerk of the Privy Council, deputy and assistant deputy minister of northern affairs, and national resources respectively.

46. The Canadian aide-mémoire took the form of a response to one from the United States on November 17, which had indicated an American willingness to meet the decade-long Canadian position that the Libby Dam be considered in the context of the development of the entire Columbia River basin.

47. The federal Cabinet also expected diplomatic level talks to continue with the United States concerning the term of any agreement between the two countries, and the nature of the national entities.

48. *The Province* (Vancouver), December 6, 1958, pp. 1–2.

49. *The Columbia River Treaty and Protocol: A Presentation*, p. 23.

50. R. G. Williston, "Hydro-Electric Power in British Columbia, An Address to the Legislative Assembly of British Columbia" (mimeographed), January 27, 1959, p. 18. Mr. Williston informed the Legislature on February 5, 1959 that a copy of this address was being forwarded immediately to Ottawa.

51. Krutilla, *The Columbia River Treaty*, p. 124.

52. Crippen-Wright Engineering Limited, *Report, Hydro-Electric Development of Columbia River Basin in Canada*, p. X–8.

53. Ibid., p. X–3. These figures assumed public utility operation, a fifty year amortization of project costs, no escalation for inflation, and a 4 percent interest rate.

54. Ibid., p. X–35.

55. Crippen-Wright Engineering Limited, "Diversion of Kootenay River into Columbia River," Interim Report no. 2 (Vancouver: 1958), p. I–2.

56. Crippen-Wright, *Report, Hydro-Electric Development of Columbia River Basin in Canada*, p. X–38.

57. Ibid., p. X–3.

58. International Columbia River Engineering Board, *Water Resources of the Columbia River Basin. Report to the International Joint Commission, United States and Canada*, p. 109.

59. Ibid., p. 72.

60. Ibid., p. 65.

61. Ibid., p. 109. Among other things, it assumed a 3 percent interest rate.

62. As did others, this British Columbian also referred to the crucial importance of sequence and timing, ignored by the ICREB, and reminded the IJC that some of the projects which had been supported by ICREB justification studies "would not be economical if added at a later stage in the sequence of development." Ibid., p. 159.

63. Mr. Alvin Hamilton recalls that an American Cabinet member agreed to this arrangement informally with him as early as September 1957. (Personal interview, March 1, 1967). One American IJC member, Mr. McWhorter, remained skeptical of the concept through most of 1958. Mr. Green formally endorsed it publicly in his December 5, 1958, public statement, and Mr. Williston announced on May 28, 1959, that this matter had been settled. (*The Province* (Vancouver), May 29, 1959, p. 2.)

Appropriating credit for settling on the fifty-fifty split has become a popular pastime. See Mr. Dill's testimony: U.S. Congress, Senate Committee on Foreign Relations, *Hearings on the Columbia River Treaty*, 87th Congress, 1st Session, 1961, pp. 62–64.

64. Dr. Krutilla argues that such ultimately was the case for one partner here. See Krutilla, *The Columbia River Treaty*, part I, chapter 3; part II, Introduction.

65. Minutes of the Second Meeting of the Canada-British Columbia Policy Liaison Committee, at Victoria, B.C., May 29, 1959, pp. 9–13.

66. Personal interview, September 9, 1965.

67. Minutes of the Second Meeting of the Canada-British Columbia Policy Liaison Committee, Victoria, May 29, 1959, p. 7.

68. Eventually Mr. Stephens was told that Mr. Green would not advance the Columbia project further, and British Columbia would veto any arrangement which required a netting procedure. In a personal interview on September 9, 1965, he said he came close to resigning at the time, and now regretted that he had not done so.

69. Minutes of the Fourth Meeting of the Canada-British Columbia Policy Liaison Committee, Victoria, October 31, 1959, p. 2.

70. Krutilla, *The Columbia River Treaty*, chapter IV.

71. *The Columbia River Treaty, Protocol, and Related Documents*, pp. 41, 43, 50.

72. Fifth Interim Report of the Canada-British Columbia Technical Liaison Committee to the Policy Liaison Committee, December 1959, p. 19.

73. The Arrow Lakes project, with no initially planned at-site generation, was primarily a storage and re-regulating facility. As the downstream benefit from it would be produced largely in the United States, and the United States claimed, would decline over time, General McNaughton did not feel it would meet his criterion of continuing usefulness to Canada. Upper Kootenay-Columbia storage, plus a diversion into the Columbia, would increase the flow over Mica and other main stream projects in Canada in perpetuity.

74. *The Province* (Vancouver), October 24, 1959, p. 21.

75. Mr. Green told the House of Commons on March 2, after describing Mr. Bennett as "a very impetuous and might I say, impatient man," that he asked him whether he intended to do anything on the Columbia.

Canada, House of Commons, *Debates*, 24th Parlt., 2nd Sess., March 2, 1959, p. 1493.

Mr. Bennett's response to this was to suggest that the two governments sign a letter of intent!

76. *The Province* (Vancouver), March 18, 1959, p. 9. He estimated the combined potential capacity of the Peace and Columbia as about 7 million kilowatts, and the province's estimated needs by 1980 as 10 million kilowatts.

77. Personal interview, W. C. Mainwaring, August 3, 1965.

78. *The Province* (Vancouver), September 30, 1959, p. 4.

79. Ibid., December 5, 1959, pp. 1, 2.

80. Ibid., December 19, 1959, p. 1. Mr. Fulton was cautious on the Peace

at this time. He doubted if there was a domestic market for parallel development, but felt the situation might change.

81. Peace River Power Development Company, Limited, *Peace River Hydro-Electric Project* (Vancouver: December 1959, 8 volumes).

82. R. L. Chantrill and J. D. Stevens, *A Report on Power Capabilities and Operating Aspects of Peace River Project and a Pacific International Power Pool*, p. 3.

83. Messrs. Chantrill and Stevens held that the main feature of the Peace development was "its ability to convert regional secondary energy into firm energy." Ibid., p. 3. Operated in coordination with rather than independently of a power pool, they maintained that the increase in pool firm energy which it would produce would be more than one million kilowatts.

When constructed after 1961 the Portage Mountain Dam was reduced in scale. Its reservoir impounds 57 million acre-feet, 30 million of them live.

Notes to Chapter 5, The Negotiation of the Treaty: Phase One

1. E. W. Bassett to A. F. Paget, December 29, 1959. Mr. Paget was also instructed to have Crippen-Wright Engineering Ltd. review their report in the light of the principles recommended by the IJC.

2. The draft had been prepared some months earlier, had been updated in the light of the impending agreement on the principles, and had been relayed to British Columbia in November 1959. It did not become the subject of inter-governmental exchanges.

3. Canada, House of Commons, *Debates*, 24th Parlt., 3rd Sess., January 14, 1960, p. 2.

4. *Vancouver Sun*, February 15, 1960, p. 17.

5. Donald Fleming to W. A. C. Bennett, January 20, 1960, p. 2.

6. Cited in *Vancouver Sun*, January 20, 1960, pp. 1–2. Mr. Green also denied Mr. Mainwaring's claim that Columbia River power was thirteen years away. Mr. Mainwaring wrote a strong letter to Messrs. Green and Fulton on January 27 in which he categorically denied that he had sought to block the Columbia.

7. The Low Arrow project was in effect that at Murphy Creek which General McNaughton had long favoured; it would not have flooded in the Arrow Lakes watershed beyond normal high water.

8. The opposition in the Arrow Lakes country was certainly mounting; Mr. Herridge, the CCF M.P. for Kootenay West, had by this time declared his intention to induce all possible resistance to a valley flooding scheme, and the Chamber of Commerce at Nakusp, the chief (but still small) town in the area had done likewise. *Vancouver Sun*, January 30, 1960, p. 8.

9. *Vancouver Sun*, February 2, 1960, p. 2. Dr. Shrum also argued that B.C. should be grateful to the backers of the Peace proposal, declaring "If the Columbia comes through, it will be as a result of this threat."

10. R. G. Williston, "The British Columbia Hydro-Power Situation, 1960"

(manuscript of Address to the British Columbia Legislative Assembly, February 3, 1960), p. 4.

11. Ibid., p. 9.

12. In justification of the company's earlier omission of a High Arrow reservoir, in its assessment of the Columbia's significance for the Peace, W. C. Mainwaring wrote on February 5: "In view of the fact that practically nothing has been said about the High Arrow Dam in recent months and that the IJC have not considered it in their studies, we had felt that Mica Creek was the important storage to include in our study."

W. C. Mainwaring to B. Gore et al., February 5, 1960, p. 1. Mr. Mainwaring, of course, was quite mistaken in his reference to the IJC's approach to High Arrow. *His comment, however, probably reflects his contact with General McNaughton, for whom Mr. Mainwaring had the highest regard.* Personal interview with Mr. Mainwaring, August 3, 1965.

13. "Report of the British Columbia-Canada Technical Liaison Committee to the Policy Committee on Columbia River Development, February 8, 1960." The report also endorsed the principle of giving the operating agencies much flexibility, and called for more investigation of Columbia River storage in Canada, and for a start on the final engineering of the High Arrow and Duncan projects.

14. There was no immediate plan for at-site generation at Arrow, and the downstream power benefit from it, as defined by the IJC (and the treaty), does decline markedly over time.

15. Minutes, Fifth Meeting, Canada-British Columbia Policy Liaison Committee on the Columbia River, Ottawa, February 9–10, 1960, p. 2.

16. This is a reference to the manner in which the law of diminishing returns applies to the value of additions of identical increments of storage in a river system. The closer the credited position to unity, the higher the attributed value.

17. Minutes, Fifth Meeting, Policy Liaison Committee, pp. 3–4. It is common federal government practice to make advances to Crown agencies on this basis.

18. On February 9 in Vancouver, meanwhile, Mr. Mainwaring held a six hour dinner and press conference during which he argued vigorously once again the merits of his company's proposal. Even with the downstream benefits, he maintained, cheap Columbia River power was a myth. *The Province* (Vancouver), February 10, 1961, p. 11.

19. E. W. Bassett, A. F. Paget, G. J. A. Kidd, "Memorandum Report on the First Canadian-American Negotiation Meeting on the Columbia River, February 11–12, 1960, for the Hon. R. G. Williston," p. 1.

20. "Canada-United States Columbia River Negotiators, First Session. February 11–12, Ottawa, Agreed Summary Record . . ." p. 5. See J. V. Krutilla, *The Columbia River Treaty*, p. 137.

21. Arguments especially relevant to the American Bruce's Eddy and Libby projects.

22. Bassett et al., "Memorandum Report . . . First . . . Negotiation Meetings," p. 13.

23. One day later the B.C. Electric Company received a discouraging assessment of the prospects of an American private utility purchase of electrical energy from British Columbia. L. E. Karrer to J. H. Steede, February 16, 1960.

24. The Seven Mile project referred to would be a run-of-the-river development on the Pend d'Oreille River in Canada, seven miles above its mouth, and upstream from the existing (but then incomplete) Waneta plant.

25. Water Rights Branch, "Economy of Mica or High Arrow: Initial Sequences for Columbia River Development," p. 5.

26. The former project had been launched with large scale federal assistance in 1958.

27. As used here, pooling means "giving the same stage credit to." Under these circumstances, the projects mentioned would all be first-added.

28. This of course was a reference to the then existing very low Bonneville Power Administration wholesale power rates, as well as to generally high domestic rates, especially in the B.C. Electric and B.C. Power Commission service areas.

29. E. W. Bassett to R. G. Williston, "Memorandum re International Columbia River Negotiations, March 9, 1960." Note the contrast between this perception and the concurrent reaction of utility personnel in Seattle to the B.C. Electric Company's market "sounding."

30. The Bull River project referred to here would be forty-two miles upstream on the Kootenay River from the International Border. A somewhat higher dam at the same site was a key element in the Kootenay to Columbia maximum diversion plan (Sequence IX A) which General McNaughton favoured.

31. *Victoria Daily Times*, March 22, 1960, p. 1. This was the first of a number of leaks or purported leaks which were to undermine federal-provincial cooperation in the course of this year.

32. External Affairs Committee, *Minutes of Proceedings and Evidence*, 24th Parlt., 3rd Sess., March 25, 1960, p. 230, March 18, 1960, pp. 178, 180.

33. *Vancouver Sun*, March 25, 1960, p. 3.

34. Krutilla, *The Columbia River Treaty*, p. 104.

35. Technical Liaison Committee, "Fifth Report to the Policy Liaison Committee, March 26, 1960," pp. 3, 4.

36. B.C. Water Rights Branch, "Sequences of Development K-2, L-1, M-1, N-1, N-2, P-3, Q-2," p. 2.

37. Minutes, Seventh Meeting, Canada-British Columbia Policy Liaison Committee, Ottawa, March 30, 1960, p. 4.

38. *Victoria Daily Times*, March 25, 1960, p. 1.

39. Cited in *The Daily Colonist* (Victoria), March 26, 1960, p. 1. Dr. Shrum was quoted by the press as agreeing with this statement.

40. *Vancouver Sun*, April 5, 1960, p. 2.

41. Ibid., April 11, 1960, p. 1.

42. Ibid., April 13, 1960, p. 23.

43. Ibid., April 21, 1960, p. 22; April 29, 1960, p. 20. The reference was to Mr. Jack D. Stevens; Mr. Mainwaring vigorously denied the charge on April 30. Ibid., April 30, p. 22.

44. Ibid., April 23, 1960, p. 6.

45. D. Fleming to W. A. C. Bennett, between May 6 and 16, 1960, p. 1.

46. Minutes, Eighth Meeting, Canada-British Columbia Policy Liaison Committee, Victoria, B.C., May 14, 1960, p. 3.

47. Which Canada had not accepted.

48. In one sense a rather understandable schizophrenia bedevilled the federal government's bargaining stance through 1960. A feature of its negotiating position during the first half of that year, in particular, was a major stress on the importance of first applying the IJC Principles (especially General Principle No. 1, which endorsed approving projects in order of their economic merit) to the initial determination of projects for cooperative development. Federal Cabinet ministers were well aware of the fact that in *systems economic terms*, all of the storage which Canada was offering was superior to anything which the United States could build in its portion of the watershed, and were convinced that their emphasis on Canadian East Kootenay as opposed to Libby storage was inevitably, in the long run, in both countries' interest. The real difficulty, however, lay in the fact that neither they nor the British Columbians placed equivalent weight on General Principle No. 2, which would have ensured that both countries enjoyed a true net benefit. Adjusting to it, fundamentally, was left to the bargaining process. In fact, as everyone around the bargaining tables soon realized, the federal government's representatives were as keen as British Columbia's to maximize the Canadian gain. The effect of their stress on General Principle No. 1, in any case, was to put them in the awkward position of seeming to claim that one could in logic maximize the net system and the Canadian benefits simultaneously. (Dr. Krutilla suggests, to a point, that they were going some way in doing this.) The provincial government, by being rather more candid with itself in this respect, found it somewhat easier ultimately to strike a bargain, and avoided the difficulties inherent in implying to other jurisdictions that it knew, better than they, what was in their own best interest.

49. Minutes, Ninth Meeting, Canada-British Columbia Policy Liaison Committee, Ottawa, June 15–16, 1960, Annex 1, pp. 2, 3.

50. Canadian Section, International Work Group, "Columbia River Negotiations: Comparative Data" (Ottawa: June 10, 1960), p. 3. This analysis pointed out that if for any reason Mica and generation downstream from it were delayed, the benefits from storage projects in Plan A "would be capable of carrying all costs of the projects for a period of at least twenty years without increasing the price of power above 4.5 mills/kwh." Under Plan B net operating deficits would continue to accumulate.

Notes to Chapter 6, The Negotiation of the Treaty: Phase Two

1. Which Mr. Williston relayed to Mr. Mainwaring along with the information that the provincial government accepted Mr. Paget's report. He added that "your company is now in the position to make the necessary applications." R. G. Williston to W. C. Mainwaring, March 23, 1960.

2. This account is based on a personal interview with W. C. Mainwaring, on August 3, 1965.

3. Minutes, Ninth Meeting, Canada-British Columbia Policy Liaison Committee, pp. 5, 8.

4. The lower the interest rate used in the calculation of the present worth of future values, the larger is the present worth sum arrived at. Already the international negotiators had jockeyed on this issue with the United States representatives seeking to use traditionally higher Canadian rates, and Canadians the reverse. At this time the Canadians agreed to seek the most favourable rate obtainable.

5. Minutes, Fifth International Negotiating Meeting on the Columbia River, Ottawa, July 14–15, 1960, p. 8.

6. The Libby flowage cost, then estimated at roughly $10 millions, was felt by Canada to have a present worth of some $600,000 annually. Mr. Bassett estimated the cost of transmitting the downstream benefit in a report to Mr. Williston at some $3.4 millions for the life of the agreement.

7. It is only after generation is installed at Mica, and downstream from it in Canada, that augmenting the flow of the Columbia's mainstream becomes particularly attractive to Canada.

8. The power was to be returned at a point near Oliver, B.C. on the International Boundary, and would then have to be transmitted some 300 miles in British Columbia to the Vancouver load-centre.

9. A preliminary (provincial) staff analysis of this American offer by July 26 indicated that Canada would be $700,000 per annum better off accepting it. E. W. Bassett, "Memorandum on the Sixth International Negotiating Meeting on the Columbia River for the Hon. R. G. Williston, July 26, 1960," p. 2.

10. Cited in *Vancouver Sun*, August 25, 1960, pp. 1, 6.

11. Ibid., September 10, 1960, p. 6.

12. *The Province* (Vancouver), August 23, 1960, p. 5.

13. *Vancouver Sun*, August 12, 1967, p. 25.

14. "Financial and Economic Implications of the Present Positions in the International Negotiations." August 15, 1960, p. 2.

15. See, however, Krutilla, *The Columbia River Treaty*, p. 109, footnote 12. Dr. Krutilla deals with the position paper on pp. 110–18.

16. "Financial and Economic Implications," p. 3.

17. Ibid., p. 4.

18. See Krutilla, *The Columbia River Treaty*, pp. 113–14. Dr. Krutilla perceives a provincial technical slippage in responding to this option.

19. He wrote to this effect, for instance, to a resident of the Arrow Lakes

Valley who was very concerned about the rumoured inclusion of a High Arrow Dam on October 5. See Donald Waterfield, *Continental Waterboy*, p. 20.

20. The Republicans were anxious to counter the claims of Senator J. F. Kennedy that they were antagonistic to an international agreement because of their reservations concerning public power development, and that the electric power production index was one in which the United States was being threatened by the USSR. *New York Times*, October 20, 1960, p. 22.

21. *The Province* (Vancouver), October 21, 1960, p. 2.

22. *Analysis by U.S. Negotiators of the Report to the Governments of the U.S. and Canada Relative to Cooperative Development of Water Resources of the Columbia River Basin*, October 1960, p. 19.

23. Ibid., p. 17d. Canadian technical advisers, more bemused than anything else by this presentation, did not miss the inclusion of Libby at-site production, and of a large block of secondary power firmed up into prime, which the negotiators had agreed would not be available for sharing purposes. They noted also that downstream benefits in Canada from Libby storage had been ignored. A none-too-successful attempt was made to put the Canadian record straight on this matter in the press release issued by the prime minister at the time of the signing of the Columbia River Treaty, January 17, 1961. See *The Columbia River Treaty, Protocol, and Related Documents*, p. 93.

24. J. Saywell, ed., *The Canadian Annual Review for 1960*, p. 93.

25. *Vancouver Sun*, October 21, 1960, p. 1.

26. Ibid., October 25, 1960, p. 11.

27. Neither a review of the official record of the negotiations nor extensive interviewing has revealed any justification for this story of Tom Gould. See *Victoria Daily Times*, October 21, 1960, p. 4.

28. *The Province* (Vancouver), October 20, 1960, p. 5.

29. W. C. Mainwaring to R. L. Chantrill, October 24, 1960, pp. 1–2. To complicate matters by this time Dr. Keenleyside had twice publicly affirmed that the Power Commission would not purchase Peace power until convinced that cheaper energy was not available elsewhere.

30. W. A. C. Bennett to D. Fleming, October 27, 1960. Mr. Bennett repeated his requests in a letter which he released to the press. *Vancouver Sun*, November 5, 1960, p. 2.

31. Mr. Bennett was rubbing in the South Saskatchewan project here. In 1960 Ottawa was expected to pay 75 percent of the cost of the dam or some $72,000,000 plus $8,500,000 for engineering, plus $1,600,000 for penstocks, and was financing Saskatchewan's 25 percent of the capital requirements.

32. His successor as the minister of northern affairs and national resources was the Honourable Walter Dinsdale.

33. See Canada, House of Commons, *Debates*, 24th Parlt., 4th Sess., December 8, 1960, p. 608.

34. Minutes, Eleventh Meeting, Canada, British Columbia Policy Liaison Committee, Ottawa, November 23–24, 1960, p. 3.

35. *Vancouver Sun*, December 7, 1960, p. 1.

36. Arrived at by adding $40 millions (⅛ percent—the federal service charge on its financial contribution—over fifty years) and $70 millions (the federal sales tax revenue likely to be generated by the construction).

37. Cited in *Vancouver Sun*, December 9, 1960, pp. 1–2.

38. Cited in *The Province* (Vancouver), December 9, 1960, p. 1.

39. Minutes, Twelfth Meeting, Canada-British Columbia Policy Liaison Committee Meeting, December 8–9, 1960, p. 4.

40. Cited in *Vancouver Sun*, December 29, 1960, p. 1. Mr. Fulton in the same speech also indicated that Ottawa accepted B.C. Hydro "as the entity to have responsibility for the physical aspects of construction and operation." The absence of a reference to financing, and to the meeting of treaty obligations here was noteworthy.

41. The Burrard Plant expected its first two units to come into service in 1962. With a total capacity of 900,000 kw it would be able to meet B.C. Electric capacity requirements over most of the decade, virtually doubling that system.

42. *The Province* (Vancouver), December 14, 1960, p. 1.

43. Personal interview, W. C. Mainwaring, August 3, 1965.

44. *The British Columbia Gazette* (Victoria: Queen's Printer, CI, no. 1, January 5, 1961), p. 1.

Since its creation in 1959 the Energy Board has received only one specific assignment, in April 1960, when it had been asked to study the feasibility and implications of a transmission grid linking all the sources of electrical energy in British Columbia.

45. *The Province* (Vancouver), December 30, 1960, pp. 1, 2.

46. Personal interview, R. G. Williston; cf. Sherman, *Bennett*, p. 242.

47. Minutes, Thirteenth Meeting, Canada-British Columbia Policy Liaison Committee Meeting, January 3–4, 1961, p. 5.

48. They emphasized the need to retain Mica's first-added position.

49. *The Province* (Vancouver), January 5, 1961, pp. 1–2.

50. Cited in *The Province* (Vancouver), January 7, 1961, p. 1.

51. External Affairs Committee, *Minutes of Proceedings and Evidence*, 26th Parlt., 2nd Sess., May 11, 1964, p. 1114.

52. Article 8 (1) dealt with the exchanges of notes relevant to any disposal of entitlement to downstream power benefits.

53. Mr. Fleming had replied to Mr. Bennett on December 21 regretting the rejection of Ottawa's "extraordinary generous" offer, suggesting that it might have been the result of a misunderstanding and hoping for the possibility of an early personal discussion.

54. Prime Minister Diefenbaker, Mr. Fulton, and Mr. A. D. P. Heeney, the Canadian ambassador to the United States, signed the treaty for Canada on January 17.

The principal features of the agreement, which has a minimal life of sixty years, and may be terminated thereafter on ten years' notice, are as follows. Canada agreed to provide by means of projects built at the outlet of the Arrow Lakes and north of Kootenay Lake (in five years after ratification) and near Mica Creek (in nine years) some 15.5 million acre-feet of storage in all. Canada agreed to operate 8,450,000 acre-feet of this storage, nearly all of it in the Arrow and Kootenay Lake drainage areas, in accordance with flood control plans, as detailed in Annex A of the treaty. She undertook also to meet periodic calls for additional flood control operation, in return for additional compensation. And she accepted a commitment to regulate the whole block of storage in accord with further operating plans, as specified in Annex B, and established five years in advance, to produce a downstream power benefit.

The United States in its turn agreed to operate its projects on the Columbia main stream so as to make the best use of this Canadian regulation. It contracted to make advance payments representing the present worth of one-half the flood control benefit provided, as each Canadian project was completed, to a total of $64.4 million (U.S.). Canada received title to one-half the downstream power benefit produced, in the United States, by its storage. This latter benefit was to be calculated in accordance with a procedure detailed in Annex B, and on the assumption that the whole of the Canadian storage would receive next-added credit to that detailed in an American base system specified in the same Annex. The power benefit was to be returned to Canada near Oliver, B.C., and the United States agreed to provide a stand-by circuit to protect its transmission to Vancouver, for $1.50 (U.S.) per kw of capacity, until a mutually satisfactory coordination agreement had been put into effect.

Provision was made for disposing of portions of the Canadian power entitlement in the United States contingent upon agreement "as evidenced by exchange of notes" between Canada and the United States. The United States received a five-year option in which to commence the construction of a dam at Libby, and the treaty recognized a Canadian right to divert approximately 20, 75, and 90 percent of the Kootenay River's flow north into the Columbia twenty, sixty, and eighty years after ratification. The two countries agreed to establish a four-man Permanent Engineering Board to report regularly on the implementation of the treaty to the two national governments concerned.

55. Personal interview, D. Fleming, August 19, 1967.

56. Personal interview, W. A. C. Bennett, December 6, 1965.

57. Personal interview, J. Diefenbaker, March 3, 1967. See also Canada, House of Commons, *Debates*, 24th Parlt., 4th Sess., May 26, 1961, p. 5405.

Notes to Chapter 7, 1961: A Year of Stalemate

1. Cited in *The Daily Colonist* (Victoria), January 19, 1961, p. 1.

2. Canada, House of Commons, *Debates*, 24th Parlt., 4th Series, January 18, 1961, pp. 1159, 1166.

3. Ibid., May 31, 1961, p. 5640.

4. *The Victoria Daily Times*, January 17, 1961, p. 1.

5. R. G. Williston, "Report on Hydro-Power" (Address to B.C. Legislature, February 8, 1961, mimeographed), p. 16.

6. cf. Howard Green at Vancouver as reported in *The Province* (Vancouver), February 17, 1961, p. 3; E. D. Fulton in the Kootenays, Ibid., February 8, 1961, p. 17.

7. See the comments of William Ryan, business editor, *The Province* (Vancouver), February 18, 1961, p. 6—and those of George Hobbs, CCF member of the Provincial Legislature from Revelstoke.

8. British Columbia Energy Board, "Interim Report on the Columbia and Peace Power Projects," March 1, 1961.

9. Canada, House of Commons, *Debates*, 24th Parlt., 4th Sess., March 3, 1961, pp. 2621–22. A reference to Messrs. A. Paget and H. Keenleyside.

10. Cited in *The Province* (Vancouver), March 4, 1961, p. 1.

11. Ibid., March 13, p. 13.

12. This official was aware of and was sensitive to Canadian embarrassment over the emerging impasse with British Columbia.

13. Special Task Force, Pacific Northwest-Pacific Southwest, *Extra-High Voltage Common Carrier Interconnection* (Washington: U.S. Department of the Interior, December 15, 1961), p. 1.

On February 9 a Bonneville Power Administration official had informed a provincial technical adviser of the fact that there appeared to be sufficient possibility of absorbing part of Canada's power entitlement to justify further talks on the subject. H. M. McIntyre to G. J. A. Kidd, February 9, 1961.

14. Cited in *The Province* (Vancouver), June 7, 1961, p. 5.

15. *The Province* (Vancouver), April 14, p. 3.

16. Ibid., May 17, p. 1, and May 20, p. 5.

17. Ibid., May 17, 1961, pp. 1, 17.

18. Ibid., May 27, 1961, pp. 1–2.

19. Subsequently provincial government spokesmen made much of this fact. Years later, reflecting on this assertion, W. C. Mainwaring did not deny that the B.C. Electric wished to expand its role in the Peace River Company, but insisted that control was not available to it. The principals he affirmed, were in no mood to disengage. Personal interview, August 3, 1965.

20. A. E. D. Grauer, "The Export of Electricity from Canada," in *Canadian Issues, Essays in Honour of Henry F. Angus*, edited by R. M. Clark, p. 283.

21. The estimates of the B.C. Electric and West Kootenay Companies were called "conservative," those of the B.C. Power Commission and the East Kootenay Power Company "normal." R. L. Chantrill, Jack Stevens, *"A Report on Power Capabilities and Operating Aspects of a British Columbia Power Pool,"* p. ii.

22. Ibid. An extraordinarily accurate estimate.

23. A consortium of three of Canada's major engineering firms: Crippen Wright Engineering, Ltd.; H. G. Acres & Co., Ltd.; The Shawinigan Engineering Company, Ltd.

24. Caseco Consultants Ltd., *Report on Columbia River Development* (Vancouver, B.C.: May 1961), pp. 1–5.

25. Actually, however, it did indicate that it was not known whether it

would be economically feasible to distribute Columbia energy to all parts of the province. Hence the load centres which the report considered were all in the centre-south: Kamloops, Trail, Oliver, Vancouver.

26. G. J. A. Kidd and A. W. Lash, "Comments on Report entitled 'Power Capabilities and Operating Aspects of a British Columbia Power Pool,'" (typewritten), June 26, 1961. (Mr. Kidd had moved to the Power Commission from the B.C. Water Resources Service, to which he returned at the end of 1962.)

27. Sherman, *Bennett*, p. 248.

28. Personal interview, W. C. Mainwaring, August 3, 1965.

29. *Victoria Daily Times*, May 29, 1961, p. 4. It was commenting on his recent endorsation of power exports on a recoverable basis.

30. L. Ladner, "The Columbia River Project and Policy" (mimeographed), p. 6.

31. G. McNabb to T. M. Patterson, May 16, 1961.

32. Cited in *The Province* (Vancouver), May 31, 1961, p. 2.

33. Ibid , July 27, 1961, p. 3.

34. British Columbia Statutes, 1961 (2nd Session), c. 4.

35. British Columbia Energy Board, *Report on the Columbia and Peace River Power Projects*, p. 29.

36. Ibid., pp. 28, 30.

37. Ibid., p. 5. Dr. Henry Angus dissented from the findings which appeared to indicate large scale economies for development under public auspices—in a desire to avoid embarrassment in his role as the chairman of the Public Utilities Commission. Further, he contended that the evidence presented to the Energy Board (of which he was a member) was "inadequate to support an opinion of this character." (Ibid., p. 31.)

38. Ibid., p. 1.

39. Ibid., pp. 19, 6.

40. The maximum compensation was based on the sum of $38 per common share—the open market price just before the premier's warning to the Legislature in February. Much of the bitterness among the investing public stemmed from the fact that a few years earlier the same shares had ranged over $50. Many holders of the B.C. Electric's preferred shares also resented the proposed exchange of these securties for fixed-interest-rate debentures. In the process they stood to lose both some appreciation in the preferred shares' value as the B.C. Electric gradually retired its indebtedness, and the 20 percent federal income tax credit on dividend payments. Some critics also referred ironically to the fact that the government had just set up a Royal Commission to investigate expropriation problems under Mr. Justice J. V. Clyne.

41. Sir Alexander Gibb and Partners, Merz and McLellan. *Columbia and Peace River Power Projects: Report on Power Costs*, p. 10. The consultants had been selected by the Energy Board (from a list supplied by W. C. Mainwaring to G. M. Shrum) because of their international reputation and their freedom from any involvement with the project work on the Columbia. The consultants' report was not made available during the Legislative session.

42. Sherman, *Bennett*, p. 249.

43. *The Province* (Vancouver), August 14, 1961, p. 1.

44. Ibid., August 30, 1961, p. 1.

45. Canada, House of Commons, *Debates*, 24th Parlt., 4th Sess., September 13, 1961, pp. 82–89.

46. Cited in *The Province* (Vancouver), September 18, 1961, p. 1.

47. This was a reference to Mr. Udall's testimony before the Committee on Foreign Relations of the U.S. Senate on March 8, 1961. U.S. Congress, Senate, Committee on Foreign Relations, *Hearing, Columbia River Treaty*, 87th Cong., 1st Session, 1961, p. 27.

48. *The Province* (Vancouver), September 18, 1961, pp. 1–2, and September 19, p. 1.

49. Cited in *The Province* (Vancouver), September 21, 1961, p. 6.

50. Ibid., October 24, 1961, p. 5.

51. Cited in *The Province* (Vancouver), November 3, 1961, p. 5. Mr. Fulton returned from this trip and a trip to British Columbia convinced that the five mill figure was unrealistic, and that putting this fact before the people was perhaps the best way of convincing them that Mr. Bennett's plan was not in the province's best interest.

52. *The Province* (Vancouver), September 19, 1961, p. 17.

53. Ibid., October 3, 1961, p. 17.

54. Ibid., November 28, 1961, p. 2.

55. These were held at Revelstoke (re Mica) on September 18, at Kaslo (re Duncan Dam) on September 21, and at Revelstoke on September 26–27, Nakusp on September 29, and Castlegar on October 3 (in connection with the High Arrow project). A final hearing was held in Victoria on November 21, 1961.

56. Comptroller of Water Rights, "Record of Proceedings, Hearings Concerning Applications to Build the Mica, Duncan and High Arrow Dams, Victoria, B.C." (September 21–November 21, 1961), mimeographed, p. 275.

57. Mr. Randolph Harding, M.L.A., for instance, emphasized the limited amount of provincial land suitable for agriculture, and suggested that prospective increases in Arrow Lakes foreshore production, which would now have to be forgone, were a real cost of the project. Ibid., p. 670.

58. Ibid., p. 404.

59. Mr. George Hobbs, M.L.A., Ibid., p. 291.

60. This point was made in an able exhibit by D. C. Waterfield, citing a letter he had received in October 1960, from Mr .Williston. Ibid., p. 721. Mr. Waterfield did not blame Mr. Williston for the change in procedure, but did argue "someone has crossed us up." (Ibid., p. 727.)

61. Cf. the results of a survey conducted for and published by *The Province* (Vancouver), October 2, 1961, pp. 1–2.

62. *The Province* (Vancouver), October 28, 1961, p. 1.

63. John Meisel, "The Formulation of Liberal and Conservative Programmes in the 1957 Canadian General Election," *The Canadian Journal of Economics and Political Science* 26, no. 4 (November 1960): 570–72.

64. Cited in H. C. McQuillan, "Energy's Administrative Framework," *Transactions of the Thirteenth British Columbia Natural Resources Conference* (Victoria, 1961), p. 30.

65. Personal interview, December 6, 1965.

66. *Montreal Gazette*, November 22, 1961, p. 1.

67. *The Province* (Vancouver), November 22, 1961, p. 1.

68. *The Province* (Vancouver), November 25, 1961, pp. 1–2.

69. *Vancouver Sun*. November 27, 1961. p. 2.

70. Cited in *Vancouver Sun*. November 27, 1961, p. 1.

71. Cited in *The Province*, November 29, 1961, pp. 2, 4.

72. He did declare that the federal plan would cost the taxpayer $750 millions over thirty-five years—which assertion Mr. Fulton described on December 12 as "cooking the books." *The Province*, December 14, 1961, p. 2.

73. *The Victoria Daily Times*, December 7, 1961, p. 1.

74. Cf. Tom Gould in *The Victoria Daily Times*, January 2, 1962, p. 1. The November 27 and December 21, 1961 letters between Mr. Bennett and Mr. Fleming were the only part of the Bennett-Fleming correspondence to be printed as appendices to the *Debates* of the House of Commons—an act which requires unanimous consent from the House. Canada, House of Commons, *Debates*, 24th Parlt., 5th Sess., January 26, 1962, pp. 281–83.

75. *The Province*, December 14, 1961, p. 2.

76. The memorandum did not actually advise disallowance as such.

Notes to Chapter 8, *The First Steps Toward a Federal-Provincial Détente*

1. The report made it clear that supporting analyses had examined the consequences of a sale and transmission to California of much of the Canadian downstream power entitlement. Both sale and non-sale circumstances had been considered. Special Task Force. U.S. Department of the Interior, *Pacific Northwest-Pacific Southwest Extra-High Voltage Common Carrier Interconnection*, December 15, 1961.

2. The Yellowknife Board of Trade in the Northwest Territories had asked Mr. Fulton on November 18, 1961, "whether or not it appears likely that you will have to invoke the appropriate clauses of the Navigable Waters Act in order to keep the B C. government from running wild." G. Bromley, president, to E. D. Fulton, November 18, 1961.

3. The B.C. Hydro and Power Authority justifies this action by referring to the legal opinion of its own and external advisers to the effect that the federal statute is not applicable to the site in question. See the prospectus accompanying the issuing of $50 millions in bonds by the Hydro Authority, dated January 11, 1967, pp. 18–19.

(Mr. Bennett constantly placed great stress on the fact that the dam was built in a formerly impassable canyon.)

4. *The Province* (Vancouver), January 17, 1962, p. 2; January 31, 1962, p. 1.

5. Ibid., January 9, 1962, p. 3, and February 21, 1962, p. 2.

6. Ibid., February 12, 1962, p. 25.

7. Ibid., January 26, 1962.

8. C. B. Bourne, J. D. Chapman, E. F. Muir, E. Ruus, A. D. Scott, H. V. Warren, E. F. Wilks, "Electrical Energy in British Columbia," February 26, 1962, p. 3 (mimeographed).

9. Ibid., pp. 5–10.

10. Ibid., p. 7.

11. The Water Resources Branch study made such points as those which follow:

The cost of the full Mica Dam had been charged to treaty storage—when this storage, in fact, was just over one-third of the project's capacity. Were the dam to serve only as a storage project, the memorandum noted, the dam would just be constructed to provide the 7 million acre-feet of storage attributed to it. The additional height would be added, and cost incurred, only when generation was required. And the cost estimates of the Peace and Columbia projects were not strictly comparable. Mica, furthermore, had been given no credit for its contribution in making the Downie and Revelstoke projects hydraulically feasible, and for providing the basic transmission-line which they would use.

12. A Vancouver-based shareholders' committee sought to insist on this approach.

13. *The Province* (Vancouver), March 14, 1962, p. 4.

14. Ibid., February 28, 1962, p. 1: March 2, 1962, p. 2.

15. Ibid., March 10, 1962, p. 11.

16. Personal interview, W. A. C. Bennett, May 13, 1966. He is well aware of the fact that, to make up for the embarrassment to Ottawa which stemmed from Mr. Udall's observations some months earlier, an account of his call was promptly relayed from Washington to the Canadian government, which promptly revealed it to a friendly reporter.

17. *The Province* (Vancouver), March 12, 1962, p. 1.

18. Ibid., March 13, p. 1.

19. The one day conference was not a major success. Ontario, clearly the major market, had real doubts about the concept of the nationwide grid. Quebec regarded the federal initiative as an intrusion on a provincial power, and boycotted the session.

20. Actually, on March 21, 1962, Mr. Williston gave some indication of the manner in which the province was modifying its earlier position in the interest of reaching an agreement with Ottawa. While addressing the provincial Legislature he suggested that the Peace River's development might be staged, that for the present perhaps only the first stage might be proceeded with to meet the needs of the years 1967–73. He suggested that energy from Mica Creek could meet provincial needs from 1973 to 1980. Thereafter the second stage of the Peace development would be brought in, followed by the Downie and High Revelstoke developments on the Columbia. *The Province* (Vancouver), March 22, 1962, p. 1.

21. G. J. A. Kidd, "Notes of Meeting between B.C. and federal officials on Columbia Project" (Victoria, April 10, 1962), p. 2. British Columbia's representatives at this meeting were Drs. Shrum and Keenleyside, who five days earlier had become co-chairmen of the new British Columbia Hydro and Power Authority, Mr. Ralph Purcell, chief engineer of the B.C. Energy Board, and Mr. G. J. A. Kidd. Present on behalf of the federal government were Mr. Gordon Robertson, one of the negotiators of the treaty, Mr. T. M. Patterson, the director of the Water Resources Branch, and Mr. Gordon McNabb, whose length of experience with Columbia planning at the federal level almost exactly matched that of Mr. Kidd, at the provincial level. The fourth federal representative was Mr. J. Parkinson, a senior officer in the Department of Finance.

22. An official British Columbia memorandum on this meeting reads rather differently, and suggests that the price was to be not higher than that obtainable via export sales to the United States.

23. Canada, House of Commons, *Debates*, 24th Parlt., 5th Sess., April 9, 1962, p. 2641; April 13, p. 2963.

24. *The Province* (Vancouver), April 14, 1962, p. 1.

25. R. G. Williston, "Power Developments in British Columbia," An Address to the Northwest Power Association, Seattle, Wash., April 17, 1963 (mimeographed), p. 3. In this address Mr. Williston also recalled that, a year earlier, the province was expecting the federal government to change its power export policy.

26. The press release is printed in *The Columbia River Treaty, Protocol, and Related Documents*, pp. 82–90; the reference in question, p. 89.

27. Power Development Act, 1961, Amendment Act, 1962. *British Columbia Statutes*, 1962, 10–11, Eliz. 11, 3, c. 50.

28. British Columbia Hydro and Power Authority Act. *British Columbia Statutes*, 1962, 10–11. Eliz. 11, c. 8.

29. Section 11, Sub-Section 4 of this act sought to free the new authority from actions pertaining to the Power Development Act of 1961 and to the 1962 Amending Act. Two of the arguments Mr. Bennett used to support the fusion of the two agencies were that it would permit a uniform "postage-stamp" rate for residential customers across the province, and that charges for all would be reduced. This was duly put into effect on April 1, with residents of the more isolated communities in the interior receiving cut-backs of up to 25 percent. *The Province* (Vancouver), April 3, 1962, p. 1.

30. Cited by H. W. Herridge, in the House of Commons. Canada, House of Commons, *Debates*, 24th Parlt., 5th Sess., April 6, 1962, p. 2586.

31. Ibid. General McNaughton's biographer declares that the general had been asked to stay on after his seventy-fifth birthday (February 5, 1962) to attend the IJC meeting at Washington on April 3–5, 1962, and that he had agreed to do so on two conditions: that his retirement not be announced until this meeting was over; and that at it he be allowed to try "as a last chance to get better terms from the Americans than those contained in the draft Columbia Treaty." (John Swettenham, *McNaughton*, III, p. 303). Both conditions

Mr. Swettenham declares were agreed to by Mr. Howard Green, and, in effect, were repudiated by Mr. Diefenbaker, who released the news of the retirement on April 3. Mr. Green observes that this account is quite incorrect, and that the general simply had no clearance to engage in a last ditch modification stand. (Personal interview, Howard Green, April 10, 1970).

32. A. G. L. McNaughton, "The Proposed Columbia River Treaty," *International Journal* 18, no. 4 (Spring, 1963) : 148–65.

33. It was, in fact, in response to questions in the House of Commons related to these assertions that Mr. Green made his statements concerning ratification on April 9 and 13.

34. *The Province* (Vancouver), May 5, 1962, pp. 1–2.

35. Cited in *The Victoria Daily Times*, May 4, 1962, p. 1.

36. *The Province* (Vancouver), June 7, 1962, p. 3.

37. Ibid., May 4, 1962, p. 8.

38. Ibid. (A reply to a position which no one had endorsed!) Dr. John Davis, who resigned from the B.C. Hydro and Power Authority to run as a Liberal candidate in Vancouver, cordially endorsed a downstream benefit power sale, again only when the price had been settled and all the tag ends tied up. Ibid., May 12, 1962, p. 6, and May 29, 1962, p. 6.

39. R. M. Strachan, "Press Release: Power-Columbia and Peace Rivers," May 4, pp. 1–4.

40. John Meisel, ed., *Papers on the 1962 Election*.

41. Mr. Bennett revealed to the press on September 1 that he had met Mr. Fleming, and with his approval, Mr. Pearson also. He declared that he expected the treaty to be ratified in the new session of Parliament if it lasted long enough, and that he was hoping for a construction start by March 31, 1963. *The Globe and Mail* (Toronto), September 3, 1962, p. 21.

42. Canada, House of Commons, *Debates*, 25th Parlt., 1st Sess., September 27, 1962, p. 9. The speech also indicated that the federal government would continue its cooperative investigation of the development possibilities of the Nelson River in Northern Manitoba, and of a national power grid.

43. e.g. Alex Young, *The Victoria Daily Times*, September 27, 1962, p. 1.

44. Interviews with E. D. Fulton, March 9, 1964, and J. G. Diefenbaker, March 3, 1967. Both confirm that the declaration in the Speech from the Throne was not meant to refer specifically to the Columbia, and was to assuage Canadian commercial opinion.

45. On October 5 the federal representatives at Portland, interestingly, had reported to Mr. Fleming that a twenty-year sale of the downstream entitlement would not finance the construction of the three treaty storages. In this they were correct. Incorrectly they went on to suggest that Mr. Bennett might be forced to realize that he had two alternatives: (a) to accelerate the Columbia by machining Mica, exporting some power to the United States, and deferring the Peace somewhat; or (b) to drop the Columbia altogether and concentrate on the Peace.

46. *The Province* (Vancouver), October 12, 1962, p. 1.

47. With Messrs. Kidd and Purcell, present from Canada.

48. G. J. A. Kidd, "Draft Summaries of Technical Discussions and Studies —With and Without the Americans," p. 5 (date not recorded).

49. Canada, House of Commons, *Debates*, 25th Parlt., 1st Sess., November 27, 1962, p. 2045.

50. Dr. Krutilla declares flatly that the prospect of this major American interconnection "largely eliminates the rationale for Columbia Treaty storage for power purposes." *The Columbia River Treaty*, p. 198.

51. Ibid., p. 197.

52. This is a point which Dr. John Krutilla, who followed the Canadian and American decision-making closely, made in a monograph which he circulated privately in mid-year, 1962: John Krutilla, "British Columbia Alternatives to the Columbia Treaty" (mimeographed July 11, 1962), pp. 22–23.

53. The reference here is to the prospect that the very large capacity of the Peace reservoir might permit a "storage" of Mica generation out of phase with provincial needs, and conversely a firming up of much of this energy. If it were thus possible to draw down the Mica reservoir to produce a large downstream benefit for the United States, and at the same time to meet Canadian energy requirements, the need for Arrow as a re-regulator of Mica's discharge was open to question, especially when, by this date, it represented an investment of well over $100 millions.

54. One of these papers was written by an employee of the B.C. Hydro and Power Authority and dated December 3, 1962. The other, drafted by a member of the province's Water Resources Service staff, was undated, but was produced either in December 1962 or early in January 1963.

55. "Memorandum to Director, Water Resources Branch, Columbia River Downstream Benefits," November 26, 1962, p. 3.

56. These included the coordination of Mica and the Canadian Columbia projects with the American system, the retention of first-added credit for its storage, the retention of Libby downstream benefits in Canada, the retention of the right to effect a limited Kootenay diversion at Canal Flats, and the United States paying for Libby flowage costs in Canada. Ibid., pp. 3–4.

57. W. D. Kennedy, G. J. A. Kidd, G. M. MacNabb, P. R. Purcell, "Evaluation of the December 1962 Proposal of the United States Representatives Relative to Implementation of Columbia River Treaty, January 11, 1963," p. V–2.

58. Ibid., Appendix 3, p. 4. Just the opposite interpretation of the tactical situation had been given by General McNaughton to a gathering of Liberal and New Democratic Party M.P.'s and senators called by the sitting members for the Kootenay (A. Herridge, Kootenay West, NDP and J. Byrne, Kootenay East, Liberal) on December 12. On this occasion the general called for the rejection of the treaty, held that the sooner this was done the better it would be for all, and reiterated his conviction that "it would not be difficult to turn back the clock with our friends in the U.S." *Winnipeg Free Press*, December 13, 1962, pp. 1, 6.

59. *The Province* (Vancouver), January 9, 1963, p. 13.

60. Personal interview, March 9, 1964. Mr. Fulton announced on November 20, 1962, that he was to be a candidate for the leadership of the British Columbia Progressive Conservative party, and was elected to that position on January 24, 1963.

61. Canada, House of Commons, *Debates*, 25th Parlt., 1st Sess., October 4, 1962, p. 204.

62. Ibid., December 12, 1962, pp. 2590–94.

63. Ibid., December 13, 1962, pp. 2613–18; 2637–41; 2643.

64. P. L. Sherman, "Columbia River Power Plan: A Special Report," *The Province*, January 24, 1963. Supporters of the provincial government found much to vindicate the province's case in his analysis.

The opposition parties were not slow to comment on a journalist being given access to information denied to them.

The Province (Vancouver), February 22, 1963, p. 5.

65. R. G. Williston, "Excerpts from an Address During Debate on the Speech from the Throne," February 7, 1963, p. 1.

66. *The Province* (Vancouver), January 29, 1963, p. 15.

67. e.g. Mr. James Byrne, M.P. Canada, House of Commons, *Debates*, December 13, 1962, p. 2642.

68. *The Province* (Vancouver), January 29, 1963, p. 15.

69. *Vancouver Sun*, February 28, 1963, p. 4.

70. Ibid., February 7, 1963, p. 11.

71. *The Province* (Vancouver), April 5, 1963, p. 2.

Notes to Chapter 9, Federal-Provincial Rapprochement

1. *The Province* (Vancouver), April 10, 1963, p. 1.

2. Ibid., April 24, 1963, p. 1.

3. L. B. Pearson, "Memorandum to the President of the United States Concerning the International Development of the Columbia River," May 10–11, 1963, p. 1.

4. Ibid. Besides an agreement on downstream benefit sales, the other items listed were:

(1) a request for clarification of the Canadian right to continue in perpetuity any Kootenay to Columbia River diversions;

(2) a request for a waiver of the stand-by transmission charges in the event of a sale;

(3) a request for a clarification of the Canadian responsibility to meet flood control calls in the post-treaty period;

(4) a request for some degree of coordination where possible without disadvantage to the United States between Libby operation and downstream Canadian plants.

5. Minutes of meetings between federal and provincial ministers and officials concerning the Columbia River Treaty held June 3 and 4, 1963 (Ottawa), p. 6.

6. Mr. Bennett had told the press on May 22 that he had enlisted Mr. Anderson, then with Lehman Brothers, during the previous November in New York. "Mr. Anderson's job," the premier declared, "was 'to get the right story across' from President Kennedy down" and to "dispel impressions put abroad . . . that B.C. was trying to sabotage the Columbia." *Victoria Daily Times*, May 22, 1963, p. 17. Actually, Mr. Bennett had been in touch with Mr. Anderson on this question for some time before November 1962. He recalls that it was Mr. Anderson who set up his meeting with President Kennedy in November 1961. Personal interview, May 13, 1966.

7. The entire agreement was published in *The Daily Colonist* (Victoria), July 11, 1963, p. 7. See also: *The Columbia River Treaty, Protocol, and Related Documents*, pp. 100–106.

8. Mr. Bennett welcomed the agreement thus: "This is the type of agreement we would have signed two or three years ago if we hadn't been frustrated by Fulton." Cited in the *Victoria Daily Times*, July 10, 1963, p. 1. Mr. Fulton sought to argue that Mr. Bennett's new line of action would mean "further lengthy delay before the treaty can be implemented and construction begins." Cited in *The Daily Colonist* (Victoria), July 11, 1963, p. 1. Generally Mr. Fulton, who on his acceptance of the provincial party leadership had endorsed the urgency of a federal-provincial agreement, and also the concept of an agreement covering the sale of genuinely surplus power to the United States, sought to concentrate on other issues. cf. *The Financial Post*, March 23, 1963, p. 24; *The Victoria Daily Times*, July 12 and 13, 1963, pp. 1–2. Mr. Perrault took the position that the federal Liberals had saved the treaty. *The Victoria Daily Times*, July 13, 1963, p. 2. Mr. Douglas for the NDP endorsed the McNaughton plan, in a valley which the general was prepared to flood.

As the Canada-British Columbia Agreement was clearly designed to facilitate the implementation of the Columbia River Treaty, its publication (on July 10) left no real grounds for a continuing belief that the two Canadian governments intended to seek an entirely new international agreement.

9. J. B. Hedley to Denis Kennedy, May 9, 1963, p. 2.

10. Without the treaty he agreed that for a few years the risks of floods on the lower Columbia and the Kootenay would remain. But the United States would save some $64 millions of payments to Canada.

11. The other two projects were Knowles and High Mountain Sheep.

12. It was included in the protocol as Article II (covering, but without a hard commitment, flood control benefits only).

13. American spokesmen in response wryly noted how either side could find ways to alter the treaty to its advantage, and how American government spokesmen had held it to be an equitable arrangement before the Senate Committee on Foreign Relations.

14. By coincidence on August 1 he became chief justice of the province, and the head of the B.C. Court of Appeal.

15. *British Columbia Power Corporation* v. *Attorney General of B.C., 1963*, W.W.R., pp. 65–356. (The three statutes invalidated were the Power Development Act of 1961, the 1962 amendment of it, and the 1962 B.C.

Hydro and Power Authority Act.) C. J. Lett advanced two basic arguments in support of his judgment. One drew attention to the fact that while the provincial Legislature had sought to vest in the Crown in the right of the province all the shares of a provincially incorporated company (the B.C. Electric Company), this concern had, in fact, been an almost wholly owned subsidiary of a holding company (the British Columbia Power Corporation) which had been incorporated by the Dominion. Thus C. J. Lett saw the expropriation as rendering nugatory status and powers federally conferred. He also argued that because of its rail and transmission-line linkages, the B.C. Electric Company was an undertaking which extended beyond the limits of the province, and, by virtue of Section 91 (29) of the British North America (1867) Act, hence fell exclusively under the jurisdiction of Parliament.

The province's compensation had amounted to $171,833,052. Before Mr. Justice Lett the Power Corporation had maintained that the sum should be at least $225 millions. The figure Mr. Lett set was $192,828,125. Ibid., p. 354.

16. Ibid., p. 171.

17. The decision of C. J. Lett in fact raises major questions concerning the provincial power to expropriate. These have been reviewed briefly but clearly by G. V. La Forest in his *Natural Resources and Public Property under the Canadian Constitution*, pp. 174–76. For a discussion of the Supreme Court of Canada's disposition of British Columbia's attempt to prevent judicial review of the contested legislation save by petition of right procedure, see B. L. Strayer, *Judicial Review of Legislation in Canada*, pp. 84–89.

18. At Victoria, September 20, 1963. Audited.

19. At Victoria, September 26, 1963. Audited.

20. *Vancouver Sun*, August 30, 1963, p. 3.

21. *The Province* (Vancouver), September 24, 1963, p. 5.

22. H. L. Keenleyside to W. A. C. Bennett, September 9, 1963, p. 2.

23. Ibid., p. 2.

24. With provincial and federal personnel equally represented. The members of it from Canada were Messrs. G. J. A. Kidd, W. D. Kennedy, G. MacNabb, and J. Parkinson.

25. Canada, House of Commons, *Debates*, 26th Parlt., 1st Sess., October 8, 1963, pp. 3300–3301.

26. The treaty provided for the use of a twenty-year stream flow record, but one covering thirty years revealed higher average annual flows, and hence a greater benefit downstream (if it were used) as a result of upstream storage in Canada.

27. Work Group no. 1, "Determination of Canadian Downstream Power Entitlement" (November 1963), p. 2.

28. W. D. Kennedy et al, memorandum for the Canadian negotiators (November 23, 1963), p. 6.

29. Even retrospective evaluation involves difficulties, for it requires the making of a series of assumptions as to the manner in which the American

system would have developed without a treaty, which assumptions are clearly untestable.

30. G. J. A. Kidd, Columbia River Development: Sale of Downstream Benefits (October 17, 1963), p. 2. *A copy of this memorandum was sent to the Water Resources Branch in Ottawa.*

31. The Americans estimated that the cost of the hiatus to them had been of the order of $50 millions—of which $10 millions were recoverable. And these figures contained no allowance for the escalation in interest rates since 1961.

32. Three Cabinet ministers now joined Messrs. Martin, Robertson, Ritchie, and Keenleyside on the Canadian "team." They were Mr. A. Laing, Mr. R. G. Williston, and Mr. R. Bonner.

33. Both Canadian governments—notwithstanding Mr. Sharp's national power policy—had been disturbed at the complications inherent in what in effect would have been an escalating sale. Both also had a real fear that an agreement of this sort might somehow devalue the Canadian downstream power entitlement.

34. Canada estimated capital costs of the storage projects at $346 millions present worth, noted that a modest 1½ percent per annum inflation would make this $375 millions, and held that probably an additional 2 percent per annum should be added to this to cover contingencies.

35. The technical problem is dealt with by Dr. Krutilla. See Krutilla, *The Columbia River Treaty and Protocol*, pp. 164–65. The result of this agreement was to increase the Canadian capacity benefit by from 5 to 7 percent.

36. The 3.75 mill figure would have been in American currency terms, would have excluded any consideration of the flood control benefit made to Canada, and would have assumed an American load factor which the Canadian technical personnel were convinced was grossly unrealistic. The Canadian figure would have been in Canadian dollar terms, would have assumed the use of a realistic load factor, and would have incorporated in the price received for the Canadian power entitlement the payment received for Canada's share of the downstream flood control benefit.

There was a major irony in this last consideration, in that allocating the flood control payment to the power benefit implied in a sense that the flood control benefit was being given away for nothing. When, however, Mr. Bennett had refused to allow the flood control payment to be attributed to reducing the cost of Columbia power at the time of the B.C. Energy Board Reference in 1960–61, he had been roundly denounced by his numerous critics for apparently tipping the scales unfairly against the Columbia. His critics were now hoist, in 1963, as a consequence of the position they had taken two years earlier.

37. "Summary of the Effects of the Columbia River Treaty Implementation Proposal," December 12, 1963, p. 1.

38. Personal interview, May 13, 1965.

39. R. W. Bonner and R. G. Williston as ministers, H. L. Keenleyside, G. J. A. Kidd, W. D. Kennedy, and Dr. Gilbert Kennedy.

40. Clause 5.

41. In Canada at the time, in the absence of special statutory provisions, no agreement between Canadian governments was enforceable through the courts, as in law it was not a contract. The Exchequer Court Act did provide that, where appropriate legislation had been passed by one or more provinces, the court had jurisdiction to resolve disputes arising out of agreements between such provinces, or between one or more of them and the federal government. But it did not apply here, for British Columbia had passed no legislation at all directly pertaining to the Columbia River's development. Furthermore, even if such legislation had existed, and had recognized a role for the Exchequer Court, the consequences of a refusal by one government to recognize proceedings subsequently instituted to enforce such an agreement, or of a default, remain obscure. See David W. Mundell, "Legal Nature of Federal and Provincial Executive Governments: Some Comments on Transactions between them," *Osgoode Hall Law Journal* 2, no. 1 (April, 1960): 56–75; Dale Gibson, "Interjurisdictional Immunity in Canadian Federalism," *The Canadian Bar Review* 47, no. 1 (March 1969): 42–59.

42. Once in the July 1963 Agreement; once earlier in this one.

43. Mr. Larratt Higgins in particular had argued that the rights to divert in Article XIII expired after 100 years. L. T. Higgins, "The Columbia River Treaty: A Reply to Professor Bourne," *International Journal* 17, no. 2 (Spring, 1962): 142–44.

44. Printed in *The Columbia River Treaty, Protocol, and Related Documents*, pp. 124–27.

45. Ibid., p. 136.

46. Cited in *The Daily Colonist* (Victoria), January 23, 1963, p. 2.

47. *The Columbia River Treaty, Protocol, and Related Documents* (Ottawa: Queen's Printer, February 1964).

48. *The Columbia River Treaty and Protocol: A Presentation* (Ottawa: Queen's Printer, April 1964).

49. Canada, House of Commons, Standing Committee on External Affairs, *Minutes of Proceedings and Evidence*, April 7, 1964, pp. 29–50.

50. Ibid., April 7, 1964, pp. 29, 30.

51. He reviewed at length the process of intergovernmental cooperation, the 1960 negotiations, and the delay after 1960, making in the process the point that the treaty was negotiated on the assumption that the downstream power benefit was to be returned to Canada, and that this was the basis on which the treaty was signed before British Columbia's "surprising contortion." (p. 1119.) He also reviewed and dismissed a number of the major criticisms advanced against the treaty as it dealt with diversion rights, operating plans, and post-treaty flood control provisions. Ibid., May 11, 1963, p. 1119. Mr. Fulton testified over two days. Ibid., May 11–12, 1963, pp. 1107–94.

52. Ibid., May 7, 1964, pp. 1026–79.

53. Ibid., May 20, 1964, pp. 1353–93; May 21, 1964, pp. 1412–31.

54. Ibid., April 7, 1964, pp. 70–123. Also included were some preliminary remarks made by General McNaughton at a meeting on July 18, 1963.

55. Mr. C. O. Cooper (Rosetown-Biggar). Canada, House of Commons, *Debates*, 26th Parlt., 1st Sess., July 12, 1963, p. 2127.

56. Cited in *The Daily Colonist* (Victoria), October 3, 1963, p. 16.

57. R. G. Williston, "Excerpts from An Address during Debate in the Speech from the Throne" (Victoria, B.C., February 6, 1964), p. 7.

58. External Affairs Committee, *Minutes of Proceedings and Evidence*, April 7, 1964, pp. 132, 135.

59. Montreal Engineering Company Ltd., *Comments on the Columbia River Treaty and Protocol*, p. 35.

60. Standing Committee on External Affairs, *Minutes of Proceedings and Evidence: Columbia River Treaty*, May 27, 1964, p. 1458.

61. Ibid., p. 1460.

62. Ibid., p. 3903.

63. Ibid, June 4, 1964, p. 3933.

64. The negotiations associated with marketing the Canadian entitlement are described in Bernard Goldhammer, "International Development of the Columbia River—Its Significance upon Western Power Developments," paper read before the Western Political Science Association, Victoria, B.C , March 19, 1965.

65. The Purchase Agreement conveyed to the CSPE the Canadian entitlement as described in Article V (1) of the treaty for thirty year periods from newly designated completion dates—April 1, 1968 (Duncan Lake), April 1, 1969 (Arrow Lakes), April 1, 1973 (Mica Creek). It contains a long detailed section (6) outlining the provisions of the compensatory arrangements in the event of a reduction of the Canadian entitlement.

66. The sum paid was $253,999,884.25 ($254.4 millions discounted at 4½ percent from October 1). In view of an undertaking of some years standing between the Canadian and American governments involving a Canadian exemption from the American Interest Equalization Tax, and a compensatory Canadian commitment not to increase unduly its holdings of United States dollars, most of the funds were actually invested in U.S. treasury bills by Ottawa, although Ottawa had to pay British Columbia the full sum immediately. A good deal was made of the cost to the government of Canada of this transaction (the consequence of lower interest rates in the United States than Canada) before the External Affairs Committee hearings. External Affairs Committee, *Minutes of Proceedings and Evidence*, April 10, 1964, pp. 261–65; April 16, 1964, pp. 488–89.

67. The Purchase Agreement, presidential proclamation, and the notes exchanged at this time are to be found in the U.S., *Department of State Bulletin*, LI, no. 1320, October 12, 1964, pp. 504–16. The American note formally relayed the information that the administrator of the Bonneville Power Administration, Department of the Interior, and the division engineer, North Pacific Division, Corps of Engineers, Department of the Army, had been named as the United States Entity (by Presidential Executive Order no. 11177). The Canadian note of September 16 repeated the salient features of

the Compensatory Section of the Purchase Agreement, the agreement concerning the operation of storages, and the filling of the Mica reservoir to 15 million acre-feet by September 1, 1975. It repeated also from the Purchase Agreement the undertaking that no modification or renewal of that agreement be effective unless approved by both governments by an exchange of notes. Finally it, and the American acceptance of it, made the dispute resolving machinery set up under Article XVI of the treaty available to the parties to the Sale Agreement. It also cited the Canadian Order-in-Council of September 4, 1964 (P.C. 1964–1967) which named the B.C. Hydro and Power Authority as the Canadian entity. Ibid., p. 512.

68. Duncan Lake, July 31, 1967; Arrow Lakes, October 10, 1968; Mica, March 29, 1973.

69. Operational for power generation, August 24, 1975.

70. It reached capacity—912,500 kw—in 1975.

71. B.C. Hydro, interestingly enough, is now arguing the wisdom of assuming, for the short-run, the accuracy of high rather than modest growth predictions. A separate issue which it has to deal with, of course, concerns the percentage of its demand to be met from hydro sources.

72. The provincial member is now Mr. B E. Marr.

73. The new (December 1975) Social Credit government quickly appointed Mr. R. W. Bonner, who had left active political life in 1968, to the chairmanship of B.C. Hydro. Its minister responsible for energy matters was Dr. Jack Davis.

74. Canada, House of Commons, *Debates*, 27th Parlt., 1st Sess., April 6, 1966, p. 3941. The terms and conditions of the licences were filed with the House of Commons in response to an enquiry from Mr. Herridge.

Notes to Chapter 10, The Policy Formation Reviewed (A)

1. The reference to computation, judgment, compromise, inspiration here is to four elements in a typology of decision issues advanced in James D. Thompson and Arthur Tuden, "Strategies, Structures, and Processes of Organizational Decision," in *Comparative Studies in Administration*, edited by J. D. Thompson (Pittsburgh: University of Pittsburgh Press, 1959), chapter XII.

2. In early theoretic speculation Lindblom was prepared to offset hierarchy versus a perfect market on this continuum on the assumption that they represented the two extremes in discretion open to decision-makers. Lindblom, "Bargaining: The Hidden Hand in Government," p. 42.

3. See Lindblom, *The Intelligence of Democracy*, pp. 197–204, and R. M. Cyert and J. G. March, *A Behavioural Theory of the Firm* (Englewood Cliffs, N.J.: Prentice Hall, Inc., 1963), p. 118.

4. Lindblom, "Bargaining: The Hidden Hand in Government," p. 21.

5. See E. S. Quade, "Methods and Procedures," in *Analysis for Military Decisions*, edited by E. S. Quade (Chicago: Rand McNally, 1964), pp. 156–76.

6. Cf. the reasoned case of C. West Churchman, *The Systems Approach* (New York: Delacorte Press, 1968).

7. Braybrooke and Lindblom, *A Strategy of Decision*, pp. 50–51.

8. Lindblom, *The Intelligence of Democracy*, chapters 11–12.

9. The phrase is Herbert Simon's. See H. A. Simon, *Models of Man* (New York: John Wiley & Sons, Inc., 1957), pp. 196–206, and his treatment of the decision-making consequences of the "limits" to man's rationality in *Administrative Behavior* (New York: The Macmillan Co., 1957, 2nd edn.), pp. 80–84.

10. See Cyert and March, *A Behavioural Theory of the Firm*, pp. 121–22.

11. See, for example, Yehezkel Dror, "Muddling Through—'Science' or Inertia?" *Public Administration Review* 24, no. 3 (September 1964): 153–57; Amitai Etzioni, "Mixed Scanning: A Third Approach to Decision-Making," *Public Administration Review* 27, no. 5 (December 1967): 389; Kenneth Boulding's review of "A Strategy of Decision: Policy Evaluation vs. a Social Process," in the *American Sociological Review*, 19 (1964): 930–31; Amitai Etzioni, *The Active Society* (New York: The Free Press, 1968), chapters 11, 12; Theodore Lowi, "Decision-Making as Policy Making: Toward an Antidote for Technocracy," *Public Administration Review* 30, no. 3 (May–June, 1970): 314–25; Abrahm Bergson, "Comments on Professor Lindblom's paper on 'Decision Making in Taxation and Expenditures,'" *Public Finances, Needs, Sources and Utilization: A Conference of the Universities-National Bureau Committee for Economic Research* (Princeton: Princeton University Press, 1965), pp. 329–34.

12. William M. Capron, "The Impact of Analysis on Bargaining in Government," in *The Politics of the Federal Bureaucracy*, edited by Alan Altschuler (New York: Dodd, Mead and Co., 1968), p. 205.

13. Cyert and March, *A Behavioural Theory of the Firm*, p. 120.

14. Lindblom, *The Policy-Making Process*, p. 112.

15. Capron, "The Impact of Analysis on Bargaining in Government," p. 200.

16. Ibid., pp. 199–200, 204.

17. Cf. Charles L. Schultze, *The Politics and Economics of Public Spending* (Washington, D.C.: The Brookings Institute, 1968), p. 64; Capron, "The Impact of Analysis on Bargaining in Government," p. 204. The reader is referred here to an interesting refinement in the thinking of analysts themselves during the last two decades with reference to policy formation involving the utilization of water as a resource. Less than two decades ago the literature was replete with prescriptions for almost unlimited comprehensiveness. Much recent thinking stresses the importance of projecting human needs on a long-term basis, but restricting the impact of decisions to as short a time horizon as possible. Compare, for example, Gilbert White, "Broad Basis for Choice: The Next and Key Move," *Perspectives on Conservation*, ed. H. Jarrett (Balti-

more: Johns Hopkins Press, 1962), and A. Maass, "System Design and the Political Process," *Design of Water Resource Systems*, ed. A. Maass (Cambridge, Mass.: Harvard University Press, 1962), with such works as the following: National Research Council, *Water and Choice in the Colorado Basin: An Example of Alternatives in Water Management*, A Report by the Committee on Water (Washington, D.C.: National Academy of Sciences, 1968); Water Resources Council, *Procedures for Evaluation of Water and Related Land Resource Projects*, A Report by the Special Task Force (Washington, D.C.: Water Resources Council, June, 1969); Gilbert F. White, *Strategies of American Water Management* (Ann Arbor: The University of Michigan Press, 1969), especially chapter VI.

18. Shultze, *The Politics and Economics of Public Spending*, pp. 65–66.

19. B.C., *Statutes*, 16–17 Elizabeth II, chapter 24, 1968. (The Libby Dam Storage Reservoir Act). This measure gave the Lieutenant-Governor-in-Council the power to appoint a department of the provincial government or a statutory agency of the Crown to take possession of land needed for the Libby storage reservoir in British Columbia.

The one qualification to this statement is that periodically by statute the provincial Legislature had approved increases in the borrowing powers of the Canadian entity, the B.C. Hydro and Power Authority.

20. The technical staffs of both Canadian governments were much impressed by the performance of Mr. Fulton and Mr. Martin, both in sessions of the Policy Liaison Committee and during the international negotiations, although their styles were quite different. Mr. Fulton expected and mastered briefings in detail; Mr. Martin left the detail to others.

21. The complete provincial technical advisory group was larger than this, but the additional members did not normally have direct access to the Cabinet.

22. Personal interview, J. Sinclair, October 6, 1965.

23. At the time of the final negotiations over the Sales Agreement and the Protocol in Ottawa late in 1963, representatives of ten American public utility districts were also brought along by the U.S. delegation and sat in on the negotiating sessions.

24. Personal interview, Ivan White, member of the U.S. negotiating team, 1960, April 22, 1964.

25. I am indebted for this observation to Ralph Purcell, who had the interesting experience of being, successively, a technical adviser to the government of Canada and the government of British Columbia during the period.

26. The writer has had access to the files of the provincial Water Resources Service for most of the period under review, and to an extensive federal working file covering the years of the Diefenbaker administration, 1957–63.

27. The Bull River Dam on the Upper Kootenay, the key element in the McNaughton Plan, as envisaged by the ICREB would have been a significantly larger project than the High Arrow and Duncan Lake structures combined. Note that the provincial technical group was not completely convinced of the merits of a High Mica project, notwithstanding the widespread public and federal Cabinet clamour for it (as opposed to smaller projects at Mica and

Surprise Rapids), until after receiving the Caseco Consultants Report to the B.C. Power Commission in 1961.

28. Two of these come to mind. One was the report of the Economic Committee on the Columbia River's development, produced under General McNaughton's chairmanship in 1958. The reservations of some committee members concerning a number of the committee's assumptions appear to have been manifest during its deliberations. The other was the report of the B.C. Energy Board, dated July 31, 1961, comparing Columbia and Peace River development. Note that reference is made here to the board's report, not that of its engineering consultants. Note also that we really move away here from the formal bureaucratic realm to the recommendations of an independent commission, made up of five men all well known for their capacity as independent thinkers. One, indeed, did dissent from one finding of the report. But the fact is that a considerable case can be made for the claim that the board's report did not, when it dealt with market areas and with total power outputs, compare "like" with "like." One member of the board, Arthur Paget, did by memorandum draw this consideration, which penalized the case for "Columbia first development," to Mr. Williston's attention by memorandum on August 4, 1961. The explanation of the willingness of the members of this board to sign this report under these circumstances appears to lie in their perception of a great general benefit which might be derived by the province from the concurrent development of both rivers, and in the manifest weakness of the federal case for proscribing significant electrical energy exports.

29. Those interviewed were Messrs. J. G. Diefenbaker, H. Green, E. D. Fulton, G. R. Pearkes, D. Fleming, A. Hamilton. None of these men raised the "alienation of the federal civil service." (Blair Fraser, *The Search for Identity*, p. 178), which numerous observers have associated with the federal policy-making environment during the "Diefenbaker years" after January 1958. This writer found no evidence that this phenomenon, whatever the extent to which it existed, affected deleteriously the staff assistance which the Diefenbaker Cabinet received apropos the Columbia River.

30. Personal interview, W. A. C. Bennett, May 13, 1966.

31. Lindblom, *The Intelligence of Democracy*, p. 34.

32. Probably the best example of this phenomenon is the extent to which the four major utilities in British Columbia were not kept in touch with developments in the late 'fifties, as they had been at the beginning of the decade.

33. Lindblom, "Bargaining: The Hidden Hand," p. 23.

34. Lindblom, *The Intelligence of Democracy*, p. 294.

35. *The Daily Colonist* (Victoria), September 1, 1965, p. 1.

36. Reference is made here to the way in which the flood control benefit accruing on the Columbia and the downstream benefit on the Canadian Kootenay below Libby and Duncan were excluded from the calculations.

37. Personal interview, W. A. C. Bennett, December 6, 1965. Mr. Bennett claims that the computer study confirmed his fears, and was the real source

of the concern which prompted his January 13, 1961 "warning" letter to Mr. Fleming.

38. They extracted a number of concessions from Canada as well.

39. *Royal Commission on Canada's Economic Prospects, Final Report* (Ottawa: Queen's Printer, November, 1957), p. 142. Earlier in 1957, in a study produced for the Gordon Commission, Dr. John Davis had dealt at length with the problem of financing hydro-electric development in the interior of British Columbia in view of the limited size of the load growth, and the fact that many interior sites required large single stage developments. John Davis, *Canadian Energy Prospects, A Study for the Royal Commission on Canada's Economic Prospects*, p. 228.

40. The September 27, 1962, declaration in the federal Speech from the Throne did not, in fact, reflect a hard decision by the Diefenbaker Cabinet, which was still debating the issue.

41. The Social Credit government also had some policy positions to reverse. Mr. Bonner had declared in 1956 that its policy and Canada's was "to insist that no electrical energy be exported from Canada save on an emergency basis such as might be contemplated in a mutually beneficial grid system." *Proceedings, Institute of Public Administration of Canada*, 1956, p. 131.

Furthermore, at the second Policy Liaison Committee meeting on May 29, 1959, Mr. Williston spoke vigorously of the competitiveness of the province's economy with that of the northwest states in a statement whose tone and import, although not its precise wording, seemed to insist that the downstream entitlement benefits should be returned to Canada in the form of power. Minutes, Second Policy Liaison Committee Meeting, Victoria, B.C., May 29, 1959, p. 4.

42. Not unreasonable projections of British Columbia's load growth put before federal Cabinet ministers in 1960 made it clear that by 1969 all of the downstream benefit energy would have been absorbed by the provincial market, and space would then open up for new energy from the Mica project.

43. E. E. Schattschneider, *The Semisovereign People* (New York: Holt, Rinehart and Winston, 1960), p. 74.

44. Cf. Patrick Nicholson, *Vision and Indecision* (Toronto: Longman's Canada Ltd., 1968), p. 31; Peter Newman, *Renegade in Power* (Toronto: McClelland and Stewart Ltd., 1963), p. 83; Peter Stursberg, *Diefenbaker: Leadership Gained, 1957–62* (Toronto: University of Toronto Press, 1975), chapter 11.

45. For a reference to Mr. Green's influence in Cabinet on other issues, and a critical assessment of him as the secretary of state for external affairs, see Peyton Lyon, *The Policy Question* (Toronto: McClelland & Stewart, 1963), pp. 113–15.

46. Mr. Donald Fleming recalls that Mr. Green made it clear at the time of the June 1962 election that his presence in British Columbia, campaigning, was not desired. Personal interview, August 19, 1967.

47. Aaron Wildavsky, *Dixon Yates: A Study in Power Politics* (New Haven: Yale University Press, 1962), pp. 304–10.

48. Mr. Bennett believes that the stubbornness of his erstwhile friends, not extraneous considerations (such as the strength of their majority prior to June 1962) explains their action, or better, inaction. Personal interview, December 6, 1965. See also John G. Diefenbaker, *One Canada: The Years of Achievement*: 1957–62 (Toronto: Macmillan of Canada, 1976), p. 156.

49. Since 1932 the CCF-NDP has constituted an exception to this generalization.

50. For an interesting study of the roles of Canadian parliamentarians during the last Diefenbaker administration see: Allan Kornberg, *Canadian Legislative Behaviour* (New York: Holt, Rinehart & Winston, 1967), p. 146. For a considerable refinement of the Kornberg analysis, dealing, this time, with the parliament which approved the Columbia River Treaty, see: David Hoffman and Norman Ward, *Bilingualism and Biculturalism in the Canadian House of Commons*, Documents of the Royal Commission on Bilingualism and Biculturalism, no. 3 (Ottawa: Queen's Printer, 1970).

51. Personal letter from Robert Thompson, September 5, 1969.

52. See Mr. Pearson's letter in Donald Waterfield, *Continental Waterboy* (Toronto: Clarke Irwin, 1970), p. 107.

53. Critics of the Columbia River Treaty refer to a press interview of Mr. Pearson's following his meeting with President Kennedy and attending a White House dinner on April 29, 1962, in which he suggested that what were needed were protocols to the existing treaty. Their claim is that any prospect of a Liberal party-inspired full-dress review of the treaty really was abandoned at this point, although the fact never was made clear. Mr. Pearson, when interviewed, did not recall the details of his comments at this time, and simply reflected that whatever he had said seems to have been grossly misunderstood, and that at the time neither he nor his party had access to the information or the technical advisers available to the federal government. (Personal interview, April 10, 1970). Cf. D. Waterfield, *Continental Waterboy*, p. 120; Swettenham, *McNaughton*, III, pp. 305–306.

54. Waterfield, *Continental Waterboy*, p. 116.

55. R. M. Strachan, "Confidential Information Bulletin to CCF MLA's," December 7, 1960, p. 2.

56. R. M. Strachan to J. Diefenbaker, June 9, 1961, p. 2.

57. General McNaughton encouraged him not to condemn the export concept. A. G. L. McNaughton to John Wood (administrative assistant to R. M. Strachan), May 12, 1962.

58. In November 1961, for instance, he insisted to his colleagues that if the treaty had been ratified before they came to power, and construction had been started, that its terms would be carried out. Letter from R. M. Strachan to his legislative colleagues, November 22, 1961.

59. In 1963 the provincial NDP MLA from Revelstoke (Mrs. George Hobbs) recalled the very real difficulty she and colleagues had had at a recent national convention in getting a resolution on the Columbia before the gathering, let alone obtaining a hearing for it.

Personal interview, August 25, 1963.

60. This consideration has led to some interesting tangles, not least over the appointment, tenure, and removal of the commissioners themselves. The reader is referred to W. R. Willoughby's excellent article, "The Appointment and Removal of Members of the International Joint Commission," *Canadian Public Administration* 30, no. 3 (Fall, 1969): 411–26.

61. Canadian Section Chairman, 1962–70.

62. See *Upper Columbia River Development, 1958*, pp. 275–79.

63. A federal Progressive Conservative Cabinet minister who had known him for years reflects that "he had a penchant for dabbling in matters one or two levels above, and, what was worse, below his own level of responsibility."

64. See, for example, his evidence before the External Affairs Committee, *Minutes of Proceedings and Evidence*, April 21, 1964, p. 545.

65. Personal interview, A. G. L. McNaughton, September 10, 1964. (These individuals do not deny that eventually their relationship with him left something to be desired, but suggest that their reservations concerning his role really date from the mid 'fifties, when, before the External Affairs Committee, he began to advance evaluations of project alternatives, such as High Arrow, significantly at variance with the results which their studies, including those conducted for the IJC, were producing.)

66. And for which, Mr. Diefenbaker believes, the general never forgave him. Personal interview, March 3, 1967.

67. D. M. Stephens, "Columbia River Notebook, November 58-12-59" (pages unnumbered—handwritten).

68. D. M. Stephens, "Memorandum to File . . . Re: Columbia River Reference," April 24, 1958, p. 2.

69. W. R. Willoughby, "The Appointment and Removal of Members of the International Joint Commission," p. 412.

70. Personal interview, September 10, 1964.

71. Krutilla, *The Columbia River Treaty*, p. 200.

72. Strictly speaking the plan which these men advanced dealt primarily with hydro electric energy which, for British Columbia, they felt to be a more reasonable source of power than thermal generation. The program which they endorsed was embodied in a nine page memorandum dated June 1957, and entitled "An Appreciation of the Electric Power Situation in British Columbia." It did not advocate the creation of a single monolithic provincial authority; rather it argued the case for pluralism to a degree. But it reviewed past experience, and suggested that the public interest would not be served if the provincial utilities (including the B.C. Power Commission) continued to be so jealously defensive of their own service areas, and so unwilling to integrate their operations on any significant scale.

In the schema thus outlined, the existing utilities would continue, but would meet much of their additional energy requirements by purchases from a new instrumentality. The new body was also perceived as a most suitable agency for entering into major international agreements. The memorandum envisaged at least ten advantages which it was felt would accrue to "centralized unbiased control of major generation and transmission" (p. 8). These included improved opportunities for planning the utilization of the province's water resources, and improved means whereby regional economic or population growth might be stimulated. Considerable economies were anticipated, in time, from major system interconnections, and from a rationalization of investment (i.e. an elimination of duplication) on new project investigation.

This, it must be observed, appears to be the plan which Mr. Bennett had in mind when he told the B.C. Power Commission in 1958 that its future energy requirements would be supplied to it. Mr. Lee Briggs' intense commitment to public power development seems to have led him to perceive the premier's observation mistakenly as one designed to permit the privately-owned utilities to "contain" his own agency.

73. Gilbert F. White, "Broader Basis for Choice," p. 222; Arthur Maass, "System Design and the Political Process," p. 585. For a good discussion of goals in the Canadian context, see Morris Miller, "The Developmental Framework for Resource Policy and its Jurisdictional-Administrative Implications," *Canadian Pacific Administration* 5, no. 2 (June 1962): 133–55.

74. ICREB, *Water Resources of the Columbia River Basin*, p. 61.

75. Crippen-Wright Engineering Ltd., *Report, Hydro-Electric Development of Columbia River Basin in Canada*, pp. 1–3.

76. External Affairs Committee, *Minutes of Proceedings and Evidence*, April 13, 1964, pp. 281–82.

77. During the international negotiations of 1960 and again of 1963, the two Canadian governments were able to draw analytic support from their own technical staffs, from these individuals meeting together under the aegis of the Technical Liaison Committee, and from them, on occasions, as member of working groups set up by the international negotiators. In 1962–63, in addition, British Columbia was able to draw upon extensive staff studies pursued by the entity-designate, the B.C. Hydro and Power Authority.

78. The broad range of studies conducted under the auspices of the federal government to assess the range of options open to Canada is summarized in "Water Power Resources in the Columbia River Basin in Canada: Investigations by the Water Resources Branch" (Ottawa: Water Resources Branch, 1964, mimeographed). For an evaluation of the two Canadian governments' technical efforts see Krutilla, *The Columbia River Treaty*, pp. 101–18, 123–31.

79. This point is one stressed by an external adviser to the government of Canada during 1960, brought in from Ontario Hydro—Mr. Matthew Ward. Personal interview, June 8, 1967.

80. This was very much the approach to planning endorsed by the eight professors from the University of British Columbia in their February 1962 monograph.

81. This concept was incorporated into the planning of the Columbia River Treaty in 1960. Although it is widely accepted in utility circles, the reader should recall that the Economic Committee disputed this contention in its 1958 report, and some articulate critics of the treaty in Canada have rejected it continuously and vigorously since 1961.

82. It is now apparent that about 6 million kw of new capacity can be installed in the Canadian watershed of the Columbia.

83. One interesting feature of this decision-making experience is the extent to which analysts within the two Canadian bureaucracies, and the B.C. Electric Co. and the B.C. Power Commission in 1960–61, tended to discount some of the argument advanced to them by the technical consultants to the Peace River Company. These latter individuals, Messrs. J. Stevens and R. Chantrill, maintained during the years 1960–61 that the flattening of the load growth curve then being experienced in the whole Pacific northwest was, for British Columbia at least, a very temporary phenomenon, and that a real explosion in provincial demand, which would provide a domestic market for the output of the two rivers developed concurrently, was in the offing. Their claims were discounted as special pleading, which in a special sense, they were. But they also turned out to be remarkably prescient over the following decade.

84. Cf. Cyert and March, *A Behavioral Theory of the Firm*, pp. 117–18.

85. Note, at the same time, the following. The substance of Dr. Krutilla's analysis is that the entire arrangement grossly violates IJC General Principle No. 2, which envisages both parties enjoying a true net gain. As a result of his simulation of the United States' system utilizing the treaty "results in a relative net loss to the United States of about $250 million to $375 million." J. Krutilla, *The Columbia River Treaty*, p. 195. In short, he concludes that the entire exercise in cooperative development added nothing to the combined gross national product of the two countries and may have produced some net loss.

86. Doubtless to the relief of the two Canadian governments directly involved, neither the members of the External Affairs Committee in 1964 nor the vast majority of the technical critics who appeared before it really grasped the potential impact of the Peace River's development on the Columbia, and the possibility it raised of dispensing with the High Arrow project. One who did raise the matter before the Committee, both in his brief, and in his testimony, was Mr. Ritchie Deane. (External Affairs Committee, *Minutes of Proceedings and Evidence*, May 7, 1964, p. 1037.) Mr. Larratt Higgins also referred to the manner in which an interconnection for Mica would provide a substitute source of most of the benefits attributed to the High Arrow Dam. He suggested linking it with the American system to attain his end. (Ibid., April 29, 1964, p. 898.) Mr. Martin and Mr. MacNabb did deal with the substitutability of an interconnection for High Arrow, albeit briefly. (Ibid., May 20, 1964, p. 1374, and May 21, 1964, p. 1437.) The committee largely concentrated on the validity of the estimated cost of High Arrow, and on its relative merit when evaluated as an alternative to East Kootenay storage. It was on this latter basis that it was so favourably endorsed by the consultant advisers to the government of Canada in 1964. (Montreal Engineering Company, *Comments on the Columbia River Treaty and Protocol*, March 1964, pp. 14–19, 23–30.)

87. Krutilla, *The Columbia River Treaty*, p. 167.

Notes to Chapter 11, The Policy Formation Reviewed (B)

1. See William Capron, "The Impact of Analysis on Bargaining in Government," p. 197.

2. Personal interview, J. V. Fisher, July 19, 1965. American economists were just as concerned as Canadian with the validity of the case for economic expansion based on the availability of cheap electricity, and about the hyperbolic claims made for it. See, for example: Bureau of Business Research, *Electrical Energy Outlook for Pacific Northwest*, Occasional Paper no. 13 (Seattle: University of Washington, 1960). When location theory was cited in British Columbia, it was directed most frequently against Mr. Bennett's dream of two-river development.

3. Simon, *Models of Man*, pp. 252–53, 272.

4. Krutilla, *The Columbia River Treaty*, p. 199. Dr. Krutilla does advance two major criticisms of British Columbia's analysis. He identifies a slippage in it with respect to the evaluation of a late-stage American offer which would have involved Canada's dropping the Duncan Lake project in return for American assistance with the costs of preparing the Libby reservoir. (An indeterminate factor here in Canadian decision-making, but possibly one of more significance than Dr. Krutilla realized, was the *ten* year option to be accorded the United States with reference to its decision to build the Libby project.) His other argument refers to the manner in which provincial analysis on Upper Kootenay-Upper Columbia Valley storage options was *not* carried on through the summer of 1960 after the provincial Cabinet had decided to write off this alternative for both economic and non-economic reasons. Dr. Krutilla has done this, and calculates that a policy choice with a present-worth to British Columbia of about $52 millions more than the one agreed upon, was thus set aside. Note, however, that this latter choice would have flooded *both* the Arrow Lakes and the Upper Columbia-Kootenay valleys. Ibid., pp. 112–18.

5. Ibid., p. 200.

6. One problem with interdepartmental committees is that their impact so often is a direct function of the ability and the aggressiveness of the membership. Tough-minded and able bureaucratic leaders in Canada, as elsewhere, are sometimes tempted to select committee members with an eye to the leverage which appointees will *not* exert on the committee's output. There is some evidence that this happened in British Columbia on this issue.

7. This would appear to be true, particularly, of British Columbia's approach to the 1959–60 intra-national bargaining.

8. Krutilla, *The Columbia River Treaty*, pp. 201–202.

9. Presumably the substantial planning sections either established in or expanded in the Office of the Prime Minister and the Privy Council Office since 1968 may provide this "extra look" in future. These planning groups have been widely held to be independent sources of policy evaluation, and an administrative reaction to incremental decision-making. And well they may be.

10. James R. Mallory, "Minister's Office Staff: An Unreformed Part of

the Public Service," *Canadian Public Administration* 10, no. 1 (March 1967): 25–34.

11. Relations left a good deal to be desired between Mr. Diefenbaker and Mr. Pearson also. Mr. Diefenbaker did agree that Mr. Bennett should brief Mr. Pearson on his objectives in August 1962.

12. C. Schultze, *The Politics and Economics of Public Spending*, p. 74.

13. A. Paget to K. Kristjanson, October 12, 1962. Mr. Paget's comments were contained in a letter replying to one from Dr. Kristjanson in which the latter relayed for Mr. Paget's perusal a draft of a paper on the subject "Planning River Basin Development." (For a modified version of the paper see K. Kristjanson and D. M. Stephens, "Planning River Basin Development," *Transactions of the Fourteenth B.C. Natural Resources Conference, 1962* (Victoria: The B.C. Natural Resources Conference, 1963), pp. 46–53.)

14. A. G. L. McNaughton orally to the writer, September 10, 1964.

15. Amitai Etzioni, "Mixed Scanning: A 'Third' Approach to Decision-Making," pp. 388–89.

16. This, in theoretic terms, is very much the position suggested by Thompson and Tuden, "Strategies, Structures, and Processes of Organized Decision," pp. 207–208.

17. Cf. J. Noel Lyon, Ronald G. Atkey (eds.), *Canadian Constitutional Law in Modern Perspective* (Toronto: University of Toronto Press, 1971), p. 1048.

18. *The Daily Colonist* (Victoria), October 15, 1957, p. 7.

19. Cf. Higgins, "The Alienation of Resources: The Case of the Columbia River Treaty," p. 234.

20. Canada, House of Commons, Standing Committee on External Affairs, *Minutes of Proceedings and Evidence: Columbia River Treaty and Protocol*, 26th Parlt., 2nd Sess., May 21, 1964, p. 1435, and May 26, 1964, p. 1460.

21. The emphasis which the federal government placed on the apparent cheapness of the downstream benefit power involved an arbitrary and debatable assumption that this power should bear the costs of the upstream Canadian storage from which it was indirectly derived only until this storage began producing energy at-site.

One little recognized consequence of the federal stress on the cheapness of the power entitlement was the effect which this policy stance had on the freedom of action of the province and the B.C. Power Commission. In the face of widely articulated projections of potential price reductions, the commission would have had great difficulty, had it so desired, in returning the benefit and selling it in the province for a high price—with the revenue thus generated being used on the one hand to offset its reliance on high cost thermal power, and on the other hand, to reduce, in time, the price of energy directly produced in the Canadian section of the Columbia watershed.

22. There is a group of constitutional lawyers in Canada who dissent today from this interpretation for a reason not yet indicated. They concede that it may well have been valid for many years, but draw attention to the manner in which provincial power systems recently have been interconnecting on a

large scale with those in other provinces as well as with those in the United States. Applying the reasoning which Mr. Justice Lett enunciated in 1963, they foresee Parliament's competence expanding considerably, both with respect to inter-provincial operations and related intra-provincial considerations. The argument is an interesting one, but it has not yet had significant intra-provicial acceptance or appreciation.

See Dale Gibson, "Constitutional Jurisdiction over Environmental Management in Canada," *University of Toronto Law Journal* 23, no. 1 (Winter, 1973): 75.

23. Neil Caplan, "Some Factors Affecting the Resolution of a Federal-Provincial Conflict," *Canadian Journal of Political Science* 2, no. 2 (June 1969): 173–86.

24. For an account of the intense in-fighting which bedevilled Progressive Conservative ranks in British Columbia during the 'forties and 'fifties, see: Edwin R. Black, "The Progressive Conservative Party in British Columbia: Some Aspects of Organization" (Master's dissertation, University of British Columbia, 1960).

25. E. R. Black and A. Cairns, "A Different Perspective on Canadian Federalism," *Canadian Public Administration* 9, no. 1 (March 1966): 41–42.

26. See, for example, Laurier L. LaPierre, "Quebec and Treaty-making," *International Journal* 20, no. 3 (Summer, 1965): 362–66. Mr. LaPierre ends up categorically asserting that the province of Quebec must be conceded the right to sign international agreements on matters falling within its jurisdiction without consulting Ottawa, with conflicts between the two settled, if necessary, by ". . . some arbitrating tribunal." (p. 366).

27. For an English-Canadian viewpoint treating the post-1963 Quebec initiatives with some equanimity, see Edward McWhinney, "The Constitutional Competence within Federal Systems for International Agreements," *Background Papers and Reports*, Ontario Advisory Committee on Confederation (Toronto: Queen's Printer of Ontario, 1967), pp. 151–57. For a concerned English-Canadian viewpoint see G. L. Morris, "The Treaty-Making Power: A Canadian Dilemma," *Canadian Bar Review* 45, no. 3 (September 1967): 478–512. A strongly revisionist argument is advanced in J. Y. Morin, "International Law—Treaty-Making Power—Constitutional Law—Position of the Government of Quebec," *Canadian Bar Review* 45, no. 1 (March 1967): 160–73.

28. W. A. C. Bennett, "Opening Statement presented to Plenary Session of the Federal-Provincial Conference, Ottawa, February 5, 1968." See also *The Victoria Daily Times*, July 15, 1967, p. 7.

29. Cf. the argument of P. E. Trudeau, *Federalism and the French Canadians*, p. 138.

30. Daniel J. Elazar, *American Federalism: A View from the States* (New York: Thomas Y. Crowell Co., 1966), p 208.

31. C. D. Tarlton, "Federalism, Political Energy, and Entropy: Implications of an Analogy," *The Western Political Quarterly* 20, no. 4 (December 1967): 866–74.

32. See, for example, M. M. Hufschmidt, "The Harvard Programme: A Summing Up," *Water Research*, ed. A. V. Kneese and S. J. Smith (Baltimore: The Johns Hopkins Press, 1966), pp. 441–56.

33. Cf. Allen V. Kneese, "Economic and Related Problems in Contemporary Water Resources Management," reprint no. 55 (Washington, D.C.: Resources for the Future, inc., November 1965), pp. 21–22.

34. Donald Stephens on the IJC was one of these Canadians, as was Arthur Paget in Victoria. Mr. Paget, however, was closer to and thus more sensitive to some of the non-technical aspects of this policy problem as it evolved over time.

35. For a comment on project selection in periods of other than full employment see Otto Eckstein, *Water Resource Development* (Cambridge: Harvard University Press, 1958), p. 281.

36. Cited in *Vancouver Sun*, May 11, 1967, p. 6.

37. The files of the Peace River Company reviewed were those in the possession of Mr. Jack Stevens, and those made available by the late W. C. Mainwaring. They were not complete, however, and this observation must be qualified accordingly.

38. Mr. Donald Stephens is also in this category. He and the others referred to, of course, may well have been privately alert to the impact of an immediate start on the Peace River development on High Arrow. Indeed, a 1961 notebook of his (date not recorded) contains a reference to the fact that if the Peace were to go ahead, an "excellent project" should be re-examined to see if it were under these circumstances super, sub, or just marginal. The notation also suggests that the IJC's offices were still available for this reassessment, and that, as far as he knew, it had not been attempted. Presumably it was the High Arrow project he had in mind.

39. He did take the position that there did not seem to be that much to choose between Peace and Columbia development, and that if the development of the Peace were assumed in a new planning exercise the Columbia projects adopted should be related to it. J. C. Davis, "Address to Water Workshop B: Benefit-Cost Analysis Applied to the Peace and Columbia River Power Programmes," *Proceedings of the Resources for Tomorrow Conference*, October 23–28, 1961 (Ottawa: Queen's Printer, 1962), III, pp. 146–54.

40. J. Krutilla, "British Columbia Alternatives to the Columbia Treaty" (unpublished, July 11, 1962).

41. See David G. Le Marquand, *International Rivers: The Politics of Cooperation* (Vancouver: Westwater Research Centre, University of British Columbia, 1977).

42. Lindblom, *The Intelligence of Democracy*, pp. 297–300.

43. Henry S. Rowen, "Bargaining and Analysis in Government," *Planning-Programming-Budgeting: Selected Comment* (U.S. Senate, Subcommittee on National Security and International Operations of the Committee on Government Operations, 90th Cong., 1st Sess., 1967, pp. 48–49).

44. Lindblom, *The Policy Making Process*, p. 106.

45. Cyert and March, *A Behavioural Theory of the Firm*, pp. 119–20.

46. Dr. Krutilla maintains that when all the superior storage on an international river is located in the upstream country, and is conceded first-added credit, dividing equally the downstream benefit derived from such storage, and determined by a grossing formula, ought to make agreement between the two states unfeasible. Krutilla, *The Columbia River Treaty*, p. 136.

47. Heinz Eulau and K. Prewitt, *Labyrinths of Democracy* (Indianapolis: Bobbs-Merril Co., Inc., 1973), chapter 11.

48. The reader is reminded again of the marked inconsistency in the approach during the 'fifties to the claims for diversionary rights and downstream benefits which Canada advanced with respect to the Upper Kootenay River, but either ignored or discounted on the Pend d'Oreille. One measure of the essential fairness in the Americans' ultimate approach to cooperative development on the Columbia can be found in the extent to which they did not turn the logic of the Canadian case on the one watershed against Canada on the other, as well they might have.

Not only do the Waneta and Seven Mile projects on the Pend d'Oreille enjoy a major unshared downstream benefit from upstream American storage, but these two sites, with 885,000 kw. of actual or projected capacity, could have been made unfeasible, and their energy directly generated in the United States, had that country applied to the Pend Oreille the strategy which General McNaughton was so keen Canada apply to the Upper Kootenay, had it insisted, in other words, on a right to divert from a reservoir within its boundary directly to the Columbia main stream. As the Pend Oreille and Kootenay cross the border running north and south respectively, the former river has two and one-half to three times the flow of the latter.

Bibliography

BOOKS AND ARTICLES

Allison, Graham T. *Essence of Decision: Explaining the Cuban Missile Crisis.* Boston: Little, Brown & Co., 1971.

Angus, Henry F. "Note on the British Columbia Election in June, 1952." *Western Political Quarterly* 5, no. 4 (December 1952): 585–91.

Armstrong, T. E., Langford, J. A. and Pennington, A. C. "The Columbia River Dispute." *Osgoode Hall Law Journal* 1, no. 1 (June 1958): 1–36.

Armstrong, W. S. "The British Columbia Water Act: The End of Riparian Rights." *University of B.C. Law Review* 1, no. 5 (April 1962): 582–94.

Austin, Jacob. "Canadian-United States Practice and Theory Respecting International Law of International Rivers: A Study of the History and Influence of the Harmon Doctrine." *The Canadian Bar Review* 37, no. 3 (September 1959): 393–443.

Bauer, Raymond A. and Gergen, Kenneth J. *The Study of Policy Formation.* New York: The Free Press, 1968.

Berber, Friedrich J. *Rivers in International Law.* Translated by R. K. Batstone. London: Oceana Publications, 1959.

Black, Edwin R. "Federal Strains within a Canadian Party." *Dalhousie Review* 45, no. 3 (Autumn, 1965): 307–23.

———. "British Columbia: The Politics of Exploitation." In *Exploiting our Economic Potential: Public Policy and the British Columbia Economy*, edited by R. Shearer. Toronto: Holt, Rinehart and Winston of Canada, Ltd., 1968, pp. 23–41.

Black, Edwin R. and Cairns, Alan C. "A Different Perspective on Canadian Federalism." *Canadian Public Administration* 9, no. 1 (March 1966): 27–44.

Bloomfield. Louis M. and Fitzgerald, Gerald F. *Boundary Waters Problems of Canada and the United States.* Toronto: Carswell, 1958.

Bourne, C. B. "Recent Developments in the Columbia River Controversy." *Bulletin No. 13.* Seattle: Institute of International Affairs—University of Washington, June 1958. (Paper read to the Pacific Northwest Regional

Meeting, American Society of International Law, Apri 118–19, 1958.)

————. "The Columbia River Controversy." *Canadian Bar Review* 37, no. 3 (September 1959) : 444–72.

————. "The Columbia River Treaty: Another View." *International Journal* 17, no. 2 (Spring, 1962) : 137–40.

————. "The Development of International Water Resources: The 'Drainage Basin Approach'." *The Canadian Bar Review* 47, no. 1 (March 1969):

Braybrooke, David and Lindblom, Charles E. *A Strategy of Decision.* New York: The Free Press, 1963.

Bullard, Oral. *Crisis on the Columbia.* Portland, Ore.: The Touchstone Press, 1968.

Burns, R. M. "Choices for Canadian Federalism." *Canadian Tax Journal* 13, no. 6 (November–December 1965) : 512–18.

Caplan, Neil. "Some Factors affecting the Resolution of a Federal-Provincial Conflict." *Canadian Journal of Political Science* 2, no. 2 (June 1969), pp. 173–86.

Capron, William M. "The Impact of Analysis on Bargaining in Government." In *The Politics of the Federal Bureaucracy*, edited by Alan A. Altschuler. New York: Dodd Mead & Co., 1968.

Chevrier, Lionel. *The St. Lawrence Seaway Authority.* Toronto: The Macmillan Company of Canada, Ltd., 1959.

Churchman, C. West. *The Systems Approach.* New York: Delacorte Press, 1968.

Cohen, Maxwell. "Canada-United States Treaty Relations, Trends and Future Problems." In *Canada-United States Treaty Relations*, edited by David R. Deener. Durham, N.C.: Duke University Press, 1963, pp. 185–94.,

————. "Columbia River: An Asset and an Irritation." *Saturday Night* 62 (September 28, 1957) : 16–17, 44–45.

————. "Some Legal and Policy Aspects of the Columbia River Dispute." *The Canadian Bar Review* 36, no. 1 (March 1958): 25–41.

Cohn, Edwin J., Jr. *Industry in the Pacific Northwest and the Location Theory.* New York: Columbia University Press, 1954.

Corbett, David C. "Hydro Power in B.C." *Canadian Forum* 35 (May 1955): 26–27.

Cyert, R. M. and March, J. G. *A Behavioural Theory of the Firm.* Englewood Cliffs, N.J.: Prentice-Hall, Inc., 1963.

Davis, John. *Canadian Energy Prospects, A Study for the Royal Commission on Canada's Economic Prospects.* Ottawa: Queen's Printer, March, 1957.

Deener, David R. "The Treaty Power in Canada." In *The Growth of Canadian Policies in External Affairs*, edited by Hugh L. Keenleyside. Durham, N.C.: Duke University Press, 1960, pp. 81–98.

Delisle, R. J. "Treaty-Making Power in Canada." In *Ontario Advisory Committee on Confederation: Background Papers and Reports.* Toronto: Queen's Printer of Ontario, 1967, pp. 115–48.

Dror, Yehezkel. "Muddling Through—'Science' or Inertia?" *Public Administration Review* 24 ,no. 3 (September 1964): 153–57.

————. *Public Policymaking Re-examined*. San Francisco: Chandler Publishing Company, 1968.

Eagleton, Clyde. "The Use of Waters of International Rivers." *The Canadian Bar Review* 33, no. 7 (August–September 1955): 1018–34.

Eayrs, James. *Canada in World Affairs, October 1955 to June 1957*. Toronto: Oxford University Press, 1959.

Eckstein, Otto. *Water Resource Development: The Economics of Project Evaluation*. Cambridge: Harvard University Press, 1958.

Etzioni, Amitai. "Mixed-Scanning: A 'Third' Approach to Decision-Making." *Public Administration Review* 27, no. 5 (December 1967): 385–92.

————. "Shortcuts to Social Change?" *The Public Interest* 12, no. 3 (Summer, 1968): 40–51.

————. *The Active Society*. New York: The Free Press, 1968.

Ferguson, G. V. "Likely Trends in Canadian-American Political Relations." *Canadian Journal of Economics and Political Science* 22, no. 4 (November 1956): 437–48.

Fesler, J. W. et al. "Government and Water Resources." *American Political Science Review* 44, no. 3 (September 1950): 575–649.

Fox, Irving K. "New Horizons in Water Resources Administration." *Public Administration Review* 25, no. 2 (March 1965): 61–69.

Fox, Irving K. and Herfindal, Orris C. "Attainment of Efficiency in Satisfying Demands for Water Resources." In *Papers and Proceedings of the American Economic Association*, May 1964, pp. 198–206. (Resources for the Future, Inc., reprint number 46.)

Fraser, Blair. *The Search for Identity, Canada 1945–1967*. Toronto: Doubleday and Co., Inc., 1967.

Fulton, E. D. "Letter in Reply to J. G. Ripley." *Engineering and Contract Record* (September 1962): 47–48.

George, Alexander L. "The Case for Multiple Advocacy in Making Foreign Policy." *American Political Science Review* 66, no. 3 (September 1972): 751–90.

Gibson, Dale. "Constitutional Jurisdiction over Environmental Management in Canada." *University of Toronto Law Journal* 23, no. 1 (Winter, 1973): 75.

Goldie, D. M. M. "Recent Developments on the Columbia Diversion." *Bulletin No. 13*. Seattle: Institute of International Affairs—University of Washington, June 1958. (Paper read to the Pacific Northwest Regional Meeting, American Society of International Law, April 18–19, 1958.)

————. "Effect of Existing Uses on the Equitable Apportionment of International Rivers II: A Canadian View." *University of B.C. Law Review* 1, no. 3 (December 1960): 399–408.

————. "International Law and the Development of International River Basins." *University of B.C. Law Review* 1, no. 6 (April 1963): 763–76.

Grauer, A. E. D. "The Export of Electricity from Canada." In *Canadian Issues, Essays in Honour of Henry F. Angus*, edited by R. M. Clark. Toronto: University of Toronto Press, 1961, pp. 248–85.

431

Haig-Brown, Roderick. "Man Tames the Wilderness." *The Atlantic Monthly* 114 (November 1964): 149–57.

———. *The Living Land.* Toronto: The Macmillan Company, 1961.

Heeney, A. D. P. "The International Joint Commission." *External Affairs* 15, no. 3 (March 1963): 141–45.

Hendry, J. M. *Treaties and Federal Constitutions.* Washington: Public Affairs Press, 1955.

Higgins, Larratt T. "Columbia River Treaty: A Critical View." *International Journal* 16, no. 4 (Autumn, 1961): 397–404.

———. "How Ottawa Can Cope with Bennett." *Saturday Night* 76 (September 16, 1961): 15–16.

———. "The Columbia River Treaty: A Reply to Professor Bourne." *International Journal* 17, no. 2 (Spring, 1962): 141–44.

———. "How Chaos Came to the Columbia." *Saturday Night* 77 (May 26, 1962): 25–27.

———. "Is the Columbia River Treaty a Sellout?" *Globe and Mail* (Toronto), January 14, 1964, p. 7.

———. "Second Deal on the Columbia: How Premier Bennett Sank Canada's Diversion Plan." *Globe and Mail* (Toronto), January 15, 1964, p. 7.

———. "Has Ottawa Learned Lessons of the Columbia River Deal?" *The Financial Post*, May 26, 1966, pp. 25–26.

———. "The Columbia River Treaty Bonanza for U.S., But What Do We Get?" *The Financial Post*, July 23, 1966, pp. 12.

———. "Much Water Down the Columbia, but Arrow Valley's Fight Lives On." *The Financial Post*, January 31, 1970, p. 15.

———. "The Alienation of Canadian Resources: The Case of the Columbia River Treaty." In *The Americanization of Canada*, edited by Ian Lumsden. Toronto: Uniiversity of Toronto Press, 1970, pp. 223–40.

Hirshman, A. O. and Lindblom, C. E. "Economic Development, Research and Development, Policy Making: Some Converging Views." *Behavioral Science* 7 (1962): 211–22.

Hodgetts, J. E. "Public Power and Ivory Power." In *Agenda, 1970*, edited by Trevor Lloyd and Jack McLeod. Toronto: University of Toronto Press, 1968.

Hufschmidt, Maynard M. "The Methodology of Water Resources System Design." In *Readings: Resource Management and Conservation*, edited by Ian Burton. Chicago: The University of Chicago Press, 1965, pp. 558–70.

Hufschmidt, Maynard M. and Fiering, Myron B. *Simulation Techniques for Water Resource Systems.* Cambridge, Mass.: Harvard University Press, 1966.

Hurst, C. K. *Water in International Affairs.* Toronto: Canadian Institute of International Affairs, 1956.

Hutchison, W. Bruce. "Coming Battle for the Columbia." *Maclean's Magazine* (September 29, 1956), pp. 11–13, 28.

———. "The Great Columbia River Foul-Up." *Maclean's Magazine* (June 3, 1961), pp. 3, 60–63.

Jewett, Pauline. "Political and Administrative Aspects of Policy Formation." In *Canadian Economic Policy*, ed. T. N. Brewis. Toronto: The Macmillan Company of Canada Ltd., 1965.

Johnson, Ralph W. "Effect of Existing Uses on the Equitable Apportionment of International Rivers I: An American View." *University of B.C. Law Review* 1, no. 3 (December 1960): 389–98.

———. "The Canada-United States Controversy over the Columbia River." *University of Washington Law Review* 41 (August 1966): 676–763.

———. "The Columbia Basin." In *The Law of International Drainage Basins*, edited by A. H. Garretson. New York: Oceana Publications, Inc., 1967.

Keate, S. "Why Bennett Took Over B.C. Power." *Saturday Night* (September 16, 1961), pp. 11–14.

Keenleyside, H. L. *Canada and the United States*. New York: A. A. Knopf, 1952.

———. "Columbia Project—A Look Back and Ahead." *Canadian Business* 37 (May 1964): 41–42.

———. "Columbia River Power Development." *Canadian Geographical Journal* 71, no. 4 (November 1965): 148–61.

Keenleyside, Hugh L. et al. *The Growth of Canadian Policies in External Affairs*. Durham, N.C.: Duke University Press, 1960.

Klein, Burton. "The Decision Making Problem in Development." *The Rate and Direction of Inventive Activity: Economic and Social Factors*, a Report of the National Bureau of Economic Research. Princeton: Princeton University Press, 1962, pp. 477–97.

Kneese, Allen V. and Smith, Stephen C., eds. *Water Research*. Baltimore: The Johns Hopkins Press, 1966.

Kristjanson, B. H. "Some Thoughts on Planning at the Federal Level." *Canadian Public Administration* 8, no. 2 (June 1965): 143–51.

Krutilla, John V. "Columbia River Development: Some Problems of International Cooperation." *Land and Water: Planning for Economic Growth—Western Resources Papers*. Edited by Harold L. Amos and Roma K. McNickle. Boulder: University of Colorado Press, 1961, pp. 97–120.

———. "The International Columbia River Treaty: An Economic Evaluation." In *Water Research*, edited by Allen V. Kneese and Stephen C. Smith. Baltimore: The Johns Hopkins Press, 1966, pp. 69–97.

———. *The Columbia River Treaty: The Economics of an International River Basin Development*. Baltimore: The Johns Hopkins Press, 1967.

Krutilla, John V. and Eckstein, Otto. *Multiple Purpose River Development*. Baltimore: Johns Hopkins Press, 1958.

Ladner, L. J. and Bourne, C. "Diversion of Columbia River Waters." *Bulletin No. 12*. Seattle: Institute of International Affairs, University of Washington, June, 1956, pp. 1–18, 26–32. (Presentation to the Pacific Northwest Regional Meeting, American Society of International Law, April 19, 1956.)

LaForest, Gerard V. *Natural Resources and Public Property under the*

Canadian Constitution. Toronto: University of Toronto Press, 1969.

La Pierre, Laurier L. "Quebec and Treaty-making." *International Journal* 20, no. 3 (Summer, 1965): 362–66.

Laskin, Bora. *Canadian Constitutional Law.* Toronto: Carswell and Company, 1960.

———. "The Provinces and International Agreements." In *Ontario Advisory Committee on Confederation: Background Papers and Reports.* Toronto: Queen's Printer of Ontario, 1967, pp. 101–14.

Le Marquand, David G. *International Rivers: The Politics of Cooperation.* Vancouver: Westwater Research Centre, University of British Columbia, 1977.

Lepawsky, Albert. "Water Resources and American Federalism." *American Political Science Review* 44, no. 3 (September 1950): 631–49.

Lesage, Jean. "Water Resources of the Columbia River Basin." *External Affairs* 7 (September 1955): 218–23.

Lindblom, Charles E. "Policy Analysis." *American Economic Review* 48, no. 3 (June 1958): 298–312.

———. "Tinbergen on Policy-Making." *Journal of Political Economy* 66, no. 6 (December 1958): 531–38.

———. "The Science of 'Muddling Through'." *Public Administration Review* 19, no. 2 (Spring, 1959): 79–88.

———. *The Intelligence of Democracy.* New York: The Free Press, 1965.

———. *The Policy-Making Process.* Englewood Cliffs, N.J.: Prentice-Hall, Inc., 1968.

Lloyd, Trevor. *Canada in World Affairs, 1957–1959.* Toronto: Oxford University Press, 1968.

Lowi, Theodore J. "Distribution, Regulation, Redistribution: The Functions of Government." In *Public Policies and Their Poltics,* edited by Randall B. Ripley. New York: W. W. Norton & Company, Inc., 1966, pp. 27–40.

———. "Decision Making as Policy Making: Towards an Antidote for Technocracy." *Public Administration Review* 30, no. 3 (May–June 1970): 314–25.

Lyon, Peyton V. *The Policy Question: A Critical Appraisal of Canada's Role in World Affairs.* Toronto: McClelland and Stewart, 1963.

———. *Canada in World Affairs 1961–1963.* Toronto: Oxford University Press, 1968.

Maass, Arthur. "System Design and the Political Process: A General Statement." In *Design of Water Resource Systems,* edited by A. Maass. Cambridge, Mass.: Harvard University Press, 1962.

Maass, Arthur et al. *Design of Water Resource Systems: New Techniques for Relating Economic Objectives, Engineering Analysis, and Governmental Planning.* Cambridge, Mass.: Harvard University Press, 1962.

McDougall, I. A. "Report on the Proposed Fraser-Columbia Water Transfer: Some Economic and Legal Implications for the Upstream Riparians," *Osgoode Hall Law Journal* 8, no. 2 (November 1970): 301–27.

————. "The Development of International Law with Respect to Trans-Boundary Water Resources: Cooperation for Mutual Advantage or Continentalism's Thin Edge of the Wedge?" *Osgoode Hall Law Journal* 9, no. 2 (November 1971): 260–311.

McInnis, Edgar W. "Neighbour to a Giant." In *Canadian Issues: Essays in Honour of Henry F. Angus*, edited by R. M. Clark. Toronto: University of Toronto Press, 1961, pp. 95–109.

McKean, Roland N. *Efficiency in Government Through Systems Analysis, With Emphasis on Water Resource Development.* New York: John Wiley and Sons, Inc., 1958.

McKinley, Charles. *Uncle Sam in the Pacific Northwest.* Berkeley: University of California Press, 1952.

McMordie, R. C. "Aspects of the Background of Columbia River Projects in Canada." *The Engineering Journal* 45 (October 1962): 47–54.

McNaughton, A. G. L. "The Proposed Columbia River Treaty." *International Journal* 18, no. 2 (Spring, 1963): 148–65.

MacNeill, J. W. *Environmental Management.* Ottawa: Information Canada, 1971.

McWhinney, Edward. "The Constitutional Competence within Federal Systems for International Agreements." *Background Papers and Reports*, Ontario Advisory Committee on Confederation. Toronto: Queen's Printer for Ontario, 1967, pp. 151–57.

Mallory, James R. "Minister's Office Staff: An Unreformed Part of the Public Service." *Canadian Public Administration* 10, no. 1 (March 1967): 25–34.

March, James G. and Simon, Herbert A. *Organizations.* New York: John Wiley and Sons, Inc., 1967 (1958).

Marshall, Hubert. "Organizing for River Basin Development." *Public Administration Review* 14, no. 3 (August 1953): 269–74.

————. "Rational Choice in Water Resources Planning." In *Readings in Resource Management and Conservation*, edited by Ian Burton. Chicago: The University of Chicago Press, 1965, pp. 529–43.

————. "Administrative Responsibility and the New Science of Management Decision." In *Toward Century 21: Technology Society and Human Values*, edited by C. S. Wallia, New York: Basic Books, Inc., 1970, pp. 257–68.

Martin, Charles E. "International Water Problems in the West: The Columbia Basin Treaty Between Canada and the United States." In *Canada-United States Treaty Relations*, edited by David Deener. Durham, N.C.: Duke University Press, 1963.

Masters, Donald C. *Canada in World Affairs, 1953 to 1955.* Toronto: University of Toronto Press, 1964.

Meisel, John. "The Formulation of Liberal and Conservative Programmes in the 1957 Canadian General Election." *The Canadian Journal of Economics and Political Science* 26, no. 4 (November 1969): 565–74.

————. *The Canadian General Election of 1957.* Toronto: The University of Toronto Press, 1962.

Meisel, John, ed. *Papers on the 1962 Election.* Toronto: University of Toronto Press, 1964.

Miller, Morris. "The Developmental Framework for Resource Policy and Its Jurisdictional-Administrative Implications." *Canadian Public Administration* 5, no. 2 (June 1962): 133–55.

Milliman, Jerome W. "Economic Considerations for the Design of Water Institutions." *Public Administration Review* 25, no. 4 (December 1965): 284–89.

Minifie, James. "Good Neighbours and Boundary Waters." *Canadian Commentator* 1 (May 1958): 14.

———. "Time to Settle Columbia Dispute." *Canadian Commentator* 2 (May 1958): 4.

Mohler, C. E. "Reservoir Storage for Hydroelectric Power." In *High Dams and Upstream Storage,* edited by A. W. Stone. Missoula, Montana: Montana State University Press, 1958.

Morin, Jacques-Yvon. "International Law-Treaty-Making Power-Constitutional Law-Position of the Government of Quebec." *Canadian Bar Review* 45, no. 1 (March 1967): 160–73.

———. "Vers un nouvel équilibre constitutionnel au Canada." In *The Future of Canadian Federalism,* edited by P. A. Crépeau and C. B. Macpherson. Toronto: University of Toronto Press, 1965, pp. 141–56.

Morris, G. L. "The Treaty-Making Power: A Canadian Dilemma." *Canadian Bar Review* 45, no. 3 (September 1967): 478–512.

Morton, W. L. *The Canadian Identity.* Madison: The University of Wisconsin Press, 1961.

Mundell, David W. "Legal Nature of Federal and Provincial Executive Governments: Some Comments on Transactions between Them." *Osgoode Hall Law Journal* 2, no. 1 (April 1960): 56–75.

Neuberger, R. L. "Power Struggle on the Canadian Border." *Harper's Magazine* 215 (December 1957): 42–49.

Newman, Peter C. "Who's Where and Why in the Great Columbia Treaty Debate." *Maclean's Magazine* 75 (November 17, 1962), pp. 2–3.

———. *Renegade in Power.* Toronto: McClelland and Stewart Limited, 1963.

———. *The Distemper of Our Times.* Toronto: McClelland and Stewart Limited, 1968.

Nicholson, Patrick. *Vision and Indecision.* Toronto: Longmans Canada Limited, 1968.

Ostrom, Vincent. "The Social Scientist and the Control and Development of Natural Resources." *Land Economics* 19, no. 2 (May 1953): 105–16.

———. "Water Resource Development: Some Problems in Economic and Political Analysis of Public Policy." In *Political Science and Public Policy,* edited by Austin Ranney. Chicago: Markham Publishing Co , 1968.

Perrow, Charles. *Organizational Analysis: A Sociological View.* Belmont, Calif.: Wadsworth Publishing Co., Inc., 1970.

Pfiffner, John M. "Administrative Rationality." *Public Administration Review* 20, no. 3 (Summer, 1960): 125–32.

Preston, Richard. *Canada in World Affairs*. Toronto: McClelland and Stewart, 1964.

Quade, Edward S. "Methods and Procedures." In *Analysis for Military Decisions*, edited by E. S. Quade. Chicago: Rand McNally, 1964.

Reuber, G. L. and Wonnacott, R. J. *The Cost of Capital in Canada—With Special Reference to Public Development of the Columbia River*. Washington: Resources for the Future, Inc., 1961.

Ripley, James G. "The Columbia River Treaty." *Engineering and Contract Record* (September 1962): 33–46.

———. "The Columbia River Scandal." *Engineering and Contract Record* (April 1964): 45–60.

Sabourin, Louis. "Politique étrangère et 'Etat du Québec'." *International Journal* 20, no. 3 (Summer, 1965): 350–61.

———. "Special International Status for Quebec." In *An Independent Foreign Policy for Canada*, edited by Stephen Clarkson. Toronto: McClelland and Stewart, 1968, pp. 97–109.

Saywell, J., ed. *Canadian Annual Review for 1960*. Toronto: University of Toroto Press, 1962. (Plus editions to 1965.)

Schultze, Charles L. *The Politics and Economics of Public Spending*. Washington: The Brookings Institution, 1968.

Scott, A. D. "The Columbia River Agreement." *Canadian Forum* 40 (March 1961), pp. 275–77.

———. "Annual Report on the Columbia Treaty." *Canadian Forum* 41 (March 1962), pp. 270–71.

Scott, Anthony D. "The Columbia River Treaty—the Economics of an International River Basin Development." Review Article. *Canadian Journal of Economics* 2, no. 4 (November 1969): 619–26.

Sewell, W. R. Derrick. "The Columbia River Treaty: Some Lessons and Implications." *Canadian Geographer* 10, no. 3 (Autumn, 1966): 145–56.

Sherman, Paddy. *Bennett*. Toronto: McClelland and Stewart, Limited, 1966.

Simeon, Richard. *Federal-Provincial Diplomacy, The Making of Recent Policy in Canada*. Toronto: University of Toronto Press, 1962.

Simon, Herbert A. *Administrative Behaviour*. New York: The Macmillan Company, 1957 (2nd ed.).

———. *The New Science of Management Decision*. New York: Harper and Brothers, 1960.

Smiley, Donald V. "Canada's Poujadists: A New Look at Social Credit." *Canadian Forum* 42 (September 1962): 121–23.

———. "The Two Themes of Canadian Federalism." *The Canadian Journal of Economics and Political Science* 31, no. 1 (February 1965): 80–97.

Soward, F. H. "External Affairs and Federalism." In *Evolving Canadian Federalism*, edited by A. Lower. Durham, N.C.: Duke University Press, 1958.

Strayer, Barry L. *Judicial Review of Legislation in Canada*. Toronto: University of Toronto Press, 1968.

437

Stursberg, Peter. *Diefenbaker: Leadership Lost.* Toronto: University of Toronto Press, 1976.

Sundborg, George. *Hail Columbia.* New York: The Macmillan Co., 1952.

Swettenham, John. *McNaughton.* Vol. III. Toronto: Ryerson Press, 1969.

Szablowski, A. J. "Creation and Implementation of Treaties in Canada." *Canadian Bar Review* 34, no. 1 (January 1956): 28–59.

Teclaff, Ludwik A. *The River Basin in History and Law.* The Hague: Martinus Nijhoff, 1967.

Thompson, James D. and Tuden, Arthur. "Strategies, Structures and Processes of Organizational Decision." In *Comparative Studies in Administration,* edited by J. D. Thompson et al. Pittsburgh, Pa.: University of Pittsburgh Press, 1959, pp. 195–212.

Van Dusen, Thomas. *The Chief.* Toronto: McGraw-Hill, 1968.

Vickers, Sir Geoffrey. *The Art of Judgment.* New York: Basic Books, 1965.

———. *Towards a Sociology of Management.* New York: Basic Books, Inc., 1967.

Warren, H. V. "Electric Energy and Future Development in British Columbia." *The B.C. Professional Engineer* (August 1967): 7–10.

Water and Choice in the Colorado River Basin. A Report of the Committee on Water, National Research Council. Washington, D.C.: National Academy of Sciences, 1968.

Waterfield, Donald. *Continental Waterboy: The Columbia River Controversy.* Toronto: Clarke Irwin and Co., Ltd., 1970.

Watkins, E. S. 'The Columbia River: A Gordian Knot." *International Journal* 12, no. 4 (Autumn, 1951): 250–61.

White, A. V. and Vick, C. J. *Water Powers of British Columbia.* Ottawa: Commission of Conservation, Canada, 1919.

White, Gilbert F. "Broader Basis for Choice: The Next and Key Move." In *Perspectives on Conservation,* edited by Henry Jarrett. Baltimore, Md.: Johns Hopkins Press, 1962.

———. *Strategies of American Water Management.* Ann Arbor: University of Michigan Press, 1969.

Wildavsky, Aaron. *Dixon-Yates: A Study in Power Politics.* New Haven: Yale University Press, 1962.

Wilensky, Harold. *Organizational Intelligence: Knowledge and Policy in Government and Industry.* New York: Basic Books Inc., 1967.

Willoughby, W. R. "The Appointment and Removal of Members of the International Joint Commission." *Canadian Public Administration* 30, no. 3 (Fall, 1969): 410–26.

———. *The St. Lawrence Waterway.* Madison: The University of Wisconsin Press, 1961.

PUBLIC DOCUMENTS, ENGINEERING AND OTHER REPORTS,
MONOGRAPHS, SUBMISSIONS TO HEARINGS AND
CONFERENCES, RECORDS OF PROCEEDINGS,
UNPUBLISHED MATERIAL

"Analysis by U.S. Negotiators of Report to the Governments of the United States and Canada Relative to Cooperative Development of Water Resources of the Columbia River Basin, October 19, 1960." 21 pp. (Mimeographed.)

Anderson, W. M., Dunsmuir, J., Shrum, G. M. "Report of the Royal Commission in the Matter of the British Columbia Power Commission." Victoria: August 14, 1959. (Mimeographed.)

Bartholomew, F. J. "Columbia River Treaty: Memorandum dealing with Sherman's Article of January 24, 1963." February 8, 1963. (Typewritten.)

Bourne, Charles B. "Recent Developments in the Columbia River Controversy." *Proceedings of the Pacific Northwest Regional Meeting*, American Society of International Law, April 18–19, 1958, pp. 1–8.

————. "Energy's Legal Framework." *Transactions of the Thirteenth British Columbia Natural Resources Conference*. Victoria: The B.C. Natural Resources Conference, 1961, pp. 32–41.

————. "Energy and A Continental Concept." *Sixth Seminar on Canadian-American Relations*. Edited by F. J. Boland. Windsor: University of Windsor, 1965, pp. 157–69.

Bourne, Charles B., Chapman, J. D., Muir, E. F., Ruus, E., Scott, A. D., Warren, H. V., and Wilks, E. F. "Electrical Energy in British Columbia." Vancouver, B.C., February 26, 1962. (Mimeographed.)

Briggs, H. L. "Brief Respecting the Trusteeship in Behalf of the People of British Columbia as Rendered through the B.C. Power Commission, 1953–1958." (Presented to the Royal Commission in the Matter of the B.C. Power Commission.) December 30, 1958.

British Columbia. Columbia River Basin Development Advisory Committee. "Minutes of Meetings, 1954." (Typewritten.)

British Columbia Department of Lands, Forests (and, post 1961, Water Resources). Water Resources Service. "Annual Review of Water Power." British Columbia, 1960–63. (Mimeographed.)

British Columbia Energy Board. *Interim Report on the Columbia and Peace Power Projects*. Victoria, B.C.: March 1, 1961.

British Columbia Energy Board. *Report on the Columbia and Peace Power Projects*. Victoria, B.C.: July 31, 1961.

British Columbia Engineering Company Ltd. *Report on An Investigation of the Columbia River in Canada*. (Prepared for the B.C. Electric Co., Ltd.) Vancouver, B.C.: 1958.

British Columbia Progressive Conservative Association. "A Factual Documented Statement of the Conservative Party's Position in British Columbia and Some of the Reasons for the Motion of No Confidence in the National Leader." Unpublished monograph, March 1955.

British Columbia. Water Resources Service. *Departmental Files, 1944–1954, 1957–1964.*

Bureau of Business Research, University of Washington. *Electrical Energy Outlook for Pacific Northwest.* (Occasional Paper no. 13.) Seattle: University of Washington, 1960.

Bureau of Governmental Research and Services, University of Washington. *The Columbia River: Main Street of the Pacific Northwest, Proceedings of the General Session of the 26th Annual Institute of Government, 1961.* Seattle: University of Washington Press, 1962.

Canada. Briefs submitted to the House of Commons, Standing Committee on External Affairs, April 7–May 27, 1964, pursuant to its hearings in the matter of a treaty between Canada and the United States relating to co-operative development of the water resources of the Columbia River Basin. Not included in the committee's Minutes of Proceedings and Evidence. (Mimeographed.)

—The Consolidated Mining and Smelting Company of Canada, Limited, April, 1964.

—F. J. Bartholomew, April, 1964.

—United Electrical, Radio and Machine Workers of America, April 24, 1964.

—International Union of Mine Mill and Smelter Workers (Canada).

—Columbia River for Canada Committee.

—United Fishermen and Allied Workers' Union.

—The Communist Party of Canada, May 6, 1964.

—The Government of Saskatchewan, May 8, 1964.

—British Columbia Federation of Labour, May 13, 1964.

—Larratt Higgins.

Canada. House of Commons. Standing Committee on External Affairs. *Minutes of Proceedings and Evidence,* Twenty-Second to Twenty-Sixth Parliaments, 1953–1964.

————. *Minutes of Proceedings and Evidence, The Columbia River Treaty and Protocol,* April 7–May 27, 1964, 26th Parliament, 2nd Session.

Canada. House of Commons. *Debates, Official Record,* Nineteenth to Twenty-Sixth Parliaments, 1944–1964.

Caseco Consultants Ltd. *Report on Columbia River Development.* Vancouver, B.C.: May 1961.

Cass-Beggs, D. "The Future of Power in Western Canada." Paper presented to the Association of Professional Engineers of Saskatchewan, February 23, 1962. Revised March 3, 1962. (Mimeographed.)

Center for Resources Policy Studies and Programs. "Procedures for Evaluation of Water and Related Land Resource Projects: An Analysis of the Water Resource Council's Task Force Report." Madison: University of Wisconsin, 1970. (Mimeographed.)

Chantrill, R. L. and Stevens, J. D. *A Report on Power Capabilities and Operating Aspects of Peace River Project and a Pacific International Power Pool.* Vancouver, B.C.: Peace River Power Development Co., Ltd., 1960.

————. *A Rate Study for the Peace River Development.* Vancouver, B.C.: Peace River Power Development Company, January 1961.

————. *A Report on Power Capabilities and Operating Aspects of a British Columbia Power Pool.* Vancouver, B.C.: Peace River Power Development Co., Ltd. and B.C. Electric Co., Ltd., May 1961.

Chapman, J. D. ed. *The International River Basin. Proceedings of a Seminar on the Development and Administration of the International River Basin.* Vancouver: University of British Columbia, 1963.

Columbia River Engineering Board, Engineering Committee and Canadian Section. "Minutes of Meetings, 1944–1956."

Columbia River Treaty Permanent Engineering Board. *Annual Report to the Governments of the United States and Canada.* Washington, D.C. and Ottawa, Ont.: 30 September, 1965–30 September, 1970.

The Columbia River Treaty and Protocol: A Presentation. Issued by the Departments of External Affairs and Northern Affairs and National Resources. Ottawa: Queen's Printer, February 1964.

The Columbia River Treaty, Protocol and Related Documents. Issued by the Departments of External Affairs and Northern Affairs and National Resources. Ottawa: Queen's Printer, April 1964.

Comptroller of Water Rights for British Columbia. "Record of Proceedings. Hearings Concerning Applications to Build the Mica, Duncan and High Arrow Dams." Victoria, B.C.: September 21–November 21, 1961. (Mimeographed.)

Corry, J. A. *Difficulties of Divided Jurisdiction: A Study Prepared for the Royal Commission on Dominion-Provincial Relations.* Ottawa: King's Printer, 1939.

Crippen-Wright Engineering Ltd. *Report, Hydro-Electric Development of Columbia River Basin in Canada.* Vancouver, B.C.: January 12, 1959. (Including eight interim reports, and one on electric power requirements in the province of B.C.—1958.)

Dales, J. H. *Canada's Energy Prospects.* Toronto: Canadian Institute of International Affairs, 1957.

Davis, John. *Canadian Energy Policy.* Toronto: Canadian Institute of International Affairs, 1959.

————. "Power Sharing in the Pacific Northwest." Address to the Pacific North West Trade Association, Sun Valley, Idaho, September 27, 1960.

————. "Presentation on Benefit-Cost Ratios with Reference to Columbia River, Peace River and Thermal Programmes in British Columbia." *Proceedings of the Resources for Tomorrow Conference, Montreal*, October 23–28, 1961, Vol. III. Ottawa: Queen's Printer, 1962, pp. 146–54.

Deane, Ritchie. "The Columbia Treaty and High Arrow Dam." (A presentation to the Standing Committee on External Affairs, House of Commons.) March 30, 1964.

Fox, Irving K. "Promising Areas for Research on Institutional Design for Water Resources Management." Presented at Chicago, Illinois, January 14, 1970. (Mimeographed.)

Fox, Irving K. and Crane, Lyle E. "Objectives and Organizational Arrangements for Multi-Purpose Development and Management of Water Resources." *Resources for Tomorrow, Conference Background Papers.* Ottawa: Queen's Printer, 1961, pp. 281–97.

Fox, Irving K., Smith, Stephen C. and Torti, T. Ufere. "Administration of International Rivers." Paper presented at the United Nations Panel of Experts on Legal and Institutional Implications of International Water Resources Development, Vienna, December 9–14, 1968.

Gibb, Sir Alexander & Partners, Merz and McLelland. *Columbia and Peace River Power Projects: Report on Power Costs.* London and Toronto, 2 vols., July 1961.

Gibson, Dale. "Water Resources Development in Canada: A Perspective." Canadian Papers: International Conference on Water for Peace. Ottawa: Department of Energy, Mines and Resources, 1967. (Mimeographed.)

Government of Canada. "Background Paper on the Columbia River Treaty." Ottawa: January 22, 1964. (Mimeographed.)

Grauer, A. E. "The Economy of British Columbia and the Power Picture." 1959. (Mimeographed.)

Higgins, Larratt T. "Resource Development: Integration or Cooperation." Paper read to the Woodsworth Foundation Conference, Toronto, November 12, 1966. (Mimeographed.)

———. "McNaughton's Last Campaign." Paper read to the Seminar on Canadian-American Relations of the University of Windsor, January 30, 1967. (Mimeographed.)

International Columbia River Engineering Board. *Kootenay River.* An Interim Report to the International Joint Commission. November 1, 1950.

———. *Libby Project: Kootenay River.* A Report on the Application of the Government of the United States for Authority to Construct the Libby Project. Submitted to the International Joint Commission, May, 1951.

———. *Libby Project: Kootenay River.* A Report . . . Submitted to the IJC, July 1951.

———. *Water Resources of the Columbia River Basin.* Report to the International Joint Commission, United States and Canada. Washington, D.C. and Ottawa, Ont : March 1, 1959.

International Joint Commission (United States and Canada). "Record of Public Hearings, Nelson and Cranbrook, B.C., March, 1951." In the Matter of the Application of the Government of the United States, Dated aJnuary 12, 1951, Re Libby Dam. (Mimeographed.)

———. "Transcript of Proceedings." Meetings of February 17, March 16–17, 1959.

Keenleyside, H. L. "Power in British Columbia." An Address Delivered in Nanaimo, B.C., December 15, 1961. (Mimeographed.)

———. "The Power Situation in British Columbia." An Address to the Canadian Club of Toronto, February 19, 1962. (Mimeographed.)

———. "The Columbia River Agreements." An Address to the Advertising and Sales Bureau of the Vancouver Board of Trade, February 10, 1964.

Kristjanson, Kris and Stephens, Donald M. "Planning River Basin Development." *Transactions of the Fourteenth B.C. Natural Resources Conference,* 1962, Victoria, B.C., pp. 46–53.

Krutilla, John V. *Sequence and Timing in River Basin Development with Special Application to Canadian-United States Columbia River Basin Planning.* Washington, D.C.: Resources for the Future, Inc., 1960.

―――. *Columbia River Development—A Study in International Cooperation.* Washington: Resources for the Future, Inc., July, 1961. (Reprint No. 42.)

―――. "Columbia River Development: Some Problems of International Cooperation." *Land and Water: Planning for Economic Growth.* Papers of the 1961 Western Resources Conference. Boulder: University of Colorado Press, 1962, pp. 91–119.

―――. "British Columbia Alternatives to the Columbia Treaty." July 11, 1962. (Mimeographed.)

―――. "The Columbia River Treaty: An International Evaluation." A lecture delivered to a lecture series jointly sponsored by the Universities of British Columbia and Washington, July 9–10, 1963. (Washington, D.C.: Resources for the Future, Inc., reprint number 42.)

Ladner, L. J., Bourne, C. B., Inglis, P., Austin, J., and MacKenzie, N. A. M. "International Law: Rivers and Marginal Seas." Vancouver: University of British Columbia, 1956. (Pamphlet.)

Laskin, Bora. "Jurisdictional Framework for Water Management." *Resources for Tomorrow, Conference Background Papers.* Ottawa: Queen's Printer, 1961, Vol. 1, pp. 211–25.

Lindblom, C. E. "Bargaining: the Hidden Hand in Government." February 1955. (Unpublished Monograph.)

McDonald, J. D. "The Columbia Treaty and High Arrow Dam." A Brief submitted to the Standing Committee on External Affairs, House of Commons, May 5, 1964.

MacLaren, G. F. "Brief on Export of Surplus Electric Power." Presented to the Export Trade Promotion Conference, Ottawa, 1960.

Maclean, H. A. "Historic Development of Water Legislation in British Columbia." *Proceedings, 8th B.C. Natural Resources Conference.* Victoria, B.C.: 1955, pp. 243–47.

MacNabb, Gordon M. "The Columbia River Treaty." *Canadian Papers: International Conference on Water for Peace.* Ottawa: Department of Energy, Mines and Resources, 1967. (Mimeographed.)

McNaughton, A. G. L. "Problems of Development of International Rivers on the Pacific Watershed of Canada and the United States." Paper presented to the Fifth World Power Conference, 1956.

―――. Press release, response to the Honourable D. Fulton, April 13, 1962. (Mimeographed.)

―――. "Statement on Proposed Columbia River Treaty made to Senators and M.P.'s in the House of Commons Committee Room," December 12, 1962. (Mimeographed.)

―――. "Address to the Association of Professional Engineers of Alberta, March 23, 1963." (Mimeographed.)

MacNeill, James W. "Law and the Agencies." *Transactions of the Fourteenth British Columbia Natural Resources Conference*, September 5–7, 1962, pp. 132–42.

McQuillan, H. C. "Energy's Administrative Framework." *Transactions of the Thirteenth British Columbia Natural Resources Conference*. Victoria: March 1961, pp. 21–32.

Maher, F. P. "A Preliminary Report on the Effects of Four Dams Proposed for the Columbia and Kootenay Rivers in British Columbia." August 1, 1961. (Mimeographed.)

Mainwaring, W. C. "What is a Power Pool? How Does it Operate? What are the Benefits?" Vancouver: Peace River Power Development Co. Ltd., 1960.

Martin, Charles E. "The Diversion of Columbia River Waters." *Proceedings of the American Society of International Law*, 51st Annual Meeting, April 25–27, 1957. Seattle: Institute of International Affairs, University of Washington, Bulletin no. 13.

Martin, Paul. *Federalism and International Relations*. Ottawa: Queen's Printer, 1968.

Montreal Engineering Company, Ltd. *Preliminary Report on the Development of Canada's Water Power Resources in the Columbia Basin*. Montreal: October 1957.

———. *Factors Affecting the Cost of Columbia River Power in Canada*. Ottawa: Dept. of Northern Affairs and National Resources, May 1961.

———. *Comments on the Columbia River Treaty and Protocol*. March 1964.

Moore, Dorothy Louise. "The Role of the International Joint Commission in Columbia River Basin Development." M.A. Thesis, University of California, Berkeley, 1962.

Muir, John F. and Ruus, E. "Engineering Research on the Fish and Power Problem." Paper no. 13 presented to the Annual Meeting of the Engineering Institute of Canada, May 1961.

———. "A Yardstick for Evaluating Costs of Electrical Energy in British Columbia." Vancouver: University of British Columbia, 1963.

Pasha, Sred Aziz. "Settlement of the Columbia River Dispute—A Contribution of the International Joint Commission Toward the Development of International River Law." Dissertation for the Degree of Doctor of Juridical Science, School of Law, New York University, 1963.

Patterson, T. M. "Administrative Framework for Water Management." *Resources for Tomorrow, Conference Background Papers*. Ottawa: Queen's Printer, 1961, pp. 227–48.

Peace River Power Development Company. *Peace River Hydro-Electric Project*. (Comprehensive Plan . . . for the Maximum Economic Development of the Hydro-Electric Potential of the Peace River in British Columbia) Vancouver, B.C.: December, 1959, 8 vols.

The President's Water Resources Policy Commission. *Ten Rivers in America's Future*. Washington, D.C.: United States Government Printing Office, 1950.

"Proceedings before A. F. Paget, Comptroller of Water Rights, in the Matter of the 'B.C. Water Act' and in the Matter of the Application of the British Columbia Power Commission to Store Water above Mica Creek, in Duncan

Lake, at Arrow Lakes." Revelstoke, September 18, 21, 26, 27; Nakusp, September 29; Castlegar, October 3, 4; Victoria, November 21, 22, 1961. 10 Vols. (Mimeographed.)

Revelstoke, City of. "Let There be Light: A Survey of the Columbia River Power Potential." August 1, 1960. (Mimeographed.)

"River Basin Development." *Transactions of the Fourteenth B.C. Natural Resources Conference, September 5–7, 1962.* Victoria, B.C.: Natural Resources Conference, 1963.

Rowen, Henry S. "Bargaining and Analysis in Government." Paper delivered at the Annual Meeting of the American Political Science Association, September 6–10, 1966. U.S. Congress. Senate. Sub-committee on National Security and International operations of the Committee on Government Operations. 90th Congress, 1st Session, Planning-Programming-Budgeting, Selected Comment. (Committee Print. 90th Cong., 1st sess., 1967, pp. 44–49). Washington, D.C.: U.S. Government Printing Office, 1967.

Royal Commission on Canada's Economic Prospects. *Final Report.* Ottawa: Queen's Printer, November 1957.

Schlesinger, James R. "Uses and Abuses of Analysis." U.S. Congress. Senate. Subcommittee on National Security and International Operations of the Committee on Government Operations. Planning-Programming-Budgeting. Committee Print. 90th Cong., 2nd Sess.

Sewell, W. R. D. et al. *Guide to Benefit-Cost Analysis: A Systematic Approach to Evaluating and Selecting Development Projects with Particular Reference to the Canadian Scene.* (Reviewed . . . at the Resources for Tomorrow Conference . . . October 23–28, 1961.) Ottawa: Queen's Printer, 1962.

Sherman, P. L. "Columbia River Power Plan—A Special Report." *The Province* (Vancouver). (Special Supplement), January 24, 1963.

Smith, George J. "Major Undeveloped Water Powers of Northern British Columbia and What They Mean to the Province." *Transactions of the 8th British Columbia Natural Resources Conference.* Victoria, B.C.: B.C. Natural Conference, 1955.

Sommers, R. E. "The Castlegar Dam Proposal." A radio address, Station CBU, November 29, 1954. (Mimeographed.)

———. "Reply to the Throne Speech." January 1955. (Mimeographed.)

Spencer, R. A. *Canadian Foreign Policy—Conservation Style.* Toronto: Canadian Institute of Public Affairs, 1968. (Monograph.)

Stephens, D. M. "Memorandum to File Re: International Joint Commission; Re: Columbia River Reference." April 24, 1958. (Mimeographed.)

———. "Power Across International Frontiers." Address to the Canadian Electrical Association, Banff, Alta., June 26, 1961. (Mimeographed.)

Stephens, Jack D. *Power Program for the Puget Sound-Cascade Region.* A Report to the Puget Sound Utilities Council, March, 1955.

U.S. Congress. Committee on Interior and Insular Affairs and a Special Subcommittee of the Committee on Foreign Relations. U.S. Senate, *Joint Hearings on Upper Columbia River Development.* March 22–23, 84th Cong., 2nd Sess., 1956.

U.S. Congress. Senate. Committee on Foreign Relations. *Hearing on the*

Columbia River Treaty. 87th Cong., 1st Sess., March 8, 1961.

U.S. Congress. Senate. Committee on Interior and Insular Affairs. *Upper Columbia River Development, Hearings.* April 21–May 7, 85th Cong., 2nd Sess., 1958.

U.S. Congress. Senate. Committee on Interior and Insular Affairs. *Columbia Basin Problems, Hearings.* May 14–23, 85th Cong., 2nd Sess., 1958.

U.S. Congress. Senate. Committee on Interior and Insular Affairs and a Special Subcommittee of the Committee on Foreign Relations. *Upper Columbia River Development, Joint Hearings.* 85th Cong., 2nd Sess., March 22–May 23, 1956.

U.S. Congress. Senate. *Message from the President of the United States Transmitting a Treaty Between the United States of America and Canada, Signed at Washington, January 17, 1961.* 87th Cong., 1st Sess., 1961.

U.S. Corps of Engineers. Department of the Army. North Pacific Division. *Review Report on Columbia River and Tributaries.* October 1, 1948.

U.S. Department of the Interior. Bureau of Reclamation. *The Columbia River.* A comprehensive departmental report on the development of the water resources of the Columbia River basin for review prior to submission to Congress, February 1947. 2 vols.

U.S. Department of the Interior. Special Task Force. *Pacific Northwest-Pacific Southwest Extra-High Voltage Common Carrier Interconnection.* Washington: U.S. Government Printing Office, December 15, 1961.

U.S. Division Engineer. U.S. Army Engineer Division, North Pacific. Water Resource Development of the Columbia River Basin. H.D. 531, 81st Cong., 2nd Sess., June 1958.

Water and Choice in the Colorado River Basin. A Report of the Committee on Water, National Research Council. Washington, D.C.: National Academy of Sciences, 1968.

"Water Resource Development in Canada: A Perspective." *Canadian Papers: International Conference on Water for Peace.* Ottawa: Department of Energy, Mines and Resources, 1967. ICWP Document 50.

Water Resources Council, *Procedures for Evaluation of Water and Related Land Resource Projects.* A Report prepared by the Special Task Force. Washington, D.C.: Water Resources Council, 1969.

West Kootenay Association of Rod and Gun Clubs. "Recreation in the Columbia River Basin of Canada: A Multiple Use Proposal." May 1961.

Williston, R. G. "Power Developments in British Columbia." An Address to the Northwest Power Association, Seattle, Washington, April 17, 1963. (Mimeographed.)

————. "Hydro-Electric Power in British Columbia," January 27, 1959; "The British Columbia Hydro-Power Situation," February 3, 1960; Subsequently annually in February to 1970, "Excerpts from an Address during the Budget Debate,"—all manuscripts of speeches to the British Columbia Legislative Assembly. (Mimeographed.)

Williston, Ray. "Excerpts from an Address during the Speech from the Throne (or the Budget) Debate." Annually, 1958–64. (Mimeographed.)

Index

committees, 103–4; effected via direct negotiation and bargaining, 354–59; in presenting the Columbia River Treaty to Parliament, 273; over protocol and power sale negotiations (1963), 257–58; since ratification of treaty, 282–84; in responding to second Libby application, 53

Canada-B.C. Policy Liaison Committee. *See* Policy Liaison Committee

Canada-B.C. relations: ambiguities over near-détente (1962), 225–26; arms-length nature of (1957–58), 90–94; asymmetric adjusting in, toward B.C.'s position, 308; B.C.'s position on the role of General McNaughton in, 113; coordinate status over treaty negotiations, 295; over creation of, and response to 1944 IJC reference, 41; debate in, over jurisdictional position of Ottawa and Victoria, 153; decision to end federal-provincial confrontation over 1955–56 winter, 68; decision to raise Columbia development deadlock to diplomatic level, 69; differing federal and provincial assumptions concerning initial international bargaining stance (1960), 130–31; differing federal and provincial responses to first Libby application, 49; disagreement over staffing IJC teams, 41–42; dispute over application of federal licensing power to Columbia River projects, 283–84; dissonance in (May–June, 1960), 152–55; fiduciary role for Ottawa in power sale, advanced by U.S., 266; final Ottawa-Victoria exchanges prior to signing of Columbia River Treaty, 181–85; financial autonomy and independence of B.C. in, 222; over financial help related to project selection, 131; over financing Columbia development, 128,

131, 136, 140, 146–47; "freeze up" of (1961), 189–93; impact on, of interacting personalities, 356; impact of two-party contest on recourse to analysis and bargaining in, 357; impact joint responsibility had over the scanning of options, 342; influence on, of broad change in direction in Canadian federal system, 356; involving weight given to considerations of economic efficiency, 328–29; legal position of federal-provincial agreements in, 413n41; mounting tension in, over B.C.'s intent re the Columbia River Treaty, 188–201; near détente in (January–April 1962), 219–25; in negotiations with the U.S.A. (1957), 72; post-ratification cooperation, 282–84; in presentation of Columbia River Treaty to Parliament, 273; over Puget Sound Utilities' Council proposal, 55–56; relationship of rivalry in, to the detailed nature of the treaty, 361; relevance to, of South Saskatchewan and New Brunswick power developments, 136; result of intermittent competition in, on federal-provincial staff relations, 343; R. G. Williston on, over 1957–58 Columbia planning, 102; role of controversial newspaper stories in, 139; September-November 1961 confrontation in, between Messrs. Fulton and Bennett on the "two river" policy, 205–12. *See also* Canadian federalism; Columbia River Treaty negotiations

Canadian-American negotiations: B.C. view of appropriate provincial role (May 1957), 74; expressed intent of (1956), 69; over principles governing the definition and division of downstream benefits, 109–15; over the Columbia River Treaty, 132–41, 143–44, 150–52, 158–61, 163–65, 179–80; over the possibilities

Douglas, T.; Strachan, R.
Coordination: varied approaches to, 3, 288–90, 295–325
Corps of Engineers (U.S. Army), 33, 40; commitment of, to Libby project, 45; perceived strength of, in U.S. policy formation, 73
Cost of electricity in B.C.: derived from Columbia development, 272–73; E. D. Fulton on, 201; need for caution in assessing, 363; R. G. Williston on (1961), 189. *See* Power costs
Credit position of storages: bargaining over, in treaty negotiations, 159; of Canadian projects, related to delay in Treaty ratification, 225; related to project timing, 6–7, 142
Crippen-Wright Report: basic recommendations of, 105–7; commissioned, 71, 385n117; emphasis of, on sequence and timing, 104; estimate by, of benefits inherent in cooperative development, 104; impact of, on federal-provincial bargaining, 308; and independent development of the Columbia, 326; perceived as a means to broadened understanding, 342
Cyert, R. M., 333, 366

Davis, Jack, 317, 318; criticism of the treaty by, 246–48; endorsement of lump sum prepayment for power benefit sale by, 235; endorsement of renegotiation of treaty by, 247; on interrelationships of Peace and Columbia development, 362; response of, to U.B.C. professors, 200
Decision-making on the Columbia: Canadian approach to, 2; Canadian goals in, 3, 8; complexity of technical issues in, 5–6; disjointed incrementalism of, 4; environment of, 3; flexibility in, of small jurisdictions, 10; measure of integrated approach to, 10–11; multiple vetoes in, 8; pace

of, 9; points of leverage in, 2; polycentric nature of, 8; problem redefinition and non-redefinition, 3; role of objectives in, 6; role of officials in, 8; role of politicians in, 8; role of technicians in, 8; roles of cabinets in, 8; strategies utilized in, 3. *See also* Policy formation process; Policy formation process (Columbia Treaty)
Decision-making strategies, 364
Deane, Ritchie, 275
Diefenbaker, John, 1; approach of, to the United States, 374; and General McNaughton, 322; indecisiveness of, 313; on parliamentary examination of Columbia River Treaty, 188; position of, concerning Columbia development, 1957 election, 77
Diefenbaker administration: absence in, of alternative assessments of ministerial policy evaluations, 348; agreement of, on priority for Columbia development, 122; agreement of, to informal sales negotiations with United States, 231, 242; alternative views of, on a joint federal-provincial developmental entity, 171–72; appreciation of, for staff assistance, 303; assumptions of, concerning signing of the Columbia River Treaty, 188; attitude of, to United States, 24; collegial approach of, to Columbia policy formation, 298; commitment of, to helping the production and transmission of electric power in the Maritimes, 81; complex pressures on (1961), 199; competition of, with government of B.C., for "political credit," 356; complexity in bargaining stance of, 396n48; concern over Peace River planning, 122; constitutional vulnerability of, re its Columbia development role, 356; decision of, to test U.S. market on prospect for downstream

of, by B.C. Energy Board, 190; relationship between specific assumptions concerning, and a precise Columbia treaty, 361

Low Arrow (Murphy Creek) project, 126, 393n7

Luce, Charles, 194, 209, 221, 235, 268

Luxor project: General McNaughton's view of, 87; profile, and location of, 89

McKay, Douglas, 85

MacNabb, Gordon: assessment by, of December 1962 U.S. power sale offer, 244–45; membership of, on Columbia River Treaty Permanent Engineering Board, 283; participation of, in 1962 bargaining with U.S.A. over a power sale, 237; testimony of, to External Affairs Committee on the treaty (1944), 274, 276; toughness of, in final bargaining with U.S.A., 280

McNaughton, A. G. L., 51, 54, 91, 325: agrees to D. Stephens' initiative, 100; asked for information by Kaiser Company, 58; assessment by, of Technical Liaison Committee, 324; assumptions of, concerning role of IJC in Columbia policy formation, 93; attempt of, to preempt provincial jurisdiction, 322; attempt to harmonize B.C. and Ottawa approaches to Columbia (November 1956), 68; chairmanship of Canadian section, IJC, 50; claims of, concerning compensation to Canada for opportunities forgone, 66; on compatibility of high dams and fish migration, 70, 86; on confusion over B.C.'s objectives, 357; contribution of, on IJC, assessed, 320–22; critical assessment by, of Libby and High Arrow projects, 86, 160; criticism by, of Chantrill-Stevens Report, 147; denunciation by, of Columbia River Treaty, 227; and federal

jurisdiction on the Columbia River, 322; first annual presentation to External Affairs Committee (1953), 53; impact of, on Diefenbaker Cabinet, 322; insensitivity of St. Laurent administration to impact of early Columbia initiatives by, 54; modification in relationship with federal and B.C. cabinets after Kaiser Dam confrontation, 64–65; on physical control of Upper Kootenay runoff, 321; as potential synthesizer of Canada-B.C. positions re Libby, 50; presentations of, to External Affairs Committee (1954), 54; (1955), 62; (1956), 70; (1957), 85–86; (1960), 140; reaction of B.C. to assumed coordinative role of, 325; reaction of, to Peace River proposal (1957), 86; on relation of thermal peaking power cost to value of Canadian storage regulation, 66; relationship of, with federal public service, 321; resistance of, to diplomatic level negotiations (1956), 69; responses of, to B.C.-Kaiser Company agreement, 59; retirement of, 227–29, 406n31; role in netting/grossing debate, 110, 111; role with Policy Liaison Committee, 324; significance of support for International Rivers Bill, 64; tactical endorsement of mini-Libby proposal (1958), 85; testimony of, before External Affairs Committee (1964), on Columbia River treaty, 275; on U.S. position re Libby (1954), 61; view of optimal project development, for Canada, 86, 87, 126; views on Canadian developmental objectives, 351. See also Diversion rights: General McNaughton's view of; East Kootenay storage/diversion

McTaggart, Sir Andrew, 158

McWhorter, R., 320

Magnuson, Warren, 262

River Treaty projects, 207–9; impact of 1961 hearings on public dialogue, 347; power of, 14; technical clearance of Portage Mountain (Peace River) project by, 144–45; water licences granted by, for Columbia River Treaty projects, 225. *See* Paget, A. F.

Waterfield, Donald, 317–18

Water resource in Canada: complexity of jurisdiction over, when an international watershed is involved, 15–16, 354–56; legislative authority of national government concerning (contrasted with American), 15; legislative authority of provinces concerning, 14; relationship of fishery and navigation powers to Ottawa's role re the Columbia, 16; significance of proprietary rights in, re hydro electric development, 356

Wenner-Gren, Axel, 82

Wenner-Gren B.C. Development Company, 82: first memorandum of agreement with B.C. Government, 82; second memorandum of agreement with B.C. Government, 83. *See also* Peace River Power Development Company

Westcoast Transmission Company: gas export plans of, related to Libby project bargaining, 53

West Kootenay Power and Light Company, 33, 342: advice of, to B.C. Government, re first Libby application, 48; interest of, in Kaiser Company proposal, 57; and storage on Kootenay Lake, 39–40

White, Ivan, 125, 262

Wildavsky, Aaron, 314

Williston, R. G.: arguments of, against use of net benefits concept, 111; assessment of General McNaughton's position by (1962), 227; assurance of, to Policy Liaison Committee, re timing of Mica, 158; basic role in Columbia policy formation of, 297;

caution of, on Canadian entity question (1959), 116; caution of, on the cost of Columbia River power, 169; closeness of, to senior provincial bureaucracy, 301; concern of, re General McNaughton's role (1958), 93; concern of, re project selection negotiations (1960), 150, 152–53, 154; and co-chairmanship of Policy Liaison Committee, 103, 142; cooperation of, with Jean Lesage (1956), 71; crucial letter of, to E. D. Fulton (January 12, 1961), 181–82; explanations of unfolding Columbia policy by, to B.C. Legislative Assembly, 127–28, 299; impact of legislative presentations by, on public dialogue, 347; indirect role in 1957 negotiations with U.S.A., 72; instructions to, over not deferring Peace River development, 330; on political parties' use of General McNaughton, 247; "problem-splitting" of, 333; and provincial preference for Libby, 148; reaction of, to unilateral federal move to open treaty negotiations (1960), 124; request of, for Canada-B.C. agreement on strategy (January 1960), 123; request of, for optional plans from provincial staff, 121; response of, to procedural views of A. G. L. McNaughton (1958), 93–94; strong support of, for "two river" policy, 128; suggestion by, of final split on downstream power benefit sale, 266–67; support of, for B.C. Energy Board Reference, 179; support of, for High Arrow, 163; testimony of, to External Affairs Committee (1964), 275; undertaking of (1960), that public hearings would precede treaty signature, 209

Willoughby, W. R., 323

Young, Alex, 145

Date Due